Good Guide to Dog Friendly Pubs, Hotels and B&Bs

Please send reports on dog friendly pubs, hotels and B&Bs to:

Dogs
FREEPOST TN1569
Wadhurst
TN5 7BR

or email us at: dogs@goodguides.com

or visit our website: www.thegoodpubguide.co.uk

Good Guide to Dog Friendly Pubs, Hotels and B&Bs 2013

5th Edition

Edited by Fiona Stapley and Alisdair Aird

Walks Consultant Tim Locke
Additional Research Fiona Wright and Patrick Stapley

EBURY PRESS
LONDON

10 9 8 7 6 5

Published in 2013 by Ebury Press, an imprint of Ebury Publishing

A Random House Group Company

Text © Random House Group Ltd 2013
Maps © PerroGraphics 2013

Alisdair Aird and Fiona Stapley have asserted their right to be identified
as the authors of this Work in accordance with the Copyright, Designs and
Patents Act 1988

The Random House Group Limited Reg. No. 954009

Addresses for companies within the Random House Group can be found
at www.randomhouse.co.uk

A CIP catalogue record for this book is available from the British Library

The Random House Group Limited supports The Forest Stewardship
Council® (FSC®), the leading international forest-certification
organisation. Our books carrying the FSC label are printed on
FSC®-certified paper. FSC is the only forest-certification scheme
supported by the leading environmental organisations, including
Greenpeace. Our paper procurement policy can be found at
www.randomhouse.co.uk/environment

To buy books by your favourite authors and register for offers
visit www.randomhouse.co.uk

Typeset from authors' files by Jerry Goldie Graphic Design
Copy editor Ruth Jarvis
Editorial assistant Roxanne Mackey

Printed and bound by CPI Group (UK) Ltd, Croydon, CR0 4YY

ISBN 9780091951498

Back cover photograph of Dylan reproduced by kind permission
of Helen Rawsthorn and Mike Beasley

Contents

Introduction

The staff who put this guide together have all owned dogs – and as we go to press a new chocolate labrador puppy, Harvey, will be joining us. We have all gone away with our dogs and really do know the kind of places that suit dog owners best. We also rely on the hundreds of dog-owner reporters who write to us regularly with their experiences.

We have chosen places that offer a real welcome to dogs and their owners. These are all establishments that we would have no hesitation in including in a 'non-dog' guidebook – indeed, many of them are distinguished entries in our sister publication, the *Good Pub Guide*. But apart from pubs, they span a tremendous range of styles, from simple B&Bs or farmhouses through venerable inns to luxurious hotels. We have put particular effort into tracking down places with plenty of good walks nearby.

Information in this Guide was correct when it was researched towards the end of 2012. Unfortunately, over the years, we have found that establishments can change their policy on welcoming dogs. One bad experience with a dog guest can be enough to cause a place to completely rescind their dog welcome. It is therefore possible that by the time you come to make a reservation, a handful of entries in the Guide will no longer welcome dogs.

Do please help us by telling us about places you have visited with your dog. Simply email us at our office (dogs@goodguides.com), or write to Dogs, FREEPOST TN1569, Wadhurst, East Sussex TN5 7BR – no stamp needed if you post in the UK, or use the pre-printed forms at the back of the book.

Ten tips for top dog holidays
Making sure your dog enjoys a break as much as you do boils down mainly to common sense and a little forethought. And do think of other people – a little consideration for staff and other visitors goes a long way.
1. Always phone the establishment to discuss with the owners or manager what their rules are regarding dogs BEFORE you book a

room. If you turn up with two large rottweilers without pre-booking, you might not get the warm reception you were hoping for. Many places set aside bedrooms that are particularly suitable for dogs, such as ground floor rooms or rooms with access to the outside. And there is often a charge for dogs – confirm this when booking.

2. Check your pet insurance to see that it covers personal liability – knocking over furniture or tripping people up, for example.

3. Check which areas your dog is allowed into, as some places will only allow them in bedrooms.

4. Many establishments do not allow dogs to be left alone in bedrooms as they could become anxious (howling or barking and annoying other guests) or bored (chewing furniture, climbing on to beds and so forth). You may, therefore, have to put your dog in the car while you're in the restaurant, for instance.

5. Make sure to take your dog's own bedding, a towel for drying muddy paws and any favourite toys. Some places do provide bowls and food but it's often best to stick to regular mealtimes and the food your pet is used to.

6. Hairy dogs need a really thorough brushing beforehand, to minimise errant hairs.

7. Obviously, you wouldn't want to take a really unsociable dog away with you. Many proprietors have dogs and other animals of their own (and children, of course), and will not want a visiting pet that is difficult with them – or with other guests.

8. Do remember to keep your dog under control all the time – we find that it's more relaxing to keep even the best-behaved dogs on leads. This is particularly relevant if you are staying on farms or estates where there is livestock.

9. When you leave, make sure that there is no evidence that your dog has been there – either inside or out.

10. If you're hoping to explore the area, most proprietors will be able to point you in the direction of good nearby walks, and some attractions have special kennels where you can leave your dog; it's worth checking this beforehand.

In the countryside with your dog

Many dogs appreciate the countryside as much as their owners do. Whether your dog likes the hills, open heaths or coastal landscapes, there's plenty of choice across Britain. However, access is by no means unlimited, and the law requires you to keep your dog under control and put it on a lead when crossing fields with livestock in. A farmer has the right to shoot dogs that are worrying his farm animals: though this not a common occurrence, it does happen from time to time. If your dog is on a lead and you are both chased by a farm animal, it's generally safer to let the dog off the lead than to risk injury to yourself.

It's considerate to carry plastic bags to clean up your dog's mess, and to make sure your dog keeps well away from birds' nests (bear in mind that some birds lay their eggs on the ground) and other wildlife.

Places you can generally walk your dog in England and Wales are:

- **Public roads**, though of course they're not always ideal.
- Most **beaches**. Some popular beaches ban dogs in the summer, and – even more than anywhere else – it's always considerate to clean up after your dog on beaches.
- Paths and tracks on **National Trust land** (apart from National Trust gardens and house estates, where you need a ticket to get in, though some of these welcome dogs on leads) that are dedicated as public land and have free access: these include areas of coast, woodlands and open land.
- **Canal towpaths** unless there's a sign to the contrary.
- Paths and tracks in areas of forest owned by the **Forestry Commission**, though note that these may be temporarily closed during felling operations.
- Areas designated as **country parks**. Many of these are owned by local authorities, and you're allowed to wander where you like within them.
- Anywhere along a **public footpath**, **public bridleway** or **public byway** (the three together are also known generically as **public rights of way**). Bridleways are also open to horse-riders and cyclists, and byways are open to all traffic, so unless these have a paved surface they can be very muddy in wet weather. Public rights of way are normally signposted from roads, and may have **waymark arrows** (red for byways, blue for bridleways and yellow for footpaths). 'Permissive paths' or 'licensed paths' cross private land and are not public rights of way; the landowner has the right to close them at any time.
- Under the Countryside and Rights of Way Act you have a 'right to roam' on **access land** in uncultivated countryside in England and Wales.

Scotland has different laws about access to the countryside. There are some legal rights of way, but not many, and they aren't indicated as such on OS maps. Access tends to be established on an informal basis: there's a general tolerance towards walkers, who can effectively go anywhere on moorland and mountains outside the grouse-shooting and deer-stalking seasons (12 August-10 December and mainly 1 July-20 October respectively). Dogs may not be welcome on moorland because of nesting game birds; look out for notices, or check locally at tourist information centres.

What the right to roam means

Right to roam grants access on foot to many areas of moors, mountains, downland, heaths and registered commons that have been designated as access land. Here you have the right to walk wherever you like without sticking to paths, although in practice the lie of the land may determine your route in places. Note that not all uncultivated land is access land, and it doesn't include farmland, woods, coast or parkland; even in areas of open-looking hills such as the South Downs, the right to roam is quite limited.

Since access areas were established in 2004, many new stiles and gates have been built to allow entry, though you do sometimes have to leave the same way you came in. Access land is marked at key points with brown and white circular pictograms depicting a walker wandering through lumpy terrain, and marked on Ordnance Survey (OS) Explorer 1:25,000 maps (see below).

Do note the restrictions: you must keep dogs on a short lead if near livestock, and at all times from March to July; dogs may also, at any time, be banned temporarily or permanently from particular areas where, for example, birds may be nesting. You are not allowed to cycle, ride a horse, light fires, camp or feed livestock; if you do, you lose your right to roam for 72 hours. There may also be local restrictions on night-time access.

Information

- **OS maps** In England and Wales, the first point of reference is the local Ordnance Survey (OS) map: both the purple-covered Landranger series (at a scale of 1:50,000, or about one and a quarter inches to the mile) and the orange-covered Explorer series (at a scale of 1:25,000, or about two and a half inches to the mile) show rights of way (crosses for byways, long dashes for bridleways and short dashes for footpaths, sometimes overprinted with diamonds to denote long-distance routes; in red on Landranger maps and in green on Explorer maps). Access land is marked with a yellow tint and a dark orange border, on Explorer maps only; they also indicate with an 'i' in an orange circle the primary access points, which have an information board; but other gates and stiles are not shown. Other areas of land that are always open (National Trust, National Trust for Scotland and Forestry Commission) are shown on Explorer and Landranger maps with purple boundaries.
- **Dog stiles and gates** Bridleways and byways use gates rather than stiles, which makes things much easier for dog walking, as dogs can find stiles baffling. Some councils and landowners are increasingly installing easily climbed stiles, or gates rather than stiles, or excellent stiles with dog gates built into them – and

there's now a legal requirement for councils to take into account the needs of the less mobile when stiles or gates are installed. In the meantime, finding out if a particular path has dog friendly crossing points isn't straightforward, and it's best to ask locally. Some local tourist information centres stock leaflets showing stile-free walks suitable for dogs.

- **Dogs on trains** are carried free of charge, and should be kept on a lead. For journey planning, see www.nationalrail.co.uk for trains, and www.traveline.org.uk for buses.
- **Guided walks** are run by all sorts of organisations. The largest of these is the Ramblers' Association, which has local clubs across the country. Leaders may or not allow dogs, so it's always worth checking first. For details of group walks and other events, as well as a wealth of information about where to walk, access rights and walking gear, see www.ramblers.org. You can try a Ramblers' Association walk for free, but will be expected to join if you go on several. There's also the splendid Butcher's Great North Dog Walk (www.cooksondogwalk.co.uk), held each June in north-east England. A major fund-raising event, it has made it into the *Guinness Book of Records* as the largest dog walk ever held, with numbers each time now well in excess of 20,000 dogs.
- Finally, although it's not really connected to dog walking, if you're into cycling and want to take your dog along with you, there are dog cycle trailers that hitch on to the back of your bike, allowing your dog to enjoy the ride. A search on www.google.co.uk for "dog cycle trailers" comes up with plenty of results.

How the *Guide* works

Each county chapter is divided into two sections – Dog Friendly Pubs, followed by Dog Friendly Inns, Hotels and B&Bs.

The maps at the back of the book will help you locate pubs that allow dogs in the bar – they are indicated with a ●. Places that have accommodation where dogs are allowed are indicated with a ◙.

Dog Friendly Pubs *(where dogs are allowed in at least one bar)*
We give opening hours and note any days that places are closed altogether, whether they have a restaurant, and if they offer bar food.

Typical food service times in pubs are 12-2pm and 7-9pm Monday to Saturday; the kitchen often closes a bit earlier on Sundays. We give specific hours for each place and also note days when no food is served, but suggest you check first before planning an expedition that depends on having a meal.

Dog Friendly Inns, Hotels and B&Bs *(where dogs are welcome in either all or some of the bedrooms)*
The price we give in each entry in this section of the Guide is the total for two people sharing a double or twin-bedded room with its own bathroom for one night. It includes a full english breakfast, VAT and any automatic service charge that we know about. We say if dinner is included in this total price, which it may be at more remote places.

We also give a price if there is a charge for dogs to stay overnight in the bedrooms. If there is no price then there is no charge.

Most places in this 'Stay' section have very good value offers all through the year – especially out of season – so it's always worth asking.

If we know that the back rooms are the quietest or the front ones have the best views or the ones in the new extension are more spacious, then we say so.

We always mention a restaurant if we know there is one and we commend food if we have information supporting a positive recommendation. Many B&Bs will recommend nearby pubs for evening meals if they do not offer an evening meal.

Let's go for a walk

Many of the places listed in this Guide are in particularly lovely countryside and some of them have great walks right on their doorsteps. This selection gives just a handful of pubs that are perfectly sited for a walk, a drink and a meal with your canine friend. We've only provided an outline to the walk itself, so you will need an OS map (1:25,000 scale Explorer sheets are the best) to help you plan and follow your exact route, though in some instances where the walks follow obvious physical features such as coastline or canals you might not need a map, and in London the A-Z will work.

BEDFORDSHIRE

Prince of Wales at Ampthill (page 27)

There's free access in Ampthill Park – a surprisingly wild expanse just north-west of Ampthill, with woodland and grassland, and once a hunting ground of Henry VIII. Car parks are on the south side, off the B530, and the park is crossed by the Greensand Ridge Walk. You can extend the stroll by walking north from the church to the ruins of Houghton House.

BERKSHIRE

Crown & Garter at Inkpen (page 33)

A few minutes' walk north-east along Great Common Road from the pub leads to Inkpen Common Nature Reserve, a patch of ancient heathland, with three types of heather and a variety of birdlife; kissing gates rather than stiles make it easy for most dogs. In total contrast, a mile south down the lane gets you to car parks at the top of the downs on either side of Walbury Hill, a really bracing place in the wind, and with huge views north. The easy chalk track along the top of the escarpment west leads past the macabre landmark of Coombe Gibbet.

BUCKINGHAMSHIRE

Red Lion at Chenies (page 41)

Although only just out of suburbia (with Chalfont & Latimer station within walking distance), Chenies is in remarkably unspoilt farmland and woodland, shared with Hertfordshire, that feels completely rural. The walks here are gentle and well signposted, with paths either side of the River Chess, and connecting Chenies with the villages of Latimer, Church End and Sarratt (striking for its extraordinarily long green). It's not difficult to devise a route that keeps off the roads.

White Horse at Hedgerley (page 44)

Around Hedgerley are some splendid broad-leafed woodlands, laced with paths and with plenty of potential for walks, at their most spectacular when carpets of bluebells appear in spring or when the leaves turn in autumn (autumn colours are especially famed at Burnham Beeches to the south-west). Almost next to the White Horse is the entrance to Church Wood RSPB Reserve (they request that you keep your dog on a lead, especially during the April to June nesting season), known for its woodland birds, including great spotted woodpeckers, nuthatches and tree creepers.

CORNWALL

Bush at Morwenstow (page 77)

The well trodden route past Morwenstow Church and to the clifftops is the obvious walk here. The eccentric 19th-century vicar Rev Hawker built the church and rectory, and buried many salvaged shipwreck victims in the churchyard: the chimney pots re-create churches in places where he had formerly lived. Ten minutes' walking brings you to the cliffs, and just before the coast path reaches Higher Sharpnose you'll find the driftwood shack, now maintained by the National Trust, where Hawker would contemplate and smoke opium.

Pandora near Mylor Bridge (page 71)

You can walk 2 miles (3.2km) around the coast southeast from the Pandora, past Weir Point and round to Mylor Creek, getting terrific views across the busy boating waters of Carrick Roads. The path eventually ends at Mylor Bridge, from where you can either take the road back to the pub or pick up a path and then a lane back to Weir Point.

CUMBRIA

Sun at Coniston (page 81)

Highly contrasting but equally rewarding walking options are found at Coniston. The easy strolling ground is along Coniston Water, reached in a few minutes from the village via Lake Road, then, where the road bends left, fork right at the signpost for the lake. The route passes the ancient-looking Coniston Hall and soon offers glorious views across the water; you can continue for up to 3 miles (5km) on a delightful lakeside path that goes in and out of woodland. Alternative expeditions for energetic dogs involve walking up to the Coppermines Valley above the west side of the village, with spectacular remnants of long-defunct mines punctuating the slopes below Coniston Old Man. The lane up from Coniston begins steeply, then rises past the Miners Bridge and waterfall.

Britannia Inn at Elterwater (page 91)

You walk straight out of this pub into some of the choicest walking country in England, with easily managed gates. Easy options follow the Cumbria Way along the river – eastwards on the way to Skelwith Force waterfall you sneak a view of the strangely elusive Elter Water, not otherwise easy to see up close. Westwards, the Great Langdale Beck enters Langdale proper: the walking is through flat fields but the views of the Langdale Pikes are hugely rewarding. Tougher dogs might enjoy the walk up to Stickle Tarn, marvellously placed beneath the Langdale Pikes summits, or an extended 9-mile (14.5km) tour of the dale taking in the lower reaches of Lingmoor Fell and scenically sited Blea Tarn, which has its own car park.

Old Dungeon Ghyll at Langdale (page 92)

Some wonderful low-level walking from here follows a bridleway section of the Cumbria Way, with easily managed gates. West of Old Dungeon Ghyll is an easily managed track along the valley of Mickleden Beck, with formidable peaks rising ahead and on either side: you can walk for about 2 miles (3km) before the terrain steepens appreciably. Eastwards, the Cumbria Way heads to the Dungeon Ghyll New Hotel, from which it's a steep, rocky climb up to Stickle Tarn, marvellously placed under the Langdale Pikes summits. Southwards is Blea Tarn (one of several Blea Tarns in the Lake District, but the most scenic), with its own car park nearby, or within reach from the pub via a steep path that starts from the campsite.

Langstrath at Stonethwaite (page 86)

You can enjoy very satisfying views of Borrowdale on an easy, level 2-mile (3.2km) circular walk from Stonethwaite – over Stonethwaite Bridge, then left along Stonethwaite Beck to the next hamlet, Rosthwaite, where you cross over and take the lane on the far side of the B5289, then left on the path by the River Derwent, over the next bridge and back on the lane to Stonethwaite.

DERBYSHIRE

Monsal Head Hotel at Monsal Head (page 105)

The view from here lures you down to the Monsal Trail, which goes over the old railway viaduct you can see below, and along a railway trackbed. It's easy going for dogs, and if you'd rather not take in the steep path from the hotel to the trail, you can start from a car park and picnic site on the A6 at the valley floor level. Either direction is beautiful: westwards extends a mile (1.6km) until you're diverted away from a tunnel entrance and past the old textile mill at Cressbrook and into Miller's Dale.

DEVON

Fountain Head at Branscombe (page 108)

The path network helps keep you and your dog off the narrow lanes, and the walkers' routes are well marked, if sometimes steep. From the little triangle of roads near the Fountain Head, a path climbs up southeast through the woods and joins the coastal path, which you can easily follow eastwards down to Branscombe Mouth for a pleasant return along the valley and then along lanes. Or carry on further along the coast from Branscombe Mouth – through the caravan park and into a strange netherworld of collapsed chalk cliffs known as Hooken Undercliff – one of the most startling coastal features in all Devon.

Rock Inn at Haytor Vale (page 125)

One of the best viewpoints in Dartmoor is nearby: drive up to the car park at Haytor Rocks, and use the groups of rocks, the abandoned quarries and the old tram tracks to guide you round the moor.

Rugglestone at Widecombe (page 119)

Good, breezy moorland strolls include eastwards up to Rugglestone Rock and the Logan Stone, and from Widecombe village to the wide ridge of Hamel Down – the latter reached by following the lane towards Natsworthy then branching up a steadily rising track, alongside a wall on the right. It can be boggy on the moor in places, but that is more than compensated for by the wonderful feeling of space.

DORSET

George at Chideock (page 133)

The busy A35 is something of a deterrent to starting a walk, but once you're away from it (best to drive the short lane to Seatown), the walk up from Seatown to Golden Cap has one of the great Dorset views, from the county's highest coastal point. You need to be careful with the cliff drops, but there's generally plenty of space for dogs at the top.

Square & Compass at Worth Matravers (page 137)

Several routes lead out to the cliffs from here: the easiest, and least interesting, is along the road west to Renscombe Farm, then left on the lane down to the atmospherically unadorned ancient chapel on the clifftop at St Aldhelm's Head (1.5 miles/2.4km total); it's more fun, but much more challenging, to keep west on a path from Renscombe Farm to join the switchback coast path above Chapman's Pool. This is wonderful in either direction, but it's not for vertigo sufferers, and there are stiles on the way. Eastwards you can edge round the coast and return to Worth Matravers along the valley floor of Winspit Bottom.

GLOUCESTERSHIRE

Bell at Sapperton (page 155)

Beneath the church, a stroll down through the meadows and into trees brings you to the ornate tunnel entrance to the overgrown, derelict Thames and Severn Canal. The locks have gone and the canal has reverted into a rather beautiful wilderness, all easily enjoyed from the canal towpath, which makes a pleasant walk to Daneway. There's more good strolling ground just north of the village, where a lane to the right of the church dips to the valley floor and you can continue on a path through woods that have a memorably heady whiff of wild garlic in early summer.

HAMPSHIRE

Royal Oak at Fritham (page 168)

You can wander at will through much of the New Forest, but beware that ponies and deer may be at large, the presence of which might either frighten your dog or encourage it to give chase. Finding a path isn't difficult; more of a problem is losing your way, as there's a huge network of paths. From the end of the public road near the Royal Oak you can step straight into the wilds, which here vary pleasantly between planted forest and open heathland.

Wykeham Arms at Winchester (page 178)

The water meadows adjoining the city make for idyllic strolling: you can join them by turning on to College Walk near Wolvesey Palace and Castle, following the signs for the Hospital of St Cross (an ancient almshouses institution), which takes about 20 minutes. A satisfying add-on for dogs that like a bit of a climb is the modest summit of St Catherine's Hill, from the entrance to the hospital. At the top are Iron Age ramparts and a mysterious 'mizmaze' cut into the turf, supposedly for knights to do penance by crawling round it; the view extends right across Winchester.

HEREFORDSHIRE

Saracens Head at Symonds Yat (page 181)

Crossing the river is half the fun here: from the Saracens Head, a rope-hoisted ferry will get you and your dog across for a small fee. On the other side, turn left along the riverside track to the 'chicken wire' bridge a mile or so downstream, then double back on the obvious riverside route along the other side. For such an easy walk, this is extraordinarily scenic and has plenty to look at, both on and away from the river; abseilers and canoeists are often in evidence. To make it more of a challenge, you could wander up to the Symonds Yat viewpoint, high above the pub, with its classic view of the river's great meander.

HERTFORDSHIRE

Valiant Trooper at Aldbury (page 185)

Adjacent to Aldbury, the glorious forests of the Ashridge Estate make ideal dog-walking terrain, with tracks that go long distances without meeting a road. Just east of the village green, a signposted bridleway leads from the road up into the woodlands and to the Bridgewater

Monument (a tall column built to honour the canal-building third Duke of Bridgewater), the major landmark hereabouts. If you prefer more open ground, head to Ivinghoe Beacon – a knob of chalk escarpment jutting out over a vast plain; it's a 3.5-mile (5.5km) walk from Aldbury and you can avoid the road virtually all the way, or you can park near the Beacon.

ISLE OF WIGHT

Red Lion at Freshwater (page 192)

Within yards of the pub you reach one of the island's great surprises: the River Yar only extends for a couple of miles but has some wonderful moments. The trackbed of a defunct railway provides an easy and stile-free way of exploring the east side of its valley, which soon has a reedy, almost East Anglian beauty, and there's an abundance of bird life as well as an impressive former tidal mill. The track takes you into Yarmouth, itself fun to explore, and for a full day's circular walk (11 miles/17.5km) for dogs with plenty of energy you can then follow the coastal path right around the island's western tip, past Alum Bay, the viewpoint above The Needles and the grassy whaleback ridge of Tennyson Down: a magnificent route that ranks among southern England's finest coastal walks.

KENT

Tiger at Stowting (page 201)

The North Downs Way, waymarked with acorn motifs, is the easiest route to follow hereabouts, and passes through the village; eastwards it climbs up on to a swathe of North Downs that are too steep for ploughing so have kept their traditional downland look. Farthing Common makes an excellent spot to aim for, or you can carry on towards Postling.

LEICESTERSHIRE

Wheatsheaf at Woodhouse Eaves (page 221)

Just west of Woodhouse Eaves are Leicestershire's mini highlands, offering lots of space and a real surprise in the heart of the Midlands. Beacon Hill rises to 803ft and even has modest crags on its moorland summit; an obvious track from the lower car park in Beacon Hill Country Park takes you up, or you can extend the walk southwards by taking a path round past Broombriggs Farm and Windmill Hill Country

Park, which has a farm trail. Further south, Bradgate Park is another hugely rewarding country park of heathland and rock outcrops – a former hunting reserve with open access and a fine view from Old Johns Tower.

LINCOLNSHIRE

Chequers at Woolsthorpe (page 225)

An uncomplicated and extremely pleasant walk for dogs of all abilities along the Grantham Canal can easily be joined from Woolsthorpe (although you may prefer to drive the unexceptional road section as far as the canal): with the pub sign on your right, follow Main Street and continue at the next junction along Sedgebrook Road, forking right at the sign for the Dirty Duck pub beyond the end of the village on a road crossing the canal. You can make a circular walk of 8.5 miles (13.5km) by following the towpath east to bridge 66, then doubling back on a field path soon skirting Denton Reservoir and carrying on through the ironstone village of Denton. At the south end of the village, a field path runs parallel to the A607 south-west until you meet the signposted Viking Way long-distance path which leads back to Woolsthorpe.

NORFOLK

White Horse at Blakeney (page 226)

All of the Norfolk Coast Path here is gloriously straightforward dog-walking terrain – easy to find, easy underfoot and plenty to enjoy looking at. From Blakeney, and many other places along the coast, the route follows the top of a grassy dyke around the marshes. Eastwards it loops around past the remains of Blakeney Chapel to Cley next the Sea (the frequent CoastHopper bus service is a useful means of getting back between Cley, Blakeney and other points on the coast; they will take dogs for no charge provided they're not a risk to other passengers; for details call 01553 776980). Westwards, the coast path heads along the landward side of the marshes to Morston, from where there's a seasonal boat service to the long coastal spit of Blakeney Point.

Orange Tree at Thornham (page 237)

A favourite spot for bird watchers, Thornham's quiet saltmarsh inlets can be followed out towards the coast via Ship Lane and Staithe Lane, where you're close to the Titchwell RSPB reserve. Then you're into a different terrain of expansive dunes as you carry on westwards past Gore Point to Holme-next-the-Sea. Either return the same way or go on to the A149 to pick up the CoastHopper bus back.

OXFORDSHIRE

Crown at Pishill (page 259)

This is in a classic part of the Chilterns, with woodlands alternating with rolling farmland. One of the many possibilities starts further east from the Buckinghamshire village of Turville, beneath its landmark windmill: well marked paths and tracks link it with Southend, Stonor and Pishill; among the country houses of which you can sneak a view are Stonor House, in its expansive deer park.

SHROPSHIRE

Royal Oak at Cardington (page 266)

The village sits on the brink of some of the loveliest hill walks in this part of the world. Your dog can experience it without climbing at all by walking along the lane west from Cardington past Willstone Farm; Caer Caradoc soon comes into view. If you want to tackle it, you'll face a steep walk up but you'll be rewarded with colossal views from its satisfyingly compact summit; easier options include the gentle moorland tracks over Hope Bowdler Hill to the south.

SOMERSET

Crown at Churchill (page 276)

The Crown is well positioned for one of the very best walks in the Mendips, around Dolebury Warren and towards Burrington Combe. From the pub, head along The Batch southwards, then fork left to cross the A38, where you'll find a lane leading past a small car park: from there it's an easily managed valley-floor track with gates: it's worth continuing for a mile (1.6km) to a junction of tracks where you can return by turning left up over Dolebury Warren – an open hill with lots of space for dogs – with far-reaching views from the Iron Age hill fort at the western end. You can extend the walk further east to take in the moorland above the limestone gorge of Burrington Combe; the road along the floor of the gorge is unfenced and pleasant to walk along.

SUFFOLK

Crown, Lord Nelson, and Swan all at Southwold
(pages 297, 298, 305)

Plenty of space on the beach and some lovely areas of common give plenty of possibilities for dog walkers. Southwold has a long beach and a spacious common: dogs are allowed on the Denes (the southern stretch of the beach) but barred from certain areas near the pier during the holiday season. From there, you can continue round to the mouth of the canalised River Blyth, where a summer ferry sometimes operates to Walberswick (giving scope for carrying on along the Dunwich river and towards Walberswick Nature Reserve); follow the river upstream to the bridge, then go right up to Southwold Common and back into the town to complete a very uncomplicated 2.5 miles (4km).

SURREY

Three Horseshoes at Thursley (page 311)

Reached by taking the Greensand Way north from Thursley is Thursley Common, one of the best Surrey heaths for walking, with sandy paths and tracks running between large expanses of heather and patches of woodland. Several ponds make attractive points to head for, and the Moat car park just off the road to Elstead is another useful starting point.

SUSSEX

Fox Goes Free at Charlton (page 315)

Just north of the village and with very much of the look of the South Downs as they were before modern agriculture, Levin Down is a nature reserve crossed by public paths, and is a habitat for numerous butterflies and chalkland wildflowers. Southwards a quiet lane and a track lead up towards Goodwood racecourse, at the west end of which is parking space giving on to The Trundle; masts mark the top of an impressive Iron Age hill fort (open access and plenty of space) with massive ramparts and a huge view extending to the Isle of Wight and Beachy Head.

Tiger at East Dean (page 318)

With the free car park adjoining the village green, this makes the perfect starting point for the finest coastal walk in the South East, taking in the grassy rollercoaster clifftops of the Seven Sisters in one direction and using the quiet tracks through Friston Forest in the other. The cliff edges are sheer and very crumbly, so you may need to keep your dog well supervised, but there's free access so you can wander some way inland. There are plenty of options for shortening it: the easiest walks include starting at Birling Gap and strolling up to Belle Tout lighthouse, or from parking at Crowlink (off the main road at Friston, just above East Dean), and walking down over the grass and on to the clifftops. The information centre is at Seven Sisters Country Park.

WORCESTERSHIRE

Nags Head at Malvern (page 359)

From the top of the long Malverns ridge there are terrific views across the Midlands and into the Welsh borders, and an almost bewildering number of paths to get you up to the top. It's all very dog friendly and somewhat more easily managed and municipal than you might expect for a range of hills that looks formidably alpine from the hazy distance, with benches sited every few paces on amiable grassy terrain. Worcestershire Beacon, the highest point, is close to the town centre of Malvern and is easily reached by walking past St Ann's Well, the original source of Malvern water.

YORKSHIRE

Lion at Blakey Ridge (page 363)

Either side of the road from here are splendid level walks through the moor, on former railway tracks that once served the ironstone quarries. On the east side, the track loops around lazily, giving effortless views over Farndale.

Bridge Inn at Grinton (page 373)

Swaledale is connoisseur's walking territory, though the number of stiles can make it tricky for dog walking, and the field crossing is often quite intricate. On the far side of the Swale from Grinton, a riverside path makes a pleasant half-mile amble, and on the open moors on all sides are opportunities for striding out. A particularly satisfying circular route could be made from Reeth, up the north side of Arkle Beck in its deep-set valley, then taking any of several paths leading up to the valley rim of Fremington Edge for an enjoyably blustery contrast

LONDON

Greenwich Union (page 384)

Greenwich's river and canine-friendly green spaces almost demand to be explored on foot, and for a bracing walk you can easily include the grassy expanse of Blackheath, although Greenwich Park has the edge scenically. The Georgian streets near the Greenwich Union are a pleasure in themselves; Crooms Hill and Hyde Vale make good strolling ground before you enter Greenwich Park, for the high-level view of the Thames. From there you could drop past the National Maritime Museum, head past the *Cutty Sark* and turn right along the riverside path to look across to the futuristic skyscape of Docklands.

SCOTLAND

Border at Kirk Yetholm (page 400)

As Kirk Yetholm is at the very end of the long-distance Pennine Way, you might like to follow it in reverse for a distance and greet walkers who have nearly made it all the way. The first stretch is along a surfaced, but virtually traffic-free, farm road. After the last building the route climbs appreciably up on to the high moors of the Cheviots, reaching a saddle between The Curr and Black Hag – a total distance from Kirk Yetholm of about 4 miles (6.5km).

Burts Hotel at Melrose (page 400)

Two objectives to join together here: one is the River Tweed, just north of Melrose, with a riverside path making the most of the Borders views. The other is the Eildon Hills, a mile or so south of Melrose, and reached by a field path. They rise just enough to feel like proper summits, and one of them – Eildon Hill North – is ringed by Iron Age ramparts, but it's only about 900ft of ascent. The view from the top takes in the Cheviots, the Moorfoots and the Lammermuir Hills. You can join the hills with the river by walking along the Tweed east to Newstead, climbing the Eildons from there, then dropping to Melrose (4.5 miles/7km).

WALES

Harp at Old Radnor (page 419)

The view from the open ground in front of the pub may well inspire you to venture on to Radnor Forest, the upland mass a few miles away. One of the most useful access points is New Radnor, from where you can climb up through forestry plantations and skirt the

prominent peak known as the Whimble or take a path through the
churchyard, round the contour and across the entrance to Harley
Dingle (used for munitions testing, but a highly scenic route skirts it).
A couple of miles west of New Radnor, along the A44, is a car park for
the 15-minute walk along a forest road to the entrance to a chasm on
the left, at the end of which is Water-Break-Its-Neck, a marvellously
tucked away waterfall that sprays appreciably after prolonged rain
and often has a show of icicles in deep winter. There are lots of sheep
on the open hills, so you need to keep your dog on a lead for much of
the way.

Pen-y-Gwryd at Llanberis (page 416)

There's really nothing here along the level, but energetic dogs may
like the walk up from here following the miners' track northwards
to the saddle between Glyder Fach and Y Foel Goch. If you choose
not to continue up to either of these summits you can just enjoy the
superlative view of Tryfan ahead.

Stackpole Inn, Stackpole (page 410)

Just to the south of the pub, Bosherston Lakes have free access, with
gorgeous walks along the water's edge, and the eastern arm is suitable
for wheelchair users. A rich wildlife haunt, it's home to numerous
species of breeding birds, dragonflies and damselflies, and in June
and July the lilies are at their showiest. At the southern end, you can
venture on to Broad Haven, a wonderfully unspoilt sandy beach. The
coast path from here eastwards is mostly level, and encompasses
St Govan's Head, near which St Govan's Chapel is an extraordinary
medieval structure ensconced beneath the cliffs.

Bedfordshire

DOG FRIENDLY PUBS

AMPTHILL
TL0338
Prince of Wales
Bedford Street (B540 N from central crossroads); MK45 2NB

Civilised with contemporary décor and up-to-date food; bedrooms

Big leather deco-style armchairs and sofas at low tables on wood-strip flooring blend a comfortable relaxed atmosphere to this open-plan bar-brasserie. It's on two levels: a slightly sunken flagstoned area with an exposed brick fireplace leads to a partly ply-panelled dining area with dark leather dining chairs set around a mixed batch of sturdy tables. Modern prints decorate the mainly cream walls (dark green and maroon accents at either end) and it's all nicely lit; background music. They have Wells & Youngs Bombardier and Eagle on handpump and good coffee, and service is brisk and helpful. There are picnic-sets out on a nicely planted two-level lawn, and a terrace by the car park.

Charles Wells ~ Lease Richard and Neia Heathorn ~ Real ale ~ Bar food (12-2.30(3 Sun), 6 30-9 30; not Sun evening) ~ Restaurant ~ (01525) 840504 ~ Children welcome ~ Dogs allowed in bar ~ Open 12-3, 6-11 (12-midnight Fri, Sat); 12-5 Sun; closed Sun evening ~ Bedrooms: £55S/£70S ~ www.princeofwales-ampthill.com

FLITTON
TL0535
White Hart
Brook Lane; MK45 5EJ

Simply furnished and friendly village pub with bar and dining area, real ales, enterprising food and seats in garden

It's worth knowing about this welcoming village pub if you're in the area and need a tasty meal. It hunkers down between Flitton Moor and a 13th-c church and has a nice garden with neat shrub borders and teak seats and tables on a terrace shaded by cedars and weeping willows. The minimally decorated front bar has been refurbished to include some dark leather tub chairs around low tables, contemporary leather and chrome seats at pedestal tables, and boldly patterned wallpaper. B&T Dragon Slayer and a guest such as Buntingford Twitchell on handpump and 18 or so wines are all available by the glass; TV. Steps lead down to a good-sized, simply furnished back dining area with red plush seats and banquettes on dark wooden floorboards.

Free house ~ Licensees Phil and Clare Hale ~ Real ale ~ Bar food (12-2(2.30 Sun), 7-9(6.30-9.30 Fri, Sat; not Sun evening, Mon)) ~ Restaurant ~ (01525) 862022 ~ Children welcome

~ Dogs allowed in bar ~ Open 12-2.30, 6-11; 12-3, 6-midnight Sat; 12-4.30 Sun; closed Sun evening, Mon ~ www.whitehartflitton.co.uk

OAKLEY   TL0053
Bedford Arms
High Street

Updated 16th-c village inn with several individual rooms, real ales and wines by the glass, popular food in two dining rooms and seats in pretty garden

There's plenty of room for both drinking and eating in this 16th-c village inn and the contemporary décor is different in each inter-connected room. Four cosy separate rooms lead off the main bar with farmhouse, ladder-back and Victorian-style chairs around all manner of wooden tables on ancient floor tiles and the two dining rooms and conservatory overlook the pretty garden.

Charles Wells ~ Tenants Tim and Yvonne Walker ~ Real ale ~ Bar food (12-2.30, 6-9.30; 12-5 Sun) ~ Restaurant ~ (01234) 822280 ~ Children welcome ~ Dogs allowed in bar ~ Open 12-11(10.30 Sun) www.bedfordarmsoakley.co.uk

OLD WARDEN   TL1343
Hare & Hounds
Village signposted off A600 S of Bedford and B658 W of Biggleswade; SG18 9HQ

Comfortable dining pub with thoughtfully prepared and presented food and lovely gardens

The four cosy beamed rooms here have dark standing timbers, and radiate out from a central servery. Cleverly blending contemporary styling with the attractive old structure, décor is in cosy reds and creams, with tweed upholstered armchairs and sofas and coffee tables on stripped flooring, light wood tables, a woodburning stove in an inglenook fireplace and fresh flowers on the bar. Prints and photographs depict historic aircraft in the famous Shuttleworth Collection just up the road. Wells & Youngs Eagle, IPA and Courage Directors are on handpump, with a dozen or so wines by the glass including some from a local vineyard; background music. The glorious sloping garden stretches up to pine woods behind.

Charles Wells ~ Lease Jane and Jago Hurt ~ Real ale ~ Bar food (12-2(3.30 Sun), 6.30-9; not Sun evening) ~ Restaurant ~ (01767) 627225 ~ Children welcome ~ Dogs allowed in bar ~ Open 12-3, 6-11; 12-10.30 Sun; closed Mon (except bank holiday lunchtimes) ~ www.hareandhoundsoldwarden.co.uk

RAVENSDEN   TL0754
Horse & Jockey
Village signed off B660 N of Bedford; pub at Church End, off village road; MK44 2RR

Contemporary comfort, with enjoyable food and good range of drinks

You're equally welcome to pop in for a drink or to linger over a thoughtfully prepared meal at this comfortable pub. Service is charming, they have some 30 wines by the glass and four guest ales from brewers such as Adnams, Cottage, Fullers and St Austell on handpump. The refurbished interior is pleasantly modern with a quiet colour scheme of olive greys and dark red, careful lighting, modern leather easy chairs in the bar, a meticulously set out wall of old local photographs, a rack of recent *Country Life* issues and daily papers; background music and board games. The bright dining room has nice chunky tables and high-backed seats, well lit prints and contemporary etched glass screen, and it overlooks a sheltered terrace with smart modern tables and chairs under cocktail parasols, a few picnic-sets on the grass beside, and the handsome medieval church in its churchyard further off.

Free house ~ Licensees Darron and Sarah Smith ~ Real ale ~ Bar food (12-2, 6-9; 12-6.30 Sun) ~ Restaurant ~ (01234) 772319 ~ Children welcome ~ Dogs allowed in bar ~ Open 12-3, 6-11; 12-11 Sat; 12-10 Sun; closed Mon, Tues in Jan ~ www.horseandjockey.info

SOULDROP   SP9861
Bedford Arms
Village signposted off A6 Rushden–Bedford; High Street; MK44 1EY

Proper country tavern with good-value homely food in cottagey dining area

Traditional in both its atmosphere and décor, this cosy relaxed place is given real heart by its lively welcoming licensees, and its handful of chatty regulars settled into the bar chairs by the counter (which has Black Sheep, Greene King IPA and Phipps Red Star on handpump alongside a guest such as Hopping Mad Brainstorm and several wines by the glass). There are just a few more seats in this small low-beamed room, including a table in a snug, low-ceilinged alcove. The cottagey dining area has more low beams (one way through is potentially a real head-cracker) and a central fireplace – and, like the rest of the pub, broad floorboards, shelves of china, and original artwork (for sale). In the evenings and at weekends, the roomy mansard-ceilinged public area (once a brew house) comes to life, with hood skittles, darts, games machine, TV and board games; it has a big inglenook fireplace, and opens on to a neat garden. The landlady is fond of her pets – look out for Poky the cat and, out in the garden, JD and Gin and Tonic the rabbits.

Free house ~ Licensees Sally Rushworth and Fred and Caroline Rich ~ Real ale ~ Bar food (12-2, 6.30-9; 12-4 Sun; not Sun evening, Mon) ~ Restaurant ~ (01234) 781384 ~ Children welcome ~ Dogs allowed in bar ~ Open 12-3, 6-12; 12-midnight Fri, Sat; 12-10 Sun; closed Mon (except bank holidays)

STEPPINGLEY   TL0135
French Horn
Off A507 just N of Flitwick; Church End; MK45 5AU

Comfortable pub with modern touches to the thoughtfully prepared food

An eclectic shabby-chic mix of comfy old armchairs, sofas and other new and old furniture works well with the light stippled-beams and fresh cream walls at this light and airy place – there are even two armchairs tucked into the old brick inglenook. Some nice old pews, lamps, cushions, pictures on the wonky walls and a couple of rugs on flagstones or floor boards keep it homely and familiar. The well stocked bar offers Greene King IPA and a Greene King guest, a farm cider, ten wines by the glass from a very good list and an interesting selection of malt whiskies; background music and TV.

Greene King ~ Lease Laurence Nelson-Boudville ~ Real ale ~ Bar food (12-3, 6-10; 12-10 Sat; 12-8 Sun) ~ Restaurant ~ (01525) 720122 ~ Children welcome ~ Dogs allowed in bar ~ Open 12-midnight; 12-12.30 Fri-Sat ~ www.thefrenchhornpub.com

DOG FRIENDLY INNS, HOTELS AND B&Bs

ASPLEY GUISE   SP9435
Best Western Moore Place
The Square, Aspley Guise, Milton Keynes, Buckinghamshire MK17 8DW (01908) 282000
www.mooreplace.com

£70; 63 well equipped, pretty rms. Elegantly restored Georgian house in attractive gardens, with bar and lounge (afternoon teas – book in advance), enjoyable food and nice breakfasts in light and airy Victorian-style conservatory restaurant, and friendly, helpful staff; 5 mins from Woburn Abbey and Safari Park; dogs in bedrooms and bar; £15

FLITWICK   TL0234
Menzies Flitwick Manor
Church Road, Flitwick, Bedford, Bedfordshire MK45 1AE (01525) 712242
www.menzies-hotels.co.uk

£145; 18 thoughtfully decorated rms with antiques and period pieces. Georgian country house surrounded by acres of rolling gardens and wooded parkland; log fire in entrance hall, comfortable, tranquil lounge and library, and smart restaurant with imaginative food using home-grown and local produce; tennis and croquet; dogs in downstairs bedrooms

HOUGHTON CONQUEST   TL0441
Knife & Cleaver
The Grove, Houghton Conquest, Bedford, Bedfordshire MK45 3LA (01234) 930789
www.theknifeandcleaver.com

£85; 9 recently refurbished rms. Comfortably civilised inn with lovely dark panelling in bar, real ales and good choice of wines by the glass, a blazing winter fire, airy white-walled conservatory dining room, enjoyable food, and tables on a terrace alongside the neatly kept, attractive garden; nearby walks; seven resident scottie dogs and one parrot; dogs in bedrooms; treats, welcome pack, bowls

H; owners Sara Fulton and Roger Baker

Berkshire

MAP 2

DOG FRIENDLY PUBS

BRAY   SU9079

Crown

1.75 miles from M4 junction 9; A308 towards Windsor, then left at Bray signpost on to B3028; High Street; SL6 2AH

Low-beamed pub with refurbished, knocked-through rooms, surprisingly pubby food (given the owner), real ales and plenty of outside seating

It's a surprisingly pubby place, given that the owner is Heston Blumenthal, where you wouldn't feel out of place just dropping in for a pint and chat and the atmosphere is friendly and informal. The partly panelled main bar has heavy old beams – some so low you may have to mind your head – plenty of timbers handily left at elbow height where walls have been knocked through, three winter log fires and neatly upholstered dining chairs and cushioned settles. Courage Best and Directors and a couple of changing guest beers on handpump and several good wines by the glass. There are modern slatted chairs and tables in the courtyard with plenty of picnic-sets in the large, enclosed back garden.

Scottish Courage ~ Lease Simon King ~ Real ale ~ Bar food (12-2.30(3 weekends), 6(7 Sun)-9.30(6.30-10 Fri and Sat)) ~ Restaurant ~ (01628) 621936 ~ Children welcome ~ Dogs allowed in bar ~ Open 11-11; 12-10.30 Sun ~ www.thecrownatbray.co.uk

BRAY   SU9079

Hinds Head

High Street; car park opposite (exit rather tricky); SL6 2AB

First class food in top gastropub, traditional surroundings, local ales, fine wines by the glass and quite a choice of other drinks, too

Of course most customers are here to enjoy the excellent food but they do keep a couple of beers from local breweries like Rebellion and Windsor & Eton on handpump and people do pop in for a drink and a chat. It's a handsome old pub and the thoroughly traditional L-shaped bar has dark beams and panelling, polished oak parquet, blazing log fires, red-cushioned built-in wall seats and studded leather carving chairs around small round tables, and latticed windows. They also keep 14 wines by the glass from an extensive list, quite a few malt whiskies, and a dozen specialist gins with interesting ways of serving them. This is under the same ownership as the nearby Crown and the renowned Fat Duck restaurant.

Free house ~ Licensee Kevin Love ~ Real ale ~ Bar food (12-2.30, 6.30-9.30; 12-4 Sun; not Sun evening) ~ Restaurant ~ (01628) 626151 ~ Children welcome ~ Dogs allowed in bar ~ Open 11-11; 12-7 Sun ~ www.hindsheadbray.com

FRILSHAM   SU5573
Pot Kiln

From Yattendon take turning S, opposite church, follow first Frilsham signpost, but just after crossing motorway go straight on towards Bucklebury ignoring Frilsham signposted right; pub on right after about half a mile; RG18 0XX

Country dining pub, bustling little bar, local beers, and imaginative bar and restaurant dishes; suntrap garden, lovely views and nearby walks

They've managed to get the balance here just right between emphasis on the interesting food and a genuinely pubby atmosphere – and it works well for all their customers. It's a bustling country inn with a warm welcome from the staff and a little bar serving West Berkshire Brick Kiln Bitter, Mr Chubbs Lunchtime Bitter and Maggs Magnificent Mild on handpump, several wines by the glass and maybe a couple of ciders. The main bar area has dark wooden tables and chairs on bare boards and a winter log fire and the extended lounge is open-plan at the back and leads into a large, pretty dining room with a nice jumble of old tables and chairs and an old-looking stone fireplace; darts and board games. It's in an idyllic spot with wide, unobstructed views from seats in a big suntrap garden and there are plenty of walks in the nearby woods.

Free house ~ Licensees Mr and Mrs Michael Robinson ~ Real ale ~ Bar food (12-2.30, 6.30-8.30; not Tues) ~ Restaurant ~ (01635) 201366 ~ Children welcome ~ Dogs allowed in bar ~ Open 12-3, 6-11; 12-11 Sat; 12-10 Sun; closed Tues ~ www.potkiln.org

HARE HATCH   SU8077
Horse & Groom

A4 Bath Road W of Maidenhead; RG10 9SB

Spreading pub with very well refurbished timbered rooms, friendly staff, enjoyable food, a fine range of drinks and seats outside

Once one of the gates into Windsor Forest, this 18th-c pub is a friendly, easy-going place. There are spacious linked areas with beams and timbering, open doorways, a pleasing variety of well spread individual tables and chairs on mahogany-stained boards, plenty of oriental rugs and some carpet to soften the acoustics, open fires in attractive tiled fireplaces, house plants and a profusion of mainly old or antique prints. The long bar counter has a splendid choice of drinks, including a good changing range of 20 wines by the glass, Brakspears Bitter and Oxford Gold and changing guests like Jennings Cumberland, Ringwood Best and Filly Drift, and Wychwood Hobgoblin on handpump, two Weston's farm ciders, lots of spirits including malts of the week, and several coffees; also several different daily papers. Busy well trained staff are kind and friendly. A sheltered back terrace has teak tables under square canvas parasols.

Brunning & Price ~ Manager Rachel Roberts ~ Real ale ~ Bar food (12-10(9.30 Sun)) ~ (0118) 940 3136 ~ Children welcome ~ Dogs allowed in bar ~ Open 12-11(10.30 Sun) ~ www.horseandgroom-harehatch.co.uk

HUNGERFORD   SU3368

Plume of Feathers

High Street; street parking opposite; RG17 0NB

Right at the heart of a bustling little town with well liked bar food and a relaxed family atmosphere

Our readers very much enjoy their visits to this well run town pub and there's always a genuinely friendly welcome to all customers. It's an open-plan place and stretches from its smallish bow-windowed façade around the island bar to an open fire in the stripped fireplace right at the back. There are armchairs and a black leather sofa around low tables under lowish beams on the left at the front and a mix of tables with padded chairs or cushioned small pews on the bare boards elsewhere. They have a fair choice of wines by the glass alongside Greene King IPA and Ruddles Best on handpump and good coffee, and the scottish landlord and his staff are unfailingly helpful. The sheltered back courtyard isn't large but is well worth knowing on a warm day: prettily planted, and with a swing seat as well as green-painted metal tables and chairs.

Greene King ~ Lease Haley and James Weir ~ Real ale ~ Bar food (12-2.30,7-9; not Sun evening) ~ (01488) 682154 ~ Children welcome ~ Dogs allowed in bar ~ Open 11-3, 5.30(6 Sat)-11; 12-4 Sun; closed Sun evening

INKPEN   SU3764

Crown & Garter

Inkpen Common: Inkpen signposted with Kintbury off A4; in Kintbury turn left into Inkpen Road, then keep on into Inkpen Common; RG17 9QR

Remote-feeling pub with appealing layout, character bars, good food and beer and particularly friendly landlady; lovely garden and nearby walks

This tucked away pub has been gently refurbished this year with contemporary paintwork throughout, original black and white or sepia photographs of local scenes on the walls, and new curtains and blinds. But the proper character of this 16th-c pub remains untouched and the friendly Mrs Hern is still very much at the helm. The low-ceilinged and relaxed panelled bar has West Berkshire Good Old Boy and a beer brewed just for the pub from the nearby Two Cocks Brewery called Gibbet Ale (it's worth asking about the name) on handpump, decent wines by the glass and several malt whiskies; a new cosy small sitting area just off here has armchairs and a leather sofa in front of the woodburning stove and books on shelves. Three original areas radiate the bar; our pick is the parquet-floored part by the raised woodburning stove which has a couple of substantial old tables and a huge old-fashioned slightly curved settle. Other parts are slate and wood with a good mix of well spaced tables and chairs, and nice lighting. The half-panelled restaurant now has comfortable, padded dark sea-green leather dining chairs around a mix of freshly scrubbed wooden tables on slate flooring. There's a front terrace for outside eating, a lovely long side garden with picnic-sets, and plenty of good downland walks nearby. In a separate single-storey building, the bedrooms (many have been redecorated recently) form an 'L' around a pretty garden. James II is reputed to have used the pub on his way to visit his mistress, who lived locally.

Free house ~ Licensee Gill Hern ~ Real ale ~ Bar food (12-2(2.30 Sun), 6.30(7.30 Sun)-9.30(9 Sun); not Mon and Tues lunchtimes) ~ Restaurant ~ (01488) 668325 ~ Children (over 7) allowed in bar only evenings and in bedrooms ~ Dogs allowed in bar ~ Open 12-3,

5.30-11; 12-5.30, 7-10.30 Sun; closed Mon and Tues lunchtimes ~ Bedrooms: £79.50B/£99B ~ www.crownandgarter.com

RUSCOMBE   SU7976

Royal Oak

Ruscombe Lane (B3024 just E of Twyford); RG10 9JN

Wide choice of popular food at welcoming pub with interesting furnishings and paintings, local beer and wine, and adjoining antiques and collectables shop

Known locally as Buratta's (which is what the pub's sign actually says so don't drive past), this remains an especially well run pub and our readers like it very much. The open-plan carpeted interior is well laid out so that each bit is fairly snug, but still manages to keep the overall feel of a lot of people enjoying themselves. A good variety of furniture runs from dark oak tables to big chunky pine ones with mixed seating to match – the two sofas facing one another are popular. Contrasting with the old exposed ceiling joists, mostly unframed modern paintings and prints decorate the walls – mainly dark terracotta over a panelled dado. Binghams (the brewery is just across the road) Brickworks and Twyford Tipple, and Fullers London Pride on handpump, champagne and a dozen wines by the glass (they stock wines from the Stanlake Park Vineyard in the village), several malt whiskies and good service. Picnic-sets are ranged around a venerable central hawthorn in the garden behind (where there are ducks and chickens); summer barbecues. The landlady's antiques and collectables shop is open during pub hours. The pub is on the Henley Arts Trail.

Enterprise ~ Lease Jenny and Stefano Buratta ~ Real ale ~ Bar food (12-2.30, 6-9.30; 12-3 Sun; not Sun or Mon evenings) ~ Restaurant ~ (0118) 934 5190 ~ Children welcome ~ Dogs allowed in bar ~ Open 12-3, 6-11; 12-3 Sun; closed Sun and Mon evenings ~ www.burattas.co.uk

SONNING   SU7575

Bull

Off B478, by church; village signed off A4 E of Reading; RG4 6UP

Pretty timbered inn in attractive spot near Thames, plenty of character in old-fashioned bars, Fullers beers, friendly staff and good food; bedrooms

So pretty when the wisteria is flowering, this is a fine black and white timbered, 16th-c inn near the Thames and our readers enjoy their visits here very much; the courtyard is bright with tubs of flowers. The two old-fashioned bar rooms have a good bustling atmosphere, plenty of chatty locals and Fullers Chiswick, Discovery, HSB, London Pride and a couple of guests on handpump served by friendly staff; good wines by the glass. There are low ceilings and heavy beams, cosy alcoves, leather armchairs and sofas, cushioned antique settles and low wooden chairs on bare boards, and open fireplaces. The dining room has a mix of wooden chairs and tables, rugs on parquet flooring and shelves of books. If you bear left through the ivy-clad churchyard opposite, then turn left along the bank of the River Thames, you come to a very pretty lock. The Thames Valley Park is close by. The bedrooms are well equipped and comfortable.

Gales (Fullers) ~ Manager Dennis Mason ~ Real ale ~ Bar food (11-9.30; 12-9 Sun) ~ Restaurant ~ (0118) 969 3901 ~ Children welcome ~ Dogs allowed in bar ~ Open 10am-11pm; 11am-10.30pm Sun ~ Bedrooms: /£99S(£125B) ~ www.fullershotels.com

STANFORD DINGLEY   SU5771
Old Boot
Off A340 via Bradfield, coming from A4 just W of M4 junction 12; RG7 6LT

Country furnishings and open fires in welcoming beamed bars, a choice of bar food, real ales, and rural views from seats in the garden

You can be sure of a warm welcome from the landlord and his staff in this stylish 18th-c pub. The beamed bar is just the place for a cosy winter drink with its two open fires (one in an inglenook) and they keep West Berkshire Good Old Boy and a guest such as Fullers London Pride on handpump and several wines by the glass. Also, fine old pews, settles, country chairs and polished tables, as well as some striking pictures and hunting prints, boot ornaments and fresh flowers. There's also a conservatory-style restaurant. From picnic-sets on the terrace and in the large, quiet garden there are pleasant rural views; a swing and a slide for children. More picnic-sets at the front are dotted between the flowering tubs.

Free house ~ Licensee John Haley ~ Real ale ~ Bar food (12-2, 7-9) ~ Restaurant ~ (0118) 974 4292 ~ Children welcome ~ Dogs allowed in bar ~ Open 11-3, 6-11; 11-11 Sat, Sun ~ www.oldbootinn.co.uk

SWALLOWFIELD   SU7364
George & Dragon
Church Road, towards Farley Hill; RG7 1TJ

Busy country pub with good nearby walks, enjoyable bar food, real ales, friendly service, and seats outside

Our readers really enjoy this comfortable, well run pub and there's always a wide mix of customers – all welcomed by the long-serving licensees. The various interconnected rooms have a thriving atmosphere and plenty of character – as well as beams and standing timbers, a happy mix of nice old dining chairs and settles around individual wooden tables, rugs on flagstones, lit candles, a big log fire and country prints on the red or bare brick walls; background music. Fullers London Pride, Ringwood Best and Sharps Doom Bar on handpump and quite a few wines by the glass served by friendly staff. There are picnic-sets on gravel or paving in the garden. They give details on their website of a circular four-mile walk that starts and ends at the pub.

Free house ~ Licensee Paul Dailey ~ Real ale ~ Bar food (12-2.30(3 Sun), 7-9.30(9 Sun)) ~ Restaurant ~ (0118) 9884432 ~ Well behaved children welcome ~ Dogs allowed in bar ~ Open 12-11(10 Sun) ~ www.georgeanddragonswallowfield.co.uk

UPPER BASILDON   SU5976
Red Lion
Off A329 NW of Pangbourne; Aldworth Road; RG8 8NG

Laid-back country pub with friendly family atmosphere, inventive food, and a good choice of drinks

'What an excellent pub' say several of our readers about this well run and genuinely friendly country pub. Of course many customers are here for the top class food but there are plenty of chatty drinkers (and maybe their dogs) and the atmosphere is relaxed and informal. There are chapel chairs, a few pews and miscellaneous stripped tables on the bare boards, a green leather chesterfield and armchair, and pale blue-grey paintwork throughout – even on the beams, ceiling and some of the top-stripped tables. Beyond a double-sided woodburning stove, a pitched-ceiling area has much the same furniture on cord carpet, but a big cut-glass chandelier and large mirror give it a slightly more formal dining feel. Brakspears Bitter, Otter Bitter, West Berkshire Good Old Boy and a weekly changing guest such as White Horse Brewery Bitter on handpump and an extensive wine list; the *Independent* and *Racing Post*, occasional background music and regular live music – usually jazz-related. There are sturdy picnic-sets in the sizeable enclosed garden, where they have summer barbecues and hog roasts.

Enterprise ~ Lease Alison Green ~ Real ale ~ Bar food (12-2.30, 6-9.30; 12-3.30, 6-9 Sun) ~ Restaurant ~ (01491) 671234 ~ Children welcome ~ Dogs allowed in bar ~ Open 11-3, 5-11; all day weekends ~ www.theredlionupperbasildon.co.uk

WHITE WALTHAM   SU8477
Beehive
Waltham Road (B3024 W of Maidenhead); SL6 3SH

Enjoyable bar food and welcoming staff at a traditional village pub

There's always a good, bustling atmosphere in this popular pub – and a friendly welcome from the landlord and his staff. To the right, several comfortably spacious areas have leather chairs around sturdy tables and there's a new brick-built room with glass doors opening on to the front terrace (the teak seats and picnic-sets here take in the pub's rather fine topiary). The neat bar to the left is brightened up by cheerful scatter cushions on its comfortable built-in wall seats and captain's chairs. Brakspears Bitter, Fullers London Pride, Greene King Abbot and a changing guest from Loddon on handpump, with ten wines by the glass and a good choice of soft drinks; background music, board games and a quiz evening on the last Thursday of the month. A good-sized sheltered back lawn has seats and tables; the village cricket field is opposite.

Enterprise ~ Lease Guy Martin ~ Real ale ~ Bar food (12-2.30, 5.30-9.30; 12-9.30(8.30 Sun) Sat) ~ Restaurant ~ (01628) 822877 ~ Well behaved children welcome ~ Dogs allowed in bar ~ Quiz night last Thurs of month ~ Open 11-3, 5-11; 11-11 Sat; 12-10.30 Sun ~ www.thebeehivewhitewaltham.co.uk

WINTERBOURNE   SU4572
Winterbourne Arms
3.7 miles from M4 junction 13; at A34 turn into Chieveley Services and follow Donnington signs to Arlington Lane, then follow Winterbourne signs; RG20 8BB

Bustling village pub with real ales, lots of wines by the glass, quite a choice of bar food and a large landscaped garden

Over 300 years old and once the village shop and post office and bakery (you can still see the remains of the bread oven), this is a pretty black and white village pub. The traditionally furnished bars have early prints and old photographs of the village on the pale washed or exposed stone walls, stools along the counter, a mix of pine dining chairs and tables, and a collection of old irons around the big fireplace; background music. Big windows take in peaceful views over rolling fields. Ramsbury Gold and a guest beer brewed by West Berkshire for the pub called Winterbourne Whistle Wetter on handpump and 20 wines by the glass including sparkling and sweet wines. There are seats outside in the large landscaped side garden and pretty flowering tubs and hanging baskets. The surrounding countryside here is lovely, with nearby walks to Snelsmore Common and Donnington Castle.

Free house ~ Licensee Frank Adams ~ Real ale ~ Bar food (12-2.30(3 Sun), 6-10(9 Sun)) ~ (01635) 248200 ~ Children welcome ~ Dogs allowed in bar ~ Open 12-3, 6-11; 12-10.30 Sun ~ www.winterbournearms.com

WOOLHAMPTON   SU5766

Rowbarge

Station Road; RG7 5SH

Carefully refurbished canalside Brunning & Price pub with lots of outside seating, rambling rooms with open fires, antiques and hundreds of prints and photographs, six real ales and good, bistro-style food

After an extensive refurbishment and under the umbrella of Brunning & Price, this is an 18th-c house next to the swing bridge on the Kennet & Avon canal. It's a fine spot in summer with good quality wooden chairs and tables on a decked terrace and lots of picnic-sets among trees by the water's edge; popular summer barbecues. Inside it's more-or-less open plan with six rambling rooms connected by open doorways and knocked-through walls: beams and timbering, plenty of nooks and crannies, open fires, and décor that's gently themed to represent the nearby canal. There are oars on walls and hundreds of prints and photographs (some of rowing and boats), old glass and stone bottles, fresh flowers, big house plants and evening candles; the many large mirrors create an impression of even more space. Throughout, there are antique dining chairs around various nice old tables, settles, built-in cushioned wall seating, armchairs, a group of high stools around a huge wooden barrel table, and rugs on polished boards, stone tiles or carpeting. Friendly, helpful staff serve Brunning & Price Bitter (brewed for them by Phoenix) and West Berkshire Good Old Boy on handpump with four guest beers such as Longdog Bunny Chaser and Golden Poacher, and Three Castles Corn Dolly and Saxon Archer, 20 wines by the glass and over 50 malt whiskies.

Brunning & Price ~ Manager Stephen Butt ~ Real ale ~ Bar food (12-9.30) ~ (0118) 971 2213 ~ Children welcome ~ Dogs allowed in bar ~ Open 11.30-11(10.30 Sun) ~ www.rowbarge.hcpr.co.uk

Chips Launder – golden cocker spaniel

DOG FRIENDLY INNS, HOTELS AND B&Bs

CHIEVELEY   SU4574

Crab at Chieveley

Wantage Road, Chieveley, Berkshire RG20 8UE (01635) 247550 www.crabatchieveley.com

£140; 14 interestingly furnished rms named after exotic locations and famous hotels, some with hot tub on private terrace. Extended and partly thatched restaurant-with-rooms famous for its top quality seafood dishes (they do non-fishy things too) with brasserie area and more formal restaurant decorated with fishing nets, floats and shells; friendly, efficient service; seats on front terrace among big flowering pots; dogs in hot tub bedrooms only

EAST GARSTON   SU3676

Queens Arms

Newbury Road, East Garston, Hungerford, Berkshire RG17 7ET (01488) 648757 www.queensarmshotel.co.uk

£100; 8 attractive rms. Smart but chatty dining pub right in the heart of racehorse training country with a roomy, opened-up bar, antique prints (many featuring jockeys), daily papers (the most prominent being the *Racing Post*), traditional pubby seats and tables on the wooden floor, local beers and a fair choice of whiskies; a lighter dining area has horse and country prints, a pleasing mix of furniture, enjoyable food served by friendly staff, and tasty breakfasts; plenty of downland walks nearby; dogs welcome anywhere

ETON   SU9677

Christopher Hotel

110 High Street, Eton, Windsor, Berkshire SL4 6AN (01753) 852359 www.thechristopher.co.uk

£145; 34 well equipped rms – those in the main house have the most character. Early 18th-c former coaching inn just across the river from Windsor Castle; the relaxed, informal half-panelled bar has sofas and armchairs on stripped floorboards and offers some sort of food all day including morning coffee and afternoon teas, and the smart restaurant serves enjoyable bistro-style meals; a small outside terrace has seats and tables and there's a field behind for dogs to exercise in; resident spaniels George and Harry, and labrador Flame; dogs in bedrooms; £10

HUNGERFORD   SU3369

Bear Hotel

41 Charnham Street, Hungerford, Berkshire RG17 0EL (01488) 682512 www.thebearhotelhungerford.co.uk

£142.50; 39 stylish, well equipped rms, some with views over the river. Civilised and carefully restored 13th-c hotel with open fires, a contemporary bar with pale wooden chairs and tables on the tiled floor, real ales and good wines by the glass, a cosy and relaxing snug with sofas and daily papers, and a beamed brasserie restaurant with a wide choice of good modern food; seats in the courtyard and riverside terrace; dog biscuits and maybe treats and doggy stockings at Christmas; walks by canal or on common two mins away; dogs in bedrooms and bar

PANGBOURNE   SU6376

Elephant

Church Road, Pangbourne, Berkshire RG8 7AR (01189) 842244 www.elephanthotel.co.uk

£155; 22 interestingly decorated rms. Victorian hotel decorated in colonial style with indian furniture on oriental rugs and bare boards, lots of elephant ornaments, a comfortable lounge with sofas and armchairs in front of the fire, a bustling friendly bar with pubby furniture, lots of prints and local beers, and an elegant restaurant; food is very good and ranges from simple to inventive, and service is helpful and cheerful; dogs welcome away from restaurant; £20

STREATLEY   SU5980

Swan at Streatley

High Street, Streatley, Reading, Berkshire RG8 9HR (01491) 878800
www.swanatstreatley.com

£115; 45 attractive rms, many overlooking the water. Well run, friendly riverside hotel with comfortable, relaxed lounges and bars, consistently good food in attractive restaurant, a popular spa with indoor pool, and flower-filled gardens where dogs may walk – other walks nearby; you can hire self-drive electric boats (not in winter) – great fun; dogs in bedrooms and most public areas (not dining room); £20

YATTENDON   SU5574

Royal Oak

The Square, Yattendon, Newbury, Berkshire RG18 0UG (01635) 201325
www.royaloakyattendon.co.uk

£85; 10 attractive rms. Handsome old inn by the village square and close to Newbury Racecourse (so it does get busy on race days); plenty of civilised character in spacious, charming rooms; beams and panelling, appealing chairs and tables on quarry tiles or wooden boards, interesting prints on brick, cream or red walls, lovely flowers, real ales (brewed in the village), carefully chosen wines, and four log fires; the food is modern and imaginative and the breakfasts delicious; dogs anywhere in the pub and in bedrooms

Buckinghamshire

DOG FRIENDLY PUBS

ADSTOCK   SP7330
Old Thatched Inn
Main Street, off A413; MK18 2JN

Pretty thatched dining pub with keen landlord, friendly staff, real ales and enjoyable food

Run with great care for both his pub and his customers, the hands-on landlord of this pretty thatched place remains as enthusiastic as ever. The pubby front bar has low beams, flagstones, high bar chairs and an open fire, and leads on to a dining area with more beams and a mix of pale wooden dining chairs around miscellaneous tables on the stripped wooden floor. There's a modern conservatory restaurant at the back. Fullers London Pride, Hook Norton Hooky Bitter, Sharps Doom Bar and Timothy Taylors Landlord on handpump, several wines by the glass and a dozen malt whiskies served by friendly staff. The sheltered terrace has tables and chairs under a gazebo. This is an attractive village.

Free house ~ Licensee Andrew Judge ~ Real ale ~ Bar food (12-2.30, 6-9.30; 12-8 Sun) ~ Restaurant ~ (01296) 712584 ~ Children welcome ~ Dogs allowed in bar ~ Open 12-midnight ~ www.theoldthatchedinn.co.uk

BOVINGDON GREEN   SU8386
Royal Oak
0.75 miles N of Marlow, on back road to Frieth signposted off West Street (A4155) in centre; SL7 2JF

A fine choice of wines by the glass, real ales, excellent food and good service at a civilised dining pub

Always friendly and welcoming, this little whitewashed pub remains as popular as ever with our readers. And while many customers are here for the imaginative food, you will be made just as welcome by the helpful staff if it's just a pint and a chat that you want. Locals tend to head for the low-beamed cosy snug, closest to the car park, which has three small tables, a woodburning stove in an exposed brick fireplace (with a big pile of logs beside it), Rebellion IPA and Smuggler (and Mutiny in summer) on handpump, 22 wines by the glass (all from Europe), nine pudding wines, a good choice of liqueurs and farm cider. Several attractively decorated areas open off the central bar: the half-panelled walls variously painted in pale blue, green or cream (though the dining room ones are red). Throughout, there's a mix of church chairs, stripped wooden tables and chunky wall seats, with rugs on the partly wooden, partly flagstoned floors, co-ordinated cushions and curtains, and a very bright, airy feel; thoughtful extra touches enhance the tone: a bowl of olives on the bar, carefully laid-out newspapers and fresh flowers or candles on the tables. Board games and background music. A sunny terrace with good solid tables leads to an appealing garden, there's a smaller side and a kitchen herb garden, and pétanque. Red kites regularly fly over.

Salisbury Pubs ~ Lease Philip Daley ~ Real ale ~ Bar food (12-2.30(3 Sat, 4 Sun), 6.30-9.30(10 Fri, Sat)) ~ Restaurant ~ (01628) 488611 ~ Children welcome ~ Dogs allowed in bar ~ Open 11-11; 12-10.30 Sun ~ www.royaloakmarlow.co.uk

CHENIES   TQ0298

Red Lion

2 miles from M25 junction 18; A404 towards Amersham, then village signposted on right; Chesham Road; WD3 6ED

Delightful pub with long-serving licensees, a bustling atmosphere, real ales and good food

Our readers love this white-painted brick house because it's smart but friendly, properly pubby and has a jovial licensee who still offers a genuinely warm welcome to all his customers after 26 years at the helm. The L-shaped bar is very traditional and unpretentious (no games machines or background music) and has comfortable built-in wall benches by the front windows, other straightforward seats and tables, and original photographs of the village and traction engines. There's also a small back snug and a neat dining extension with more modern décor. Well kept Lion Pride is brewed for the pub by Rebellion and served on handpump alongside Vale Best Bitter and a couple of changing guests like Thwaites Best Bitter and Wadworths 6X, and they have up to ten wines by the glass and some nice malt whiskies. The hanging baskets and window boxes are pretty in summer, there are picnic-sets on a small side terrace, and good local walks. They now call themselves an autarkic (self-sufficient) free house. No children.

Free house ~ Licensee Mike Norris ~ Real ale ~ Bar food (12-2,7-10(9.30 Sun)) ~ Restaurant ~ (01923) 282722 ~ Dogs allowed in bar ~ Open 11-2.30, 5.30-11; 12-3, 6.30-10.30 Sun ~ www.theredlionchenies.co.uk

COLESHILL   SU9594

Harte & Magpies

E of village on A355 Amersham–Beaconsfield, by junction with Magpie Lane; HP7 0LU

Friendly, professionally run roadside dining pub with enjoyable all-day food, well kept local ales and seats in big garden

With plenty of nearby walks, it's really useful that this bustling pub serves food all day – from 10am for breakfast. It's a big, open-plan place but its rambling collection of miscellaneous pews, high-backed booths and some quite distinctive tables and chairs and cosy boltholes over to the right give it a pleasantly snug feel; as we went to press they were taking up the carpets and polishing the old floorboards underneath. There's a profusion of vigorously patriotic antique prints, candles in bottles and Scrumpy Jack the self-possessed young labrador, who adds a relaxed country touch – as does the jar of dog treats. Chiltern Ale, Rebellion Smuggler and a changing guest beer on handpump and a good choice of other drinks, too; service is friendly and civilised. Outside, a terrace has picnic-sets by a tree picturesquely draped with wisteria and a big sloping informal garden has more trees and more tables on wood chippings. This is under the same ownership as the Royal Standard of England at Forty Green.

Free house ~ Licensee Stephen Lever ~ Real ale ~ Bar food (10-9.45; 12-8 Sun) ~ (01494) 726754 ~ Children welcome ~ Dogs allowed in bar ~ Live music Sat evening ~ Open 10am-11pm; 11-10 Sun ~ www.magpiespub.com

DENHAM   TQ0487

Swan

Village signed from M25 junction 16; UB9 5BH

Double-fronted, civilised dining pub in pretty village with stylish furnishings in several bars, open fires, interesting food and a fine choice of drinks

In a quiet and lovely village, this is a handsome Georgian pub that cleverly manages to appeal to both diners and drinkers. The rooms are stylishly furnished with a nice mix of antique and old-fashioned chairs and solid tables, individually chosen pictures on the cream and warm green walls, rich heavily draped curtains, inviting open fires, newspapers to read and fresh flowers. Caledonian Flying Scotsman and Rebellion IPA and a summer guest beer on handpump, 22 european wines by the glass, plus nine pudding wines and a good choice of liqueurs; background music. The extensive garden is floodlit at night, and leads from a sheltered terrace with tables to a more spacious lawn; the wisteria is beautiful in May. It can get busy at weekends and parking may be not be easy then.

Salisbury Pubs ~ Lease Mark Littlewood ~ Real ale ~ Bar food (12-2.30(3 Sat, 4 Sun), 6.30-9.30(10 Fri, Sat)) ~ Restaurant ~ (01895) 832085 ~ Children welcome ~ Dogs allowed in bar ~ Open 11-11; 12-10.30 Sun ~ www.swaninndenham.co.uk

FINGEST   SU7791

Chequers

Off B482 Marlow–Stokenchurch; RG9 6QD

Friendly, spotlessly kept old pub with big garden, real ales and interesting food

Surrounded by good walks, this 15th-c pub is just the place for a pre- or post-walk break. As well as an unaffected public bar with real country charm, the other neatly kept old-fashioned rooms are warm, cosy and traditional, with large open fires, horsebrasses, pewter tankards and pub team photographs on the walls. Brakspears Bitter and Special and a guest like Banks's Sunbeam on handpump alongside quite a few wines by the glass and several malt whiskies; board games. French doors from the smart back dining extension open to a terrace (plenty of picnic-sets), which leads on to the big garden with fine views over the Hambleden valley. Over the road is a unique Norman twin-roofed church tower – probably the nave of the original church.

Brakspears ~ Tenants Jaxon and Emma Keedwell ~ Real ale ~ Bar food (12-2(3 Sat, 4 Sun), 7-9(9.30 Fri, Sat)) ~ Restaurant ~ (01491) 638335 ~ Children welcome ~ Dogs allowed in bar ~ Open 12-3, 5.30-11; 12-11 Sat; 12-10.30 Sun ~ www.chequersfingest.com

FORD   SP7709

Dinton Hermit

SW of Aylesbury; HP17 8XH

Thoughtfully furnished dining pub with enjoyable food, big inglenook in the bar, cosy restaurant and seats in pretty garden; nicely decorated bedrooms in main building and converted barn

This is a carefully extended 16th-c stone inn with pretty summer window boxes and flower-filled wooden tubs; there are picnic-sets under parasols in the quiet back garden and lots of walks in the surrounding countryside. Inside, the little bar has timbered walls, a happy mix of chairs and wooden tables on the nice old black and red tiled floor, white-painted plaster on thick uneven stone walls, an old print of John Bigg, the supposed executioner of King Charles I and the man later known as the Dinton Hermit, and a huge inglenook fireplace. The back dining area has similar furniture on quarry tiles and church candles. Adnams Bitter and a guest from Vale on handpump and several wines by the glass. The contemporary bedrooms are comfortable and some are in the converted barn.

Free house ~ Licensee David White ~ Real ale ~ Bar food (12-2(3 Sun), 7-9(6.30-8.30 Sun)) ~ Restaurant ~ (01296) 747473 ~ Children welcome ~ Dogs allowed in bar ~ Open 11am-midnight; 11-10.30(8.30 winter) Sun ~ Bedrooms: /£110S ~ www.dintonhermit.co.uk

FORTY GREEN   SU9291

Royal Standard of England

3.5 miles from M40 junction 2, via A40 to Beaconsfield, then follow sign to Forty Green, off B474 0.75 miles N of New Beaconsfield; keep going through village; HP9 1XT

Ancient place with fascinating antiques in rambling rooms, and good choice of drinks and food

Yet another feather in the cap for this especially well run pub is that they now brew their own beer – as we went to press they just had Britannia Pale Ale on offer. This is joined by six changing guests from other breweries such as Brakspears, Chiltern, Rebellion, and Windsor & Eton; there's also a carefully annotated list of bottled beers and malt whiskies, farm ciders, perry, somerset brandy and around a dozen wines by the glass. Our readers love this old place for its history (it's been trading for nearly 900 years and they have an interesting leaflet documenting the pub's history), for the consistently warm welcome, all-day food and the many fascinating things to look at; it's also used regularly for filming programmes such as Midsomer Murders. The rambling rooms have huge black ship's timbers, lovely worn floors, finely carved old oak panelling, roaring winter fires with handsomely decorated iron firebacks and cluttered mantelpieces, and there's a massive settle apparently built to fit the curved transom of an Elizabethan ship. Nooks and crannies are filled with a collection of antiques, including rifles, powder-flasks and bugles, ancient pewter and pottery tankards, lots of tarnished brass and copper, needlework samplers and richly coloured stained glass; board games. You can sit outside in a neatly hedged front rose garden or under the shade of a tree.

Own brew ~ Licensee Matthew O'Keeffe ~ Real ale ~ Bar food (11.30am-10pm) ~ (01494) 673382 ~ Children welcome ~ Dogs allowed in bar ~ Open 11-11; 12-10.30 Sun ~ www.rsoe.co.uk

FULMER

SU9985

Black Horse

Village signposted off A40 in Gerrards Cross, W of its junction with A413; Windmill Road; SL3 6HD

Appealingly reworked dining pub, friendly and relaxed, with enjoyable up-to-date food, exemplary service and pleasant garden

Dating from the 17th c when these cottages were built for craftsmen, this extended dining pub has a lot of character and a warm welcome for all. There's a proper bar area on the left – three smallish rooms with low black beams, parquet floor or a rug on bare boards, very mixed tables and chairs, Greene King IPA and Old Speckled Hen and a changing guest beer on handpump; 22 european wines by the glass, nine pudding wines and a good range of liqueurs; service is prompt, friendly and efficient. The main area on the right is set for dining with comfortable, modern dining chairs on a beige carpet and the rest of the pub has a relaxed and contented atmosphere; background music. The good-sized back terrace, below the church, has teak and wrought-iron tables and chairs, with picnic-sets on the sheltered grass beyond. This is a charming conservation village.

Salisbury Pubs ~ Lease Richard Coletta ~ Real ale ~ Bar food (12-2.30(3 Sat, 4 Sun), 6.30-9.30(10 Fri and Sat)) ~ Restaurant ~ (01753) 663183 ~ Children welcome ~ Dogs allowed in bar ~ Open 11-11; 12-10.30 Sun ~ www.blackhorsefulmer.co.uk

GREAT MISSENDEN

SP9000

Nags Head

Old London Road, E – beyond Abbey; HP16 0DG

Well run and pretty inn with beamed bars, an open fire, a good range of drinks and good modern cooking; comfortable bedrooms

Built in the late 15th c as three small cottages, this pretty brick and flint inn was used by Roald Dahl as his local and there are several of his limited edition prints in the dining areas; the Roald Dahl Museum and Story Centre is just a stroll away. It's a quietly civilised and neatly kept place with a low beamed area on the left, a loftier part on the right, a mix of small pews, dining chairs and tables on the carpet, Quentin Blake prints on the cream walls and a log fire in a handsome fireplace. Fullers London Pride, Sharps Doom Bar and a changing guest from Tring, Rebellion or Vale on handpump from the unusual bar counter (the windows behind face the road) and a dozen wines by the glass from an extensive list. There's an outside dining area under a pergola and seats on the extensive back lawn. The beamed bedrooms are well equipped and attractive.

Free house ~ Licensee Adam Michaels ~ Real ale ~ Bar food (12-2.30(3.30 Sun), 6.30-9.30(8.30 Sun)) ~ (01494) 862200 ~ Children welcome ~ Dogs allowed in bar ~ Open 12-11(10.30 Sun) ~ Bedrooms: /£95B ~ www.nagsheadbucks.com

HEDGERLEY

SU9687

White Horse

2.4 miles from M40 junction 2; at exit roundabout take Slough turn-off following alongside M40; after 1.5 miles turn right at T junction into Village Lane; SL2 3UY

Old-fashioned drinkers' pub with lots of beers tapped straight from the cask, regular beer festivals, home-made lunchtime food and a cheery mix of customers

You'd never believe this little country gem is in the Gerrards Cross commuter belt – it feels a world away. Thankfully, little changes here and you can still be sure of a warmly friendly welcome and a marvellous choice of up to eight real ales. As well as Rebellion IPA they keep up to seven daily changing guests, sourced from all over the country and tapped straight from casks kept in a room behind the tiny hatch counter. Their Easter, May, Spring and August bank holiday beer festivals (they can get through about 130 beers during the May one) are a highlight of the local calendar. This fine range of drinks extends to three farm ciders, still apple juice, a perry, belgian beers, ten or so wines by the glass and winter mulled wine. The cottagey main bar has plenty of unspoilt character, with lots of beams, brasses and exposed brickwork, low wooden tables, standing timbers, jugs, ballcocks and other bric-a-brac, a log fire, and a good few leaflets and notices about village events. A little flagstoned public bar on the left has darts and board games. A canopy extension leads out to the garden where there are tables and occasional barbecues, and there are lots of hanging baskets and a couple more tables in front of the building overlooking the quiet road. Good walks nearby, and the pub is handy for the Church Wood RSPB reserve and popular with walkers and cyclists; it can get crowded at weekends.

Free house ~ Licensees Doris Hobbs and Kevin Brooker ~ Real ale ~ Bar food (lunchtime only) ~ (01753) 643225 ~ Children in canopy extension area ~ Dogs allowed in bar ~ Open 11-2.30, 5-11; 11-11 Sat; 12-10.30 Sun

HUGHENDEN VALLEY

SU8697

Harrow

Warrendene Road, off A4128 N of High Wycombe; HP14 4LX

Little roadside pub near pleasant walks, traditional furnishings in two bars, a separate dining room, woodburning stove, real ales, home-cooked food, friendly staff and seats outside

In a nice spot at the start of Chilterns valley walks, this is a small brick and flint roadside cottage with traditional furnishings. There's a tiled-floor bar on the left with black beams and joists, a woodburner in the big fireplace with pewter mugs on its high mantelbeam, lots of country pictures on the white walls and wall seats, dining chairs and stools around a mix of tables. The bigger right-hand bar is similarly furnished with sizeable dining tables on the brick floor and there's a carpeted dining room at the back. The atmosphere throughout is cheerful and easy-going. Courage Best, Fullers London Pride and Shepherd Neame Spitfire on handpump served by friendly staff. In front of the building there are plenty of picnic-sets, with more on a back lawn; children's play area and disabled access.

S&N ~ Lease Fiona Brocklebank ~ Real ale ~ Bar food (12-2.30, 6.30-9.30; 12-9.30(5 Sun) Sat; not Sun evening) ~ Restaurant ~ (01494) 564105 ~ Children welcome ~ Dogs allowed in bar ~ Quiz night Tues 9pm ~ Open 12-11(10.30 Sun) ~ www.harrowhughenden.co.uk

LONG CRENDON

SP6908

Eight Bells

High Street, off B4011 N of Thame; car park entrance off Chearsley Road, not 'Village roads only'; HP18 9AL

Good beers and sensibly priced pubby food in nicely traditional village pub with charming garden

The little garden at the back of this unassuming pub is a joy in summer and there are well spaced picnic-sets among a colourful variety of shrubs and flowers; aunt sally. Inside, it's a friendly place with an unassuming and unchanging character and the little bare-boards bar on the left has well kept Hel's Bells (brewed for the pub) and Wadworths IPA on handpump and three changing guests tapped from the cask such as Jennings Bitter, Northumberland St James' Park Bitter and White Horse Champion the Wonder Horse; they also have a decent choice of wines by the glass. A bigger low-ceilinged room on the right has a log fire, daily papers, darts and a pleasantly haphazard mix of tables and simple seats on its ancient red and black tiles; one snug little hidey-hole with just three tables is devoted to the local morris men – frequent visitors; service is cheerful. The interesting old village is known to many from TV's Midsomer Murders.

Free house ~ Licensee Helen Copleston ~ Real ale ~ Bar food (12-2(2.30 Sun), 6-9; not Sun evening or all day Mon) ~ (01844) 208244 ~ Children welcome ~ Dogs allowed in bar ~ Open 12-3, 5.30-11; 12-11 Sun and Sat; closed Mon lunchtime ~ www.eightbellspub.com

PENN   SU9093
Old Queens Head
Hammersley Lane/Church Road, off B474 between Penn and Tylers Green; HP10 8EY

Stylishly updated pub with imaginative woodland walks nearby

After a walk through the ancient beechwoods of Common or Penn Woods, this extended dining pub, with its 17th-c heart, is just the place to head for. It's open-plan and decorated in a stylish mix of contemporary and chintz, with well spaced tables in a variety of linked areas, a modicum of old prints, and comfortably varied seating on flagstones or broad dark boards. Stairs take you up to an attractive (and popular) two-level dining room, part carpeted, with stripped rafters. The active bar side has Greene King IPA and Ruddles County on handpump, 22 wines by the glass, eight pudding wines and quite a few liqueurs; the turntable-top bar stools let you swivel to face the log fire in the big nearby fireplace. There are lots of daily papers and well reproduced background music. The sunny terrace overlooks the church of St Margaret's and there are picnic-sets on the sheltered L-shaped lawn.

Salisbury Pubs ~ Lease Tina Brown ~ Real ale ~ Bar food (12-2.30(3 Sat, 4 Sun), 6.30-9.30(10 Fri, Sat)) ~ Restaurant ~ (01494) 813371 ~ Children welcome ~ Dogs allowed in bar ~ Open 11-11; 12-10.30 Sun ~ www.oldqueensheadpenn.co.uk

PRESTWOOD   SP8799
Polecat
170 Wycombe Road (A4128 N of High Wycombe); HP16 0HJ

Enjoyable food, real ales and a chatty atmosphere in several smallish civilised rooms; attractive sizeable garden

Civilised and rather smart, this well run country pub has a quietly chatty atmosphere and helpful, friendly staff. Several smallish rooms, opening off the low-ceilinged bar, have a slightly chintzy décor: an assortment of tables and chairs, various stuffed birds, stuffed white polecats in one big cabinet, small country pictures, rugs on bare boards or red tiles, and a couple of antique housekeeper's chairs by a good open fire. Brakspears Bitter, Greene King Old Speckled Hen, Marstons Pedigree and Ringwood Best on handpump, 16 wines by the glass, 20 malt whiskies and home-made summer elderflower pressé. The garden is most attractive with lots of spring bulbs and colourful summer hanging baskets and tubs, and herbaceous plants; quite a few picnic-sets under parasols on neat grass out in front beneath a big fairy-lit pear tree, with more on a big well kept back lawn. They don't take bookings at lunchtime (except for tables of six or more) so you do need to arrive promptly at weekends to be sure of a table.

Free house ~ Licensee John Gamble ~ Real ale ~ Bar food (12-2, 6.30-9 (not Sun evening)) ~ (01494) 862253 ~ Children in gallery or drovers' bar only ~ Dogs allowed in bar ~ Open 11.30-2.30, 6-11; 12-3 Sun; closed Sun evening.

SKIRMETT   SU7790

Frog

From A4155 NE of Henley take Hambleden turn and keep on; or from B482 Stokenchurch–Marlow take Turville turn and keep on; RG9 6TG

Bustling pub with modern cooking in a traditional atmosphere, fine choice of drinks, lovely garden and nearby walks; bedrooms

Although many customers visit this 18th-c coaching inn for the imaginative food, the public bar is still very much the heart of the place. There's a winter log fire in the brick fireplace with lots of little framed prints above it, a cushioned sofa and leather-seated bar stools around a low circular table on the wooden floor, and high bar chairs by the counter; background music. Rebellion IPA, Gales Seafarer and a changing guest beer on handpump, a dozen wines by the glass (including champagne) and around two dozen carefully sourced malt whiskies. The two dining rooms are quite different in style – one is light and airy with country kitchen tables and chairs and the other is more formal with dark red walls, smarter dining chairs and tables and candlelight. Outside, a side gate leads to a lovely garden with a large tree in the middle and the unusual five-sided tables are well placed for attractive valley views. Plenty of nearby hikes (Henley is close by) and just down the road is the delightful Ibstone windmill. There's a purpose-built outdoor heated area for smokers. The breakfasts are good (though it might be worth asking for a bedroom that isn't right above the bar).

Free house ~ Licensees Jim Crowe and Noelle Greene ~ Real ale ~ Bar food (12-2.30, 6.30-9.30; not winter Sun evenings) ~ Restaurant ~ (01491) 638996 ~ Children welcome ~ Dogs allowed in bar ~ Open 11.30-3, 6-11; 12-4, 6-10.30 Sun; closed Sun evening Oct-May ~ Bedrooms: £60B/£80B ~ www.thefrogatskirmett.co.uk

WENDOVER   SP8609

Village Gate

Aylesbury Road (B4009); HP22 6BA

Well run country pub with plenty of outside seating, friendly bar and several dining rooms, real ales and well liked food

In warm weather there's plenty of outside seating around this neatly kept cream-painted brick dining pub: grey high-backed wicker or modern metal chairs and picnic-sets on a roped-off decked area covered by a giant parasol, on terracing, on a raised decked area and on gravel – and there are long-reaching country views at the back. Inside, the interconnected rooms have contemporary paintwork and furnishings and the atmosphere is easy-going and friendly. The bar has red leather tub chairs around log tables with polished tops in front of the woodburning stove in its brick fireplace, chunky leather stools and a mix of dining chairs around various tables, and animal prints on the walls above the half-panelling. High leather bar chairs sit against the modern bar counter with its unusual metal decoration and they keep Fullers London Pride with guests like Greene King IPA and St Austell Tribute on handpump. The other rooms are laid out for eating with high-backed plush, wooden or leather dining chairs around a mix of tables on oak boarding (some carpeting and stone tiling, too); one of the rooms has rafters and beams in a very high ceiling and long swagged curtains.

Free house ~ Licensee John Johnston ~ Real ale ~ Bar food (12-3, 6-10; 12-8 Sun) ~ Restaurant ~ (01296) 623884 ~ Children welcome ~ Dogs allowed in bar ~ Occasional live bands ~ Open 12-11.30(midnight Fri, Sat); 12-10.30 Sun ~ www.villagegatewendover.com

WOOBURN COMMON   SU9187

Chequers

From A4094 N of Maidenhead at junction with A4155 Marlow road keep on A4094 for another 0.75 miles, then at roundabout turn off right towards Wooburn Common and into Kiln Lane; if you find yourself in Honey Hill, Hedsor, turn left into Kiln Lane at the top of the hill; OS Sheet 175 map reference 910870; HP10 0JQ

Busy and friendly hotel with a bustling bar, four real ales and more elaborate food and refurbished restaurant; comfortable bedrooms

The same friendly family have run this 17th-c former coaching inn for over 35 years and despite much emphasis being placed on the bustling hotel side, its heart is still the main bar, which continues to thrive as a welcoming local. It feels nicely pubby with low beams, standing timbers and alcoves, characterful rickety furniture and comfortably lived-in sofas on bare boards, a bright log-effect gas fire, pictures, plates, a two-man saw and tankards. In contrast, the bar to the left, with its dark brown leather sofas at low tables on wooden floors, feels plain and modern; the restaurant has been recently refurbished. They keep Greene King Old Speckled Hen, Rebellion Smuggler, XT4 from the new XT Brewing Company and a changing guest on handpump, have a good sizeable wine list (with a dozen by the glass) and a fair range of malt whiskies and brandies; background music. The spacious garden, set away from the road, has seats around cast-iron tables, and summer barbecues.

Free house ~ Licensee Peter Roehrig ~ Real ale ~ Bar food (12-2.30, 6-9.30; all day weekends) ~ Restaurant ~ (01628) 529575 ~ Children welcome ~ Dogs allowed in bar ~ Open 11am-midnight(11pm Sun) ~ Bedrooms: £99.50B/£107.50B ~ www.chequers-inn.com

DOG FRIENDLY INNS, HOTELS AND B&Bs

AYLESBURY   SP7812

Hartwell House

Oxford Road, Aylesbury, Buckinghamshire HP17 8NL (01296) 747444
www.hartwell-house.com

£370; 30 extremely comfortable rms and suites in main house over three floors and 6 rms and 10 suites in restored 18th-c stables with private garden and statues. Elegant Grade I listed building with Jacobean and Georgian façades, wonderful decorative plasterwork and panelling, fine paintings and antiques, a marvellous gothic central staircase, splendid morning room, a library, fine wines and excellent food in three dining rooms, and exceptional service; 90 acres of parkland with ruined church, lake and statues, and spa with indoor swimming pool, saunas, gym and beauty rooms, and a café and bar; tennis, croquet and fishing; dog walking in grounds and on nearby footpaths; dogs in Hartwell Court suites only

BENNETT END

SU7897

Three Horseshoes

Horseshoe Road, Bennett End, High Wycombe, Buckinghamshire HP14 4EB (01494)
483273 www.thethreehorseshoes.net

£90; 6 comfortable rms in attic or annexe. Nicely converted country pub in lovely quiet spot – seemingly off the beaten track but handy for M40; flagstoned snug bar with soft lighting and a log fire in the raised fireplace, original brickwork and bread oven, two further sitting areas, one with a long winged settle, the other enclosed by standing timbers, and a stone-floor dining room with big windows overlooking the garden (where there are seats by a pond with ducks and a sunken red telephone box); real ales, wines by the glass and good modern cooking; walks in nearby big field, by the Thames and on the Red Kite Walk and Chiltern Way; dogs in bar and bedrooms; bowls and biscuits provided

MARLOW

SU8586

Macdonald Compleat Angler

Bisham Road, Marlow, Buckinghamshire SL7 1RG (0844) 879 9128
www.macdonald-hotels.co.uk/compleatangler

£197; 64 pretty, stylish rms named after fishing flies and overlooking garden or river. Famous Thames-side hotel with oak-panelled, 400-year-old bar, comfortable lounge, spacious beamed restaurant and conservatory-style brasserie with riverside terrace, imaginative food using the best produce, and courteous, helpful service; tennis, croquet, coarse fishing and private launches and boats for hire; dogs in bedrooms with treats and in bar/lounge; £10

TAPLOW

SU9185

Cliveden

Taplow, Maidenhead, Berkshire SL6 0JF (01628) 668561 www.clivedenhouse.co.uk

£255; plus £10.10 to National Trust (doggy break packages available, too); 38 luxurious rms and suites named after a prominent guest or figure from Cliveden's past. Superb Grade I listed stately home with gracious, comfortable public rooms, antiques, fine paintings, and lovely flower arrangements, and a surprisingly unstuffy atmosphere; lovely views over the magnificent Thames-side parkland and formal gardens; exceptional food in two restaurants with lighter meals in the conservatory, super breakfasts, and impeccable staff; Pavilion Spa with heated indoor and outdoor pools, canadian hot tubs, whirlpool spas, separate men's and ladies' steam rooms and sauna and treatment rooms; tennis, squash, croquet, and boats for river trips; dogs can walk in most parts of the 250 acres of grounds; dogs anywhere except dining rooms and spa; beds, bowls and special menu

WINSLOW

SP7627

Bell

Market Square, Winslow, Buckingham, Buckinghamshire MK18 3AB (01296) 714091
www.thebell-hotel.com

£79; 41 rms, some with four-posters. Elegant black and white timbered inn overlooking the market square, with beams and open fires, a plush hotel bar, all-day coffee lounge, enjoyable bar food, and good lunchtime and evening carvery in restaurant; dogs in seven bedrooms; £10

Cambridgeshire

MAP 5

DOG FRIENDLY PUBS

BALSHAM
Black Bull
TL5850

Village signposted off A11 SW of Newmarket, and off A1307 in Linton; High Street; CB21 4DJ

Pretty thatched pub with bedroom extension – a good all-rounder – enjoyable food, too

This thatched 17th-c inn has a good mix of both locals and visitors all welcomed by the friendly landlord. The beamed bar spreads around a central servery where they keep Adnams Bitter, Greene King IPA, Woodfordes Wherry and a guest beer like Nethergate Augustinian on handpump and a good choice of wines by the glass. Dividers and standing timbers break up the space, which has an open fire, floorboards, low black beams in the front part and seating including small leatherette-seated dining chairs. A restaurant extension with pitched rafters and timbered ochre walls was being refurbished as we went to press. The front terrace has teak tables and chairs by a long, pleasantly old-fashioned verandah and there are more seats in a small sheltered back garden. Bedrooms are in a neat single-storey extension. This pub is under the same good ownership as the Red Lion at Hinxton.

Free house ~ Licensee Alex Clarke ~ Real ale ~ Bar food (12-2(2.30 Fri-Sun), 6.30(7 Sun)-9(9.30 Fri and Sat) ~ Restaurant ~ (01223) 893844 ~ Well behaved children welcome ~ Dogs allowed in bar ~ Jazz singer first Sat of month ~ Open 11-3.30, 6-11.30; 8.30am-11.30pm Sat; 8.30am-4.30, 7-10.30 Sun ~ Bedrooms: £79B/£99B ~ www.blackbull-balsham.co.uk

CAMBRIDGE
Free Press
TL4558

Prospect Row; CB1 1DU

Quiet and unspoilt with interesting local décor, up to six real ales and good value food

Away from the tourist trail in a pretty little back street, this is just the place for a quiet pint by the warm log fire with no noisy mobile phones, background music or games machines to disturb the peace. In a nod to the building's history as home to a local newspaper, the walls of the characterful bare-boarded rooms are hung with old newspaper pages and printing memorabilia, as well as old printing trays that local customers are encouraged to top up with little items. Greene King IPA, Abbot and Mild and regularly changing guests such as Brains

Milkwood, Titanic 1912 and York Guzzler on handpump, 25 malt whiskies, a dozen wines by the glass, and lots of rums, gins and vodkas; assorted board games. There are seats in the sheltered and paved suntrap garden and perhaps summer morris men. Wheelchair access.

Greene King ~ Lease Craig Bickley ~ Real ale ~ Bar food (12-2(2.30 Sat, Sun), 6(7 Sun)-9) ~ (01223) 368337 ~ Children welcome ~ Dogs allowed in bar ~ Open 12-2.30, 6-11; 12-11 Fri and Sat; 12-3, 7-10.30 Sun ~ www.freepresspub.com

ELSWORTH   TL3163

George & Dragon

Off A14 NW of Cambridge, via Boxworth, or off A428; CB3 8JQ

Popular dining pub with quite a choice of enjoyable food served by efficient staff, three real ales and several wines by the glass

It's best to book in advance to be sure of a table as this very well run and neatly kept dining pub is always busy. There's a civilised but friendly atmosphere and the pleasant panelled main bar, decorated with a fishy theme, opens on the left to a slightly elevated dining area with comfortable tables and a good woodburning stove. The garden room has tables overlooking attractive terraces and on the right is a more formal restaurant. Greene King IPA and Old Speckled Hen and a guest beer on handpump and decent wines served by courteous, attentive staff.

Free house ~ Licensees Paul and Karen Beer ~ Real ale ~ Bar food (12-2, 6-9.30; all day Sun) ~ Restaurant ~ (01954) 267236 ~ Children welcome ~ Dogs allowed in bar ~ Open 12-3, 6-11; 12-10.30 Sun ~ www.georgeanddragon-elsworth.co.uk

ELTON   TL0894

Crown

Off B671 S of Wansford (A1/A47), and village signposted off A605 Peterborough–Oundle; Duck Street; PE8 6RQ

Lovely thatched inn in charming village with interesting food, several real ales, well chosen wines and a friendly atmosphere; stylish bedrooms

Our readers feel this lovely thatched stone inn is really rather special and enjoy their visits very much; if you stay overnight, the breakfasts are especially good. The layout is most attractive and the softly lit beamed bar, which will have been refurbished by the time the Guide is published, has an open fire in the stone fireplace, good pictures and pubby ornaments on pastel walls, and cushioned settles and chunky farmhouse furniture on the tartan carpet. The beamed main dining area has fresh flowers and candles and similar tables and chairs on stripped boards; a more formal, circular, conservatory-style restaurant is open at weekends. Golden Crown (brewed for them by Tydd Steam), Greene King IPA and a guest beer like Oakham JHB or Slaters Top Totty on handpump, well chosen wines by the glass and farm cider. There are tables outside on the front terrace. Elton Mill and Lock are a short walk away.

Free house ~ Licensee Marcus Lamb ~ Real ale ~ Bar food (12-2(3 Sun), 6.30-9; not Sun evening, not Mon lunchtime) ~ Restaurant ~ (01832) 280232 ~ Children welcome ~ Dogs allowed in bar ~ Open 12-11 (Mon 5-11); closed Mon lunchtime ~ Bedrooms: £55B/£75B ~ www.thecrowninn.org

FEN DRAYTON   TL3468
Three Tuns
Off A14 NW of Cambridge at Fenstanton; High Street; CB4 5SJ

Welcoming landlady in charming old pub, traditional furnishings in bar and dining room, real ales, tasty food and seats in garden

It's thought that this well preserved ancient thatched building, in a particularly delightful village, may once have housed the guildhall, and the heavy-set moulded Tudor beams and timbers certainly give the impression of solidity and timelessness. The rooms are more or less open-plan with an open fire in the relaxed and friendly bar and a mix of burgundy cushioned stools, nice old dining chairs and settles. The dining room has framed prints of the pub on the walls and wooden dining chairs and tables on the red-patterned carpet. Greene King IPA and Morlands Old Speckled Hen and guests like Brains Milkwood and J W Lees Bitter on handpump and 16 wines by the glass; friendly service. A well tended lawn at the back has seats and tables, a covered dining area and a play area for children.

Greene King ~ Tenant Sam Fuller ~ Real ale ~ Bar food (12-2, 6-9(9.30 Fri, Sat); not Sun evening) ~ (01954) 230242 ~ Children welcome ~ Dogs allowed in bar ~ Open 10.30-2.30, 6-11; 12-3, 6-11 Sat; 12-3 Sun; closed Sun evening ~ www.the3tuns.co.uk

HELPSTON   TF1205
Blue Bell
Woodgate; off B1443; PE6 7ED

Bustling pub with friendly landlord and cheerful staff, quickly changing beers and good value, tasty food

There's always a cheerful, happy atmosphere in this exceptionally (and deservedly) popular pub, and the professional, hands-on landlord and his helpful staff make all their customers feel genuinely welcomed. The lounge, parlour and snug have comfortable cushioned chairs and settles, plenty of pictures, ornaments, mementos and cartwheel displays, and a homely atmosphere. The dining extension is light and airy with a sloping glass roof. Grainstore John Clare (exclusive to this pub) and quickly changing guests such as Adnams Sole Star, Greene King Ruddles Best Bitter, Shepherd Neame Bishops Finger and a changing guest beer on handpump, nine wines by the glass and summer scrumpy cider. They may have marmalade and jam for sale; background music, cribbage and TV. A sheltered and heated terrace has cafe-style chairs and tables, an awning and pretty hanging baskets; wheelchair access. The poet John Clare lived in the cottage next door, which is open to the public.

Free house ~ Licensee Aubrey Sinclair Ball ~ Real ale ~ Bar food (12-2(3 Sun), 6.30-9; not Sun evening or Mon) ~ Restaurant ~ (01733) 252394 ~ Children welcome away from bar ~ Dogs allowed in bar ~ Open 11.30-2.30, 5(6 Sat)-11(midnight Sat); 12-6 Sun; closed Sun evening

HEMINGFORD ABBOTS   TL2870

Axe & Compass

High Street; village signposted off A14 W of Cambridge; PE28 9AH

Thriving proper village community pub, popular too for good value food

The central island servery has Greene King IPA, Sharps Doom Bar and Thwaites Wainwright on handpump, and 13 wines by the glass. Various linked rooms around it have mainly traditional pub furnishings on tiled floors, with cheery pictures and an inglenook fireplace in one red-walled room, heavy black Tudor beams and local photographs in another, and a well lit pool table and TV on the left. Around the back are an old leather sofa and comfortable library chairs by shelves of books and a dresser with their own chutneys and jams for sale; darts, pool, TV and board games. Leading off is a long dining room decorated with biggish prints, and the garden between the pretty thatched pub and the tall-spired church has swings, a play area and a chicken run.

Enterprise ~ Lease Nigel Colverson ~ Real ale ~ Bar food (12-2.30(3 weekends), 6-9; not Sun evening) ~ (01480) 463605 ~ Children in bar until 5pm and in dining area after that ~ Dogs allowed in bar ~ Occasional live music ~ Open 12(10 weekends)-11(10 Sun) ~ Bedrooms: /£70S ~ www.axeandcompass.co.uk

HEMINGFORD GREY   TL2970

Cock

Village signposted off A14 eastbound, and (via A1096 St Ives road) westbound; High Street; PE28 9BJ

Imaginative food in pretty pub, extensive wine list, four interesting beers, a bustling atmosphere and a smart restaurant

'After each visit, we start planning the next one,' one of our enthusiastic readers tells us. And this well run, pretty pub is just the sort of place that customers do return to again and again as it cleverly manages to appeal to both drinkers and diners. The bar rooms have dark or white-painted beams, lots of contemporary pale yellow and cream paintwork, artwork here and there, fresh flowers and church candles, and throughout a really attractive mix of old wooden dining chairs, settles and tables. They've sensibly kept the traditional public bar on the left for drinkers only: an open woodburning stove on the raised hearth, bar stools, wall seats and a carver, steps that lead down to more seating, Brewsters Hophead, Great Oakley Wagtail and Welland Valley Mild and Tydd Steam Barn Ale on handpump, 17 wines by the glass and local farm cider; they hold a beer festival every August bank holiday weekend. In marked contrast, the stylishly simple spotless restaurant on the right – you must book to be sure of a table – is set for dining with flowers on each table, pale wooden floorboards and another woodburning stove. There are seats and tables among stone troughs and flowers in the neat garden and lovely hanging baskets.

Free house ~ Licensees Oliver Thain and Richard Bradley ~ Real ale ~ Bar food (12-2.30, 6.30(6 Fri, Sat)-9(8.30 Sun)) ~ Restaurant ~ (01480) 463609 ~ Children allowed in bar lunchtime only; must be over 5 in evening restaurant ~ Dogs allowed in bar ~ Open 11.30-3, 6-11; 12-4, 6.30-10.30 Sun ~ www.thecockhemingford.co.uk

HINXTON
TL4945

Red Lion

2 miles off M11 junction 9 northbound; take first exit off A11, A1301 N, then left turn into village – High Street; a little further from junction 10, via A505 E and A1301 S; CB10 1QY

16th-c pub, handy for the Imperial War Museum at Duxford, with friendly staff, interesting bar food, real ales and a big landscaped garden; comfortable bedrooms

A new terrace for both drinkers and diners has been added just outside the porch door of this extended pink-washed old inn – there's a huge parasol for sunny days. The low-beamed bar has oak chairs and tables on wooden floorboards, two leather chesterfield sofas, an open fire in the dark green fireplace, an old wall clock and a relaxed, friendly atmosphere. Adnams Bitter, Greene King IPA, Woodfordes Wherry and a guest such as Brandon Rusty Bucket on handpump, 12 wines by the glass (they have regular wine tastings), a dozen malt whiskies and first class service. An informal dining area has high-backed settles and the smart dry-pegged oak-raftered restaurant is decorated with various pictures and assorted clocks. The neatly kept big garden has a pleasant terrace with teak tables and chairs, picnic-sets on grass, a dovecote and views of the village church. The bedrooms are in a separate flint and brick building. They also own the Black Bull in Balsham just up the road.

Free house ~ Licensee Alex Clarke ~ Real ale ~ Bar food 12-2(2.30 Fri, Sun), 6.30(7 Sun)-9.30(9 Sun); all day Sat (restricted 2.30-6.30) ~ Restaurant ~ (01799) 530601 ~ Well behaved children welcome ~ Dogs allowed in bar ~ Open 11-11; 12-4, 7-10.30 Sun ~ Bedrooms: £90B/£135S(£115B) ~ www.redlionhinxton.co.uk

KEYSTON
TL0475

Pheasant

Just off A14 SE of Thrapston; brown sign to pub down village loop road, off B663; PE28 0RE

Good civilised country dining pub with appealing décor and attractive garden

The main bar has pitched rafters high above, dating no doubt from its long-gone days as the village smithy, with lower dark beams in side areas. The more or less central serving area has dark flagstones, with hop bines above the handpumps for Adnams Southwold and Broadside and Nene Valley ESB, a tempting array of wines by the glass, and padded stools along the leather-quilted counter. Nearby are armchairs, a chesterfield, quite a throne of a seat carved in 17th-c style, other comfortable seats around low tables, and a log fire in a lofty fireplace. The rest of the pub is mostly red-carpeted with dining chairs around a variety of polished tables, and large sporting prints – even hunting-scene wallpaper in one part. Lighted candles and tea-lights throughout, and the attentive attitude of neat friendly staff, add to the feeling of wellbeing. The attractively planted and well kept garden behind has tables on its lawn and terrace; from the picnic-table sets out in front of the pretty thatched building you may see the neighbours' hens pottering about by the very quiet village lane.

Free house ~ Licensee Simon Cadge ~ Real ale ~ Bar food (12-2, 7-9.30; not Sun evening or Mon) ~ (01832) 710241 ~ Children welcome ~ Dogs allowed in bar ~ Open 12-3, 6-11; closed Sun evening and all day Mon ~ www.thepheasant-keyston.co.uk

KIMBOLTON

New Sun

High Street; PE28 0HA

TL0967

Interesting bars and rooms, tapas menu plus other good food and a pleasant back garden

Neatly kept and always busy with a good mix of customers, this is an interesting town pub with reliably enjoyable food and a genuine welcome from the friendly, efficient staff. The cosiest room is perhaps the low-beamed front lounge with a couple of comfortable armchairs and a sofa beside the log fire, standing timbers and exposed brickwork, and books on shelves. This leads into a narrower locals' bar with Wells & Youngs Bombardier and Eagle and a weekly changing guest on handpump, and 15 wines by the glass (including champagne and pudding wines); background music, board games, piano and quiz machine. The traditionally furnished dining room opens off here. The airy conservatory with high-backed leather dining chairs has doors leading to the terrace where there are smart seats and tables under giant umbrellas. Do note that some of the nearby parking spaces have a 30-minute limit. This high street is lovely.

Charles Wells ~ Lease Stephen and Elaine Rogers ~ Real ale ~ Bar food (12-2.15(2.30 Sun), 7-9.30; not Sun or Mon evenings) ~ Restaurant ~ (01480) 860052 ~ Children welcome ~ Dogs allowed in bar ~ Open 11.30-11(10.30 Sun); 11.30-2.30, 5-11 Mon-Thurs in winter ~ www.newsuninn.co.uk

LITTLE WILBRAHAM

Hole in the Wall

High Street; A1303 Newmarket Road to Stow cum Quy off A14, then left at The Wilbrahams signpost, then right at Little Wilbrahams signpost; CB1 5JY

TL5458

Charming tucked-away dining pub – quite a find

Much emphasis is placed on the imaginative food in this friendly country pub but there is a proper bar with real ales and the welcome is as warm for those dropping in for a pint and chat as it is for those dining. The carpeted ochre-walled bar on the right is cosy for a robust no-nonsense pub lunch, with logs burning in the big brick fireplace, 15th-c beams and timbers, snug little window seats and other mixed seating around scrubbed kitchen tables. For more of an occasion, either the similar middle room (with another fire in its open range) or the rather plusher main dining room (yet another fire here) is the place to head for. Local ales include beer from the new Fellowes Brewery, there might be Brandon Rusty Bucket, Potton Shannon IPA and Woodfordes Sundew on handpump, ten wines by the glass, and unusual soft drinks such as pomegranate and elderflower pressé; helpful service. The neat side garden has good teak furniture and a little verandah. It's a very quiet hamlet, with an interesting walk to nearby unspoilt Little Wilbraham Fen.

Free house ~ Licensee Alex Rushmer ~ Real ale ~ Bar food (12-2, 7-9) ~ Restaurant ~ (01223) 812282 ~ Well behaved children welcome ~ Dogs allowed in bar ~ Open 11.30-3, 6.30-11; 12-3 Sun; closed Sun evening, all day Mon; 2 weeks in Jan ~ www.holeinthewallcambridge.co.uk

THRIPLOW

TL4346

Green Man

3 miles from M11 junction 10; A505 towards Royston, then first right; Lower Street; SG8 7RJ

Comfortable and cheery with pubby food and changing ales

Run by a friendly, hands-on landlady, this is a cheerful village pub with honest home-cooked food and well kept beer. There are always plenty of customers and it's all comfortably laid out with modern tables and attractive high-backed dining chairs and pews; there are beer mats on the ceiling and champagne bottles on high shelves. Two arches lead through to a restaurant on the left. The regularly changing real ales might include Oakham Citra, Slaters Premium, Titanic Anchor Bitter and Woodfordes Wherry on handpump. There are tables in the pleasant garden and the vivid blue paintwork makes an excellent backdrop for the floral displays.

Free house ~ Licensee Mary Lindgren ~ Real ale ~ Bar food (not Sun evening or Mon) ~ (01763) 208855 ~ Children welcome ~ Dogs allowed in bar ~ Open 12-3, 7-11; closed Sun evening, all day Mon ~ www.greenmanthriplow.co.uk

UFFORD

TF0904

White Hart

Main Street; S on to Ufford Road off B1443 at Bainton, then right; PE9 3BH

Friendly village pub with lots of interest in bar and restaurants, real ales, interesting food and large garden; bedrooms

This is a friendly 17th-c stone pub in a pretty village with 3 acres of gardens at the back; as well as a sunken dining area with plenty of chairs and tables and picnic-sets on the grass, there are steps and various quiet corners and lovely flowers and shrubs. Inside, the bar has an easy-going, chatty atmosphere, railway memorabilia, farm tools and chamber pots, high-backed settles and a leather sofa by the woodburning stove, exposed stone walls, and stools against the counter where they serve Adnams Bitter, Black Sheep, Grainstore Ten Fifty and Oakham JHB on handpump and quite a few wines by the glass. There's also a beamed restaurant and a light and airy little orangery. Four of the comfortable bedrooms are in the pub itself with two more in a converted cart shed.

Free house ~ Licensee Sue Olver ~ Real ale ~ Bar food (12-2.30, 6-9; 12-6 Sun) ~ Restaurant ~ (01780) 740250 ~ Children welcome ~ Dogs allowed in bar ~ Open 12-11(9 Sun) ~ Bedrooms: /£100S ~ www.whitehartufford.co.uk

DOG FRIENDLY INNS, HOTELS AND B&Bs

BUCKDEN   TL1967

George

High Street, Buckden, St Neots, Cambridgeshire PE19 5XA (01480) 812300
www.thegeorgebuckden.com

£120; 12 charming rms. Handsome and stylish Georgian-faced hotel with a
bustling, informal bar, fine fan beamwork, leather and chrome chairs on parquet
or stone flooring, a log fire, real ales and lots of wines including champagne by
the glass from the chrome-topped counter, a good choice of teas and coffees,
contemporary food in popular brasserie with smart cream dining chairs around
carefully polished tables, and well trained staff; seats outside in the pretty
sheltered terrace; dogs in bedrooms; £6

ELY   TL5480

Lamb

2 Lynn Road, Ely, Cambridgeshire CB7 4EJ (01353) 663574 www.thelamb-ely.com

£90; 31 comfortable rms. Pleasant, neatly kept 15th-c coaching inn near
the cathedral, with a crackling log fire in a reception room, an attractive bar
with high-backed chairs around a mix of tables and scatter cushions along a
leather-seated wall bench, wooden flooring, real ales and wines by the glass,
and enjoyable food served by friendly staff in the smart restaurant; limited car
parking; walks nearby; dogs welcome anywhere; bowls

HUNTINGDON   TL2471

Old Bridge

1 High Street, Huntingdon, Cambridgeshire PE29 3TQ (01480) 451591
www.huntsbridge.com

£160; 24 very comfortable rms, some overlooking the river. Georgian hotel by the
River Great Ouse with seats on waterside terrace and a landing stage for visiting
boats; a proper pubby bar with a wide mix of chatty customers, comfortable sofas
and wooden tables on polished floorboards, a log fire, an exceptional wine list
and local beers, and first class service; enticing food is served in the Terrace room
and the more formal panelled restaurant, and breakfasts are delicious; dogs in
bedrooms, bar and lounge; not dining areas

WANSFORD   TL0799

Haycock

London Road, Wansford, Peterborough, Cambridgeshire PE8 6JA (01780) 782223
www.macdonaldhotels.co.uk

£110; 48 individually decorated rms. 16th-c golden stone inn with relaxed,
comfortable lounges, a pubby bar with real ales and wines by the glass, a smart,
stylish restaurant, a conservatory, and contemporary british food using top quality
local produce served by friendly, efficient staff; seats in the pretty garden with
boules and fishing, and dogs can walk in the grounds – plenty of nearby country
walks too; dogs in garden bedrooms

Cheshire

MAP 7

DOG FRIENDLY PUBS

ALDFORD   SJ4259

Grosvenor Arms
B5130 Chester–Wrexham; CH3 6HJ

Spacious place with buoyantly chatty atmosphere, impressive range of drinks, wide-ranging imaginative menu and good service; lovely big terrace and gardens

One of the most consistent pubs in the Guide, this flagship in the Brunning & Price chain has had terrific reports from the first day of its inclusion. It retains plenty of individuality and its friendly staff engender a welcoming atmosphere. Spacious cream-painted areas are sectioned by big knocked-through arches with a variety of wood, quarry tile, flagstone and black and white tiled floor finishes – some richly coloured turkish rugs look well against these natural materials. Good solid pieces of traditional furniture, plenty of interesting pictures and attractive lighting keep it all intimate enough. A handsomely boarded panelled room has tall bookshelves lining one wall; good selection of board games. Lovely on summer evenings, the airy terracotta-floored conservatory has lots of gigantic low-hanging flowering baskets and chunky pale wood garden furniture. It opens out to a large elegant suntrap terrace, and a neat lawn with picnic-sets, young trees and an old tractor. Attentive staff dispense a wide range of drinks from a fine-looking bar counter, including 20 wines by the glass and over 80 whiskies, distinctive soft drinks such as peach and elderflower cordial and Willington Fruit Farm pressed apple juice, as well as half a dozen real ales including Brunning & Price Original (brewed for them by Phoenix) and Weetwood Eastgate, with guests from brewers such as Derby, Moorhouses and Spitting Feathers.

Brunning & Price ~ Manager Tracey Owen ~ Real ale ~ Bar food (12-9.30(10 Fri, Sat; 9 Sun)) ~ (01244) 620228 ~ Children welcome ~ Dogs allowed in bar ~ Open 11.30-11; 12-10.30 Sun ~ www.grosvenorarms-aldford.co.uk

ASTON   SJ6146

Bhurtpore
Off A530 SW of Nantwich; in village follow Wrenbury signpost; CW5 8DQ

Fantastic range of drinks (especially real ales) and a varied menu in warm-hearted pub with some unusual artefacts; big garden

With the terrific range of drinks at this lovingly run place, including 11 real ales, it's no surprise that tables reserved for drinkers in the comfortable public bar are put to good use. They usually run through over 1,000 superbly kept real ales a year, sourced from an enterprising range of brewers from around the UK such as All Gates, Brecon, Derby, Foxfield, Hobsons, Pennine, Rowton, Salopian, Tatton and Wapping. They also stock dozens of unusual bottled beers and fruit beers, a great many bottled ciders and perries, over 100 different whiskies, carefully selected soft drinks and wines from a good list; summer beer festival. The pub is named to commemorate the siege of Bhurtpore (a town in India) during which local landowner Sir Stapleton Cotton (later Viscount Combermere) was commander in chief. The connection with India also explains some of the quirky artefacts in the carpeted lounge bar – look out for the sunglass-wearing turbaned figure behind the counter; also good local period photographs and some attractive furniture; board games, pool, TV and games machine. Cheery staff usually cope well with the busy weekends.

Free house ~ Licensee Simon George ~ Real ale ~ Bar food (12-2, 7-9.30; 12-9.30 Sat (9 Sun)) ~ Restaurant ~ (01270) 780917 ~ Children welcome till 8.30pm ~ Dogs allowed in bar ~ Open 12-2.30, 6.30-11.30; 12-midnight Fri, Sat; 12-11 Sun ~ www.bhurtpore.co.uk

BICKLEY MOSS   SJ5550
Cholmondeley Arms

Cholmondeley; A49 5.5 miles N of Whitchurch; the owners would like us to list them under Cholmondeley village, but as this is rarely marked on maps we have mentioned the nearest village which appears more often; SY14 8HN

Imaginatively converted high-ceilinged schoolhouse with decent range of real ales and wines, well presented food and a sizeable garden

Recent refurbishments have gloriously brought a quirkily baronial feel to the interior of this former schoolhouse with its lofty ceilings, stripped brick walls and massive stag's head by the cosy fire, though its high gothic windows, huge old radiators and various old school paraphernalia (look out for hockey sticks, tennis rackets and trunks) are all testament to its former identity. Plenty of attention to detail in the shape of fresh flowers and church candles. Warmly coloured rugs on bare boards, big mirrors, armchairs by the fire and a comfy mix of dining chairs keep it all feeling friendly and well cared for; background music. Their impressive range of 87 gins look well with the attractively carved dark wood counter, and their Cholmondeley Best and Teachers Tipple (both Weetwood beers) and three guests from brewers such as Coach House, Dunham Massey and Salopian are usefully described on little boards propped up in front of the taps. There's plenty of seating outside on the sizeable lawn, which drifts off into open countryside, and more in front overlooking the quiet road. The pub is handily placed for Cholmondeley Castle Gardens.

Free house ~ Licensee Steven Davies ~ Real ale ~ Bar food (12-9.30(9.45 Sat, 8.45 Sun)) ~ (01829) 720300 ~ Children under 10 till 7pm in pub, 9pm in garden ~ Dogs welcome ~ quiz monthly ~ Open 12-11(11.30 Sat, 10.30 Sun) ~ Bedrooms: £80B/£110B ~ www.cholmondeleyarms.co.uk

BUNBURY   SJ5658
Dysart Arms

Bowes Gate Road; village signposted off A51 NW of Nantwich; and from A49 S of Tarporley – coming in this way on northernmost village access road, bear left in village centre; CW6 9PH

Civilised chatty dining pub attractively filled with good furniture in thoughtfully laid out rooms; very enjoyable food, lovely garden with pretty views

A steady flow of enthusiastic reader reports confirm that this village pub is on terrific form. Although opened up and gently refurbished, its rooms retain a cosy cottagey feel and have an easy-going sociable atmosphere – there's a genuinely friendly welcome here. Neatly kept, they ramble gently around the pleasantly lit central bar. Cream walls keep it all light, clean and airy, with deep venetian red ceilings adding cosiness, and each room (some with good winter fires) is nicely furnished with an appealing variety of well spaced sturdy wooden tables and chairs, a couple of tall filled bookcases and just the right amount of carefully chosen bric-a-brac, properly lit pictures and plants. Flooring ranges from red and black tiles to stripped boards and some carpet. Service is efficient and friendly. Phoenix Brunning & Price Original, Timothy Taylors Landlord and three guests such as Adnams, Caledonian Deuchars IPA and Fullers London Pride are on handpump alongside a good selection of 17 wines by the glass from a list of about 70 bottles, and just over 20 malts. Sturdy wooden tables on the terrace and picnic-sets on the lawn in the neatly kept slightly elevated garden are lovely in summer, with views of the splendid church at the end of this pretty village, and the distant Peckforton Hills beyond.

Brunning & Price ~ Manager Greg Williams ~ Real ale ~ Bar food (12-9.30(9 Sun)) ~ Restaurant ~ (01829) 260183 ~ Children welcome ~ Dogs allowed in bar ~ Open 11.30am-11pm; 12-10.30 Sun ~ www.dysartarms-bunbury.co.uk

BURLEYDAM   SJ6042
Combermere Arms
A525 Whitchurch–Audlem; SY13 4AT

Roomy and attractive beamed pub successfully mixing a good drinking side with imaginative all-day food

The attractive but understated interior of this popular 18th-c place has been cleverly opened up to give a light and spacious feel, though its many different areas still seem intimate. Décor and furnishings take in a laid-back mix of wooden chairs at dark wood tables, rugs on wood (some old and some new oak) and stone floors, prints hung frame to frame on cream walls, deep red ceilings, panelling and open fires. Friendly staff extend an equally nice welcome to drinkers and diners, with both aspects of the business seeming to do well. Alongside Black Sheep, Phoenix Brunning & Price Original and Weetwood Cheshire Cat, three or four guests might be from brewers such as McMullen and Stonehouse. They also stock around 60 whiskies and a dozen wines by the glass from an extensive list; a few board games. Outside there are good solid wood tables in a pretty, well tended garden.

Brunning & Price ~ Manager Lisa Hares ~ Real ale ~ Bar food (12-9.30; 12-10 Thurs-Sat; 12-9 Sun) ~ (01948) 871223 ~ Children welcome ~ Dogs allowed in bar ~ Open 11.30am-11pm(10.30 Sun) ~ www.combermerearms-burleydam.co.uk

CHELFORD   SJ8175
Egerton Arms
A537 Macclesfield–Knutsford; SK11 9BB

Well organised and welcoming, with something for everyone; food all day

This big rambling place is nicely broken up, with dark beams, an appealingly varied mix of tables and chairs, including some attractive wicker dining chairs, carved settles and a wooden porter's chair by a grandfather clock. At one end a few steps take you down into a super little raftered games area, with tempting squishy sofas and antique farm-animal prints on stripped-brick walls, as well as pool, darts, games machines and sports TV; background music. Staff are cheerful and helpful, making for a good relaxed atmosphere, and Copper Dragon Golden Pippin, Wells & Youngs Bombardier and five guests from brewers such as Mobberley, Redwillow and Tatton are served from handpumps on the long counter. An outside deck has canopied picnic-sets, with more on the grass by a toddlers' play area. There's a warm welcome for both dogs and children.

Free house ~ Licensees Jeremy and Anne Hague ~ Real ale ~ Bar food (12-9) ~ (01625) 861366 ~ Children welcome ~ Dogs allowed in bar ~ Open 12-11(10.30 Sun) ~ www.chelfordegertonarms.co.uk

CHESTER   SJ4066
Albion
Albion Street; CH1 1RQ

Strongly traditional pub with comfortable Edwardian décor and captivating World War I memorabilia; pubby food and good drinks

Most unusually, this peaceful Victorian pub is an officially listed site of four war memorials to soldiers from the Cheshire Regiment and its homely interior is entirely dedicated to the Great War of 1914-18. It's been run by the same friendly sincere licensees for over 40 years and there's something inimitably genuine about its lovely old-fashioned atmosphere. Throughout its tranquil rooms you'll find an absorbing collection of World War I memorabilia, from big engravings of men leaving for war and similarly moving prints of wounded veterans, to flags, advertisements and so on. The post-Edwardian décor is appealingly muted, with dark floral William Morris wallpaper (designed on the first day of World War I), a cast-iron fireplace, appropriate lamps, leatherette and hoop-backed chairs and cast-iron-framed tables. You might even be lucky enough to hear the vintage 1928 Steck pianola being played; there's an attractive side dining room, too. Service is friendly, though groups of race-goers are discouraged (opening times may be limited during meets), and they don't like people rushing in just before closing time. A good range of drinks includes Adnams and a couple of guests from brewers such as Hook Norton and Titanic on handpump, new world wines, fresh orange juice, organic bottled cider and fruit juice, over 25 malt whiskies and a good selection of rums and gins. Dog owners can request a water bowl and cold sausage for their pets. Bedrooms are small but comfortable and furnished in keeping with the pub's style (free parking for residents and a bottle of house wine if dining).

Punch ~ Lease Michael Edward Mercer ~ Real ale ~ Bar food (12-2(2.30 Sat), 5-8 (6-8.30 Sat, not Sun)) ~ Restaurant ~ No credit cards ~ (01244) 340345 ~ Dogs allowed in bar ~ Open 12-3, 5(6 Sat)-11; closed Sun evening ~ Bedrooms: £70B/£85B ~ www.albioninnchester.co.uk

CHESTER   SJ4166
Old Harkers Arms
Russell Street, down steps off City Road where it crosses canal – under Mike Melody Antiques; CH3 5AL

Well run spacious canalside building with lively atmosphere, great range of drinks (including lots of changing real ales) and good tasty food

The striking industrial interior of this high-ceilinged early Victorian warehouse is divided into user-friendly spaces by brick pillars. Cheery staff spread a happy bustle, attractive lamps add cosiness and the mixed dark wood furniture is set out in intimate groups on stripped-wood floors. Walls are covered with old prints hung frame-to-frame, there's a wall of bookshelves above a leather banquette at one end and the Shropshire Union Canal flows just metres away from the tall windows that run the length of the main bar; selection of board games. You'll find a very wide range of drinks taking in around nine real ales on handpump including Phoenix Brunning & Price, Flowers Original and Weetwood Cheshire Cat, and half a dozen regularly changing guests from brewers such as Brimstage, Bradfield, Northumberland, Salopian and Titanic, over 100 malt whiskies, 50 well described wines (around half of them available by the glass), eight or so farmhouse ciders and local apple juice.

Brunning & Price ~ Manager Paul Jeffery ~ Real ale ~ Bar food (12-9.30) ~ (01244) 344525 ~ Children over 10 welcome ~ Dogs allowed in bar ~ Open 11.30-11; 11.30-10.30 Sun ~ www.harkersarms-chester.co.uk

COTEBROOK   SJ5765
Fox & Barrel
A49 NE of Tarporley; CW6 9DZ

Attractive property with stylishly airy décor, an enterprising menu and good wines

There's a gentle elegance to this warmly welcoming place which has been subtly refurbished to make the most of the building's nice old character. Much enjoyed by readers, it's run with attention to detail and appeals to drinkers and diners alike. The tiled bar is dominated by a big log fireplace and has stools along its counter. A bigger uncluttered dining area has attractive rugs and an eclectic mix of period tables on polished oak floorboards, with extensive wall panelling hung with framed old prints. The terrace and in the garden have plentiful seating, old fruit trees and a tractor. Real ales include Caledonian Deuchars IPA, Weetwood Eastgate and a couple of guests from brewers such as Beartown and Tatton; good array of wines, with about 20 by the glass.

Free house ~ Licensee Gary Kidd ~ Real ale ~ Bar food (12-9.30(9 Sun)) ~ (01829) 760529 ~ Children welcome but no pushchairs ~ Dogs allowed in bar ~ Open 12-11(10.30 Sun) ~ www.foxandbarrel.co.uk

KETTLESHULME   SJ9879
Swan
B5470 Macclesfield–Chapel-en-le-Frith, a mile W of Whaley Bridge; SK23 7QU

Charming 16th-c cottagey-pub with enjoyable food (especially fish), good beer and an attractive garden

The interior of this pretty white wisteria-clad cottage, under its heavy stone roof, is snug and cosy, with latticed windows, very low dark beams hung with big copper jugs and kettles, timbered walls, antique coaching and other prints and maps, ancient oak settles on the turkish carpet and log fires. They have well kept Marstons on handpump with a couple of guest beers such as Abbeydale Moonshine and Marble Lagonda IPA, and very good food; service is polite and efficient. The front terrace has teak tables, a second two-level terrace has further tables and steamer benches under parasols, and there's a sizeable streamside garden.

Free house ~ Licensee Robert Cloughley ~ Real ale ~ Bar food (12-2, 6-8.30 Tues; 12-9

Weds, Sat; 12-7 Thurs, Fri; 12-4 Sun; not Mon) ~ (01663) 732943 ~ Children welcome ~ Dogs allowed in bar ~ Open 12-11; closed Mon lunchtime ~ www.verynicepubs.co.uk/swankettleshulme

LANGLEY   SJ9569
Hanging Gate

Meg Lane, Higher Sutton; follow Langley signpost from A54 beside Fourways Motel, and that road passes the pub; from Macclesfield, heading S from centre on A523 turn left into Byrons Lane at Langley, Wincle signpost; in Sutton (0.5 miles after going under canal bridge, ie before Langley) fork right at Church House Inn, following Wildboarclough signpost, then 2 miles later turn sharp right at steep hairpin bend; OS Sheet 118 map reference 952696; SK11 0NG

Remotely set old place with fires in traditional cosy rooms, tasty food and lovely views from airy extension and terrace

First licensed in 1621 this low-beamed old drovers' pub has an interesting history. The landlady tells us that prisoners were led from here out to the gallows outside (hence the name of the pub) with the last hanging taking place here in 1958. It's tucked on to the side of a hill high up in the Peak District with stunning panoramic views from its terrace, traditional pub rooms and airy glass-doored dining room over a patchwork of valley pastures to distant moors – on a clear day you can see Liverpool's Anglican Cathedral and Snowdonia. Still in their original layout, the three cosy little low-beamed rooms are simply furnished. The tiny little snug bar, at its pubbiest at lunchtime, has a welcoming log fire in a big brick fireplace, just one single table, plain chairs and cushioned wall seats and a few old pub pictures and seasonal photographs on its creamy walls. The second room, with just a section of bar counter in the corner, has five tables, and there's a third appealing little oak-beamed blue room. Beers served include well kept Hydes Original and a Hydes seasonal beer with a couple of guests such as Charles Wells Bombardier on handpump; also quite a few malt whiskies and ten wines by the glass; background music, board games, dominoes, books. It can get busy so it's best to book a table in advance at weekends. Walkers are made to feel welcome with tap water and there's a dog bowl outside and free camping if you eat at the pub.

Hydes ~ Tenants Ian and Luda Rottenbury ~ Real ale ~ Bar food (12-2(3 Sat, Sun); 6-9) ~ Restaurant ~ (01260) 252238 ~ Children in lounge bar and restaurant till 7pm ~ Dogs allowed in bar ~ Open 11-3, 6-11; 11-11 Sat; 10-10 Sun ~ www.thehanginggateincheshire.co.uk

MACCLESFIELD   SJ9271
Sutton Hall

Leaving Macclesfield southwards on A523, turn left into Byrons Lane signposted Langley, Wincle, then just before canal viaduct fork right into Bullocks Lane; OS Sheet 118 map reference 925715; SK11 0HE

Historic building set in attractive grounds, with a fine range of drinks and impressive food

The gardens of this rather splendid 16th-c manor house are particularly lovely, with spaciously laid out tables, some on their own little terraces, sloping lawns and fine mature trees. The original hall that forms the heart of the building is beautifully impressive, particularly in its entrance space. Quite a series of delightful bar and dining areas, some divided by tall oak timbers, are warm and cosy with plenty of character, antique oak panelling, warmly coloured rugs on broad flagstones, board and tiled floors, lots of frame-to-frame pictures and a raised open fire – all very Brunning & Price. The atmosphere has just enough formality, with bubbly staff and an enjoyable mix of customers including dog walkers keeping it nicely relaxed. A good range of drinks includes Flowers Original, Phoenix Brunning & Price, Wincle Lord Lucan and a couple of guests from brewers such as Rebellion and Titanic and well over a dozen wines by the glass from an extensive list.

Brunning & Price ~ Manager Syd Foster ~ Real ale ~ Bar food (12-10(9.30 Sun)) ~ (01260) 253211 ~ Children welcome ~ Dogs allowed in bar ~ Open 11.30-11; 12-10.30 Sun ~ www.suttonhall.co.uk

MOBBERLEY   SJ7879
Bulls Head
Mill Lane; WA16 7HX

Terrific all rounder just over six miles from the M6 and with interesting food

There's nothing overblown about the recent refurbishments here. It's been kept nice and pubby with just a touch of modernity, and a good villagey welcome. There's plenty of room round the counter (three Weetwood beers and three guests from brewers such as local Merlin and local Mobberley with useful tasting notes) for a chat, and dogs are particularly welcome – one reader counted three water bowls, and the friendly staff dispense doggie biscuits from a huge jar. Its several rooms, lively with the sound of happy customers, are furnished quite traditionally with an unpretentious mix of wooden tables and chairs on characterful old tiling. Black and pale grey walls contrast well with warming red lampshades, pink stripped-brick walls and pale stripped-timber detailing.

Free house ~ Licensees Jenny and Shane Boushell ~ Real ale ~ Bar food (12-9(9.45 Sat, 8.45 Sun)) ~ (01565) 873395 ~ Children over 10 till 7pm in pub, till 9pm in garden ~ Dogs allowed in bar ~ quiz monthly, jazz alternate Sundays ~ Open 12-11(11.30 Sat, 10.30 Sun) ~ www.thebullsheadpub.com

PEOVER HEATH   SJ7973
Dog
Off A50 N of Holmes Chapel at the Whipping Stocks, keep on past Parkgate into Wellbank Lane; OS Sheet 118 map reference 794735; note that this village is called Peover Heath on the OS map and shown under that name on many road maps, but the pub is often listed under Over Peover instead; WA16 8UP

Homely pub with interesting range of beers and generously served food; bedrooms

Gently old fashioned and comfortably cottagey, the neatly kept bar here has tied-back floral curtains at little windows, a curved cushioned banquette built into a bay window and mostly traditional dark wheelbacks arranged on a patterned carpet. A coal fire, copper pieces and pot plants add to the homely feel. A genuine local atmosphere is kept up by areas that are set aside for drinkers. Hydes (very good value at £2.30 a pint) and two beers from Weetwood are on handpump. They also have a good range of malt whiskies and wines by the glass; games room with darts, pool, a games machine, dominoes, board games and TV, background music. Friendly efficient staff cope well when it's busy. There are picnic-sets beneath colourful hanging baskets on the peaceful lane, and more out

in a pretty back garden. It's a pleasant walk from here to the Jodrell Bank Centre
and Arboretum.

Free house ~ Licensee Steven Wrigley ~ Real ale ~ Bar food (12-2.30, 6-9; 12-9 Sat; 12-8.30
Sun) ~ Restaurant ~ (01625) 861421 ~ Children welcome ~ Dogs allowed in bar ~ Live
music last Fri in month ~ Open 11.30-3, 4.30-11; 11.30-midnight Sat, Sun ~ Bedrooms:
£60B/£80B ~ www.thedoginnatpeover.co.uk

SANDBACH   SJ7560
Old Hall

1.2 miles from M6 junction 17: A534 into town, then right into High Street; CW11 1AL

**Stunning mid-17th-c hall house with impressive original features, plenty
of drinking and dining space, six real ales and imaginative food**

This magnificent Grade I listed manor house – a masterpiece of timbering
and fine carved gable-ends – was a challenging two-year restoration
project completed by Brunning & Price in 2011. There are many lovely original
architectural features, particularly in the room to the left of the entrance hall
which is much as it has been for centuries, with a Jacobean fireplace, oak
panelling and priest's hole. This leads into the Oak Room, divided by standing
timbers into two dining rooms – heavy beams, oak flooring and reclaimed
panelling. Other rooms in the original building have more hefty beams and
oak boards, three open fires and a woodburning stove; the cosy snugs are
carpeted. The newly built Garden Room is big and bright, with reclaimed
quarry tiling and exposed A-frame oak timbering, and opens on to a suntrap
back terrace with teak tables and chairs among flowering tubs. Throughout,
the walls are covered with countless interesting prints, there's an appealing
mix of antique dining chairs and tables of all sizes, and plenty of rugs,
bookcases and plants. From the handsome bar counter they serve Phoenix
Brunning & Price, Redwillow Feckless, Three Tuns XXX and three guests from
brewers such as Oakham, Storm and Titanic on handpump, 15 good wines by
the glass and 40 malt whiskies. There are picnic-sets in front of the building by
rose bushes and clipped box hedging.

Brunning & Price ~ Manager Chris Button ~ Real ale ~ Bar food (12-10(9 Sun)) ~
(01270) 758170 ~ Children welcome ~ Dogs allowed in bar ~ Open 11.30-11; 12-10.30 Sun ~
www.oldhall-sandbach.co.uk

SPURSTOW   SJ5657
Yew Tree

*Off A49 S of Tarporley; follow Bunbury 1, Haughton 2 signpost into Long Lane;
CW6 9RD*

**Great place, a top-notch all-rounder with a good deal of individuality and
frequently changing food**

The décor at this thriving place is genuinely individual and entertaining. Giant
Timorous Beasties' bees are papered on to the bar ceiling and a stag's head
looms proudly out of the wall above a log fire. Nicely simple pale grey, off-white
and cream surfaces explode into striking bold wallpaper; there's a magnified
hunting print and surprisingly angled bright tartans. The island bar has half a
dozen well kept and sensibly priced ales such as Acorn Barnsley Gold, Merlins
Gold, Redwillow Wreckless, Stonehouse Station, Weetwood Eastgate and Woods
Shropshire Lass on handpump, a beer of the month, a local cider, over two dozen
malts and a good range of wines by the glass from an interesting bin ends list of

about 50. The informal service is quick even when they are busy. A more dining-oriented area shares the same feeling of relaxed bonhomie (our favourite table there was snugged into a stable-stall-style alcove of stripped wood). A terrace outside has teak tables, with more on the grass.

Free house ~ Licensees Jon and Lindsay Cox ~ Real ale ~ Bar food (12-2.30, 6-9.30 (10 Fri); 12-10 Sat; 12-8 Sun) ~ (01829) 260274 ~ Children welcome ~ Dogs allowed in bar ~ Open 12-11; 11-10.30 Sun ~ www.theyewtreebunbury.com

SWETTENHAM   SJ7967
Swettenham Arms
Off A54 Congleton–Holmes Chapel or A535 Chelford–Holmes Chapel; CW12 2LF

Big old country pub in lovely setting with shining brasses, four real ales, enjoyable food and early bird menu

Beware of your Sat Nav when seeking out this spacious country pub – it may direct you to the middle of the local ford. Said to be as old as the interesting village church (which dates in part from the 13th c), the three communicating areas of this former nunnery are still nicely traditional, with dark heavy beams, individual furnishings, a polished copper bar, three welcoming open fires and plenty of shiny brasses, a sweep of fitted turkey carpet, a variety of old prints – military, hunting, old ships, reproduction Old Masters and so forth. Friendly efficient staff serve four beers from brewers such as Hydes, Sharps, Thwaites and Timothy Taylor; background music. Outside behind, there are tables on a lawn that merges into a lovely sunflower and lavender meadow; handy for Quinta Arboretum.

Free house ~ Licensees Jim and Frances Cunningham ~ Real ale ~ Bar food (12-2.30, 5-9.30; 12-9.30 Sat, Sun) ~ No credit cards ~ (01477) 571284 ~ Children welcome ~ Dogs allowed in bar ~ Open 11.30-11 ~ www.swettenhamarms.co.uk

THELWALL   SJ6587
Little Manor
Bell Lane; WA4 2SX

Recently restored manor house with plenty of character in the beamed rooms, lots to look at, well kept ales and interesting bistro-style food; seats outside

After an extensive six-month renovation, this handsome place – originally built in the 17th c for the Percival family – has been opened by Brunning & Price. A great deal of character has been carefully preserved in the nooks and crannies of the six beamed rooms, all linked by open doorways and standing timbers. Flooring ranges from rugs on wood through carpeting to some fine old black and white tiles. There are leather armchairs by open fires (the carved wooden one is lovely), all manner of antique dining chairs around small, large, circular or square tables, and lighting from lamps, standard lamps and metal chandeliers. As well as fresh flowers and house plants, the décor includes hundreds of interesting prints and photographs covering the walls, books on shelves and lots of old glass and stone bottles on windowsills and mantelpieces. Drinks include Coach House Cromwell, Phoenix Brunning and Price, Wincle Sir Philip and three guests from brewers such as Beartown, Merlin and Salopian, about 15 wines by the glass and around 60 whiskies. Helpful young staff. In fine weather you can sit at the chunky teak chairs and tables on the terrace; some are under a gazebo.

Brunning & Price ~ Manager Andrew Cloverly ~ Real ale ~ Bar food (12-10(9.30 Sun)) ~
(01925) 261703 ~ Children welcome ~ Dogs allowed in bar ~ Open 10.30-11(10.30 Sun) ~
www.littlemanor-thelwall.co.uk

WRENBURY   SJ5947
Dusty Miller

Cholmondeley Road; village signed from A530 Nantwich–Whitchurch; CW5 8HG

**Generous food and views of busy canal from bars and terrace of big mill
conversion**

The atmosphere at this well converted 19th-c corn mill is low-key restauranty,
with some emphasis on the generously served food, though drinkers are
welcome. The very spacious modern-feeling main bar is comfortably furnished
with a mixture of seats (including tapestried banquettes, oak settles and
wheelback chairs) around rustic tables. Further in, a quarry-tiled area by the bar
counter has an oak settle and refectory table. Friendly staff serve four well kept
Robinsons beers on handpump and a farm cider; eclectic background music.
Tables by a series of tall glazed arches and picnic-sets among rose bushes on a
gravel terrace are great vantage points for the comings and goings of craft along
the Shropshire Union Canal, which runs immediately outside, and passes beneath
a weighted drawbridge. Inside you can still see the old lift hoist up under the
rafters.

Robinsons ~ Tenant Neil Clarke ~ Real ale ~ Bar food (12-3, 6-9(10 Fri); 12-10(8 Sun) Sat)
~ (01270) 780537 ~ Children welcome ~ Dogs allowed in bar ~ Open 11.30-11; 12-10.30 Sun;
closed Mon in winter ~ www.dustymiller-wrenbury.co.uk

DOG FRIENDLY INNS, HOTELS AND B&Bs

BEESTON   SJ5559
Wild Boar Hotel

Whitchurch Road, Beeston, Tarporley, Cheshire CW6 9NW (01829) 260309
www.wildboarhotel.com

£155; 38 comfortably modern rms. Striking timbered 17th-c former hunting
lodge, much extended over the years, with manicured lawns and fine views,
beams and standing timbers in relaxed bars and lounges, original features mixed
in with bold contemporary furnishings, all manner of attractive chairs and tables
and sofas on carpeting, a sleek brasserie, good, bistro-style meals, and friendly,
helpful service; lots of nearby walks; dogs in ground-floor bedrooms; £10

BICKLEY MOSS   SJ5450
Cholmondeley Arms

Cholmondeley, Malpas, Cheshire SY14 8HN (01829) 720300
www.cholmondeleyarms.co.uk

£79.95; 6 rms in recently refurbished headmaster's house. Imaginatively
converted former schoolhouse with lofty ceilings, stripped brick walls, sofas
and a massive stag's head by the cosy fire, huge old radiators, various school
paraphernalia (hockey sticks, tennis rackets and so forth), rugs on bare boards,

fresh flowers and church candles; real ales, 87 different gins, wines by the glass, and well presented modern food, hearty breakfasts; handy for Cholmondeley Castle gardens; dogs anywhere in the pub and in bedrooms

BURWARDSLEY   SJ5256
Pheasant

Burwardsley, Chester, Cheshire CH3 9PF (01829) 770434 www.thepheasantinn.co.uk

£85; 12 attractive rms. 17th-c half-timbered, sandstone pub with fantastic views across the Cheshire plains and a great stop if you're walking the scenic Sandstone Trail along the Peckforton Hills; the airy, modern-feeling spreading rooms have low beams, comfortable leather armchairs and nice old chairs on wooden floors, a log fire in a huge fireplace, local beers and ciders, and enjoyable food (snacks served all day); dogs anywhere in the pub and in bedrooms

EATON   SJ8765
Plough

Eaton, Congleton, Cheshire CW12 2NH (01260) 280207 www.theploughinnateaton.co.uk

£75; 18 appealing rms in converted stables. Neat 17th-c village pub with beams, exposed brickwork and snug alcoves in carefully converted bar, comfortable armchairs and cushioned wall seats on red patterned carpets, a big stone fireplace, four interesting beers, ten wines by the glass, and decent traditional food; the restaurant is in a heavily raftered bar, and there are seats in a big garden with views of the Peak District – walks from the door; dogs in bedrooms

FULLERS MOOR   SJ4854
Frogg Manor

Nantwich Road, Broxton, Chester, Cheshire CH3 9JH (01829) 782629
www.froggmanorhotel.co.uk

£112.75; 8 lavishly decorated rms with thoughtful extras. Enjoyably eccentric Georgian manor house full of ornamental frogs and antique furniture, open fires and ornate dried-flower arrangements, a restful upstairs sitting room, cosy little bar, a large collection of 1930s/40s records, good english cooking in elegant dining room leading to a conservatory overlooking the gardens, and super breakfasts; resident mini yorkshire terrier; walks in 10 acres of grounds and nearby; dogs in bedrooms and bar lounge; £15

KNUTSFORD   SJ7479
Longview

51-55 Manchester Road, Knutsford, Cheshire WA16 0LX (01565) 632119
www.longviewhotel.com

£125; 32 individually decorated rms. Friendly family-run Victorian hotel with attractive period and reproduction furnishings, open fires in original fireplaces, a cosy cellar bar and well presented modern european food in the elegant restaurant; dogs can walk on the heath directly opposite hotel; dogs in bedrooms; £10

POTT SHRIGLEY   SJ9478
Shrigley Hall
Shrigley Park, Pott Shrigley, Macclesfield, Cheshire SK10 5SB (01625) 575757
www.pumahotels.co.uk

£107; 148 well equipped smart rms, some with country views. In over 262 acres of parkland, this impressive country house has many original features, a splendid entrance hall with several elegant rooms and the Courtyard bar leading off, enjoyable food in the Oakridge restaurant, and good service from friendly staff; championship golf course, fishing, tennis, beauty rooms and a health club; dogs can walk in grounds and in Lyme Park (must not chase the deer); dogs in bedrooms; £15

SANDIWAY   SJ5968
Nunsmere Hall
Tarporley Road, Oakmere, Northwich, Cheshire CW8 2ES (01606) 889100
www.primahotels.co.uk

£145; 36 rms plus 8 suites with antiques and fine fabrics. Luxurious Victorian hotel on a wooded peninsula bounded on three sides by a 60-acre lake, and in lovely gardens; elegantly furnished lounge and library, an oak-panelled bar with maritime memorabilia, very good modern cooking in the Crystal restaurant, and a warm welcome from courteous staff; dogs in two ground floor bedrooms

TARPORLEY   SJ5562
Swan
50 High Street, Tarporley, Cheshire CW6 0AG (01829) 733838
www.theswanhotel-tarporley.co.uk

£95; 16 comfortable rms (6 in converted coach house). Handsome Georgian inn with a good mix of individual tables and chairs in attractive bar, four real ales, decent wines and quite a few malt whiskies, traditional british food with some french touches, nice breakfasts and afternoon teas, friendly staff; dogs in coach-house annexe bedrooms; £20

WARMINGHAM   SJ7061
Bears Paw
School Lane, Warmingham, Sandbach, Cheshire CW11 3QN (01270) 526317
www.thebearspaw.co.uk

£105; 17 well equipped rms. Refurbished Victorian inn with a maze of rooms of individual character – two little panelled sitting rooms, comfortable leather furniture and woodburning stoves in magnificent fireplaces, light, airy dining areas with an eclectic mix of wooden furniture on stripped floorboards, and half a dozen real ales, 12 wines by the glass, and well thought of food served by cheerful staff; seats in a small front garden; dogs in bedrooms and bar

Cornwall

MAP 1

DOG FRIENDLY PUBS

BLISLAND   SX1073

Blisland Inn
Village signposted off A30 and B3266 NE of Bodmin; PL30 4JF

Village local by the green with fine choice of real ales, beer-related memorabilia, pubby food and seats outside

The friendly licensees run this extremely popular local as an old-fashioned, traditional place with a fine collection of beers and honest home cooking. Every inch of the beams and ceiling is covered with beer badges (or a particularly wide-ranging collection of mugs), and the walls are similarly filled with beer-related posters and the like. Tapped from the cask or on handpump, the ales include two brewed for the pub by Sharps – Blisland Special and Bulldog – as well as five or six quickly changing guests; also, farm cider, fruit wines and real apple juice; good service. The carpeted lounge has a number of barometers on the walls, toby jugs on the beams and a few standing timbers, and the family room has pool, table skittles, euchre, cribbage and dominoes; background music. Plenty of picnic-sets outside. The popular Camel Trail cycle path is close by – though the hill up to Blisland is pretty steep. As with many pubs in this area, it's hard to approach without negotiating several single-track roads.

Free house ~ Licensees Gary and Margaret Marshall ~ Real ale ~ Bar food (12-2, 6.30-9) ~ (01208) 850739 ~ Children in family room only ~ Dogs allowed in bar ~ Open 11.30-11.30(midnight Sat); 12-10.30 Sun

BOSCASTLE   SX0991

Cobweb
B3263, just E of harbour; PL35 0HE

Heavy beams, flagstones, lots of old jugs and bottles, a cheerful atmosphere, several real ales, straightforward food and friendly staff

You can be sure of a warm welcome in this tall stone pub, close to the tiny steeply cut harbour and pretty village. It's an interesting place with two bars featuring heavy beams hung with hundreds of bottles and jugs, lots of historic pictures, quite a mix of seats (from settles and carved chairs to more pubby furniture) and cosy log fires. They keep four real ales such as St Austell Tribute, Sharps Doom Bar, Tintagel Harbour Special and a guest on handpump and a local cider and, especially at peak times, there's a cheerful, bustling atmosphere; games machine, darts and pool. The restaurant is upstairs. There are picnic-sets and benches outside – some under cover. They have a self-catering apartment for rent.

Free house ~ Licensees Ivor and Adrian Bright ~ Real ale ~ Bar food (11.30-2.30, 6-9.30) ~ Restaurant ~ (01840) 250278 ~ Children welcome ~ Dogs allowed in bar ~ Live music Sat evenings and some Sun afternoons ~ Open 10.30am(11 Sun)-11pm ~ www.cobwebinn.co.uk

MYLOR BRIDGE   SW8137
Pandora

Restronguet Passage: from A39 in Penryn, take turning signposted Mylor Church, Mylor Bridge, Flushing and go straight through Mylor Bridge following Restronguet Passage signs; or from A39 further N, at or near Perranarworthal, take turning signposted Mylor, Restronguet, then follow Restronguet Weir signs, but turn left down hill at Restronguet Passage sign; TR11 5ST

Beautifully placed waterside inn with seats on long floating pontoon, lots of atmosphere in beamed and flagstoned rooms, and some sort of food all day

After a dreadful fire and a year of careful restoration, this lovely medieval thatched pub is open again. It's in an idyllic waterside position – best enjoyed from the picnic-sets in front or on the long floating jetty – and many customers do arrive by boat. Inside, several rambling, interconnecting rooms have low wooden ceilings (mind your head on some of the beams), beautifully polished big flagstones, cosy alcoves with leatherette benches built into the walls, old race posters, model boats in glass cabinets, and three large log fires in high hearths (to protect them against tidal floods). St Austell HSD, Proper Job, Trelawny and Tribute on handpump and a dozen wines by the glass. Upstairs, there's now a new dining room with exposed oak vaults and dark tables and chairs on pale oak flooring. The inn gets very crowded and parking is extremely difficult at peak times; wheelchair access.

St Austell ~ Tenant John Milan ~ Real ale ~ Bar food (12-9(9.30 Fri and Sat)) ~ Restaurant ~ (01326) 372678 ~ Children welcome away from bar area ~ Dogs allowed in bar ~ Open 10.30am-11pm ~ www.pandorainn.co.uk

PERRANUTHNOE   SW5329
Victoria

Signed off A394 Penzance–Helston; TR20 9NP

Carefully furnished inn close to Mount's Bay beaches, friendly welcome, local beers, interesting fresh food and seats in pretty garden; bedrooms

'Not to be missed if you are in this part of Cornwall,' says one of our enthusiastic readers about this well run and friendly pub – and many others agree with him. There's a good bustling atmosphere and a cheerful mix of both regulars and visitors in the L-shaped bar, as well as various cosy corners, exposed joists, a woodburning stove, an attractive mix of dining chairs around wooden tables on the oak flooring, china plates, all sorts of artwork on the walls and fresh flowers. The restaurant is separate. Sharps Doom Bar and Skinners Betty Stogs on handpump and several wines by the glass; background music. The pub labrador is called Bailey. The pretty tiered garden has white metal furniture under green parasols and the beaches of Mount's Bay are a couple of minutes' stroll away. The bedrooms are light and airy (we'd love to hear from readers who have stayed here) and they have a cottage to rent in nearby St Hilary.

Pubfolio ~ Lease Anna and Stewart Eddy ~ Real ale ~ Bar food (12-2(3 Sun), 6.30-9; not
Sun evening or winter Mon) ~ Restaurant ~ (01736) 710309 ~ Children welcome ~ Dogs
allowed in bar ~ Open 12-2.30(3.30 Sun), 5.30-midnight; closed Sun evening, winter Mon, 1
week in Jan ~ Bedrooms: £50S/£75S ~ www.victoriainn-penzance.co.uk

PERRANWELL   SW7739
Royal Oak
Village signposted off A393 Redruth–Falmouth and A39 Falmouth–Truro; TR3 7PX

**Welcoming and relaxed with helpful, friendly landlord, well presented
food, real ales and thoughtful wines**

This is a splendid little pub with a friendly hands-on landlord and a cheerful,
welcoming atmosphere. The roomy, carpeted bar has a gently upmarket but
relaxed feel, horsebrasses and pewter and china mugs on its black beams and
joists, plates and country pictures on the cream-painted stone walls and cosy wall
and other seats around candlelit tables. It rambles around beyond a big stone
fireplace (with a winter log fire) into a snug little nook of a room behind, with
just a couple more tables. Sharps Doom Bar and IPA and Skinners Betty Stogs on
handpump, as well as good wines by the glass and farm cider.

Free house ~ Licensee Richard Rudland ~ Real ale ~ Bar food (12-2.30, 6.30-9.30) ~
Restaurant ~ (01872) 863175 ~ Children welcome ~ Dogs allowed in bar ~ Open 11-3, 6-11;
12-4, 6-11 Sun

POLPERRO   SX2050
Blue Peter
Quay Road; PL13 2QZ

**Friendly pub overlooking pretty harbour, with fishing paraphernalia,
paintings by local artists and carefully prepared food**

Now opening at 8.30am for breakfast (which could be anything from a full
english to crab omelette), this busy harbourside pub is as reliably well run
and friendly as ever – and there's always a good mix of both locals and visitors.
The cosy low-beamed bar has a chatty, relaxed atmosphere, St Austell Tribute,
Sharps Doom Bar and guests like Bays Gold and Otter Ale on handpump, and
traditional furnishings that include a small winged settle and a polished pew
on the wooden floor, fishing paraphernalia, photographs and pictures by local
artists, lots of candles and a solid wood bar counter. One window seat looks
down on the harbour and another looks out past rocks to the sea. Families must
use the upstairs room; background music. There are a few seats outside on the
terrace and more in an upstairs amphitheatre-style area. The pub is quite small,
so it does get crowded at peak times. They have a cash machine (there's no
bank in the village).

Free house ~ Licensees Steve and Caroline Steadman ~ Real ale ~ Bar food (12-2.30, 6.30-
8.30; food all day in peak season) ~ (01503) 272743 ~ Children in upstairs family room only
~ Dogs allowed in bar ~ Live music weekends ~ Open 10.30(11.30 Sun)-11.30 ~
www.thebluepeter.co.uk

PORTHTOWAN   SW6948
Blue
Beach Road, East Cliff; car park (fee in season) advised; TR4 8AW

Informal, busy bar right by wonderful beach with modern food and drinks; lively staff and customers

Of course, this is not a traditional pub. It's a cheerful bar right by a fantastic beach, which makes it incredibly popular with customers of all ages – and their dogs. The atmosphere is easy and informal and huge picture windows look across the terrace to the huge expanse of sand and sea. The front bays have built-in pine seats and the rest of the large room has chrome and wicker chairs around plain wooden tables on the stripped wood floor, quite a few high-legged chrome and wooden bar stools and plenty of standing space around the bar counter; powder blue-painted walls, ceiling fans, some big ferny plants and fairly quiet background music; pool table. St Austell Tribute on handpump, several wines by the glass, cocktails and shots, and giant cups of coffee all served by perky, helpful young staff.

Free house ~ Licensees Tara Roberts and Luke Morris ~ Real ale ~ Bar food (12-9 though menu reduced between 3-6) ~ (01209) 890329 ~ Children welcome ~ Dogs allowed in bar ~ Acoustic music Sat evening ~ Open 10am-11pm(10pm Sun) ~ www.blue-bar.co.uk

ST MERRYN   SW8874
Cornish Arms
Churchtown (B3276 towards Padstow); PL28 8ND

Busy roadside pub, liked by locals and holiday makers, with bar and dining rooms, real ales, good food, friendly service and seats outside

Part of the Rick Stein stable (but under tenancy from St Austell), this bustling roadside pub naturally places strong emphasis on the good food, but also remains a local with darts and euchre teams; it does get pretty busy in summer so it's best to arrive early to be sure of a table. The main door leads into a sizeable, informal area with a pool table, plenty of cushioned wall seating and a shelf of paperbacks, and to the left of this is a light and airy dining room overlooking the terrace. There's an unusual modern, upright woodburner with tightly packed logs to each side, photographs of the sea and of past games teams, and pale wooden dining chairs around tables on the quarry tiles. You can walk from here through to two more linked rooms with ceiling joists; the first with an open fire in a stone fireplace, some black and white photographs and pubby furniture on huge flagstones and then on to the end room with more cushioned wall seating and contemporary seats and tables on parquet flooring. St Austell Proper Job, Trelawny and Tribute on handpump, friendly service, background music and TV. In summer, the window boxes are pretty and there are picnic-sets on a side terrace and more on grass.

St Austell ~ Tenant Luke Taylor ~ Real ale ~ Bar food (12-2, 6-9) ~ Restaurant ~ (01841) 532700 ~ Children welcome ~ Dogs allowed in bar ~ live music winter Fri evenings ~ Open 11.30-11 ~ www.rickstein.com/The-Cornish-Arms.html

DOG FRIENDLY INNS, HOTELS AND B&Bs

BOSCASTLE   SX1291
Old Rectory
St Juliot, Boscastle, Cornwall PL35 0BT (01840) 250225 www.stjuliot.com

£75; 4 pretty, light and airy rms. Carefully restored Victorian house (run along
the warmly welcoming owners' green policies) where Thomas Hardy met his wife
– Hardy memorabilia is displayed in the dining room; comfortable lounge with
a winter woodburning stove and french windows opening on to the verandah, a
conservatory for evening meals (by arrangement) and delicious breakfasts using
their rare-breed pigs for the bacon and sausages, home-grown fruit, free-range
eggs (their own chickens and ducks) and their own honey; 3 acres of lovely
gardens with seats; dogs in stable bedroom

CADGWITH   SW7214
Cadgwith Cove Inn
Cadgwith, Ruan Minor, Helston, Cornwall TR12 7JX (01326) 290513
www.cadgwithcoveinn.com

£82.70; 6 rms overlooking the sea. Bustling local at the bottom of a fishing cove
village with fine coastal walks in either direction; plainly furnished and cosy front
rooms with lots of local photos, cases of naval hat ribands and fancy rope-work,
ships' shields on beams and a log fire, a back bar with a big colourful fish mural,
real ales on handpump, pubby food, and breakfasts using their own jams; dogs
welcome anywhere; bowls and treats; £10

CAMELFORD   SX1486
Pendragon Country Hotel
Davidstow, Camelford, Cornwall PL32 9XR (01840) 261131
www.pendragoncountryhouse.com

£84; 7 deeply comfortable, thoughtfully equipped rms. Former Victorian
rectory with charming, helpful young owners, two lounges with antiques, leather
chesterfields by open fires, books and board games, an honesty bar, a downstairs
games room with a full-size pool table, and seats in the garden; very good evening
meals using local produce and smashing breakfasts with home-made bread and
preserves; beaches and walks nearby; dogs in downstairs bedroom and one
lounge; towel/bowl on request; £5

CARNE BEACH   SX0655
Nare Hotel
Carne Beach, Veryan, Truro, Cornwall TR2 5PF (01872) 501279 www.narehotel.co.uk

£363; 36 lovely rms to suit all tastes – some stylish ones look over garden and
out to sea. Attractively decorated and furnished hotel run by staff who really
care, in magnificent clifftop position with secluded gardens, outdoor and indoor
swimming pools, tennis, sailboarding, and fishing; antiques, fresh flowers and log
fires in the airy, spacious day rooms, very good food in two restaurants (one less

formal with a more relaxed atmosphere), wonderful breakfasts; there's a safe sandy beach below; dogs welcome away from restaurants; from £16 including chef's special dog meals

CONSTANTINE   SW7328
Trengilly Wartha
Constantine, Falmouth, Cornwall TR11 5RP (01326) 340332 www.trengilly.co.uk

£90; 8 cottagey rms. Tucked away inn with 6 acres of pretty surrounding gardens, with a sociable main bar, four real ales, 20 wines by the glass, 60 malt whiskies and a woodburning stove, a bright family conservatory, enjoyable food served by courteous staff in the cosy bistro, and smashing breakfasts; resident dog, Tara; nearby walks; dogs in bedrooms and bar; £3

CONSTANTINE BAY   SW8674
Treglos Hotel
Constantine Bay, Padstow, Cornwall PL28 8JH (01841) 520727 www.tregloshotel.com

£192; 42 light rms, some with dramatic coastal views. Quiet and relaxed hotel close to a good sandy beach, and in the same family for over 40 years, with comfortable traditional furnishings in light and airy lounges and bar, open fires, enjoyable food using plenty of local fish and shellfish in attractive restaurant (jackets or ties after 7pm), and friendly helpful staff; indoor swimming pool, spa and treatment rooms, games room, sheltered garden, 18-hole golf course, self-catering apartments and lovely surrounding walks; dogs in bedrooms; not in public areas; £9.50

COVERACK   SW7818
Bay Hotel
North Corner, Coverack, Helston, Cornwall TR12 6TF (01326) 280464 www.thebayhotel.co.uk

£136; 13 airy, restful rms with fine sea views over Coverack Bay. Family-run hotel by a beach on the Lizard Peninsula, with a well stocked cosy bar, a comfortable lounge with an open fire, books and a telescope, very good modern food (delicious local fish and shellfish) in candlelit conservatory, tasty cornish breakfasts and afternoon cream teas on the terrace; dogs in bedrooms; not in public rooms; £8

FALMOUTH   SW7932
Best Western Penmere Manor
Mongleath Road, Falmouth, Cornwall TR11 4PN (01326) 211411 www.penmere.co.uk

£142; 35 spacious rms. Quietly set, family-run Georgian manor house in 5 acres of gardens and woodland, with an indoor swimming pool, Jacuzzi and leisure centre; a convivial and informal bar, comfortable, relaxing lounge, friendly staff, and enjoyable food using local produce in smart restaurant; dogs in some bedrooms only; £10

FALMOUTH
Rosemary

SW8131

22 Gyllyngvase Terrace, Falmouth, Cornwall TR11 4DL (01326) 314669
www.therosemary.co.uk

£89; 10 well equipped, pretty rms, many looking over the water. Family-run
Edwardian house (designed by England's first female architect) with sea views
and two-minute walk to the beach; helpful, welcoming owners, comfortable
lounge with books and magazines, a small, cosy bar, enjoyable hearty breakfasts
(cream teas and picnics, too), and seats on sundeck in south-facing garden; well
behaved dogs in some bedrooms; £5

LAMORNA
Cove Hotel

SW4424

Lamorna, Cornwall TR19 6XH (01736) 731411 www.thecovecornwall.com

£195; 15 spacious apartments (can self-cater too). Chic boutique hotel decorated
in sea colours of white and aqua with lots of glass, contemporary art, good,
interesting modern food in fireside restaurant, a poolside bar, plenty of loungers
on the terrace around the infinity pool and sea views; lots of coastal walks;
restaurant closed end Nov-Easter; small dogs welcome anywhere; £10

LANLIVERY
Crown

SX0759

Lanlivery, Bodmin, Cornwall PL30 5BT (01208) 872707 www.wagtailinns.com

£89.95; 9 recently refurbished rms. Pretty 12th-c inn in tranquil gardens and
close to the Eden Project; traditional rambling rooms with pubby furniture on big
flagstones, a log fire in the huge fireplace, a lit-up well with a glass top, popular
food in the dining conservatory and quite a choice of drinks; dogs in bedrooms
and bar

LOOE
Talland Bay Hotel

SX2251

Porthallow, Looe, Cornwall PL13 2JB (01503) 272667 www.tallandbayhotel.co.uk

£120; 20 charming rms with sea or country views. Down a little lane between
Looe and Polperro, this restful partly 16th-c country house has lovely subtropical
gardens just above the sea, a comfortable, contemporary sitting room with log
fire, a cosy brasserie, quite a choice of good, modern food (lots of local fish) in
elegant oak-panelled dining room, and courteous, friendly service; heated outdoor
swimming pool, putting and croquet, and coastal and beach walks; dogs welcome
away from main dining room; welcome pack, bedding and treats; £10

MAWNAN SMITH
Meudon Hotel

SW7828

Mawnan Smith, Falmouth, Cornwall TR11 5HT (01326) 250541 www.meudon.co.uk

£140; 29 newly refurbished rms. Old stone mansion, with a newer wing, set in
beautiful subtropical gardens laid out 200 years ago by R W Fox; lovely views

from dining room, comfortable lounge with log fire and fresh flowers, cosy bar, helpful staff and enjoyable food; walks in own grounds and along coastal footpath at bottom of garden; dogs in bedrooms; not in public rooms; £12

MITHIAN   SW7450
Rose-in-Vale Country House Hotel

Mithian, St Agnes, Cornwall TR5 0QD (01872) 552202 www.rose-in-vale-hotel.co.uk

£110; 24 well equipped comfortable rms including 2 suites. Secluded and quietly set Georgian house in 4 acres of neatly kept gardens, with comfortable sofas and open fires, a friendly atmosphere and enjoyable modern food in dining room that overlooks the grounds; ducks on ponds, a trout stream, and an outdoor swimming pool; dogs in bedrooms and lounge; £7.50

MORWENSTOW   SS2015
Bush

Crosstown, Morwenstow, Bude, Cornwall EX23 9SR (01288) 331242
www.bushinn-morwenstow.co.uk

£87.50; 4 rms with lovely views. 13th-c pub near one of the grandest parts of the Cornish coast – super walks; a busy, characterful bar with a woodburning stove in the big stone fireplace and lots of horse tack and brass, and airy dining rooms with carefully sourced produce for well liked, all-day food; self-catering, too; dogs in bedrooms and bar; £6.50

MULLION   SW6618
Mullion Cove Hotel

Mullion Cove, Lizard Peninsula, Cornwall TR12 7EP (01326) 240328
www.mullion-cove.co.uk

£160; 30 comfortable rms, many with sea views. Sizeable clifftop Victorian hotel overlooking fishing cove and harbour with wonderful uninterrupted sea views; several lounges, a convivial bar, genuinely friendly staff, good, daily-changing food in bistro and restaurant and extensive breakfast choice; seats in garden and solar-heated swimming pool; dogs in bedrooms and one doggy lounge; welcome pack and helpful info; £7

MULLION   SW6718
Polurrian Hotel

Mullion, Helston, Cornwall TR12 7EN (01326) 240421 www.polurrianhotel.com

£195; 41 rms, some with memorable sea views. White clifftop hotel in 12 acres of lovely gardens with a path down to the sheltered private cove below; comfortable contemporary lounges and bar, good food using fresh local ingredients in airy restaurant (stunning sea views), and enjoyable breakfasts; gym, indoor and outdoor swimming pools, tennis, and coastal path walks; dogs in bedrooms; blanket and bowl; £10

PADSTOW   SW9175
St Petroc's Hotel & Bistro
4 New Street, Padstow, Cornwall PL28 8EA (01841) 532700 www.rickstein.com

£150; 10 pretty little rms. Attractive white Georgian hotel with a stylish lounge looking over a small courtyard, a quiet reading room, an airy dining room, good food quickly served from a short bistro-type menu (plenty of fish), a sensible wine list and a friendly, informal atmosphere; dogs in bedrooms; bowl and big fleece blanket; £20 (£5 each additional night)

PENZANCE   SW4730
Abbey Hotel
Abbey Street, Penzance, Cornwall TR18 4AR (01736) 366906 www.theabbeyonline.co.uk

£150; 9 charming rms. Stylish little 17th-c house close to harbour with marvellous views, a relaxed atmosphere in comfortable chintzy drawing room, flowers, antiques, paintings and a winter log fire, and breakfasts in cream-painted, panelled dining room with a second open fire (the Abbey restaurant next door is not connected); pretty walled garden and park nearby for walks and beaches (out of season); dogs are welcome anywhere and get a sausage for breakfast

PORT ISAAC   SX0080
Port Gaverne Hotel
Port Gaverne, Port Isaac, Cornwall PL29 3SQ (01208) 880244 www.portgavernehotel.co.uk

£120; 16 rms. Bustling inn with a low beamed and flagstoned bar, chatty customers, real ales and log fires, interesting antiques in comfortable lounge, quite a choice of food in the 'Captain's Cabin' (a little room where everything is shrunk to scale) and restaurant, seats in the terraced garden and splendid clifftop and beach walks all around; dogs welcome away from dining room; £4

PORTSCATHO   SW8736
Rosevine
Porthcurnick Beach, Portscatho, Cornwall TR2 5EW (01872) 580206 www.rosevine.co.uk

£199; 12 apartment suites including 4 courtyard studios. Imposing house set above a fine beach with an attractive, semi-tropical garden, a club-like bar with leather armchairs, a relaxing drawing room with sofas in front of the woodburning stove, and sunny dining room serving modern food ranging from brunches through tapas to full evening meals; indoor swimming pool; and walks all around; self-catering house, too; dogs in studios

ST MAWES   SW8432
Tresanton
Lower Castle Road, St Mawes, Truro, Cornwall TR2 5DR (01326) 270055 www.tresanton.com

£245; 31 rms all with individual furnishings and sea views. Hidden away behind a discreet entrance, with elegant terraces (heating for cool weather), a little bottom bar, steps up to the main building and its stylish lounge with deeply comfortable sofas and armchairs, big bowls of flowers, log fire, daily papers and sophisticated but relaxed atmosphere; good modern food in airy restaurant, a fine wine list and friendly informal service; several boats for hire including the beautiful 48-ft yacht Pinuccia; dogs in four bedrooms (Room 1 is super); bowls, baskets and blankets; £20

TREVAUNANCE COVE   SW7251

Driftwood Spars

Trevaunance Cove, St Agnes, Cornwall TR5 0RT (01872) 552428
www.driftwoodspars.com

£86; 15 comfortable, attractive rms, some with sea views. Friendly old inn with plenty of history just up the road from a beach and its dramatic cove; timbered bars with massive ships' spars, lots of nautical and wreck memorabilia, a woodburning stove, seven real ales (and two or three own brews), good wines by the glass and helpful staff, a modern dining room serving tasty, seasonally changing food, and seats in the garden; the coastal footpath passes the door; dogs in bedrooms; £3

TRURO   SW8345

Alverton Manor

Tregolls Road, Truro, Cornwall TR1 1ZQ (01872) 276633 www.alvertonmanor.co.uk

£130; 33 antique-filled rms. Elegant sandstone hotel, formerly a convent, in 6 acres of pretty grounds and close to the city centre; comfortable public rooms including a great hall, library and former chapel, friendly service, and enjoyable food using local, seasonal produce served in the smart restaurant; seats on the terrace; dogs in bedrooms; £5

ISLES OF SCILLY

ST MARTIN'S   SV9116

St Martin's on the Isle

Lower Town, St Martin's, Isles of Scilly TR25 0QW (01720) 422092
www.stmartinshotel.co.uk

£350 including dinner for two; 30 attractively decorated rms, most with fine sea views. Stone-built hotel set idyllically on a white sand beach, with stunning sunsets; comfortable, light and airy split-level bar-lounge with doors opening on to the terrace, genuinely friendly professional staff, sophisticated food in the main restaurant (lighter lunches in the bar), and a fine wine list; fantastic walks (the island is car free), launch trips to other islands and good bird-watching; small swimming pool; closed Oct-end March; dogs in bedrooms only; £15 including food

Cumbria

DOG FRIENDLY PUBS

AMBLESIDE
NY3704

Golden Rule

Smithy Brow; follow Kirkstone Pass signpost from A591 on N side of town; LA22 9AS

Simple town local with a cosy, relaxed atmosphere and real ales

All customers – including walkers and their dogs – are made welcome in this no-frills town local; nothing changes at all, which is just the way its regulars like it. The bar area has built-in wall seats around cast-iron-framed tables (one with a local map set into its top), horsebrasses on the black beams, assorted pictures on the walls, a welcoming winter fire and a relaxed atmosphere. Robinsons Cumbria Way, Dark Mild, Dizzy Blonde, Double Hop, Enigma and Hartleys XB on handpump. A brass measuring rule hangs above the bar (hence the pub's name). There's also a back room with TV (not much used), a left-hand room with darts and a games machine, a further room, down a couple of steps on the right, with lots of seating. The backyard has benches and a covered heated area, and the window boxes are especially colourful. There's no car park.

Robinsons ~ Tenant John Lockley ~ Real ale ~ No credit cards ~ (015394) 32257 ~ Children welcome away from bar and must leave by 9pm ~ Dogs allowed in bar ~ Open 11am-midnight ~ www.goldenrule-ambleside.co.uk

BEETHAM
SD4979

Wheatsheaf

Village (and inn) signed off A6 S of Milnthorpe; LA7 7AL

17th-c inn with handsome timbered cornerpiece, lots of beams, interesting food and quite a choice of drinks

In a quiet village and opposite a pretty 14th-c church, this is a striking old coaching inn with friendly licensees. It's recently been refurbished in traditional style throughout with a mix of high-backed wooden, leather and fabric-covered dining chairs around an attractive mix of dark wooden tables on tartan carpet with pictures and photographs of local scenes in gold frames on cream-painted walls, burgundy-patterned silk curtains and chandeliers. There's an opened-up front lounge bar with lots of exposed beams and joists, a main bar (behind on the right) with an open fire, two upstairs dining rooms and a residents' lounge. Cross Bay Nightfall, Tirril Queen Jean and a guest beer on handpump, several wines by the glass and quite a few malt whiskies. Plenty of surrounding walks.

Free house ~ Licensees Mr and Mrs Skelton ~ Real ale ~ Bar food (9am-9pm) ~ Restaurant ~ (015395) 62123 ~ Children welcome ~ Dogs allowed in bar ~ Open 11-11; 12-10.30 Sun ~ Bedrooms: £55B/£75B ~ www.wheatsheafbeetham.com

BROUGHTON MILLS   SD2190

Blacksmiths Arms

Off A593 N of Broughton-in-Furness; LA20 6AX

Friendly little pub with imaginative food, local beers and open fires; fine surrounding walks

Tucked away in a little hamlet in peaceful countryside, this bustling pub is just the place to relax after a day on the fells. The four little bars, with warm log fires, have a relaxed, friendly atmosphere and are simply but attractively decorated with straightforward chairs and tables on ancient slate floors. Barngates Cracker Ale, Cumberland Corby Blonde and Hawkshead Bitter on handpump, nine wines by the glass and summer farm cider; darts, board games and dominoes. The hanging baskets and tubs of flowers in front of the building are very pretty in summer and there are seats and tables under parasols on the back terrace.

Free house ~ Licensees Mike and Sophie Lane ~ Real ale ~ Bar food (12-2, 6-9; not Mon) ~ (01229) 716824 ~ Children welcome · Dogs allowed in bar ~ Open 12-11(5-11 Mon); 12-10.30 Sun; 12-2.30, 5-11 Tues-Fri in winter; closed Mon lunchtime ~ www.theblacksmithsarms.co.uk

CARLETON   NY5329

Cross Keys

A686, off A66 roundabout at Penrith; CA11 8TP

Friendly refurbished pub with several connected seating areas, real ales and popular food

Always bustling and friendly, this well run pub has a healthy mix of both drinkers and diners – and the atmosphere is relaxed and informal. The beamed main bar has pubby tables and chairs on the light wooden floorboards, modern metal wall lights and pictures on the bare stone walls, and Theakstons Black Bull, Tirril 1823 and a changing guest on handpump. Steps lead down to a small area with high bar stools around a high drinking table and then upstairs to the restaurant – a light, airy room with big windows, large wrought-iron candelabra hanging from the vaulted ceiling, pale solid wooden tables and chairs and doors to a verandah. At the far end of the main bar, there are yet another couple of small connected bar rooms with darts, games machine, pool, juke box and dominoes; TV and background music. There are fell views from the garden.

Free house ~ Licensee Paul Newton ~ Real ale ~ Bar food (12-2.30, 6(5.30 Fri and Sat)-9(8.30 Sun)) ~ Restaurant ~ (01768) 865588 ~ Children welcome ~ Dogs allowed in bar ~ Open 12-3, 5-midnight; 12-1am(midnight Sun) Sat ~ www.kyloes.co.uk

CONISTON   SD3098

Sun

Signed left off A593 at the bridge; LA21 8HQ

Lovely position for extended old pub with a lively bar, plenty of dining space, real ales, well liked food and seats outside; comfortable bedrooms

This 16th-c pub is in a spectacular position surrounded by dramatic bare fells; seats and tables on the terrace and in the big tree-sheltered garden make the most of the lovely views. The heart of the place is the cheerful bar, which has a good mix of customers (and their dogs), exposed stone walls, beams and timbers, flagstones and a Victorian-style range. Also, cask seats, old settles and cast-iron-framed tables and quite a few Donald Campbell photographs (this was his headquarters during his final attempt on the world water speed record). Eight real ales from breweries such as Barngates, Black Sheep, Coniston, Copper Dragon, Cumbrian Legendary, Hawkshead, Keswick and Yates on handpump, eight wines by the glass, two farm ciders and 20 malt whiskies. Above the bar is a new room, open to the ceiling, with extra seating for families and larger groups, and there's a sizeable side lounge that leads into the dining conservatory; pool, darts and TV. A front terrace has more tables and chairs. The bedrooms are quiet and comfortable and the views are pretty special.

Free house ~ Licensee Alan Piper ~ Real ale ~ Bar food (12-2.30, 5.30-8.30) ~ Restaurant ~ (015394) 41248 ~ Children in eating area of bar and restaurant ~ Dogs allowed in bar ~ Open 11am-midnight ~ Bedrooms: £40S/£80S(£90B) ~ www.thesunconiston.com

CROSTHWAITE   SD4491
Punch Bowl
Village signed off A5074 SE of Windermere; LA8 8HR

Smart dining pub with a proper bar and several other elegant rooms, real ales, a fine wine list, imaginative food and friendly staff; seats on terrace overlooking the valley; lovely bedrooms

As well as being a lovely place to stay with stylish and comfortable bedrooms and excellent food, this civilised dining pub has a proper bar with real ales and locals do pop in for a pint and a chat. This public bar is raftered and hop-hung with a couple of eye-catching rugs on flagstones, bar stools by the slate-topped counter, Barngates Westmorland Gold, Coniston Bluebird and Hawkshead Bitter on handpump, 22 wines by the glass and around a dozen malt whiskies; friendly, helpful staff. To the right are two linked carpeted and beamed rooms with well spaced country pine furniture of varying sizes, including a big refectory table, and walls painted in restrained neutral tones with an attractive assortment of prints; winter log fire, woodburning stove, lots of fresh flowers and daily papers. On the left, the wooden-floored restaurant area (also light, airy and attractive) has comfortable high-backed leather dining chairs. Throughout, the pub feels relaxing and nicely uncluttered. There are some tables on a terrace stepped into the hillside overlooking the lovely Lyth Valley. This is sister pub to the Plough at Lupton (in this same chapter).

Free house ~ Licensees Richard Rose and co-owner ~ Real ale ~ Bar food (12-9) ~ Restaurant ~ (015395) 68237 ~ Children welcome ~ Dogs allowed in bar ~ Open 11-11 ~ Bedrooms: £94B/£140B ~ www.the-punchbowl.co.uk

GREAT SALKELD   NY5536
Highland Drove
B6412, off A686 NE of Penrith; CA11 9NA

Bustling place with a cheerful mix of customers, good food in several dining areas, fair choice of drinks and fine views from the upstairs verandah; bedrooms

'This well run place provides every element of the perfect village pub,' one of our readers tells us – and many others agree. The hard-working, hands-on landlord is always there to greet his customers and everything is spotlessly kept. The chatty main bar has sandstone flooring, stone walls, cushioned wheelback chairs around a mix of tables and an open fire in a raised stone fireplace. The downstairs eating area has more cushioned dining chairs around wooden tables on the pale wooden floorboards, stone walls and ceiling joists and a two-way fire in a raised stone fireplace that separates this room from the coffee lounge with its comfortable leather chairs and sofas. There's also an upstairs restaurant (best to book to be sure of a table). Theakstons Black Bull, John Smiths and a guest beer on handpump, several wines by the glass and 30 malt whiskies; background music, juke box, darts, pool and dominoes. The lovely views over the Eden Valley and the Pennines are best enjoyed from seats on the upstairs verandah. There are more seats on the back terrace.

Free house ~ Licensees Donald and Paul Newton ~ Real ale ~ Bar food (12-2, 6(5.30 Fri and Sat)-9(8.30 Sun); not Mon lunchtime) ~ Restaurant ~ (01768) 898349 ~ Children welcome ~ Dogs allowed in bar ~ Open 12-3, 6-11; 12-midnight Sat; closed Mon lunchtime ~ Bedrooms: £42.50S/£75S ~ www.kyloes.co.uk

HAWKSHEAD   NY3501
Drunken Duck

Barngates; the hamlet is signposted from B5286 Hawkshead–Ambleside, opposite the Outgate Inn; or it may be quicker to take the first right from B5286, after the wooded caravan site; OS Sheet 90 map reference 350013; LA22 0NG

Stylish small bar, several restaurant areas, own-brewed beers and bar meals as well as innovative restaurant choices; lovely bedrooms, stunning views

This is a civilised dining pub with beautifully appointed bedrooms but at lunchtime there's much more of an informal, pubby feel and it's extremely popular for lunch after, or before, a walk. The small, smart bar has leather bar stools by the slate-topped bar counter, leather club chairs, beams and oak floorboards, photographs, coaching prints and hunting pictures on the walls, and horsebrasses and some kentish hop bines as decoration. From their Barngates brewery, there might be Cat Nap, Cracker, Red Bull Terrier, Tag Lag and Westmorland Gold on handpump as well as 17 wines by the glass from a fine list, 18 malt whiskies and belgian and german draught beers. The three restaurant areas are elegant. Outside, wooden tables and benches on grass opposite the building offer spectacular views across the fells, and there are thousands of spring and summer bulbs.

Own brew ~ Licensee Steph Barton ~ Real ale ~ Bar food (12-4, 6.30-9) ~ Restaurant ~ (015394) 36347 ~ Children welcome ~ Dogs allowed in bar ~ Open 11.30-11; 12-10.30 Sun ~ Bedrooms: £71.25B/£95B ~ www.drunkenduckinn.co.uk

LANGDALE   NY2806
Old Dungeon Ghyll

B5343; LA22 9JY

Straightforward place in lovely position with real ales, traditional food and fine walks; bedrooms

Full of character and atmosphere, this traditional pub is a real fell-walkers' and climbers' haven and the setting is pretty dramatic as it's right at the heart of the Great Langdale Valley. The whole feel of the place is basic but cosy and there's no need to remove boots or muddy trousers – you can sit on seats in old cattle stalls by the big warming fire and enjoy the fine choice of six real ales on handpump: Dent Bitter, Jennings Cumberland, Theakston Old Peculier, Thwaites Lancaster Bomber and Yates Best Bitter; also, around 20 malt whiskies. It may get lively on a Saturday night (there's a popular National Trust campsite opposite).

Free house ~ Licensee Neil Walmsley ~ Real ale ~ Bar food (12-2, 6-9) ~ Restaurant ~ (015394) 37272 ~ Children welcome ~ Dogs allowed in bar ~ Open 11-11(10.30 Sun) ~ Bedrooms: £58S/£116S ~ www.odg.co.uk

LEVENS   SD4987

Strickland Arms

4 miles from M6 junction 36, via A590; just off A590, by Sizergh Castle gates; LA8 8DZ

Friendly, open-plan pub with much enjoyed food, local ales and a fine setting; seats outside

Overlooking the entrance to Sizergh Castle, this well run and extremely popular pub is a civilised place for a drink or a meal. It's largely open-plan with a light and airy feel, and the bar on the right has oriental rugs on the flagstones, a log fire, Cumbrian Legendary Langdale and Loweswater Gold and four quickly changing guest beers on handpump, several malt whiskies and nine wines by the glass. On the left are polished boards and another log fire, and throughout there's a nice mix of sturdy country furniture, candles on tables, hunting scenes and other old prints on the walls, heavy fabric for the curtains and some staffordshire china ornaments; it's best to book ahead if you want to eat downstairs but there is a further dining room upstairs. Background music and board games. The flagstoned front terrace has plenty of seats. The castle, a lovely partly medieval house with beautiful gardens, is open in the afternoon (not Friday or Saturday) from April to October. They have disabled access and facilities.

Free house ~ Licensee Martin Ainscough ~ Real ale ~ Bar food (12-2, 7-9) ~ (015395) 61010 ~ Children welcome ~ Dogs allowed in bar ~ Open 12-11(10.30 Sun); 12-2, 5-11 in in winter ~ www.thestricklandarms.com

LITTLE LANGDALE   NY3103

Three Shires

From A593 3 miles W of Ambleside take small road signposted The Langdales, Wrynose Pass; then bear left at first fork; LA22 9NZ

Fine valley views from seats on the terrace, local ales, quite a choice of food and comfortable bedrooms

This is a lovely spot with views over the valley from seats on the terrace to the partly wooded hills below; there are more seats on a neat lawn behind the car park, backed by a small oak wood, and award-winning summer hanging baskets. The comfortably extended back bar has a mix of green Lakeland stone and homely red patterned wallpaper (which works rather well), stripped timbers and a beam and joist stripped ceiling, antique oak carved settles, country-kitchen chairs and stools on its big dark slate flagstones, and Lakeland photographs. Coniston Old Man, Hawkshead Bitter, Jennings Cumberland, and a guest beer on handpump, over 50 malt whiskies and a decent wine list. The front restaurant has chunky leather dining chairs around solid tables on the wood flooring, fresh flowers, and wine bottle prints on the dark red walls; a snug leads off here; darts, TV and board games. The three shires are the historical counties of Cumberland, Westmorland and Lancashire, which meet at the top of the nearby Wrynose Pass.

Free house ~ Licensee Ian Stephenson ~ Real ale ~ Bar food (12-2, 6-9) ~ Restaurant ~ (015394) 37215 ~ Children welcome ~ Dogs allowed in bar ~ Open 11-10.30(11 Sat) ~ Bedrooms: /£114S ~ www.threeshiresinn.co.uk

STAVELEY   SD4798
Beer Hall at Hawkshead Brewery
Staveley Mill Yard, Back Lane; LA8 9LR

Hawkshead Brewery showcase in glass-fronted building on two levels serving their whole range, a huge choice of bottled beers, knowledgeable staff, brewery memorabilia, interesting food and brewery tours

This spacious, modern glass-fronted building is the showcase for the full range of real ales from the Hawkshead Brewery: Bitter, Brodies Prime, Lakeland Gold and Lager, Pure Brewed Organic Stout, Red, Triple X Brodies Prime, Windermere Pale and seasonal beers on 14 handpumps; they also keep an extensive choice of bottled beers and whiskies with an emphasis on independent producers – all served by friendly, interested staff. The main bar is on two levels with the lower level dominated by the stainless steel fermenting vessels. There are high-backed chairs around light wooden tables, benches beside long tables and nice dark leather sofas around low tables (all on new oak floorboards) and a couple of walls are almost entirely covered with artistic photos of barley and hops and the brewing process; darts. You can buy T-shirts, branded glasses and mini casks and polypins and there are brewery tours; they have regular beer festivals, too. Parking can be tricky at peak times.

Own brew ~ Licensee Alex Brodie ~ Real ale ~ Bar food (12-3; 12-7(6 Sun) Fri and Sat) ~ (01539) 822644 ~ Children welcome away from bar ~ Dogs allowed in bar ~ Open 12-5(6 Tues-Thurs); 12-11 Fri and Sat; 12-8 Sun ~ www.hawksheadbrewery.co.uk

STAVELEY   SD4797
Eagle & Child
Kendal Road; just off A591 Windermere–Kendal; LA8 9LP

Welcoming inn with warming log fires, a good range of local beers and enjoyable food; bedrooms

'This is just what a pub should be,' says one reader enthusiastically, and many others agree. It's a really warmly welcoming little place in a lovely spot and makes a perfect base for exploring the area – it's on the Dales Way. There's a log fire under an impressive mantelbeam, a friendly, bustling atmosphere, and a roughly L-shaped flagstoned main area with plenty of separate parts to sit in, furnished with pews, banquettes, bow window seats and high-backed dining chairs around polished dark tables. Also, police truncheons and walking sticks, some nice photographs and interesting prints, a few farm tools, a delft shelf of bric-a-brac and another log fire. The five real ales on handpump come from breweries such as Coniston, Cumbrian Legendary, Hawkshead and Yates, and they keep several wines by the glass, 30 malt whiskies and farm cider; background music, darts and board games. An upstairs barn-themed dining room (with its own bar for functions) doubles as a breakfast room. There are picnic-sets under cocktail parasols in a sheltered garden by the River Kent, with more on a good-sized back terrace and a second garden behind.

Free house ~ Licensees Richard and Denise Coleman ~ Real ale ~ Bar food (12-2.30; 6-9) ~ Restaurant ~ (01539) 821320 ~ Children welcome ~ Dogs allowed in bar ~ Open 11-11 ~ Bedrooms: £50S/£70S ~ www.eaglechildinn.co.uk

STONETHWAITE   NY2513
Langstrath
Off B5289 S of Derwentwater; CA12 5XG

Civilised little place in lovely spot, traditional food with a modern twist, four real ales, good wines and malt whiskies, and seats outside; bedrooms

A warm haven on a cold, wet day, this is a civilised little inn with friendly licensees. The neat and simple bar (at its pubbiest at lunchtime) has a welcoming log fire in a big stone fireplace, new rustic tables, plain chairs and cushioned wall seats, and walking cartoons and attractive Lakeland mountain photographs on its textured white walls. Four real ales on handpump from breweries like Black Sheep, Hawkshead, Hesket Newmarket and Jennings and 25 malt whiskies; background music and board games. The small room on the left (actually the original cottage built around 1590) is a residents' lounge; the restaurant has fine views. Outside, a big sycamore shelters several picnic-sets with views up to Eagle Crag. There are fine surrounding walks as the pub is in a lovely spot in the heart of Borrowdale and en route for the Cumbrian Way and the Coast to Coast path.

Free house ~ Licensees Guy and Jacqui Frazer-Hollins ~ Real ale ~ Bar food (12-2.30 (snacks 2.30-4), 6-9; not Mon or Dec and Jan) ~ Restaurant ~ (017687) 77239 ~ Children over 10 in restaurant but only before 7.30pm ~ Dogs allowed in bar ~ Open 12-10.30; closed Mon, closed Dec and Jan (except New Year); best to phone for Feb hours ~ Bedrooms: /£110S(£117B) ~ www.thelangstrath.com

TALKIN   NY5457
Blacksmiths Arms
Village signposted from B6413 S of Brampton; CA8 1LE

Neatly kept and welcoming with tasty bar food, several real ales and good surrounding walks; bedrooms

This early 18th-c blacksmith's, now a pub with several neatly kept, traditionally furnished rooms, is attractively set on a village green and has plenty of walks right from the door or just a short drive away. You can be sure of a warm welcome from the licensees and their staff. The warm lounge on the right has a log fire, upholstered banquettes and wheelback chairs around dark wooden tables on the patterned red carpeting, and country prints and other pictures on the walls. The restaurant is to the left, and there's a long lounge opposite the bar, with another room up a couple of steps at the back. Black Sheep Bitter, Cumberland Corby Ale, Geltsdale Brampton Bitter and Yates Bitter on handpump, 20 wines by the glass and 35 malt whiskies; background music, darts and board games. There are a couple of picnic-sets outside the front door with more in the back garden. This is a quiet and comfortable place to stay.

Free house ~ Licensees Donald and Anne Jackson ~ Real ale ~ Bar food (12-2, 6-9) ~ Restaurant ~ (016977) 3452 ~ Children welcome ~ Dogs allowed in bar ~ Open 12-3, 6-11; 12-12 Sat; 12-4, 6-11 Sun ~ Bedrooms: £50S/£70S ~ www.blacksmithstalkin.co.uk

THRELKELD   NY3225

Horse & Farrier

A66 Penrith–Keswick; CA12 4SQ

Well run and friendly 17th-c fell-foot dining pub with good food and drinks; bedrooms

A happy mix of locals and tourists can be found in this attractive 17th-c inn, enjoying the real ales and hearty food. The neat, mainly carpeted bar has sturdy farmhouse and other nice tables, seats from comfortably padded ones to pubby chairs and from stools to bigger housekeeper's chairs and wall settles, country pictures on its white walls, one or two stripped beams and some flagstones; several open fires. Jennings Bitter, Cumberland, Mild and Sneck Lifter on handpump and several wines by the glass; friendly, efficient service. The partly stripped-stone restaurant is smart and more formal, with quite close-set tables. There are a few picnic-sets outside. If you plan to stay, the rooms in the inn itself are the best bet. The views towards Helvellyn range are stunning and there are walks straight from the door. Good disabled access and facilities.

Jennings (Marstons) ~ Lease Ian Court ~ Real ale ~ Bar food (12-9) ~ Restaurant ~ (017687) 79688 ~ Children welcome ~ Dogs allowed in bar ~ Open 7.30am-midnight ~ Bedrooms: £50B/£80B ~ www.horseandfarrier.com

YANWATH   NY5128

Gate Inn

2.25 miles from M6 junction 40; A66 towards Brough, then right on A6, right on B5320, then follow village signpost; CA10 2LF

Emphasis on imaginative food but with local beers and thoughtful wines, a pubby atmosphere and a warm welcome from the helpful staff

Once again, we've had nothing but praise for this civilised and immaculately kept 17th-c dining pub. There's a cosy bar of charming antiquity with country pine and dark wood furniture, lots of brasses on the beams, church candles on all the tables and a good log fire in the attractive stone inglenook. Friendly, courteous staff serve Barngates Tag Lag, Hesket Newmarket Doris's 90th Birthday Ale and Tirril Old Faithful on handpump and around a dozen good wines by the glass, 12 malt whiskies and Weston's Old Rosie cider. Two restaurant areas have oak floors, panelled oak walls and heavy beams; background music. There are seats on the terrace and in the garden. They have a self-catering cottage to let and the pub is handy for Ullswater.

Free house ~ Licensee Matt Edwards ~ Real ale ~ Bar food (12-2.30, 6-9) ~ Restaurant ~ (01768) 862386 ~ Children welcome ~ Dogs allowed in bar ~ Open 12-11 ~ www.yanwathgate.com

DOG FRIENDLY INNS, HOTELS AND B&Bs

ALSTON NY7646

Lovelady Shield Country House

Nenthead Road, Alston, Cumbria CA9 3LF (01434) 381203 www.lovelady.co.uk

£130; 12 rms. In a lovely setting with the River Nent running along bottom of the sizeable garden, this handsome country house has a tranquil atmosphere, courteous staff, log fires in the comfortable bar, lounge and library, and delicious modern british food (excellent breakfasts, too) in the elegant, formal dining room; resident cat; fine walks from the door; dogs in bedrooms only; £10

AMBLESIDE   NY3703

Regent

Waterhead Bay, Ambleside, Cumbria LA22 0ES (015394) 32254 www.regentlakes.co.uk

£119; 30 well equipped contemporary rms. Family-run hotel opposite a slipway on to Lake Windermere with pretty gardens, a bar lounge with sofas, a quiet snug with books, a split-level restaurant in shades of browns and cream, good, brasserie-style food, marvellous breakfasts and helpful staff; indoor heated pool, lots to do nearby and plenty of walks; dogs in courtyard bedrooms; £10

BARBON   SD6282

Barbon Inn

Barbon, Carnforth, Cumbria LA6 2LJ (015242) 76233

£80; 10 simple but comfortable rms, some with own bthrm. Small, friendly 17th-c village inn in a quiet spot below the fells, with relaxing bar and traditional lounge, open log fires, hearty meals in candlelit dining room, and helpful service; lots of good tracks and paths all around; dogs in bar and bedrooms; £10

BASSENTHWAITE LAKE   NY2032

Armathwaite Hall Hotel

Bassenthwaite Lake, Keswick, Cumbria CA12 4RE (017687) 76551
www.armathwaite-hall.com

£200; 46 lovely rms with views of the lake, gardens or park. Turreted 17th-c mansion, in 400 acres of deer park and woodland, with handsome public rooms, fine panelling, antiques and flowers, log fires in handsome fireplaces, a bustling bar-brasserie with all-day food, good french and english cooking using local seasonal produce in more formal restaurant, a super wine list and helpful staff; spa, indoor swimming pool and lots of outside activities – fishing shooting, bike and quad bike hire; resident belgian shepherds; many surrounding walks; dogs in bedrooms by prior arrangement; bed and treats; £15

BASSENTHWAITE LAKE

NY1930

Pheasant

Bassenthwaite Lake, Cockermouth, Cumbria CA13 9YE (017687) 76234
www.the-pheasant.co.uk

£140; 15 comfortable rms. Smart hotel with delightfully old fashioned pubby bar serving real ales and light lunches, restful lounges with open fires, antiques, fresh flowers and comfortable armchairs, a front bistro and more formal back restaurant with first class food, and interesting gardens merging into surrounding fellside woodland; lots of walks all around; dogs in bar and in Garden Lodge bedrooms; £5

BOUTH

SD3285

White Hart

Bouth, Ulverston, Cumbria LA12 8JB (01229) 861229 www.whitehart-lakedistrict.co.uk

£70; 5 comfortable rms. Cheerful, bustling inn with Lakeland feel, bars with sloping ceilings and floors, old local photos, farm tools and a collection of long-stemmed clay pipes, two woodburning stoves, six real ales and 25 malt whiskies, and generously served food using local lamb and beef; seats in the garden and fine surrounding walks; dogs in bedrooms and bar

BOWLAND BRIDGE

SD4189

Hare & Hounds

Bowland Bridge, Grange-Over-Sands, Cumbria LA11 6NN (015395) 68333
www.hareandhoundsbowlandbridge.co.uk

£85; 3 comfortable rms. 17th-c inn close to Lake Windermere and with fine valley views from spacious garden; log fire, daily papers and interesting ales in little bar, appealing furniture and more open fires in rooms leading off here, very good food using meat from local farms, and super breakfasts. The resident collie is called Murphy; dogs in bedrooms and bar; treats and bowl

BRAMPTON

NY5760

Farlam Hall

Hallbankgate, Brampton, Cumbria CA8 2NG (01697) 746234 www.farlamhall.co.uk

£340 including dinner; 12 smart and comfortable rms. Very civilised, mainly 19th-c country house with log fires in ornately Victorian lounges, excellent attentive service, good country-house-style meals at 8pm in friendly but formal restaurant, marvellous breakfasts and peaceful, spacious grounds with croquet lawn and small pretty lake; plenty of nearby walks; dogs in bedrooms and elsewhere but must be in car during mealtimes

BUTTERMERE

NY1716

Bridge

Buttermere, Cockermouth, Cumbria CA13 9UZ (017687) 70252 www.bridge-hotel.com

£70; 21 comfortable rms. Surrounded by some of the best steep countryside in the county and run by the same family for 30 years, this friendly hotel has a lounge and a walkers' bar, open fires, deep armchairs and books in residents' lounge, hearty food in separate restaurant, and an easy-going atmosphere; self-catering also; dogs in some bedrooms; £10

CARTMEL   SD3879QQ

Aynsome Manor

Cartmel, Grange-Over-Sands, Cumbria LA11 6HH (01539) 536653
www.aynsomemanorhotel.co.uk

£99; 12 attractive rms. Lovely old manor house, in the same family for 30 years and surrounded by countryside with plenty of surrounding walks; relaxing, homely sitting room with sofas by a log fire, a cosy, well stocked bar, interesting daily-changing food in the oak-panelled restaurant, and a warm, friendly atmosphere throughout; resident cats; closed Jan; dogs in bedrooms; not in public rooms; £4.50

CARTMEL   SD3977

Uplands

Haggs Lane, Cartmel, Grange-Over-Sands, Cumbria LA11 6HD (01539) 536848
www.uplandscartmel.co.uk

£80; 5 pretty rms. Comfortable Edwardian house in 2 acres of grounds (plenty of wildlife) with views over to Morecambe Bay; large, attractively decorated lounge, welcoming owners, an informal atmosphere, very good modern food (including light lunches and afternoon teas) in the restaurant, and super breakfasts; walks from the front door; dogs welcome away from public rooms; £10

CARTMEL FELL   SD4189

Masons Arms

Cartmel Fell, Grange-Over-Sands, Cumbria LA11 6NW (015395) 68486
www.strawberrybank.com

£84; 5 stylish suites and 2 cottages. Well run pub in an unrivalled setting with wonderful views and good surrounding walks; a beamed and flagstoned main bar with much character and several real ales, other small rooms with panelling, oak furniture and an open range, and inventive, enjoyable food in the upstairs dining room; dogs in bedrooms and in bar (after 9pm)

CLIFTON   NY5326

George & Dragon

Clifton, Penrith, Cumbria CA10 2ER (01768) 865381
www.georgeanddragonclifton.co.uk

£95; 12 smart rms. 18th-c former coaching inn with attractive bars, leather or farmhouse chairs around wooden tables on flagstones, bright rugs here and there, open fires, sheep and fell pictures on grey and yellow walls, and real ales and wines by the glass; a sizeable restaurant serving imaginative food from the open kitchen and using rare-breed meat from nearby estate, and a resident patterdale terrier, Porter; dogs in bedrooms and bar

CROOK
SD4395
Wild Boar
Crook, Windermere, Cumbria LA23 3NF (015394) 45225
www.englishlakes.co.uk/the-wildboar-inn

£96; 17 individually decorated rms, some with woodburning stoves and brass baths. Open-plan rooms with ladder-back chairs around dark tables, rugs on floorboards, painted beams, real ales and 50 malt whiskies, helpful, friendly service and interesting bistro-style food using their own smokehouse; very nice breakfasts; dogs in bedrooms; £10

DERWENT WATER
NY2618
Lodore Falls
Borrowdale, Keswick, Cumbria CA12 5UX (017687) 77285 www.lodorefallshotel.co.uk

£188; 69 refurbished rms with lakeside or fell views. Imposing hotel in 40 acres of gardens and overlooking Derwentwater and with fantastic walks from the front door; courteous, friendly staff, comfortable lounges, bar and café with lake views and open fire, and imaginative food, morning coffees and afternoon teas; tennis court, outdoor and indoor swimming pools, a hot tub, squash court, a sauna, gym and spa; you can hire kayaks, canoes and sailing boats; dogs in bedrooms and side bar; bowl and basket; £10;

ELTERWATER
NY3204
Britannia Inn
Elterwater, Ambleside, Cumbria LA22 9HP (015394) 37210 www.britinn.co.uk

£95; 9 rms. Simple charmingly traditional pub in fine surroundings close to the central lakes and tracks over the fells; small front and back bars with coal fires, oak benches and settles, good ales and whiskies, a comfortable lounge, and dining room with generously served, honest food (book in advance); smashing breakfasts; dogs in bedrooms and bar

ENNERDALE BRIDGE
NY0615
Shepherds Arms
Ennerdale, Cleator, Cumbria CA23 3AR (01946) 861249

£89.50; 8 rms. Set on the popular Coast to Coast path and with wonderful surrounding walks, this welcoming inn has a convivial bar, a woodburning stove, a main bar with a coal fire and traditional seats and tables, a conservatory, cheerful staff, well kept ales and substantial bar food; dogs in bedrooms

FAR SAWREY
SD3895
Cuckoo Brow
Far Sawrey, Ambleside, Cumbria LA22 0LQ (015394) 43425 www.cuckoobrow.co.uk

£100; 14 refurbished rms. Friendly hotel well placed at the foot of Claife Heights and surrounded by lovely scenery and walks, with nice wooden tables and chairs on bare boards, open fires and woodburning stoves, local ales and hearty food using the best local produce, and good breakfasts; seats outside; resident dog,

Poppy; dogs welcome anywhere as long as well behaved and on lead; treats and bowls; £10

GRASMERE

NY3308

Swan

Keswick Road, Grasmere, Ambleside, Cumbria LA22 9RF (0844) 8799120
www.macdonaldhotels.co.uk/our-hotels/swan-hotel

£75; 38 rms, most with fine views. Smart and friendly 17th-c former coaching inn in beautiful fell-foot surroundings, with beams and winter log fires in inglenooks, comfortable lounges, a walkers' bar, a wide range of enjoyable food in the elegant dining room, and seats in the attractive sheltered garden; lovely walks close by; dogs welcome away from restaurant; £15

INGS

SD4498

Watermill

Ings, Kendal, Cumbria LA8 9PY (01539) 821309 www.lakelandpub.co.uk

£79; 8 comfortable rms. Busy, cleverly converted pub with a fantastic range of real ales including their own brews, 40 malt whiskies and scrumpy cider; lively bars with traditional furnishings, open fires and interesting photos and cartoons, and popular food using their own-reared beef; good walking country; dogs in bedrooms and bar; biscuits; £4 to a dog charity

Ralf; owner Paul Smith

IREBY   NY2335
Overwater Hall
Ireby, Carlisle, Cumbria CA5 1HH (017687) 76566 www.overwaterhall.co.uk

£150; 11 individually decorated rms with fell or garden views. Turreted Georgian
hotel in 18 acres of gardens and woodland – lots of walks, too; log fire in
traditionally furnished, comfortable drawing room, a well stocked panelled bar,
good imaginative food in cosy dining room, hearty breakfasts, and tasty afternoon
teas, and genuinely helpful, friendly service; two resident black labradors and one
cat; closed 2 weeks from New Year; dogs in bedrooms, bar and one lounge; they
have a dog of the day photo on website

LANGDALE   NY2806
Old Dungeon Ghyll
Great Langdale, Ambleside, Cumbria LA22 9JY (015394) 37272 www.odg.co.uk

£116; 12 rms, some with shared bthrm. Friendly, simple and cosy walkers' and
climbers' inn dramatically surrounded by fells, wonderful views and terrific walks
straight from the front door; cosy residents' lounge and popular food in dining
room – best to book for dinner if not a resident; dogs in bedrooms only; £5

LORTON   NY1522
New House Farm
Lorton, Cockermouth, Cumbria CA13 9UU (01900) 85404 www.newhouse-farm.co.uk

£65; 5 rms with wonderful hillside views. Friendly 17th-c house in 15 acres of
grounds, with beams and rafters, flagstones, farming artefacts and open fires in
residents' lounges, very good three- or five-course traditional meals served in the
dining room and smashing breakfasts with fresh-baked croissants and freshly
squeezed orange juice; two resident terriers; lots of walks; dogs in bedrooms; not
dining room; £7

LOWESWATER   NY1421
Kirkstile Inn
Loweswater, Cockermouth, Cumbria CA13 0RU (01900) 85219 www.kirkstile.com

£99; 11 cottagey rms. Busy, well run in with stunning peak views and surrounded
by walks of all levels; friendly, low-beamed bar with own-brew beers, nine wines
by the glass, a roaring log fire and cushioned small settles and pews, a slate shove-
ha'penny board and board games, and hearty food using lots of seasonal game;
dogs in annexe bedroom and bar at lunchtime; £5

LUPTON   SD5581
Plough
Cow Brow, Lupton, Carnforth, Lancashire LA6 1PJ (015395) 67700
www.theploughatlupton.co.uk

£165; 5 well equipped, lovely rms. Stylish18th-c inn with fine walks all around,
spreading open-plan rooms with leather sofas and armchairs in front of a big
woodburning stove, antique tables and chairs, rugs on bare boards, real ales, daily

papers and top class food served all day by helpful staff; very good breakfasts; dogs in one bedroom and bar; £10

MUNGRISDALE

NY3630

Mill Inn

Mungrisdale, Penrith, Cumbria CA11 0XR (017687) 79632 www.the-millinn.co.uk

£75; 6 rms. Friendly 17th-c Lakeland inn with seats in the garden by the water and marvellous surrounding walks; neatly kept bar with a log fire in the stone fireplace, traditional dark wooden furnishings, hunting pictures, good real ales, and tasty food in the separate dining room; dogs in bedrooms and bar; not restaurant; £5

NEAR SAWREY

SD3795

Tower Bank Arms

Near Sawrey, Ambleside, Cumbria LA22 0LF (015394) 36334
www.towerbankarms.com

£93; 4 nice rms. Busy little inn, backing on to Beatrix Potter's farm (the pub features in The Tale of Jemima Puddleduck), with genuinely welcoming staff in the low-beamed main bar; lots of rustic charm, a log fire, fresh flowers and a grandfather clock, popular food using local produce and particularly good breakfasts; dogs in bedrooms and bar

NEWBIGGIN-ON-LUNE

NY7005

Brownber Hall Country House

Newbiggin-on-Lune, Kirkby Stephen, Cumbria CA17 4NX (01539) 623208
www.brownberhall.co.uk

£80; 10 comfortable rms. Victorian country house in mature grounds with marvellous spreading views, a relaxing atmosphere, many original features in two traditionally furnished sitting rooms, and good breakfasts; inns and restaurants nearby for evening meals; seats on the terrace look over the countryside; dogs welcome by prior arrangement; £5

RAVENSTONEDALE

NY7203

Black Swan

Ravenstonedale, Kirkby Stephen, Cumbria CA17 4NG (015396) 23204
www.blackswanhotel.com

£85; 15 comfortable rms. Family-run Victorian hotel with thriving bar and a happy mix of customers; lots of original period features, plush furnishings and fresh flowers, real ales, wines by the glass and 20 malt whiskies, enjoyable food using seasonal local produce, and tables in sheltered streamside garden; this is serious walking country and they have leaflets describing the routes; dogs in some bedrooms, bar and lounge; £10

SCALES   NY3326

Scales Farm

Scales, Threlkeld, Cumbria CA12 4SY (01768) 779660 www.scalesfarm.com

£70; 6 comfortable, well equipped rms, 3 with ground-floor access. Converted 17th-c farmhouse with wide-stretching views, a friendly welcome, a woodburning stove and wide screen TV in homely beamed lounge, traditional english breakfasts in large dining room (good pub next door for evening meals), and packed lunches on request; they keep chickens; fine walks all around; dogs in bedrooms; £4, bring own bedding

SEATOLLER   NY2413

Seatoller House

Borrowdale, Keswick, Cumbria CA12 5XN (017687) 77218 www.seatollerhouse.co.uk

£90; 10 spotless, comfortable rms. Friendly house-party atmosphere in 17th-c house – a guest house for over 100 years; comfortable sitting room and library, a bar for hot and cold drinks, snacks and a daily home-made cake, and a dining room with two large oak tables for the four-course 7pm evening meal and for breakfasts; 2 acres of grounds and many walks from doorstep (the house is at the foot of Honister Pass); closed Dec-Feb; dogs welcome in bedrooms and one of the lounges

SHAP   NY5614

Greyhound

Shap, Penrith, Cumbria CA10 3PW (01931) 716474 www.greyhoundshap.co.uk

£85; 11 rms. Former coaching inn with fell views and handy for the M6; usefully open all day, the big open-plan bar has a log fire, seats ranging from armchairs and a sofa to straightforward dining tables and chairs, and up to eight real ales; friendly staff, honest food in separate dining rooms, and hearty breakfasts; resident alsatian, Glen, and cat, Biscuit; dogs in bedrooms and bar

SKELWITH BRIDGE   NY3403

Skelwith Bridge Hotel

Skelwith Bridge, Ambleside, Cumbria LA22 9NJ (015394) 32115
www.skelwithbridgehotel.co.uk

£100; 28 attractive rms with fine views. Carefully extended 17th-c former farmhouse in quiet countryside (only 2 miles to Ambleside) with beams and other original features, open fire in comfortable sitting room, antiques and fresh flowers, oak-panelled Library bar and convivial little Talbot bar, and enjoyable food in restaurant overlooking gardens and river; self-catering cottage, too; dogs in bedrooms (not to be left unattended); welcome pack, blankets, towels; £5

TIRRIL   NY5026

Queens Head

Tirril, Penrith, Cumbria CA10 2JF (01768) 863219 www.queensheadinn.co.uk

£75; 7 rms. 18th-c pub a couple of miles from Ullswater with several bars, an open fire in inglenook fireplace, low beams, black panelling and flagstones, an attractive mix of tables and chairs, and real ales; speciality pies (and other food choices) are served in two dining rooms; they also run the village shop; dogs in bedrooms and bars; £5

TORVER   SD2894
Church House

Torver, Coniston, Cumbria LA21 8AZ (015394) 41282 www.churchhouseinntorver.com

£70; 5 rms. Rambling 14th-c coaching inn with splendid hill views from seats in big garden and close to Coniston Water – they can advise on walks; bustling beamed bar with a fine log fire in large stone fireplace, Lakeland bric-a-brac, traditional furniture on slate flooring and well kept local ales, and interesting food served in comfortable lounge and dining room; resident jack russell Molly loves catching beer mats; dogs in bedrooms and bar; bowls in bar and outside; £5

TROUTBECK   NY4103
Queens Head

Troutbeck, Windermere, Cumbria LA23 1PW (015394) 32174
www.queenshoteltroutbeck.co.uk

£150; 15 highly thought of rms in inn or converted barn. Rather smart and warm-hearted, extended pub with several rambling, beamed rooms, log and coal fires, interesting settles, chairs and tables on flagstones, musical instruments, stuffed pheasants and country pictures on stone walls, a good choice of ales and wines by the glass and imaginative food served by courteous staff; countless nearby walks; resident dog; dogs in two bedrooms and bar; £20

ULVERSTON   SD3177
Bay Horse

Canal Foot, Ulverston, Cumbria LA12 9EL (01229) 583972
www.thebayhorsehotel.co.uk

£120; 9 rms. Civilised and nicely placed hotel overlooking Morecambe Bay with a relaxed, smart bar, comfortable seating, an open fire in the handsomely marbled grey slate fireplace, a huge stone horse's head, real ales and 16 wines by the glass; interesting lunchtime bar food (restaurant only in evening); walks on beach; dogs in bedrooms and lounge bar

WASDALE HEAD   NY1607
Wasdale Head Hotel

Wasdale Head, Seascale, Cumbria CA20 1EX (019467) 26229 www.wasdale.com

£118; 9 simple but warmly comfortable pine-clad rms, with 3 more luxurious ones in farmhouse annexe. Old flagstoned and gabled walkers' and climbers' inn in magnificent setting surrounded by steep fells and wonderful walks; micro-brewery (tours available), civilised day rooms, residents' lounge with books and games, popular home cooking, good wine list, huge breakfasts and cheerfully busy public bar; steam room; self-catering cottages, too; dogs welcome away from restaurant; biscuits and towels; £10

WATERMILLOCK
NY4523
Rampsbeck Country House
Watermillock, Penrith, Cumbria CA11 0LP (017684) 86442 www.rampsbeck.co.uk

£90; 19 attractive, traditional rms, many with stunning views. Fine Victorian hotel in wonderful lakeside setting with 18 acres of formal gardens and parkland; open fire in the cosy sitting room, french windows into the garden from the plush, comfortable lounge, friendly attentive staff, and carefully prepared food in the attractive dining room; croquet, and lots to do nearby; dogs in some bedrooms and hall lounge

WINDERMERE
NY3902
Holbeck Ghyll
Holbeck Lane, Windermere, Cumbria LA23 1LU (015394) 32375 www.holbeck-ghyll.co.uk

£210; 25 opulent rms, 6 in lodge, 5 in cottages. Warmly friendly country house in 15 acres of grounds with tennis and putting and close to Lake Windermere – lots of walks; amazing views from two gracious, comfortable lounges, antiques, panelling and log fires, and well reputed food in oak-panelled restaurant; health spa; resident golden retriever, Daisy; dogs in bedrooms and beside inglenook; welcome pack, beds, biscuits, towels; £25

WINDERMERE
SD4095
Linthwaite House
Crook Road, Windermere, Cumbria LA23 3JA (015394) 88600 www.linthwaite.com

£239; 30 light rms decorated in both contemporary and traditional styles. Edwardian house set in 14 acres of grounds with lovely views over Lake Windermere and their own fishing tarn; an attractive, airy conservatory and sunny terrace overlooking the water, a cosy lounge with roaring fire and afternoon teas, a convivial bar, imaginative modern cooking, an eclectic wine list and warmly friendly, helpful service; croquet, lovely walks from the door and plenty to see nearby; dogs in two rooms with outside access; £9

WITHERSLACK
SD4482
Derby Arms
Witherslack, Grange-over-sands, Cumbria LA11 6RH (015395) 52207 www.thederbyarms.co.uk

£65; 6 comfortable rms. Bustling country inn with sporting prints, big rugs on floorboards, hops strung over the counter where they keep six real ales on handpump, and an open fire, a larger room with political cartoons and local castle prints, another open fire and quite a bit of china, and two further similarly furnished room; quite a choice of highly thought of food served by friendly staff; Levens Hall and Sizergh Castle are nearby; dogs anywhere in the pub and in bedrooms

Derbyshire

MAP 7

DOG FRIENDLY PUBS

ALDERWASLEY   SK3153

Bear

Left off A6 at Ambergate on to Holly Lane (turns into Jackass Lane) then right at end
(staggered cross roads); DE56 2RD

Unspoilt country inn with beamed cottagey rooms, good range of real
ales, tasty food and a peaceful garden; bedrooms

This characterful tavern has lovely dark low-beamed rooms with warming open
fires and a cheerful miscellany of antique furniture including high-backed
settles and locally made antique oak chairs with derbyshire motifs. One little
room is filled right to its built-in wall seats by a single vast table. Other décor
includes staffordshire china ornaments, old paintings and engravings. There's no
obvious front door – you get in through the plain back entrance by the car park,
and as it can get busy you may need to book. Bass, Derby Blue Bear, Hartington
IPA, Thornbridge Jaipur and Timothy Taylors Landlord are on handpump
alongside a guest or two, and they do several wines by the glass from a decent
list, as well as malt whiskies. Well spaced picnic-sets out in a lovely garden have
wonderful country views. Please call before you visit to check opening times.

Free house ~ Licensee Pete Buller ~ Real ale ~ Bar food (12-3, 6-9; 12-9 Fri-Sun) ~
Restaurant ~ (01629) 822585 ~ Children welcome ~ Dogs allowed in bar ~ Open 12-
11(10.30 Sun) ~ Bedrooms: /£75B ~ www.bear-hotel.com

BRASSINGTON   SK2354

Olde Gate

Village signed off B5056 and B5035 NE of Ashbourne; DE4 4HJ

Lovely old interior, candlelit at night, with tasty, fair-priced food, real
ales and country garden

The charming interior of this unspoilt listed building (just a few minutes' drive
from Carsington Water) is full of attractive old architectural features, from
mullioned windows to a Georgian panelled room. Fine old furnishings include
an ancient wall clock, rush-seated old chairs and antique settles, among them a
lovely ancient example in black solid oak. Log fires blaze away, gleaming copper
pots sit on a 17th-c kitchen range, pewter mugs hang from a beam, and a side
shelf boasts a collection of embossed Doulton stoneware flagons. To the left of
a small hatch-served lobby, a cosy beamed room has stripped panelled settles,
scrubbed-top tables and a blazing fire under a huge mantelbeam. Marstons

Pedigree and two guests from the Marstons stable of brewers such as Jennings and Ringwood are on handpump, and they keep a good selection of malt whiskies; cribbage, dominoes, cards, and maybe Sunday evening boules in summer. A very inviting garden has a good number of tables looking out to idyllic silvery-walled pastures and there are some benches in the small front yard; please ring to check opening times.

Marstons ~ Lease Peter Scragg ~ Real ale ~ Bar food (12-2(2.30 Sun), 6.30-8.45 Tues-Sat; not Sun evening) ~ (01629) 540448 ~ Children welcome ~ Dogs allowed in bar ~ Open 12-2.15(3 Sun), 6-11; 12-3, 6-10 Sun; closed Mon (except bank holidays), Tues lunchtime, Sun evening in winter ~ www.oldgateinnbrassington.co.uk

BRETTON   SK2078
Barrel

Signposted from Foolow, which itself is signposted from A623 just E of junction with B6465 to Bakewell; can also be reached from either the B6049 at Great Hucklow, or the B6001 via Abney, from Leadmill just S of Hathersage; S32 5QD

Remote dining pub with traditional décor, popular food and friendly staff

This magnificently situated stone-roofed turnpike inn dates back to 1597. Being the highest pub in Derbyshire (so we're told), at the top of Bretton Clough, it enjoys glorious sweeping views over five counties – seats out on the front terrace by the road and a courtyard garden are nicely sheltered from the inevitable breeze at this height. Inside, stubs of massive knocked-through stone walls divide it into several areas. The cosy dark oak-beamed bar is charmingly traditional with its gleaming copper and brass, warming fire, patterned carpet, low doorways and stools lined up at the counter, which has Marstons Pedigree and EPA and Wychwood Hobgoblin on handpump, and tankards hanging above. Everything here is kept spic and span and the friendly staff are smartly dressed; background radio.

Free house ~ Licensee Philip Cone ~ Real ale ~ Bar food (12-2, 6-9; 12-9 Sun) ~ (01433) 630856 ~ Well behaved children welcome ~ Dogs allowed in bar ~ Open 11-11; 11-3, 6-11 Mon-Fri Oct-March ~ Bedrooms: £50S/£85B ~ www.thebarrelinn.co.uk

CHELMORTON   SK1170
Church Inn

Village signposted off A5270, between A6 and A515 SE of Buxton; keep on up through village towards church; SK17 9SL

Cosy, convivial traditional inn beautifully set in High Peak walking country – good value food

This welcoming pub is in a quiet spot at the end of a road up to the moors. It's opposite a largely 18th-c church and prettily tucked into woodland with fine views over the village and hills beyond from good teak tables on its two-level terrace. The warm can-do hospitable greeting from the licensees and staff really sets a friendly atmosphere in the chatty low-ceilinged tiled bar. It has a warming fire and is traditionally furnished with cushioned built-in benches and simple chairs around polished cast-iron-framed tables – one or two still with their squeaky sewing treadles. Shelves of books, Tiffany-style lamps and house plants in the curtained windows, atmospheric Dales photographs and prints, and a coal-effect stove in the stripped-stone end wall all add a cosy feel. Adnams, Marstons Bitter and Pedigree and a couple of guests from brewers such as Buxton and

Thornbridge might be on handpump; darts in a tiled-floor games area on the left; TV, background music and board games.

Free house ~ Licensees Julie and Justin Satur ~ Real ale ~ Bar food (12-2.30, 6-8.30; 12-9 Fri-Sun) ~ (01298) 85319 ~ Children welcome ~ Dogs allowed in bar ~ Open 12-3, 6-midnight; 12-midnight Fri-Sun ~ Bedrooms: £50S/£75S ~ www.thechurchinn.co.uk

GREAT LONGSTONE   SK1971

Crispin
Main Street; DE45 1TZ

Spotless traditional pub with emphasis on good, fairly priced pubby food; good drinks choice, too

You can be sure of a good homely welcome and cheerful service at this well established family-run pub in the heart of the Peak District. Décor throughout is thoroughly traditional, running from some brass or copper implements, decorative plates, a collage of regulars' snapshots and horsebrasses on the beams in the red ceiling, to cushioned built-in wall benches and upholstered chairs and stools around polished tables on red carpet, and a fire. A corner area is snugly partitioned off, and on the right is a separate, more formal dining room; darts, board games and maybe faint background music. Welcoming staff serve a good choice of wines and whiskies as well five Robinsons beers on handpump. There are picnic-sets out in front, set well back above the quiet lane (one under a heated canopy), and more in the recently redesigned garden.

Robinsons ~ Tenant Paul Rowlinson ~ Real ale ~ Bar food (12-2.30, 6-9) ~ Restaurant ~ (01629) 640237 ~ Children welcome ~ Dogs allowed in bar ~ Open 12-3, 6-midnight; 12-midnight Sat; 12-11 Sun ~ www.thecrispin.co.uk

HASSOP   SK2272

Eyre Arms
B6001 N of Bakewell; DE45 1NS

Comfortable, neatly kept comfortable pub with decent food and beer, and pretty views from the garden

The metre-thick walls of this 17th former coaching inn are completely swathed in vines, and in autumn, when they turn a vibrant orange, the building appears to glow. Inside it's snug and cosy with cheery log fires warming the low-ceilinged oak beamed rooms. Traditional furnishings include cushioned oak settles, comfortable plush chairs, a long-case clock, old pictures and lots of brass and copper. The small public bar has an unusual collection of teapots, as well as Black Sheep, Chatsworth Gold and Peak Ales Swift Nick on handpump, and several wines by the glass; background classical music, darts. The dining room is dominated by a painting of the Eyre coat of arms above the stone fireplace. The delightful garden, with its gurgling fountain, looks straight out into fine Peak District countryside.

Free house ~ Licensees Nick and Lynne Smith ~ Real ale ~ Bar food (12-2, 6.30-9; 12-3, 6-9 Sat, Sun) ~ (01629) 640390 ~ Children welcome ~ Dogs allowed in bar ~ Open 11-3, 6.30-11; 11-11 Sat; 11-10.30 Sun; closed Mon evening ~ www.eyrearms.com

HOPE   SK1783
Cheshire Cheese
Off A6187, towards Edale; S33 6ZF

Cosy multi-level stone pub, with good real ales and pubby food and in an attractive Peak District village; bedrooms

There's plenty of traditional atmosphere in the two snug oak-beamed rooms at this popular honey-coloured 16th-c inn. Arranged on different levels, they are cosy with warming fires, red carpets or stone floors, traditional dark wood furnishings and gleaming brasses. It's a well liked place and often fills to capacity with locals as well as tourists, all welcomed equally by the friendly barman and staff. Bradfield Farmers Blonde, Kelham Island Easy Rider, Peak Ales Swift Nick and two guests such as Bradfield Farmers Brown Cow and Peak Ales Chatsworth Gold are on handpump and they've a dozen malts. There's a glorious range of local walks near here, taking in the summits of Lose Hill and Win Hill, or the cave district of the Castleton area, and the village of Hope itself is worth a stroll; parking is limited.

Enterprise ~ Lease Laura Offless ~ Real ale ~ Bar food (12-2(3 Sat, 4 Sun), 6-9) ~ Restaurant ~ (01433) 620381 ~ Children welcome ~ Dogs allowed in bar ~ Open 12-3, 6-11; 12-11 Sat, 12-6 Sun; closed Sun evening, Mon ~ Bedrooms: £45B/£70B ~ www.cheshirecheeseinn.co.uk

INGLEBY   SK3427
John Thompson
NW of Melbourne; turn off A514 at Swarkestone Bridge or in Stanton by Bridge; can also be reached from Ticknall (or from Repton on B5008); DE73 7HW

Own-brew pub that strikes the right balance between attentive service, roomy comfort and good value lunchtime food

Friendly staff serve the two beers that are brewed at the back of this relaxed and unchanging pubby place, alongside a guest such as Timothy Taylors Landlord. Simple but comfortable and immaculately kept, the big modernised lounge has ceiling joists, some old oak settles, button-back leather seats, sturdy oak tables, antique prints and paintings and a log-effect gas fire; background music. A couple of smaller, cosier rooms open off; piano, games machine, board games, darts, TV, and pool in the conservatory. There are lots of tables by flower beds on the neat lawns, or you can sit on the partly covered terrace, surrounded by pretty countryside and near the River Trent. Breakfast is left in your fridge if you stay in one of their self-catering detached chalet lodges. The pub takes its name from the licensee's father.

Own brew ~ Licensee Nick Thompson ~ Real ale ~ Bar food (12-2) ~ Restaurant ~ (01332) 862469 ~ Children welcome in main bar till 6pm, in conservatory till 9pm ~ Dogs allowed in bar ~ Open 11-2.30, 6-11; 11-11 Sat; 12-10.30 Sun; closed Mon lunchtime except bank holidays ~ www.johnthompsoninn.com

MONYASH
Bulls Head
B5055 W of Bakewell; DE45 1JH

SK1566

Unpretentious local with tasty home cooking

This rambling multi roomed stone pub extends a genuinely friendly welcome to visitors and locals alike. Its high-ceilinged rooms are gently unassuming, with a good log fire, straightforward traditional furnishings including plush stools lined along the bar, horse pictures and a shelf of china. A small back bar room has darts, board games and pool, and the newly decorated more cottagey feeling restaurant is cosy with leather high backed dining chairs on heated stone floors; quiet background music. Black Sheep and a couple of guests such as Bradfield Farmers Blonde are on handpump. A gate from the pub's garden leads into an entertaining village play area, and this is fine walking country.

Free house ~ Licensee Sharon Barber ~ Real ale ~ Bar food (12-9; 12-2, 5.30-9 weekdays in winter) ~ Restaurant ~ (01629) 812372 ~ Children welcome ~ Dogs allowed in bar ~ Open 12-2.30, 5-11; 12-11 Fri-Sun ~ www.thebullsheadmonyash.co.uk

STANTON IN PEAK
Flying Childers
Village signposted from B6056 S of Bakewell; Main Road; DE4 2LW

SK2364

Top-notch beer and inexpensive simple bar lunches in warm-hearted unspoilt pub – a delight

Besides his regular Wells & Youngs Bombardier, the friendly landlord at this homely village pub (named after an unbeatable racehorse of the early 18th c) keeps a couple of constantly changing guests from brewers such as Abbeydale and Storm. The room to enjoy them best in is the snug little right-hand bar, virtually built for chat, with its dark beam-and-plank ceiling, dark wall settles,

Frankie – wire-haired, miniature dachshund

single pew, plain tables, a hot coal and log fire, a few team photographs, and dominoes and cribbage; background music. There's a bigger equally unpretentious bar on the right. A well tended garden at the back has picnic-sets and there are a couple more out in front; this beautiful steep stone village overlooks a rich green valley, and there are good walks in most directions.

Free house ~ Licensees Stuart and Mandy Redfern ~ Real ale ~ Bar food (lunchtimes only) ~ No credit cards ~ (01629) 636333 ~ Children welcome ~ Dogs allowed in bar ~ Open 12-2(3 Sat, Sun), 7-11; closed Mon, Tues lunchtimes ~ www.flyingchilders.com

DOG FRIENDLY INNS, HOTELS AND B&Bs

ASHBOURNE   SK1746
Callow Hall
Mappleton Road, Ashbourne, Derbyshire DE6 2AA (01335) 300900
www.callowhall.co.uk

£200; 16 lovely individually furnished rms. Quietly smart and friendly Victorian mansion up a long drive through 35 acres of grounds and surrounded by marvellous countryside walks; heavy drapes, antiques, open fires and fresh flowers, plenty of original features, a comfortable drawing room and informal bar, extremely good modern food in the elegant restaurant, delicious breakfasts and kind staff; dogs in some bedrooms; £25

ASHBOURNE   SK2742
Mercaston Hall
Mercaston, Ashbourne, Derbyshire DE6 3BL (01335) 360263 www.mercastonhall.com

£75; 3 comfortable rms. Quietly set and handsome 17th-c house on working sheep farm, with friendly owners, a comfortable and homely beamed lounge with a woodburning stove, hearty breakfasts, and tennis court; good surrounding walks; two resident border collies; dogs in bedrooms (not to be left unattended); not in dining room; £2

ASHOVER   SK3462
Old Poets Corner
Butts Road, Ashover, Chesterfield, Derbyshire S45 0EW (01246) 590888
www.oldpoets.co.uk

£75; 5 attractive rms. Characterful village pub with cosy lived-in feel in friendly bar, interesting ales (some own-brewed) and ciders, two roaring fires, lots of knick-knacks and hops, a pile of board games by piano and generous helpings of honest food; newspapers and vintage comics in smaller room and regular live acoustic, folk and blues music; self-catering cottage also; miles of walks from doorstep; resident cocker spaniels, Rosy and Lilly, and Ruby the brewery cat; dogs in bedrooms and bar; not main dining room; water bowls inside and outside; £5

BEELEY

SK2667

Devonshire Arms

The Beeches, Beeley, Matlock, Derbyshire DE4 2NR (01629) 733259
www.devonshirebeeley.co.uk

£199; 14 stylishly comfortable rms. Handsome stone inn on the fringes of Chatsworth Estate with contemporary colours contrasting well with attractive traditional furnishings in various bar rooms; lots of prints and floral arrangements, black beams and flagstones, cheerful log fires, six real ales and well chosen wines, and inventive food using seasonal produce from the estate; dogs in cottage bedrooms

BIGGIN-BY-HARTINGTON

SK1559

Biggin Hall

Biggin-by-Hartington, Buxton, Derbyshire SK17 0DH (01298) 84451
www.bigginhall.co.uk

£102; 21 spacious rms with antiques, some in converted 18th-c stone building and in bothy. Cheerfully run 17th-c house in 8 acres of quiet grounds with a very relaxed atmosphere, two comfortable sitting rooms, one with a library, the other with a woodburning stove in the inglenook fireplace, and an attractive dining room serving interesting country-house-style food using local and free range produce; two resident collies, one cat, geese, chickens and horses; plenty of trails and dales to walk; dogs in courtyard and bothy bedrooms, not restaurant

GRINDLEFORD

SK2478

The Maynard

Main Road, Nether Padley, Grindleford, Hope Valley, Derbyshire S32 2HE (01433) 630321 www.themaynard.co.uk

£100; 10 refurbished rms. Comfortable hotel with log fire and good Peak District views from the first-floor lounge, a welcoming bar, interesting modern food in the smart restaurant, generous breakfasts, afternoon cream teas and particularly attentive service; walks in the garden and nearby through Padley Gorge; dogs in bedrooms and bar; £10

HATHERSAGE

SK2380

Plough

Leadmill, Hathersage, Hope Valley, Derbyshire S32 1BA (01433) 650319
www.theploughinn-hathersage.co.uk

£95; 8 rms. Immaculately kept old dining pub with traditional dark tables and chairs on tartan and oriental patterned carpets, a big log fire and a woodburner, lots of decorative plates on terracotta walls, pewter tankards hanging from beams, a fine choice of drinks and enterprising food; the 9 acres of gardens slope down to the River Derwent and the inn is usefully placed for exploring the Peak District; dogs anywhere in the pub and in bedrooms; £15

MATLOCK BATH   SK2958
Hodgkinsons Hotel

150 South Parade, Matlock Bath, Matlock, Derbyshire DE4 3NR (01629) 582170
www.hodgkinsons-hotel.co.uk

£105; 8 comfortable rms with fine views (the ones at the back are the quietest).
Dating from 1770 and keeping many original features, this warmly friendly hotel is
traditionally furnished and has an open fire, portraits and figurines in the lounge,
a good choice of drinks in the small bar, and good, modern cooking and excellent
breakfasts in the restaurant; this is a pretty village with fine surrounding walks;
dogs in bedrooms; not in public rooms; £10

MONSAL HEAD   SK1871
Monsal Head Hotel

Monsal Head, Buxton, Derbyshire DE45 1NL (01629) 640250 www.monsalhead.com

£100; 7 good rms, some with outstanding views. Comfortable and enjoyable
small hotel in marvellous setting high above the River Wye, with a horsey theme
in the little bar (converted from old stables), freshly prepared enjoyable food
using seasonal produce in popular restaurant, open fires, well kept real ales and
good service; resident dog; lots of trails and walks from the hotel; dogs welcome
away from restaurant; treats and bowls; £10

OVER HADDON   SK2066
Lathkil

Over Haddon, Bakewell, Derbyshire DE45 1JE (01629) 812501 www.lathkil.co.uk

£90; 4 rms. Comfortable inn with stunning views and plenty of surrounding walks
(muddy boots must be left in lobby); nice fire in carved fireplace, old-fashioned
settles and upholstered chairs, a delft shelf of plates and well kept real ales in
airy bar, and a sunny, spacious dining area that doubles as an evening restaurant
serving good, popular food; dogs in two bedrooms and bar; £5

ROWSLEY   SK2565
Peacock

Rowsley, Matlock, Derbyshire DE4 2EB (01629) 733518 www.thepeacockatrowsley.com

£155; 16 comfortable rms. Smart 17th-c country-house hotel by River Derwent
(private fishing in season), with neat gardens (where dogs may walk) and close
to the moors; friendly staff, an interesting and pleasant old-fashioned inner
bar, a spacious and comfortable lounge, and very popular restaurant; dogs in
bedrooms; £10

Devon

MAP 1

DOG FRIENDLY PUBS

AVONWICK   SX6958

Turtley Corn Mill

0.5 miles off A38 roundabout at SW end of South Brent bypass; TQ10 9ES

Careful conversion of tall mill house with interestingly furnished areas, local beers, modern bar food and huge garden; bedrooms

The spreading series of linked areas in this carefully converted watermill are decorated with some individuality. There are bookcases, fat church candles and oriental rugs in one area, dark flagstones by the bar, a strategically placed woodburning stove dividing off one area, a side enclave with a modern pew built in around a really big table. Lighting is good, with plenty of big windows looking out over the grounds, and there's a pleasant array of prints, a history of the mill and framed 78rpm discs on pastel-painted walls, elderly wireless sets and house plants dotted about and a mix of comfortable dining chairs around heavy baluster-leg tables. Dartmoor Legend, St Austell Tribute, Sharps Doom Bar and Summerskills Tamar on handpump, nine wines by the glass and around 30 malt whiskies. The extensive garden has plenty of well spaced picnic-sets, a giant chess set and a small lake with interesting ducks. This is under the same ownership as the Finnygook at Crafthole (in Cornwall). The bedrooms are comfortable and the breakfasts good.

Free house ~ Licensees Lesley and Bruce Brunning ~ Real ale ~ Bar food (12-9.30) ~ (01364) 646100 ~ Children welcome ~ Dogs allowed in bar ~ Open 11-11; 12-10.30 Sun ~ Bedrooms: /£89S ~ www.turtleycornmill.com

AXMOUTH   SY2591

Harbour Inn

B3172 Seaton–Axminster; EX12 4AF

Family-run thatched pub by the Axe estuary with heavily-beamed bars, plenty of boating memorabilia, real ales and well liked food

Overlooking the Axe estuary, this thatched pub is family-run and friendly with a bustling atmosphere and plenty of happy customers. There's an entrance hall with seats on huge flagstones that leads into two heavily-beamed connected bar rooms with a lot of character: brass-bound cask seats, a high-backed oak settle and one or two smaller ones, leather-topped bar stools and all manner of tables on bare floorboards, fat pots hanging from pot-irons in the huge inglenook fireplace, glass balls in nets, a large turtle shell and lots of model boats and accounts of shipwrecks. There are also two dining rooms with more heavy beams, a little snug alcove leading off, built-in blue cushioned wall, window and other seats, and more model yachts, ships in bottles, pulleys and blocks; they hope to install a big scale model of HMS Victory in a large cabinet. Badger Best, First Gold, Pickled Partridge and Tanglefoot on handpump and several wines by the glass; pool, skittle alley. There are contemporary-style seats and tables on the front terrace and plenty of picnic-sets on grass. The handsome church opposite has some fine stone gargoyles. This is sister pub to the Wheelwright in Colyford.

Badger ~ Lease Gary and Toni Valentine ~ Real ale ~ Bar food (9am-9.30pm) ~ Restaurant ~ (01297) 20371 ~ Children welcome ~ Dogs allowed in bar ~ Open 9am-11.30pm(midnight Sat; 11pm Sun) ~ www.theharbour-inn.co.uk

BAMPTON   SS9622

Quarrymans Rest

Briton Street; EX16 9LN

Bustling village pub with friendly staff, several real ales, comfortable bars and enjoyable bar food cooked by the landlord; bedrooms

This is a comfortable place to stay (the breakfasts are good) and there's plenty to do and see in the area, too. It's well run and friendly and the licensees and their staff offer a warm welcome to all their customers – regulars or visitors. The beamed and carpeted main bar has leather sofas in front of the inglenook woodburning stove, dining chairs and some housekeepers' chairs around a mix of wooden tables set with church candles. Exe Valley Dobs Best Bitter, Exmoor Fox, Otter Ale, and Sharps Doom Bar on handpump, any wine by the glass from their list of around 40 and 15 malt whiskies. A couple of steps lead up to the comfortable stripped-stone dining room with high-backed leather chairs and heavy pine tables. There are daily papers, a shelf of paperbacks, pool and a games machine. The prettily planted back garden has some picnic-sets and there are a few more in front of the building.

Free house ~ Licensees Donna and Paul Berry ~ Real ale ~ Bar food (12-2, 6-9.30; 12-4 Sun; not Sun evening) ~ Restaurant ~ (01398) 331480 ~ Children welcome but must leave bar area by 7pm ~ Dogs allowed in bar ~ Open 11-11 (11.45 Fri and Sat); 12-10.30 Sun ~ Bedrooms: £55S(£65B)/£75S(£85B) ~ www.thequarrymansrest.co.uk

BEESANDS   SX8140

Cricket

About 3 miles S of A379, from Chillington; in village turn right along foreshore road; TQ7 2EN

Welcoming pub with enjoyable food (especially fish) and real ales; clean, airy bedrooms

The light and airy new england-style interior is not what you'd expect of this busy inn, given its slightly unassuming exterior. It's a good all rounder – the sort of place that grows on you the longer you stay – with locals chatting to the cheery landlord and his wife at one end of the counter, enjoyable bedrooms with sea views, and very good food cooked by the landlord's son. It's also on a particularly lovely part of the South Devon Coastal Path – head west for the nicest section which takes you past the remains of a village that was swept away by the sea. Big solid light wood tables with dark wood or leather chairs are well spaced on stripped wooden flooring by the bar and light brown patterned carpet in the restaurant. Big TV screens at either end roll through old local photographs, sport or the news. Otter Ale and Bitter and St Austell Tribute on handpump, several wines by the glass and local cider.; background music. The cheerful black labrador is called Brewster. There are picnic-sets beside the sea wall (a little bleak but essential protection) with pebbly Start Bay beach just over the other side.

Heavitree ~ Tenant Nigel Heath ~ Real ale ~ Bar food (12-2.30, 6-8.30) ~ Restaurant ~ (01548) 580215 ~ Children welcome ~ Dogs allowed in bar ~ Open 11-11; 11-3, 6-10.30 weekdays in winter ~ Bedrooms: £80S/£100S ~ www.thecricketinn.com

BRAMPFORD SPEKE   SX9298
Lazy Toad
Off A377 N of Exeter; EX5 5DP

Well run dining pub in pretty village, delicious food, real ales, friendly service and pretty garden; bedrooms

' A cracking little pub' is how one of our readers describes this 18th-c inn and we have plenty of enthusiastic reports from other readers, too. It's a carefully restored dining pub with beams, standing timbers and slate floors in the connected rooms, a comfortable armchair and rocking chair (much prized in winter) by the open log fire, and cushioned wall settles and high-backed wooden dining chairs around a mix of tables; the cream-painted brick walls are hung with lots of pictures and there's a rather fine grandfather clock. Otter Ale, Amber and a beer named for the pub from Otter on handpump and nice wines by the glass are served by the friendly, attentive staff; the resident cocker spaniel is called Sam. There are green-painted picnic-sets in the courtyard (once used by the local farrier and wheelwright) and in the walled garden. As we went to press, they were just opening their bedrooms. This is a pretty village of thatched cottages and there are lovely walks along the banks of the River Exe and on the Exe Valley Way and Devonshire Heartland Way.

Free House ~ Licensees Clive and Mo Walker ~ Real ale ~ Bar food (12-2(2.30 Sun), 6.30-9; not Sun evening or Mon) ~ (01392) 841591 ~ Children welcome ~ Dogs allowed in bar ~ Open 11.30-11; 12-3 Sun; 11.30-2.30, 6-11 in winter; closed Sun evening, Mon ~ Bedrooms: £55S(£65B)/£75S(£95B) ~ www.thelazytoadinn.co.uk

BRANSCOMBE   SY1888
Fountain Head
Upper village, above the robust old church; village signposted off A3052 Sidmouth–Seaton, then from Branscombe Square follow road up hill towards Sidmouth, and after about a mile turn left after the church; OS Sheet 192 map reference SY188889; EX12 3BG

Old-fashioned and friendly, with own-brewed beers and reasonably priced, well liked food

O ne of our readers describes this friendly and unpretentious 14th-c pub as 'exactly as a real pub should be' and we know exactly what he means. The helpful staff make everyone welcome – whether you're a local or a visitor – and the atmosphere is unchanging and nicely old-fashioned; there are no games machines, background music or TV. The room on the left (formerly a smithy) has forge tools and horseshoes on the high oak beams, and there's a log fire in the original raised firebed with its tall central chimney, cushioned pews and mate's chairs. They brew their own Branscombe Vale Branoc, Summa That and a changing guest beer which they keep on handpump and their annual beer festival is held in June; several wines by the glass and local cider. On the right, an irregularly shaped, more orthodox snug room has another log fire, a white-painted plank ceiling with an unusual carved ceiling-rose, brown-varnished panelled walls and rugs on its flagstone-and-lime-ash floor. Local artists' paintings and greeting cards are for sale; darts and board games. You can sit outside on the front loggia and terrace listening to the little stream gurgling under the flagstoned path and the surrounding walks are very pleasant.

Free house ~ Licensees Jon Woodley and Teresa Hoare ~ Real ale ~ Bar food (12-2, 6.30-9) ~ Restaurant ~ (01297) 680359 ~ Children welcome away from main bar area ~ Dogs allowed in bar ~ Live music on summer Sun evenings ~ Open 11-3, 6-11; 12-3, 6-10.30 Sun ~ www.fountainheadinn.com

BUCKLAND MONACHORUM   SX4968
Drake Manor
Off A386 via Crapstone, just S of Yelverton roundabout; PL20 7NA

Nice little village pub with snug rooms, popular food, quite a choice of drinks and pretty back garden; bedrooms

Our readers enjoy staying in the comfortable bedrooms of this delightful little village pub which also has an attractive self-catering apartment. It's run by a welcoming landlady who has now been here for 22 years and loves the place as much as she did when she arrived. The heavily beamed public bar on the left has brocade-cushioned wall seats, prints of the village from 1905 onwards, some horse tack and a few ship badges on the wall and a woodburning stove in a really big stone fireplace; a small door leads to a low-beamed cubbyhole. The snug Drakes Bar has beams hung with tiny cups and big brass keys, a woodburning stove in another stone fireplace, horsebrasses and stirrups and a mix of seats and tables (note the fine stripped pine high-backed settle with its hood). On the right is a small, beamed dining room with settles and tables on flagstones. Shove-ha'penny, darts, euchre and board games. Dartmoor Jail Ale, Otter Bitter, St Austell Tribute and Sharps Doom Bar on handpump, ten wines by the glass and 20 malt whiskies. There are picnic-sets in the prettily planted and sheltered back garden and the front floral displays are much admired.

Punch ~ Lease Mandy Robinson ~ Real ale ~ Bar food (12-2(2.30 weekends), 7-10(9.30 Sun)) ~ Restaurant ~ (01822) 853892 ~ Children in restaurant and area off main bar ~ Dogs allowed in bar ~ Open 11.30-2.30, 6.30-11; 11.30-11.30 Sat; 12-11 Sun ~ Bedrooms: /£90B ~ www.drakemanorinn.co.uk

CLAYHIDON   ST1817
Merry Harriers
3 miles from M5 junction 26: head towards Wellington; turn left at first roundabout signposted Ford Street and Hemyock, then after a mile turn left signposted Ford Street; at hilltop T-junction, turn left towards Chard – pub is 1.5 miles on right; at Forches Corner NE of the village itself; EX15 3TR

Bustling and friendly dining pub with imaginative food, several real ales and quite a few wines by the glass; sizeable garden

Always deservedly busy, this is a particularly well run and friendly pub and our readers love it. The hands-on, hard-working licensees and their staff will always make you welcome – even when rushed off their feet. Several small linked newly carpeted areas have a cheerful, bustling atmosphere, comfortably cushioned pews and farmhouse chairs, a sofa beside the woodburning stove, candles in bottles, horsey and hunting prints and local wildlife pictures. Two dining areas have a brighter feel with quarry tiles and lightly timbered white walls. Cotleigh Golden Seahawk, Exmoor Ale and Otter Head on handpump, 14 wines by the glass, two local ciders, 25 malt whiskies, 6 rums and a good range of other spirits; skittle alley (newly refurbished this year), chess and solitaire. There are plenty of tables and chairs in the sizeable garden and on the terrace, and they have a wendy house and other play equipment for children; there are good surrounding walks.

Free house ~ Licensees Peter and Angela Gatling ~ Real ale ~ Bar food (12-2(2.15 Sun), 6.30-9; not Sun evening or Mon) ~ Restaurant ~ (01823) 421270 ~ Children welcome ~ Dogs allowed in bar ~ Open 12-3, 6.30-11; 12-3.30 Sun; closed Sun evening, all day Mon ~ www.merryharriers.co.uk

COCKWOOD SX9780

Anchor

Off, but visible from, A379 Exeter–Torbay road, after Starcross; EX6 8RA

Busy dining pub specialising in seafood (other choices available), with five real ales, too

To be sure of a table in this extremely popular pub it's best to book in advance as there are often queues to get in at peak times. As well as an extension made up of mainly reclaimed timber and decorated with over 300 ship emblems, brass and copper lamps and nautical knick-knacks, there are several small, low-ceilinged, rambling rooms with black panelling and good-sized tables in various alcoves; the snug has a cheerful winter coal fire. Otter Ale and St Austell Tribute with guests like Dartmoor Jail Ale, Gales Seafarers Ale and O'Hanlons Yellowhammer on handpump, eight wines by the glass and 80 malt whiskies; background music, darts, cards and shove-ha'penny. From the tables on the sheltered verandah you can look across the road to the inlet (which is a pleasant spot to wander around).

Heavitree ~ Lease Malcolm and Katherine Protheroe, Scott Hellier ~ Real ale ~ Bar food (all day) ~ Restaurant ~ (01626) 890203 ~ Children welcome if seated and away from bar; no facilities for them ~ Dogs allowed in bar ~ Open 11-11; 11.30-10.30 Sun ~ www.anchorinncockwood.com

COLEFORD SS7701

New Inn

Just off A377 Crediton–Barnstaple; EX17 5BZ

Ancient thatched inn with interestingly furnished areas, well liked food and real ales, and welcoming licensees; bedrooms

As well as being an enjoyable place to stay (and the breakfasts are particularly good), our readers love dropping into this 800-year-old inn for either a drink and a chat or a leisurely meal – and Mr and Mrs Cowie are always warmly welcoming. It's a U-shaped building with the servery in the 'angle' and interestingly furnished areas leading off it: ancient and modern settles, cushioned stone wall seats, some character tables – a pheasant worked into the grain of one – and carved dressers and chests. Also, paraffin lamps, antique prints on the white walls and landscape plates on one of the beams, with pewter tankards on another. Captain, the chatty parrot, may greet you with a 'hello' or even a 'goodbye'. Otter Ale, Sharps Doom Bar and a guest like Hunters Pheasant Plucker or Skinners Betty Stogs on handpump, local cider, 14 wines by the glass and a dozen malt whiskies; background music, darts and board games. There are chairs and tables on decking under a pruned willow tree by the babbling stream and more in a covered dining area.

Free house ~ Licensees Carole and George Cowie ~ Real ale ~ Bar food (12-2, 6.30-9.39) ~ Restaurant ~ (01363) 84242 ~ Children welcome ~ Dogs allowed in bar ~ Open 12-3, 6-11(10.30 Sun); closed 25 and 26 Dec ~ Bedrooms: £65B/£85B ~ www.thenewinncoleford.co.uk

COLYFORD   SY2592

Wheelwright

Swan Hill Road (A3052 Sidmouth–Lyme Regis); EX24 6QQ

Thatched dining pub with plenty of room, real ales and friendly staff, quite a choice of popular food and seats outside

Usefully open all day and serving some kind of food from midday until 9.30pm, this is an attractive thatched dining pub with friendly staff and an easy-going atmosphere. The bar has red leather armchairs and a chesterfield at one end, cushioned wall seating, farmhouse chairs and chunky wooden tables on the stripped floorboards, a pair of giant bellows, a big cartwheel and all sorts of interesting knick-knacks, and a warming woodburning stove. From the ornate bar counter under its thatched roof, helpful staff serve Badger Bitter and First Gold and a guest beer on handpump and nice wines by the glass. The two dining rooms have high rafters and high-backed black dining chairs around a mix of tables and there's a snug room that's just right for a private party. On the way to a large, further dining room with a chandelier made of wine glasses, is their charming gift shop selling all sorts of soaps, candles, pot pourri and so forth; it's rather fun to find this in a pub. Outside on the front terrace are plenty of seats. This is sister pub to the bustling Harbour Inn at Axmouth.

Badger ~ Lease Gary and Toni Valentine ~ Real ale ~ Bar food (12-3, 6-9.30; light lunches 3 6) Restaurant ~ (01297) 552585 ~ Children welcome ~ Dogs allowed in bar ~ Open 10.30am-11pm ~ www.wheelwright-inn.co.uk

DALWOOD   ST2400

Tuckers Arms

Village signposted off A35 Axminster–Honiton; keep on past village; EX13 7EG

13th-c thatched inn with friendly, hard-working young licensees, real ales and interesting bar food

'What an excellent pub', say several of our readers – and with its smart new thatched roof, it looks picture-postcard pretty. You can be sure of a warm welcome from the enthusiastic, hands-on licensees who make all their many customers, locals or visitors, feel at home. The beamed and flagstoned bar has a relaxed atmosphere, traditional furnishings including various dining chairs, window seats and wall settles, and a log fire in the inglenook fireplace with lots of horsebrasses on the wall above it. The back bar has an enormous collection of miniature bottles and there's also a more formal dining room; lots of copper implements and platters. Branscombe Vale Branoc, Otter Bitter and a changing local guest beer on handpump, several wines by the glass and up to 20 malt whiskies; background music and a double skittle alley. In summer, the hanging baskets are pretty and there are seats in the garden. Apart from the church, this is the oldest building in the parish.

Free house ~ Licensee Tracey Pearson ~ Real ale ~ Bar food (12-2, 6.30-9) ~ Restaurant ~ (01404) 881342 ~ Children in restaurant but must be well behaved ~ Dogs allowed in bar ~ Open 11.30-3, 6.30(6 Sat)-11.30; 12-4, 7-10.30 Sun ~ Bedrooms: £45S/£70S ~ www.tuckersarms.com

DARTMOUTH   SX8751

Floating Bridge

Opposite Upper Ferry, use Dart Marina Hotel car park; Coombe Road (A379); TQ6 9PQ

Quayside pub with seats by the water and on roof-top terrace, some boating memorabilia and friendly staff

As we went to press, new licensees had just taken over this bustling quayside pub. Obviously some refurbishment will take place but what can't change is the position right by the River Dart and the little car ferry; prized seats include picnic-sets by the water and tables and chairs up on the sizeable roof terrace. The bar has lots of stools by the windows to make the most of the view, oak chairs and tables, a few model boats and black and white photographs of local boating scenes on the walls, St Austell Tribute and Sharps Doom Bar on handpump, and several wines by the glass; background music. The dining room on the left is lighter with leather-backed dining chairs around a mix of wooden tables on bare boards and more black and white photographs. They've opened up a back family room with access to the roof terrace. The window boxes are pretty against the white-painted building.

Enterprise ~ Lease Alison Hogben ~ Real ale ~ Bar food (12-9.30) ~ Restaurant ~ (01803) 832354 ~ Children welcome away from main bar ~ Dogs allowed in bar ~ Open 11-11

DODDISCOMBSLEIGH   SX8586

Nobody Inn

Off B3193; EX6 7PS

Busy old pub with plenty of character, a fine range of drinks, friendly staff and well liked bar food; bedrooms

This 17th-c inn is full of character and run by the welcoming licensees and their friendly staff. The two rooms of the beamed lounge bar have handsomely carved antique settles, windsor and wheelback chairs, quite a mix of wooden tables, guns and hunting prints in a snug area by one of the big inglenook fireplaces and fresh flowers. The restaurant is more formal. A beer named for the pub from Branscombe Vale and two changing guests such as Branscombe Vale Branoc and Exe Valley Bitter on handpump, 250 whiskies, 29 wines by the glass and local cider. There are picnic-sets in the pretty garden with views of the surrounding wooded hill pastures. The medieval stained glass in the local church is some of the best in the west country.

Free house ~ Licensee Susan Burdge ~ Real ale ~ Bar food (12-2(3 Sun), 6.30(7 Sun)-9(9.30 Fri and Sat)) ~ Restaurant ~ (01647) 252394 ~ Children welcome away from main bar ~ Dogs allowed in bar ~ Open 11-11; 12-10.30 Sun ~ Bedrooms: £65S/£90S ~ www.nobodyinn.co.uk

FROGMORE

SX7742

Globe

A379 E of Kingsbridge; TQ7 2NR

Extended and neatly refurbished inn with a bar and several seating and dining areas, real ales and nice wines by the glass, helpful staff, popular food and seats outside; comfortable bedrooms

Much extended and refurbished since our last visit some years ago, this is a white-painted inn with lovely summer flowering window boxes. The neatly kept bar has a double-sided woodburner with horsebrass-decorated stone pillars on either side, another fireplace filled with logs, cushioned settles, chunky farmhouse chairs and built-in wall seating around a mix of tables on the wooden floor, and a copper diving helmet. Attentive staff serve Otter Bitter, Skinners Betty Stogs, and South Hams Eddystone on handpump and several wines by the glass. The slate-floored games room has a pool table and darts and there's also a comfortable lounge with an open fire, cushioned dining chairs and tables on red carpeting, a big leather sofa, a model yacht and a large yacht painting; spot the clever mural of a log pile. The back terrace has teak tables and chairs and steps lead up to another level with picnic-sets. The bedrooms are comfortable and well equipped.

Free house ~ Licensees John and Lynda Horsley ~ Real ale ~ Bar food (12-2, 6(6.30 Sun)-9) ~ Restaurant ~ (01548) 531351 ~ Children in family room ~ Dogs allowed in bar ~ Open 12-2.30(3 Sun), 6-11.30; 12-3, 6(6.30 in winter)-10.30 Sun; closed Mon lunchtime 1 Oct-end June (except bank holidays) ~ Bedrooms: £50S/£80S ~ www.theglobeinn.eclipse.co.uk

GEORGEHAM

SS4639

Rock

Rock Hill, above village; EX33 1JW

Beamed family pub, good food cooked by the landlord, up to six real ales on handpump, plenty of room inside and out and a relaxed atmosphere

Always busy and cheerful with a good mix of both chatty drinkers and diners, this is a neatly kept pub with a 17th-c heart. There are plenty of heavy beams and the sizeable bar is separated into two areas by a step. The pubby top part has an open woodburning stove in a stone fireplace, captain's and farmhouse chairs around wooden tables on the quarry tiles and half-planked walls, and the lower bar has panelled wall seats, some built-in settles forming a cosy booth, old local photographs and ancient flat irons. Leading off here is a red-carpeted dining room with attractive black and white photographs of people from North Devon. Friendly young staff serve Exmoor Ale, Fullers London Pride, St Austell Tribute, Sharps Doom Bar and Timothy Taylors Landlord on handpump and they keep around a dozen wines by the glass; background music and board games. The light and airy back dining conservatory has high-backed wooden or modern dining chairs around tables under the growing vine, with a little terrace beyond. They have wheelchair access. Beside the pretty hanging baskets and tubs in front of the pub are some picnic-sets.

Punch ~ Lease Darren Stocker and Daniel Craddock ~ Real ale ~ Bar food (all day Jun-Sept (and all day Sun); 12-2.30, 6-9.30 Oct-May) ~ Restaurant ~ (01271) 890322 ~ Children welcome ~ Dogs allowed in bar ~ Open 11am-11.30pm; 12-11 Sun ~ www.therockgeorgeham.co.uk

HONITON
Holt

High Street, W end; EX14 1LA

Friendly, informal pub run by two brothers with super tapas and other interesting food and a fine range of Otter beers

After a gentle refurbishment, this charming little pub is even more appealing. There's just one room downstairs with elm tables surrounded by chunky pine chairs on the slate flooring, a bar with high stools where you can enjoy the delicious tapas, a couple of brown leather sofas at one end facing each other across a circular table and a coal-effect woodburner in the brick fireplace with a shelf of books to one side; the windows are shuttered (and one looks down on to a small stream). Brewing has been in the McCaig family for three generations and indeed they founded the Otter Brewery, so it's not surprising that the full range of Otter beers are kept on handpump: Ale, Amber, Bitter, Bright and Head. Upstairs, a bigger, brighter room now has elegant, high-backed elm tables and chairs on pale floorboards and small, very attractive musician prints, much larger contemporary pictures and an old Chamonix travel poster on the pale grey or maroon walls; background music and friendly staff. It's all very relaxed and informal. The black cat is called Dangermouse. They also run a café and patisserie almost next door called Post.

Free house ~ Licensees Joe and Angus McCaig ~ Real ale ~ Bar food (12-2, 6.30-9; not Sun or Mon) ~ Restaurant ~ (01404) 47707 ~ Well behaved children welcome ~ Dogs allowed in bar ~ Music festival four times a year ~ Open 11-3, 5.30-11; closed Sun and Mon ~ www.theholt-honiton.com

KING'S NYMPTON
Grove

Off B3226 SW of South Molton; EX37 9ST

Thatched 17th-c pub in remote village, local beers, highly thought of bar food and cheerful licensees

In a lovely conservation village, this thatched 17th-c pub is much enjoyed by our readers for its local beers and excellent food. It's run by friendly, cheerful licensees and the low-beamed bar has lots of bookmarks hanging from the ceiling, simple pubby furnishings on the flagstoned floor, bare stone walls, a winter log fire and Clearwater Proper Ansome, Cotleigh Barn Owl Premium Ale, and Exmoor Ale on handpump; also, 26 wines (and champagne) by the glass, 60 malt whiskies, local cider, darts, shove-ha'penny and dominoes. They have a self-catering cottage to rent and the pub is surrounded by quiet rolling and wooded countryside.

Free house ~ Licensees Robert and Deborah Smallbone ~ Real ale ~ Bar food (not Sun evening or winter Mon lunchtime) ~ Restaurant ~ (01769) 580406 ~ Children welcome but must be well behaved ~ Dogs allowed in bar ~ Open 12-3, 6-11; 12-4 Sun; closed Sun evening, Mon lunchtime (except bank holidays) ~ www.thegroveinn.co.uk

KINGSBRIDGE
Dodbrooke Inn

Church Street, Dodbrooke (parking some way off); TQ7 1DB

Chatty, bustling local, genuinely welcoming licensees, good mix of customers, and honest food and drink

In warm weather, the attractive covered eating area in the courtyard of this quaint little local is very popular – especially at night when it's candlelit. The long-serving and friendly licensees are sure to make you welcome and there's always a mix of locals (and visitors) of all ages. The atmosphere is comfortably traditional and the bar has plush stools and straightforward built-in cushioned stall seats around pubby tables, ceiling joists, some horse harness, old local photographs and china jugs, and a log fire. Bass, Bath Ales Gem Bitter, and Sharps Cornish Coaster and Doom Bar on handpump and local farm cider. There's also a simply furnished dining room.

Free house ~ Licensees Michael and Jill Dyson ~ Real ale ~ Bar food (12-1.30, 5.30(7 Sun)-8.30(9 Fri and Sat); not Mon or Tues lunchtimes) ~ (01548) 852068 ~ Children welcome if over 5 ~ Dogs allowed in bar ~ Open 12-2, 5-11; 12-2(2.30), 7-10.30 Sun; closed Mon and Tues lunchtimes

LUSTLEIGH   SX7881
Cleave
Off A382 Bovey Tracey–Moretonhampstead; TQ13 9TJ

In a popular beauty spot so best to arrive early at this thatched pub with its roaring log fire and popular food and drink; pretty summer garden

Picture-postcard pretty, this thatched 15th-c pub has a lovely sheltered summer garden with plenty of seats and lots of hanging baskets and flower beds. Inside, you can be sure of a genuinely warm welcome from the landlord and his friendly staff and our readers often describe the place as a 'gem'. The low-ceilinged lounge bar has a roaring log fire, attractive antique high-backed settles, cushioned wall seats and wheelback chairs around the tables on its patterned carpet and granite walls. A second bar has similar furnishings, a large dresser, harmonium, an HMV gramophone, and prints and there's a family room with toys for children. Otter Ale and Bitter and a couple of guests such as Dartmoor Jail Ale and Skinners Betty Stogs on handpump, quite a few malt whiskies, several wines by the glass and local organic soft drinks.

Heavitree ~ Tenant Ben Whitton ~ Real ale ~ Bar food (11-9; 12-8.30 Sun) ~ Restaurant ~ (01647) 277223 ~ Children welcome ~ Dogs allowed in bar ~ Open 11-11 ~ www.thecleavelustleigh.com

MARLDON   SX8663
Church House
Off A380 NW of Paignton; TQ3 1SL

Spreading bar plus several other rooms in this pleasant inn, particularly good food, fine choice of drinks and seats on three terraces

Very popular locally – always a good sign – this bustling pub is neatly kept and run by a friendly landlord and his helpful staff. The attractively furnished spreading bar with its woodburning stove has several different areas that radiate off the big semi-circular bar counter: unusual windows, some beams, dark pine and other nice old dining chairs around solid tables and yellow leather bar chairs. Leading off here is a cosy little candlelit room with just four tables on the bare-boarded floor, a dark wood dado and stone fireplace. There's also a restaurant with a large stone fireplace and at the other end of the building, a similarly interesting room is split into two parts with a stone floor in one and a wooden floor in the other (which has a big woodburning stove). The old barn holds yet another restaurant with displays by local artists. Bays Gold, Otter Ale and St Austell Dartmoor Best and Tribute on handpump, 15 wines by the glass and several malt whiskies; background music. There are picnic-sets on three carefully maintained grassy terraces behind the pub.

Enterprise ~ Lease Julian Cook ~ Real ale ~ Bar food (12-2(2.30 Sun), 6.30-9.30(9 Sun)) ~ Restaurant ~ (01803) 558279 ~ Children welcome ~ Dogs allowed in bar ~ Open 11.30-2.30, 5-11(5.30-11.30 Sat); 12-3, 5.30-10.30 Sun ~ www.churchhousemarldon.com

PARKHAM   SS3821
Bell
Rectory Lane; EX39 5PL

A proper village pub with chatty locals, welcoming landlord, neatly kept bars, four real ales and well liked food

This is a cheerful 13th-c thatched village pub and very much the heart of the community. The three connected rooms are spotlessly kept and full of chatty locals and you can be sure of a first-rate welcome from the landlord and his staff. There are beams and standing timbers hung with horsebrasses, a woodburning stove in the main bar and a small coal fire in the lower one, brass and copper jugs here and there, nice old photos of the pub and the village, a grandfather clock and pubby tables and seats (mates' and other straightforward chairs and burgundy or green plush stools) on the red-patterned carpet. There are some model ships and lanterns above the bar where Cotleigh Barn Owl, Jollyboat Mainbrace, Sharps Doom Bar and Skinners Betty Stogs are on handpump; darts. The covered and fairy-lit back terrace has some picnic-sets.

Free house ~ Licensees Michael and Rachel Sanders ~ Real ale ~ Bar food (12-1.30, 6-8.30) ~ Restaurant ~ (01237) 451201 ~ Children welcome ~ Dogs allowed in bar ~ Open 12-2.30(3 Sun), 5.30(5 Fri and Sat, 6 Sun)-11 ~ www.thebellinnparkham.co.uk

PORTGATE   SX4185
Harris Arms
Leave A30 E of Launceston at Broadwoodwidger turn-off (with brown Dingle Steam Village sign), and head S; Launceston Road (old A30 between Lewdown and Lifton); EX20 4PZ

Enthusiastic, well travelled licensees in roadside pub with exceptional wine list and interesting food

The wines are chosen very carefully here as both Mr and Mrs Whiteman are qualified award-winning wine-makers. There are around 22 of their favourites by the glass and detailed, helpful notes with each wine; you can buy them to take home, too. The bar has a woodburning stove, some rather fine photographs, burgundy end walls and cream ones in between, and afghan saddle-bag cushions scattered around a mixture of dining chairs and along a red plush built-in wall banquette. On the left, steps lead down to the dining room with elegant beech dining chairs (and more afghan cushions) around stripped-wood tables, and there are some unusual paintings on the walls. Bays Topsail and Otter Bitter on handpump, local cider and Luscombe organic soft drinks; there may be a pile of country magazines. On a heated decked area there are seats among pots of lavender and plenty of picnic-sets in the sloping back garden looking out over the rolling hills. They are growing 24 vines.

Free house ~ Licensees Andy and Rowena Whiteman ~ Real ale ~ Bar food (12-2, 6-9; not Sun evening or Mon) ~ Restaurant ~ (01566) 783331 ~ Well behaved children welcome

~ Dogs allowed in bar ~ Open 12-3, 6-11; 12-3 Sun; closed Sun evening, Mon ~ www.harrisarms.co.uk

POSTBRIDGE   SX6780

Warren House

B3212 0.75 miles NE of Postbridge; PL20 6TA

Straightforward old pub, relaxing for a drink or meal after a Dartmoor hike

Remote on Dartmoor (and a valuable refuge after a walk), this friendly place has a lot of local character and is something of a focus for the scattered moorland community. The cosy bar is straightforward with simple furnishings such as easy chairs and settles under the beamed ochre ceiling, old pictures of the inn on the partly panelled stone walls and dim lighting (powered by the pub's own generator); one of the fireplaces is said to have been kept alight almost continuously since 1845. There's also a family room. Adnams Broadside, Otter Ale and Sharps Doom Bar and one or two guest beers on handpump, local farm cider and malt whiskies; background music, darts and board games. The picnic-sets on both sides of the road have moorland views.

Free house ~ Licensee Peter Parsons ~ Real ale ~ Bar food (12-9(8.30 Sun); winter Mon and Tues 12-4.30) ~ (01822) 880208 ~ Children in family room ~ Dogs allowed in bar ~ Open 11-11; 11-5 Mon and Tues during Nov-Feb; 12-10.30 Sun ~ www.warrenhouseinn.co.uk

RATTERY   SX7461

Church House

Village signposted from A385 W of Totnes, and A38 S of Buckfastleigh; TQ10 9LD

One of Britain's oldest pubs with plenty to look at, a friendly landlord, a good range of drinks, and popular bar food; peaceful views

The original building here probably housed the craftsmen who built the Norman church, and may then have served as a hostel for passing monks. There are some fine original features – notably the spiral stone steps behind a little stone doorway, on your left as you come in which date from about 1030. It's a charming place with particularly helpful, friendly staff and plenty of character: massive oak beams and standing timbers in the homely open-plan bar, large fireplaces (one with a little cosy nook partitioned off around it), traditional pubby chairs and tables on the patterned carpet, some window seats and prints and horsebrasses on the plain white walls. The dining room is separated from this room by heavy curtains and there's a lounge area, too. Dartmoor Jail Ale and Legend, Exmoor Ale and Fullers/Gales Seafarers on handpump, 15 malt whiskies and ten wines by the glass. The garden has picnic-sets on the large hedged-in lawn and peaceful views of the partly wooded surrounding hills.

Free house ~ Licensee Ray Hardy ~ Real ale ~ Bar food (11.30-2, 7-9) ~ Restaurant ~ (01364) 642220 ~ Children welcome ~ Dogs allowed in bar ~ Open 11-2.30, 6-11; 12-3, 6-10.30 Sun ~ www.thechurchhouseinn.co.uk

SIDBURY

SY1496

Hare & Hounds

3 miles N of Sidbury, at Putts Corner; A375 towards Honiton, crossroads with B3174; EX10 0QQ

Large, well run roadside pub with log fires, beams and attractive layout, popular daily carvery, efficient staff and a big garden

As we went to press, a new dining extension was being built on to this sizeable roadside pub which will have a central open fire surrounded by dining chairs and tables and doors opening out onto a decked area; seats from here and picnic-sets in the big garden have marvellous views down the Sid Valley to the sea at Sidmouth. It's a large place with two log fires (and rather unusual wood-framed leather sofas complete with pouffes), heavy beams and fresh flowers, plenty of tables with red plush-cushioned dining chairs, window seats and leather sofas, and is mostly carpeted with bare boards and stripped-stone walls at one end. From a long bar with high bar chairs, they offer Otter Bitter and Ale and St Austell Tribute tapped from the cask and several wines by the glass.

Heartstone Inns ~ Managers Graham Cole and Lindsey Chun ~ Real ale ~ Bar food (all day) ~ (01404) 41760 ~ Children welcome away from bar ~ Dogs allowed in bar ~ Open 10am-11pm(10.30pm Sun) ~ www.hareandhounds-devon.co.uk

SIDFORD

SY1389

Blue Ball

A3052 just N of Sidmouth; EX10 9QL

Big, popular inn with friendly staff, four real ales, good food and a neat garden; bedrooms

With coastal walks just ten minutes away, it's useful that this handsome thatched pub is open all day for food. There's a good bustling atmosphere and the friendly family (who have been here 100 years now) offer a warm welcome to all their customers. The central bar covers three main areas and has light beams, bar stools and a nice mix of wooden dining chairs around circular tables on the patterned carpet, three log fires, prints, horsebrasses and plenty of bric-a-brac on the walls, and Bass, Otter Bitter, St Austell Tribute and Sharps Doom Bar on handpump; cheerful service. The public bar has darts, games machine and board games; skittle alley and background music. There are seats on a terrace and in the flower-filled garden and a well designed wooden smokers' gazebo.

Punch ~ Lease Roger Newton ~ Real ale ~ Bar food (8-10 for breakfast, 12-2.30, 6-9; 12-3, 5.30-8.30 Sun) ~ Restaurant ~ (01395) 514062 ~ Children welcome away from bar ~ Dogs allowed in bar ~ Open 8am-11pm ~ Bedrooms: £60B/£95B ~ www.blueballinn.net

TOTNES

SX8059

Steam Packet

St Peters Quay, on W bank (ie not on Steam Packet Quay); TQ9 5EW

Seats outside overlooking quay, interesting layout and décor inside, and popular food and drink; bedrooms

On a fine day, it's best to get to this busy pub early if you're hoping to bag one of the seats and tables on the front terrace overlooking the River Dart; there are walks along the river bank from here. Inside, it's interestingly laid out with bare stone walls and wooden flooring and one end has an open log fire, a squashy leather sofa with lots of cushions against a wall of books, a similar seat built into a small curved brick wall (which breaks up the room) and a TV. The main bar has built-in wall benches and plenty of stools and chairs around traditional pub tables and a further area has a coal fire and dark wood furniture. Dartmoor Jail Ale, Sharps Doom Bar and a guest from Hunters named for the pub on handpump and several wines by the glass. The conservatory restaurant has high-backed leather dining chairs around wooden tables and smart window blinds.

Buccaneer Holdings ~ Manager Richard Cockburn ~ Real ale ~ Bar food (12-2.30, 6-9) ~ Restaurant ~ (01803) 863880 ~ Children welcome ~ Dogs allowed in bar ~ Open 11-11; 12-10.30 Sun ~ Bedrooms: £59.50B/£79.50B ~ www.steampacketinn.co.uk

WIDECOMBE SX7276

Rugglestone

Village at end of B3387; pub just S – turn left at church and National Trust church house, OS Sheet 191 map reference 720765; TQ13 7TF

Unspoilt local near busy tourist village, with a couple of bars, cheerful customers, friendly staff, four real ales and traditional pub food

Just a walk from the busy tourist village, this is a charming, cottagey pub with a warm welcome for both locals and visitors. The unspoilt bar has only four tables, a few window and wall seats, a one-person pew built into the corner by the nice old stone fireplace (where there's a woodburner), and a good mix of customers. The rudimentary bar counter dispenses Butcombe Bitter and Dartmoor Legend and a couple of guests like Otter Bright and Teignworthy Gun Dog tapped from the cask; local farm cider and a decent small wine list. The room on the right is a bit bigger and lighter-feeling with another stone fireplace, a beamed ceiling, stripped-pine tables and a built-in wall bench, and there's also a small dining room. There are seats in the field across the little moorland stream and tables and chairs in the garden. They have a holiday cottage for rent.

Free house ~ Licensees Richard and Vicki Palmer ~ Real ale ~ Bar food (12-2, 6-9) ~ Restaurant ~ (01364) 621327 ~ Children allowed but must be away from bar area ~ Dogs allowed in bar ~ Open 11.30-3, 6-11.30(5-midnight Fri); 11.30am-midnight Sat; 12-11 Sun ~ www.rugglestoneinn.co.uk

WINKLEIGH SS6308

Kings Arms

Fore Street; off B3220 Crediton–Torrington; EX19 8HQ

Friendly pub with woodburning stoves in beamed main bar, west country beers and popular food

With friendly licensees and chatty locals, this thatched village pub hasn't changed much – which is just how our readers like it. The most character can be found in the cosy beamed main bar with old-fashioned built-in wall settles and benches around scrubbed pine tables on flagstones and a woodburning stove in a cavernous fireplace; another woodburning stove separates the bar from the green or red-painted dining rooms (one has military memorabilia and a glass-covered old mine shaft). Butcombe Bitter, Otter Bitter and Sharps Doom Bar on handpump and two local ciders; board games. There are seats in the garden.

Enterprise ~ Lease Cheryl and Denis MacDonald ~ Real ale ~ Bar food (all day) ~ Restaurant ~ (01837) 83384 ~ Children welcome ~ Dogs allowed in bar ~ Open 11-11; 12-10.30 Sun ~ www.thekingsarmswinkleigh.co.uk

WOODBURY SALTERTON
SY0189
Diggers Rest

3.5 miles from M5 junction 30: A3052 towards Sidmouth, village signposted on right about 0.5 miles after Clyst St Mary; also signposted from B3179 SE of Exeter

Bustling village pub with real ales, well liked food, and lovely views from the terraced garden

The oldest part of this thatched pub is 500 years old and the main bar has antique furniture, local art on the walls and a cosy seating area by the open fire with its extra large sofa and armchair. The modern extension is light and airy and opens on to the garden with its lovely countryside views. Bays Topsail and Otter Ale and Bitter on handpump, 13 wines by the glass and Westons cider; background music, darts, TV and board games. The window boxes and flowering baskets are pretty.

Heartstone Inns ~ Licensee Ben Thomas ~ Real ale ~ Bar food (12-2(2.15 Sun), 6-9(8.30 Sun)) ~ Restaurant ~ (01395) 232375 ~ Well behaved children welcome ~ Dogs allowed in bar ~ Open 11-3, 5.30-11; 12-3.30, 5.30-10.30 Sun - www.diggersrest.co.uk

DOG FRIENDLY INNS, HOTELS AND B&Bs

ASHPRINGTON
SX8056
Watermans Arms

Tuckenhay Road, Bow Bridge, Ashprington, Totnes, Devon TQ9 7EG (01803) 732214 www.thewatermansarms.net

£80; 15 comfortable rms. Bustling pub in quiet spot by Bow Creek with plenty of riverside seats; several beamed, rambling rooms with lots to look at (stone bottles, copper implements, stuff fish, fishing rods, oars and so forth), a log fire and a woodburning stove, all manner of tables and chairs, and a good choice of drinks; friendly staff serve tasty all-day food using local free-range and organic produce and enjoyable breakfasts (available to non-residents, too); three resident dogs – Emma, Bow and Benson, three cats, chicken; lots of nearby walks; dogs anywhere in the pub and in bedrooms; snacks and water any time; £3

ASHWATER
SX3697
Blagdon Manor

Ashwater, Beaworthy, Devon EX21 5DF (01409) 211224 www.blagdon.com

£150; 6 pretty rms. Standing in rolling countryside, this carefully restored and tranquil 17th-c manor has 20 acres of grounds including 3 acres of gardens; beams and flagstones, antiques and paintings, log fires and fresh flowers in the bar and lounge, a comfortable library, delicious, beautifully presented food using the best local produce in smart but informal restaurant, big breakfasts in airy conservatory, and a genuinely warm welcome; two resident chocolate labradors, Cassia and Mace; dogs welcome away from restaurant; biscuits, bowl, bed; £8.50

BAMPTON   SS9221

Bark House

Oakford Bridge, Bampton, Devon EX16 9HZ (01398) 351236 www.thebarkhouse.co.uk

£90; 5 cottagey rms. Charming hotel with lovely rural views, a garden with croquet, and plenty of surrounding walks; caring, hospitable owners, open fires and low beams in comfortable homely sitting and dining rooms, very good food using local produce, a thoughtful wine list and super breakfasts; self-catering cottage, too; well behaved dogs welcome in bedrooms

BIGBURY-ON-SEA   SX6544

Henley

Folly Hill, Bigbury-on-Sea, Kingsbridge, Devon TQ7 4AR (01548) 810240
www.thehenleyhotel.co.uk

£135; 5 recently refurbished rms. Renovated Edwardian cottage with fine views of the Avon estuary, Burgh Island, and beyond; lounge and conservatory dining room with magnificent sea views, deep wicker chairs and polished furniture, binoculars and books, good, enjoyable food from a small menu, super breakfasts, and steep, private path down the cliff to a sandy bay where dogs may walk; dogs in bedrooms only; bring own bedding; £5

BOLBERRY   SX6939

Port Light

Bolberry, Salcombe, Devon TQ7 3DY (01548) 561384 www.portlight.co.uk

£96; 7 pleasant rms with lovely views. Clifftop former RAF radar station (an easy walk from Hope Cove) with a warmly friendly welcome, good home-made food (super fresh fish) in attractive bar and restaurant, a warm woodburning stove, and good outdoor children's play area; 20 acre National Trust field borders the garden; dogs welcome in bedrooms (not to be left unattended) and conservatory; bring own bedding

BOVEY TRACEY   SX8078

Edgemoor Hotel

Haytor Road, Bovey Tracey, Newton Abbot, Devon TQ13 9LE (01626) 832466
www.edgemoor.co.uk

£140; 17 charming rms. Family-run, ivy-covered country house in neatly kept gardens on the edge of Dartmoor, with a comfortable lounge and cosy bar, log fires, good modern english cooking using seasonal local produce in elegant restaurant, afternoon teas; walks in grounds and on Dartmoor; dogs in Woodland Wing bedrooms with back door leading to private terrace

BRADWORTHY   SS3214

Lake Villa

Bradworthy, Devon EX22 7SQ (01409) 241962 www.lakevilla.co.uk

£76; 2 rms with garden or country views. 300-year-old farmhouse with friendly owners offering a warm welcome to well behaved pets (and their owners); good breakfasts, packed lunches on request and pubs very nearby for evening meals; gardens, tennis court and barbecue equipment, and nearby common for dog exercise; walking holidays arranged, and self-catering cottages, too; dogs by prior arrangement

BURRINGTON   SS6218
Northcote Manor

Burrington, Umberleigh, Devon EX37 9LZ (01769) 560501 www.northcotemanor.co.uk

£225; 16 individually decorated rms. Country-house hotel In the Taw Valley with far-reaching views and surrounding walks; comfortable lounges with big murals and lots of house plants, a well stocked bar, open fires, rugs on floorboards, interesting modern, well presented food in the elegant restaurant (more large murals), and genuinely helpful, courteous staff; dogs in bedrooms; not in lounge or restaurant; treats and bowls; £10

CHAGFORD   SX7189
Easton Court

Sandy Park, Chagford, Newton Abbot, Devon TQ13 8JN (01647) 433469 www.easton.co.uk

£85; 5 comfortable rms. Extended Tudor thatched longhouse in 4 acres of gardens and paddocks, with a relaxed and informal atmosphere, hearty breakfasts in guest lounge/breakfast room, helpful, friendly owners, and lots to do nearby; plenty of surrounding pubs and restaurants for evening meals; dogs in one bedroom if small and well behaved; £2.50

CHILLINGTON   SX7942
Whitehouse

Chillington, Devon TQ7 2JX (01548) 580505 www.whitehousedevon.co

£210; 6 individually decorated, well equipped rms. Georgian house with a peaceful back garden, an easy-going, friendly atmosphere, comfortable leather sofas and armchairs on bare boards in the sitting room, a snug study with daily papers and magazines and an open fire, good, modern food in airy dining room overlooking the terrace, a bar serving all-day drinks and snacks, and delicious breakfasts; dogs allowed but on lead in public rooms

CLAWTON   SX3499
Court Barn Hotel

Clawton, Holsworthy, Devon EX22 6PS (01409) 271219 www.hotels-devon.com

£95; 7 individually furnished rms. Charming house in 5 acres of pretty gardens with croquet, a nine-hole putting green, small chip-and-putt course, and tennis and badminton courts; two comfortable lounges with log fires, a bar, an elegant breakfast room, an antique-filled restaurant offering country-house-style evening meals, and a quiet, relaxed atmosphere; walks in grounds and surrounding country lanes; dogs in bedrooms; bowls and treats; £6

COUNTISBURY   SS7449
Blue Ball Inn
Countisbury, Lynton, Devon EX35 6NE (01598) 741263 www.exmoorsandpiper.com

£78; 15 good rms. 13th-c inn surrounded by fine scenery and nearby coastal walks – they have leaflet of four circular routes; rambling, heavy beamed rooms, three ales including one brewed for the pub, handsome log fires, generous local food in bar and restaurant and friendly service; two residents dogs, Poppy and Molly; dogs welcome anywhere; bring own bedding; home-made treats for sale; £8

CULMSTOCK   ST1013
Culm Valley
Culmstock, Cullompton, Devon EX15 3JJ (01884) 840354 www.culmvalleyinn.co.uk

£65; 3 rms. Quirky, friendly dining pub with charming if slightly off-beat landlord, an enjoyable and informal atmosphere, lots of chatty locals and visitors, a hotchpotch of modern and unrenovated furnishings, knick-knacks and paintings to do with racing on the walls, a big fireplace and a really interesting choice of drinks; there's also a dining room, a small conservatory and an oak-floored room with views into the kitchen; food is imaginative and highly enjoyable and uses local game and fish; seats overlook the River Culm; dogs welcome anywhere

DARTMOUTH   SX8752
Dart Marina
Sandquay Road, Dartmouth, Devon TQ6 9PH (01803) 832580 www.dartmarina.com

£185; 49 well equipped neat rms, all with river views. Well run hotel beside the River Dart with a contemporary bar/lounge, genuinely friendly, helpful staff, first class food using the best local seasonal produce in light, airy restaurant (panoramic views, white cloths, crystal, and candlelight), lighter choices in the bistro, and lovely breakfasts; seats on the terrace, luxury spa, gym and swimming pool; self-catering apartments, too; dogs in ground floor bedrooms; not in public rooms at mealtimes; £10;

DARTMOUTH   SX8751
Royal Castle
11 The Quay, Dartmouth, Devon TQ6 9PS (01803) 833033 www.royalcastle.co.uk

£160; 25 charming rms, many with harbour views. 17th-c hotel at the heart of a lovely town, with a lot of character and a thriving atmosphere; two quite different bars – one traditional with fine antiques and maritime pieces and a Tudor fireplace and the other contemporary and rather smart with regular live acoustic music; the more formal restaurant overlooks the water, and particularly friendly staff serve enjoyable, all-day food; dogs anywhere in the hotel and in some bedrooms; bed provided; £20

EAST ALLINGTON
SX7648

Fortescue Arms

East Allington, Totnes, Devon TQ9 7RA (01548) 521215 www.fortescue-arms.co.uk

£60; 3 rms. Pretty village pub, carefully refurbished recently, with an informal, friendly atmosphere, a good choice of real ales and wines, comfortable armchairs by the open fire, church candles, and some brewery memorabilia; enjoyable food in separate dining room and helpful staff; dogs anywhere in the pub and in bedrooms

EXETER
SX9292

Magdalen Chapter

Magdalen Street, Exeter, Devon EX2 4HY (01392) 281000
www.themagdalenchapter.com

£150; 59 beautifully furnished rms and lovely bthrms. Cleverly converted Victorian eye hospital with a new lounge, modern furnishings and a stunning botanical wall painting, a library with lots of books and an open fire, excellent imaginative food from the theatre-style kitchen in the stylish open-plan restaurant, morning coffee and afternoon tea, spa with an inside-out swimming pool, and plenty of seats on the terrace in the walled garden; Friday jazz; dogs in bedrooms; beds, bowls, treats

EXMINSTER
SX9686

Turf Hotel

Exminster, Exeter, Devon EX6 8EE (01392) 833128 www.turfpub.net

£80; 2 rms. Remote, friendly pub reached on foot beside the ship canal, by bicycle or by boat (from Topsham quay); enormously popular in fine weather and plenty of seating in the big garden – the summer barbecues are very good indeed; simply furnished rooms with pine tables and chairs, a woodburning stove, local beers, cider and wine, and enjoyable food using their own produce; lots of walks nearby; two resident jack russells; closed Oct-mid Feb; dogs welcome anywhere; treats on bar

GITTISHAM
SY1497

Combe House

Gittisham, Honiton, Devon EX14 3AD (01404) 540400 www.combehousedevon.com

£215; 16 individually decorated pretty rms with lovely views. Peaceful, Grade I listed, Elizabethan country hotel in gardens with 400-year-old cedar of Lebanon, and walks around the 3,500-acre estate; a hall with a roaring fire, elegant sitting rooms with fine panelling, antiques, portraits and fresh flowers, a happy relaxed atmosphere, beautifully presented food in the restaurant using their own-grown produce, chickens, pigs and sheep, and excellent breakfasts; dogs in some bedrooms and public rooms (not restaurant); £10

GULWORTHY
SX4473

Horn of Plenty

Gulworthy, Tavistock, Devon PL19 8JD (01822) 832528 www.thehornofplenty.co.uk

£125; 10 lovely rms with personal touches, 6 in Garden House annexe with french windows to walled gardens. Luxury small country-house hotel in 6 acres of gardens and orchards with wonderful views over the Tamar Valley (direct access to Tamar Valley trails); drawing room with log fires and fresh flowers, separate bar lounge, delicious modern cooking (and super breakfasts) using produce from Devon and Cornwall in smart, airy restaurant and a friendly, relaxed atmosphere; dogs in Garden Rooms; £10

HAWKCHURCH
SY3499

Fairwater Head Country House

Hawkchurch, Axminster, Devon EX13 5TX (01297) 678349
www.fairwaterheadhotel.co.uk

£145; 16 rms most with country views. Edwardian hotel in quiet, flower-filled gardens with genuinely friendly, attentive staff, an open fire in the comfortable lounge hall, a well stocked bar and wine cellar, and enjoyable brasserie-style food in the bustling restaurant; croquet; walks directly from the door; resident springer/cocker spaniel Mocca and labradors Lolly and Barney; closed Jan; dogs welcome anywhere except restaurant; welcome biscuits and info pack

HAYTOR VALE
SX7777

Rock Inn

Haytor Vale, Newton Abbot, Devon TQ13 9XP (01364) 661305 www.rock-inn.co.uk

£99; 9 individual rms. Civilised former coaching inn on the edge of Dartmoor National Park that's at its most informal at lunchtime; two neat communicating bars have courteous staff, lots of dark wood and red plush, candles and fresh flowers, a thoughtful choice of drinks and warming log fires; there's a residents' lounge and a spacious dining room serving extremely good food; super breakfasts; dogs in bedrooms; not in public rooms; £8.50

HEXWORTHY
SX6572

Forest Inn

Hexworthy, Princetown, Yelverton, Devon PL20 6SD (01364) 631211
www.theforestinn.co.uk

£75; 10 cosy rms. Country inn in fine Dartmoor setting, popular with walkers, riders, canoeists and anglers; convivial bar with real ales and a relaxed atmosphere, a lounge area with a log fire, tasty pubby food and hearty breakfasts in separate restaurant, and friendly staff; dogs welcome anywhere; bowls and towels

HORNDON
SX5280
Elephants Nest
Horndon, Mary Tavy, Tavistock, Devon PL19 9NQ (01822) 810273
www.elephantsnest.co.uk

£87.50; 3 nicely furnished rms. Isolated old inn surrounded by lots of Dartmoor walks; simply furnished bar with farm ciders, real ales and several wines by the glass, two other rooms with modern dark wood tables and chairs on flagstones, three woodburning stoves, bare stone walls, changing bar food using local produce, and super breakfasts (devilled kidneys and kedgeree); resident grand bassett griffon vendeen, Louis, and glen of imaal terrier, Bertie; dogs welcome anywhere; £5

HORNS CROSS
SS3823
Hoops
Horns Cross, Bideford, Devon EX39 5DL (01237) 451222 www.hoopsinn.co.uk

£105; 13 well equipped rms. Striking thatched inn, a former smugglers' haunt, with plenty of character and a cheerful mix of customers; bars have traditional furniture, log fires in sizeable fireplaces, standing timbers and partitioning, a more formal restaurant has another open fire, real ales, wines by the glass, and enterprising food served all day from 8am; 2 acres of gardens, and resident black labradors, Scout and Skye; dogs in coach-house bedrooms and bar

IDDESLEIGH
SS5608
Duke of York
Iddesleigh, Winkleigh, Devon EX19 8BG (01837) 810253 www.dukeofyorkdevon.co.uk

£70; 8 charming, timbered rms, 3 in separate building. Originally four cottages built for craftsmen rebuilding the church, this is long and thatched and dates from the 15th-c; the unspoilt bar has homely character, rocking chairs and built-in wall benches, banknotes pinned to beams, a log fire in a big fireplace and chatty customers, and the separate dining room has an inglenook and serves honest, fairly priced food; and seats in a small back garden; dogs in bedrooms and bar; £5

ILFRACOMBE
SS5146
Strathmore
57 St Brannocks Road, Ilfracombe, Devon EX34 8EQ (01271) 862248
www.the-strathmore.co.uk

£72; 8 pretty rms. Victorian hotel close to the town centre and beach with a comfortable and well stocked lounge bar, hearty breakfasts in attractive dining room, welcoming owners and staff, and a terraced garden; plenty of nearby walks; dogs in bedrooms; bacon/sausage for breakfast; £6.50 (half to a local dog trust)

ILSINGTON
SX7776
Ilsington Country House
Ilsington, Newton Abbot, Devon TQ13 9RR (01364) 661452 www.ilsington.co.uk

£120; 25 country-style rms, 8 on ground floor. Family-run extended hotel in 10

acres of gardens surrounded by Dartmoor National Park with its rolling hills and ancient woodland; a friendly, easy-going atmosphere throughout the traditionally decorated public rooms (fine views too), interesting modern food using the best local produce in the green carpeted restaurant, informal meals in the attached Blue Tiger inn and helpful, courteous service; indoor swimming pool; dogs in ground floor bedrooms and in conservatory; £8

LEWDOWN   SX4586
Lewtrenchard Manor
Lewdown, Okehampton, Devon EX20 4PN (01566) 783256 www.lewtrenchard.co.uk

£170; 14 luxurious rms with period furniture. Lovely family-run Jacobean manor house in gardens with a fine dovecote and surrounded by a peaceful estate; dark panelling, ornate ceilings, antiques, fresh flowers and log fires in the public rooms, a relaxed atmosphere, a friendly welcome, and a candlelit restaurant with very good imaginative food; very good afternoon teas and breakfasts, too; resident dog, Spencer; walks in the grounds and on many nearby footpaths; dogs in bedrooms (must not be left alone) and lounges; £15

LIFTON   SX3885
Arundell Arms
Fore Street, Lifton, Devon PL16 0AA (01566) 784666 www.arundellarms.com

£179; 21 well equipped rms. Carefully renovated old coaching inn with 20 miles of its own waters – salmon and trout fishing and a long-established fly-fishing school; shooting, and deer stalking also; comfortable sitting room, log fires, super food in both bar and elegant restaurant, carefully chosen wines, and kind service from local staff; attractive terraced garden (where dogs may walk) and walks in nearby playing fields; dogs anywhere except restaurant; bowls; £10

LODDISWELL   SX7252
Hazelwood House
Loddiswell, Kingsbridge, Devon TQ7 4EB (01548) 821232 www.hazelwoodhouse.com

£85; 14 rms, 7 with own bthrm. Relaxed and informal Victorian hotel in 67 acres of river valley – lots of wildlife and fine walks; bold paintwork and eclectic art throughout, open fire in comfortable drawing room, a hall lounge with a piano and a woodburning stove, and enjoyable breakfasts, light lunches, afternoon teas and evening meals in dining room or on wisteria-covered verandah; resident jack russell, Lily, and cat, Daisy (who does not like being chased); regular music, art and dance events; self-catering cottages, too; walks on the coast and on Dartmoor; dogs in bedrooms but not dining room; on lead elsewhere; £10

MALBOROUGH   SX7039
Soar Mill Cove Hotel
Malborough, Salcombe, Devon TQ7 3DS (01548) 561566 www.soarmillcove.co.uk

£200; 22 comfortable rms that open on to garden. Neatly kept single-storey, family-run hotel in idyllic spot by a peaceful and very beautiful cove on National Trust coast – lovely views and 10 acres of grounds; refurbished bars, a coffee shop and lounge with an informal, easy-going atmosphere (and lovely views), good, enjoyable food in the restaurant (more fine views) and well trained, kind staff; excellent walks all around and they also have a dog walk map; spa, indoor pool, snooker, pitch and putt and tennis; self-catering, too; dogs in bedrooms and coffee shop

MOLLAND   SS8028
London
Molland, South Molton, Devon EX36 3NG (01769) 550269 www.londoninnmolland.co.uk

£75; 2 cottagey rms. A proper Exmoor inn tucked away down narrow lanes and hardly changed in 50 years; two small rooms with local stag-hunting pictures, tough carpeting or rugs on flagstones, plain furniture, a friendly, easy-going atmosphere, real ales and tasty, reasonably priced food; look out for the particularly good game bird prints in the panelled dining room and the original Victorian mahogany and tiling in the lavatories; the church next door has some untouched early 18th-c box pews; dogs in bedrooms and bar; £10

MORETONHAMPSTEAD   SX7386
Great Sloncombe Farm
Moretonhampstead, Newton Abbot, Devon TQ13 8QF (01647) 440595 www.greatsloncombefarm.co.uk

£40; 3 comfortable country rms. Lovely 13th-c farmhouse on a working stock farm, with friendly owners, carefully polished old-fashioned furniture in oak-beamed lounge with woodburning stove in inglenook, games and books, hearty breakfasts with sausages from their pigs and eggs from their hens, and a relaxed atmosphere; they will make up picnics and have bikes for hire – good nearby walking and bird-watching – and three resident scottish terriers and one bearded collie; dogs in bedrooms; £5

NORTHAM   SS4528
Yeoldon House
Durrant Lane, Northam, Bideford, Devon EX39 2RL (01237) 474400 www.yeoldonhousehotel.co.uk

£125; 10 individually decorated rms, 5 with water views. Quietly set hotel in 2 acres of grounds by the River Torridge, with a warmly friendly and relaxed atmosphere, an open fire and fresh flowers in the comfortable lounge, imaginative food cooked by the chef/patron in the attractive dining room and helpful service; one resident dog; plenty of walks; lots to do nearby; dogs in bedrooms (not to be left unattended); £5

POSTBRIDGE   SX6578
Lydgate House
Postbridge, Yelverton, Devon PL20 6TJ (01822) 880209 www.lydgatehouse.co.uk

£90; 7 rms. Friendly and relaxed Victorian country house in a secluded wild Dartmoor valley spot (lots of wildlife), with a log fire in the comfortable sitting room, good, simple modern cooking in candlelit conservatory dining room, fine breakfasts – and picnic lunches on request; good walks from the door; resident dogs and cats; dogs in bedrooms (not to be left unattended); £3

SALCOMBE

SX7338

Tides Reach

Cliff Road, South Sands, Salcombe, Devon TQ8 8LJ (01548) 843466
www.tidesreach.com

£144; 35 rms, many with estuary views. Unusually individual resort hotel – run by the same family for three generations – in a pretty wooded cove by the sea; airy, comfortable lounges and sun lounge (overlooking the water), a cocktail bar with a big sea aquarium, very good breakfasts, light lunches, afternoon teas and evening meals all using the best local produce, and friendly efficient service; indoor pool, gym and spa, squash, snooker and table tennis, and lots of coastal walks; dogs in bedrooms (not to be left unattended); £9

SANDFORD

SS8202

Lamb

Sandford, Crediton, Devon EX17 4LW (01363) 773676 www.lambinnsandford.co.uk

£85; 6 well equipped, comfortable modern rms. Bustling, 16th-c village inn with much genuine character, beams and standing timbers in bar and connected dining room, red leather sofas in front of the log fire (there's also a woodburner), cushioned settles and window seats, interesting animal prints (done by the landlord's wife), real ales, decent wines and 20 malts; a skittle alley doubles as a cinema, the food is highly enjoyable and the breakfasts nice, and staff are cheerful and helpful; the jack russell is called Tiny and the collie, Bob; dogs anywhere in the pub and in bedrooms; £5

SANDY PARK

SX7189

Mill End

Sandy Park, Chagford, Newton Abbot, Devon TQ13 8JN (01647) 432282
www.millendhotel.com

£140; 15 charming, peaceful rms, 3 have direct garden access. Quietly set former flour mill, with original waterwheel, in 15 acres of neatly kept grounds below Dartmoor – wonderful surrounding walks; three lounges with comfortable sofas, fresh flowers and open fires, excellent british cooking in elegant restaurant, fine breakfasts and cream teas on the lawn, and good service; dogs in bedrooms; £8

SHEEPWASH

SS4806

Half Moon

Sheepwash, Beaworthy, Devon EX21 5NE (01409) 231376
www.halfmoonsheepwash.co.uk

£95; 11 rms, some in converted stables. Civilised heart-of-Devon hideaway with 12 miles of private salmon, sea trout and brown trout fishing on the Torridge and plenty of walks; simply furnished main bar, lots of beams and a big log fire, real ales and wines by the glass, enjoyable food in extended dining room and a friendly atmosphere; two resident dogs, Boris and Bertie; dogs welcome in annexe bedrooms and bar; not restaurant; treats

SIDFORD
SY1389

Salty Monk

Church Street, Sidford, Exeter, Devon EX10 9QP (01395) 513174
www.saltymonk.co.uk

£120; 6 cottagey rms, some with spa baths. 16th-c former salt house (monks trading in salt stayed here on their way to Exeter) with comfortable sofas and fresh flowers in sitting room, good food using local produce cooked by the owners in restful restaurant, nice breakfasts and cream teas, and seats in the quiet garden; yoga suite/fitness room and mini spa; resident spinone, Isca, and irish water spaniel, Finn; fantastic walks all around; closed 1 week in Nov, all Jan; dogs in bedrooms and lounge (on lead); not restaurant; welcome pack, maps; £20

SLAPTON
SX8245

Tower

Slapton, Kingsbridge, Devon TQ7 2PN (01548) 580216 www.thetowerinn.com

£85; 3 cosy, refurbished rms. 14th-c century inn built for masons erecting the next door chantry; a low-ceilinged, beamed bar with a friendly, relaxed atmosphere, log fire, settles and scrubbed oak tables on flagstones or bare boards, well kept beers, wines by the glass and impressive food; seats in pretty back garden and resident cockapoo, Bella, and westie, Tavi; dogs in bedrooms and bar

STAVERTON
SX7964

Sea Trout

Staverton, Totnes, Devon
TQ9 6PA (01803) 762274
www.theseatroutinn.co.uk

£102; 10 cottagey rms. Comfortable, partly 15th-c pub in quiet hamlet near River Dart with sea trout and salmon flies and stuffed fish on the walls of the rambling beamed lounge, simpler locals' bar with more stuffed fish, a stag's head, lots of horsebrasses and a woodburning stove, and a smarter panelled restaurant and conservatory with very popular, enjoyable food; lots to do nearby (plenty of walks) including fishing on the river (daily tickets available); dogs in bedrooms and bar; treats; £5

Rufus – irish soft-coated wheaten terrier

THURLESTONE   SX6742

Thurlestone Hotel

Thurlestone, Kingsbridge, Devon TQ7 3NN (01548) 560382 www.thurlestone.co.uk

£240; 64 comfortable rms, many with sea or country views. Owned by the same family since 1896, this well run hotel is in 19 acres of subtropical gardens and just 5 minutes from the sea; stylish and spacious lounges, a convivial bar, imaginative food in the light, attractive restaurant with views over Bigbury Bay, enjoyable light lunches, afternoon teas and first class breakfasts, and courteous helpful staff; they also own the pub, the Village Inn; outdoor swimming pool, tennis, squash and badminton courts, a golf course and a new spa with indoor swimming pool; nearby beaches and walks; dogs in some bedrooms; £8

TORQUAY   SX9265

Cary Arms

Babbacombe Beach, Torquay, Devon TQ1 3LX (01803) 327110 www.caryarms.co.uk

£270; 8 lovely New England-style rms. Charming and unusual higgledy-piggledy boutique hotel at the bottom of a tortuously steep lane – glorious sea views; a beamed, grotto-effect bar with alcoves, rustic hobbit-style red leather cushioned chairs around carved wooden tables on slate or bare boards, an open woodburning stove, local beers and cider, and enjoyable, interesting food; comfortable residents' lounge, smashing breakfasts and wonderful terraces with steps leading down to the quay; self-catering, too; dogs in bar and bedrooms; treats, bowl and bed

TORQUAY   SX9267

Orestone Manor

Rockhouse Lane, Maidencombe, Torquay, Devon TQ14SX (01803) 328098
www.orestonemanor.com

£150; 11 individually decorated rms, most with sea views. Elegant family-run country house in a fine setting surrounded by mature gardens and overlooking Lyme Bay; comfortable public rooms, a chatty bar with local ales and cider, a relaxed atmosphere, attentive staff and particularly good modern british cooking using home-grown produce and local seafood in the bistro, restaurant and terrace bar; resident cat and rabbits; outdoor swimming pool; lots of nearby walks; closed Jan; dogs in Garden Suite; £15

TWO BRIDGES   SX6274

Prince Hall

Two Bridges, Yelverton, Devon PL20 6SA (01822) 890403 www.princehall.co.uk

£130; 8 attractive, spacious rms. Surrounded by Dartmoor National Park, this tranquil 18th-c country house is run by caring, friendly owners and their helpful staff; lovely views from convivial bar, a comfortable sitting room, a smart, cosy dining room, open fires, inventive food using local, seasonal produce, enjoyable breakfasts and delicious cream teas; lots of fine walks; Polo, Portia and Cee Cee are the resident dogs; dogs very welcome anywhere; doggy treats and so forth

Dorset

DOG FRIENDLY PUBS

CERNE ABBAS   ST6601

New Inn
Long Street; DT2 7JF

Newly refurbished former coaching inn with character bar and two dining rooms, friendly licensees, local ales and inventive food; lovely bedrooms

Just re-opening as we went to press after an extensive and sympathetic refurbishment, this is, at its heart, still a charming 16th-c former coaching inn with friendly, hands-on licensees. The bar now has a new solid oak counter, an attractive mix of nice old dining tables and chairs on the slate or polished wooden floors, settles built into various nooks and crannies, and a woodburner in the opened-up yorkstone fireplace; throughout the lovely mullioned windows and the heavy oak beams remain untouched. Palmers Copper, Dorset Gold and IPA on handpump, a dozen wines by the glass, several malt whiskies and local cider. The two dining rooms are furnished in similar style. There are seats on the terrace and picnic-sets under mature fruit trees or parasols in the back garden. The newly furnished bedrooms are smart, well equipped and comfortable – some in the inn itself and some in converted stables. You can walk from the attractive stone-built village up and around the prehistoric Cerne Abbas Giant chalk carving and on to other nearby villages.

Palmers ~ Tenant Jeremy Lee ~ Real ale ~ Bar food (12-2.15, 6.30-8.45) ~ Restaurant ~ (01300) 341274 ~ Children welcome ~ Dogs allowed in bar ~ Open 11-3, 6-11; 11-11 Sun and Sat ~ Bedrooms: £75S/£110S ~ www.thenewinncerneabbas.co.uk

CHIDEOCK   SY4191

Anchor
Off A35 from Chideock; DT6 6JU

Dramatically set pub offering lovely sea and cliff views from large terrace, simple snug bars and fair value food

This strikingly sited pub nestles dramatically beneath the 188-metre Golden Cap pinnacle, just a few steps from the cove beach and very near the Dorset Coast Path. It's ideally placed for the lovely sea and cliff views, so get here early in summer for a table on the spacious front terrace (and a parking space). In winter, when the sometimes overwhelming crowds have gone, the little bars feel especially snug, with low white-planked ceilings, roaring winter fires, some sea pictures, lots of interesting local photographs, a few fossils and shells, simple but comfortable seats around neat tables. Friendly, efficient staff serve well kept Palmers 200, IPA and Copper on handpump (kept under light blanket pressure in winter), and there's a decent little wine list; background, mainly classical, music.

Palmers ~ Tenant Paul Wiscombe ~ Real ale ~ Bar food (12-9; 12-2.30(5.30 Sun), 6-9 (not Sun evening) Nov-March) ~ (01297) 489215 ~ Children welcome ~ Dogs allowed in bar ~ Open 11-11; 11.30-10.30 Sun ~ www.theanchorinnseatown.co.uk

CHIDEOCK   SY4292
George
A35 Bridport–Lyme Regis; DT6 6JD

Comfortably traditional local with well liked food

While working for Hugh Fearnley-Whittingstall, the young couple who own this thatched village pub, developed a love for the area and decided to stay. The interior is still nicely traditional and the cosy low-ceilinged carpeted bar is just as you'd hope, with four Palmers beers on handpump, warm log fires, brassware and pewter tankards hanging from dark beams. There are wooden pews and long built-in tongue and groove banquettes, tools on the cream walls and high shelves of bottles, plates and mugs; background music, TV, bar billiards, table skittles and board games. The garden room opens on to a pretty walled garden with a terrace and wood-fired oven.

Palmers ~ Tenants Mr and Mrs Steve Smith ~ Real ale ~ Bar food (12-2.30, 6-9.30) ~ Restaurant ~ (01297) 489419 ~ Children welcome ~ Dogs allowed in bar ~ Live music Weds, Sat evenings in summer ~ Open 12-3, 6-11 ~ www.georgeinnchideock.co.uk

MUDEFORD   SZ1792
Ship in Distress
Stanpit; off B3059 at roundabout; BH23 3NA

Wide choice of fish dishes, quirky nautical décor and friendly staff in a cheerful cottage pub

The light-hearted interior of this former smugglers' pub is full of amusing seaside themed paraphernalia, the most eye-catching of which are the brightly painted fish cut-outs swimming across the walls. There's everything from rope fancywork and brassware through to lanterns and oars, an aquarium, model boats and the odd piratical figure; darts, games machine, board games, big screen TV, background music and a winter woodburning stove. Besides a good few boat pictures, the room on the right has tables with masses of snapshots of locals caught up in various waterside japes under the glass tabletops. Ringwood Best and a guest or two such as Sharps Doom Bar are on handpump alongside several wines by the glass. A spreading two-room restaurant area, as cheerful in its way as the bar, has a fish tank, contemporary works by local artists for sale and a light-hearted mural sketching out the impression of a window opening on to a sunny boating scene. There are seats and tables out on the suntrap back terrace and a covered heated area for chillier evenings. The pub is near to Mudeford Quay and Stanpit Nature Reserve is close by.

Punch ~ Lease Maggie Wheeler ~ Real ale ~ Bar food (12-2, 7-9) ~ Restaurant ~ (01202) 485123 ~ Children welcome ~ Dogs allowed in bar ~ Open 11am-midnight(11pm Sun) ~ www.ship-in-distress.co.uk

NETTLECOMBE SY5195

Marquis of Lorne

Off A3066 Bridport–Beaminster, via West Milton; DT6 3SY

Attractive country pub with enjoyable food and drink, friendly licensees and seats in the large mature garden; bedrooms

The comfortably traditional bars and dining rooms at this attractive pub are named after local hills – Nettlecombe is in an area of lovely unspoilt countryside, within walking distance of Eggardon Hill, one of Dorset's most spectacular Iron Age forts. The comfortable, bustling main bar has a log fire, mahogany panelling and old prints and photographs around its neatly matching chairs and tables. Two dining areas lead off, the smaller of which has another log fire. The wooden-floored snug (liked by locals) has board games, table skittles and background music. Palmers Best, Copper and 200 are on handpump with a dozen wines by the glass from a decent list. A lovely big mature garden has an array of pretty herbaceous borders, picnic-sets under apple trees, and a rustic-style play area.

Palmers ~ Tenants Stephen and Tracey Brady ~ Real ale ~ Bar food (12-2, 6-9) ~ Restaurant ~ (01308) 485236 ~ Children welcome ~ Dogs allowed in bar ~ Open 12-2.30, 6-11(10 Sun) ~ Bedrooms: £65S/£90S(£90B) ~ www.themarquisoflorne.co.uk

PLUSH ST7102

Brace of Pheasants

Village signposted from B3143 N of Dorchester at Piddletrenthide; DT2 7RQ

16th-c thatched pub with friendly service, three real ales, lots of wines by the glass, generously served food and decent garden; good nearby walks; comfortable bedrooms

Charmingly tucked away in a pretty hamlet in a fold of hills surrounding the Piddle Valley, this handsome thatched place was once the village smithy and two cottages. The welcoming beamed bar has a mix of locals (and maybe their dogs) and visitors, windsor chairs around good solid tables on the patterned carpet, a few standing timbers, a huge heavy-beamed inglenook at one end with cosy seating inside, and a good warming log fire at the other. Flack Manor Double Drop, Sharps Doom Bar and a guest such as Palmers Gold are tapped from the cask by the friendly licensees, and they offer a fine choice of wines with 18 by the glass, and two proper farm ciders; A decent-sized garden includes a terrace and a lawn sloping up towards a rockery. The pub is well placed for walks – an attractive bridleway behind goes to the left of the woods and over to Church Hill. The bedrooms are nicely fitted out and comfortable.

Free house ~ Licensees Phil and Carol Bennett ~ Real ale ~ Bar food (12-2, 7-9) ~ (01300) 348357 ~ Children welcome ~ Dogs allowed in bar ~ Open 12-3, 7-11(10.30 Sun) ~ Bedrooms: £105B/£115B ~ www.braceofpheasants.co.uk

SHERBORNE ST6316

Digby Tap

Cooks Lane; park in Digby Road and walk round corner; DT9 3NS

Regularly changing ales in simple alehouse, open all day with very inexpensive beer and food

One couple told us that this simple back street tavern was the sort of pub they thought had died out. It's the lively local atmosphere, friendly welcome and unspoilt interior, with little changing from one year the next, that makes this old-fashioned alehouse special. The simple flagstoned bar, with its cosy corners, is full of understated character, the small games room has pool and a quiz machine, and there's a TV room. Bass, Otter Bitter, Teignworthy Neap Tide and a local guest are on handpump, with several wines by the glass and a choice of malt whiskies. There are some seats outside and Sherborne Abbey is just a stroll away.

Free house ~ Licensees Oliver Wilson and Nick Whigham ~ Real ale ~ Bar food (12-1.45, not Sun) ~ No credit cards ~ (01935) 813148 ~ Children welcome ~ Dogs allowed in bar ~ Open 11-11; 12-11 Sun ~ www.digbytap.co.uk

SYDLING ST NICHOLAS   SY6399

Greyhound

Off A37 N of Dorchester; High Street; DT2 9PD

Former coaching inn in pretty streamside village with good balance of imaginative food, regular locals and country décor; bedrooms

Though the food at this charming place is quite upmarket, there's still a good local atmosphere in the beamed and flagstoned serving area, with drinkers gathered for a pint and a chat. There are plenty of bar stools by the counter, and the carpeted bar has a comfortable mix of straightforward tables and chairs, some country decorations and a warm fire in a handsome Portland stone fireplace. Butcombe Bitter, St Austel Dartmoor Best and a changing guest such as Dorset Hardy Pool are on handpump and they keep a farm cider. The cosy dining room is a little smarter with fresh cream walls, white table cloths and a glass-covered well set into the floor from which coachmen used it to pull up buckets of water for their horses. A conservatory has attractive rustic furniture around scrubbed wooden tables and a green leather chesterfield. The small front garden has picnic-sets and a children's play area.

Free house ~ Licensees Alice Draper and Helena Boot ~ Real ale ~ Bar food (12-2, 6.30-9) ~ Restaurant ~ (01300) 341303 ~ Children welcome ~ Dogs allowed in bar ~ Open 12-3, 6-11; 12-3 Sun; closed Sun evening ~ Bedrooms: £80B/£90B ~ www.thegreyhound.net

WEST BAY   SY4690

West Bay

Station Road; DT6 4EW

Relaxed seaside inn with emphasis on seafood

If you like fish you should be delighted by the extensive choice at this well run seaside pub where you can enjoy a relaxing meal in an informal, welcoming atmosphere. An island servery separates the fairly simple bare-boards front part (with coal-effect gas fire and a mix of sea and nostalgic prints) from a cosier carpeted dining area with more of a country kitchen feel; background music. Though its spaciousness means it never feels crowded, booking is virtually essential in season. Palmers 200, Best, Copper Ale and Dorset Gold are served on handpump alongside good house wines (with ten by the glass) and several malt whiskies. There are tables in the small side garden, with more in a large garden. Several local teams meet to play in the pub's 100-year-old skittle alley. The bedrooms are quiet and comfortable.

Palmers ~ Tenants Paul Crisp and Tracy McCulloch ~ Real ale ~ Bar food (12-2(3 Sun); 6-9) ~ Restaurant ~ (01308) 422157 ~ Children welcome till 8pm ~ Dogs allowed in bar ~ Open 12-11; 12-3, 6-11 (Mon-Thurs) in winter in winter ~ Bedrooms: /£85(£100B) ~ www.thewestbayhotel.co.uk

WEST STOUR   ST7822

Ship
A30 W of Shaftesbury; SP8 5RP

Civilised and pleasantly updated roadside dining inn, offering a wide range of food

During his summer beer festival, the landlord at this well cared for roadside inn puts a stage up in the garden and showcases a dozen beers and ten ciders, all from the West Country. At other times you'll find Dartmoor IPA and three guests from brewers such as Butcombe, Fullers and Sharps on handpump, good wines by the glass, a farm cider, elderflower pressé and organic apple juices. The smallish bar on the left is airy with big sash windows looking beyond the road and car park to rolling pastures, cream décor and a mix chunky farmhouse furniture on dark boards. The smaller flagstoned public bar has a good log fire and low ceilings. On the right, two carpeted dining rooms with stripped pine dado, stone walls and shutters are similarly furnished in a pleasantly informal style, and have some attractive contemporary cow prints; TV, darts, lots of board games and background music. The bedlington terriers are called Douglas and Toby. The five bedrooms have just been refurbished.

Free house ~ Licensee Gavin Griggs ~ Real ale ~ Bar food (12-2.30, 6-9; not Sun evening) ~ Restaurant ~ (01747) 838640 ~ Children welcome ~ Dogs allowed in bar ~ Open 12-3, 6-11; 12-11 Sun ~ Bedrooms: £60B/£90B ~ www.shipinn-dorset.com

WEYMOUTH   SY6878

Red Lion
Hope Square; DT4 8TR

Cheery place with sunny terrace, great range of drinks including loads of whiskies and rums, and good value pubby food

Opposite the redeveloped brewery (now shops and so forth) in Weymouth's pedestrianised Old Harbour, and sharing its Victorian architecture, this lively place has an outside seating area that enjoys all the local bustle and is warmed by the sun well into the evening – during the summer months it turns one of Weymouth's smallest pubs into one of its biggest. You can warm up here nicely, too, in winter as they stock an impressive range of over 60 rums, well over 100 whiskies and whiskeys displayed behind the bar. Real ales (with helpful tasting notes), pulled by the cheery irish landlord, include Tring Lifeboat, Dorset Red Lion Pride and three guests from brewers such as Dorset, Hop Back and Sharps. The refurbished bare-boards interior is kept cosy with candles, has just enough bric-a-brac to add interest, and some nice contemporary touches like the woven timber wall and loads of mirrors wittily overlapping on stripped brick walls; board games, background music.

Free house ~ Licensee Brian McLaughlin ~ Real ale ~ Bar food (12-9; 12-3, 6-8.30 in winter) ~ (01305) 786940 ~ Children welcome ~ Dogs allowed in bar ~ Live music Fri evenings, summer Sun afternoons ~ Open 12-11(midnight Sat, 10.30 Sun) ~ www.theredlionweymouth.co.uk

WIMBORNE MINSTER

SZ0199

Green Man

Victoria Road at junction with West Street (B3082/B3073); BH21 1EN

Cosy, warm-hearted town pub with simple food at bargain prices

This cheerful local is a proper community pub with regulars popping in and out throughout the day, but as a visitor you'll get just as warm a welcome from the friendly landlord. The four small linked areas have maroon plush banquettes and polished dark pub tables, copper and brass ornaments, red walls and Wadworths IPA, 6X and Bishops Tipple on handpump. One room has a log fire in a biggish brick fireplace, another has a coal-effect gas fire, and they have two dart boards, a silenced games machine, background music and TV; in summer the Barn houses a pool table. The award-winning window boxes, flowering tubs and hanging baskets at the front are a fantastic sight in summer – there are more on the heated back terrace. Their little border terrier is called Cooper.

Wadworths ~ Tenant Andrew Kiff ~ Real ale ~ Bar food (10-2; not evenings) ~ Restaurant ~ (01202) 881021 ~ Children welcome until 7.30pm ~ Dogs allowed in bar ~ Open 10am-11.30pm(12.30 Sat) ~ www.greenmanwimborne.com

WORTH MATRAVERS

SY9777

Square & Compass

At fork of both roads signposted to village from B3069; BH19 3LF

Unchanging country tavern with masses of character, in the same family for many years; lovely sea views and fine nearby walks

For most of our readers this 'blissfully eccentric place' is 'worth a huge detour', though its simple offerings are not to everyone's taste, and it can get very busy. The Newman family first took on this fine old pub over 100 years ago and to this day, there's no bar counter. Palmers Copper and guests from brewers such as Bowmans, Otley and Wessex and up to 13 ciders are tapped from a row of casks and passed to you in a drinking corridor through two serving hatches; also about 20 malt whiskies. A couple of basic unspoilt rooms have simple furniture on the flagstones, a woodburning stove and a loyal crowd of friendly locals; darts and shove-ha'penny. From benches (made from local stone) out in front there's a fantastic view down over the village rooftops to the sea around St Aldhelm's Head and there may be free-roaming hens, chickens and other birds clucking around your feet. A little museum (free) exhibits local fossils and artefacts, mostly collected by the current friendly landlord and his father. There are wonderful walks from here to some exciting switchback sections of the coast path above St Aldhelm's Head and Chapman's Pool – you will need to park in the public car park 100 metres along the Corfe Castle road (which has a £1 honesty box).

Free house ~ Licensee Charlie Newman ~ Real ale ~ Bar food (all day) ~ No credit cards ~ (01929) 439229 ~ Children welcome ~ Dogs allowed in bar ~ Live music some Fri and Sat evenings and Sun lunchtime ~ Open 12-11; 12-3, 6-11 Mon-Thurs in winter ~ www.squareandcompasspub.co.uk

DOG FRIENDLY INNS, HOTELS AND B&Bs

BEAMINSTER
SU1401

Bridge House

3 Prout Bridge, Beaminster, Dorset DT8 3AY (01308) 862200 www.bridge-house.co.uk

£150; 13 rms, more spacious in main house. Seven hundred years old and a former house for priests, this friendly place has an open fire in the cosy, comfortable sitting room, a convivial bar, a breakfast room overlooking the attractive walled garden (where dogs may walk), good, modern cooking in the Georgian dining room and an informal, relaxed atmosphere; dogs in coach-house bedrooms; £15

BOURNEMOUTH
SZ1091

Langtry Manor

26 Derby Road, Eastcliff, Bournemouth, Dorset BH1 3QB (01202) 290550 www.langtrymanor.com

£145; 27 individually refurbished, pretty rms, some in the manor, some in the lodge. Built by Edward VII for Lillie Langtry and with lots of memorabilia, this family-run hotel has plenty of fine original features in the comfortable lounges, open fires, helpful friendly staff and first class contemporary food in the elegant restaurant with its minstrel's gallery and stained glass windows (they offer a six-course Edwardian banquet every Saturday); resident boxer, Tyson; walks for dogs in grounds and some fine walks in the area; closed first 2 weeks in Jan; dogs in bedrooms only

BOURNEMOUTH
SZ1491

White Topps

Southbourne, Bournemouth, Dorset BH6 4BB (01202) 428868 www.whitetopps.co.uk

£80; 5 rms, shared bthrms. Homely Edwardian house that is 100% dog oriented and all guests bring at least one dog; two lounges, one with a bar and one with a fridge for guests (used for storing dog food), traditional meals (and vegetarian choices) in dining room, and lots of doggy pictures and ornaments; four resident dogs; walks on nearby beach; closed Nov-Feb; dogs welcome anywhere and ground floor rooms for elderly or disabled dogs

BRIDPORT
SY4691

Britmead House

West Bay Road, Bridport, Dorset DT6 4EG (01308) 422941 www.britmeadhouse.co.uk

£74; 9 clean rms. Extended Victorian hotel with lots to do nearby, a comfortable lounge overlooking the garden, attractive dining room serving good breakfasts, and kind helpful service; fields at back of the grounds to walk dogs and a nearby beach; dogs in bedrooms (must not be left unattended) by prior arrangement; £5

BRIDPORT
SY4893
Orchard Barn
Bradpole, Bridport, Dorset DT6 4AR (01308) 455655 www.lodgeatorchardbarn.co.uk

£69.50; 3 lovely rms. Run by professional, genuinely caring hotel keepers, this first class place is built on the site of an old farm and set beside the River Asker (walks close by); an open log fire and a gallery in the comfortable lounge with french windows to the terrace and garden, dining room offering excellent breakfasts using home-made marmalades and jams, and afternoon teas with home-made cake; evening snacks on request but lots of places nearby; three resident dogs and one cat; dogs welcome (not in dining room); £10

CERNE ABBAS
ST6601
New Inn
14 Long Street, Cerne Abbas, Dorchester, Dorset DT2 7JF (01300) 341274
www.thenewinncerneabbas.co.uk

£110; 12 lovely, well equipped rms. Newly refurbished former coaching inn with character bar and two dining rooms, mullioned windows, heavy beams, attractive old furniture on slate or polished wooden floors, various nooks and crannies and a woodburning stove; local ales and cider, friendly licensees and inventive food; you can walk from the village up and around the prehistoric Cerne Abbas Giant chalk carving and on to other nearby villages; dogs anywhere in the pub and in bedrooms

EAST KNIGHTON
SY8185
Countryman
East Knighton, Dorchester, Dorset DT2 8LL (01305) 852666
www.thecountrymaninndorset.com

£85; 8 cosy rms. Attractively converted and newly refurbished pair of old cottages with open fires and plenty of character in the main bar which opens into several smaller areas; real ales, an extensive menu including a popular carvery and nice breakfasts in the large restaurant, and courteous staff; resident dog and cat; walks in garden and nearby; dogs in bedrooms; treats, bowls and meals

EVERSHOT
ST5704
Summer Lodge
Evershot, Dorchester, Dorset DT2 0JR (01935) 482000 www.summerlodgehotel.com

£335; 24 beautifully decorated rms, some in thatched cottages. Spotlessly kept and peacefully set former dower house with a cosy whisky bar, an airy conservatory, a smart, elegant dining room, a carefully chosen wine list, excellent english cooking with contemporary touches and using home-grown and best quality local produce, delicious breakfasts and afternoon teas, and personal, caring service; spa and indoor swimming pool, tennis, croquet and giant chess; dogs on a lead in garden and nearby walks; dogs in some bedrooms and some public rooms; £20

FARNHAM
ST9514

Museum Inn

Farnham, Blandford Forum, Dorset DT11 8DE (01725) 516261 www.museuminn.co.uk

£110; 8 rms. Rather smart 17th-c thatched inn with comfortably cushioned furnishings in the bustling beamed and flagstoned small bar, an inglenook fireplace and fine antique dresser in the dining room, another room like a contemporary baronial hall with dozens of antlers and a stag's head looking down on a long refectory table, real ales, good wines, particularly good modern cooking and attentive service; walks in the surrounding fields; dogs welcome away from restaurant; treats; £10

HAZELBURY BRYAN
ST7409

Old Causeway Bakery

Hazelbury Bryan, Sturminster Newton, Dorset DT10 2BH (01258) 817228 www.oldcausewaybakery.co.uk

£85; 3 comfortable rms. Plenty of antiques, paintings and guidebooks in comfortable sitting room/dining room, bold coloured walls, friendly, helpful owners and good, generous breakfasts; resident dogs Henry the black labrador and Bertie the working cocker spaniel; good nearby walks and beaches; dogs welcome anywhere, except on beds; food and bedding on request; water bowls inside and out

LOWER BOCKHAMPTON
SY7290

Yalbury Cottage

Lower Bockhampton, Dorchester, Dorset DT2 8PZ (01305) 262382 www.yalburycottage.com

£120; 8 rms overlooking garden or fields. Very attractive family-run 16th-c thatched house with a relaxed friendly atmosphere, candlelight, low beams, exposed stone walls and woodburning stoves in inglenook fireplaces in comfortable lounge and restaurant, carefully cooked and beautifully served imaginative food, good wines, and seats on pretty terrace overlooking fields; dogs in bedrooms; not in public rooms; £7.50

MIDDLEMARSH
ST6607

Hunters Moon

Middlemarsh, Sherborne, Dorset DT9 5QN (01963) 210966 www.hunters-moon.org.uk

£75; 8 comfortable rms. Cheerfully run former coaching inn with friendly hands-on licensees, a pubby atmosphere in the comfortably traditional beamed bars, quite a variety of tables and chairs on red patterned carpets, plenty of bric-a-brac, three log fires, local beers and good food; seats on a neat lawn; dogs in bedrooms and bar (on lead); £10

STUDLAND
SZ0383

Knoll House

Studland, Swanage, Dorset BH19 3AH (01929) 450450 www.knollhouse.co.uk

£220; 80 comfortable rms. Spacious, well run hotel owned by the same family for over 50 years and set in 100 acres with marvellous views of Studland Bay and direct access to the fine 3-mile beach; comfortable spreading lounges with open fires, paintings and plenty of armchairs and sofas, a cocktail bar, enjoyable meals in airy restaurant and lots to do – tennis, table tennis, pool and table football, heated outdoor pool and health spa, small private golf course and nearby sea fishing, riding, walking, sailing and windsurfing; resident dogs; dogs welcome away from dining rooms, pool and spa; £5 including food

STURMINSTER NEWTON
ST7711

Plumber Manor

Hazelbury Bryan Road, Plumber, Sturminster Newton, Dorset DT10 2AF (01258) 472507 www.plumbermanor.co.uk

£220; 16 very comfortable rms, 6 in the house and 10 in the restored stone barn with river and garden views. Handsome 17th-c house (owned and run by the same family since it was built) in quiet countryside, with a convivial well stocked bar, antiques, fresh flowers and open fires in the lounge, good interesting english/french food in three dining rooms, smashing breakfasts, a relaxed atmosphere and exceptionally friendly, helpful service; tennis; closed Feb; dogs in ground floor bedrooms only; £10

TARRANT MONKTON
ST9408

Langton Arms

Tarrant Monkton, Blandford, Dorset DT11 8RX (01258) 830225 www.thelangtonarms.co.uk

£90; 10 comfortable rms. Charming thatched pub in a pretty village with nearby walks, a beamed bar with wooden tables and chairs on flagstones, lots of black and white photos, local beers, and an inglenook fireplace; the attractive restaurant and conservatory are in a converted barn and the well liked food is carefully prepared using some own-grown produce; seats in the nice back garden and a children's play area; dogs in bedrooms and bar

WINTERBORNE ZELSTON
SY9097

Huish Manor

Winterborne Zelston, Blandford Forum, Dorset DT11 9ES (01929) 459065

£55; 2 large, comfortable rms. Handsome 18th-c house with open fires, antiques, marine paintings and fresh flowers in the drawing room and elegant pink-walled dining room, excellent breakfasts cooked by the hostess, and a friendly, relaxed atmosphere; seats on the front lawn and in the walled garden and an adjoining small orchard and paddocks; dogs welcome by prior arrangement

Essex

DOG FRIENDLY PUBS

AYTHORPE RODING   TL5915
Axe & Compasses
B184 S of Dunmow; CM6 1PP

Appealing free house, nice balance of eating and drinking and friendly welcome

Attention to detail goes into all aspects of this lovely old weatherboard pub. Although popular with diners, locals do pop in for a pint of the Sharps Doom Bar or three guests from local brewers such as Colchester, Nethergate and Wibblers which are on handpump or racked behind the counter in temperature-stabilised casks; also up to three Weston's farm ciders on handpump. Everything is neatly kept and warm and cosy with bent old beams and timbers in stripped red brick walls, comfortable bar chairs at the counter, leatherette settles and stools and dark country chairs around a few pub tables on pale boards and turkish rugs. The original part on the left has a two-way fireplace marking off a snug little raftered dining area which has sentimental prints on dark masonry and a big open-faced clock; background music. The small garden behind has stylish modern tables and chairs.

Free house ~ Licensee David Hunt ~ Real ale ~ Bar food (12-2.30, 6-9.30; 12-8 Sun) ~ Restaurant ~ (01279) 876648 ~ Children welcome ~ Dogs allowed in bar ~ Open 11-11(12 Fri, Sat); 12-10.30 Sun ~ www.theaxeandcompasses.co.uk

FEERING   TL8720
Sun
Just off A12 Kelvedon bypass; Feering Hill (B1024 just W of Feering proper); CO5 9NH

Striking 16th-c timbered and jettied pub with good beer and food, and pleasant garden

So handsome outside, the Sun lives up to its promise inside, with handsomely carved black beams and timbers galore, and attractive wildflower murals in a frieze above the central timber divider. The spreading carpeted bar is relaxed, unpretentious and civilised, with two big woodburning stoves, one in the huge central inglenook fireplace, another by an antique winged settle on the left. They have half a dozen Shepherd Neame ales in fine condition on handpump – on our most recent visit, Bitter, Kents Best, Spitfire, Early Bird, Amber and Bishops Finger, and hold summer and winter beer festivals; cheerful service, daily papers, board games. A brick-paved back courtyard has tables, heaters and a shelter, and the garden beyond has tall trees shading green picnic-sets.

Shepherd Neame ~ Tenant Andy Howard ~ Real ale ~ Bar food (12-2.30, 6-9.30; 12-8 Sun) ~ (01376) 570442 ~ Children welcome ~ Dogs allowed in bar ~ Open 12-3, 5.30-11; 12-11.30 Sat; 12-10.30 Sun ~ www.suninnfeering.co.uk

GOSFIELD   TL7829
Kings Head
The Street (A1017 Braintree-Halstead); CO9 1TP

Comfortable dining pub with proper public bar and good value food

A well supported whisky club meets four times a year for tastings and to choose the impressive list of 70 internationally sourced single malts that are on offer at this ancient pub. Adnams Southwold, Timothy Taylors Landlord and Sharps Doombar on handpump, around a dozen wines by the glass and organic soft drinks are also served. Bright splashes of warm contemporary colour brighten the modernised interior of the softly lit beamed main bar, which has red panelled dado and ceiling, neat modern black leather armchairs, bucket chairs and a sofa, as well as sturdy pale wood dining chairs and tables on dark boards, and a log fire in a handsome old brick fireplace with big bellows. Black timbers mark off a red carpeted and walled dining area with red furnishings that opens into a carpeted conservatory; background music, daily papers. The good-sized quite separate public bar, with a purple pool table, games machine, darts and TV, has its own partly covered terrace; the main terrace has round picnic-sets.

Enterprise ~ Lease Mark Bloomfield ~ Real ale ~ Bar food (12-2, 7-9; 12-6 Sun) ~ Restaurant ~ (01787) 474016 ~ Children welcome ~ Dogs allowed in bar ~ Open 12-11(1am Sat, 10.30 Sun) ~ www.thekingsheadgosfield.co.uk

HATFIELD BROAD OAK   TL5416
Dukes Head
B183 Hatfield Heath-Takeley; High Street; CM22 7HH

Relaxed, well run dining pub with enjoyable food, attractive layout of nicely linked separate areas

Various intimate seating areas ramble pleasantly around the central feature woodburner and side servery at this comfortable village pub. Seating is mainly good solid wooden dining chairs around a variety of more or less chunky stripped and sealed tables, with a comfortable group of armchairs and a sofa down one end, and a slightly more formal area at the back on the right. Cheerful prints on the wall and occasional magenta panels in the mainly cream décor, make for quite a buoyant mood, as does the lively attitude of the friendly, helpful staff; well kept Fullers London Pride, Greene King IPA and St Austell Tribute on handpump and over a dozen wines by the glass from a good list; background music. Sam the dog welcomes other dogs and there are always dog biscuits behind the bar. The back garden, with a sheltered terrace and an end wendy house, has comfortable chairs around teak tables under cocktail parasols; there are also some picnic-sets in the front angle of the building, which has some nice pargeting.

Enterprise ~ Lease Liz Flodman ~ Real ale ~ Restaurant ~ (01279) 718598 ~ Children welcome ~ Dogs allowed in bar ~ Open 12-3, 6-11.30; 12-11.30 Sat; 12-10.30 Sun ~ www.thedukeshead.co.uk

LITTLE WALDEN
TL5441

Crown

B1052 N of Saffron Walden; CB10 1XA

Bustling 18th-c cottage pub with a warming log fire, hearty food and bedrooms

This homely low-ceilinged local looks fairly unassuming from the exterior – it's the particularly warm and cheery welcome from the licensees and their staff that make it so appealing, plus they serve tasty food and a good pint, too. Four changing beers are tapped straight from casks racked up behind the bar – normally Adnams Best, Greene King IPA, Woodfordes Wherry and a guest such as Nethergate. The interior is traditional, with book room-red walls, floral curtains, bare boards, navy carpeting, cosy warm fires and an unusual walk-through fireplace. A higgledy-piggledy mix of chairs ranges from high-backed pews to little cushioned armchairs spaced around a good variety of closely arranged tables, mostly big, some stripped. The small red-tiled room on the right has two small tables; TV, disabled access. Tables out on the terrace take in views of surrounding tranquil countryside.

Free house ~ Licensee Colin Hailing ~ Real ale ~ Bar food (11.30-3, 6-11; 12-8 Sun) ~ Restaurant ~ (01799) 522475 ~ Children welcome ~ Dogs allowed in bar ~ Open 11.30-3, 6-12; 12-11 Sun ~ Bedrooms: £65S/£65S ~ www.thecrownlittlewalden.co.uk

MARGARETTING TYE
TL6801

White Hart

From B1002 (just S of A12/A414 junction) follow Maldon Road for 1.3 miles, then turn right immediately after river bridge, into Swan Lane, keeping on for 0.7 miles; The Tye; CM4 9JX

Fine choice of ales tapped from the cask in cheery country pub with good food and a family garden

The cottagey interior of this unpretentious weatherboard pub is as fresh and neatly kept as its pristine cream exterior suggests. Walls and wainscoting are painted in chalky traditional colours that look well with its dark old timbers and mix of old wooden chairs and tables, mostly ready for diners to arrive. A stuffed deer head is mounted on the chimneybreast above the woodburning stove. The neat carpeted back conservatory is similar in style, and the front lobby has a charity paperback table; darts, quiz machine, skittles, board games and background music. Friendly informative staff serve an impressive range of eight real ales tapped straight from the cask. Besides Adnams Best and Broadside, Mighty Oak IPA and Oscar Wilde and Red Fox Hunters Gold they bring on a constant stream of nationwide guest beers, available to take away and have interesting bottled beers, too, during their popular June and October beer festivals might have up to 60 kinds a day; winter mulled wine. There are plenty of picnic-sets out on grass and terracing around the pub, with a sturdy play area, a safely fenced duck pond and pens of rabbits, guinea-pigs and a pygmy goat.

Free house ~ Licensee Elizabeth Haines ~ Real ale ~ Bar food (12-2(2.30 Sat, 4.30 Sun), 6.30(6 Fri, Sat)-9(8.30 Sun); not Mon evening) ~ (01277) 840478 ~ Well behaved children welcome ~ Dogs allowed in bar ~ Open 11.30-3, 6-midnight; 11.30-midnight Sat; 12-midnight Sun ~ Bedrooms: /£80B ~ www.whitehartmargarettingtye.com

SOUTH HANNINGFIELD
TQ7497
Old Windmill
Off A130 S of Chelmsford; CM3 8HT

Extensive but invitingly converted Brunning & Price pub with interesting food and good range of drinks

The rambling interior of this knocked-through place contains a forest of stripped standing timbers, making it feel at once open-plan and intimate. Décor is comfortably inviting, with an agreeable mix of highly polished old tables and chairs, frame-to-frame pictures on cream walls, woodburning stoves and homely pot plants. Deep green or dark red dado and one or two old rugs dotted on the glowing wood floors provide splashes of colour; other areas are more subdued with beige carpeting. Phoenix Brunning & Price Original and five guests from brewers such as Crouch Vale, Mighty Oak, Timothy Taylor and Wibblers are on handpump, with 20 wines by the glass, farm cider, 70 malts and a good range of spirits; background music. A back terrace has tables and chairs and there are picnic-sets on the lawn here and a few out in front.

Brunning & Price ~ Manager Julia Palmer ~ Real ale ~ Bar food (12-10(9.30 Sun)) ~ (01268) 712280 ~ Children welcome ~ Dogs allowed in bar ~ Open 11.30-11; 12-10.30 Sun ~ www.oldwindmillpub.co.uk

STOCK
TQ6999
Hoop
B1007; from A12 Chelmsford bypass take Galleywood, Billericay turn-off; CM4 9BD

Happy weatherboarded pub with interesting beers, nice food and a large garden

Simple wood fixtures and fittings, including stripped floors, wooden tables and brocaded wooden settles, keep the interior of this old weatherboard pub feeling appropriately down-to-earth and pubby – just the right setting for the cheery locals and visitors enjoying the happy bustle and real ales here. Adnams is kept alongside three guests from brewers such as Bishop Nick, Crouch Vale and Mighty Oak, and during the eight days of their late May beer festival (when they open all day) they can get through over 200 real ales and 80 ciders and perries. Standing timbers and beams in the open-plan bar hint at the building's great age and its original layout as a row of three weavers' cottages. In winter, a warming fire burns in a big brick-walled fireplace. A restaurant up in the timbered eaves – very different in style, with a separate à la carte menu – is light and airy with pale timbers set in white walls and more wood flooring. Prettily bordered with flowers, the large sheltered back garden has picnic-sets and a covered seating area. Parking is limited, so it's worth getting here early.

Free house ~ Licensee Michelle Corrigan ~ Real ale ~ Bar food (12-3(5 Sun), 6-9; 12-9 Sat; not Sun evening) ~ Restaurant ~ (01277) 841137 ~ Children welcome if eating ~ Dogs allowed in bar ~ Open 11-11; 12-10.30 Sun ~ www.thehoop.co.uk

DOG FRIENDLY INNS, HOTELS AND B&Bs

BURNHAM-ON-CROUCH   TQ9595
White Harte
The Quay, Burnham-on-Crouch, Essex CM0 8AS (01621) 782106
www.whiteharteburnham.co.uk

£85; 11 rms, 4 with shared bthrm, many overlooking the water. Comfortably
old-fashioned hotel overlooking the River Crouch with picnic-sets on the jetty and
riverside walks from the door; informal bars with assorted nautical bric-a-brac
and real ales, and other traditionally furnished high-ceilinged rooms with oak
furniture on polished parquet flooring, sea pictures, big winter log fires and pubby
food; dogs anywhere except restaurant; £5

GREAT CHESTERFORD   TL5042
Crown House
Great Chesterford, Saffron Walden, Essex CB10 1NY (01799) 530515/530257
www.crownhousehotel.com

£99.50; 18 individually decorated rms, some in restored stable block. Carefully
restored, imposing Georgian coach house in lovely gardens, with plenty of
original features, an open fire and comfortable leather seating in the attractive
lounge bar, good, bistro-style food in the smart, panelled restaurant, and pleasant,
efficient staff; dogs in ground floor annexe bedrooms; £5

HORNDON-ON-THE-HILL   TQ6783
Bell
High Road, Horndon-on-the-Hill, Stanford-le-Hope, Essex SS17 8LD (01375) 642463
www.bell-inn.co.uk

£70; 16 attractive rms. Lovely Tudor inn, run by the same family for 70 years,
with a heavily beamed bar, antique high-backed settles and benches on polished
oak floorboards and flagstones, a curious collection of ossified hot cross buns
hanging along a beam, an impressive range of drinks and quite an emphasis on
the top notch food; seats in pretty flower-filled courtyard; resident black labrador,
Floyd and shar pei, Stella; dogs in bedrooms and bar; £10

MISTLEY   TM1131
Mistley Thorn
High Street, Mistley, Manningtree, Essex CO11 1HE (01206) 392821
www.mistleythorn.com

£90; 8 well equipped rms, four with Stour Estuary views. 18th-c former coaching
inn with a contemporary open-plan interior, modern paintwork and art on the
walls, a convivial small bar, a woodburning stove in an inglenook fireplace in
the smart dining room, quite a choice of interesting food (lots of fish speciality
dishes) and nice breakfasts; they also run a pizzeria in town (Lucca's); walks
on the nearby Essex Way; dogs welcome; bedding, bowls, treats and breakfast
sausage; £10

Gloucestershire

DOG FRIENDLY PUBS

BLAISDON   SO7016
Red Hart
*Village signposted off A4136 just SW of junction with A40 W of Gloucester; OS Sheet 162
map reference 703169; GL17 0AH*

**Busy pub with cheerful landlord, bustling atmosphere, some interesting
bric-a-brac in attractive rooms, popular bar food and several real ales**

Run by an enthusiastic, cheerful landlord and his attentive staff, this village pub
has a bustling atmosphere and a happy mix of both locals and visitors. The
flagstoned main bar has cushioned wall and window seats, traditional pub tables,
a big sailing-ship painting above the log fire, Hook Norton Bitter and guests from
Bath Ales, Malvern Hills and RCH on handpump, several wines by the glass and
local cider; background music and bar billiards. Spotty the jack russell is now 15
years old and makes the occasional appearance. On the right, there's an attractive
beamed restaurant with interesting prints and bric-a-brac, and on the left, you'll
find additional dining space for families. There are some picnic-sets in the garden
and a children's play area, and at the back of the building is a terrace for popular
summer barbecues. The little church above the village is worth a visit.

Free house ~ Licensee Guy Wilkins ~ Real ale ~ Bar food (12-2, 7-9) ~ Restaurant ~
(01452) 830477 ~ Well behaved children welcome ~ Dogs allowed in bar ~ Open 11.30-3
(4 Sun), 6(7 Sun)-11(midnight Sat)

BLEDINGTON   SP2422
Kings Head
B4450; OX7 6XQ

**Beams and atmospheric furnishings in 16th-c former cider house, super
wines by the glass, real ales and delicious food; smart bedrooms**

Our readers love this well run and civilised old inn and for many, it's an
absolute favourite. You can be sure of a genuine welcome, the food and beer
are first rate and the courtyard bedrooms are smart and comfortable. The main
bar is full of ancient beams and other atmospheric furnishings (high-backed
wooden settles, gateleg or pedestal tables) and there's a warming log fire in the
stone inglenook with its bellows and big black kettle; sporting memorabilia of
rugby, racing, cricket and hunting. To the left of the bar, a drinking area for locals
has built-in wall benches, stools and dining chairs around wooden tables, rugs
on bare boards and a woodburning stove. Hook Norton Best and guests from

breweries such as Butcombe, Purity and Wye Valley on handpump, an excellent wine list with ten by the glass and 25 malt whiskies; background music and darts. There are seats in front of the inn and more in the back courtyard garden and resident ducks and chickens. This is a pretty setting in a tranquil village, just back from the green, which has a brook running through it. The same first class licensees also run the Swan at Swinbrook (Oxfordshire).

Free house ~ Licensees Nicola and Archie Orr-Ewing ~ Real ale ~ Bar food (12-2, 7-9) ~ Restaurant ~ (01608) 658365 ~ Children welcome ~ Dogs allowed in bar ~ Open 11(12 Sun)-11 ~ Bedrooms: £75B/£95B ~ www.kingsheadinn.net

BROCKHAMPTON   SP0322
Craven Arms

Village signposted off A436 Andoversford–Naunton – look out for inn sign at head of lane in village; can also be reached from A40 Andoversford–Cheltenham via Whittington and Syreford; GL54 5XQ

Friendly village pub with tasty bar food, real ales, seats in a big garden and nice surrounding walks

After enjoying one of the fine surrounding walks, this attractive 17th-c pub is just the place to head for – and it's in a pretty spot with plenty of seats in the large garden and lovely views. Inside, the bars have low beams, thick roughly coursed stone walls and some tiled flooring, and though much of it has been opened out to give a sizeable eating area off the smaller bar servery, it's been done well to give a feeling of several communicating rooms. The furniture is mainly pine with some comfortable leather sofas, wall settles and tub chairs, and there are gin traps and various stuffed animal trophies, and a warm log fire. Otter Bitter and a couple of changing guests from breweries like Butcombe and Cotswold Spring on handpump and several wines by the glass; board games. The dog is called Max and the cat Polly.

Free house ~ Licensees Barbara and Bob Price ~ Real ale ~ Bar food (not Sun evening or Mon) ~ Restaurant ~ (01242) 820410 ~ Children welcome ~ Dogs allowed in bar ~ Open 12-3, 6-11; 12-11 Sat; 12-6 Sun; Mon in winter; closed Sun evening and Mon ~ www.thecravenarms.co.uk

CHEDWORTH   SP0512
Seven Tuns

Village signposted off A429 NE of Cirencester; then take second signposted right turn and bear left towards church; GL54 4AE

Enjoyable little pub with several open fires, lots of wines by the glass, popular bar food and plenty of outside seats

In a charming village and handy for the nearby famous Roman villa, this is a friendly little 17th-c pub with a bustling atmosphere. The small snug lounge on the right has comfortable seats and decent tables, sizeable antique prints, tankards hanging from the beam over the serving bar, a partly boarded ceiling, and a good winter log fire in a big stone fireplace. Down a couple of steps, the public bar on the left has an open fire and this leads into a dining room with yet another open fire. Wells & Youngs Bitter and guests like Otter Ale and Sharps Doom Bar on handpump, up to 14 wines by the glass and 19 malt whiskies; background music and skittle alley. One sunny terrace has a boules pitch and across the road there's another little walled, raised terrace with a waterwheel and a stream; plenty of tables and seats. There are nice walks through the valley.

Youngs – Tenant Alex Davenport-Jones ~ Real ale ~ Bar food (12-2.30(3 Sat, Sun), 6.30-9.30(9 Sun)) ~ Restaurant ~ (01285) 720242 ~ Children welcome ~ Dogs allowed in bar ~ Open 12-3, 6-11; all day in July and Aug; 12-midnight(10.30 Sun) Sat ~ www.seventuns.co.uk

CHIPPING CAMPDEN   SP1539
Eight Bells
Church Street (which is one way – entrance off B4035); GL55 6JG

Handsome inn with massive timbers and beams, log fires, quite a choice of bar food, real ales and seats in the large terraced garden; handy for the Cotswold Way; bedrooms

This handsome old inn has been serving customers since it was built as a hostel for workmen building the nearby church. The bars have heavy oak beams, massive timber supports and stripped-stone walls with cushioned pews, sofas and solid dark wood furniture on the broad flagstones and log fires in up to three restored stone fireplaces. Inset into the floor of the dining room is a glass panel showing part of the passage from the church by which Roman Catholic priests could escape from the Roundheads. Hook Norton Best, Goffs Jouster, Purity Mad Goose and a guest such as Wye Valley HPA on handpump from the fine oak bar counter, quite a few wines by the glass and Old Rosie cider. background music and board games. There's a large terraced garden with plenty of seats, and striking views of the almshouses and church. The pub is handy for the Cotswold Way walk, which takes you to Bath.

Free house ~ Licensee Neil Hargreaves ~ Real ale ~ Bar food (12-2(2.30 Fri, Sat, 2.15-Sun), 6.30-9(9.30 Fri, Sat, 8.45 Sun)) ~ Restaurant ~ (01386) 840371 ~ Well behaved children welcome but only in dining room after 6pm ~ Dogs allowed in bar ~ Open 12(11 Sat)-11(10.30 Sun) ~ Bedrooms: £65B/£100B ~ www.eightbellsinn.co.uk

CLIFFORD'S MESNE   SO6922
Yew Tree
From A40 W of Huntley turn off at May Hill 1, Clifford's Mesne 2.5 signpost, then pub eventually signed up steep narrow lane on left; Clifford's Mesne also signposted off B4216 S of Newent, pub then signed on right; GL18 1JS

Unusual dining pub nicely tucked away on slopes of May Hill, with inventive food using home-reared pigs, and wine bargains

The provincial french wines from small producers served in this well run dining pub come in three glass sizes, in a 500ml jug and of course, by the bottle. They have a seating area in their small informal wine shop making it a sort of wine bar with nibbles and if you buy a bottle with your meal, they charge just the shop price plus £6 which represents excellent value especially at the top end. They also have Battledown Natural Selection, Sharps Own and a guest like Cotswold Spring Ambler on handpump, local farm cider and perry and good value winter mulled wine; service is prompt and genial. The smallish two-room beamed bar has an attractive mix of small settles, a pew and character chairs around interesting tables including antiques, rugs on an unusual stone floor, and a warm woodburning stove. You can eat more formally up a few steps, in a carpeted dining room beyond a sofa by a big log fire; newspapers and unobtrusive nostalgic pop music. Teak tables on a side terrace are best placed for the views and there are steps down to a sturdy play area. Plenty of nearby walks.

Free house ~ Licensees Mr and Mrs Philip Todd ~ Real ale ~ Bar food (12-2, 6-9; 12-4 Sun; not Mon or Tues lunchtimes) ~ (01531) 820719 ~ Children welcome ~ Dogs allowed in bar

~ Open 12-2.30, 6-11; 12-5 Sun; closed Sun evening, Mon and Tuesday lunchtimes ~
www.yewtreeinn.com

COATES   SO9600

Tunnel House

Follow Tarlton signs (right then left) from village, pub up rough track on right after
railway bridge; OS Sheet 163 map reference 965005; GL7 6PW

Friendly pub with interesting décor, lots of character, popular food and
drink, and seats in the sizeable garden; at entrance to derelict canal
tunnel

The stretch of the old Thames and Severn Canal nearby is known as the Kings
Reach to commemorate a visit by King George III in 1788; the big garden
slopes down to the derelict entrance tunnel and there are seats and tables
on the terrace in front of this eccentric bow-fronted stone house with a fine
views. The atmosphere inside is cheerful and easy-going and there's always a
good mix of customers – the place is especially popular with students from the
Royal Agricultural College. The rambling rooms have beams, flagstones, a mix
of furnishings including massive rustic benches and seats built into the sunny
windows, lots of enamel advertising signs, racing tickets and air travel labels, a
stuffed wild boar's head and owl, plenty of copper and brass and an upside-down
card table complete with cards and drinks fixed to the beams; there's a winter
log fire with sofas in front (but you have to arrive early to grab them). The more
conventional dining extension and back conservatory fill up quickly at mealtimes.
Otter Bright, Prescott Hill Climb, Sharps Doom Bar and Uley Bitter on handpump,
several wines by the glass and two draught ciders; background music. Good
walks nearby; disabled lavatories.

Free house ~ Licensee Michael Hughes ~ Real ale ~ Bar food (12-9.30) ~ Restaurant ~
(01285) 770280 ~ Children welcome ~ Dogs allowed in bar ~ Open 12-midnight ~
www.tunnelhouse.com

COOMBE HILL   SO8926

Gloucester Old Spot

A mile from M5 junction 10 (access from southbound and to northbound carriageways
only); A4019 towards A38 Gloucester–Tewkesbury; GL51 9SY

The country local comes of age – a model for today's country pubs

Carefully restored while keeping its essential simplicity – and avoiding the all-
too-common trap of a surfeit of cheap leather furniture – this country local
has a companionable quarry-tiled beamed bar, softly lit, with chapel chairs and
other seats around mixed tables, one in a bow-windowed alcove, and opens into a
lighter partly panelled area with cushioned settles and stripped kitchen tables. They
sometimes have their own-brewed cider or perry (Black Rat if not), as well as well
kept ales such as Gwynt y Ddraig Happy Daze, Hop Back GFB, Purity Mad Goose
and Skinners Betty Stogs on handpump, and seven decent wines by the glass; the
young staff are friendly without being pushy, and decoration is in unobtrusive good
taste, with winter log fires. A separate dark-flagstoned dining room, handsome with
its tall stripped brick walls and candlelight, has similar country furniture. There are
picnic-table sets under cocktail parasols on the terrace behind.

Free house ~ Licensees Simon Daws and Hayley Cribb ~ Real ale ~ Bar food (12-2, 6-9; all
day Sat; 12-6 Sun; not Sun evening) ~ Restaurant ~ (01242) 680321 ~ Children welcome ~
Dogs allowed in bar ~ Open 10.30am-11pm ~ www.thegloucesteroldspot.co.uk

DIDMARTON   ST8187
Kings Arms
A433 Tetbury road; GL9 1DT

Bustling pub with knocked-through rooms, several real ales, tasty bar food and pleasant back garden; bedrooms and self-catering cottages

If you stay in the comfortable bedrooms of this 17th-c former coaching inn, the breakfasts are very good; they also have self-catering cottages in a converted barn and stable block. The several knocked-through beamed bar rooms work their way around a big central counter, with deep terracotta walls above a dark green dado in some, yellow and cream paintwork in others, an attractive mix of wooden tables and chairs on bare boards, quarry tiles and carpet, fresh flowers, and a big stone fireplace. There's also a smart restaurant. Brakspears Bitter, Butcombe Gold and Uley Bitter on handpump and several wines by the glass; darts. There are seats out in the pleasant back garden and boules. The pub is handy for Westonbirt Arboretum.

Free house ~ Licensee Steve Payne ~ Real ale ~ Bar food (12-2, 6-9; 12-7.45 Sun) ~ Restaurant ~ (01454) 238245 ~ Children welcome ~ Dogs allowed in bar ~ Open 11-11; 12-10.30 Sun ~ Bedrooms: £65S/£90S ~ www.kingsarmsdidmarton.co.uk

DURSLEY   ST7598
Old Spot
Hill Road; by bus station; GL11 4JQ

Unassuming and cheery town pub with up to 11 real ales and regular beer festivals, and good value lunchtime food

Enthusiasm never wanes for this particularly well run town local – our readers enjoy their every visit. Mr Herbert is a genuinely friendly landlord who welcomes both regulars and visitors alike and keeps a fantastic range of up to 11 real ales on handpump. This always includes Uley Old Rick plus guests from breweries such as Bath Ales, Butcombe, Moles, Otter, Sawbridgeworth, Severn Vale, Springhead, Wickwar and Wye Valley; they also hold four annual beer festivals and stock quite a few malt whiskies, too. The front door opens into a deep pink small room with stools on shiny quarry tiles along its pine-boarded bar counter and old enamel beer advertisements on the walls and ceiling; there's a profusion of porcine paraphernalia. A small room on the left leads off from here and the little dark wood-floored room to the right has a stone fireplace. A step takes you down to a cosy Victorian tiled snug and (to the right) the meeting room. There are seats in the heated and covered garden.

Free house ~ Licensee Steve Herbert ~ Real ale ~ Bar food (12-3; no evening meals except Monday (6.30-9)) ~ (01453) 542870 ~ Children in family room only (best to book) ~ Dogs allowed in bar ~ Open 11(12 Sun)-11 ~ www.oldspotinn.co.uk

FORD   SP0829
Plough
B4077 Stow–Alderton; GL54 5RU

16th-c inn in horse racing country, with lots of horse talk, a bustling atmosphere, first class service, good food and well kept beer; bedrooms

Even when this lively, enjoyable pub is packed to the gunnels (which it always is on race meeting days), the friendly hands-on landlord and his helpful staff remain courteous and efficient; it's certainly worth booking ahead to be sure of a table. There's always a chatty atmosphere and the beamed and stripped-stone bar has racing prints and photos on the walls (many of the customers here are from the racing fraternity and well known racehorse trainer's yard is opposite), old settles and benches around the big tables on uneven flagstones, oak tables in a snug alcove and open fires and woodburning stoves (a couple are the real thing). Darts, TV (for the races) and background music. Donnington BB and SBA on handpump. There are some picnic-sets under parasols and pretty hanging baskets at the front of the stone building and a large back garden with a play fort for children. The Cotswold Farm Park is nearby. The comfortable bedrooms away from the pub are the quietest and there are views of the gallops.

Donnington ~ Tenant Craig Brown ~ Real ale ~ Bar food (12-2, 6-9; all day Fri-Sun) ~ Restaurant ~ (01386) 584215 ~ Children welcome ~ Dogs allowed in bar ~ Open 9am-11pm ~ Bedrooms: £60S/£80S ~ www.theploughinnatford.co.uk

GUITING POWER   SP0924
Hollow Bottom
Village signposted off B4068 SW of Stow-on-the-Wold (still called A436 on many maps); GL54 5UX

Popular old inn with lots of racing memorabilia, a good bustling atmosphere, real ales and enjoyable food

Although there are lots of racing folk here and live horse-racing is shown on the TV, our non-horsey readers tell us they always enjoy their visits to this snug old stone cottage very much and are warmly welcomed by the helpful, friendly staff. The comfortable beamed bar has plenty of atmosphere, lots of racing memorabilia including racing silks, tunics, photographs, race badges, framed newspaper cuttings and horseshoes (their local horse won the Cheltenham Gold Cup in 2010 and they have dedicated an area in the bar to him); there's a winter log fire in an unusual pillar-supported stone fireplace. The public bar has flagstones and stripped-stone masonry; newspapers to read, darts, board games and background music. Battledown Tipster, Donnington SBA and a beer named for the pub on handpump, several wines (including champagne) by the glass and a dozen malt whiskies. From the pleasant garden behind the pub there are views towards the sloping fields; decent nearby walks.

Free house ~ Licensees Hugh Kelly and Charles Pettigrew ~ Real ale ~ Bar food (all day) ~ Restaurant ~ (01451) 850392 ~ Children welcome ~ Dogs allowed in bar ~ Open 9am-midnight ~ Bedrooms: £75B/£90B ~ www.hollowbottom.com

KILCOT   SO6925
Kilcot Inn
2.3 miles from M50 junction 3; B4221 towards Newent; GL18 1NG

Attractively reworked small country inn, kind staff, enjoyable local food and drink

Reopened in summer 2011 after sympathetic renovation by Weston's, the cider people, this has their Old Rosie, The Governor and Perry on handpump, with more by the bottle, as well as Marstons Pedigree and EPA and Wye Valley Butty Bach, and local wine and organic fruit juice. It's open-plan, with stripped beams, bare boards and dark flagstones, sunny bay-window seats, homely armchairs by one of the two warm woodburning stoves, tables with padded dining chairs, and daily papers; big-screen TV, may be background music. The front terrace has picnic-table sets under cocktail parasols, with more out behind. We have not yet heard from readers using the four new bedrooms, but would expect this to be a nice place to stay – and there's a smart new bicycle shed.

Free house ~ Licensee Mark Lawrence ~ Real ale ~ Bar food (12-3, 6-9; breakfast 7-11.30am; afternoon tea 3-5) ~ Restaurant ~ (01989) 720707 ~ Children welcome ~ Dogs allowed in bar ~ Occasional live music – best to phone ~ Open 11-11 ~ Bedrooms: /£80S ~ www.kilcotinn.com

LEIGHTERTON   ST8290
Royal Oak
Village signposted off A46 S of Nailsworth; GL8 8UN

Handsome country pub elegantly refurbished, good choice of drinks, imaginative food and kind staff

The rambling bar has plenty of nice touches, from the pair of log fireplaces facing each other (you have to look twice to be sure it's not a mirror) to the splendid heavy low-loading antique trolley with the daily papers – including the Racing Post. Part parquet, part broad boards, with some stripped stone and some pastel paintwork, it has carefully chosen furniture from stylish strung-seat dining chairs to soft sofas. They have some interesting wines by the glass and local farm cider, as well as O'Hanlons Royal Oak Best, Wadworths IPA and Wye Valley O'er the Sticks on handpump, and helpful smartly dressed staff. There's good disabled access. A sheltered side courtyard has mainly teak and metal tables and chairs, and there are good walks near the quiet village, with Westonbirt Arboretum not far off.

Free house ~ Licensees Paul and Antonia Whitbread ~ Real ale ~ Bar food (12-2.30, 6-9.30; not Sun evening) ~ Restaurant ~ (01666) 890250 ~ Children welcome ~ Dogs allowed in bar ~ Open 11-3, 5.30-11; 11-11 Sat; 12-10.30 Sun ~ www.royaloakleighterton.co.uk

NAILSWORTH   ST8699
Weighbridge
B4014 towards Tetbury; GL6 9AL

Super two-in-one pies served in cosy old-fashioned bar rooms, a fine choice of drinks, friendly service and a sheltered garden

Dating in part from the 17th c, this neatly kept place was once run by a landlord who also operated the nearby weighbridge – hence the pub's name. The relaxed bar has three cosily old-fashioned rooms with open fires, stripped-stone walls and antique settles, country chairs and window seats. The black beamed ceiling of the lounge bar is thickly festooned with black ironware – sheep shears, gin traps, lamps and a large collection of keys, many from the old Longfords Mill opposite the pub. Upstairs is a raftered hayloft with an engaging mix of rustic tables. No noisy games machines or background music. Uley Old Spot and Wadworths 6X and a couple of guest beers like Great Western Maiden Voyage and Timothy Taylors Landlord on handpump, 18 wines (and champagne and prosecco) by the glass, Weston's cider and 14 malt whiskies; staff are welcoming and helpful. A sheltered landscaped garden at the back has picnic-sets under umbrellas. Good disabled access and facilities.

Free house ~ Licensee Howard Parker ~ Real ale ~ Bar food (12-9.30) ~ Restaurant ~ (01453) 832520 ~ Children allowed away from the bars ~ Dogs allowed in bar ~ Open 12-11(10.30 Sun) ~ www.2in1pub.co.uk

NETHER WESTCOTE   SP2220
Feathered Nest
Off A424 Burford–Stow-on-the-Wold; OX7 6SD

Caring service, happy atmosphere, attractive surroundings, beautifully presented, inventive food and drink, nice bedrooms

We rather liked this place when we first knew it, as the New Inn and then the Westcote Inn, but since its refurbishment and reopening under new management in 2010 it's become really special. Service is top-notch – friendly and individual, making sure that everyone's enjoying themselves. The softly lit largely stripped-stone bar is a companionable place, with real saddles as bar stools (some of the best racehorse trainers live around here), a carved settle among other carefully chosen seats, dark flagstones and low beams. They have 25 wines by the glass from an impressive list, and a couple of guest beers on handpump as well as Hook Norton. The bar opens into an inner ochre-walled high-raftered room with deeply comfortable sofas by a vast log fire. Two attractively decorated dining rooms, both on two levels, have a pleasing mix of antique tables in varying sizes, but a lively up-to-date atmosphere. A flagstoned terrace and heated shelter have teak tables and wicker armchairs, and a spreading lawn bounded by floodlit trees has groups of rustic seats, with the Evenlode Valley beyond. If you stay, you get a very good breakfast.

Free house ~ Licensee Amanda Timmer ~ Real ale ~ Bar food (12-2.30, 6.30-9; 12-3.30 Sun; not Sun evening, not Mon) ~ Restaurant ~ (01993) 833030 ~ Children welcome ~ Dogs allowed in bar ~ Occasional live jazz ~ Open 11-11(9 Sun); closed Mon (except bank holidays) ~ Bedrooms: £90S(£105B)/£130(£180S)(£165B) ~ www.thefeatherednestinn.co.uk

NEWLAND   SO5509
Ostrich
Off B4228 in Coleford; or can be reached from the A466 in Redbrook, by turning off at the England–Wales border – keep bearing right; GL16 8NP

Liked by walkers and their dogs with a friendly feel in spacious bar, great choice of beers, open fire, daily papers and smashing food

In a charmingly picturesque village close to the River Wye, this is a fine old pub with a warmly welcoming landlady; it's much enjoyed by walkers and their dogs. The atmosphere is chatty and relaxed and the low-ceilinged bar is spacious but cosily traditional with creaky floors, window shutters, candles in bottles on the tables, miners' lamps on the uneven walls and comfortable furnishings such as cushioned window seats, wall settles and rod-backed country-kitchen chairs. There's a big fireplace, newspapers to read, perhaps quiet background jazz, and board games. There are between four and eight real ales on handpump: Archers Best Bitter, Badger Bitter, Gales Seafarers, Greene King Abbot, Otter Bitter, RCH Pitchfork, Uley Pigs Ear, and Wye Valley Butty Bach. They also have several wines by the glass and Old Rosie cider. The pub lurcher is called Alfie. There are picnic-sets in a walled garden behind and more out in front; the church, known as the Cathedral of the Forest, is worth a visit.

Free house ~ Licensee Kathryn Horton ~ Real ale ~ Bar food (12-2.30, 6.30(6 Sat)-9.30) ~ Restaurant ~ (01594) 833260 ~ Children welcome ~ Dogs allowed in bar ~ Open 12-3, 6.30-11; 12-3, 6-midnight Sat; 12-4, 6.30-10.30 Sun ~ www.theostrichinn.com

OLDBURY-ON-SEVERN

ST6092

Anchor

Village signposted from B4061; BS35 1QA

Friendly country pub with tasty bar food, a fine choice of drinks and a pretty garden with hanging baskets

Always deservedly busy with a good mix of drinkers and diners, this is an enjoyable pub with friendly, cheerful staff. The neatly kept lounge has a big winter log fire, modern beams and stonework, a variety of tables including an attractive oval oak gateleg, cushioned window seats, winged seats against the wall, and oil paintings by a local artist. The bar has old photographs and farming and fishing bric-a-brac on the walls. Diners can eat in the lounge or bar area or in the dining room at the back (good for larger groups); the menu is the same in all rooms. Bass, Butcombe Bitter, Otter Bitter and a changing guest like Great Western Maiden Voyage on handpump well priced for the area; 85 malt whiskies (the tasting notes are really helpful) and a dozen wines by the glass. In summer, you can eat in the pretty garden and the hanging baskets and window boxes are lovely then; boules. They have wheelchair access and a disabled lavatory. Plenty of walks to the River Severn and along the many footpaths and bridleways, and St Arilda's church nearby is interesting on its odd little knoll with wild flowers among the gravestones (the primroses and daffodils in spring are quite a show).

Free house ~ Licensees Michael Dowdeswell and Mark Sorrell ~ Real ale ~ Bar food (12-2(2.30 Sat, 3 Sun), 6-9) ~ Restaurant ~ (01454) 413331 ~ Children in dining room only ~ Dogs allowed in bar ~ Open 11.30-3, 6-11; 11-midnight Sat; 12-11 Sun ~ www.anchorinnoldbury.co.uk

SAPPERTON

SO9403

Bell

Village signposted from A419 Stroud–Cirencester; OS Sheet 163 map reference 948033; GL7 6LE

Super pub with beamed cosy rooms, a really good mix of customers, delicious food, local ales and very pretty outside dining areas

'A treasure – we love it,' says one of our enthusiastic readers – and many agree with her. It's a fine old pub with a good mix of both locals and visitors and the hands-on, hard-working licensees continue to tweak things here and there to keep it all running as smoothly as ever. Harry's Bar has big cushion-strewn sofas, benches and armchairs where you can read the daily papers with a pint in front of the woodburning stove – or simply have a pre-dinner drink. The two other cosy rooms have beams, a nice mix of wooden tables and chairs, country prints and modern art on stripped-stone walls, one or two attractive rugs on the flagstones, fresh flowers and open fires. Bath Ales Gem, Otter Bitter, St Austell Tribute and Uley Old Spot on handpump, 22 wines by the glass and carafe from a large and diverse wine list (with very helpful notes; they now have more organic and bio dynamic wines), 20 malt whiskies, farm cider and local soft drinks. The gents' has schoolboy humour cartoons on the walls. Their young springer spaniel is called William and welcomes other dogs. There are armchairs and tables out on a small front terrace, with more in a mediterranean-style back courtyard garden with an old live tree, herb-filled pots and a colourful, heated loggia. Horses have their own tethering rail (and bucket of water) and there are plenty of surrounding hacking trails and walks.

Free house ~ Licensees Paul Davidson and Pat LeJeune ~ Real ale ~ Bar food (12-2.15(2.30 Sun), 7-9.30(9 Sun)) ~ (01285) 760298 ~ Children allowed but must be over 10 in evening ~ Dogs allowed in bar ~ Open 11-3, 6.30-11; 12-10.30 Sun; closed Sun evenings in Jan and Feb ~ www.foodatthebell.co.uk

SHEEPSCOMBE   SO8910

Butchers Arms

Village signed off B4070 NE of Stroud; or A46 N of Painswick (but narrow lanes); GL6 7RH

Bustling country pub with enjoyable bar food, real ales, friendly young licensees and fine views

This is the sort of friendly, relaxed pub where a wide mix of customers mingle happily in the chatty atmosphere. The bustling lounge bar has beams, wheelback chairs, cushioned stools and other comfortable seats around simple wooden tables, built-in cushioned seats in the big bay windows, interesting oddments like assorted blow lamps, irons and plates, and a woodburning stove. The restaurant has an open log fire. Butcombe Rare Breed, Otter Bitter and a guest like Wye Valley Butty Bach on handpump, several wines by the glass and Weston's cider or perry; darts, chess, cribbage and draughts. The view over the lovely surrounding steep beechwood valley is terrific and there are seats outside to make the most of it. It's thought that this area was once a royal hunting ground for Henry VIII. Walkers and cyclists can pre-book their food orders.

Free house ~ Licensees Mark and Sharon Tallents ~ Real ale ~ Bar food (12-2.30, 6.30-9.30; all day weekends; no food after 6pm Sun Jan/Feb) ~ Restaurant ~ (01452) 812113 ~ Children welcome ~ Dogs allowed in bar ~ Open 11.30-3, 6.30-11; 11.30-11.30 Sat; 12-10.30 Sun ~ www.butchers-arms.co.uk

SOUTHROP   SP2003

Swan

Off A361 Lechlade–Burford; GL7 3NU

Creeper-covered pub with proper village bar, two dining rooms, imaginative food and an impressive choice of drinks

The first class food in this 17th-c creeper-covered inn is extremely highly thought of by our readers and you can be sure of a warm welcome, too. The chatty public bar is very much for those wanting a pint and a natter: it's got stools against the counter, simple tables and chairs, Hook Norton Hooky Bitter, Sharps Doom Bar and a beer named for the pub on handpump, 16 wines by the glass from a carefully chosen list and daily non-alcoholic cocktails. The low-ceilinged front dining rooms have open fires, all manner of leather dining chairs around a nice mix of old tables, cushions on settles, rugs on flagstones, nightlights, candles and lots of fresh flowers. There's a skittle alley and tables in the sheltered back garden. They have self-catering cottages to let.

Free house ~ Licensees Sebastian and Lana Snow ~ Real ale ~ Bar food (12-3, 6-10; not Sun evening) ~ Restaurant ~ (01367) 850205 ~ Children welcome ~ Dogs allowed in bar ~ Open 12-3, 6-11; 12-11 Sat; 12-3 Sun; closed Sun evenings ~ www.theswanatsouthrop.co.uk

UPPER ODDINGTON   SP2225

Horse & Groom

Village signposted from A436 E of Stow-on-the-Wold; GL56 0XH

Pretty 16th-c Cotswold inn with enterprising food, lots of wines by the glass, local beers and other local drinks and comfortable, character bars; lovely bedrooms

We get enthusiastic reports on every aspect of this particularly well run and attractive stone pub. It's a lovely place to stay (and the breakfasts are very good), there's a fine choice of wines by the glass and well kept real ales, the food is first class and Mr Jackson is genuinely welcoming and helpful landlord. The bar has pale polished flagstones, a handsome antique oak box settle among other more modern seats, some nice armchairs at one end, oak beams in the ochre ceiling, stripped-stone walls and a log fire in the inglenook fireplace; the comfortable lounge is similarly furnished. Box Steam Piston Broke, Prescott Hill Climb and Wye Valley Bitter on handpump, 25 wines (including champagne and sweet wines) by the glass, 20 malt whiskies, local apple juice and elderflower pressé, and cider and lager brewed by Cotswold. There are seats and tables under green parasols on the terrace and in the pretty garden.

Free house ~ Licensees Simon and Sally Jackson ~ Real ale ~ Bar food (12-2, 6.30 (7 Sun)-9) ~ Restaurant ~ (01451) 830584 ~ Children welcome ~ Dogs allowed in bar ~ Open 12-3, 5.30-11; 12-3, 6-10.30 Sun ~ Bedrooms: £79S/£99S(£105B) ~ www.horseandgroom.uk.com

DOG FRIENDLY INNS, HOTELS AND B&Bs

ARLINGHAM   SO7010

Old Passage

Passage Road, Arlingham, Gloucestershire GL2 7JR (01452) 740547
www.theoldpassage.com

£80; 3 airy rms with river views. Civilised seafood restaurant-with-rooms overlooking the River Severn, with sofas and magazines in the small lounge, local artwork on green walls, plenty of dining space – simple, innovative cooking using sustainably sourced fish plus set midweek lunch menus – and excellent breakfasts; seats in the garden; dogs in bedrooms by arrangement; not in restaurant; £10

BARNSLEY   SP0705

Village Pub

Barnsley, Cirencester, Gloucestershire GL7 5EF (01285) 740421 www.thevillagepub.co.uk

£125; 6 individually decorated and newly refurbished rms. Smart, civilised country pub with communicating rooms, a wide mix of customers (often with their dogs), contemporary paintwork, polished candlelit tables on flagstones or oak floorboards, oil paintings, three open fires, real ales and an extensive wine list, super breakfasts with their own conserves and home-made bread, and extremely good, imaginative food; seats in sheltered back courtyard; dogs anywhere in the pub and in bedrooms

BIBURY SP1106
Bibury Court

Bibury, Cirencester, Gloucestershire GL7 5NT (01285) 740337 www.biburycourt.com

£185; 18 individual rms, some overlooking the garden. Lovely peaceful mansion dating from Tudor times set in 7 acres of beautiful gardens (where dogs may walk); an informal friendly atmosphere, a chatty bar, an oak panelled drawing room with a huge log fire and antiques, an airy conservatory and more formal restaurant, and delicious food from breakfast through light lunches to afternoon teas and contemtporary evening meals; seats on the terrace; dogs in some bedrooms (but must not be left unattended); £15

BIBURY SP1106
Swan

Bibury, Cirencester, Gloucestershire GL7 5NW (01285) 740695
www.cotswold-inns-hotels.co.uk

£170; 22 very pretty individually decorated rms. Handsome creeper-covered hotel on the River Coln, with private fishing and attractive formal garden (where dogs may walk); lovely flowers and log fires in carefully furnished comfortable lounges, a cosy parlour, an opulent dining room, stylish modern brasserie/bar, modern, european-style cooking and smashing breakfasts, and attentive staff; country walks; dogs in bedrooms and public rooms but not restaurant; £10

CHELTENHAM SO9421
Montpellier Chapter

Bayshill Road, Cheltenham, Gloucestershire GL50 3AS (01242) 527788
www.themontpellierchapterhotel.com

£200; 48 large, stylish and well equipped rms. White-painted Regency hotel with contemporary furnishings in the chatty bar, restaurant and Garden Room, lots of art on pale walls, log fires, enjoyable modern cooking from an open-plan kitchen including first class breakfasts, light lunches and afternoon teas, and friendly, willing staff; seats on the terrace and in the courtyard; dogs in bedrooms by prior arrangement and bar; bowl and bed; £25

COLN ST ALDWYNS SP1405
New Inn

Coln St Aldwyns, Cirencester, Gloucestershire GL7 5AN (01285) 750651
www.new-inn.co.uk

£147.50; 14 strikingly decorated rms. Partly 16th-c ivy-covered inn with recently renovated rooms – a cheerful bar with an easy-going and chatty atmosphere and a weekday happy hour (5-7pm), open fires, a wide choice of enjoyable food in the attractive restaurant, good breakfasts and friendly staff; seats on the terrace and in the garden, and walks in the surrounding countryside; dogs in ground floor bedroom; £15

CORSE LAWN   SO8330

Corse Lawn House

Corse Lawn, Gloucester, Gloucestershire GL19 4LZ (01452) 780771
www.corselawn.com

£160; 18 well equipped, chintzy rms. Handsome Queen Anne building
surrounded by 12 acres of gardens and fields and in the same family for many
years; a friendly, relaxed atmosphere in two comfortable drawing rooms, a large
bistro bar, a distinguished restaurant, quite a choice of highly thought of french-
influenced cooking (meals in the bistro are simpler), a carefully chosen wine list,
and good breakfasts served by helpful, long-serving staff; heated indoor pool,
croquet and tennis; dogs in bedrooms

COWLEY   SO9714

Green Dragon

Cockleford, Cowley, Cheltenham, Gloucestershire GL53 9NW (01242) 870271
www.green-dragon-inn.co.uk

£95; 9 comfortable, well appointed rms. 17th-c former cider house with plenty of
character in two beamed bars, chairs (look out for Robert Thompson's designs,
which have little mice running all over them) around candlelit tables on big
flagstones or floorboards, winter log fires in two stone fireplaces, tasty food in
the little upstairs restaurant, generous breakfasts and seats on terraces; good
surrounding walks; dogs in bedrooms and bar; £10

ENGLISH BICKNOR   SO5714

Dryslade Farm

English Bicknor, Coleford, Gloucestershire GL16 7PA (01594) 860259
www.drysladefarm.co.uk

£68; 3 homely rms. 18th-c farmhouse owned by same family for 100 years and
part of a working farm – lots of walks; friendly and relaxed atmosphere, cosy
guest lounge with a winter log fire, and traditional breakfasts in light and airy
conservatory (cake and tea on arrival); resident springer spaniel and cavalier
king charles spaniel; well behaved dogs in bedrooms; towels and washing
facilities

EWEN   SU0097

Wild Duck

Ewen, Cirencester, Gloucestershire GL7 6BY (01285) 770310
www.thewildduckinn.co.uk

£135; 12 pretty, well equipped rms. 16th-c inn with stylishly old-fashioned
furnishings and pictures in high-beamed log-fire main bar, a lounge with a
handsome Elizabethan fireplace and antiques, a residents' lounge with another
log fire, plenty of bold paintwork, six real ales, interesting food, and tables in a
neatly kept heated courtyard; four resident dogs; surrounded by over 100 lakes
for walks; dogs in bedrooms and bar; free pig's ear; £10

FOSSEBRIDGE   SP0711

Fossebridge Inn

Fossebridge, Cheltenham, Gloucestershire GL54 3LS (01285) 720721
www.fossebridgeinn.co.uk

£85; 9 smart rms, self-catering, too. Partly Tudor and partly Georgian inn with 4 acres of riverside gardens, a 15th-c bar with chatty locals, cider and real ales, two other rooms with beams, arches, stripped-stone walls and nice old flagstones, a happy mix of chairs and tables, copper implements, open fires, candles and fresh flowers, and a couple of rather grand dining rooms serving reliably good food; the National Trust Roman villa at Chedworth is nearby; lots of nearby walks; dogs anywhere in the pub and in bedrooms; on lead in grounds (free-range fowl); treats; £15

GREAT RISSINGTON   SP1917

Lamb

Great Rissington, Cheltenham, Gloucestershire GL54 2LN (01451) 820388
www.thelambinn.com

£75; 14 rms each with a teddy bear and views of village or fields. Civilised 17th-c inn overlooking the Windrush Valley with surrounding walks in stunning countryside; the two-roomed bar has high-backed leather and farmhouse chairs around polished tables, a woodburning stove in the stone fireplace and some interesting things to look at (a Wellington bomber crashed in the garden in 1943); there's another woodburner and agricultural tools in the restaurant and bistro-style food using local produce; the village church is idyllic; circular walk from pub door; dogs in bedrooms and bar; £7

GUITING POWER   SP0924

Guiting Guest House

Post Office Lane, Guiting Power, Cheltenham, Gloucestershire GL54 5TZ (01451) 850470
www.guitingguesthouse.com

£90; 7 pretty rms with thoughtful extras (and a teddy). 16th-c Cotswold stone former farmhouse with inglenook fireplaces, beams and rugs on flagstones or elm floorboards, two sitting rooms, enjoyable breakfasts in beamed dining room (evening meals by prior arrangement), attentive owners and a very relaxed atmosphere; self-catering cottage, also; dogs in some bedrooms

KEMPSFORD   SU1596

Kempsford Manor

High Street, Kempsford, Fairford, Gloucestershire GL7 4EQ (01285) 810131
www.kempsfordmanor.com

£70; 4 antique-filled rms. Lovely 17th-c house surrounded by fine gardens leading to a canal walk; Warmly friendly owners, a restful atmosphere in gracious sitting room with panelling, comfortable seats on rug-covered floorboards and an open fire, two pianos (occasional music evenings), a well stocked library and delicious breakfasts and suppers using home-grown produce; resident whippet; dogs in bedrooms; bowls and bedding; £10;

LOWER SLAUGHTER   SP1522

Lower Slaughter Manor

Lower Slaughter, Cheltenham, Gloucestershire GL54 2HP (01451) 820456
www.lowerslaughter.co.uk

£225; 19 luxurious rms. Grand 17th-c manor house in 4 neatly kept acres
of gardens and grounds with a 15th-c dovecote, all-weather tennis court and
croquet; sitting rooms with open fires, fine plaster ceilings, antiques and
paintings, excellent modern cooking in the elegant, stylish dining room, fine
breakfasts and afternoon teas, and attentive welcoming staff; dogs in Coach
House bedrooms; £10

LOWER SLAUGHTER   SP1622

Slaughter Country Inn

Lower Slaughter, Cheltenham, Gloucestershire GL54 2HS (01451) 822143
www.theslaughtersinn.co.uk

£155; 30 individually decorated, spacious rms, some in cottage suites. Honey-
coloured stone hotel by the River Eye in 4 acres of neat grounds where dogs may
walk (nearby local walks, too); comfortable and charming lounges, beams, open
fires and persian rugs on polished parquet floors, stone mullioned windows, and
delicious modern cooking in light airy restaurant; super breakfasts, light bar
lunches and afternoon teas; dogs in some bedrooms and bar; £10

Jack and Bruno; owner Fiona MacIntyre

MORETON-IN-MARSH

SP2032

Manor House

High Street, Moreton-in-Marsh, Gloucestershire GL56 0LJ (0608) 50501
www.cotswold-inns-hotels.co.uk/manor

£158; 35 luxurious rms. 16th-c manor house with pretty gardens and a chic, contemporary interior that blends well with the lovely original features; a convivial bar, comfortable lounge and library, an airy brasserie for lighter meals and elegant restaurant for the first class, inventive food (breakfasts are excellent too), and courteous, helpful staff; walks in the grounds; dogs in bedrooms and some public areas; £10

MORETON-IN-MARSH

SP2032

White Hart Royal

High Street, Moreton-in-Marsh, Gloucestershire GL56 0BA (01608) 650731
www.whitehartroyal.co.uk

£130; 28 stylish rms, some in converted stable block. Partly 15th-c former coaching inn with interesting Civil War history; comfortable beamed lounge areas with open fires, exposed stone walls, big gilt mirrors, paintings and artefacts, all manner of attractive chairs and tables on rugs and polished boards, real ales, bistro-style food and an easy-going atmosphere; seats in attractive courtyards; lots of surrounding Cotswold walks; dogs anywhere except restaurant; treats

NORTH CERNEY

SP0208

Bathurst Arms

North Cerney, Cirencester, Gloucestershire GL7 7BZ (01285) 831281
www.bathurstarms.com

£90; 6 comfortable rms. Handsome old inn with a beamed and panelled bar, a good mix of visitors, an open fire and a woodburning stove at each end of the room, nice old furniture on flagstones, real ales and wines that you can choose yourself from their wine room; there's also an oak-floored room, a restaurant with leather sofas and another woodburner, and enjoyable food; Cerney House Gardens are worth a visit and there are lots of nearby walks; dogs in bedrooms and bar; £10

NORTHLEACH

SP1114

Wheatsheaf

West End, Northleach, Cheltenham, Gloucestershire GL54 3EZ (01451) 860244
www.cotswoldswheatsheaf.com

£160; 14 stylish rms. Handsome 17th-c former coaching inn by fine market square in lovely Cotswold town; big-windowed linked rooms with antique and contemporary artwork, church candles, fresh flowers, attractive chairs and tables on flagstones or wooden floors, three open fires, a fantastic wine list, local beers and cider, enterprising food and excellent breakfasts; seats in the pretty back garden and they can arrange fishing on the River Coln; lots of nearby walks; dogs anywhere in the pub and in bedrooms; beds, bowl, treats, maybe a pig's ear; £10

PARKEND
SO6108

Edale House

Folly Road, Parkend, Lydney, Gloucestershire GL15 4JF (01594) 562835
www.edalehouse.co.uk

£67; 6 rms. Georgian house opposite a cricket green and backing on to Nagshead Nature Reserve; comfortable, homely sitting room, honesty bar, good food in the attractive dining room and a relaxed atmosphere; resident dog; nearby walks; dogs in ground floor rooms, not public areas; £10

STOW-ON-THE-WOLD
SP1925

Old Stocks

The Square, Stow-on-the-Wold, Cheltenham, Gloucestershire GL54 1AF (01451) 830666
www.oldstockshotel.co.uk

£92; 18 pretty rms. 16th-c Cotswold stone hotel overlooking the market square with a cosy welcoming small bar, beams and open fires, a comfortable lounge with books and games, good food in two restaurant areas, friendly staff and seats in the terraced garden; resident golden retriever, Alfie; nearby walks; closed 2 weeks in Jan; dogs in garden bedrooms and some public rooms but not restaurant; £5

THORNBURY
ST6390

Thornbury Castle

Castle Street, Thornbury, Bristol BS35 1HH (01454) 281182 www.thornburycastle.co.uk

£190; 27 opulent rms, some with big Tudor fireplaces or fine oriel windows. Impressive and luxuriously renovated early 16th-c castle with antiques, tapestries, huge fireplaces and mullioned windows in the baronial public rooms, three dining rooms (one in the base of a tower), fine modern cooking using home-grown and local produce, an extensive wine list (including wine from their own vineyard), thoughtful friendly service, and vast grounds including the oldest Tudor gardens in England; nearby fields for walks; dogs in bedrooms and lounges; £10

WESTONBIRT
ST8690

Hare & Hounds

Westonbirt, Tetbury, Gloucestershire GL8 8QL (01666) 880233

£158; 43 newly and attractively refurbished rms. Cotswold stone hotel in lovely gardens and woodland with two tennis courts and plenty of nearby walks; a contemporary, convivial bar with an open fire and high-backed brown leather dining and other nice old wooden chairs around a mix of tables on flagstones or wooden flooring, a comfortable lounge with plenty of sofas and armchairs and another log fire, enjoyable light lunches and afternoon teas, and an elegant restaurant with original features serving interesting modern food using the best local seasonal produce; dogs in some bedrooms, public areas (not restaurant) and grounds on a lead; £10

Hampshire

MAP 2

DOG FRIENDLY PUBS

BANK   SU2806

Oak

Signposted just off A35 SW of Lyndhurst; SO43 7FE

New Forest pub with a good mix of customers, well liked food and interesting décor

Tucked away at the heart of the New Forest, this well run pub is popular with walkers and cyclists; it's best to book in advance to be sure of a table. On either side of the door in the bay windows of the L-shaped bar are built-in red-cushioned seats, and on the right there are two or three little pine-panelled booths with small built-in tables and bench seats. The rest of the bare-boarded bar has some low beams and joists, candles in individual brass holders on a line of stripped old and newer blond tables set against the wall and all manner of bric-a-brac: fishing rods, spears, a boomerang, old ski poles, brass platters, heavy knives and guns. There are cushioned milk churns along the bar counter and little red lanterns among hop bines above the bar. Fullers London Pride and Gales HSB and Seafarers on handpump and a dozen wines by the glass; background music. The pleasant side garden has picnic-sets and long tables and benches by the big yew trees.

Fullers ~ Manager Martin Sliva ~ Real ale ~ Bar food (12-2.30, 6-9.30; all day weekends) ~ (023) 8028 2350 ~ Children welcome but all under-10s must leave by 6pm ~ Dogs allowed in bar ~ Open 11.30-3, 6-11; 11.30-11 Sat; 12-10.30 Sun; 11.30-3, 6-11 weekdays in winter

BENTWORTH   SU6740

Sun

Sun Hill; from the A339 coming from Alton, the first turning takes you there direct; or in village follow Shalden 2¼, Alton 4¼ signpost; GU34 5JT

Smashing choice of real ales, generously served food and welcoming landlady in popular country pub; nearby walks

Many of our readers describe this bustling 17th-c place as the perfect country pub. The long-serving landlady and her helpful staff make all their customers welcome and the atmosphere is chatty and easy-going. The two little traditional communicating rooms have high-backed antique settles, pews and schoolroom chairs, olde-worlde prints and blacksmith's tools on the walls, and bare boards and scrubbed deal tables on the left; three big fireplaces with log fires make it especially snug in winter. An arch leads to a brick-floored room with another open fire. There's a fine choice of half-a-dozen real ales on handpump: Andwell Resolute Bitter, Bowman Swift One, Fullers London Pride, Hook Norton Old Hooky, Itchen Valley Hampshire Rose, and Sharps Doom Bar. There are seats out in front and in the back garden; pleasant nearby walks.

Free house ~ Licensee Mary Holmes ~ Real ale ~ Bar food (12-2, 7-9.30) ~ (01420) 562338 ~ Children welcome ~ Dogs allowed in bar ~ Open 12-3, 6-11; 12-11 Sun ~ www.thesuninnbentworth.co.uk

BOLDRE
SZ3198

Red Lion

Off A337 N of Lymington; SO41 8NE

Friendly pub on the edge of the New Forest, lots of bygones in five beamed rooms, four real ales, interesting food and seats outside

Our readers love this well run pub – there's a warm welcome for all from the friendly licensees, the beers are well kept and the food is extremely good. The five black-beamed rooms reveal an entertaining collection of bygones, with heavy-horse harness, gin traps, ferocious-looking man traps, copper and brass pans and rural landscapes, as well as a dainty collection of old bottles and glasses in the window by the counter. Seating is on pews, sturdy cushioned dining chairs and tapestried stools. There's a fine old cooking range in the cosy little bar, and three good log fires. Banks's Bitter, Brakspears Oxford Gold and Ringwood Best and Fortyniner on handpump and16 wines by the glass. The pub is opposite the village green and on the edge of the New Forest and in summer there are seats outside among the flowering tubs and hanging baskets with more tables out in the back garden. They have a sunny self-catering apartment for rent.

Eldridge Pope ~ Lease Alan and Amanda Pountney ~ Real ale ~ Bar food (12-2.30, 6-9.30; all day Sun and summer Sat) ~ Restaurant ~ (01590) 673177 ~ Children welcome ~ Dogs allowed in bar ~ Open 11-3, 5.30-11; 11-11 Sat; 12-10.30 Sun; 11-3, 5.30-11 Sat in in winter ~ www.theredlionboldre.co.uk

BRANSGORE
SZ1997

Three Tuns

Village signposted off A35 and off B3347 N of Christchurch; Ringwood Road, opposite church; BH23 8JH

Interesting food in pretty thatched pub with proper old-fashioned bar and good beers, as well as a civilised main dining area

On the edge of the New Forest Country Park, this 17th-c thatched pub is full of cheerful customers – all welcomed by the friendly landlord and his staff. The roomy low-ceilinged and carpeted main area has a fireside 'codgers' corner', as well as a good mix of comfortably cushioned low chairs around a variety of dining tables. On the right is a separate traditional regulars' bar that seems almost taller than it is wide, with an impressive log-effect stove in a stripped brick hearth, some shiny black panelling and individualistic pubby furnishings. Ringwood Best and Fortyniner and Timothy Taylors Landlord and guests like Otter Bitter and St Austell Tribute on handpump and nine wines by the glass. The Grade II listed barn is popular for parties. In summer, the hanging baskets are lovely and there's an attractive, extensive shrub-sheltered terrace with picnic-sets on its brick pavers; beyond that are more tables out on the grass looking over pony paddocks.

Enterprise ~ Lease Nigel Glenister ~ Real ale ~ Bar food (12-2.15, 6-9.15; all day weekends) ~ Restaurant ~ (01425) 672232 ~ No children in lounge bar after 6pm (can use bar and restaurant) ~ Dogs allowed in bar ~ Open 11-11; 12-10.30 Sun ~ www.threetunsinn.com

CRAWLEY   SU4234
Fox & Hounds
Village signed from A272 and B3420 NW of Winchester; SO21 2PR

Attractive building, three roaring winter log fires, several real ales and impressive food; bedrooms

This is a solidly constructed mock-Tudor building where each timbered upper storey successively juts further out, with lots of pegged structural timbers in the neat brickwork and elaborately carved steep gable-ends. New licensees took over just as we went to press but don't plan any major changes and the neat and attractive linked rooms have a mix of attractive wooden tables and chairs on polished floors, lots of bottles along a delft shelf and three log fires. The traditional little bar has built-in wall seats and Ringwood Best and Fortyniner, Wadworths 6X and Wychwood Hobgoblin on handpump, and several wines by the glass. There are picnic-sets in the gardens and the bedrooms, in converted outbuildings, are named after the ducks on the village pond (this may change). The inn is one of the most striking buildings in a village of fine old houses.

Enterprise ~ Lease Alex and Sally Wood ~ Real ale ~ Bar food (12-2.30, 7-9.30; 12-4; not Sun evening) ~ Restaurant ~ (01962) 776006 ~ Children welcome ~ Dogs allowed in bar ~ Open 11-3, 6-11; 11-11 Sat; 12-8(4 in winter) Sun; 11-3, 6-11 Sat in winter in winter; closed Sun evening ~ Bedrooms: /£72.50B ~ www.foxandhoundscrawley.co.uk

DROXFORD   SU6018
Bakers Arms
High Street; A32 5 miles N of Wickham; SO32 3PA

Attractively opened-up and friendly pub with well kept beers, good, interesting cooking and cosy corners

In a pretty village at the heart of the Meon Valley, this is a bustling pub with friendly licensees. It's attractively laid-out and although the interesting food does play a big part, the central bar is kept as the main focus: Bowman Swift One and Wallops Wood on handpump, Stowford Press cider, and a careful short choice of wines by the glass. Well spaced mixed tables on carpet or neat bare boards spread around the airy L-shaped open-plan bar, with low leather chesterfields and an assortment of comfortably cushioned chairs down at one end; a dark panelled dado, dark beams and joists and a modicum of country oddments emphasise the freshness of the crisp white paintwork. There's a good log fire and board games. To one side, with a separate entrance, is the village post office. There are picnic-sets outside.

Free house ~ Licensees Adam and Anna Cordery ~ Real ale ~ Bar food (12-2, 7-9; not Sun evening or Mon) ~ (01489) 877533 ~ Well behaved children welcome ~ Dogs allowed in bar ~ Open 11.45-2.30, 6-11; 12-3 Sun; closed Sun evening and Mon ~ www.thebakersarmsdroxford.com

DROXFORD

SU6118

Hurdles

Brockbridge, just outside Soberton; from A32 just N of Droxford take B2150 towards Denmead; SO32 3QT

Roomy, smartly updated country dining pub with enticing, good value food and local ales

On the edge of the Meon Valley, this handsome Victorian brick building is always deservedly busy and our readers are full of praise for the genuinely warm welcome from the attentive young staff and for the reliably delicious meals. It's been brought very suitably up to date inside, from the dark grey leather chesterfield and armchairs by the log fire in one room with elegant columnar lamps in its big windows, to the dining areas on the right, with their stylish figured wallpaper, toning stripey chairs around shiny modern tables, and glittering mirrors. There are high ceilings and stripped boards throughout. Bowmans Wallops Wood and Swift One and a changing guest on handpump, decent wines by the glass and good coffee; unobtrusive background pop music. It's a peaceful spot, with wood and metal tables on neat terraces (one covered and heated), and a long flight of steps up to picnic-sets on a sloping lawn by tall trees.

Enterprise ~ Lease Gareth and Sarah Cole ~ Real ale ~ Bar food (12-3, 6-9.30; 12-7.30 Sun) ~ Restaurant ~ (01489) 877451 ~ Children welcome ~ Dogs allowed in bar ~ Open 11-11; 12 10.30 Sun ~ www.thehurdlesdroxford.co.uk

EASTON

SU5132

Chestnut Horse

3.6 miles from M3 junction 9: A33 towards Kings Worthy, then B3047 towards Itchen Abbas; Easton then signposted on right – bear left in village; SO21 1EG

Cosy dining pub with log fires, fresh flowers and candles, deservedly popular food and friendly staff; Itchen Valley walks nearby

In a pretty village of thatched cottages, this smart 16th-c dining pub is just the place to head for after a walk in the nearby Itchen Valley. The open-plan interior manages to have a pleasantly rustic and intimate feel with a series of cosily separate areas, and the snug décor takes in candles and fresh flowers on the tables, log fires in cottagey fireplaces and comfortable furnishings. The black beams and joists are hung with all sorts of jugs, mugs and chamber-pots, and there are lots of attractive pictures of wildlife and the local area. Badger K&B and Hopping Hare on handpump, several wines by the glass and 30 malt whiskies; the landlady and her staff are friendly and efficient. There are seats and tables out on a smallish sheltered decked area with colourful flower tubs and baskets, and some picnic-sets in front.

Badger ~ Tenant Karen Wells ~ Real ale ~ Bar food (12-2.30, 6-9.30; 12-8 Sun) ~ Restaurant ~ (01962) 779257 ~ Children welcome ~ Dogs allowed in bar ~ Open 12-4, 5.30-11.30; 12-11.30 Fri and Sat ~ www.thechestnuthorse.com

EVERSLEY

SU7861

Golden Pot

B3272; RG27 0NB

Bustling and friendly village pub with comfortable interlinked rooms, woodburning stoves, beers from smaller breweries, good food and seats outside

Dating back to the 1700s and at the heart of a village, this is a busy little brick pub with a friendly landlord. There's a comfortable atmosphere in the different spreading areas, a couple of woodburning stoves, sofas, cushioned settles, mates' and farmhouse kitchen chairs around wooden tables on carpeting, brass implements, sizeable mirrors and fresh flowers. High chairs line the counter where they keep three quickly changing real ales only from small local breweries such as Andwell, Bowman, Rebellion and Windsor & Eton on handpump; several wines by the glass. Monday evenings are fun with live music and a rösti menu. There are seats and tables at the front of the building under the colourful hanging baskets with more seats among flowering tubs and a view over fields at the back.

Free house ~ Licensee John Calder ~ Real ale ~ Bar food (12-2(3 Sun), 6-9; not Sun evening) ~ Restaurant ~ (0118) 973 2104 ~ Pianist/vocalist/guitarist Mon evening ~ Dogs allowed in bar ~ Open 11-3, 6-10.30; 12-3.30 Sun; closed Sun evening ~ www.golden-pot.co.uk

FRITHAM   SU2314
Royal Oak
Village signed from M27 J1; SO43 7HJ

Rural New Forest spot and part of a working farm; traditional rooms, log fires, seven real ales and simple lunchtime food

'This lovely country pub never disappoints' is just one of the enthusiastic comments from our readers about this charming brick and cob thatched pub. It's part of a working farm so there are ponies and pigs out on the green and plenty of livestock nearby. Three neatly kept black beamed rooms are straightforward but full of proper traditional character, with prints and pictures involving local characters on the white walls, restored panelling, antique wheelback, spindleback and other old chairs and stools with colourful seats around solid tables on the oak flooring and two roaring log fires; both the chatty locals and the hard-working staff are genuinely friendly. The back bar has quite a few books. Up to seven real ales are tapped from the cask: Bowman Wallops Wood, Flack Manor Double Drop, Hop Back Summer Lightning, Ringwood Best and Fortyniner, and Stonehenge Sign of Spring. Also, ten wines by the glass (mulled wine in winter) and a September beer festival. Summer barbecues may be put on in the neatly kept big garden which has a marquee for poor weather and a pétanque pitch. It's always busy whatever the season but is especially popular at weekends with walkers, cyclists and families.

Free house ~ Licensees Neil and Pauline McCulloch ~ Real ale ~ Bar food (12-2.30(3 weekends); not evenings) ~ No credit cards ~ (023) 8081 2606 ~ Well behaved children welcome ~ Dogs allowed in bar ~ Open 11-11; 12-10.30 Sun; 11-3, 6-11 weekdays in winter

HOOK   SU7153
Hogget
1.1 miles from M3 junction 5; A287 N, at junction with A30 (car park just before traffic lights); RG27 9JJ

Well run and accommodating, a proper pub moving with the times and giving good value

This bustling pub is just the place to escape the boredom of both the M3 and A30 and they are usefully open all day at weekends. As well as plenty of visitors, it's locally popular too, and the rooms ramble right round the central server so there's plenty of room for all. The lighting, wallpaper and carpet pattern, and the leather sofas and tub chairs over on the right at the back, give a friendly and homely feel, as does the way it provides several smallish distinct areas. Ringwood Best, Wychwood Hobgoblin and a guest beer on handpump, decent wines by the glass, and plenty of staff in neat but informal black uniforms. A sizeable terrace had sturdy tables and chairs, with some in a heated covered area.

Marstons ~ Lease Tom Faulkner ~ Real ale ~ Bar food (12-2.30, 6.30-9; all day Sat; 12-6 Sun; not Sun evening) ~ Restaurant ~ (01256) 763009 ~ Children welcome but not after 7pm Fri and Sat evenings ~ Dogs allowed in bar ~ Open 12-3, 5.30-11; 12-11(10.30 Sun) Sat ~ www.hogget.co.uk

HORDLE
SZ2996
Mill at Gordleton
Silver Street; SO41 6DJ

Charming tucked-away country inn with friendly bar, exceptional food and drink and delightful waterside gardens; comfortable bedrooms

The gardens here are very special, an extensive series of interestingly planted areas looping about pools and a placid winding stream, dotted with intriguing art objects (and an entertaining duck family), and with plenty of places to sit, from intimate pairs of seats to the nicely lit teak or wrought iron tables of the main waterside terraces close by the inn. The small main panelled bar on the right is informal and relaxed: casually dressed local regulars perhaps with their dogs, friendly helpful staff, well kept Ringwood Best and a guest like Oakleaf Quercus Folium on handpump, good wines by the glass, a rack of daily papers, leather armchairs and Victorian-style mahogany dining chairs on the parquet floor, a little feature stove and a pretty corner china cupboard. This overflows into a cosy lounge, and there's a roomy second bar by the sizeable beamed restaurant extension – an attractive room with contemporary art and garden outlook. The bedrooms are comfortable and individual, with excellent breakfasts; good walks here. They also offer tours to local breweries.

Free house ~ Licensee Liz Cottingham ~ Real ale ~ Bar food (12-2, 7-9; 12-3, 6.30-8.30) ~ Restaurant ~ (01590) 682219 ~ Children welcome ~ Dogs allowed in bar ~ Open 11-11; 12-10.30 Sun ~ Bedrooms: £95S/£150S ~ www.themillatgordleton.co.uk

LONGPARISH
SU4244
Plough
B3048, off A303 just E of Andover; SP11 6PB

Bustling, upmarket dining pub with friendly staff, real ales, attractive bars, popular food and seats in garden

Although many customers are here to enjoy the good food, there's a comfortable little area for drinkers and you can be sure of a genuinely friendly welcome from the helpful staff. The various rooms are kept spic and span and have flagstones and oak flooring, elegant high-backed wooden dining chairs and pews around a mix of tables, some beams and standing timbers, contemporary paintwork, and open fireplaces. The cosy snug has black leather bar chairs against the counter where they serve Ringwood Best and Boondoggle and Timothy Taylors Landlord on handpump, and they have a walk-in wine cellar (and several wines by the glass). On the decking outside are lots of seats, with more under parasols in the garden. The pub makes a good break from the A303.

Enterprise ~ Lease James Durrant ~ Real ale ~ Bar food (12-2.30(4.30 Sun), 6-9.30; not Sun evening) ~ (01264) 720358 ~ Children welcome ~ Dogs allowed in bar ~ Open 12-11(10.30 Sun) ~ www.theploughinn.info

LOWER WIELD   SU6339

Yew Tree

Turn off A339 NW of Alton at Medstead, Bentworth 1 signpost, then follow village signposts; or off B3046 S of Basingstoke, signposted from Preston Candover; SO24 9RX

Bustling country pub with a hard-working, hands-on landlord, relaxed atmosphere and super choice of wines and food; sizeable garden and nearby walks

This is a smashing little pub run by a first class (and always enthusiastic) landlord and his friendly, helpful staff. There's a small flagstoned bar area on the left with pictures above its stripped-brick dado, a steadily ticking clock and a log fire. Around to the right of the serving counter – which has a couple of stylish wrought-iron bar chairs – it's carpeted; throughout there's a mix of tables, including some quite small ones for two, and miscellaneous chairs. Twelve wines by the glass from a well chosen list which may include summer rosé and Louis Jadot burgundies from a shipper based just along the lane and Longdog Bunny Chaser and a beer from Triple fff named after the pub on handpump (and very reasonably priced for the area). There are solid tables and chunky seats out on the front terrace, picnic-sets in a sizeable side garden, pleasant views and a cricket field across the quiet lane; nearby walks.

Free house ~ Licensee Tim Gray ~ Real ale ~ Bar food (12-2, 6.30-9(8.30 Sun); not Mon) ~ Restaurant ~ (01256) 389224 ~ Children welcome ~ Dogs allowed in bar ~ Open 11-3, 6-11; 12-10.30 Sun; closed Mon; first 2 weeks in Jan ~ www.the-yewtree.org.uk

NORTH WALTHAM   SU5645

Fox

3 miles from M3 junction 7: A30 southwards, then turn right at second North Waltham turn, just after Wheatsheaf; pub also signed from village centre; RG25 2BE

Traditional flint country pub, very well run, with good food and drink, nice garden

This is a proper pub with a traditional bar for locals and those wanting a drink and a chat and a separate restaurant, too. This bar on the left is low-ceilinged with a chatty and relaxed atmosphere and Brakspears Bitter, Sharps Doom Bar, West Berkshire Good Old Boy and a guest beer on handpump and lots of bottled ciders as well as Aspell's cider on draught; ten wines by the glass, 22 malt whiskies and quite a collection of miniatures. The big woodburning stove, parquet floor, simple padded country-kitchen chairs, and poultry and 'Beer is Best' prints above the dark dado, all give a comfortably old-fashioned feel – in which perhaps the vital ingredient is the polite and friendly efficiency of the hands-on landlord. There may be very faint background music. The separate dining room, with high-backed leather chairs on a blue tartan carpet, is rather larger. The garden, colourful in summer with its pergola walkway up from the gate on the lane, and with immaculate flower boxes and baskets, has picnic-sets under cocktail parasols in three separate areas, and overlooks rolling farmland (with a glimpse of the distant M3). Walks include a nice one to Jane Austen's church at Steventon.

Free house ~ Licensees Rob and Izzy MacKenzie ~ Real ale ~ Bar food (12-3, 6.30-9) ~ Restaurant ~ (01256) 397288 ~ Children welcome ~ Dogs allowed in bar ~ Open 11-11(midnight Sat, 10.30 Sun) ~ www.thefox.org

NORTH WARNBOROUGH
SU7352
Mill House

A mile from M3 junction 5: A287 towards Farnham, then right (brown sign to pub) on to B3349 Hook Road; RG29 1ET

Converted mill with an attractive layout, inventive modern food, good choice of drinks and lovely waterside terraces

There are several linked areas on the main upper floor of this old heavy-beamed and raftered mill building: lots of well spaced tables in a variety of sizes and styles, rugs on polished boards or beige carpet, coal-effect gas fires in pretty fireplaces, and a profusion of often interesting pictures. A section of glass floor shows the rushing water and mill wheel below, and a galleried part on the left looks down into a dining room on that level, given a more formal feel by its panelling. The well stocked bar has an interesting changing range of malt whiskies, a good choice of wines, and well kept B&P Original (the house beer, brewed by Phoenix), Andwells King John, Hook Norton Double Stout, Stonehenge Sign of Spring, and Three Castles Saxon Archer on handpump; the young staff are cheerful and effective, and the atmosphere is relaxed and comfortable. In warm weather a very big plus is the extensive garden, attractively landscaped around a sizeable millpond, with plenty of solid tables and chairs on various terraces; there are swings on a neatly kept stretch of grass.

Brunning & Price ~ Lease Ashley Harlow ~ Real ale ~ Bar food (all day) ~ Restaurant ~ (01256) 702953 ~ Children welcome ~ Dogs allowed in bar ~ Open 11.30-11(10.30 Sun) ~ www.millhouse-hook.co.uk

PETERSFIELD
SU7227
Trooper

From A32 (look for staggered crossroads) take turning to Froxfield and Steep; pub 3 miles down on left in big dip; GU32 1BD

Charming landlord, popular food, decent drinks and little persian knick-knacks and local artists' work; comfortable bedrooms

There's always a good mix of customers in this well run, popular pub and the friendly Mr Matini offers a warm welcome to all. The bar has all sorts of cushioned dining chairs around dark wooden tables, old film star photos and paintings by local artists (for sale) on the walls, little persian knick-knacks here and there, quite a few ogival mirrors, lots of lit candles, fresh flowers and a log fire in the stone fireplace; there's a sun room with lovely downland views, carefully chosen background music and newspapers and magazines to read. Bowman Swift One and Ringwood Best on handpump and several wines by the glass or carafe. The attractive raftered restaurant has french windows to a paved terrace with views across the open countryside, and there are lots of picnic-sets on an upper lawn. The horse rail in the car park is reserved 'for horses, camels and local livestock'. Our readers enjoy staying in the comfortable bedrooms.

Free house ~ Licensee Hassan Matini ~ Real ale ~ Bar food (12-3(3.30 Sun), 6-9.30; not Sun evening or Mon lunchtime) ~ Restaurant ~ (01730) 827293 ~ Children must be seated and supervised by an adult ~ Dogs allowed in bar ~ Open 12-3, 6-11; 12-3.30 Sun; closed Sun evening, Mon lunchtime ~ Bedrooms: £69B/£89B ~ www.trooperinn.com

PETERSFIELD

SU7129

White Horse

*Up on an old downs road about halfway between Steep and East Tisted, near Priors Dean
– OS Sheet 186 or 197 map reference 715290; GU32 1DA*

**Unchanging and much-loved old place with a great deal of simple
character, friendly licensees and up to ten real ales**

Happily unchanging for many years and with up to ten real ales, it's not
surprising that this remote 17th-c country pub is so loved by its many
customers. The two charming and idiosyncratic parlour rooms (candlelit at night)
have open fires, oak settles and a mix of dark wooden dining chairs, nice old tables
(including some drop-leaf ones), various pictures, farm tools, rugs, a longcase
clock, a couple of fireside rocking chairs, and so forth. The beamed dining room is
smarter with lots more pictures on the white or pink walls. On handpump, the ales
might include two named for the pub, plus Butcombe Bitter, Fullers London Pride,
Ringwood Best and Fortyniner and guests such as Adnams Bitter, Gales Spring
Sprinter, Holt IPA, and Ringwood Boondoggle, and lots of country wines. They
hold a beer festival in June and a cider festival in September. There are some rustic
seats outside and they have camping facilities. If trying to find it for the first time,
keep your eyes skinned – not for nothing is this known as the Pub With No Name.

Gales (Fullers) ~ Managers Georgie and Paul Stuart ~ Real ale ~ Bar food (12-2.30, 6-9.30;
some cold food all day weekdays) ~ Restaurant ~ (01420) 588387 ~ Children welcome ~
Dogs allowed in bar ~ Open 12-11 ~ www.pubwithnoname.co.uk

PRESTON CANDOVER

SU6041

Purefoy Arms

B3046 Basingstoke–Alresford; RG25 2EJ

First class food and wines in gently upmarket village pub

If you love wine and chocolates, then this friendly and civilised pub is just the
place for you. Every Tuesday they hold a Wine Club evening where for just
£5 corkage you can bring a special wine of your own to eat with your meal and
talk about with other interested customers; they also hold regular wine tasting
events. The delicious truffles and chocolates that they sell are all made by the
landlord's father. There are two pairs of smallish linked rooms, all with an easy-
going country pub feel. On the left, the airy front bar has chunky tables, including
ones so tall as to need bar stools, and a corner counter serving a fine changing
choice of wines, as well as Andwell Spring Twist and Flack Manor Double Drop
on handpump; this opens into a jute-floored back area with four dining tables and
characterful mixed seats including old settles. The right-hand front room has red
leather sofas and armchairs by a log fire, and goes back into a bare-boards area
with three or four sturdy pale pine tables. An understated contemporary décor
in grey and puce goes nicely with the informal friendliness of the service; there
may be unobtrusive background pop music. The sizeable sloping garden has well
spaced picnic-sets, a wendy house and perhaps a big hammock slung between
two of its trees; there are teak tables on a terrace sheltered by the pub. This is an
attractive village, with nearby snowdrop walks in February.

Free house ~ Licensees Andres and Marie-Louise Alemany ~ Real ale ~ Bar food (12-3, 6-10;
not Sun evening or Mon) ~ Restaurant ~ (01256) 389777 ~ Well behaved children welcome
~ Dogs allowed in bar ~ Open 12-3, 6-11; 12-4 Sun; closed Sun evening, all day Mon ~
www.thepurefoyarms.co.uk

ROCKBOURNE
SU1118

Rose & Thistle
Signed off B3078 Fordingbridge–Cranborne; SP6 3NL

Pretty pub with hands-on landlady and friendly staff, informal bars, real ales, good food and seats in garden

Even on a cold wet day, this 16th-c thatched pub is buzzing with customers; it's best to book in advance to be sure of a table. It's run with friendliness and efficiency by a first class, hands-on landlady, and the bar has homely dining chairs, stools and benches around a mix of old pubby tables, Fullers London Pride, Palmers Copper Ale and Timothy Taylors Landlord on handpump, a dozen wines (and prosecco) by the glass and Weston's cider. The two-roomed restaurant has a log fire in each (one is a big brick inglenook), old engravings and cricket prints and an informal and relaxed atmosphere. There are benches and tables under the pretty hanging baskets at the front of the building, with picnic-sets under parasols on the grass; good nearby walks. This is a pretty village on the edge of the New Forest.

Free house ~ Licensee Kerry Dutton ~ Real ale ~ Bar food (12-2.30, 7-9.30; not Sun evening) ~ Restaurant ~ (01725) 518236 ~ Children welcome ~ Dogs allowed in bar ~ Open 11-3, 6-11; 11-11 Sat; 12-10.30(8 in winter) Sun ~ www.roseandthistle.co.uk

SPARSHOLT
SU4331

Plough
Village signposted off B3049 (Winchester–Stockbridge), a little W of Winchester; SO21 2NW

Neat, well run dining pub with interesting furnishings, an extensive wine list and highly thought of bar food; garden with children's play fort

Our readers enjoy their visits to this particularly well run country pub very much indeed – and it's the sort of place customers tend to return to again and again. It's always deservedly busy (you must book a table in advance) but you can be sure of a friendly welcome from the courteous licensees and their staff. The main bar has an interesting mix of wooden tables and chairs with farm tools, scythes and pitchforks attached to the ceiling, and they keep Wadworths IPA, 6X, Bishops Tipple, Horizon and Swordfish on handpump and quite a few wines and champagne by the glass from an extensive list. Outside, there are plenty of seats on the terrace and lawn and a children's play fort; disabled access and facilities.

Wadworths ~ Tenants Richard and Kathryn Crawford ~ Real ale ~ Bar food (12-2, 6-9(9.30 Fri, Sat, 8.30 Sun)) ~ (01962) 776353 ~ Children welcome ~ Dogs allowed in bar ~ Open 10-3, 6-11; 10-11 Sun

STEEP
SU7525

Harrow
Take Midhurst exit from Petersfield bypass, at exit roundabout take first left towards Midhurst, then first turning on left opposite garage, and left again at Sheet church; follow over dual carriageway bridge to pub; GU32 2DA

Unchanging, simple place with long-serving landladies, beers tapped from the cask, unfussy food and a big free-flowering garden; no children inside

Our readers love this tiny, unspoilt and quite unchanging pub and many of them have been coming here for years. It's been in the same family for 83 years and there's no pandering to modern methods – no credit cards, no waitress service, no restaurant, no music and outside lavatories. Everything revolves around village chat and the friendly locals who will probably draw you into light-hearted conversation. There are adverts for logs next to calendars of local views being sold in support of local charities and news of various quirky competitions. The little public bar has hops and dried flowers hanging from the beams, built-in wall benches on the tiled floor, stripped-pine wallboards, a good log fire in the big inglenook, and wild flowers on the scrubbed deal tables; board games. Ringwood Best and Bowman Swift One are tapped straight from casks behind the counter, and they've local wine and apple juice; staff are polite and friendly, even when under pressure. The big garden is left free-flowering so that goldfinches can collect thistle seeds from the grass, but there are some seats on paved areas. The Petersfield bypass doesn't intrude on this idyll, though you will need to follow the directions above to find the pub. No children inside and dogs must be on lead.

Free house ~ Licensees Claire and Denise McCutcheon ~ Real ale ~ Bar food (not summer Sun evening) ~ No credit cards ~ (01730) 262685 ~ Dogs allowed in bar ~ Open 12-2.30, 6-11; 11-3, 6-11 Sat; 12-3, 7-10.30 Sun ~ www.harrow-inn.co.uk

SWANMORE   SU5815
Rising Sun
Droxford Road; signed off A32 N of Wickham and B2177 S of Bishops Waltham), at Hillpound E of village centre; SO32 2PS

Proper country pub with friendly staff, good beers and popular food

They now offer a takeaway menu in this 17th-c coaching inn on Sunday-Thursday evenings and it's proving very popular. The low-beamed carpeted bar has some easy chairs and a sofa by its good log fire and a few tables with pubby seats. Beyond the fireplace on the right is a pleasant much roomier dining area (with similarly unpretentious furnishings) running back in an L past the bar; one part of this has stripped brick barrel vaulting. Jennings Tizzie Wizzie, Ringwood Best, Sharps Doom Bar and Timothy Taylors Landlord on handpump and 13 wines by the glass. There are picnic-sets out on the side grass with a play area and the Kings Way long-distance path is close by.

Free house ~ Licensees Mark and Sue Watts ~ Real ale ~ Bar food (12-2(2.30 Sun), 6-9(8.30 Sun)) ~ Restaurant ~ (01489) 896663 ~ Children welcome ~ Dogs allowed in bar ~ Open 11.30-3, 5.30-11; 12-4, 5.30-10.30 Sun ~ www.risingsunswanmore.co.uk

DOG FRIENDLY INNS, HOTELS AND B&Bs

BUCKLERS HARD   SU4000
Master Builders House
Bucklers Hard, Beaulieu, Brockenhurst, Hampshire SO42 7XB (01590) 616253 www.themasterbuilders.co.uk

£130; 9 lovely rms. Sizeable hotel with character bar in lovely spot overlooking the river in charming village; a small gate at the bottom of the garden leads to a walkway beside the river; the original yachtsman's bar is on two levels with a warm winter log fire, benches and cushioned wall seats around long tables, rugs on bare boards, mullioned windows, real ales and steps down to the lower room with a fireplace at each end; some sort of bar food served all day (including afternoon cream teas), more elaborate restaurant food, smashing summer barbecues and good breakfasts; dogs anywhere in the hotel and in bedrooms; £20

CHERITON   SU5828

Flower Pots

Cheriton, Alresford, Hampshire SO24 0QQ (01962) 771318 www.flowerpots-inn.co.uk

£85; 3 rms. Unspoilt and quietly comfortable village local run by a very friendly family, with two pleasant little bars, log fire, decent bar food, super own-brew beers and old-fashioned seats on the pretty lawns; resident dog, George; lots of walks nearby; well behaved dogs on lead in bedrooms and bars

EAST TYTHERLEY   SU2927

Star

East Tytherley Road, Lockerley, Romsey, Hampshire SO51 0LW (01794) 340225 www.starinn.co.uk

£80; 3 rms overlooking the cricket pitch. Spic-and-span country pub with friendly licensees, a bar with comfortable sofas and tub armchairs, bookshelves on rich red walls, a log fire, well kept beers and cider, popular food in the attractive restaurant, tasty breakfasts and seats outside; lots of nearby walks; dogs on lead in bedrooms and bar

EMSWORTH   SU7405

36 On the Quay

47 South Street, Emsworth, Hampshire PO10 7EG (01243) 375592 www.36onthequay.co.uk

£120; 6 rms, 1 in cottage decorated in browns and creams, with waterside views. Restaurant-with-rooms facing the harbour with views from the windows over the yachts; contemporary bar with blue tub seats on pale wooden floorboards, a comfortable lounge area and most emphasis on the faultless, beautifully presented food in the formally laid out dining room; good continental breakfasts in your room or breakfast room; dogs in cottage by arrangement

HURSTBOURNE TARRANT   SU3954

Esseborne Manor

Hurstbourne Tarrant, Andover, Hampshire SP11 0ER (01264) 736444 www.esseborne-manor.co.uk

£125; 19 individually decorated rms. Small stylish family-run Victorian manor with a relaxed, friendly atmosphere, a comfortable lounge and snug little bar, good modern cooking and log fires in formally laid-out dining room, and courteous staff; 3 acres of neat gardens (where dogs may walk, paths nearby too) with tennis and croquet, and they have a special arrangement with a local golf club and health and leisure centre; dogs in annexe bedrooms

LONGSTOCK
SU3537

Peat Spade

Longstock, Stockbridge, Hampshire SO20 6DR (01264) 810612
www.peatspadeinn.co.uk

£95; 7 stylish, contemporary rms. Former coaching inn just 100 metres from the River Test, with a friendly landlady, a nice, bustling atmosphere in the bars, lots of stuffed fish and hunting pictures on dark red or green walls, wine bottles, old stone bottles and soda siphons on shelves and windowsills, an upstairs room with comfortable sofas and armchairs, and good bar food; seats on the terrace and in garden, and plenty of surrounding walks; dogs in bar and bedrooms; £5

LOWER FROYLE
SU7643

Anchor

Lower Froyle, Alton, Hampshire GU34 4NA (01420) 23261
www.anchorinnatlowerfroyle.co.uk

£120; 5 stylish rms. Civilised but informal pub with blazing fires, a good bustle of cheerful customers, various bars with low beams and standing timbers, genuinely interesting knick-knacks and paintings, contemporary paintwork mixing well with nice old chairs and tables, and extremely good food served by helpful staff; breakfasts are first class; dogs in bedrooms and bar; £5

LYMINGTON
SZ3094

Efford Cottage

Milford Road, Everton, Lymington, Hampshire SO41 0JD (01590) 642315
www.effordcottage.co.uk

£65; 3 comfortable rms. Spacious Georgian cottage in an acre of garden that has a special doggy area marked out; marvellous breakfasts with home-baked bread and home-made preserves served in charming dining room, and friendly, helpful owners; resident dog; good parking; walks on nearby beach, footpaths, and in the New Forest; dogs in bedrooms but must not be left unattended; £2

LYMINGTON
SZ3295

Stanwell House

High Street, Lymington, Hampshire SO41 9AA (01590) 677123 www.stanwellhouse.com

£140; 29 lovely rms. Handsome town house – a boutique hotel – with an attractively furnished lounge, a cosy little bar, contemporary european food in the stylish bistro overlooking the walled back garden, and first class fish and seafood in the smart main restaurant; New Forest nearby for walks; dogs in garden bedrooms by prior arrangement; £15

NORTHINGTON
SU5737

Woolpack

Totford, Northington, Hampshire SO24 9TJ (01962) 734184
www.thewoolpackinn.co.uk

£85; 7 rms named after game birds. Nicely refurbished, clean and comfortable roadside inn with a raised open fire, smart split-level dining room, real ales, good food from bar snacks to restaurant dishes, excellent breakfasts, efficient service, and good walks nearby; three resident dogs; dogs welcome in bedrooms

OWER   SU3318

Ranvilles Farm House

Pauncefoot Hill, Romsey, Hampshire SO51 6AA (023) 80814481 www.ranvilles.com

£75; 4 attractively decorated, cottagey rms. Dating from the 13th c when Richard de Ranville came from Normandy and settled with his family, this Grade II* listed house is in 5 quiet acres of gardens and paddock; warmly friendly owners, lots of antiques and paintings in the deeply comfortable two-level sitting room, and enjoyable breakfasts – no evening meals; two resident dogs; walks in the grounds and in the New Forest; dogs in bedrooms; bedding, bowls, treats; first dog free, second dog £3

PETERSFIELD   SU7023

Langrish House

Langrish, Petersfield, Hampshire GU32 1RN (01730) 266941
www.langrishhouse.co.uk

£139; 13 pretty, themed rms with country views. Family home dating back to the 17th c and set in lovely gardens; genuinely helpful and friendly staff, a drawing room for afternoon tea, a vaulted, candlelit bar and imaginative, prettily presented food in the small, cosy restaurant with its log fire; resident dog, cats and fowl; dogs welcome away from restaurant; bed, bowls and blankets; £10

ROTHERWICK   SU7155

Tylney Hall

Rotherwick, Basingstoke, Hampshire RG27 9AZ (01256) 764881 www.tylneyhall.com

£220; 112 well equipped rms with heavy drapes and antiques. Grand Victorian mansion in 66 acres of lovely gardens and parkland; gracious rooms with oak panelling, oil paintings, log fires in big ornate fireplaces, fresh flowers, and spectacular ceilings, a relaxed library and bar, innovative modern cooking in splendid candlelit restaurant, super afternoon teas and good attentive service; tennis, croquet, golf, spa with treatment rooms, gym, and indoor and outdoor swimming pools; dogs in garden bedrooms with own basket, blanket, bowl and chewy toy; £25

SPARSHOLT   SU4431

Lainston House

Sparsholt, Winchester, Hampshire SO21 2LT (01962) 776088
www.lainstonhouse.co.uk

£207; 50 sumptuous rms. Close to Winchester, this elegant William and Mary hotel stands in 63 acres of parkland, with tennis court, croquet, fishing, falconry, archery and clay pigeon shooting; a cosy panelled bar with leather seating, an open fire and a fine view down the avenue of lime trees, a relaxing, deeply comfortable drawing room with fresh flowers and paintings where the delicious afternoon teas are taken, and an elegant restaurant serving first class food using much home-grown produce and home-reared pigs; dogs in bedrooms; special dog menu, bowls, etc; £50

STUCKTON   SU1613
Three Lions

Stuckton, Fordingbridge, Hampshire SP6 2HF (01425) 652489
www.thethreelionsrestaurant.co.uk

£125; 7 rms, 3 in newish courtyard block. Friendly family-run restaurant-with-rooms on the edge of the New Forest with 2-acre gardens and paddock where dogs may walk – plus woods and fields; a cosy bar, comfortable little lounge, airy conservatory, particularly good english/french food in cottagey restaurant and enjoyable breakfasts; hot tub and sauna; resident cat; closed last 2 weeks of Feb; dogs in bedrooms and dining conservatory only; bowls and treats; £10

WINCHESTER   SU4729
Hotel du Vin

14 Southgate Street, Winchester, Hampshire SO23 9EF (01962) 841414
www.hotelduvin.com

£185; 24 smart clubby rms. Engaging early 18th-c town house with a comfortable sitting room, lots of prints on panelled walls, all manner of dark wooden tables and chairs on bare floorboards, two relaxed and pretty eating areas with imaginative bistro-style cooking and an exceptional wine list; seats under parasols in the pretty walled garden; dogs in bedrooms; £10

WINCHESTER   SU4828
Wykeham Arms

75 Kingsgate Street, Winchester, Hampshire SO23 9PE (01962) 853834 www.
wykehamarmswinchester.co.uk

£139; 14 lovely rms, some with four-posters. Very well run and smart old town inn, close to the cathedral, with all sorts of interesting collections dotted about in several bustling rooms, three log fires, 19th-c oak desks retired from nearby Winchester College, five real ales, lots of wines by the glass and several malt whiskies; there's also a snug back room plus a panelled one and tables on a covered back terrace; the food is imaginative and the breakfast smashing; water meadows for walking nearby; dogs in one bedroom and bar; bowls and treats; £15

Herefordshire

DOG FRIENDLY PUBS

CAREY   SO5631

Cottage of Content

Village signposted from good back road between Ross-on-Wye and Hereford E of A49,
through Hoarwithy; HR2 6NG

Country furnishings in a friendly rustic cottage, interesting food, real
ales and seats on terraces; quiet bedrooms

This cosy medieval inn is in a lovely peaceful spot and was originally three labourers' cottages with its own integral cider and ale parlour. The building has kept much of its old character, with a multitude of beams and country furnishings such as stripped-pine kitchen chairs, long pews by one big table and various old-fashioned tables on flagstones or bare boards. Hobsons Best and Wye Valley Butty Bach on handpump and a local cider, and the friendly landlady serves a local cider during the summer months; background music. There are picnic-sets on the flower-filled front terrace and in the rural-feeling garden at the back. This is a nice place to stay.

Free house ~ Licensees Richard and Helen Moore ~ Real ale ~ Bar food (12-2, 6.30-9) ~ Restaurant ~ (01432) 840242 ~ Children welcome ~ Dogs allowed in bar ~ Open 12-2, 6-11; 12-3 Sun; closed Sun evening, Mon, Tues lunchtime Jan-March, 2 weeks in Oct ~ Bedrooms: £55(£65B)/£65(£75B) ~ www.cottageofcontent.co.uk

EARDISLEY   SO3149

Tram

Corner of A4111 and Woodseaves Road; HR3 6PG

Food a growing focus in character village pub – village itself a big
draw, too

Since the arrival of the present young couple, the pink-walled hatch-served room on the right has been turned into a small dining room and the pool table has gone. The beamed bar on the left happily keeps its warmly local character, especially in the cosy back enclave behind sturdy standing timbers, where regulars congregate on the bare boards by the counter – which has well kept Hobsons Best, Ludlow Gold and Wye Valley Butty Bach on handpump and local organic ciders. The rest of it has antique red and ochre floor tiles, a handful of nicely worn tables and chairs, a pair of long cushioned pews enclosing one much longer table, a high-backed settle, old country pictures and a couple of pictorial Wye maps; background music. The outside gents' is one of the most stylish we have ever seen; the sizeable neatly planted garden has picnic-sets on its lawn, and a very comfortable shelter complete with sofas. The handsome old building suits this famous black-and-white village well.

Free house ~ Licensees Mark and Kerry Vernon ~ Real ale ~ Bar food (12-3, 6-9; not Sun evening) ~ Restaurant ~ (01544) 327251 ~ Children welcome ~ Dogs allowed in bar ~ Open 12-3, 6-midnight(7-11 Sun); closed Mon (except spring and summer bank holidays) ~ www.thetraminn.co.uk

KILPECK   SO4430
Kilpeck Inn
Village and church signposted off A465 SW of Hereford; HR2 9DN

Imaginatively extended country inn in fascinating and peaceful village

The nearby castle ruins are interesting, the unique romanesque church even more so. In its way the inn itself is rather special, too, sensitively reworked and reopened a couple of years ago. The softly lit dark-beamed bar, with dark slate flagstones, rambles happily around to give several tempting corners, for instance one with an antique high-backed settle, one with high stools around a matching chest-high table, one with a sheepskin thrown casually and invitingly over a seat. This opens into three cosily linked dining rooms on the left, with high panelled wainscoting. Throughout the mood is thoroughly up-to-date, with clean-cut décor and furnishings; well reproduced background music. They have a good choice of wines by the glass, well kept Wye Valley Butty Bach on handpump, and Weston's cider. The neat back grass has picnic-sets (and there's a bicycle rack). We haven't yet heard from readers staying here, but the four bedrooms look nice – they're very eco-minded, with a biomass boiler and rainwater recycling system.

Licensee Catherine Carleton-Smith ~ Real ale ~ Bar food (12-2, 7-9) ~ Restaurant ~ (01981) 570464 ~ Children welcome ~ Dogs allowed in bar ~ Open 12-2.30, 5.30-11; 12-11 Sun; closed Sun evening in winter in winter ~ www.kilpeckinn.com

SELLACK   SO5526
Lough Pool
Off A49; HR9 6LX

Charming cottage pub with individual furnishings in beamed bars, a good choice of food and drinks, and lots of seats outside in the pretty garden

The garden in front of this lovely 17th century black and white cottage is peacefully rural, and if you're lucky you'll catch sight of local jockeys out training on their racehorses. The charmingly simple and timeless interior is complete with cheery locals, beams, standing timbers, flagstones, rustic furniture and fires burning in the two woodburners at either end of the bar on all but the warmest days. Wye Valley Bitter and Butty Bach and a guest such as Butcombe are on handpump alongside local farm ciders and perries and several wines by the glass from a thoughtful wine list. The restaurant enjoys views over the lovely garden.

Free house ~ Licensees Jim Watson and Jo Morgan ~ Real ale ~ Bar food (12-3, 6.30-9) ~ Restaurant ~ (01989) 730888 ~ Children welcome ~ Dogs allowed in bar ~ Open 12-3, 6-11; closed Sun evening, Mon ~ www.theloughpoolinn.co.uk

SYMONDS YAT   SO5616

Saracens Head

Symonds Yat E; HR9 6JL

Lovely riverside spot with a fine range of drinks in friendly inn, interesting food and seats on waterside terraces; comfortable bedrooms

Steps lead up from the River Wye to picnic-sets on the waterside terrace at this friendly pub which is in a stunning position at the epicentre of the most scenic stretch of the Wye gorge, far below the celebrated Symonds Yat viewpoint. An entertaining riverside walk crosses the Wye a little downstream by a bouncy wire bridge at Biblins and recrosses at the pub by the long-extant hand-hauled chain ferry that one of the pub staff operates. Even when the weather is inclement, the bustling bar tends to be packed with happy customers enjoying the buoyant, welcoming atmosphere. Cheerful staff serve Theakstons Old Peculier, Wye Valley Butty Bach and HPA from handpump, a couple of local guests such as Kingstone Gold, Mayfields Copper Fox and Otley 01, a dozen wines by the glass and a local cider; TV, background music and board games. There's also a cosy lounge and a modernised bare-boards dining room. As well as bedrooms in the main building, there are two contemporary ones in the boathouse annexe.

Free house ~ Licensees P K and C J Rollinson ~ Real ale ~ Bar food (12-2.30, 6.30-9) ~ Restaurant ~ (01600) 890435 ~ Children welcome ~ Dogs allowed in bar ~ Open 11-11 ~ Bedrooms: £59B/£89B ~ www.saracensheadinn.co.uk

TILLINGTON   SO4645

Bell

Off A4110 NW of Hereford; HR4 8LE

Friendly and relaxed, with snug character bar opening into civilised dining areas – good value

Lulu Roberts; cavachon – a cross between a king charles spaniel and a bichon frise

The snug parquet-floor bar on the left has a variety of bucket armchairs around low chunky mahogany-coloured tables, brightly cushioned wall benches, team photographs and shelves of books – and on our visit its black beams were strung with Six Nations flags as well as their usual dried hops, and there was a big roll-down screen for the rugby. They have Sharps Doom Bar, Wye Valley and a guest such as Worthington Red Shield on handpump, and staff are notably cheerful and welcoming; daily papers, unobtrusive background music. The bar opens into a comfortable bare-boards dining lounge with stripey plush banquettes and a coal fire; beyond that is a pitched-ceiling restaurant area with more banquettes and big country prints; its slatted blinds look out on to a sunken terrace with contemporary tables and a garden with teak tables, picnic-sets and a play area.

Free house ~ Licensee Glenn Williams ~ Real ale ~ Bar food (12-2.15(2.45 Sun), 6-9.15; not Sun evening) ~ Restaurant ~ (01432) 760395 ~ Children welcome ~ Dogs allowed in bar ~ Open 11-11; 12-10.30 Sun ~ www.thebellinntillington.co.uk

UPPER COLWALL   SO7643

Chase

Chase Road, brown sign to pub off B4218 Malvern-Colwall, first left after hilltop on bend going W; WR13 6DJ

Gorgeous sunset views from cheerful country tavern's garden, good drinks and cost-conscious food

Tables out on the steep series of small, pretty terraces behind the pub have sweeping views from this western slope of the Malvern Hills, right out over Herefordshire and on a clear day as far as the Black Mountain and even the Brecon Beacons; there are good walks all around. Inside is chatty and companionable, with quite a pack of gilt cast-iron-framed and treadle sewing tables, seats in great variety from a wooden-legged tractor seat to a carved pew, an old black kitchen range and plenty of decorations – china mugs, blue glass flasks, lots of small pictures. They have half a dozen changing well kept ales on handpump, such as Bathams Best, Hobsons Mild, Jennings Cocker Hoop, Sharps Doom Bar and Woods Shropshire Lad, and several wines by the glass; friendly, helpful staff. There may be free sandwiches in the early evening.

Free house ~ Licensee Andy Lannie ~ Real ale ~ Bar food (12-2(2.30 weekends),6.30-9) ~ Restaurant ~ (01684) 540276 ~ Children welcome ~ Dogs allowed in bar ~ Open 12-3,5-11; 12-11 Sat; 12-10.30 Sun ~ www.thechaseinnuppercolwall.co.uk

WOOLHOPE   SO6135

Butchers Arms

Off B4224 in Fownhope; HR1 4RF

Pleasant country inn in peaceful setting, with an inviting garden, excellent food and a fine choice of real ales

Standards are consistently high and attention is paid to every detail at this welcoming 16th-c timber-framed pub. It's down a country lane in lovely countryside, surrounded by a pretty garden with picnic-sets beside a stream. Inside, the bar has very low beams (some with hops), built-in, red-cushioned wall seats, farmhouse chairs and red-topped stools around a mix of old tables (some set for dining) on the red patterned carpet, hunting and horse pictures on the cream walls and an open fire in the big fireplace; there's also a little beamed dining room, similarly furnished. Wye Valley Bitter and Butty Bach are kept alongside a couple of guests from brewers such as Breconshire on handpump and there's a well annotated wine list with several by the glass. To enjoy some of the best of the surroundings, turn left as you come out of the pub and take the tiny left-hand road at the end of the car park; this turns into a track and then into a path, and the view from the top of the hill is quite something.

Free house ~ Licensee Stephen Bull ~ Real ale ~ Bar food (12-2, 7-9) ~ (01432) 860281 ~ Children welcome ~ Dogs allowed in bar ~ Open 12-3, 6-11(midnight Sat); 12-3 Sun; closed Sun evening, Mon, 1 week in Jan ~ www.butchersarmswoolhope.com

DOG FRIENDLY INNS, HOTELS AND B&Bs

BODENHAM   SO5454
Englands Gate
Bodenham, Hereford, Herefordshire HR1 3HU (01568) 797286 www.englandsgate.co.uk

£68; 7 smart, modern rms and suites in converted coach house. Comfortable 16th-c inn with a rambling, open-plan interior, heavy beams and joists, an attractive mix of furnishings on well worn flagstones, open fires, real ales on handpump, a wide choice of good, pubby food, and seats under parasols on the terrace and in the garden; dogs in bedrooms and bar

GLEWSTONE   SO5622
Glewstone Court
Glewstone, Ross-on-Wye, Herefordshire HR9 6AW (01989) 770367
www.glewstonecourt.com

£125; 8 smart, chintzy rms. Elegant, partly Georgian and partly Victorian country house set in neat grounds with a fine cedar of Lebanon and views over Ross-on-Wye; long-standing, warmly welcoming owners and staff, comfortable and relaxing bar and lounges, paintings, chandeliers, and open fires, and good food in antique-filled dining room; croquet; resident working cocker spaniel, Benji; walks in the grounds and in surrounding countryside; dogs in bedrooms; blanket and towel provided; £7

LEDBURY   SO7137
Feathers
25 High Street, Ledbury, Herefordshire HR8 1DS (01531) 635266
www.feathers-ledbury.co.uk

£140; 22 carefully decorated rms making the most of the old beams and timbers. Very striking, mainly 16th-c black and white hotel with convivial back bar-brasserie, cosy leather sofas and armchairs by the fire at one end, contented diners in its main part and comfortable bays of banquettes and other seats; masses of hop bines on long beams, prints and antique sale notices on stripped panelling, real ales, wines by the glass from an extensive list and three dozen malts; a sedate lounge has daily papers, a big log fire and good afternoon teas and the more formal restaurant serves enjoyable bistro-style food; dogs in bedrooms and bar

ROSS-ON-WYE   SO5924
Kings Head
8 High Street, Ross-on-Wye, Herefordshire HR9 5HL (01989) 763174
www.kingshead.co.uk

£90; 15 good rms. Market-town hotel dating from the 14th c with traditional pubby furnishings on stripped boards, a log-effect fire and real ales in little beamed and panelled bar, a lounge bar with some timbering and soft leather seating, and a big carpeted dining room serving very fair value lunches, afternoon snacks and more elaborate evening meals; good breakfasts; can walk along nearby river paths; dogs in bedrooms and bar

ROSS-ON-WYE   SO5824
Wilton Court

Wilton Lane, Ross-on-Wye, Herefordshire HR9 6AQ (01989) 562569
www.wiltoncourthotel.com

£135; 10 pretty, chintzy rms. 16th-c riverside building with friendly owners, lots of original features like leaded windows, heavy beams, and sloping floors, a comfortable sitting room, a bar with an open fire and river views, lovely breakfasts and imaginative food using the best local, seasonal produce in pretty, country-style restaurant, and 2 acres of grounds; fishing; dogs in bedrooms; £10

SYMONDS YAT   SO5417
Norton House

Whitchurch, Symonds Yat, Herefordshire HR9 6DJ (01600) 890046
www.norton-house.com

£80; 3 attractive rms. 300-year-old farmhouse with charming, friendly owners, plenty of original features, flagstones, beams, inglenook fireplaces, and stripped pine shutters and doors, a residents' sitting room and a homely lounge, fine breakfasts taken around an antique mahogany table in the beamed dining room with its farmhouse dresser, and cake and tea on arrival; dogs in bedrooms; £15

TITLEY   SO3359
Stagg

Titley, Kington, Herefordshire HR5 3RL (01544) 230221 www.thestagg.co.uk

£115; 7 rms either above pub or in Georgian vicarage close by. One of Britain's top dining pubs but still very much a pub rather than pure restaurant; welcoming, courteous staff, a small hospitable bar with 200 jugs hanging from the ceiling, real ales, local potato and apple vodkas, and fine wines, and extensive dining rooms with truly excellent, inventive food using their own-grown produce and eggs; first class breakfasts, a 2-acre garden and lovely surrounding countryside (lots of walks); closed first 2 weeks of Nov, 1 week in Jan/Feb; dogs in bedrooms and bar

Hertfordshire

DOG FRIENDLY PUBS

ALDBURY   SP9612
Valiant Trooper
Trooper Road (towards Aldbury Common); off B4506 N of Berkhamsted; HP23 5RW

Cheery, traditional all-rounder with appealing interior, six real ales, generous helpings of pubby food and garden

Readers praise the friendly welcome and attentive, helpful staff at this pleasant old country pub. It's a relaxing place with an easy-going atmosphere throughout its series of unpretentiously appealing old rooms. The first is beamed and tiled in red and black, with built-in wall benches, a pew and small dining chairs around attractive country tables, and an inglenook fireplace. Further in, the middle bar has spindleback chairs around tables on a wooden floor and some exposed brickwork. The far room has nice country kitchen chairs around a mix of tables, and a woodburning stove, and the back barn has been converted to house a restaurant; dominoes, cribbage and bridge on Monday evenings. They keep a jolly decent range of half a dozen well kept changing beers on handpump from brewers such as Hook Norton, Red Squirrel and Tring, alongside local Millwhite's cider. The enclosed garden has a wooden adventure playground, and the pub is well placed for walks through the glorious beech woods of the National Trust's Ashridge Estate.

Free house ~ Licensee Wendy Greenall ~ Real ale ~ Bar food (12-3, 6-9; 12-9 Sat; 12-4 Sun; not Mon evening) ~ Restaurant ~ (01442) 851203 ~ Children in restaurant ~ Dogs allowed in bar ~ Open 11-11; 12-10.30 Sun ~ www.valianttrooper.co.uk

BARNET   TQ2599
Duke of York
Barnet Road (A1000); EN5 4SG

Big place with reasonably priced bistro-style food and nice garden

This Brunning & Price pub opened just as went to press but we had no qualms about including it as we know you can depend on this thriving group to get things just right. The garden is particularly nice, with plenty of tables on a tree-surrounded terrace and lawn, and a tractor in the good children's play area. Though big, the interior is nicely sectioned, giving some intimate areas, with big windows and plenty of mirrors keeping it all light and airy. An eclectic mix of furniture creates a relaxed atmosphere and nice touches such as table lamps, fireplaces, books, rugs and pot plants keep it all homely. There are stools at the impressive counter, where friendly staff serve Phoenix Brunning & Price Original (brewed for them by Phoenix) and Tring Side Pocket on handpump alongside three guests from brewers such as Adnams, Dark Star and Red Squirrel, 25 wines by the glass and about 80 whiskies; background music.

Brunning & Price ~ Manager Kit Lett ~ Real ale ~ Bar food (12-10(9.30 Sun)) ~ (020) 8449 0297 ~ Children welcome ~ Dogs allowed in bar ~ Open 11.30-11; 12-10.30 Sun ~ www.brunningandprice.co.uk/dukeofyork

BATFORD   TL1415

Gibraltar Castle

Lower Luton Road; B653, S of B652 junction; AL5 5AH

Pleasantly traditional pub with interesting militaria displays, some emphasis on food (booking advised); pretty terrace

Seats on the front terrace of this neatly kept pub look over a nature reserve and there are more tables on a large pretty decked back area with lots of flowers and in a tree-lined garden to one side. Inside, the traditional long carpeted bar is decked out with an impressive collection of military memorabilia – everything from rifles to swords, medals, uniforms and bullets (with plenty of captions to read) and pictures depicting various moments in Gibraltar's history. In one area the low beams give way to soaring rafters and there are comfortably cushioned wall benches and a couple of snugly intimate window alcoves, one with a fine old clock, several board games are piled on top of the piano, and a pleasant old fireplace. Fullers London Pride, ESB and a guest beer on handpump; background music.

Fullers ~ Tenant Hamish Miller ~ Real ale ~ Bar food (12-2.30, 6-9; 12-9(8 Sun) Sat) ~ Restaurant ~ (01582) 460005 ~ Children welcome ~ Dogs allowed in bar ~ Open 11.30-11(12 Fri, Sat); 12-10.30 Sun ~ www.gibraltarcastle.co.uk

FLAUNDEN   TL0101

Bricklayers Arms

4 miles from M25 junction 18; village signposted off A41 – from village centre follow Boxmoor, Bovingdon road and turn right at Belsize, Watford signpost into Hogpits Bottom; HP3 0PH

Cosy country restaurant with fairly elaborate food; very good wine list

Carefully prepared food is served in a calmly civilised atmosphere and not overblown surroundings at this neatly kept virginia creeper-covered dining pub. Meals tend to be a considered affair (with prices to match) so it's not really the place for a quick bargain lunch. Stubs of knocked-through oak-timbered wall indicate the layout of the original rooms in its fairly open-plan interior. The well refurbished low-beamed bar is snug and comfortable, with a roaring log fire in winter. The extensive wine list includes about 20 by the glass, and they have Rebellion IPA, Fullers London Pride, a beer from Tring and a guest or two such as Sharps Doom Bar on handpump. This is a lovely peaceful spot in summer, when the terrace and beautifully kept old-fashioned garden with its foxgloves against sheltering hedges comes into its own. Just up the Belsize road there's a path on the left which goes through delightful woods to a forested area around Hollow Hedge.

Free house ~ Licensee Alvin Michaels ~ Real ale ~ Bar food (12-2.30(3.30 Sun); 6.30-9.30(8.30 Sun)) ~ Restaurant ~ (01442) 833322 ~ Children welcome ~ Dogs allowed in bar ~ Open 12-11.30(12.30 Sat, 10.30 Sun) ~ www.bricklayersarms.com

FRITHSDEN   TL0109
Alford Arms

A4146 from Hemel Hempstead to Water End, then second left (after Red Lion) signed Frithsden, then left at T junction, then right after 0.25 miles; HP1 3DD

Thriving dining pub with a chic interior, good food from imaginative menu and a thoughtful wine list

This pretty Victorian pub stands by a village green and is surrounded by lovely National Trust woodland. It's usually full to the brim with cheerful diners – though you might still find a few locals chatting at the bar. The fashionably elegant but understated interior has simple prints on pale cream walls, with blocks picked out in rich Victorian green or dark red, and an appealing mix of good antique furniture (from Georgian chairs to old commode stands) on bare boards and patterned quarry tiles. It's all pulled together by luxuriously opulent curtains; darts and background jazz. All the wines on their list are european, with most of them available by the glass, and they have Sharps Doom Bar, Rebellion Smuggler and a guest brewer such as Tring on handpump. There are plenty of tables outside.

Salisbury Pubs ~ Lease Darren Johnston ~ Real ale ~ Bar food (12-2.30(3 Sat, 4 Sun), 6.30(7 Sun)-9.30(10 Fri, Sat)) ~ Restaurant ~ (01442) 864480 ~ Children welcome ~ Dogs allowed in bar ~ Open 11-11; 12-10.30 Sun ~ www.alfordarmsfrithsden.co.uk

HERTFORD HEATH   TL3510
College Arms

London Road; B1197; SG13 7PW

Light and airy rooms with contemporary furnishings, friendly service, good, interesting food and real ales; seats outside

Very popular locally but with a warm welcome for visitors too, this nicely refurbished pub is on the edge of a village and backed by woodland – handy for walks. Clearly run with care and attention to detail, it's light and airy throughout with comfortable contemporary furnishings. The bar has some high chairs around equally high tables, long cushioned wall seating and pale leather dining chairs around tables on rugs or wooden floorboards, and a modern bar counter where they serve Sharps Doom Bar and Woodfordes Wherry on handpump and 16 wines by the glass; background jazz. There's an area with long button-back wall seating, an open fireplace piled up with logs and a doorway that leads to a charming little room with brown leather armchairs and a couple of cushioned pews, a small woodburning stove in an old brick fireplace, another rug on more wooden boards and hunting-themed wallpaper. The elegant partly carpeted dining room has a real mix of antique dining chairs and tables and a couple of large house plants. There are seats and tables and a long wooden bench among flowering pots on the back terrace and a children's play house.

Punch ~ Lease Tim Lightfoot ~ Real ale ~ Bar food (12-3(5 Sat, 7 Sun), 6-10; not Sun evening) ~ Restaurant ~ (01992) 558856 ~ Children welcome ~ Dogs allowed in bar ~ Open 12-11(10.30 Sun) ~ www.thecollegearmshertfordheath.com

PRESTON   TL1824

Red Lion

Village signposted off B656 S of Hitchin; The Green; SG4 7UD

Homely village local with changing beers, fair-priced food and neat colourful garden

This welcoming place (one of the first community-owned pubs in the country) is pubbily simple but cheery. The grey wainscoted main room on the left has sturdy well varnished pub furnishings including padded country-kitchen chairs and cast-iron-framed tables on a patterned carpet, a generous window seat, a log fire in a brick fireplace and foxhunting prints. The somewhat smaller room on the right has steeplechasing prints, some varnished plank panelling and brocaded bar stools on flagstones around the servery; darts and dominoes. As well as Fullers London Pride and Wells & Youngs, three regularly changing interesting guests might be from brewers such as Brewsters, Marston Moor and Red Squirrel. They also tap farm cider from the cask, have several wines by the glass (including an english house wine), a perry and mulled wine in winter. A few picnic-sets out on the front grass face across to lime trees on a peaceful village green. At the back, a pergola-covered terrace gives way to many more picnic-sets (with some shade from a tall ash tree) and, beyond, a good-sized sheltered garden with a colourful herbaceous border.

Free house ~ Licensee Raymond Lamb ~ Real ale ~ Bar food (12-2, 7-8.30; not Sun evening or Tues) ~ (01462) 459585 ~ Children welcome ~ Dogs allowed in bar ~ Open 12-2.30(3.30 Sat), 5.30-11(12 Sat); 12-3.30, 7-10.30 Sun ~ www.theredlionpreston.co.uk

REDBOURN   TL1011

Cricketers

3.2 miles from M1 junction 9; A5183 towards St Albans, bear right on to B487, first right into Chequer Lane, then third right into East Common; AL3 7ND

Good food and beer in a nicely placed, attractively updated pub

This nicely refurbished place is appropriately situated opposite the cricket pitch. The front bar, which was knocked into quite an unusual shape during restyling of the building, is snugly civilised with leather tub armchairs, plush banquettes and some leather cube stools on its pale carpet. It leads back into an attractive and comfortably modern dining room, also gaining from the unusual shape of the building. Friendly efficient staff serve four thoughtfully sourced guests, alongside Greene King IPA, which might come from brewers such as Aylesbury, Church End, Tring and Sharps. They also serve local Millwhite's Rum Cask cider and about two dozen wines by the glass along with decent coffees; well reproduced background music. There are picnic-sets out on the side grass and sheltered benches by the front door and a map board by the next-door local museum describes some interesting nearby walks.

Free house ~ Licensees Colin Baxter and Andy Stuart ~ Real ale ~ Bar food (12-3, 6-9 (10 Fri, Sat); 12-5 Sun; not Sun evening) ~ Restaurant ~ (01582) 620612 ~ Children welcome ~ Dogs allowed in bar ~ Open 12-11(midnight Sat, 10.30 Sun) ~ www.thecricketersofredbourn.com

SARRATT   TQ0498

Cock

Church End: a very pretty approach is via North Hill, a lane N off A404, just under a mile W of A405; WD3 6HH

Plush pub popular with older dining set at lunchtime and families outside during summer weekends; Badger beers

At lunchtime you're likely to find an older set making the most of the good value OAP meals on offer at this comfortably traditional place. The latched front door opens straight into the homely tiled snug with a cluster of bar stools, vaulted ceiling and original bread oven. Through an archway, the partly oak-panelled cream-walled lounge has a lovely log fire in an inglenook, pretty Liberty-style curtains, red plush chairs at dark oak tables, lots of interesting artefacts, and several namesake pictures of cockerels. Badger Best, Sussex, Tanglefoot and a seasonal Badger guest are on handpump; background music. The restaurant is in a nicely converted barn. In summer, children can play in the bouncy castle and play area, leaving parents to take in the open country views from picnic-sets on the pretty, sheltered lawn and terrace. There are more picnic-sets in front that look out across a quiet lane towards the churchyard.

Badger ~ Tenants Brian and Marion Eccles ~ Real ale ~ Bar food (12-2.30, 6-9; 12-6 Sun) ~ Restaurant ~ (01923) 282908 ~ Children welcome ~ Dogs allowed in bar ~ Open 12-11(11.30 Sat, 9 Sun) ~ www.cockinn.net

SARRATT   TQ0499

Cricketers

The Green; WD3 6AS

Charming pub by village green with rambling, interconnected rooms, lots to look at, six real ales, good wines, helpful staff and enjoyable food; seats outside

Made up of three charming old cottages by the village green and duck pond, this is another fine pub from the Brunning & Price stable. The interlinked rooms have been refurbished with much character and it's certainly worth wandering around before you decide where you want to sit – you can choose from little snugs and alcoves that are perfect for a quiet drink or several dining areas, connected or more private. Throughout, there's plenty of cricketing memorabilia, fresh flowers, large plants and church candles, all manner of antique dining chairs and tables on rugs or stripped floorboards, comfortable armchairs or tub seats, cushioned pews and wall seats and two open fires in raised fireplaces. Phoenix

Dipper; owner Fergus McMullen

Brunning and Price is on handpump alongside five guests from brewers such as Batemans, Fullers, Mauldens and Tring, good wines by the glass and 50 whiskies; background music and board games. Several sets of french windows open on to the terrace where there are tables and chairs, with picnic-sets on grass next to a colourfully painted tractor.

Brunning & Price ~ Licensee David Stowell ~ Real ale ~ Bar food (12-3, 5.30-10; 12-4, 5-9.30 Sun) ~ Restaurant ~ (01923) 270877 ~ Children welcome ~ Dogs allowed in bar ~ Open 12-11(10.30 Sun) ~ www.cricketers-sarratt.co.uk

TRING   SP9211
Robin Hood
Brook Street (B486); HP23 5ED

Really welcoming pub with good beer and popular pubby food

The pubby menu at this pleasingly traditional place is particularly good value – it's the sort of place where diners who are in for a good value meal happily co-exist with regulars on stools along the counter enjoying the half a dozen Fullers ales. It's a carefully run place with a homely atmosphere and genial service in its several immaculately kept smallish linked areas. The main bar has banquettes and standard pub chairs on spotless bare boards or carpets. Towards the back, you'll find a conservatory with a vaulted ceiling and woodburner. The licensees' two little yorkshire terriers are called Buddy and Sugar; background music. There are tables out on the small pleasant back terrace.

Fullers ~ Tenants Terry Johnson and Stewart Canham ~ Real ale ~ Bar food (12-2.15, 7-9; 12-9.15 Sat; not Sun evening) ~ (01442) 824912 ~ Children welcome ~ Dogs allowed in bar ~ Open 11.30-3, 5.30-11(11.30-11 Fri); 12-11.30 Sat; 12-11 Sun ~ www.therobinhoodtring.co.uk

DOG FRIENDLY INNS, HOTELS AND B&Bs

BISHOP'S STORTFORD   TL5213
Down Hall Country House
Matching Road, Hatfield Heath, Bishop's Stortford, Hertfordshire CM22 7AS (01279) 731441 www.downhall.co.uk

£109; 99 stylish, comfortable rms, some on ground floor with individual access. Fine italianate mansion dating from 14th c in 110 acres of gardens and grounds; ornate décor, a relaxing atmosphere, comfortable lounges with log fires and afternoon teas, a well stocked cosy cocktail bar, imaginative cooking in the modern bistro and smarter restaurant, an outside terrace restaurant and genuinely helpful, friendly staff; snooker and indoor swimming pool; dogs in bedrooms; treats and bowl; £10

Isle of Wight

MAP 2

DOG FRIENDLY PUBS

ARRETON   SZ5386
White Lion
A3056 Newport-Sandown; PO30 3AA

Friendly local with good value pubby food

The neatly kept beamed lounge at this unchanging white-painted village house is comfortably old fashioned and cosy, with a genuinely warm welcome, dark pink walls or stripped brick above a stained pine dado, gleaming brass and horse tack and lots of cushioned wheelback chairs on the patterned red carpet. The background music tends to be very quiet, and the public bar has a TV, games machine, darts and board games. Three changing real ales on handpump might be Wells & Youngs Eagle, Sharps Doom Bar and Timothy Taylors Landlord; also a farm cider and draught pear cider. There's also a restaurant (no children in here) and family room. The pleasant garden has a small play area.

Enterprise – Lease Chris and Kate Cole ~ Real ale ~ Bar food (12-9) ~ (01983) 528479 ~ Children welcome ~ Dogs allowed in bar ~ Open 11(12 Sun)-11 ~ www.white-lion-arreton.com

BEMBRIDGE   SZ6587
Crab & Lobster
Foreland Fields Road, off Howgate Road (which is off B3395 via Hillway Road); PO35 5TR

Clifftop views from terrace and delicious seafood; bedrooms

There can't be much that's more summery than a seafood meal out on the terrace of this coastal pub, with its terrific Solent views; the dining area and some of the bedrooms share the same aspect. Perched on low cliffs within yards of the shore it's not surprising that it's such a popular summer destination (picnic-sets outside fill up quickly and service can slow down) so do arrive early for a table. Inside it's roomier than you might expect and is done out a little like a parlour, with lots of yachting memorabilia, old local photographs and a blazing winter fire; darts, dominoes and cribbage. Goddards Fuggle-Dee-Dum, Greene King IPA and Sharps Doom Bar are on handpump, with a dozen wines by the glass, 16 malt whiskies and good coffee.

Enterprise ~ Lease Caroline and Ian Quekett ~ Real ale ~ Bar food (12-2.30, 6-9(9.30 Fri, Sat) with limited menu 2.30-5.30 weekends and holidays) ~ Restaurant ~ (01983) 872244 ~ Children welcome ~ Dogs allowed in bar ~ Open 11-11; 12-10.30 Sun – Bedrooms: £50S(£55B)/£85S(£90B) ~ www.crabandlobsterinn.co.uk

FISHBOURNE

SZ5592

Fishbourne Inn

From Portsmouth car ferry turn left into Fishbourne Lane no through road; PO33 4EU

Attractively refurbished pub with a contemporary feel, several inter-connected rooms, real ales, a good number of wines by the glass and all-day food; bedrooms

This half-timbered pub is handy for the Wightlink ferry terminal. It's been give an attractive contemporary make-over inside and the open-plan rooms are connected by knocked-through doorways. There's a mix of wooden and high-backed dining chairs around square tables on the slate floor, a red-painted area off the bar with a big model yacht and two leather sofas facing each other, a woodburning stove in a brick fireplace with an ornate mirror above it, and a smart dining room with leather high-backed chairs around circular tables on the new wood flooring and another model yacht on the window-sill; one comfortable room has huge brown leather sofas, and throughout there are country pictures on the partly panelled walls.

Enterprise ~ Lease Richard Morey ~ Real ale ~ Bar food (12-9.30; 12-2.30, 6-9.30 winter weekdays) ~ (01983) 882823 ~ Children welcome ~ Dogs allowed in bar ~ Open 9am-11pm(10.30 Sun) ~ Bedrooms: /£90S ~ www.thefishbourne.co.uk

FRESHWATER

SZ3487

Red Lion

Church Place; from A3055 at E end of village by Freshwater Garage mini-roundabout follow Yarmouth signpost, then take first real right turn signed to Parish Church; PO40 9BP

Good mix of locals and visiting diners, good food and composed atmosphere

Although the food is quite a draw at this civilised place, you're likely to find a row of chatty locals occupying stools along the counter, enjoying the Flowers Original, Goddards Best and Fuggle-Dee-Dum and Sharps Doom Bar. Steady and reliable, this is a longstanding stalwart of the Guide, with a nicely grown-up pubby atmosphere. The comfortably furnished open-plan bar has fires, low grey sofas and sturdy country-kitchen-style furnishings on mainly flagstoned floors and bare boards. Outside, there are tables (some under cover) in a carefully tended garden beside the kitchen's herb and vegetable patch. A couple of picnic-sets in a quiet square at the front have pleasant views of the church. The pub is virtually on the Freshwater Way footpath that connects Yarmouth with the southern coast at Freshwater Bay.

Enterprise ~ Lease Michael Mence ~ Real ale ~ Bar food (12-2, 6-9) ~ (01983) 754925 ~ Children over 10 at the landlord's discretion ~ Dogs allowed in bar ~ Open 11.30-3, 5.30-11; 11.30-4, 6-11 Sat; 12-3, 7-10.30 Sun

NINGWOOD

SZ3989

Horse & Groom

A3054 Newport-Yarmouth, a mile W of Shalfleet; PO30 4NW

Spacious family dining pub with fairly priced all-day food, excellent play area and crazy golf

This is a neatly kept and carefully extended pub with a friendly, helpful licensee and an easy-going atmosphere. The roomy interior has been thoughtfully arranged with comfortable leather sofas grouped around low tables and a nice mix of sturdy tables and chairs, well spaced for a relaxing meal. Walls are pale pink, which works nicely with the old flagstone flooring. Greene King IPA, Ringwood Best and a guest like Adnams Lighthouse on handpump and a dozen wines by the glass; background music, games machine and board games. Children and families will find plenty to keep them occupied outside where there are ample tables in the garden, a bouncy castle, crazy golf and a fully equipped play area.

Enterprise ~ Lease Steve Gilbert ~ Real ale ~ Bar food (12-9) ~ (01983) 760672 ~ Children welcome ~ Dogs allowed in bar ~ Open 11-11(midnight Fri-Sun) ~ www.horse-and-groom.com

SEAVIEW   SZ5992

Boathouse

On B3330 Ryde Seaview; PO34 5BW

Contemporary décor in well run pub by the beach, real ales, quite a choice of food, a friendly welcome and seats outside; bedrooms

Just across the road from the beach, this extended, blue-painted Victorian pub usefully serves food all day at weekends and all day on weekdays too from April to October. The décor is appealing and contemporary, with light, fresh paintwork and a mix of polished bare boards, flagstones and carpet, and you can be sure of a warm welcome from the friendly staff. The bar has sturdy leather stools and blue, tub-like chairs around circular wooden tables, a large model yacht on the mantelpiece above the open fire with a huge neat stack of logs beside it, fresh flowers and candles, and Ringwood Best and Sharps Doom bar on handpump from the pale wooden counter; another room has a dinghy with oars in it leaning against the wall. The dining room has a mix of elegant dining chairs, more wooden tables, some portraits on pale blue walls and an ornate mirror over another open fire; background music. There are picnic-sets and white tables and chairs outside, some under parasols, that look across to the sea. The double bedrooms overlook the water.

Punch ~ Tenant Martin Bullock ~ Real ale ~ Bar food (12-9.30; limited between 2.30-6) ~ (01983) 810616 ~ Children welcome ~ Dogs allowed in bar ~ Open 9am-11pm(10.30 Sun) ~ Bedrooms: /£110S ~ www.theboathouseiow.co.uk

SHALFLEET   SZ4089

New Inn

A3054 Newport-Yarmouth; PO30 4NS

Happy pub with seafood specialities, good beers and wines, too

Readers enjoy the genuinely cheerful atmosphere at this nice old 18th-c former fishermen's haunt, and we think it gets better and better, with more attention to detail, from one year to the next. Its rambling rooms have plenty of character with warm fires, yachting photographs and pictures, boarded ceilings and scrubbed-pine tables on flagstone, carpet and slate floors. Sharps Doom Bar and a couple of guests such as Goddards Ale of Wight and Yates Golden are on handpump, and they stock over 60 wines; background music. As it's popular, you will need to book and there may be double sittings in summer; dogs are only allowed in areas with stone floors.

Enterprise ~ Lease Mr Bullock and Mr McDonald ~ Real ale ~ Bar food (9-11, 12-2.30, snacks 2.30-5 Fri, Sat, 6-9.30) ~ (01983) 531314 ~ Children welcome ~ Dogs allowed in bar ~ Open 9-11(10.30 Sun) ~ www.thenew-inn.co.uk

SHORWELL   SZ4582

Crown

B3323 SW of Newport; PO30 3JZ

Popular pub with an appealing streamside garden and play area, pubby food and several real ales

In summer, the tree-sheltered garden around this pretty pub is very appealing with its little stream that broadens into a small trout-filled pool. There are plenty of closely spaced picnic-sets and white garden chairs and tables on grass, and a decent children's play area. Inside, four pleasant opened-up rooms spread around a central bar, with either carpet, tiles or flagstones, and chatty regulars lending some local character. Adnams Broadside and Explorer, Goddards Fuggle-Dee-Dum, St Austell Tribute and Sharps Doom Bar on handpump. The beamed knocked-through lounge has blue and white china on an attractive carved dresser, old country prints on stripped-stone walls and a winter log fire with a fancy tile-work surround. Black pews form bays around tables in a stripped-stone room off to the left with another log fire; background music and board games.

Enterprise ~ Lease Nigel and Pam Wynn ~ Real ale ~ Bar food (12-9.30) ~ (01983) 740293 ~ Children welcome ~ Dogs allowed in bar ~ Open 10.30(11.30 Sun)-11 ~ www.crowninnshorwell.co.uk

VENTNOR   SZ5677

Spyglass

Esplanade, SW end; road down is very steep and twisty, and parking nearby can be difficult – best to use the pay-and-display (free in winter) about 100 metres up the road; PO38 1JX

Interesting waterside pub with appealing seafaring bric-a-brac, four well kept beers and enjoyable food

The terrific seaside location of this cheery, bubbling place seems to draw the crowds whatever the season. It's perched just above the beach, and tables in the bar and outside on a terrace have lovely views over the sea. Inside, the snug quarry-tiled old interior is charmingly done out with a fascinating jumble of seafaring memorabilia (anything from ship's wheels to stuffed seagulls); background music. Ringwood Best and Fortyniner are well kept alongside a couple of guests from brewers such as Banks and Yates. There are strolls westwards from here along the coast towards the Botanic Garden, as well as heftier hikes up on to St Boniface Down and towards the eerie shell of Appuldurcombe House. No children in the bedrooms.

Free house ~ Licensees Neil and Stephanie Gibbs ~ Real ale ~ Bar food (12-9.30) ~ (01983) 855338 ~ Children welcome ~ Dogs allowed in bar ~ Live bands every day in summer and Weds-Sun in winter ~ Open 10.30am-11pm ~ Bedrooms: /£80B ~ www.thespyglass.com

DOG FRIENDLY INNS, HOTELS AND B&Bs

BONCHURCH   SZ5777
Lake Hotel
Bonchurch, Ventnor, Isle of Wight PO38 1RF (01983) 852613 www.lakehotel.co.uk

£100; 20 rms. Early 19th-c country house in 2 acres of pretty gardens just 400 metres from beach, and run by the same family for 45 years; airy, comfortable lounges – some homely and one recently refurbished with white tub chairs on pale floorboards – a well stocked bar, and hearty, healthy breakfasts using local produce in the light, contemporary dining room; walks in part of the grounds and on the beach; dogs in bedrooms; bring own bedding; £8

SEAVIEW   SZ6390
Priory Bay Hotel
Priory Croft, Priory Road, Seaview, Isle of Wight PO34 5BU (01983) 613146
www.priorybay.co.uk

£200; 18 individually furnished rms with 10 in cottages. Former Tudor farmhouse with Georgian and more recent additions in a 70-acre estate that leads to a fine sandy private beach with a beach bar (good for lunch); lovely day rooms with comfortable sofas, books and magazines on coffee tables, and pretty flower arrangements, imaginative food in the classically decorated Island Restaurant and delicious fish and shellfish in the more contemporary Priory Oyster, and excellent breakfasts; outdoor swimming pool, tennis, croquet, and a nine-hole par three golf course; resident dog; dogs in cottages in grounds; £20

SEAVIEW   SZ6291
Seaview Hotel
High Street, Seaview, Isle of Wight PO34 5EX (01983) 612711 www.seaviewhotel.co.uk

£135; 28 attractively decorated rms and suites, some with sea views. Friendly and spotlessly kept hotel with fine naval photographs and artefacts in the chatty and relaxed front lounge bar, an interesting old-fashioned back bar with real ales and a pubby feel, and good imaginative food in the pretty restaurant; self-catering cottage, also; dogs in bedrooms; £20

TOTLAND   SZ3286
Sentry Mead
Totland Bay, Isle of Wight PO39 0BJ (01983) 753212 www.sentrymead.co.uk

£100; 11 pretty rms. Victorian country-house guest house in flower-filled gardens overlooking the Solent and 120 metres from the beach; traditionally furnished rooms – an open fire in the lounge, a bar area and an airy conservatory, caring, attentive staff, super breakfasts using local produce and home-made jams and marmalade in the stylish restaurant, and all-day bar snacks; good nearby walks; dogs in bedrooms and on lead, away from the dining room; £10

Kent

MAP 3

DOG FRIENDLY PUBS

BEKESBOURNE   TR1856

Unicorn

Bekesbourne Hill, off Station Road; village E of Canterbury; CT4 5ED

Small, friendly pub, simply furnished bars, local beer and pubby food

The licensees at this friendly little pub are particularly welcoming and clearly enjoy their work. It's a simple place with just a few scrubbed old pine tables and wooden pubby chairs on worn floorboards, a nice old leather sofa beside the open fire, a canary yellow ceiling and walls above a dark green dado, minimal décor and a handful of bar stools against the neat counter; background music and board games. They make a point of serving only Kentish beers from brewers such as Ramsgate and Westerham on handpump, alongside Biddenden cider. A side terrace is prettily planted and there's a garden with benches and bat and trap in summer. Parking in front is tricky but there's a large car park at the back reached from the small track at the end of the adjacent terrace of cottages. More reports please.

Free house ~ Licensee Martin Short ~ Real ale ~ Bar food (12-2.30, 6.30-9; 12-5 Sun; not Mon) ~ (01227) 830210 ~ Well behaved children welcome ~ Dogs allowed in bar ~ Folk or acoustic music Sun ~ Open 12-3, 6-11; 12-10.30 Sun; closed Mon ~ www.pubunicorn.com

BIDDENDEN   TQ8238

Three Chimneys

A262, a mile W of village; TN27 8LW

Pubby beamed rooms of considerable individuality, log fires, imaginative food and pretty garden

The simple huddled down exterior of this appealingly civilised place, with its low-slung roof and little windows, is absolutely delightful, and its little low-beamed rooms have exactly the charmingly timeless feel you'd hope for. They are simply done out with plain wooden furniture and old settles on flagstones and coir matting, some harness and sporting prints on the stripped-brick walls and good log fires. The public bar on the left is quite down-to-earth, with darts, dominoes and cribbage. Adnams Best and Old and a guest from a brewer such as Franklins tapped straight from casks racked behind the counter, several wines by the glass, local Biddenden cider and apple juice and several malt whiskies. But don't be misled into thinking this place is in any way old fashioned. In fact, the candlelit bare-boards restaurant though rurally rustic in its décor is chatty and alive with customers and the style of dining is completely up to date. French windows open from the restaurant to a conservatory and garden. Sissinghurst Gardens are nearby.

Free house ~ Licensee Craig Smith ~ Real ale ~ Bar food (12-2(2.30 Sat, Sun), 6.30-9(9.30 Fri, Sat)) ~ Restaurant ~ (01580) 291472 ~ Children welcome ~ Dogs allowed in bar ~ Open 11.30-3.30, 5.30-11; 12-4, 6-10.30 Sun ~ www.thethreechimneys.co.uk

BOUGH BEECH   TQ4846
Wheatsheaf
B2027, S of reservoir; TN8 7NU

Former hunting lodge with lots to look at, fine range of local drinks, popular food and plenty of seats in appealing garden

This ancient ivy-clad building is thought to have originated as a 15th-century royal hunting lodge, and is full of characterful historic detail. Its neat central bar and long front bar (which has an attractive old settle carved with wheatsheaves) have unusually high ceilings with lofty oak timbers, a screen of standing timbers and a revealed king post. Divided from the central bar by two more rows of standing timbers – one formerly a exterior wall – are the snug and another bar. On the walls and above the massive stone fireplaces, there are quite a few horns and heads as well as african masks, a sword from Fiji, crocodiles, stuffed birds, swordfish spears and a matapee. Look out, too, for the piece of 1607 graffiti, 'Foxy Holamby', who is thought to have been a whimsical local squire. Thoughtful touches include piles of smart magazines, board games, tasty nibbles and winter chestnuts to roast. Harveys Best, Westerham Brewery Grasshopper and a guest are on handpump and they've three ciders (including one from local Biddenden), a decent wine list, several malt whiskies, summer Pimms and winter mulled wine. Outside is appealing, too, with plenty of seats, flowerbeds and fruit trees in the sheltered side and back gardens. Shrubs help divide the garden into various areas, so it doesn't feel too crowded even when it's full.

Enterprise ~ Lease Liz and David Currie ~ Real ale ~ Bar food (12-10) ~ (01732) 700254 ~ Dogs allowed in bar ~ Open 12-11.30(midnight Sat, 11 Sun)

BROOKLAND   TQ9724
Woolpack
On A259 from Rye, about a mile before Brookland, take the first right turn signposted Midley where the main road bends sharp left, just after the expanse of Walland Marsh; OS Sheet 189 map reference 977244; TN29 9TJ

15th-c pub with simple furnishings, massive inglenook fireplace, big helpings of tasty food and large garden

Being fairly near Camber Sands, this aged place can get busy at weekends and during the school holidays with families looking for a good value meal. Steeped in the atmosphere of days gone by, it's said to have been the haunt of local smugglers. Its ancient entrance lobby has a lovely uneven brick floor and black-painted pine-panelled walls and, to the right, the simple quarry-tiled main bar has basic cushioned plank seats in the massive inglenook fireplace and a painted wood-effect bar counter hung with lots of water jugs. Low-beamed ceilings incorporate some very early ships' timbers (maybe 12th c) thought to be from local shipwrecks. A long elm table has shove-ha'penny carved into one end and there are other old and newer wall benches, chairs at mixed tables with flowers and candles and photographs of locals on the walls. The two pub cats, Liquorice and Charlie Girl, are often toasting themselves around the log fire. The dining room to the left is traditional with carpets and dark wheelback chairs; background music and games machine. Shepherd Neame Master Brew and Spitfire and a seasonal brew on handpump. There are plenty of picnic-sets under parasols in the garden, and it's all nicely lit up in the evenings.

Shepherd Neame ~ Tenant Scott Balcomb ~ Real ale ~ Bar food (12-2.30, 6-9; all day Sat, Sun, bank holidays, school holidays) ~ Restaurant ~ (01797) 344321 ~ Children welcome ~ Dogs welcome ~ Open 11-3, 6-11; 12-11 Sat, Sun, bank holidays and school holidays

ICKHAM   TR2258

Duke William

Off A257 E of Canterbury; The Street; CT3 1QP

Relaxing family-owned village pub with airy bar, dining conservatory, enjoyable bar food and plenty of seats outside; bedrooms

There's a very enjoyable pubby atmosphere in the big spreading bar of this friendly village pub. It has huge new oak beams and stripped joists, a fine mix of seats from settles to high-backed cushioned dining chairs, dark wheelback and bentwood chairs around all sorts of wooden tables on the stripped wooden floor, a log fire with a couple of settles and a low barrel table in front of it, a central bar counter with high stools and brass coat hooks and a snug little area with one long table, black leather high-backed dining chairs, a flat-screen TV and a computer if you need it; daily papers, quiet background music, cheerful modern paintings and large hop bines. Brains IPA and a guest such as Shepherd Neame Master Brew on handpump alongside some decent wines. Staff are chatty and attentive. A low-ceilinged dining room leads off to the left with dark wood chairs, tables and more cushioned settles and paintings and mirrors on the walls. At the back of the pub, there's a light-filled dining conservatory with all manner of interesting paintings, prints and heraldry on the walls and similar furniture on the stone floor. Doors lead from here to a big terrace with a covered area to one side, plenty of wooden and metal tables and chairs, and a lawn with picnic-table sets, some swings and a slide.

Free house ~ Licensees Louise and Nicola White ~ Real ale ~ Bar food (12-3, 6-9.30) ~ Restaurant ~ (01227) 721308 ~ Children welcome ~ Dogs allowed in bar ~ Open 11-11(midnight Sat, 10 Sun) ~ Bedrooms: /$70S ~ www.dukewilliam.biz

LANGTON GREEN   TQ5439

Hare

A264 W of Tunbridge Wells; TN3 0JA

Interestingly decorated Edwardian pub with a fine choice of drinks and imaginative, bistro-style food

The décor at this roomy mock-Tudor former hotel is more or less in period with the building, which is dated at 1901. Its high-ceilinged rooms have plenty of light flooding through large windows (especially in the front bar where drinkers tend to gather) dark-painted dados below light walls that are covered in old photographs and prints, 1930s oak furniture, light brown carpet and turkish-style rugs on stained wooden floors, old romantic pastels and a huge collection of chamber-pots hanging from beams. Greene King IPA, Abbot alongside a couple of guests from brewers such as Titanic are on handpump alongside two dozen wines by the glass, over 60 whiskies and a fine choice of vodkas and other spirits; board games. French windows open on to a big terrace with pleasant views of the tree-ringed village green. Parking is limited and on the road so best to arrive early.

Brunning & Price ~ Manager Rob Broadbent ~ Real ale ~ Bar food (12-9.30 (10 Fri, Sat; 9 Sun)) ~ Restaurant ~ (01892) 862419 ~ Children welcome (away from bar after 6pm) ~ Dogs allowed in bar ~ Open 12-11(midnight Sat, 10.30 Sun) ~ www.hare-tunbridgewells.co.uk

PENSHURST   TQ5142
Bottle House

Coldharbour Lane; leaving Penshurst SW on B2188 turn right at Smarts Hill signpost, then bear right towards Chiddingstone and Cowden; keep straight on; TN11 8ET

Low-beamed, connected bars in country pub, friendly service, chatty atmosphere, real ales and decent wines, popular bar food and sunny terrace; nearby walks

'Everything pleases,' says one reader about his visit to this cottagey dining pub, which seems to have cosy woodwork everywhere. There are standing timbers separating the open-plan rooms into intimate areas, all sorts of beams and joists (one or two of the especially low ones are leather padded), pine wall boards, and bar stools ranged along the timber clad copper topped counter – Harveys Best and Larkins Traditional on handpump, a local bottled ale, local apple juice and nearly a dozen wines by the glass from a good list. A nice hotchpotch of wooden tables (most with fresh flowers and candles) and chairs are fairly closely spaced on dark boards or coir and warmed by a woodburning stove; background music. There are photographs of the pub and local scenes on the walls (some of which are stripped stone). The sunny, brick-paved terrace has green-painted picnic-sets under parasols and some olive trees in white pots; parking is limited. Good surrounding walks in this charming area of rolling country.

Free house ~ Licensee Paul Hammond ~ Real ale ~ Bar food (12-10(9 Sun)) ~ Restaurant ~ (01892) 870306 ~ Children welcome ~ Dogs allowed in bar ~ Open 11-11(10.30 Sun) ~ www.thebottlehouseinnpenshurst.co.uk

PLUCKLEY   TQ9243
Dering Arms

Pluckley station, which is signposted from B2077; or follow Station Road (left turn off Smarden Road in centre of Pluckley) for about 1.3 miles S, through Pluckley Thorne; TN27 0RR

Fine fish dishes plus other good food in handsome building, stylish main bar, carefully chosen wines and roaring log fire; comfortable bedrooms

James Buss, the long-standing landlord here, injects individuality and maintains sound traditional standards at this striking pub. Formerly a hunting lodge and part of the Dering Estate, it was built in the 1840s as a mini replica of the manor house. Hence its imposing frontage, mullioned arched windows and dutch gables. The high-ceilinged and stylishly plain main bar has a solid country feel with a variety of wooden furniture on the flagstone floors, a roaring log fire in the great fireplace, country prints and some fishing rods. The smaller half-panelled back bar has similar dark wood furnishings, and an extension to this area has a woodburning stove, comfortable armchairs, sofas and a grand piano; board games. Though emphasis tends to be on the food here, the bar is characterful and comfortable and they do keep a beer named for the pub from Goachers on handpump as well as a very good wine list of around 100 wines; 50 malt whiskies, 20 brandies and an occasional local cider. Classic car meetings (James has a couple of classics) are held here on the second Sunday of the month. Readers very much enjoy staying here – and the breakfasts are excellent.

Free house ~ Licensee James Buss ~ Real ale ~ Bar food (12-2.30, 7-9; 12-3 Sun) ~ Restaurant ~ (01233) 840371 ~ Children welcome ~ Dogs allowed in bar ~ Open 11.30-3, 6-11; 12-4 Sun; closed Sun evening ~ Bedrooms: £60(£80S)/£70(£90S) ~ www.deringarms.com

SEVENOAKS   TQ5352
White Hart
Tonbridge Road (A225 S, past Knole); TN13 1SG

Well run and bustling old coaching inn with a civilised atmosphere in many bar rooms, a thoughtful choice of drinks, enjoyable modern food and friendly, helpful staff

This seemingly endless early 18th-c coaching inn is popular with both drinkers and diners. Its many rooms are interconnected by open doorways and steps and there are several open fires and woodburning stoves. All manner of nice wooden dining chairs around tables of every size sit on warming rugs or varnished bare floorboards, the cream walls are hung with lots of prints and old photographs (many of local scenes or schools) and there are fresh flowers and plants, daily papers to read, board games and a bustling, chatty atmosphere. Friendly, efficient staff serve Brunning & Price Original (brewed for the pub by Phoenix), Fullers London Pride, Harveys Best, Old Dairy Blue Top and three guests from brewers such as Belhaven, Sharps and Westerham, and they keep over 25 good wines by the glass, a fair choice of ciders and over 75 whiskies. It's all very civilised. At the front of the building there are picnic-sets under parasols.

Brunning & Price ~ Manager Chris Little ~ Real ale ~ Bar food (12-10(9.30 Sun)) ~ (01732) 452022 ~ Children welcome away from bar ~ Dogs allowed in bar ~ Open 12-11; 12-10.30 Sun ~ www.bandp.co.uk/whitehart

SPELDHURST   TQ5541
George & Dragon
Village signed from A264 W of Tunbridge Wells; TN3 0NN

Fine old pub, beams, flagstones and huge fireplaces, local beers, good food and attractive outside seating areas

The rambling interior of this half-timbered building, which is based around a medieval manorial hall, conjures up a great sense of antiquity with its ancient beams and winter log fire burning in a huge sandstone fireplace in the main room. To the right of the rather splendid entrance hall (where there's a water bowl for thirsty dogs), the half-panelled room is set for dining with a mix of old wheelback and other dining chairs and a cushioned wall pew around several tables, a few little pictures on the walls, horsebrasses on one huge beam and a sizeable bar counter with Harveys Best, Larkins Traditional Ale and an ale from Westerham Brewery on handpump, 16 wines by the glass and local organic cordials; friendly, efficient staff. A doorway leads through to another dining room with similar furnishings and another big inglenook. Those wanting a drink and a chat tend to head to the room on the left of the entrance (though people do eat in here, too), where there's a woodburning stove in a small fireplace, high-winged cushioned settles and various wooden tables and dining chairs on the wood-strip floor;

background music. There's also an aged-feeling upstairs restaurant. In front of the pub are teak tables, chairs and benches on a nicely planted gravel terrace, while at the back there's a covered area with big church candles on more wooden tables and a lower terrace with seats around a 300-year-old olive tree; more attractive planting here and some modern sculpture.

Free house ~ Licensee Julian Leefe-Griffiths ~ Real ale ~ Bar food (12-2.30(3 Sat, 3.30 Sun), 7-9.30; not Sun evening) ~ Restaurant ~ (01892) 863125 ~ Children welcome ~ Dogs allowed in bar ~ Open 12-11(11.30 Sat, 10.30 Sun) ~ www.speldhurst.com

STALISFIELD GREEN   TQ9552
Plough
Off A252 in Charing; ME13 0HY

Ancient country pub with rambling rooms, open fires, interesting local ales, smashing bar food and friendly licensees

The genuinely cheerful licensees at this ancient country pub – said to date back to 1350 – put in plenty of loving care to make it a winner, and it's the combination of terrific food and local beers served in a lovely cosy atmosphere that makes it so appealing. Its several hop-draped rooms, relaxed and easy-going, ramble around, up and down, with open fires in brick fireplaces, interesting pictures on green- or maroon-painted walls, books on shelves, farmhouse and other nice old dining chairs around a mix of pine or dark wood tables on bare boards and the odd milk churn dotted about. Dixie, the pub cat, likes to find a cosy lap to lie on. Beers come from kentish brewers such as Gadds, Goachers, Old Dairy and Whitstable and they stock kentish lagers, wines, water, fruit juices and cider. The pub appears to perch up on its own amid downland farmland, and picnic-sets on a simple terrace overlook the village green below. They have a site for caravans.

Free house ~ Licensees Robert and Amy Lloyd ~ Real ale ~ Bar food (12-2.30(3 Sun), 6-9; 12-9 Sat) ~ Restaurant ~ (01795) 890256 ~ Children welcome away from main bar ~ Dogs allowed in bar ~ Live music Fri monthly ~ Open 12-3, 6-11; 12-12 Sat(6 Sun) Sat; closed Mon, Tues lunchtime, Sun evening ~ www.stalisfieldgreen.com

STOWTING   TR1241
Tiger
3.7 miles from M20 junction 11; B2068 N, then left at Stowting signpost, straight across crossroads, then fork left after 0.25 miles and pub is on right; coming from N, follow Brabourne, Wye, Ashford signpost to right at fork, then turn left towards Posting and Lyminge at T junction; TN25 6BA

Peaceful pub with helpful staff, traditional furnishings, well liked food, several real ales and open fires; good walking country

Nicely down to earth and cheerily friendly, this 17th-c inn is cosily traditional with a relaxed mix of wooden tables and chairs and built-in cushioned wall seats on wooden floorboards and woodburning stoves at each end of the bar. There's an unpretentious array of books, candles in bottles, brewery memorabilia and paintings, lots of hops and some faded rugs on the stone floor towards the back of the pub. As well as Shepherd Neame Master Brew three or four guests from local brewers such as Hot Fuzz, Old Dairy Brewery and lots of malt whiskies, several wines by the glass, local Biddenden cider and local fruit juice. On warmer days you can sit out on the front terrace and there are plenty of nearby walks along the Wye Downs and North Downs Way.

Free house ~ Licensees Emma Oliver and Benn Jarvis ~ Real ale ~ Bar food (12(4 Mon)-9(9.30 Fri, Sat, 8 Sun)) ~ Restaurant ~ (01303) 862130 ~ Children welcome ~ Dogs allowed in bar ~ Open 12(4 Mon)-11; closed Mon lunchtime, Tues ~ www.tigerinn.co.uk

TUNBRIDGE WELLS   TQ5839
Sankeys
Mount Ephraim (A26 just N of junction with A267); TN4 8AA

Pubby, street-level bar, informal downstairs brasserie (wonderful fish and shellfish), real ales and good wines, a chatty atmosphere and seats on sunny back terrace

If it's the fantastic fish menu you're after at this well known place, head down the steps by the entrance to the chatty and informal restaurant which has an oyster bar and lobster tank on display. Unfussy bistro-style decor includes big mirrors on rustic stripped-brick walls and pews or chairs around sturdy tables on rustic flagstones. French windows open on to an inviting suntrap deck with wicker and chrome chairs and wooden tables. The laid-back street-level bar is light and airy with comfortably worn, informal leather sofas and pews around all sorts of tables on bare wooden boards. The walls are covered with a fine collection of rare enamel signs and antique brewery mirrors as well as old prints, framed cigarette cards and lots of old wine bottles and soda siphons. Goachers, Westerham Brewery Joeys Bite and a guest from a brewery such as Meantime are on handpump, alongside fruit beers, american and british craft beers and several wines by the glass from a good list; big flat-screen TV for sports (not football and it's very busy here when there's a major rugby match) and background music.

Free house ~ Licensee Matthew Sankey ~ Real ale ~ Bar food (12-3(4 Sun), 6-10(8 Sun, Mon)) ~ Restaurant ~ (01892) 511422 ~ Children welcome ~ Dogs allowed in bar ~ Open 12-1am(3am Sat) ~ www.sankeys.co.uk

ULCOMBE   TQ8550
Pepper Box
Fairbourne Heath; signposted from A20 in Harrietsham, or follow Ulcombe signpost from A20, then turn left at crossroads with sign to pub, then right at next minor crossroads; ME17 1LP

Friendly country pub with lovely log fire, well liked food, fair choice of drinks and seats in a pretty garden

Nicely placed on high ground above the Weald, this cosy and traditional country inn is a friendly place with helpful licensees. The homely bar has standing timbers and a few low beams (some hung with hops), copper kettles and pans on window sills and two leather sofas by the splendid inglenook fireplace (nice horsebrasses on the bressumer beam) with its lovely log fire. A side area, furnished more functionally for eating, extends into the opened-up beamed dining room with a range in another inglenook and more horsebrasses. Shepherd Neame Master Brew and Spitfire and a seasonal beer on handpump, with local apple juice and several wines by the glass; background music. The two cats are called Murphy and Jim. There's a hop-covered terrace and a garden with shrubs and fine views. The name of the pub refers to the pepperbox pistol – an early type of revolver with numerous barrels; the village church is worth a look and the Greensand Way footpath runs close by.

Shepherd Neame ~ Tenant Sarah Pemble ~ Real ale ~ Bar food (12-2.15(3 Sun), 6.30-9.30; not Sun evening) ~ Restaurant ~ (01622) 842558 ~ Dogs allowed in bar ~ Open 11-3,

6-midnight; 11-11 Sat; 12-5 Sun; 11-3, 6-midnight Sat in in winter; closed Sun evening ~
www.thepepperboxinn.co.uk

WHITSTABLE

TR1066

Pearsons Arms

*Sea Wall off Oxford Street after road splits into one way system; public parking on left as
road divides; CT5 1BT*

**Seaside pub with an emphasis on interesting food, several local ales and
good mix of customers**

Always busy with a good mix of both locals and visitors, this weatherboarded
pub overlooks a pebble beach and the sea. The two front bars are
divided by a central chimney and have cushioned settles, captain's chairs and
leather armchairs on the stripped-wood floor, driftwood walls and big flower
arrangements on the bar counter where they serve Harveys Best, Hop Back
Summer Lightning, Ramsgate Gadds No 3, and Whitstable East India Pale Ale on
handpump; background music. A cosy lower room has trompe l'oeil bookshelves
and a couple of big chesterfields and dining chairs around plain tables on
the stone floor. Up a couple of flights of stairs, the restaurant has sea views,
mushroom paintwork, contemporary wallpaper, more driftwood, and church
chairs and pine tables on nice wide floorboards.

Enterprise ~ Lease Richard Phillips ~ Real ale ~ Bar food (12-3.30, 6.30-10; not Mon, not
Tues evening) ~ Restaurant ~ (01227) 272005 ~ Children welcome ~ Dogs allowed in bar ~
live music Tues and Sun ~ Open 12-midnight ~ www.pearsonsarmsbyrichardphillips.co.uk

Tango; owner Emily Auclair

DOG FRIENDLY INNS, HOTELS AND B&Bs

BOUGHTON LEES   TR0147

Eastwell Manor

Eastwell Park, Boughton Lees, Ashford, Kent TN25 4HR (01233) 219955
www.eastwellmanor.co.uk

£120; 23 prettily decorated rms in hotel and 39 in courtyard cottages (some have their own garden and can also be booked on self-catering basis). Fine Jacobean-style manor (actually rebuilt in the 1920s) in 62 acres of grounds and surrounded by a 3,000 acre estate – lots of walks; grand oak-panelled rooms, open fires, comfortable leather seating, antiques and fresh flowers, courteous helpful service and extremely good, creative food in several restaurants; health and fitness spa with 20-metre indoor pool – plus croquet, tennis, boules, golf and outdoor swimming pool; dogs in mews cottages only; £10

BROOKLAND   TQ9825

Royal Oak

High Street, Brookland, Romney Marsh, Kent TN29 9QR (01797) 344215
www.royaloakbrookland.co.uk

£95; 5 comfortable rms. Lovely old building tucked away on Romney Marsh with an airy bar, pews and leather upholstered chairs around oak tables on flagstones, floorboards and ancient bricks, horse racing watercolours on white panelled walls, a woodburning stove, chatty locals by the granite counter, real ales and 17 wines by the glass; the beamed restaurant has Cecil Aldin prints, a big inglenook fireplace and interesting food using carefully sourced produce; lots of surrounding walks; closed Sun evening, Mon; dogs in bedrooms and bar only

CANTERBURY   TR1557

Cathedral Gate

36 Burgate, Canterbury, Kent CT1 2HA (01227) 464381 www.cathgate.co.uk

£90; 27 rms, 12 with own bthrm and some overlooking cathedral. 15th-c hotel that predates the adjoining sculpted cathedral gateway; bow windows, massive oak beams, sloping floors, antiques and fresh flowers in the quiet reading lounge, pubby-style meals and continental breakfast (you can pay extra for full english) in the little dining room, and a restful atmosphere; municipal car parks a few minutes away; dogs in bedrooms

CANTERBURY   TR1457

Thanington Hotel

140 Wincheap, Canterbury, Kent CT1 3RY (01227) 453227 www.thanington-hotel.co.uk

£100; 15 recently refurbished, pretty rms. Thoughtfully run and warmly welcoming family-run hotel with elegant little rooms, a good-sized bar with a huge choice of malt whiskies, a cosy residents' lounge, two elegant dining rooms serving enjoyable breakfasts, a sun-trap walled garden, and an indoor swimming pool; dogs in bedrooms

DOVER
TR3241

Hubert House

9 Castle Hill Road, Dover, Kent CT16 1QW (01304) 202253 www.huberthouse.co.uk

£80; 6 pleasant rms. Fine Georgian building just beneath the castle and close to the beach, ferry and clifftop walks; enjoyable breakfasts and home-baked croissants in smart coffee house (open all day) and friendly owners; resident dog; walking area nearby; forecourt parking; resident slovakian rough-haired pointer; dogs in some bedrooms; £8

ST MARGARET'S AT CLIFFE
TR3444

Wallett's Court

Dover Road, Westcliffe, Dover, Kent CT15 6EW (01304) 852424 www.wallettscourt.com

£150; 17 rms, some in converted stable block. Fine, family-run old manor house in wild landscape, with 13th-c cellars, beams, antiques, comfortable seating and a winter open fire in the lounge, good, interesting food using the best local produce in the conservatory and restaurant (all day light meals and afternoon teas, too), particularly friendly and helpful service, and seats on the terrace; swimming pool, spa and gym, and tennis; handy for the ferries; dogs in some bedrooms and lounge

THURNHAM
TQ8057

Black Horse

Pilgrims Way, Thurnham, Maidstone, Kent ME14 3LD (01622) 737185 www.wellieboot.net

£85; 16 pretty rms in separate annexe. Family-run, 18th-c inn beneath the North Downs (good nearby walks) with a characterful bar with hops, beams, real ales, daily papers and an open log fire, a wide choice of enjoyable food in the neat, airy restaurant, friendly staff and a pleasant garden with partly covered back terrace, water features and nice views; dogs in bedrooms, bring own bedding; £6

TUNBRIDGE WELLS
TQ5839

Hotel du Vin

Crescent Road, Tunbridge Wells, Kent TN1 2LY (01892) 526455 www.hotelduvin.com/hotels/tunbridge-wells

£160; 34 well equipped, chic rms. Handsome sandstone building with a relaxed atmosphere and comfortable sofas and chairs in two lounge rooms, good modern cooking in the airy, high-ceilinged and informal bistro-style restaurant (the french-style Sunday brunch is proving popular), and particularly good wines; seats on the terrace and in garden; dogs in bedrooms; bowls and beds available

Lancashire
with Greater Manchester and Merseyside

MAP 7

DOG FRIENDLY PUBS

BISPHAM GREEN   SD4813
Eagle & Child
Maltkiln Lane (Parbold–Croston road, off B5246); L40 3SG

Successful all-rounder with antiques in stylishly simple interior, enterprising food, an interesting range of beers, appealing rustic garden

Charming and stylish, this is a carefully run country pub with a friendly, civilised atmosphere. It's largely open-plan and discerningly furnished with a lovely mix of small old oak chairs, an attractive oak coffer, several handsomely carved antique oak settles (the finest apparently made partly from a 16th-c wedding bed-head), old hunting prints and engravings, and low hop-draped beams. There are red walls and coir matting up a step and oriental rugs on ancient flagstones in front of the fine old stone fireplace and counter; the pub's dogs are called Betty and Doris. Friendly young staff serve Thwaites Original alongside five guests from brewers such as Copper Dragon, George Wright and Phoenix, a farm cider, decent wines and around 30 malt whiskies. They hold a popular beer festival over the first May bank holiday weekend. The gently rustic spacious garden has a well tended but unconventional bowling green, and beyond this, a wild area that is home to crested newts and moorhens. Selling interesting wines and pottery, the terrific shop housed in the handsome side barn includes a proper butcher and a deli.

Free house ~ Licensee David Anderson ~ Real ale ~ Bar food (12-2, 5.30-8.30(9 Fri, Sat); 12-8.30 Sun) ~ (01257) 462297 ~ Children welcome ~ Dogs allowed in bar ~ Open 12-3, 5.30-11; 12-11 Sat; 12-10.30 Sun ~ www.ainscoughs.co.uk

GREAT MITTON   SD7139
Three Fishes
Mitton Road (B6246, off A59 NW of Whalley); BB7 9PQ

Stylish modern revamp, tremendous attention to detail, excellent regional food with contemporary twist, interesting drinks

Readers have high praise for all aspects of this particularly attractive and imaginatively converted pub. Despite its size it's cleverly laid out with plenty of intimate corners; the areas closest to the bar are elegantly traditional with a couple of big stone fireplaces, rugs on polished floors and upholstered stools. Then there's a series of individually furnished and painted rooms with exposed stone walls, careful spotlighting and wooden slatted blinds, ending with another impressive fireplace. Staff are young and friendly and there's a good chatty atmosphere. The long bar counter (with elaborate floral displays) serves Thwaites Nutty Black, Original and Wainwright, a dozen wines by the glass and unusual soft drinks such as locally made sarsaparilla and dandelion and burdock. Overlooking the Ribble Valley, the garden and terrace have tables and perhaps their own summer menu. You write your name on a blackboard when you arrive and they find you when a table becomes free – the system works surprisingly well.

Free house ~ Licensee Andy Morris ~ Real ale ~ Bar food (12-8.30(9 Fri, Sat, 8 Sun)) ~ (01254) 826888 ~ Children welcome ~ Dogs allowed in bar ~ Open 12-11(10.30 Sun) ~ www.thethreefishes.com

LATHOM   SD4510
Ring o' Bells
In Lathom, turn right into Ring o' Bells Lane; L40 5TE

Bustling family-friendly canalside pub, interconnected rooms with antique furniture, six real ales, some sort of food all day and children's inside and outside play areas

Handy for the M6, this red brick Victorian pub is usefully open for some sort of food all day – starting with morning coffee and cakes – and there's a good mix of customers, with some emphasis on families. Several interconnected rooms of all sizes lead from the handsome central bar counter with its pretty inlaid tiles, and throughout there are all manner of antique dining chairs and carved settles around some lovely old tables, comfortable sofas, rugs on flagstones, lots of paintings and prints of the local area, of sporting activities and of plants, and large mirrors, brass lanterns and standard lamps; staffordshire dogs and decorative plates sit on mantelpieces above open fires. Cumbrian Legendary, Thwaites Nutty Black and Wainwright and guests from brewers such as George Wright, Liverpool Organic and Prospect on handpump, good wines by the glass and over 25 whiskies; background music, TV, darts, board games. Downstairs, there's a more plainly furnished room and indoor and outdoor children's play areas. As we went to press, they had all sorts of plans for their 4 acres of land such as a football pitch, a vegetable garden, a cider orchard – and of course seats and tables by the Liverpool to Leeds Canal.

Free house ~ Licensee Anna Gervasoni ~ Real ale ~ Bar food (12-2, 5-9; 12-9 Sat; 12-8 Sun) ~ Restaurant ~ (01704) 893157 ~ Children welcome ~ Dogs allowed in bar ~ Open 11-11(10 Sun) ~ www.ainscoughs.co.uk

NETHER BURROW   SD6175
Highwayman
A683 S of Kirkby Lonsdale; LA6 2RJ

Substantial and skilfully refurbished old stone house with country interior serving carefully sourced food; lovely gardens

Our readers enjoy their visits to this friendly pub very much and tend to go back again and again. Although large, the stylishly simple flagstoned 17th-c interior is nicely divided into intimate corners, with a couple of big log fires and informal wooden furnishings. Black and white wall prints and placemats show the local farmers and producers used in the cooking and a map on the menu even locates these 'regional food heroes'. Bowland Hen Harrier, Moorhouses Black Cat and Thwaites Bitter and Wainwright on handpump, several wines by the glass, around a dozen whiskies and a particularly good range of soft drinks. They don't take bookings at the weekend (except for groups of six or more), but write your name on a blackboard when you arrive, and they'll find you when a table is free. Service is busy, welcoming and efficient. French windows open to a big terrace and lovely gardens.

Thwaites ~ Lease Andy Morris and Craig Bancroft ~ Real ale ~ Bar food (12-2, 5.30-8.30(8 Sun); reduced menu 2-5.30) ~ (01254) 826888 ~ Children welcome ~ Dogs allowed in bar ~ Open 12-11(10.30 Sun) ~ www.highwaymaninn.co.uk

PLEASINGTON   SD6528
Clog & Billycock

Village signposted off A677 Preston New Road on W edge of Blackburn; Billinge End Road; BB2 6QB

Carefully sourced local food in appealingly modernised stone-built village pub

Even when this skilfully refurbished and extended village pub is at its busiest (which it often deservedly is) staff remain friendly and efficient and the atmosphere is chatty and easy-going. It has the feel of an upmarket barn conversion and is light and airy with flagstoned floors and pale grey walls; a cosier room has high-backed settles and a fireplace at the end. The whole pub is packed with light wooden tables, and although you may find them all full on arrival, such is the size of the place that you probably won't have to wait long in the little bar area for one to come free. Thwaites Lancaster Bomber, Original, Wainwright and a seasonal guest on handpump and a good choice of wines. There are some tables outside, beside a small garden.

Thwaites ~ Lease Andy Morris and Craig Bancroft ~ Real ale ~ Bar food (12-8.30(9 Fri, Sat, 8 Sun)) ~ (01254) 201163 ~ Children welcome ~ Dogs allowed in bar ~ Open 12-11(10.30 Sun) ~ www.theclogandbillycock.com

SAWLEY   SD7746
Spread Eagle

Village signed just off A59 NE of Clitheroe; BB7 4NH

Nicely refurbished pub with imaginative food and riverside restaurant

At the heart of the Ribble Valley and just across a country lane from the river, this is an attractive coaching inn and a lovely place for a drink or a meal. The interior has a lot of character and a pleasing mix of nice old and quirky modern furniture – anything from an old settle and pine tables to new low chairs upholstered in animal print fabric, all set off well by the grey rustic stone floor. Low ceilings, cosy sectioning, a warming fire and cottagey windows keep it all feeling intimate. The dining areas are more formal, with modern stripes, and, as a bit of a quip on the decorative trend for walls of unread books, a bookshelf mural – much easier to keep dust free; background music. Moorhouses Pride of Pendle, Theakstons Lightfoot Bitter, Thwaites Wainwright and a beer named for the pub on handpump and several wines by the glass. They have two smoking porches, and individually furnished, comfortable bedrooms. The pub is handy for exhilarating walks in the Forest of Bowland and close to the substantial ruins of a 12th-c cistercian abbey.

Free house ~ Licensee Kate Peill ~ Real ale ~ Bar food (12-2, 6 9.30; 12-7.30 Sun) ~
Restaurant ~ (01200) 441202 ~ Children welcome ~ Dogs allowed in bar ~ Singer Fri nights
~ Open 11-11(10.30 Sun) ~ www.spreadeaglesawley.co.uk

TUNSTALL
SD6073

Lunesdale Arms

A683 S of Kirkby Lonsdale; LA6 2QN

Emphasis on good imaginative food, separate area with traditional games

Bare boards and lively acoustics give the opened-up interior of this bustling
dining pub a cheerful atmosphere. A white-walled area has a good mix of
stripped dining tables and blue sofas facing each other across a low table (with
daily papers) by a woodburning stove in a solid stone fireplace. Another area has
pews and armchairs (some of the big unframed oil paintings are for sale) and, to
one end, an airy games section with pool, table football, board games and TV. A
snugger little flagstoned back part has another woodburning stove. Black Sheep
and a guest such as Lancaster Blonde on handpump alongside a farm cider. The
church in this Lune Valley village has Brontë associations.

Free house ~ Licensee Emma Gillibrand ~ Real ale ~ Bar food (12-2(2.30 weekends), 6-9) ~
(01524) 274203 ~ Children welcome ~ Dogs allowed in bar ~ Open 11-3, 6-midnight; 11-3.30,
6-1am Sat; 12-4, 6-midnight Sun; closed Mon except bank holidays ~ www.thelunesdale.co.uk

UPPERMILL
SD0006

Church Inn

*From the main street (A607), look out for the sign for Saddleworth Church, and turn off
up this steep narrow lane – keep on up!; OL3 6LW*

**Lively, good value community pub with big range of own-brew beers
at unbeatable bargain prices, lots of pets and good food; children very
welcome**

Next to an isolated church on a steep slope high up on the moors, this
enjoyably quirky pub with fine views down the valley, has plenty of
individual character. The horse-collar on the wall of the bar is worn by the
winner of their annual gurning (face-pulling) championship which is held
during the lively traditional Rush Cart Festival, which is usually over the August
bank holiday. Local bellringers arrive on Wednesdays to practise with a set of
handbells that is kept here, while anyone is invited to join the morris dancers
who meet here on Thursdays. When the water levels from the spring aren't high
enough for brewing, they bring in guest beers such as Black Sheep and Timothy
Taylors Landlord. At other times, you might find up to 11 of their own-brew
Saddleworth beers, usually starting at just £1.20 a pint. Some of the seasonal
ones (look out for Ruebens, Ayrtons, Robyns and Indya) are named after the
licensee's children, only appearing around their birthdays; dark lager on tap, too.
The big unspoilt L-shaped main bar has high beams and some stripped stone,
settles, pews, a good individual mix of chairs and lots of attractive prints and
staffordshire and other china on a high delft shelf, jugs, brasses and so forth; TV
(when there's sport on) and unobtrusive background music; the conservatory
opens on to a terrace. Children will enjoy the burgeoning menagerie of animals,
which includes rabbits, chickens, dogs, ducks, geese, alpacas, horses, 14
peacocks in the next-door field and some cats resident in an adjacent barn; dogs
are made to feel very welcome.

Own brew ~ Licensee Christine Taylor ~ Real ale ~ Bar food (12-2.30, 5.30-9; 12-9 Fri-Sun

and bank holidays) ~ Restaurant ~ (01457) 820902 ~ Children welcome ~ Dogs allowed in
bar ~ Open 12-12(1am Sat) ~ www.thechurchinn.co.uk

WADDINGTON   SD7243

Lower Buck

Edisford Road; BB7 3HU

**Hospitable village pub with reasonably priced, tasty food and five
real ales**

This pretty 18th-c village pub has a chatty, friendly atmosphere and is tucked
away behind the church. There are several small, neatly kept cream-painted
bars and dining rooms, each with a warming coal fire and good solid wood
furnishings on stripped boards. Staff and other customers are chatty and
welcoming and they keep up to five real ales such as Bowland Hen Harrier and
Sawley Tempted, Moorhouses Premier Bitter and Blond Witch, and Timothy
Taylors Landlord on handpump, around a dozen malt whiskies and several
wines by the glass; darts and pool. There are picnic-sets out on cobbles at the
front and in the sunny back garden, and the pub is handily placed for walks in
the Ribble Valley.

Free house ~ Licensee Andrew Warburton ~ Real ale ~ Bar food (12-2.30, 6-9; 12-9 Sat, Sun
and bank holidays) ~ (01200) 423342 ~ Children welcome ~ Dogs allowed in bar ~ Open
11(12 Sun)-11(midnight Sat) ~ www.lowerbuckinn.co.uk

WHALLEY   SD7336

Swan

King Street; BB7 9SN

**Bustling old town inn with cheerful bar, lots of customers and good value
food and drink; bedrooms**

There's always a good mix of customers in this friendly 17th-c former coaching
inn and good value food and beer, too. The cheerful bar is big and nicely
decorated in mushroom, beige and cream with colourful blinds, some modern
artwork, simple dark leather dining chairs around deco-look pedestal tables,
Bowland Hen Harrier and Sawley Tempted and Timothy Taylors Landlord on
handpump and several wines by the glass. A quieter room leads off here with
leather sofas and armchairs on neat bare floorboards; unobtrusive background
music, games machine, and maybe a Wednesday quiz night; service is helpful and
efficient. There are picnic-sets on a back terrace and on grass strips by the car
park. The bedrooms are named after nearby rivers and attractions.

Enterprise ~ Lease Louise Clough ~ Real ale ~ Bar food (12-8.45) ~ Restaurant ~ (01254)
822195 ~ Children welcome ~ Dogs allowed in bar ~ Occasional live music weekends ~
Open 12-11 ~ Bedrooms: £50S/£78S ~ www.swanhotelwhalley.co.uk

DOG FRIENDLY INNS, HOTELS AND B&Bs

BLACKPOOL   SD3037
Imperial Hotel
North Promenade, Blackpool, Lancashire FY1 2HB (01253) 623971
www.pumahotels.co.uk/hotels/northern-england/barcelo-blackpool-imperial-hotel

£107; 180 well equipped rms, many with sea views. Fine Victorian hotel
overlooking the sea, with spacious and comfortable lounges, a bustling, convivial
bar, lots of period features, enjoyable food and fine wines in the smart restaurant
, and a full health and leisure club with indoor swimming pool, gym, sauna and so
forth; lots to do nearby; dogs can walk in the grounds on lead and on the nearby
beach; dogs in bedrooms; not allowed near food areas; £15

COWAN BRIDGE   SD6475
Hipping Hall
Cowan Bridge, Kirkby Lonsdale, Carnforth, Lancashire LA6 2JJ (01524) 271187
www.hippinghall.com

£120; 9 light rms decorated in pretty, pale colours, some overlooking the garden.
Relaxed country-house atmosphere in sensitively furnished hotel – open fires,
big portraits and plenty of comfortable armchairs and sofas in lounges, a lovely
beamed Great Hall with minstrels' gallery, an elegant 15th-c dining room with an
open fire, stripped bare boards, chandeliers and excellent, beautifully presented
food, and a carefully chosen wine list; 4 acres of walled gardens and walks from
front door; dogs in two cottage bedrooms

HURST GREEN   SD6938
Shireburn Arms
Whalley Road, Hurst Green, Clitheroe, Lancashire BB7 9QJ (01254) 826678
www.shireburnarmshotel.co.uk

£75; 22 comfortable rms. Refurbished 17th-c hotel with Ribble Valley views,
a beamed and flagstoned lounge bar with armchairs, sofas and a log fire, well
kept ales, wines by the glass, daily papers, enjoyable food from traditional to
contemporary dishes in the light and airy restaurant, friendly staff and a lovely,
neatly kept garden with an attractive terrace; pretty walks nearby; dogs anywhere
except main restaurant; treats

MANCHESTER   SJ8498
Malmaison
Piccadilly, Manchester M1 3AQ (0161) 278 1000
www.malmaison.com/locations/manchester

£222; 167 chic modern rms. Stylishly contemporary hotel with comfortable
furniture, exotic flower arrangements, bright paintings, very efficient service, an
opulent cocktail bar, a grill serving brasserie-style food, generous breakfasts and
spa; dogs in bedrooms; £30

MORECAMBE
Midland

SD4364

Marine Road West, Morecambe, Lancashire LA4 4BU (01524) 424000
www.englishlakes.co.uk/hotels/lancashire-hotels/the-midland-hotel-morecambe

£130; 44 boutique-style rms. Carefully restored and famous art deco showpiece hotel beside the sea, with chic, minimalist décor, an informal terrace café serving drinks, coffees and snacks all day, an airy, modern restaurant with a glass frontage making the most of the sea views and serving contemporary food using the best local produce (lighter lunches and afternoon teas also), genuinely friendly, helpful staff and a bustling, informal atmosphere; dogs in bedrooms; £10

WADDINGTON
Waddington Arms

SD7243

Clitheroe Road, Waddington, Clitheroe, Lancashire BB7 3HP (01200) 423262
www.waddingtonarms.co.uk

£85; 6 rms. Classic pub with plenty of character and a friendly atmosphere in four linked rooms; low beams, a woodburning stove in huge fireplace, ancient flagstones, antique prints, vintage motor-racing posters and contemporary Laurie Williamson prints, carefully chosen furniture, a good choice of drinks, and enjoyable country cooking; seats on the front terrace look across to the attractive church; good walks (the pub is on the edge of the Forest of Bowland); dogs in bedrooms and bar

WHITEWELL
Inn at Whitewell

SD6546

Dunsop Road, Whitewell, Clitheroe, Lancashire BB7 3AT (01200) 448222
www.innatwhitewell.com

£150; 23 luxury rms, many with open fires. Elegant manor house on the River Hodder with several miles of trout, salmon and sea trout fishing and 6 acres of grounds with valley views; several bars with antique settles, oak tables and sonorous clocks, big attractive prints on powder blue walls, a pubby main room with roaring log fires, daily papers, local maps and guidebooks, an extraordinary wine list and five real ales; well presented bar food, a more elaborate restaurant menu and hearty breakfasts; resident working labradors and spaniels; dogs in bedrooms and bar but not restaurant

Leicestershire
and Rutland

MAPS 4, 7 & 8

DOG FRIENDLY PUBS

BREEDON ON THE HILL   SK4022
Three Horse Shoes
Main Street (A453); DE73 8AN

Comfortable pub with friendly licensees and emphasis on popular food

We particularly enjoyed the interior of this agreeable 18th-c pub. It's been nicely restored and decorated to make the best of its attractive structure. The clean-cut central bar has a stylishly simple feel with heavy worn flagstones, green walls and ceilings, a log fire, pubby tables and a dark wood counter, Marstons Pedigree on handpump, 30 malt whiskies and decent house wines. Beyond here, a dining room has maroon walls, dark pews and cherry-stained tables. The two-room dining area on the right has a comfortably civilised chatty feel with big antique tables set quite closely together on seagrass matting and colourful modern country prints and antique engravings on canary yellow walls. Even at lunchtime there are lighted candles in elegant modern holders. Look out for the quaint conical village lock-up opposite.

Free house ~ Licensees Ian Davison, Jennie Ison, Stuart Marson ~ Real ale ~ Bar food (12-2, 5.30-9) ~ Restaurant ~ (01332) 695129 ~ Dogs allowed in bar ~ Open 11.30-2.30, 5.30-11; 12-3 Sun; closed Sun evening ~ www.thehorseshoes.com

BUCKMINSTER   SK8822
Tollemache Arms
B676 Colsterworth–Melton Mowbray; Main Street; NG33 5SA

Emphasis on good food in stylishly updated pub recently reopened by two enthusiastic young couples

This well run place with its quick and attentive service is notable for both its good food and its keen prices. The stone and brick building is surprisingly stately for a village pub, and the refurbishments suit it well. One rather elegant corner room has comfortable easy chairs around its log fire, and quite a library of books. The series of other linked areas contain a dark leather chesterfield by a low table of magazines and newspapers in another fireside corner, and otherwise a mix of wheelback, dining and stripped kitchen chairs, and some rather nice specially made small pews, around tables set on floorboards; table lamps and standard lamps, big bunches of flowers, and a shelf of board games add a homely touch, and they don't turn up their noses at dogs or muddy boots. There's a good choice of wines by the glass and changing ales from local brewers such as Belvoir, Grainstore and Oakham on handpump, and perhaps discreet nostalgic background music. There are teak tables out on the back grass, by a clump of sycamores; beyond is a small herb and salad garden, and a swing.

Free house ~ Licensees Matt and Amanda Wrisdale ~ Real ale ~ Bar food (12-2 (2.30 Sun), 6.30-9; not Sun evening, Mon) ~ Restaurant ~ (01476) 860477 ~ Children welcome ~ Dogs allowed in bar ~ Open 12-3, 5-11; 12-4 Sun; closed Sun evening, Mon, first week in Jan ~ www.tollemache-arms.co.uk

COLEORTON   SK4117
George
Loughborough Road (A512 E); LE67 8HF

Attractively traditional homely pub with dining area, honest food and drink and large garden

The welcoming atmosphere at this unassumingly comfortable pub is generated by the hands-on friendly licensee couple here. The bar on the right is nicely laid out to give the feel of varied and fairly small separate areas: dark leather sofa and tub chairs by a woodburning stove in front, scatter-cushioned pews and mixed chairs below shelves of books in one corner, and other mixed seating elsewhere. This room has lots of local photographs on its ochre or dove-grey walls, black beams and joists, and a dark-panelled dado. A bigger room on the left, broadly similar and again with plenty to look at, has another woodburning stove, and more of a dining-room feel. Burton Bridge XL, Marstons Pedigree and Timothy Taylors Landlord are on handpump. The spreading garden behind has sturdy wooden furniture among sizeable trees, and a play area.

Free house ~ Licensees Mark and Janice Wilkinson ~ Real ale ~ Bar food (12-2.30(3 Sun), 6-9(9.30 Fri, Sat); not Sun evening, Mon) ~ Restaurant ~ (01530) 834639 ~ Well behaved supervised children welcome ~ Dogs allowed in bar ~ Open 12-3.30, 5.30-11; 12-11 Sat; 12-4 Sun; closed Sun evening, Mon ~ www.georgeinncoleorton.co.uk

COTTESMORE   SK9013
Sun
B668 NE of Oakham; LE15 7DH

Nice village pub with friendly staff and reasonably priced food

This attractive 17th-c thatched and white-painted village pub is run by friendly licensees. Décor is simple and homely, with stripped pine and plush stools on flagstones, an inglenook fire and lots of pictures and ornaments. The carpeted back restaurant has white walls and dark wheelback chairs. Friendly staff serve Everards Tiger, a seasonal Everards beer, a guest from a brewer such as Oakham and a farm cider; background music. There are picnic-sets in front of the building with more in the large garden.

Everards ~ Tenants Neil and Karen Hornsby ~ Real ale ~ Bar food (12-2, 6-9; 12-4 Sun) ~ Restaurant ~ (01572) 812321 ~ Children welcome ~ Dogs allowed in bar ~ Open 11.30-11(10 Sun) ~ www.everards.co.uk

LEICESTER   SK5804
Rutland & Derby Arms
Millstone Lane; nearby metered parking; LE1 5JN

Neatly kept modern town bar with interesting food from deli counter, impressive drinks range, sheltered courtyard

The neat cream-walled courtyard at this city tavern shelters some sunny picnic-sets and there are more on an upper terrace. It's fairly staid on the outside, but the open-plan interior has a pleasing clean-cut modernity. There are comfortable bar chairs by the long counter, padded high seats including one unusual high banquette by chunky tall tables, a few small prints of classic film posters and the like; apart from some stripped brick, décor in shades of ochre and coffee. Cocktails (they have an impressive array of spirits), and soft drink cocktails are offered, and there are various foreign beers on tap alongside Adnams Broadside, four Everards beers and a guest such as Charles Wells Bombardier on handpump, a farm cider, 20 wines by the glass and 20 whiskies; bright pleasant service, well reproduced background music, games machine.

Everards ~ Tenant Samuel Hagger ~ Real ale ~ Bar food (12-8) ~ (0116) 2623299 ~ Children welcome ~ Dogs allowed in bar ~ Open 12-11 (2am Sat); closed Sun ~ http://www.everards.co.uk/pubs/rutland__derby_122/

OAKHAM   SK8509
Grainstore
Station Road, off A606; LE15 6RE

Super own-brewed beers in a converted railway grain warehouse, friendly staff, cheerful customers and pubby food

Most of this former Victorian grain store's customers are here to try the own-brewed beers and the friendly staff will happily let them taste a sample or two before they decide. There are ten real ales which are served traditionally at the left end of the bar counter and through swan necks with sparklers on the right. As per the traditional tower system of production, the beer is brewed on the upper floors of the building, directly above the down-to-earth bar. During working hours you'll hear the busy noises of the brewery workings rumbling above your head. The décor is plain and functional with wide well worn floorboards, bare ceiling boards above massive joists supported by red metal pillars, a long brick-built bar counter with cast-iron bar stools, tall cask tables and simple elm chairs; games machine, darts, board games, giant Jenga and bottle-walking. In summer they pull back the huge glass doors, opening the bar up to a terrace with picnic-sets, often stacked with barrels. You can tour the brewery by arrangement, they do takeaways, and hold a real ale festival with over 80 real ales and live music during the August bank holiday weekend; disabled access.

Own brew ~ Licensee Peter Atkinson ~ Real ale ~ Bar food (11.30-3; no evening food except Weds; all day Sat-Sun) ~ (01572) 770065 ~ Children welcome till 8pm ~ Dogs allowed in bar ~ Open 11-11(midnight Fri); 9am-midnight Sat; 9am-10.30pm Sun ~ www.grainstorebrewery.com

OAKHAM   SK8608

Lord Nelson
Market Place; LE15 6DT

Splendidly restored as proper relaxed grown-up pub, full of interest; open all day from 9am and with excellent pizzas (choose your own toppings)

Taken deftly in hand by Michael Thurlby, who redeveloped the Tobie Norris in Stamford so successfully that it won our Newcomer of the Year Award in 2012, this handsome old building now has over half a dozen rooms spread over two floors, giving plenty of companionable places for chatty relaxation. It's worth having a good look round before you decide where to sit: you can choose from cushioned church pews, leather elbow chairs, long oak settles, sofas, armchairs – or, to watch the passing scene, a big bow window seat; carpet, bare boards, or ancient red and black tiles; paintwork in soft shades of ochre, canary yellow, sage or pink, or William Morris wallpaper. There's plenty to look at, too, from intriguing antique Police News and other prints – plenty of Nelson, of course – to the collections of mullers, copper kettles and other homely bric-a-brac in the heavy-beamed former kitchen with its Aga. But the main thing is simply the easy-going good-natured atmosphere. They have well kept Adnams Southwold and Castle Rock Harvest Pale on handpump, with three good guests on our visit – Exmoor Fox, Gales Spring Sprinter and Newby Wyke HM Queen Elizabeth; also Weston's farm cider, and a good changing choice of wines by the glass. Staff are helpful and efficient, and clearly love working here. The resident king charles spaniel is called Buzz.

Free house ~ Licensee Adam Dale ~ Real ale ~ Bar food (12-2.30,6-9; not Sun evening) ~ (01572) 868340 ~ Over-4s allowed till 8pm away from bar; no pushchairs ~ Dogs allowed in bar ~ Open 9am-11pm(midnight Fri and Sat); 12-11 Sun ~ www.thelordnelsonoakham.com

PEGGS GREEN   SK4117

New Inn
Signposted off A512 Ashby–Shepshed at roundabout, then turn immediately left down Zion Hill towards Newbold; pub is 100 metres down on the right, with car park on opposite side of road; LE67 8JE

Intriguing bric-a-brac in unspoilt pub, friendly welcome, good value food and drinks; cottagey garden

With its genial irish licensees and chatty locals, this simple and unspoilt little pub is a real gem – one reader tells us this it's 'probably the most friendly pub we've ever been in'. Quirky and quite unique-feeling, the two cosy tiled front rooms are filled with a diverting collection of old bric-a-brac that covers almost every inch of the walls and ceilings. The little room on the left, a bit like an old kitchen parlour (they call it the Cabin), has china on the mantelpiece, lots of prints and photographs and little collections of this and that, three old cast-iron tables, wooden stools and a small stripped kitchen table. The room to the right has nice stripped panelling and more appealing bric-a-brac. The small back Best room, with a stripped-wood floor, has a touching display of old local photographs including some colliery ones. Bass, Caledonian Deuchars IPA and Marstons Pedigree on handpump; background music and board games. There are plenty of seats in front of the pub, with more in the peaceful back garden. Do check their unusual opening times below carefully.

Enterprise ~ Lease Maria Christina Kell ~ Real ale ~ Bar food (12-2, Mon, Fri and Sat, 6-8 Mon; filled baps might be available at other times) ~ (01530) 222293 ~ Children welcome ~ Dogs allowed in bar ~ Quiz Thurs, folk club monthly second Mon ~ Open 12-2.30, 5.30-11; 12-3, 6.30-11 Sat; 12-3, 7-10.30 Sun; closed Tues-Thurs lunchtimes ~ www.thenewinnpeggsgreen.co.uk

SILEBY   SK6015

White Swan

Off A6 or A607 N of Leicester; in centre turn into King Street (opposite church), then after mini-roundabout turn right at Post Office signpost into Swan Street; LE12 7NW

Exemplary town local, a boon to its chatty regulars, its good honest home cooking luring others from further afield

In the same hands for nearly 30 years now, this solidly built red-brick pub has all the touches that marked the best of between-the-wars estate pub design, such as its deco-tiled lobby, the polychrome-tiled fireplaces, the shiny red anaglypta ceiling and the comfortable layout of linked but separate areas including a small restaurant (now lined with books). It's packed with bric-a-brac from bizarre hats to decorative plates and lots of prints, and quickly draws you in with its genuinely bright and cheerful welcome; this, along with its food and the can-do attitude of the helpful staff, is what sets it above the thousands of other good locals. Fullers London Pride is on handpump, and they stock good value house wines.

Free house ~ Licensee Theresa Miller ~ Real ale ~ Bar food (12-1.30, 6-8.30; not Sat lunchtime, Sun evening, Mon) ~ (01509) 814832 ~ Children welcome ~ Dogs allowed in bar ~ Open 12-2, 6-11; 12-3 Sun; closed Sat lunchtime, Sun evening and Mon and 1-6 Jan ~ www.whiteswansileby.co.uk

STATHERN   SK7731

Red Lion

Off A52 W of Grantham via the brown-signed Belvoir road (keep on towards Harby -Stathern signposted on left); or off A606 Nottingham–Melton Mowbray via Long Clawson and Harby; LE14 4HS

Fine range of drinks and popular food in country-style dining pub with open fires and good garden with a play area; own shop, too

You'll find the same high standards at this rather civilised dining pub as you will at its sister pub, the Olive Branch in Clipsham. It's decorated in a charming rustic style, staff are welcoming and the atmosphere throughout is relaxed and informal. The yellow room on the right, with its collection of wooden spoons and lambing chairs, has a simple country-pub feel. The lounge bar has sofas, an open fire and a big table with books, newspapers and magazines. It leads off the smaller, more traditional flagstoned bar with terracotta walls, another fireplace with a pile of logs beside it and lots of beams and hops. A little room with tables set for eating leads to the long, narrow, main dining room, and out to a nicely arranged suntrap lawn and terrace with good hardwood furnishings; background music. Red Lion Ale (from Grainstore) and a couple of guests such as Batemans XB and Caledonian Deuchars IPA are on handpump, with draught belgian and continental bottled beers, several ciders and a varied wine list (several by the glass). There's an unusually big play area behind the car park with swings, climbing frames and so on.

Free house ~ Licensees Sean Hope and Ben Jones ~ Real ale ~ Bar food (12-2(4 Sun), 7-9;

not Sun evening, Mon) ~ Restaurant ~ (01949) 860868 ~ Children welcome ~
Dogs allowed in bar ~ Open 12-3, 6-11; 12-11 Sat; 12-8 Sun; closed Mon ~
www.theredlioninn.co.uk

STRETTON   SK9415

Jackson Stops

Rookery Lane; a mile or less off A1, at B668 (Oakham) exit; follow village sign, turning off Clipsham Road into Manor Road, pub on left; LE15 7RA

Attractive thatched former farmhouse with good food, just off A1

This 16th-c stone inn has one of the only two nurdling benches left in Britain.
It's a place of great character and the rooms meander around filled with lots
of lovely period features. The black-beamed country bar down on the left has wall
timbering, a couple of bar stools, a cushioned wall pew and an elderly settle on
the worn tile and brick floor, and a coal fire in one corner. Phipps IPA made for
them by Grainstore and Oakham JHB on handpump alongside several wines by
the glass. The smarter main room on the right is light and airy with a nice mix of
ancient and modern tables on dark blue carpet, and another coal fire in a stone
corner fireplace. Past the bar, is the dining room with stripped-stone walls, a tiled
floor and an old open cooking range, and there's a second smaller dining room;
background music.

Free house ~ Licensee Robert Reid ~ Real ale ~ Bar food (12-2.30, 6.30-9; not Sun
evening, Mon) ~ Restaurant ~ (01780) 410237 ~ Children welcome ~ Dogs allowed in bar
~ Open 12-3, 6-1.30(11 Fri and Sat); 12-5 Sun; closed Sun evening and Mon ~
www.thejacksonstops.com

WYMONDHAM   SK8518

Berkeley Arms

Main Street; LE14 2AG

Pleasant village pub with interesting food and sunny terrace

Feeling a little like home-from-home, this friendly golden stone 16th c inn has
a welcoming relaxed feel with its knick-knacks, magazines, table lamps and
cushions. At one end two wing chairs are set on the patterned carpet beside a
low coffee table and a cosy log fire. The red-tiled dining area, dense with stripped
beams and standing timbers is furnished with kitchen-style with light wood tables
and red-cushioned chunky chairs, or you can eat in the smarter dining area with
its dark leather chairs. Real ales include Greene King IPA, Marstons Pedigree and
a guest such as Hopback Glass Hopper; ten wines are offered by the glass, and
they keep a local cider. Outside in front, on small terraces to either side of the
entrance, picnic-sets benefit from the sun nearly all day.

Free house ~ Licensee Louise Hitchen ~ Real ale ~ Bar food (12-2(3 Sun), 6-9 Tues-
Thurs; 6-9.30 Fri, Sat; not Sun evening, Mon lunchtime) ~ Restaurant ~ (01572) 787587 ~
Children welcome ~ Dogs allowed in bar ~ Open 12-3(5 Sun), 6-11; closed Sun evening, Mon
lunchtime, first 2 weeks of Jan, 1 week in summer ~ www.theberkeleyarms.co.uk

DOG FRIENDLY INNS, HOTELS AND B&Bs

CLIPSHAM   SK9616
Olive Branch
Main Street, Clipsham, Oakham, Rutland LE15 7SH (01780) 410355
www.theolivebranchpub.com

£175; 6 lovely rms in Beech House just opposite. Civilised inn with various small
but charmingly attractive bars, rustic chairs around candlelit tables, dark joists
and beams, a log fire in the stone inglenook, lots of books (sometimes for sale),
a carefully chosen range of drinks (a fine choice of whiskies, armagnacs and
cognacs), extremely highly thought of food, delicious breakfasts, seats on a pretty
terrace with more on a neat lawn; dogs in ground floor bedrooms and bar; £10

EXTON   SK9211
Fox & Hounds
19 The Green, Exton, Oakham, Rutland LE15 8AP (01572) 812403
www.foxandhoundsrutland.co.uk

£70; 4 spotlessly clean rms. Handsome and friendly, this well run place has a
traditionally civilised lounge bar with red plush seats around pine tables, fresh
flowers, a winter log fire in a big stone fireplace, and real ales and wines served
by helpful staff; the popular food is cooked by the landlord and the breakfasts are
very good; Rutland Water and the gardens at Barnsdale are both close by; dogs in
bedrooms and bar

HINCKLEY   SP4292
Sketchley Grange
Sketchley Lane, Hinckley, Burbage, Leicestershire LE10 3HU (01455) 251133
www.sketchleygrange.co.uk

£97.50; 95 attractive modern rms. In its own grounds with country views, this
mock-Tudor hotel is a friendly, relaxed place with a lounge and bar for morning
coffees, light lunches, afternoon teas and evening cocktails, a main restaurant
overlooking the garden with a wide range of cosmopolitan food, and a leisure
club with a sauna, spa and indoor swimming pool; small dogs in bedrooms; £10

LYDDINGTON   SP8797
Marquess of Exeter
52 Main Street, Lyddington, Oakham, Leicestershire LE15 9LT (01572) 822477
www.marquessexeter.co.uk

£89.50; 17 rms. Carefully re-worked inside, this friendly stone inn has attractive
historic features like flagstones, thick walls, beams and exposed stonework, and
the spacious open-plan areas have stylish furnishings, several open fires, real ales
and a dozen wines by the glass, and excellent food cooked by the landlord; seats
in the tree-sheltered gardens seem to merge with the countryside beyond; the
charming village is worth strolling around; dogs in bedrooms and bar; £10

MELTON MOWBRAY   SK7319
Sysonby Knoll
Asfordby Road, Melton Mowbray, Leicestershire LE13 0HP (01664) 563563
www.sysonby.com

£98; 30 individually styled rms. Family-run Edwardian brick house on the edge of a bustling market town, with period-style furnishings in the reception and lounge areas, winter open fires, friendly owners and excellent service, a wide choice of brasserie-style food in the airy restaurant or bar, and 5 acres of landscaped gardens and meadows (where dogs may walk) leading down to the River Eye where guests can fish; walks from the door, too; dogs welcome away from restaurant; one dog free, additional dogs £5

OAKHAM   SK9110
Barnsdale Lodge Hotel
The Avenue, Oakham, Leicestershire LE15 8AH (01572) 724678
www.barnsdalelodge.co.uk

£120; 44 individually decorated rms. 18th-c former farmhouse on the north shore of Rutland Water, with a relaxed atmosphere in the comfortable lounge and bar, conservatory and smart main dining room, very good food from smashing breakfasts, nibbles and quick bites and light lunches to more formal evening choices using home-grown vegetables and their own eggs and other top quality, seasonal local produce, and friendly, helpful staff; seats under parasols on the terrace; dogs in bedrooms; £10

ROTHLEY   SK5712
Rothley Court
Westfield Lane, Rothley, Leicestershire LE7 7LG (0116) 237 4141
www.oldenglishinns.co.uk

£80; 30 rms of individual character, some in court annexe. Mentioned in the Domesday Book, this carefully run manor house with its beautifully preserved 13th-c chapel has some fine oak panelling, open fires, stained glass windows, suits of armour, a comfortable bar and lounge, a conservatory, a beamed restaurant with a huge stone fireplace, a wide choice of good food, and courteous staff; seats out on the terrace and in the neatly kept gardens; walks in nearby Charnwood Forest; dogs in ground floor and annexe rooms; £10

STAPLEFORD   SK8118
Stapleford Park
Stapleford, Melton Mowbray, Leicestershire LE14 2EF (01572) 787522
www.staplefordpark.com

£288; 55 individually designed rms in main house or in cottages. Luxurious country house, extravagantly restored, in 500 acres of grounds with riding, shooting, falconry, and an 18-hole championship golf course; lots of opulent furnishings, fine oil paintings and an impressive library, delicious food in the smart restaurant or more informal dining areas, and warmly welcoming staff; health spa with treatment rooms and pool complex; dogs in bedrooms (not to be left unattended) and most public areas; £15

UPPINGHAM   SP8699

Lake Isle

16 High Street East, Uppingham, Oakham, Rutland LE15 9PZ (01572) 822951
www.lakeislehotel.co.uk

£80; 12 lovely, well equipped rms. In a charming market town, this 18th-c restaurant-with-rooms has an open fire in the attractive lounge, a comfortable bar, good, imaginative food, enjoyable afternoon teas and excellent breakfasts, a carefully chosen wine list and a small, pretty garden; dogs in bedrooms; £10

WING   SK8902

Kings Arms

Top Street, Wing, Oakham, Rutland LE15 8SE (01572) 737634
www.thekingsarms-wing.co.uk

£100; 7 rms. Neatly kept old place with lots of chatty customers, an attractive low-beamed bar with two big log fires and various nooks and crannies, stripped stone walls and flagstoned or wood-strip floors, real ales and a super choice of wines by the glass; the cooking is inventive and modern (they have their own smokehouse – you can buy produce to take away as well) and the breakfasts are good; there's a medieval turf maze just up the road; walks all around; dogs in bedrooms, bar, snug, reception; dog menu; £10

WOODHOUSE EAVES   SK5313

Wheatsheaf

90 Brand Hill, Woodhouse Eaves, Loughborough, Leicestershire LE12 8SS (01509) 890320
www.wheatsheafinn.net

£80; 2 well equipped rms. Smart and hospitable country inn with traditionally furnished bar areas, log fires, interesting motor-racing, family RAF and flying memorabilia, real ales and decent wines by the glass; a cosy dining area serves tasty pubby dishes and the atmosphere is cheerful and easy-going; lots of seats on the floodlit, heated terrace; resident dogs; dogs in bedrooms and bar

Lincolnshire

MAP 8

DOG FRIENDLY PUBS

DRY DODDINGTON   SK8546

Wheatsheaf

Main Street; 1.5 miles off A1 N of Grantham; NG23 5HU

Happy, bustling pub with good food cooked by chef/patron; handy for A1

The welcome at this 16th-c colour-washed village pub is consistently warm and friendly. It's well run by an enthusiastic young couple – the landlord is the chef. Popular with visitors and locals alike, the front bar is basically two rooms, with a woodburning stove, a variety of settles and chairs, and tables in the windows facing across to the green and the lovely 14th-c church with its crooked tower. The serving bar on the right has Batemans XB, Greene King Abbot, Timothy Taylors Landlord and a guest on handpump, and a nice choice of over a dozen wines by the glass. A slight slope takes you down to the extended dining room, comfortable with its thick carpet and relaxing red and cream décor. Once a cow byre, this part is even more ancient than the rest of the building, perhaps dating from the 13th c; background music. The front terrace has neat dark green tables under cocktail parasols, among tubs of flowers; disabled access at the side.

Free house ~ Licensees Dan and Kate Bland ~ Real ale ~ Bar food (12-2.30(4 Sun),6-9 (5-7 Sun); not Sun evening, Mon) ~ Restaurant ~ (01400) 281458 ~ Children welcome ~ Dogs allowed in bar ~ Open 12-3, 5-11; 12-11 Sat, Sun; closed Mon except bank holidays ~ www.wheatsheaf-pub.co.uk

GREAT CASTERTON   SK9909

Plough

B1081, just off A1 N of Stamford (coming from the S or returning to A1 southbound, use A606 junction instead); Main Street; PE9 4AA

Cheerful atmosphere and good food in well run comfortably modernised pub, handy for A1

The landlady keeps a kindly eye on everything at this homely pub, so as well as good service and tasty food the details work well too: good coffee, for instance, and unusual bar nibbles such as warmed chorizo. A good choice of wines by the glass and Greene King IPA and a guest such as Wychwood Hobgoblin on handpump are served from a counter with comfortable leather-and-chrome bar stools. The unassuming carpeted bar on the left is small and quite brightly decorated with colourful scatter cushions on seats built into the wall, and light and airy with its big bow window. There may be unobtrusive background music (Peggy Lee and the like) and board games. The main lounge bar, also carpeted, has a mix of dark pub tables and some banquette seating as well as dining chairs. The good-sized garden, like the pub itself kept very neatly, has well spaced picnic-sets by a big weeping willow, with swings and a rabbit hutch; there are also tables on a small wood-screened terrace.

Punch ~ Tenants Peter Lane and Amy Thompson ~ Real ale ~ Bar food (12-2.30(3 Sun), 6-9.30; not Sun evening, Mon) ~ Restaurant ~ (01780) 762178 ~ Children welcome ~ Dogs allowed in bar ~ Open 12-3, 6-11(11.30 Sat); closed Sun evening, Mon, 1 week in Jan ~ www.theplough-greatcasterton.co.uk

HEIGHINGTON   TF0369
Butcher & Beast
High Street; LN4 1JS

Traditional village pub with terrific range of drinks, pubby food and a pretty garden by a stream

It's the friendly, hard-working licensees that make this homely pub so enjoyable. You can be sure of a warm welcome, and there's always something going on here, with events ranging from beer festivals and quizzes to themed food evenings. The simply furnished bar has button-back wall banquettes, pubby furnishings and stools along the counter where they keep half a dozen real ales including Batemans XB, XXXB, Victory and three guests from brewers such as Blue Monkey, Castle Rock and Everards, a dozen bottled beers, four ciders, two dozen malt whiskies and 20 gins; occasional TV. The Snug now has red-cushioned wall settles and high-backed wooden dining chairs, and the refurbished, beamed dining room is neatly set with proper tablecloths and napkins; throughout, the cream walls are hung with old village photos and country pictures. There are picnic-sets on a lawn that runs down to a stream and the award-winning hanging baskets and tubs are very pretty in summer.

Batemans ~ Tenants Mal and Diane Gray ~ Real ale ~ Bar food (12-2, 5.30-8; 12-4 Sun; not Sun evening) ~ Restaurant ~ (01522) 790386 ~ Children welcome away from bar area ~ Dogs allowed in bar ~ Quiz Thurs ~ Open 12-11(10.30 Sun) ~ www.butcherandbeast.co.uk

STAMFORD   TF0307
Tobie Norris
St Pauls Street; PE9 2BE

Great period atmosphere in a warren of ancient rooms, splendid choice of drinks, nice pub food, pleasant courtyard

Centuries old, beautifully restored and full of character, this lovely place is a quite charming series of little rooms. Add careful attention by friendly staff, a fine changing range of wines, well kept Adnams and (from the owner's microbrewery) Ufford White Hart on handpump, three guest beers including ones from Adnams and Ufford, and Weston's organic farm cider, and you get a most enjoyable, relaxed and easy-going atmosphere – particularly liked by the two labradoodles Fraggle and Sprocket, it appears. Refurbishments really have made the made the most of the building's age – worn flagstones, meticulously stripped stonework, huge hearth for one room's woodburning stove, and steeply pitched rafters in one of the two upstairs rooms. Furnishings here run from pews and heavy leatherette wall settles to comfortable armchairs, with flickering church candles, and abundant books and antique prints. Downstairs, several linked rooms include a handsomely panelled shrine to Nelson and the Battle of Trafalgar on the left. These open off a spinal corridor, glass-roofed at the far end, to make a snug conservatory that opens to a narrow but sunny two-level courtyard with cast-iron tables, hanging baskets and plant tubs.

Free house ~ Licensee William Fry ~ Real ale ~ Bar food (12-2.30, 6-9; not Sun evening) ~ (01780) 753800 ~ Children over 10 at lunchtimes ~ Dogs allowed in bar ~ Open 11-11(midnight Fri, Sat); 12-10.30 Sun ~ www.tobienorris.com

DOG FRIENDLY INNS, HOTELS AND B&Bs

STAMFORD   TF0306
George of Stamford

High Street, St Martins, Stamford, Lincolnshire PE9 2LB (01780) 750750
www.georgehotelofstamford.com

£150; 47 lovely rms. Ancient former coaching inn, civilised and relaxed, with a surprisingly pubby bar, various other rooms with leather, cane and antique wicker seats and soft sofas and armchairs, a particularly striking central lounge with heavy beams, sturdy timbers, broad flagstones and massive stonework, and quite a choice of impressive food, served by professional staff in the Garden Room, sedate panelled formal restaurant and in the lovely courtyard (partly covered); good morning coffees, afternoon teas and breakfasts; the walled garden is immaculately kept and there's a sunken lawn where croquet is often played; dogs in bedrooms and bar

WASHINGBOROUGH   TF0170
Washingborough Hall

Church Hill, Washingborough, Lincoln, Lincolnshire LN4 1BE (01522) 790340
www.washingboroughhall.com

£135; 12 rms, some contemporary with bold wallpaper and some with four-posters. Lovely and elegant family-run Georgian house in 3 acres of gardens, with carefully restored rooms – a convivial bar, deeply comfortable reception/lounge, open fires and woodburning stoves, enjoyable food in elegant dining rooms and smart restaurant overlooking the grounds, and seats under parasols on the terrace; dogs in bedrooms; £10

WINTERINGHAM   SE9322
Winteringham Fields

1 Silver Street, Winteringham, Scunthorpe, Lincolnshire DN15 9ND (01724) 733096
www.winteringhamfields.co.uk

£200; 11 pretty rms (3 off courtyard). Family-run restaurant-with-rooms in 16th-c manor house with comfortable and attractive Victorian furnishings, beams and open fires, excellent, inventive and beautifully presented food, super breakfasts, friendly service, and an admirable wine list; miles of walks directly from door; dogs in courtyard bedrooms (not to be left unattended); £10

WOODHALL SPA
TF1963

Petwood

Stixwould Road, Woodhall Spa, Lincolnshire LN10 6QG (01526) 352411
www.petwood.co.uk

£100; 53 smart rms. Sizeable Edwardian house in 30 acres of mature woodland and gardens, with a putting green and croquet lawn; many original features including a fine main staircase, an informal bar where light lunches are served overlooking the terrace and grounds, a traditionally furnished restaurant and comfortable lounge, enjoyable food from breakfasts to afternoon teas and evening meals, and helpful, courteous service; dogs in bedrooms and public rooms (not during food service); £20

WOOLSTHORPE
SK8334

Chequers

Main Street, Woolsthorpe, Grantham, Lincolnshire NG32 1LU (01476) 870701
www.chequersinn.net

£70; 4 simply furnished rms. 17th-c former coaching inn with views of Belvoir Castle from seats outside; a heavily beamed bar with two huge oak tables surrounded by handsome leather chairs and banquettes, a big boar's head above a log fire in the brick fireplace, cartoons on the walls, real ales, 50 malts and 35 wines by the glass, and interesting modern food in both the dining room (once the village bakery) and the airy restaurant; miles of open country walks on the Belvoir Estate; resident springer spaniels, Hector and Ruby; dogs in bedrooms and bar; £5

Toby – cockerpoo; owners Martin and Jan Jones

Norfolk

DOG FRIENDLY PUBS

BLAKENEY   TG0243
White Horse
Off A149 W of Sheringham; High Street; NR25 7AL

Cheerful small hotel with popular dining conservatory, interesting food and drinks and helpful staff; bedrooms

The new landlord has given this bustling former coaching inn a stylish make-over and made some other gentle changes, too. The informal long bar has cream-coloured walls above a pale grey dado hung with fine art equestrian prints and paintings from a local gallery, high-backed brown leather dining and other chairs around light oak tables on the new black and white striped carpet and natural coloured linen window blinds; Adnams Bitter, Broadside, Ghost Ship and a seasonal guest on handpump and a dozen wines by the glass. There's also an airy conservatory. The suntrap courtyard and pleasant paved garden both have plenty of tables, and the inn is just a stroll from the small tidal harbour. This area is a haven for bird-watchers and sailors.

Free house ~ Licensee Francis Guildea ~ Real ale ~ Bar food (12-2.15, 6-9) ~ Restaurant ~ (01263) 740574 ~ Children welcome ~ Dogs allowed in bar ~ Open 11-11 ~ Bedrooms: /£100S ~ www.blakeneywhitehorse.co.uk

BURSTON   TM1383
Crown
Village signposted off A140 N of Scole; Mill Road; IP22 5TW

Relaxed village pub usefully open all day, with a warm welcome, real ales and well liked bar food

As this village pub is open all day, there are always customers dropping in and out and the atmosphere is easy-going and friendly. Locals tend to gather in an area by the bar counter, with its high bar chairs, where they serve Adnams Bitter, Greene King Abbot and guests such as Elmtree Norfolks 80 Shilling Ale and Nethergate Britains Best on handpump, two farm ciders and several wines by the glass. In cold weather, the best place to sit in this heavy-beamed, quarry-tiled room is on the comfortably cushioned sofas in front of the big log fire in its huge brick fireplace, and there are also some stools by the low chunky wooden table and newspapers and magazines to read. The public bar on the left has a nice long table and panelled settle on an old brick floor in one alcove, another sofa, straightforward tables and chairs on the carpet by the pool table, games machine and juke box, and up a step, more tables and chairs. Both of these cream-painted rooms are hung with cheerful naive local character paintings; background music and board games. The simply furnished, beamed dining room has another big brick fireplace. Outside, there's a smokers' shelter, a couple of picnic-sets in front of the old brick building and more seats in a hedged-off area with a barbecue.

Free house ~ Licensees Bev and Steve Kembery and Jonathan Piers-Hall ~ Real ale ~ Bar food (12-2(4 Sun), 6.30-9; not Sun evening) ~ Restaurant ~ (01379) 741257 ~ Children welcome ~ Dogs allowed in bar ~ Open 12-11(10.30 Sun) ~ www.burstoncrown.com

CASTLE ACRE   TF8115
Ostrich
Stocks Green; PE32 2AE

Friendly old coaching inn with original features, fine old fireplaces, real ales and tasty food

Wandering around the various rooms in this handsome 16th-c former coaching inn you can still see some of the original masonry and beams and trusses in the lofty ceilings, although the place was largely rebuilt in the 18th-c. The L-shaped low-ceilinged front bar (on two levels) has a woodburning stove in a huge old fireplace, lots of wheelback chairs and cushioned pews around pubby tables on the wood-strip floor and gold patterned wallpaper; a step leads up to an area in front of the bar counter where there are similar seats and tables and a log fire in a brick fireplace. Greene King IPA, Abbot and Old Speckled Hen and a seasonal guest beer on handpump, a dozen wines (including fizz) by the glass and several malt whiskies. There's a separate dining room with another brick fireplace. The sheltered garden has picnic-sets under parasols and the inn faces the tree-lined village green. There are some remains of a Norman castle in the village as well as a cluniac monastery.

Greene King ~ Tenant Tiffany Turner ~ Real ale ~ Bar food (12-3, 6-9; 12-3 Sun; not Sun evening) ~ Restaurant ~ (01760) 755398 ~ Children welcome ~ Dogs allowed in bar ~ Open 10am-11pm; 10-12.30am(11.30 Sun) Sat ~ Bedrooms: /£80B ~ www.ostrichcastleacre.com

HINGHAM   TG0202
White Hart
Market Place, just off B1108 W of Norwich; NR9 4AF

Carefully and interestingly furnished pub in attractive town square with thoughtful furnishings, a good choice of drinks and imaginative modern cooking

Bustling and friendly, this is a well run place with a civilised but informal atmosphere. The rooms, arranged over two floors, have a great deal of character: stripped floorboards, a few oriental and other colourful rugs, an attractive variety of chairs and tables (some rather fine), a few beams and standing timbers, lots of prints and photographs and objects such as antique hanging scales on walls painted in mushroom and cream, several woodburning stoves, and quiet corners with comfortable sofas. Lighting is good from ceiling spots to interesting lanterns and even – in one rather grand room with a barrel-vaulted ceiling – antler chandeliers. The galleried long room up steps from the main bar with its egyptian frieze is just right for a sizeable party. Their own JoC's Norfolk Kiwi beer and Adnams Bitter on handpump and up to 20 wines by the glass. There are some modern benches and seats in the gravelled courtyard. This is part of the Flying Kiwi Inns group.

Flying Kiwi Inns ~ Manager Chris Coubrough ~ Real ale ~ Bar food (12-2.30, 6.30-9.30(9 Sun)) ~ (01953) 850214 ~ Children welcome ~ Dogs allowed in bar ~ Open 11am-11.30pm ~ www.whitehartnorfolk.co.uk

LETHERINGSETT   TG0638
Kings Head
A148 (Holt Road) W of Holt; NR25 7AR

Comfortably contemporary areas in neat country house, friendly young staff, real ales, good wines by the glass, bistro-type food and plenty of outside seating

Our readers enjoy their visits to this large, country-house-style pub very much – it's certainly wise to book a table in advance as it does get busy at peak times. The atmosphere is informal and civilised, and to the right of the main door, a small room has dining chairs around scrubbed wooden tables, bookshelves beside a black fireplace, a flat-screen TV and apple-green paintwork. The main bar, to the left, is comfortable with daily papers and an open fire, big leather armchairs and sofas, stools and various dining chairs, reproduction hunting and coaching prints on the mushroom paintwork, rugs on quarry tiles and their own-brewed JoC's Norfolk Kiwi and Adnams Best on handpump; quite a choice of wines by the glass and good coffee. The dining room has a skylight, built-in white-painted planked wall seating with maroon cushions and a mix of dining chairs around wooden tables, rugs on stripped floorboards, and a few farm tools and cabinets of taps and spiles on the cream-painted flint and cob walls. A back area, under a partly pitched ceiling with painted rafters, has more comfortable leather sofas and armchairs in front of another big flat-screen TV; scrabble and background music. Outside, there are lots of picnic-sets under parasols on the front gravel with many more on a grass side lawn (where there's also a play fort under tenting).

Flying Kiwi Inns ~ Licensee Chris Coubrough ~ Real ale ~ Bar food (12-2.30, 6.30-9.30; cake and coffee 8-12, 3-6 daily) ~ (01263) 712691 ~ Children welcome ~ Dogs allowed in bar ~ Open 11am-11.30pm ~ www.letheringsettkingshead.co.uk

MORSTON   TG0043
Anchor
A149 Salthouse–Stiffkey; The Street; NR2 7AA

Quite a choice of rooms filled with bric-a-brac and prints, real ales and some sort of food all day

In a small seaside village, this is a bustling pub with an easy-going atmosphere and friendly young licensees. On the right, there are three traditional rooms with pubby seating and tables on original wooden floors, coal fires, local 1950s beach photographs and lots of prints and bric-a-brac. Adnams Bitter, local Winters Golden and Woodfordes Wherry on handpump and several wines by the glass. The contemporary airy extension on the left has groups of deep leather sofas around low tables, grey-painted country dining furniture, fresh flowers and fish pictures. There are tables and benches out in front of the building. You can book seal-spotting trips from here and the surrounding area is wonderful for bird-watching and walking.

Free house ~ Licensees Harry Farrow and Rowan Glennie ~ Real ale ~ Bar food (12-3, 6-9; light snacks all afternoon) ~ Restaurant ~ (01263) 741392 ~ Children welcome ~ Dogs allowed in bar ~ Open 9am-11pm ~ www.morstonanchor.co.uk

NORTH CREAKE   TF8538

Jolly Farmers

Burnham Road; NR21 9JW

Friendly village local with three cosy rooms, open fires and woodburners, well liked food and several real ales

Even when this yellow-painted pub is really busy, you can be sure of a friendly welcome from the cheerful licensees – our readers enjoy their visits very much. There are three cosy and relaxed rooms and the main bar has a large open fire in a brick fireplace, a mix of pine farmhouse and high-backed leather dining chairs around scrubbed pine tables on the quarry-tiled floor and pale yellow walls. Beside the wooden bar counter are some high bar chairs and they keep Woodfordes Nelsons Revenge and Wherry and a guest like Adnams Southwold on handpump or tapped from the cask, eleven wines by the glass and a dozen malt whiskies. There's also a cabinet of model cars. A smaller bar has pews and a woodburning stove and the red-walled dining room has similar furniture to the bar and another woodburning stove. There are seats outside on the terrace. This is a charming flint-stone village.

Free house ~ Licensees Adrian and Heather Sanders ~ Real ale ~ Bar food (not Mon or Tues) ~ (01328) 738185 ~ Children welcome ~ Dogs allowed in bar ~ Open 12-2.30, 7-11; 12-3, 7-10.30 Sun; closed Mon and Tues ~ www.jollyfarmersnorfolk.co.uk

NORWICH   TG2207

Eagle

Newmarket Road (A11, between A140 and A147 ring roads); NR2 2HN

Popular pub with a variety of seating areas for both drinking and dining, real ales, lots of coffees, wines by the glass and quite a choice of fairly priced food

At peak times, this well run pub is extremely busy so it's lucky that there are lots of different seating areas both downstairs and upstairs. As well as comfortable sofas and armchairs by the open fire in its ornate fireplace, there are white-painted chairs around pine tables on tiled or stripped-wood flooring, cream paintwork above a red dado and more sofas and straightforward pubby seating in a cosy end room. There's also a low-ceilinged dining room and a spiral staircase in the bar leading to another dining room with high-backed brown leather chairs around various tables on pale floorboards. Greene King IPA, Sharps Doom Bar and a house beer from Bass called Eagles Nest on handpump and decent wines; background music. A 'conservatory' with chrome and bentwood chairs and wooden tables leads on to a sunny terrace with picnic-sets and a smart barbecue, and there are more seats on grass.

Free house ~ Licensee Nigel Booty ~ Real ale ~ Bar food (12-2.30(4 Sun), 6-9) ~ Restaurant ~ (01603) 624173 ~ Children welcome ~ Dogs allowed in bar ~ Open 11-11 ~ www.theeaglepub.co.uk

NORWICH

TG2109

Fat Cat

West End Street; NR2 4NA

A place of pilgrimage for beer lovers, and open all day; lunchtime baps and pies

A visit to this enormously popular and friendly pub is a bit like coming to a private beer festival and the knowledgeable landlord and his helpful staff keep an amazing range of up to 30 quickly changing real ales. On handpump or tapped from the cask in a stillroom behind the bar – big windows reveal all – are their own beers, Fat Cat Brewery Tap Bitter, Cougar, Hell Cat, Honey Ale, Marmalade Cat and Wild Cat, as well as Adnams Bitter, Batemans Salem Porter, Burton Bridge Festival Ale, Crouch Vale Yakima Gold, Dark Star American Pale Ale, Elgoods Black Dog Mild, Epping (Pitfield) Pale Ale, Fullers ESB, Grain Redwood, Greene King Abbot, Milestone Dark Galleon, Oakham Bishops Farewell, St Peters Golden Ale, Stonehenge Old Smokey, Thornbridge Jaipur, Timothy Taylors Landlord, and Woodfordes Wherry. You'll also find imported draught beers and lagers, over 50 bottled beers from around the world plus ciders and perries. There's a lively bustling atmosphere at busy times, with maybe tranquil lulls in the middle of the afternoon, and a good mix of cheerful customers. The no-nonsense furnishings include plain scrubbed pine tables and simple solid seats, lots of brewery memorabilia, bric-a-brac and stained-glass. There are tables outside.

Own brew ~ Licensee Colin Keatley ~ Real ale ~ Bar food (filled baps available until sold out; not Sun) ~ No credit cards ~ (01603) 624364 ~ Children allowed until 6pm ~ Dogs allowed in bar ~ Open 12-11; 11-midnight Sat ~ www.fatcatpub.co.uk

SALTHOUSE

TG0743

Dun Cow

A149 Blakeney–Sheringham (Purdy Street, junction with Bard Hill); NR25 7XA

Relaxed seaside pub, a good all-rounder and with enterprising food

Picnic-table sets out on the front grass look across the bird-filled salt marshes towards the sea, and there are more tables in a sheltered back courtyard, with yet more in an orchard garden beyond. The flint-walled bar consists of a pair of high-raftered rooms opened up into one area, stone tiles in the back half where regulars congregate by the serving counter, carpet matting at the front. There are log fireplaces each end, scrubbed tables, one very high-backed settle as well as country kitchen chairs and elegant little red-padded dining chairs, with big sailing-ship and other prints. With well kept Adnams Southwold, Greene King IPA and Woodfordes Wherry on handpump, and quick service by friendly helpful staff, it has a good relaxed atmosphere. There is pool in a separate games room. We have not yet heard from readers who have stayed in their self-catering bedrooms.

Punch ~ Lease Daniel Goff ~ Real ale ~ Bar food (12-9) ~ (01263) 740467 ~ Children welcome ~ Dogs allowed in bar ~ Open 11-11 ~ Bedrooms: /£65B ~ www.salthouseduncow.com

STANHOE
TF8037

Duck

B1155 Docking–Burnham Market; PE31 8QD

Smart candlelit country dining pub, good food (especially fish), appealing layout and attentive staff; bedrooms

Past the village duck pond and surrounded by quiet farmland, this is smart and neatly kept dining pub and close to the beaches of Brancaster and Holkham. The original bar is charming and atmospheric and now forms three cosy dining areas with beams, country kitchen chairs and pews around wooden tables on bare boards or black slate flooring, a couple of woodburning stoves, and original oil paintings by local artists. Elgoods Cambridge and Pageant on handpump from a fine slab-topped counter and several wines by the glass; good service. There's also a garden room and seats under apple trees in the pretty garden. As well as well appointed bedrooms they have a site for touring caravans. This is sister pub to the Bell in Wiveton.

Elgoods ~ Tenant Berni Morritt ~ Bar food (12-2.15, 6-9.15; not Sun evening, not Mon) ~ (01485) 518330 ~ Children welcome ~ Dogs allowed in bar ~ Open 12-11 ~ Bedrooms: /£95S ~ www.duckinn.co.uk

SWANTON MORLEY
TG0217

Darbys

B1147 NE of Dereham; NR20 4NY

Unspoilt country local with six real ales, plenty of farming knick-knacks, tasty bar food, and children's play area

Once a pair of 18th-c cottages, this creeper-covered brick pub has a fine choice of changing real ales and a friendly atmosphere. The long bare-boarded country-style bar has a comfortable lived-in feel with big stripped-pine tables and chairs, lots of gin traps and farming memorabilia, a good log fire (with the original bread oven alongside) and tractor seats with folded sacks lining the long, attractive serving counter. Adnams Bitter and Broadside, Beeston Afternoon Delight, Woodfordes Wherry and two guests like Beeston Squirrels Nuts and Woodfordes Nelsons Revenge tapped from the cask, several wines by the glass and quite a few coffees; good, efficient service. A step up through a little doorway by the fireplace takes you through to the attractive dining room with neat, dark tables and chairs on the wooden floor; the children's room has a toy box and a glassed-over well, floodlit from inside. Background music, TV and board games. There are picnic-sets and a children's play area in the back garden. Plenty to do locally (B&B is available in carefully converted farm buildings a few minutes away) as the family also own the adjoining 720-acre estate. They also have a well equipped camping site.

Free house ~ Licensees John Carrick and Louise Battle ~ Real ale ~ Bar food (12-2.15, 6.30-9.45; all day weekends) ~ Restaurant ~ (01362) 637647 ~ Children welcome ~ Dogs allowed in bar ~ monthly live music ~ Open 11.30-3, 6-11; 11.30-11 Fri and Sat; 12-10.30 Sun ~ Bedrooms: £35S(£40B)/£60(£70S)(£75B) ~ www.darbysfreehouse.com

WEST BECKHAM
TG1439

Wheatsheaf

Church Road; off A148 Holt–Cromer; NR25 6NX

Traditional pub with several real ales, proper home cooking and seats in the garden

This is a warmly friendly brick-built pub in a quiet village. There's a genuine welcome for all – dogs included – and the newish landlord works hard at making all his customers feel at home. The bars have beams, standing timbers, cottagey doors, lots of horsebrasses and a couple of roaring winter log fires, and the furnishings are pleasantly traditional with plenty of wheelback chairs, settles and comfortably cushioned wall seats around dark wood pubby tables. Greene King IPA and Old Speckled Hen and Woodfordes Wherry on handpump and quite a few wines by the glass. The charming garden has a covered terrace and seats both here and on the grass.

Free house ~ Licensee Matt Lock ~ Real ale ~ Bar food (12-2,6-9(8 Sun)) ~ (01263) 822110 ~ Children welcome ~ Dogs allowed in bar ~ Open 12-3, 6-11(may open all day in summer); 12-10.30 Sun ~ www.thewheatsheafwestbeckham.co.uk

WIVETON
TG0442

Bell

Blakeney Road; NR25 7TL

Busy, open-plan dining pub, drinkers welcomed too, local beers, fine food and seats outside; bedrooms

Even when this well run dining pub is really busy – which it deservedly usually is – you can be sure of a warm welcome from the helpful landlord and his friendly staff. It's mainly open plan throughout and there are some fine old beams, an attractive mix of dining chairs around wooden tables on the stripped wooden floor, as log fire and prints on the yellow walls. The sizeable conservatory has smart beige dining chairs around wooden tables on the coir flooring and the atmosphere is chatty and relaxed. Elgoods Cambridge Bitter, Woodfordes Wherry and Yetmans Red on handpump, and several wines by the glass. Outside, there are picnic-sets on grass in front of the building looking across to the church, and at the back, stylish wicker tables and chairs on several decked areas are set among decorative box hedging. The bedrooms are comfortable and they also have a self-catering cottage to let.

Free house ~ Licensee Berni Morritt ~ Real ale ~ Bar food (12-2.15, 6-9) ~ Restaurant ~ (01263) 740101 ~ Children welcome ~ Dogs allowed in bar ~ Open 12-11 ~ Bedrooms: /£95S ~ www.wivetonbell.co.uk

DOG FRIENDLY INNS, HOTELS AND B&Bs

BLAKENEY   TG0243
Blakeney Hotel
Blakeney, Holt, Norfolk NR25 7NE (01263) 740797 www.blakeneyhotel.co.uk

£202; 63 very comfortable rms, many with views over the salt marshes and some with their own little terrace. Overlooking the harbour and the estuary, this friendly hotel has light and airy, appealing public rooms, good food served in the bar, restaurant and on the terrace, and very pleasant staff; indoor swimming pool, sauna, steam room and mini gym; dogs in ground floor bedrooms; £5

BRANCASTER STAITHE   TF8044
White Horse
Main Road, Brancaster Staithe, King's Lynn, Norfolk PE31 8BY (01485) 210262 www.whitehorsebrancaster.co.luk

£170; 15 rms, 8 with their own terrace and access to the Norfolk Coastal Path. Looking over the salt marshes (wonderful sunsets) this well run hotel has an informal front locals' bar with real ales, a middle area with comfortable sofas and newspapers and a big dining conservatory with enjoyable food (lots of fish) and good breakfasts; helpful, friendly staff; dogs in annexe bedrooms; £10

BURNHAM MARKET   TF8342
Hoste Arms
Market Place, Burnham Market, King's Lynn, Norfolk PE31 8HD (01328) 738777 www.thehoste.com

£149; 58 stylish rms with views over the garden or village green. Handsome and civilised 17th-c inn – most emphasis on the smart hotel and restaurant side but with a proper bustling bar with panelling, a log fire, nice watercolours, real ales and an exceptional wine list; a conservatory has comfortable leather sofas and armchairs, there's a lounge for afternoon tea and several restaurants serving delicious modern food (from simple bar lunches upwards); the pretty walled garden has lots of seats and a covered moroccan-style dining area; lovely beaches nearby for walking; dogs in bedrooms and bar; £15

CLEY NEXT THE SEA   TG0443
George
High Street, Cley, Holt, Norfolk NR25 7RN (01263) 740652 www.thegeorgehotelatcley.co.uk

£90; 13 refurbished rms, some with fine views. Busy pub in quiet village overlooking the salt marshes (fantastic bird watching); little public bar with photos of wherries and local scenes, simple seats and tables, a table of daily papers, good local beers and lots of wines by the glass, two dining rooms with candlelight, pale wooden cushioned dining chairs around a mix of tables, and a woodburning stove, and enjoyable food; dogs in bedrooms and bar; £10

EAST RUDHAM
Crown
TF8228

The Green, East Rudham, King's Lynn, Norfolk PE31 8RD (01485) 528530
www.crowninnnorfolk.co.uk

£110; 6 warm, comfortable rms. Civilised and friendly inn with stylish open-plan areas, winter log fires, all manner of seating from comfortable sofas through leather dining chairs to pubby built-in cushioned wall benches, a cosy back sitting room, interesting décor, first class contemporary cooking, and friendly young staff; dogs anywhere in the pub and in bedrooms; £10

ERPINGHAM
Saracens Head
TG1732

Wolterton, Norwich, Norfolk NR11 7LZ (01263) 768909 www.saracenshead-norfolk.co.uk

£100; 5 comfortable modern rms. Remote inn with an easy-going atmosphere, a two-roomed bar with a good mix of seats and tables, fresh flowers, log fires, real ales, a six-table parlour with another big open fire, and inventive, popular food; seats out in a charming, old-fashioned gravelled stable yard; dogs in bedrooms and back bar

GREAT BIRCHAM
Kings Head
TF7632

Great Bircham, King's Lynn, Norfolk PE31 6RJ (01485) 578265
www.thekingsheadhotel.co.uk

£100; 12 attractive, contemporary rms. Rather grand looking Edwardian hotel with a bustling and attractively modern bar with a log fire and comfortable sofas, good innovative food in the light, airy restaurant, hearty breakfasts, friendly staff, and seats out in front and at the back with rustic views; dogs in bedrooms and bar; £10

GREAT MASSINGHAM
Dabbling Duck
TF7922

11 Abbey Road, Great Massingham, King's Lynn, Norfolk PE32 2HN (01485) 520827
www.thedabblingduck.co.uk

£85; 6 rms, named after famous local sportsmen and airmen from the WW2 air base in Massingham. Bustling inn, overlooking a sizeable village green with big duck ponds, relaxed bars with leather sofas and armchairs, roaring log fires, antique dining chairs and tables on flagstones or stripped wooden floors, quirky 18th- and 19th-c prints and cartoons, local beers, imaginative food using local produce and nice breakfasts; dogs anywhere in the pub and in bedrooms; £10

HOLKHAM
Victoria
TF8943

Park Road, Holkham, Wells-next-the-sea, Norfolk NR23 1RG (01328) 711008
www.victoriaatholkham.co.uk

£140; 10 rms (extensive refurbishment soon), some overlooking the marshes.

Stylish hotel just a few minutes from Holkham Beach with an eclectic mix of furnishings in the engaging bar – deep sofas, chunky candles, an open log fire, fresh flowers and real ales, an airy dining room serving enjoyable food with emphasis on game and beef from the Holkham Estate, fresh fish and shellfish and other seasonal local produce, friendly staff, and seats in the sheltered courtyard; walks to the nature reserve salt marshes and the sea; dogs in some bedrooms; £15

MORSTON   TG0043

Morston Hall

The Street, Morston, Holt, Norfolk NR25 7AA (01263) 741041 www.morstonhall.com

£320 including dinner; 7 comfortable rms with country views. Attractive 17th-c flint-walled house with lovely quiet gardens, two small lounges (one with an antique fireplace), a conservatory and hard-working friendly young owners; exceptional modern cooking (they also run cookery demonstrations and courses), a thoughtful small wine list and super breakfasts and afternoon teas; croquet; coastal path for walks right outside; dogs in bedrooms; bring own bedding; £5

MUNDFORD   TL8093

Crown

Crown Street, Mundford, Thetford, Norfolk IP26 5HQ (01842) 878233
www.the-crown-hotel.co.uk

£79.50; 40 good rms. Unassuming old pub, warmly welcoming, with heavy beams and huge fireplaces, interesting local memorabilia, real ales, sensibly priced and enjoyable food in two dining areas, and seats on a back terrace and in the garden; well behaved dogs in some bedrooms; £10

NORTH WALSHAM   TG2730

Beechwood

Cromer Road, North Walsham, Norfolk NR28 0HD (01692) 403231
www.beechwood-hotel.co.uk

£130; 17 individually decorated, pretty rms. Creeper-covered Georgian house, once Agatha Christie's Norfolk hideaway, with a comfortable lounge and bar, charming owners and super staff, good, imaginative modern cooking in attractive dining room, nice breakfasts and lovely garden where dogs may walk – there's also a park nearby and beaches, too; dogs in three bedrooms; £10

SEDGEFORD   TF7036

King William IV

Heacham Road, Sedgeford, Hunstanton, Norfolk PE36 5LU (01485) 571765
www.thekingwilliamsedgeford.co.uk

£100; 9 comfortable rms. Carefully run inn with enthusiastic owners, a homely, relaxed bar, several cosy dining areas and a newly refurbished restaurant, log fires, paintings of the north Norfolk coast, high-backed leather dining chairs around pine tables on slate tiles, real ales, popular food and rather special breakfasts; lots of seats outside plus a covered dining area; several nearby beaches, fantastic bird-watching, walks on the Peddars Way and Sandringham Estate; dogs in bedrooms and bar/sitting area; £7.50

SNETTISHAM   TF6834

Rose & Crown

Old Church Road, Snettisham, King's Lynn, Norfolk PE31 7LX (01485) 541382
www.roseandcrownsnettisham.co.uk

£90; 16 comfortable rms decorated in seaside colours. Particularly well run old pub with three bars, log fires and interesting furnishings, floor tiles and coir carpeting, beams and nice old prints of King's Lynn and Sandringham, an airy Garden Room with inviting wicker-based chairs, a lounge with squashy sofas and armchairs and newspapers and magazines to read, a thoughtful choice of drinks, and interesting, highly thought of food served by neat, courteous staff; dogs anywhere in the pub and in bedrooms; £12

STIFFKEY   TF9643

Red Lion

44 Wells Road, Stiffkey, Wells-next-the-sea, Norfolk NR23 1AJ (01328) 830552
www.stiffkey.com

£110; 10 airy rms with own balconies or terraces. Cheerful, eco-friendly pub with an appealing layout and a perky atmosphere, cushioned pews and settles and other pubby seats, candlelit tables, two back dining rooms (one almost a flint-walled conservatory), local landscape photos, good wines by the glass, two dozen malts and local beers, tasty food and chatty, helpful staff; nice coastal walks nearby; dogs anywhere in the pub and in bedrooms; £5

SWAFFHAM   TF8109

Strattons

Ash Close, Swaffham, Norfolk PE37 7NH (01760) 723845 www.strattonshotel.co.uk

£190; 14 interesting and opulent rms, including suites. Environmentally-friendly Palladian-style villa with individual and comfortably decorated rooms filled with sculptures, ornaments and original paintings, log fires, imaginative food using local organic produce from a short daily-changing menu, and good breakfasts using their own eggs and home-baked bread; a new café and deli; plenty of nearby walks; dogs in some bedrooms (not to be left unattended); bowl and walk map; £6.50

THORNHAM   TF7343

Lifeboat

Ship Lane, Thornham, Hunstanton, Norfolk PE36 6LT (01485) 512236
www.lifeboatinnthornham.com

£130; 13 smart rms, many with sea views. Rambling inn facing coastal sea flats and with many surrounding walks; several character bars with beams, open fires and woodburning stoves, reed-slashers and other antique farm tools on the walls, seats ranging from low settles and pews to more ornate dining chairs, fresh flowers and candles, real ales and wines by the glass, and highly thought of food using seasonal local produce; steps up from the conservatory lead to a sunny terrace; dogs in bedrooms and bars; £10

THORNHAM   TF7343

Orange Tree

Church Street, Thornham, Hunstanton, Norfolk PE36 6LY (01485) 512213
www.theorangetreethornham.co.uk

£85; 6 contemporary courtyard rms. Friendly village centre pub with comfortable
leather and basket-weave chairs on tiled floors, stripped beams in low ceilings,
a log fire, real ales, 24 wines by the glass and a chatty atmosphere; the two-part
dining area is cheerfully contemporary in style and the food is interesting and
inventive; resident labrador, Poppy; dogs in bedrooms and bar; £10

THORPE MARKET   TG2434

Gunton Arms

Cromer Road, Thorpe Market, Norwich, Norfolk NR11 8TZ (01263) 832010
www.theguntonarms.co.uk

£130; 8 rms with original fittings. Stately place in a 1,000-acre deer park with
impressive rooms and an easy-going atmosphere; huge entrance hall, pubby bar
with simple furnishings, a log fire, beers served from big mahogany counter,
and pool table, dining room with vast antlers on the walls and a second huge
log fire (they often cook over this), a lounge with comfortable leather sofas and
armchairs in front of yet another fire, and a formal restaurant; food is robust and
contemporary and uses their own venison, local fish, foraged plants and seashore
vegetables; dogs in bedrooms and bar; £10

TITCHWELL   TF7543

Titchwell Manor Hotel

Main Road, Titchwell, King's Lynn, Norfolk PE31 8BB (01485) 210221
www.titchwellmanor.com

£130; 25 light, pretty rms. Comfortable hotel, handy for nearby RSPB reserve,
and with lots of walks and footpaths nearby; roaring log fire, magazines and good
naturalists' records of the wildlife, a cheerful bar, attractive brasserie restaurant
with french windows on to lovely sheltered walled garden, good breakfasts, and
particularly helpful licensees and staff; dogs in ground floor bedrooms and bar;
towel, bowl, walk map and biscuits; £8

WARHAM   TF9441

Three Horseshoes

The Street, Warham, Wells-next-the-Sea, Norfolk NR23 1NL (01328) 710547

£70; 3 rms in former post office next to the pub and with own residents' lounge.
Basic but cheerful local with marvellously unspoilt traditional atmosphere in its
three friendly gas-lit rooms, simple furnishings, a log fire, very tasty generous
bar food, decent wines, and very well kept real ales; plenty of surrounding walks
– in field opposite pub, on Warham marshes and nearby Holkham beach; dogs
welcome anywhere; bowls, biscuits, treats, tinned food

WELLS-NEXT-THE-SEA

Globe

TF9143

The Buttlands, Wells-next-the-Sea, Norfolk NR23 1EU (01328) 710206
www.holkham.co.uk/globe

£120; 7 airy rms. Handsome Georgian inn just a short walk from the quay, with several opened-up rooms with contemporary furnishings, comfortable sofas and armchairs in relaxed front bar, quirky fish and shellfish drawings on driftwood, good ales and wines, and enjoyable food; seats in attractive heated back courtyard; dogs anywhere in the pub and in bedrooms; £10

WINTERTON-ON-SEA

Fishermans Return

TG4919

The Lane, Winterton-on-Sea, Great Yarmouth, Norfolk NR29 4BN (01493) 393305
www.fishermans-return.com

£80; 3 rms reached by a tiny staircase. Traditional 300-year-old pub in quiet village, close to the beach (fine walking), with warmly welcoming and helpful owners, a relaxed lounge bar with well kept real ales, open fire, good home-made food (fine fish dishes), enjoyable breakfasts and sheltered garden; dogs in bedrooms and bar

Dizzy; owners Donald and Angie Clay

Northamptonshire

DOG FRIENDLY PUBS

BULWICK   SP9694

Queens Head
Off A43 Kettering–Duddington; NN17 3DY

Honey-coloured 17th-c stone pub with five ales, good interesting food and friendly licensees

This pretty 600-year-old stone cottage has been carefully refurbished by its newish owners. The beamed bar has exposed stone walls, contemporary paintwork, cushioned walls seats and wooden dining chairs, stone floors and a woodburning stove – and still has the feel of a traditional village pub; the bellringers continue to pop in after their Wednesday practice. The dining room has high-backed black or brown leather dining chairs around light wooden tables on floor tiles, another fireplace and quite a few interesting little knick-knacks. Digfield Barnwell, Oakham JHB, Shepherd Neame Spitfire and a couple of guest beers from local breweries such as Brewsters, Great Oakley, and Potbelly on handpump. Outside, there are rattan tables and chairs under a pergola and on the terrace and a pizza oven; this is a lovely spot, with the summer sounds of swallows and house martins, sheep in the adjacent field and bells ringing in the nearby church.

Free house ~ Licensees Julie Barclay and Robert Windeler ~ Real ale ~ Bar food (12-2, 6-9; 12-3 Sun; not Sun evening or Mon) ~ Restaurant ~ (01780) 450272 ~ Children welcome ~ Dogs allowed in bar ~ Open 12-3, 6-11; 12-7 Sun; closed Sun evening; Mon ~ www.thequeensheadbulwick.co.uk

FARTHINGSTONE   SP6155

Kings Arms
Off A5 SE of Daventry; village signed from Litchborough; NN12 8EZ

Individual place with cosy traditional interior, carefully prepared food using own produce and lovely gardens

The licensees at this quirky gargoyle-embellished 18th-c stone country pub give wildlife talks here and are passionate about their wildlife-friendly garden. With a surprise around every corner, it's laid out in a series of tucked away little nooks, and the tranquil terrace is charmingly decorated with hanging baskets, flower and herb pots, plant-filled painted tractor tyres and recycled art. Inside, the timelessly intimate flagstoned bar has a huge log fire, comfortable homely sofas and armchairs near the entrance, whisky-water jugs hanging from oak beams, and lots of pictures and decorative plates on the walls. A games room at the far end has darts, dominoes, cribbage, table skittles and board games. Three changing beers might be from brewers such as Black Sheep, Charles Wells and St Austell Tribute, they have a short but decent wine list and quite a few country wines. Look out for the interesting newspaper-influenced décor in the outside gents'. This is a picturesque village and there are good walks near here including the Knightley Way. It's worth ringing ahead to check the opening and food serving times and do note that they don't take credit cards.

Free house ~ Licensees Paul and Denise Egerton ~ Real ale ~ Bar food (12-2.30 Sat, Sun only; 7.15-9.30 last Fri evening of month) ~ (01327) 361604 ~ Children welcome ~ Dogs allowed in bar ~ Open 7-11.30; 6.30-midnight Fri; 12-4, 7-midnight Sat; 12-4, 9-11 Sun; closed Mon and weekday lunchtimes

FOTHERINGHAY   TL0593

Falcon

Village signposted off A605 on Peterborough side of Oundle; PE8 5HZ

Upmarket dining pub, good range of drinks and interesting food from snacks up and attractive garden

Readers have only praise for this beautifully kept, civilised pub. Staff here are exceptionally friendly and polite, creating a delightful atmosphere for the good inventive food they serve – not cheap, but the consensus is that it's worth it. Everything is neatly turned out, with fresh flower arrangements and sedate cushioned slatback arm and bucket chairs, and good winter log fires in stone fireplaces. The pretty conservatory restaurant and charming lavender-surrounded terrace have lovely views of the vast church behind, and an attractively planted garden. Surprisingly, given the emphasis on dining, it does have a thriving little locals' tap bar and a darts team. The very good range of drinks includes three changing beers from brewers such as Fullers and Nene Valley on handpump, good wines (most available by the glass), Aspall's cider, organic cordials and fresh orange juice. The village is lovely, with mooring on the Nene, and the ruins of Fotheringhay Castle, where Mary Queen of Scots was executed, not far away.

Free house ~ Licensee Sally Facer ~ Real ale ~ Bar food (12-2.15(3 Sun), 6.15-9.15(8.30 Sun)) ~ Restaurant ~ (01832) 226254 ~ Children welcome ~ Dogs allowed in bar ~ Open 12-11(10.30 Sun) ~ www.thefalcon-inn.co.uk

GREAT BRINGTON   SP6664

Althorp Coaching Inn

Off A428 NW of Northampton, near Althorp Hall; until recently known as the Fox & Hounds; NN7 4JA

Friendly golden stone thatched pub with great choice of real ales, tasty popular food and sheltered garden

Cheerful staff serve around nine real ales at this lovely old coaching inn. On handpump, these might include Fullers London Pride, Greene King IPA and Abbot, St Austell Tribute, Sadlers Worcester Sorcerer, Warwickshire Shakespeare's County, and guests from breweries such as Abbeydale, Goffs, Quartz and Saltaire. The extended dining area gives views of the 30 or so casks racked in the cellar; also, eight wines by the glass and a decent range of malt whiskies. The ancient bar has all the traditional features you'd wish for, from a dog or two sprawled out by the huge log fire, to old beams, sagging joists and an attractive mix of country chairs and tables (maybe with fresh flowers) on its broad flagstones and bare boards. There are plenty of snug alcoves and nooks and crannies with some stripped-pine shutters and panelling, two fine log fires and an eclectic medley of bric-a-brac from farming implements to an old clocking-in machine and country pictures. One of the bars is used for pub games and an old garden cottage adjoins the lovely little paved courtyard (also accessible by the old coaching entrance) which has sheltered tables and tubs of flowers; more seating in the side garden.

Free house ~ Licensee Michael Krempels ~ Real ale ~ Bar food (12-3, 6.30-9.30(10 Fri, Sat); 12-5, 6-8 Sun) ~ Restaurant ~ (01604) 770651 ~ Children welcome ~ Dogs allowed in bar ~ Live music Tues evening ~ Open 11-11.30; 12-10.30 Sun ~ www.althorp-coaching-inn.co.uk

NETHER HEYFORD   SP6658

Olde Sun

1.75 miles from M1 junction 16: village signposted left off A45 westbound; Middle Street; NN7 3LL

Unpretentious place handy for M1 with diverting bric-a-brac, reasonably priced pubby bar food and garden with play area

All manner of entertaining bric-a-brac hangs from the ceilings and is packed into nooks and crannies in the several small linked rooms of this lively 18th-c golden stone pub. It includes brassware (one fireplace is a grotto of large brass animals), colourful relief plates, 1930s cigarette cards, railway memorabilia and advertising signs, World War II posters and rope fancywork. The nice old cash till on one of the two counters where the friendly landlord and staff serve well kept Banks's, Greene King Ruddles, Marstons Pedigree and a guest such as Charles Wells Eagle is wishfully stuck at one and a ha'penny. Most of the furnishings are properly pubby, with the odd easy chair. There are beams and low ceilings (one painted with a fine sunburst), partly glazed dividing panels, steps between some areas, rugs on parquet, red tiles or flagstones, a big inglenook log fire, and up on the left a room with full-sized hood skittles, a games machine, darts, Sky TV, cribbage and dominoes; background music. In the garden you'll find antiquated hand-operated farm machines, some with plants in their hoppers and the first thing that will catch your eye when you arrive will probably be a row of bright blue grain kibblers along the edge of the fairy-lit front terrace (with picnic-sets).

Free house ~ Licensees P Yates and A Ford ~ Real ale ~ Bar food (12-2(4 Sun), 7-9; not Sun evening) ~ Restaurant ~ (01327) 340164 ~ Children welcome ~ Dogs allowed in bar ~ Open 12-2.30, 5-11; 12-midnight Sat; 12-11 Sun

NORTHAMPTON   SP7559

Malt Shovel

Bridge Street (approach road from M1 junction 15); no parking in nearby street, best to park in Morrisons central car park, far end – passage past Europcar straight to back entrance; NN1 1QF

Friendly well run real ale pub with bargain lunches and over a dozen varied beers

Beer lovers will be in heaven at this pubby place where they serve an astonishing 13 real ales from a battery of handpumps lined up on the long counter, with even more during beer festivals. As well as their three Great Oakley house beers, Frog Island Natterjack and Fullers London Pride, they run through quickly changing guests from the likes of Bridestones, Elland, Mallinsons, Millstone, Oakham and Ruddles. They also have belgian draft and bottled beers, over 40 malt whiskies, english country wines and Rich's farm cider. This is home to quite an extensive collection of carefully chosen brewing memorabilia, some from Phipps Northampton Brewery Company which was once across the road – the site is now occupied by Carlsberg Brewery. Look out for the rare Phipps Northampton Brewery Company star, displayed outside the pub, and some high-mounted ancient beer engines from the Carlsberg Brewery. Staff are cheery and helpful; darts, daily papers, disabled facilities, may be background music. The secluded backyard has tables and chairs, a smokers' shelter and occasional barbecues.

Free house ~ Licensee Mike Evans ~ Real ale ~ Bar food (12-2; not evenings or Sun) ~ (01604) 234212 ~ Well behaved children welcome ~ Dogs allowed in bar ~ Blues Weds evening ~ Open 11.30-3, 5-11.30; 11.30-11 Fri, Sat; 12-10.30 Sun ~ www.maltshoveltavern.com

DOG FRIENDLY INNS, HOTELS AND B&Bs

BADBY   SP5558

Windmill

Main Street, Badby, Daventry, Northamptonshire NN11 3AN (01327) 311070
www.windmillinn-badby.com

£75; 8 refurbished rms. Carefully modernised and warmly welcoming thatched stone inn with beams, flagstones and huge inglenook fireplace in the front bar, a cosy comfortable lounge, a relaxed and civilised atmosphere, good generously served bar and restaurant food, and decent wines; resident chocolate labrador, Bailey; fine views of the pretty village from car park, and woods to walk in a mile away; dogs in bedrooms and bar; £5

CRANFORD   SP9277

Dairy Farm

12 St Andrews Lane, Cranford, Kettering, Northamptonshire NN14 4AQ (01536) 330273
www.olddairyfarmguesthouse.co.uk

£40; 4 comfortable rms. Charming 17th-c manor house of great character on an arable and sheep farm, with oak beams and inglenook fireplaces, good homely cooking using home-grown fruit and vegetables, kind, attentive owners, and garden with a charming summer house and ancient dovecote; walks half a mile away; dogs in annexe bedrooms; £5

DAVENTRY   SP5656

Fawsley Hall

Fawsley, Daventry, Northamptonshire NN11 3BA (01327) 892000 www.fawsleyhall.com

£225; 58 fine rms, all with their own character. Lovely Tudor hotel with Georgian and Victorian additions set in quiet gardens designed by Capability Brown and surrounded by 2,000 acres of parkland (where dogs may walk); smart, beautifully furnished antique-filled reception rooms with impressive décor, open fires, a Great Hall for afternoon tea, excellent food in the restaurant based in the original Tudor kitchens, a spa with treatment rooms and an indoor swimming pool, a gym, tennis and fishing; dogs in ground floor bedrooms

GREAT OXENDON   SP7383
George
Harborough Road, Great Oxendon, Market Harborough, Leicestershire LE16 8NA
(01858) 465205

£65.50; 3 clean rms. Elegant 16th-c inn with a convivial bar, well kept ales, green leather bucket chairs around small tables, a big log fire, a tiled-floor entrance with easy chairs, a carpeted conservatory, good bar food, friendly staff and seats in the big shrub-sheltered garden; dogs in bedrooms and bar

---

OLD   SP7873
Wold Farm
Harrington Road, Old, Northampton, Northamptonshire NN6 9RJ (01604) 781258
www.woldfarm.co.uk

£68; 5 rms. 18th-c farmhouse in a quiet village, with spacious interesting rooms, antiques and fine china, an open log fire, hearty breakfasts in the beamed dining room, attentive welcoming owners and two pretty gardens where dogs may walk; dogs in bedrooms; £4

OUNDLE   TL0388
Ship
18 West Street, Oundle, Peterborough, Northamptonshire PE8 4EF (01832) 273918
www.theshipinn-oundle.co.uk

£69; 14 charming rms. Bustling down-to-earth town pub with interesting beers and a good range of malt whiskies; heavily beamed lounge with leather and other seats around sturdy tables, a log fire in a stone inglenook and good value traditional food, and a wooden-floored public bar with board games, a cheerful, chatty feel and probably the pub cat, Midnight; dogs in bedrooms and bar; £6

Charlie; owners Sara Fulton and Roger Baker

Northumbria
(County Durham, Northumberland and Tyneside)

MAP 10

DOG FRIENDLY PUBS

CATTON   NY8257
Crown
B6295, off A686 S of Haydon Bridge; NE47 9QS

Good value food and good drinks in attractive and welcoming pub, usefully open all day

With charming and efficient service, local Allendale Golden Plover and Wagtail on handpump, and a decent choice of wines by the glass, this is a friendly pub liked by our readers. The stripped-stone bare-boards inner bar feels relaxed and civilised, with soft lighting from coloured lanterns and comfortable mate's chairs, dining chairs and a sturdy traditional wall settle around dark polished tables. A partly carpeted extension is rather lighter in décor, and both rooms have interesting local photographs including one of the Allendale Wolf, shot nearby in 1905 and a key ingredient in some hair-raising folk tales. Charming and efficient service, picnic-sets on a side terrace and neat small lawn, plenty of good nearby walks.

Free house ~ Licensee Emma Carrick-Thomson ~ Real ale ~ Bar food (12-2, 6-9; 12-3 Sun; not Sun evening or Mon) ~ (01434) 683447 ~ Children welcome ~ Dogs allowed in bar ~ Open 12-2, 6-11; 12-11 Fri, Sat, Sun; closed Mon (except bank holidays) ~ www.crownatcatton.co.uk

HALTWHISTLE   NY7166
Milecastle Inn
Military Road; B6318 NE – OS Sheet 86 map reference 715660; NE49 9NN

Close to Hadrian's Wall and some wild scenery, with cosy little rooms warmed by winter log fires and straightforward bar food; fine views and walled garden

As it's open all day in summer this sturdy stone-built pub, just 500 metres from Hadrian's Wall and some of its most celebrated sites, is a handy refreshment stop, and in winter you can warm-up nicely by the two log fires. The snug little rooms of the beamed bar are decorated with brasses, horsey and local landscape prints and attractive fresh flowers; at lunchtime, the small, comfortable restaurant is used as an overflow. Three Big Lamp beers are on handpump and they stock several malt whiskies. There are tables and benches in the big sheltered big walled garden, with a dovecote and rather stunning views; two self-catering cottages and a large car park.

Free house ~ Licensees Clare and Kevin Hind ~ Real ale ~ Bar food (12-8.45; 12-2.30, 6-8.30 in winter) ~ Restaurant ~ (01434) 321372 ~ Children welcome ~ Dogs allowed in bar ~ Open 12-11(midnight Sat); 12-3, 6-11 in winter ~ www.milecastle-inn.co.uk

HAYDON BRIDGE   NY8364
General Havelock
A69 Corbridge–Haltwhistle; NE47 6ER

Bustling, chatty riverside dining pub with local beers and interesting food cooked by the landlord

Just a short stroll downstream from Haydon Bridge itself, this old stone terraced house is well run and friendly. The attractively lit L-shaped bar is imaginatively decorated in shades of green. It's at its best in the back part with a stripped-pine chest of drawers topped with bric-a-brac, colourful cushions on long pine benches and a sturdy stripped settle, interestingly shaped mahogany-topped tables and good wildlife photographs. Mordue Five Bridge Bitter and a local guest such as Geltsdale Tarn on handpump, ten wines by the glass and a fair choice of juices; board games and boules. Both the stripped-stone barn dining room and the terrace enjoy fine South Tyne river views.

Free house ~ Licensees Gary and Joanna Thompson ~ Real ale ~ Bar food (12-2.30, 7-9; not Sun evening, not Mon) ~ Restaurant ~ (01434) 684376 ~ Children welcome ~ Dogs allowed in bar ~ Open 12-3, 7-midnight; 12-5, 7.30-10.30 Sun; closed Mon lunchtime ~ www.generalhavelock.co.uk

NEWTON-BY-THE-SEA   NU2424
Ship
Village signed off B1339 N of Alnwick; NE66 3EL

In a charming square of fishermen's cottages close to the beach, good simple food and a fine spread of drinks; best to check winter opening times

Tables outside this row of converted fishermen's cottages look across the sloping village green to the sandy beach – not surprisingly given this idyllic location it can get extremely busy at peak times so it's best to book in advance – and be aware that there might be a queue for the bar. Inside, the plainly furnished but cosy bare-boards bar on the right has nautical charts on dark pink walls and another simple room on the left has beams, hop bines, some bright modern pictures on stripped-stone walls and a woodburning stove in the stone fireplace; darts, dominoes. They started making their own beers here four years ago and if the brewer is in he will happily chat about the five or so they usually have on. There's no nearby parking, but there's a car park up the hill.

Own brew ~ Licensee Christine Forsyth ~ Real ale ~ Bar food (12-2.30, 7-8 (check in winter)) ~ No credit cards ~ (01665) 576262 ~ Children welcome ~ Dogs allowed in bar ~ Open 11-11; 12-10.30 Sun; phone for opening hours in winter ~ www.shipinnnewton.co.uk

WARK

NY8676

Battlesteads

B6320 N of Hexham; NE48 3LS

Eco pub with good local ales, fair value interesting food and a relaxed atmosphere; comfortable bedrooms

The welcoming owners of this popular stone hotel are conscientious about the environment and gently weave their beliefs into the business. They run a biomass boiler, have a charging point in the car park for electric cars and grow all their own produce, and encouraging birds into the garden is a priority when they do any planting. This last is clearly a success, as they tell us there is good bird-watching from their conservatory, and they've laid out binoculars on the windowsills so that you can enjoy it. The pub is an enjoyable all-rounder with a relaxed unhurried atmosphere. The nicely restored carpeted bar has a woodburning stove with a traditional oak surround, low beams, comfortable seats including some comfy deep leather sofas and easy chairs, and old Punch country life cartoons on the terracotta walls above its dark dado. As well as a dozen or so wines by the glass, four good changing local ales such as Black Sheep Best, Durham Magus, High House Farm Nel's Best and beers from guest brewers such as Hadrian & Border Secret Kingdom are on handpumps on the heavily carved dark oak bar counter. This leads through to the restaurant and spacious conservatory; good coffee, cheerful service and background music. There are tables on a terrace in the beautifully maintained walled garden. Disabled access to some of the ground floor bedrooms, and they are licensed to hold civil marriages.

Free house ~ Licensees Richard and Dee Slade ~ Real ale ~ Bar food (12-3, 6.30-9) ~ (01434) 230209 ~ Children welcome ~ Dogs allowed in bar ~ Open 11-11 ~ Bedrooms: £60S/£105B ~ www.battlesteads.com

DOG FRIENDLY INNS, HOTELS AND B&Bs

CARTERWAY HEADS

NZ0452

Manor House Inn

Kiln Pit Hill, Shotley Bridge, Consett, County Durham DH8 9LX (01207) 255268
www.themanorhouseinn.com

£75; 4 attractive rms. Simple slate-roofed stone inn with stunning views over Derwent reservoir and lots of nearby walks; the plain, heart-warming locals' bar has wooden tables and chairs and an old-fashioned feel, the carpeted lounge has a woodburning stove and picture windows make the most of the lovely setting; five real ales, 20 malts, farm cider and bar food (usefully served all day) using local game and meat; dogs in bedrooms, bar and lounge

CORNHILL-ON-TWEED

NT8842

Tillmouth Park

Cornhill-on-Tweed, Northumberland TD12 4UU (01890) 882255
www.tillmouthpark.co.uk

£165; 14 spacious, pretty rms with period furniture. Solid stone-built country house in 15 acres of parkland (where dogs may walk), with comfortable, relaxing panelled lounges, antiques and stained glass windows, open fires, a galleried hall, over 60 malt whiskies, good, thoughtfully prepared food in the candlelit restaurant, afternoon teas and hearty breakfasts, and a carefully chosen wine list; nearby golf and shooting; lots to do nearby; dogs in bedrooms and on lead in bar; £10

CROOKHAM   NT9138

Coach House

Crookham, Cornhill-on-Tweed, Northumberland TD12 4TD (01890) 820293
www.coachhousecrookham.com

£90; 10 individual rms with nice views. 17th-c farm buildings around a sunny courtyard, with helpful and friendly staff, an airy beamed lounge with comfortable sofas and big arched windows, good breakfasts with home-made preserves (which you can also take home), afternoon tea and enjoyable dinners using local seasonal produce; paddocks and footpaths for walking and lots to do nearby; closed mid Nov-mid-Feb; dogs in bedrooms (not to be left unattended); £5

DURHAM   NZ2742

Victoria

86 Hallgarth Street, Durham, County Durham DH1 3AS (0191) 386 5269
www.victorianinn-durhamcity.co.uk

£72; 6 recently refurbished rms. Lovingly preserved inn run by the same friendly family for over 30 years; three small rooms with typical Victorian décor that takes in mahogany, etched and cut glass and mirrors, colourful William Morris wallpaper over a high panelled dado, and plush seating; coal fires in handsome iron and tile fireplaces, lots of period prints and engravings of Queen Victoria, and staffordshire figurines of her and the Prince Consort, local ales, over 40 irish whiskeys, and food limited to toasties (they do hearty breakfasts); exercise area 20 metres away; dogs anywhere in the pub and in bedrooms

GRETA BRIDGE   NZ0813

Morritt Arms

Greta Bridge, Barnard Castle, County Durham DL12 9SE (01833) 627232
www.themorritt.co.uk

£125; 27 rms. Striking 17th-c country-house hotel where Charles Dickens stayed in 1838 to research for Nicholas Nickleby – one of the interesting bars has a colourful Dickensian mural; comfortable lounges with sofas and open fires, enjoyable, attractively presented food in the smart restaurant served by knowledgeable staff, and seats in the pleasant garden; lots of surrounding walks, and coarse fishing; dogs in courtyard rooms and bar; bring own bedding; £10

HEADLAM   NZ1818

Headlam Hall

Headlam, Darlington, County Durham DL2 3HA (01325) 730238
www.headlamhall.co.uk

£75; 39 comfortable rms, in the main house and adjacent coach house. Peaceful, family-run Jacobean mansion in 4 acres of carefully kept gardens with a little trout lake, tennis court, and croquet lawn; elegantly updated rooms, a fine carved oak fireplace in the main hall, stylish food in the restaurant's three individually decorated rooms, and courteous staff; spa with swimming pool, sauna, gym and treatment rooms; nine-hole golf course, driving range and shop; owners' dogs Fred and Purdy (labradors) and Mabel (jack russell); walks in grounds and surrounding footpaths; dogs in ground floor bedrooms (not to be left unattended), on lead in brasserie; treats, bowl and mat

LONGFRAMLINGTON   NU1301

Embleton Hall

Longframlington, Morpeth, Northumberland NE65 8DT (01665) 570249
www.embletonhall.com

£105; 13 comfortable, pretty and individually decorated rms. Charming, family-run hotel in lovely grounds surrounded by fine countryside, with a particularly friendly, relaxed atmosphere and courteous staff; log fires in all rooms, a tranquil lounge, a convivial bar with good pubby food and real ales, and an attractive dining room serving very good food using home-grown fruit and vegetables; seats in the garden; resident welsh springer, Tory; dogs welcome anywhere

Harvey – chocolate labrador puppy; owner Fiona Stapley

LONGHORSLEY
Macdonald Linden Hall

Longhorsley, Morpeth, Northumberland NE65 8XF (0844) 879 9084
www.macdonaldhotels.co.uk/lindenhall

£125; 50 comfortable, contemporary rms. Georgian hotel in 450 acres of landscaped park with an 18-hole golf course; open fires and fresh flowers, a clubby pub room, a friendly cocktail bar, an airy drawing room, and good, modern cooking served by courteous staff in the smart, plush restaurant; spa and health club; dogs in ground floor bedrooms only; £10

ROMALDKIRK
Rose & Crown

Romaldkirk, Barnard Castle, County Durham DL12 9EB (01833) 650213
www.rose-and-crown.co.uk

£150; 12 charming rms, 5 in the courtyard. Smart and interesting old coaching inn with a cosily traditional beamed bar, old-fashioned seats facing a warming log fire, a Jacobean oak settle, a grandfather clock and plenty of interesting farm tools and photographs; a smart brasserie-style room, an oak-panelled restaurant and an interestingly decorated hall all serving imaginative food using their own eggs and local seasonal produce and super breakfasts; the exceptional Bowes Museum and High Force waterfall are close by; can walk on nearby disused railway line; dogs in bedrooms and bar; £5

STANNERSBURN
Pheasant

Stannersburn, Hexham, Northumberland NE48 1DD (01434) 240382
www.thepheasantinn.com

£95; 8 tastefully decorated rms. Beautifully located, unpretentious 17th-c stone inn close to Kielder Water and its quiet forests; traditional, comfortable beamed lounge with stripped stone, panelling and straightforward furnishings, a simpler public bar, and a further cosy seating area with more beams and panelling, local beers, 36 malts and courteous staff; bar food is good, breakfasts are nice, and there are seats in the streamside garden; dogs in bedrooms only; £5

WELDON BRIDGE
Anglers Arms

Weldon Bridge, Longframlington, Morpeth, Northumberland NE65 8AX (01665) 570271
www.anglersarms.com

£90; 7 recently refurbished rms. Sizeable place with a comfortable two-part bar at its heart; oak panelling, beams hung with copper pants, a profusion of fish memorabilia, some nice old prints, a shelf of staffordshire cats, a sofa by a coal fire, large helpings of food in a carefully converted railway dining car, and friendly staff; fishing on the River Coquet; self-catering flat, also; dogs in bedrooms and bar; £5

Nottinghamshire

MAP 7

DOG FRIENDLY PUBS

CAYTHORPE   SK6845
Black Horse

Turn off A6097 0.25 miles SE of roundabout junction with A612, NE of Nottingham; into Gunthorpe Road, then right into Caythorpe Road and keep on; NG14 7ED

Quaintly old-fashioned little pub brewing its own beer, simple interior and enjoyable homely food; no children, no credit cards

Peacefully free of games machines, children and swearing, this timeless 300-year-old country local has been run by the same friendly family for three generations. Its uncluttered carpeted bar has just five tables, decorative plates on a delft shelf, a few horsebrasses on the ceiling joists, brocaded wall banquettes and settles, and a coal fire. Cheerful regulars might occupy the few bar stools to enjoy the Caythorpe Dover Beck (named after the stream that runs past the pub) and One Swallow that are brewed in outbuildings here and served alongside a couple of guests from Adams or Greene King Abbot. Off the front corridor is a partly panelled inner room with a wall bench running right the way around three unusual long copper-topped tables, and there are quite a few old local photographs; darts and board games. Down on the left, an end room has just one huge round table. There are some plastic tables outside, and the River Trent is fairly close for waterside walks.

Own brew ~ Licensee Sharron Andrews ~ Real ale ~ Bar food (12-2, 7-9; not Sat evening, Sun or as pub closed times below) ~ Restaurant ~ No credit cards ~ (0115) 966 3520 ~ Dogs allowed in bar ~ Open 12-2.30, 6-11.30; 12-5, 8-11.30 Sun; closed Mon (except bank holidays) and Tues lunchtime after the third Mon of month and bank holidays

UPTON   SK7354
Cross Keys

A612; NG23 5SY

17th-c pub in fine spot with welcoming licensees and tasty well liked food and drink

Friendly, hard-working new licensees have recently taken over this bustling 17th-c pub, but early reports from readers suggested that things are going well. The rambling, heavy-beamed bar has lots of alcoves, a log fire in the brick fireplace, some brass and copper implements, dark wooden cushioned dining chairs around a mix of tables on the traditional red and white floor tiles and Greene King Ruddles H&H Bitter, Wells & Youngs Bombardier and a guest beer on handpump and several wines by the glass. A back extension has a long carved pew, and there's a room for private hire upstairs. The decked terrace outside has plenty of seats, and the pub is opposite the British Horological Institute.

Free house ~ Licensees Roy and Laura Wood ~ Bar food (12-2.30, 6-8 (maybe earlier); not Mon evening) ~ Restaurant ~ (01636) 813269 ~ Children welcome ~ Dogs allowed in bar ~ Live music Sun and Mon evenings ~ Open 12-3,5.30(6 Sat)-11(midnight Sat); 12-10.30 Sun ~ www.crosskeysupton.co.uk

DOG FRIENDLY INNS, HOTELS AND B&Bs

LANGAR   SK7234
Langar Hall
Church Lane, Langar, Nottingham, Nottinghamshire NG13 9IIG (01949) 860559
www.langarhall.com

£130; 13 lovely, pretty rms. Fine family-run country house in spacious grounds and with 30 acres of surrounding fields for walks; a friendly, informal atmosphere, a convivial bar, a homely drawing room and library with antiques, comfortable sofas and armchairs and fresh flowers, a conservatory offering light meals and afternoon teas, and a pillared, candlelit restaurant with imaginative meals served by willing young staff; small dogs in two bedrooms; £20

Lenny – working cocker spaniel; owners Donald and Angie Clay

NOTTINGHAM
SK5639
Harts

Standard Hill, Park Row, Nottingham, Nottinghamshire NG1 6FN (0115) 988 1900
www.hartsnottingham.co.uk

£145; 32 well appointed, quiet rms with fine views. Adjacent to the well known restaurant of the same name, this is a smart and stylish purpose-built hotel in a traffic-free cul-de-sac on the site of the city's medieval castle; charming, friendly staff, an airy bar/breakfast room (breakfasts are very good) and excellent modern british cooking in Hart's restaurant next door; small exercise room, and seats in the courtyard garden; dogs in bedrooms (not to be left unattended); £5

NOTTINGHAM
SK5739
Lace Market

29-31 High Pavement, Nottingham, Nottinghamshire NG1 1HE (0115) 852 3232
www.lacemarkethotel.co.uk

£80; 42 modern, comfortable rms. Next to a lovely church, this Georgian town house has a relaxed atmosphere, friendly young staff, a convivial bar with daily papers, wood-strip floors and strong but subtle colours, a relaxed lounge and a boudoir-style restaurant serving good, brasserie-style food and enjoyable breakfasts; small dogs in bedrooms; £15

SOUTHWELL
SK7053
Old Forge

Burgage Lane, Southwell, Nottinghamshire NG25 0ER (01636) 812809
www.southwell-online.co.uk/localpages/oldforge.html

£80; 5 rms. In a quiet but central spot with its own parking, this 200-year-old former blacksmith's house has a welcoming owner, interesting furnishings, super breakfasts in the conservatory overlooking the minster, and a pretty terrace; resident collie cross, Jake; the Southwell Trail half a mile away is good for walks; dogs in bedrooms; bring own bedding; £2

Oxfordshire

MAPS 2 & 4

DOG FRIENDLY PUBS

BANBURY   SP4540

Olde Reindeer

Parsons Street, off Market Place; OX16 5NA

Plenty of shoppers and regulars in this interesting town pub, fine real ales, simple generous food and roaring log fires

'The best type of town pub' is how one reader describes this well run and unpretentious tavern, and there's a good bustling atmosphere and plenty of customers keen to enjoy the real ales and fair value lunchtime food served by the friendly, helpful staff. The welcoming front bar has heavy 16th-c beams, very broad polished oak floorboards, magnificent carved overmantel for one of the two roaring log fires and traditional solid furnishings. It's worth looking at the handsomely proportioned Globe Room used by Oliver Cromwell as his base during the Civil War. Quite a sight, it still has some very fine carved 17th-c dark oak panelling. Hook Norton Bitter, Hooky Dark, Hooky Gold, Old Hooky and a changing guest beer on handpump, wines by the glass, and several malt whiskies; maybe background music. The little back courtyard has tables and benches under parasols, aunt sally and pretty flowering baskets.

Hook Norton ~ Tenant Marc Sylvester ~ Real ale ~ Bar food (11-4, 6-9) ~ Restaurant ~ (01295) 264031 ~ Children welcome ~ Dogs allowed in bar ~ Open 11-11 ~ www.yeoldereindeer.co.uk

BESSELS LEIGH   SP4501

Greyhound

A420 Faringdon–Botley; OX13 5PX

Handsome 400-year-old stone pub with knocked-through rooms, plenty of character and interest, half a dozen real ales, lots of wines by the glass and enjoyable interesting food

Several of our readers use this handsome former coaching inn as a civilised break on the A420 Oxford to Swindon road and there are plenty of locals dropping in and out too, creating a bustling and chatty atmosphere. The knocked-through rooms give plenty of space and interest and the half-panelled walls are covered in all manner of old photographs and pictures. The individually chosen cushioned dining chairs, leather-topped stools and dark wooden tables are grouped on carpeting or rug-covered floorboards and there are books on shelves, glass and stone bottles on windowsills, big gilt mirrors, three fireplaces (one housing a woodburning stove), and sizeable pot plants dotted about. Wooden bar stools sit against the counter where they serve Brunning & Price Original (brewed for the company by Phoenix), Hook Norton Hooky Bitter, White Horse Wayland Smithy and three changing guest beers on handpump, 15 wines by the glass and 80 malt whiskies. By the back dining extension there's a white picket fence-enclosed garden with picnic-sets under green parasols.

Brunning & Price ~ Manager Emily Waring ~ Real ale ~ Bar food (12-10(9.30 Sun)) ~ (01865) 862110 ~ Children welcome ~ Dogs allowed in bar ~ Open 12-11(10.30 Sun) ~ www.greyhound-besselsleigh.co.uk

BRIGHTWELL BALDWIN   SU6594
Lord Nelson

Off B480 Chalgrove–Watlington, or B4009 Benson–Watlington; OX49 5NP

Attractive inn with several different character bars, real ales, good wines by the glass and enjoyable well thought of food; bedrooms

In a quiet village and set opposite the church, this 300-year-old inn is best known as a well run dining pub – but they do keep Black Sheep Best, Brakspears Bitter and Rebellion IPA on handpump, around 14 wines (including champagne) by the glass and winter mulled wine. There are wheelback and other dining chairs around a mix of dark tables, candles and fresh flowers, wine bottles on window sills, horsebrasses on standing timbers, lots of paintings on the white or red walls and a big brick inglenook fireplace. One cosy room has cushions on comfortable sofas, little lamps on dark furniture, ornate mirrors and portraits in gilt frames; background music. The back terrace has seats and tables with more in the willow-draped garden.

Free house ~ Licensees Roger and Carole Shippey ~ Real ale ~ Bar food (12-2.30(3 Sun), 6-10(7-9.30 Sun)) ~ Restaurant ~ (01491) 612497 ~ Children welcome ~ Dogs allowed in bar ~ Open 12-3, 6-11; 12-10.30 Sun ~ Bedrooms: £70B/£90B ~ www.lordnelson-inn.co.uk

CHIPPING NORTON   SP3127
Chequers

Goddards Lane; OX7 5NP

Busy, friendly town pub open all day with several real ales, popular bar food, a cheerful mix of customers and simple bars

Tucked away in a quiet part of town, this cheerful pub has a good mix of both locals and visitors. The three softly lit beamed rooms have no frills, but are clean and comfortable with low ochre ceilings, lots of character, and a blazing log fire. Quick staff serve up to eight real ales on handpump: Fullers Chiswick, Discovery, ESB, HSB, London Pride, and Seafarers Ale and a couple of changing guest beers. They also have good house wines – 15 by the glass. The conservatory restaurant is light and airy and used for more formal dining. The theatre is next door.

Fullers ~ Lease Jim Hopcroft ~ Real ale ~ Bar food (12-2.30, 6-9.30; 12-4 Sun; not Sun evening) ~ Restaurant ~ (01608) 644717 ~ Children welcome ~ Dogs allowed in bar ~ Live music monthly and Sun evening quiz ~ Open 11(11.30 Sun)-11(midnight Sat) ~ www.chequers-pub.com

EAST HENDRED   SU4588

Eyston Arms

Village signposted off A417 E of Wantage; High Street; OX12 8JY

Attractive bar areas with low beams, flagstones, log fires and candles, imaginative food and helpful service

There are a few tables for drinkers and seats at the bar and locals do pop in for a pint and chat, but most customers come to this well run and pleasant dining pub to enjoy the good, interesting food. It's a busy, welcoming place and there are several separate-seeming areas with contemporary paintwork and modern country-style furnishings. Also, low ceilings and beams, stripped timbers, the odd standing timber, an inglenook fireplace, nice tables and chairs on the flagstones and carpet, some cushioned wall seats, candlelight and a piano; background music. Cheerful staff serve Fullers London Pride and Hook Norton Hooky Bitter on handpump and several wines by the glass. Picnic-sets outside overlook the pretty lane and there are seats in the back courtyard garden.

Free house ~ Licensees George Dailey and Daisy Barton ~ Real ale ~ Bar food (12-2, 7-9; 12-9 Fri and Sat; 11.30-3; not Sun evening) ~ Restaurant ~ (01235) 833320 ~ Children welcome but must be well behaved ~ Dogs allowed in bar ~ Open 12-3, 6-11; 11-11 Fri and Sat; 11.30-11 Sun; closed Sun evening ~ www.eystonarms.co.uk

FERNHAM   SU2991

Woodman

A420 SW of Oxford, then left into B4508 after about 11 miles; village a further 6 miles on; SN7 7NX

A good choice of real ales and interesting highly thought of bar food in a charming old-world country pub

This is a smashing pub, particularly well run by the friendly landlord and his attentive staff – and our readers enjoy their visits here very much. The heavily beamed main rooms have the most character and are full of an amazing assortment of old objects like clay pipes, milkmaids' yokes, leather tack, coach horns, an old screw press, some original oil paintings and good black and white photographs of horses. Comfortable seating includes cushioned benches, pews and windsor chairs, and the candlelit tables are simply made from old casks; a big wood fire, too. As well as some comfortable newer areas, there's a large room for Sunday lunches. The four real ales are from breweries such as Greene King, Oakham, Sharps, Timothy Taylors, Wadworths 6X and White Horse and are tapped from the cask and they keep several wines by the glass and 16 malt whiskies; background music. There are seats outside on the terrace. Disabled lavatories.

Free house ~ Licensee Steven Whiting ~ Real ale ~ Bar food (12-2(2.30 weekends), 6.30-9.30) ~ Restaurant ~ (01367) 820643 ~ Children welcome ~ Dogs allowed in bar ~ Open 11-11 ~ www.thewoodmaninn.net

HIGHMOOR   SU6984

Rising Sun

Witheridge Hill, signposted off B481; OS Sheet 175 map reference 697841; RG9 5PF

Thoughtfully run, pretty pub with a mix of diners and drinkers and well liked interesting food

Y ou can be sure of a warm welcome from the friendly licensees and their staff in this pretty black and cream village pub – whether you're a local or a visitor and looking for a chatty drink or a leisurely meal. On the right by the bar, there are wooden tables and chairs and a sofa on the stripped wooden floors, cream and terracotta walls and an open fire in the big brick inglenook fireplace. The main area spreading back from here has shiny bare boards and a swathe of carpeting with well spaced tables and attractive pictures on the walls. Brakspears Bitter and Oxford Gold on handpump, ten wines by the glass and Weston's cider; background music and board games. There are seats and tables in the pleasant back garden; boules. As this is the heart of the Chilterns, there are plenty of surrounding walks.

Brakspears ~ Tenant Simon Duffy ~ Real ale ~ Bar food (12-2, 6.30-9; some sort of food all day Sat; till 7 Sun evening) ~ Restaurant ~ (01491) 640856 ~ Children allowed under strict supervision in dining areas only ~ Dogs allowed in bar ~ Open 12-3, 5.30-11; 12-11(7 Sun) Sat; closed Sun evening ~ www.risingsunwitheridgehill.co.uk

KINGSTON LISLE   SU3287
Blowing Stone
Village signposted off B4507 W of Wantage; OX12 9QL

Easy-going chatty country pub with up-to-date blend of simple comfort, good interesting food and drink

T he heart of this friendly village pub with its easy country informality is the central bar, where broad tiles by the log fire suit the muddy riding boots of the cheerful young people in from nearby training stables. They have the Racing Post alongside other daily papers, and most of the photographs on the pale sage walls are of racehorses, often spectacularly coming to grief over jumps. Several separate areas radiate off, most of them carpeted, quite small and snug, though a back dining conservatory is more spacious. Apart from a couple of high-backed winged settles, most of the furniture is an unfussy mix of country dining tables each with its own set of matching chairs, either padded or generously cushioned. Greene King Morland Original, Ramsbury Gold and West Berkshire Mr Chubbs Lunchtime Bitter on handpump, ten decent wines by the glass, and chilled manzanilla and oloroso sherry; service is attentive and there may be unobtrusive background music. The pretty front terrace has a couple of picnic-sets under cocktail parasols with more on the back lawn by a rockery; the Ridgeway and Uffington White Horse are both nearby.

Free house ~ Licensees Angus and Steph Tucker ~ Real ale ~ Bar food (12-2, 6.30-9; not Sun evening (except summer Sun for freshly made pizzas)) ~ Restaurant ~ (01367) 820288 ~ Children welcome ~ Dogs allowed in bar ~ Open 12-midnight(11pm Sun) ~ www.theblowingstone.co.uk

KIRTLINGTON   SP4919
Oxford Arms
Troy Lane, junction with A4095 W of Bicester; OX5 3HA

Civilised and friendly stripped-stone pub with enjoyable food using local produce and good wine choice

T he chef/landlord and his charming young staff ensure a genial atmosphere in this neatly kept stone pub with its pretty, geranium-filled window boxes. A long line of linked rooms is divided by a central stone hearth with a great round stove – and by the servery itself, with Brakspears Bitter and St Austell Tribute on handpump, an interesting range of 13 wines in two glass sizes, 14 malt whiskies, and a good choice of soft drinks. Past the bar area with its cushioned wall pews, creaky beamed ceiling and age-darkened floor tiles, dining tables on parquet have neat red chairs, and beyond that leather sofas cluster round a log fire at the end; there are church candles, fresh flowers and plenty of stripped stone. A sheltered back terrace has teak tables under giant parasols with heaters, and beyond are picnic-sets on pale gravel.

Punch ~ Lease Bryn Jones ~ Real ale ~ Bar food (12-2.30, 6.30-9.30, not Sun evening) ~ (01869) 350208 ~ Well behaved children welcome ~ Dogs allowed in bar ~ Open 12-3, 6-11; 12-3 Sun; closed Sun evening ~ www.oxford-arms.co.uk

LANGFORD   SP2402
Bell
Village signposted off A361 N of Lechlade, then pub signed; GL7 3LF

Civilised pub with beams, flagstones and log fire, friendly service, well chosen wines and beer, and extremely good food

Once they've discovered this enjoyable country dining pub, our readers tend to return again and again. It's a friendly place with an informal country atmosphere, with simple low-key furnishings and décor adding to the appeal. The main bar has just six sanded-down tables on grass matting, a variety of chairs, three nice cushioned window seats, an attractive carved oak settle, polished broad flagstones by a big stone inglenook fireplace with a good log fire, low beams and butter-coloured walls with two or three antique engravings. A second even smaller room on the right is similar in character; daily papers on a little corner table. Hook Norton Hooky Bitter, Sharps Cornish Coaster and St Austell Tribute on handpump and a dozen wines by the glass. The bearded collie is called Madison. There are two or three picnic-sets in the small garden with a play house; aunt sally. The village is quiet and charming.

Free house ~ Licensees Paul and Jackie Wynne ~ Real ale ~ Bar food (12-1.45, 7-9; not Sun evening or Mon) ~ Restaurant ~ (01367) 860249 ~ Children welcome but no under 4s after 7pm ~ Dogs allowed in bar ~ Open 12-3, 7-11 (midnight Fri, 11.30 Sat); 12-3.30 Sun; closed Sun evening, all day Mon ~ www.bellatlangford.co.uk

LONG HANBOROUGH   SP4214
George & Dragon
A4095 Bladon–Witney; Main Road; OX29 8JX

Substantial well organised pub, something for everyone; wide choice of enjoyable food

Busy and very well run by its friendly and efficient hands-on licensees, this is almost best thought of as two separate places. The original two-room bar, 17th-c or older, is all stripped stone, low beams and soft lighting, with thoroughly traditional pubby feel and furnishings to suit – including two stoves (one very elaborate). It forms an L with a roomy thatched restaurant extension, which has comfortably padded dining chairs around the sturdy tables on floorboards, plenty of pictures on deep pink walls, and decorative plates on the beams. Neat black-uniformed staff are friendly and efficient; they have well kept Courage Directors and Wells & Youngs Bombardier and Eagle IPA on handpump, Weston's farm cider and a good range of wines; there may be soft background music. The peaceful back garden has cream-painted picnic-sets among attractive shrubs, tables beneath a big dark canopy on a separate sheltered terrace, and further areas where you'll find rabbits and guinea-pigs.

Charles Wells ~ Lease Mr A and Mrs J Willett ~ Real ale ~ Bar food (12-2(3 Sun), 6.30-9(9.30 Fri, Sat); not Sun evening) ~ Restaurant ~ (01993) 881362 ~ Children welcome ~ Dogs allowed in bar ~ Open 12-3, 6-midnight; 12-4, 6.30-11 Sun ~ www.menublackboard.com

LONGWORTH   SU3899

Blue Boar

Tucks Lane; OX13 5ET

Smashing old pub with a friendly welcome for all, good wines and beer, and fairly priced reliable food; Thames-side walks nearby

From outside, this is pretty much the classic image of an english country pub in a charming village. Inside, you can be sure of a warm welcome from the friendly staff and a bustling but easy-going atmosphere – helped by a healthy mix of both diners and chatty locals. The three low-beamed, characterful little rooms are properly traditional with well worn fixtures and furnishings and two blazing log fires, one beside a fine old settle. Brasses, hops and assorted knick-knacks like skis and an old clocking-in machine line the ceilings and walls, there are fresh flowers on the bar and scrubbed wooden tables, and faded rugs on the tiled floor; benches are firmly wooden rather than upholstered. The main eating area is the red-painted room at the end and there's a quieter restaurant extension, too. Brakspears Bitter, Fullers London Pride and a guest like Sharps Doom Bar on handpump, 20 malt whiskies, a dozen wines by the glass, summer Pimms and quite a few brandies and ports. There are tables in front and on the back terrace, and the Thames is a short walk away.

Free house ~ Licensee Paul Dailey ~ Real ale ~ Bar food (12-2.30(3 Sun), 6.30-9.30(10 Fri, Sat, 9 Sun); pizzas all day) ~ Restaurant ~ (01865) 820494 ~ Children welcome ~ Dogs allowed in bar ~ Open 11.30-11(midnight Sat) ~ www.blueboarlongworth.co.uk

OXFORD   SP5106

Bear

Alfred Street/Wheatsheaf Alley; OX1 4EH

Delightful pub with friendly staff, two cosy rooms, six real ales and well liked bar food

Tucked away off the tourist trail, this charming little pub is the oldest drinking house in the city. There are two small low-ceilinged, beamed and partly panelled rooms, not over-smart and often packed with students, with a bustling chatty atmosphere, winter coal fires, thousands of vintage ties on walls and up to six real ales from handpumps on the fine pewter bar counter: Fullers Chiswick, ESB, Gales HSB and London Pride and a couple of guests beers such as Shotover Prospect and Scholar. Staff are friendly and helpful. There are seats under parasols in the terraced back garden where summer barbecues are held.

Fullers ~ Manager James Verneade ~ Real ale ~ Bar food (all day) ~ (01865) 728164 ~ children until 9pm ~ Dogs allowed in bar ~ acoustic night Wed ~ Open 11-11(midnight Fri and Sat); 11-11 Sun

OXFORD   SP5005

Punter

South Street, Osney (off A420 Botley Road via Bridge Street); OX2 0BE

Friendly, relaxed pub overlooking the water with lots of character and enjoyable modern food

Actually on Osney Island and with views over the Thames, this easy-going pub is run with great enthusiasm by the young landlord. The lower area has attractive rugs on flagstones and an open fire and the upper room has more rugs on floorboards and a single big table surrounded by oil paintings – just right for a private party. Throughout there are all manner of nice old dining chairs around an interesting mix of tables, affordable art on white-washed walls and one rather fine stained-glass window. Adnams Bitter and Broadside on handpump from the tiled counter, several wines by the glass and friendly service; board games.

Greene King ~ Lease Tom Rainey ~ Real ale ~ Bar food (all day) ~ Restaurant ~ (01865) 248832 ~ Children welcome ~ Dogs allowed in bar ~ Open 12-midnight(11.30 Sun) ~ www.thepunteroxford.com

PISHILL   SU7190

Crown

B480 Nettlebed–Wattlington; RG9 6HH

Fine old inn with attractive beamed bars, winter fires, real ales, several wines by the glass and enjoyable hearty food; bedrooms

Kept spotlessly clean, this mainly 15th-c red brick and flint pub is in the heart of the Chilterns. Our readers enjoy their visits here very much and always receive a friendly welcome from the helpful, professional staff. The partly-panelled walls in the beamed bars are hung with old local photographs and maps, there are nice old chairs around a mix of wooden tables, candles everywhere, Black Sheep Best Bitter, Brakspears Bitter, and Rebellion IPA on handpump and nine wines by the glass. The knocked-through back area has standing oak timbers, and there are three roaring log fires in winter; there's a priest's hole said to be one of the largest in the country. The beautiful thatched barn used for parties and functions, is some 500 years old. In warm weather, there are lots of seats and tables under neat blue parasols in the pretty garden; nearby walks. A self-contained cottage can be rented by the night (breakfast provided).

Free house ~ Licensee Lucas Wood ~ Real ale ~ Bar food (12-2.30(3 Sun), 6.30-9(9.30 Fri, Sat)) ~ (01491) 638364 ~ Children welcome ~ Dogs allowed in bar ~ Open 12-3, 6-11; 12-10 Sun ~ Bedrooms: /£80B ~ www.thecrowninnpishill.co.uk

RAMSDEN   SP3515

Royal Oak

Village signposted off B4022 Witney–Charlbury; OX7 3AU

Busy pub with long-serving licensees, large helpings of varied food, carefully chosen wines and seats outside; bedrooms

There are no noisy games machines or background music to spoil the relaxed atmosphere in this 17th-c cotswold stone pub. The unpretentious rooms have a mix of wooden tables, chairs and settles, cushioned window seats, exposed stone walls, bookcases with old and new copies of Country Life and, when the weather gets cold, a cheerful log fire. Hook Norton Old Hooky, Stonehenge

Heelstone and Wye Valley HPA on handpump, and ten wines by the glass from a carefully chosen list. There are tables and chairs out in front and on the terrace behind the restaurant (folding back doors give easy access). The bedrooms are in separate cottages and there are some fine surrounding walks.

Free house ~ Licensee Jon Oldham ~ Real ale ~ Bar food (12-2, 7-9) ~ Restaurant ~ (01993) 868213 ~ Children in restaurant with parents ~ Dogs allowed in bar ~ Open 11.30-3, 6.30-11; 12-3, 7-10.30 Sun ~ Bedrooms: £60S/£80S ~ www.royaloakramsden.com

ROTHERFIELD GREYS   SU7282

Maltsters Arms

Can be reached off A4155 in Henley, via Greys Road passing Southfields long-stay car park; or follow Greys Church signpost off B481 N of Sonning Common; RG9 4QD

Well run, civilised country pub in the Chilterns with well liked, fairly priced food, nice scenery and walks

With Greys Court (National Trust) not far away and two good footpaths passing close by, this civilised pub is just the place for lunch; the friendly helpful staff make you feel quickly at home. The maroon-carpeted front room has comfortable wall banquettes and lots of horsebrasses on its black beams, Brakspears Bitter and Oxford Gold and a guest such as Jennings Cumberland on handpump, a dozen wines by the glass and decent coffee; there's a warm winter open fire and maybe soft background music. Beyond the serving area, which has hop bines and pewter tankards hanging from its joists, a back room has cricketing prints on dark red walls over a shiny panelled dado, and a mix of furnishings from pink-cushioned pale wooden dining chairs to a pair of leatherette banquettes forming a corner booth. The chocolate Labradors have been here as long as the licensees – 14 years. Terrace tables under a big heated canopy are set with linen for meals, and the grass behind has picnic-sets under green parasols, looking out over paddocks to rolling woodland beyond.

Brakspears ~ Tenants Peter and Helen Bland ~ Real ale ~ Bar food (12-2.15, 6.15-9.15; not Sun evening) ~ (01491) 628400 ~ Children welcome ~ Dogs allowed in bar ~ Open 11.45-3, 6-11(midnight Sat); 12-9(5.30 winter) Sun; closed winter Sun evening ~ www.maltsters.co.uk

SHILTON   SP2608

Rose & Crown

Just off B4020 SE of Burford; OX18 4AB

Simple and appealing little village pub, with a relaxed civilised atmosphere, real ales and good food cooked by the landlord

There's a warm welcome from the very nice landlord and his staff for all their customers, whether visitors or locals. It's a pretty and cosy 17th-c stone-built pub with an unassuming feel – in a subtly upmarket way. The small front bar has low beams and timbers, exposed stone walls, a log fire in a big fireplace and half a dozen or so kitchen chairs and tables on the red tiled floor. There are usually a few locals at the planked counter where they serve Hook Norton Old Hooky, Wells & Youngs Bitter and a guest like Stonehenge Heelstone on handpump, along with ten wines by the glass; big cafetières of coffee. A second room, similar but bigger, is used mainly for eating, with flowers on the tables and another fireplace. At the side, an attractive garden has picnic-sets.

Free house ~ Licensee Martin Coldicott ~ Real ale ~ Bar food (12-2(2.45 weekends and bank holidays), 7-9) ~ Restaurant ~ (01993) 842280 ~ Well behaved children welcome until 7pm ~ Dogs allowed in bar ~ Open 11.30-3, 6-11; 11.30-11 Fri and Sat; 12-10 Sun ~ www. roseandcrownshilton.com

STANFORD IN THE VALE

SU3393

Horse & Jockey

A417 Faringdon–Wantage; Faringdon Road; SN7 8NN

Friendly traditional village local with real character, highly thought of good value food and well chosen wines

Prices are very fair here with main courses (apart from steaks) under £10 – and we've given them one of our Bargain Awards this year. Big Alfred Munnings' racecourse prints, card collections of Grand National winner and other horse and jockey pictures reflect not just the pub's name but the fact that this is racehorse training country – which so often seems to guarantee a relaxed and comfortably welcoming atmosphere. Greene King Morlands Original, Old Speckled Hen and Ruddles County on handpump and carefully chosen wines in a sensible choice of glass sizes. The main area, with flagstones, a low ochre ceiling and a woodburning stove in its big fireplace, has several old high-backed settles and a couple of bucket armchairs. On the right is a carpeted area with a lofty raftered ceiling, a lattice-windowed inner gallery and some stripped stone, and at the back a spacious bare-boards dining room. As well as tables out under a heated courtyard canopy, there's a separate enclosed and informal family garden with a play area and picnic-sets on the grass; aunt sally. The bedrooms are comfortable.

Greene King ~ Lease Charles and Anna Gaunt ~ Real ale ~ Bar food (12-2.15(2.30 Sun), 6.30-9(9.30 Fri, Sat, 8.30 Sun)) ~ Restaurant ~ (01367) 710302 ~ Children welcome ~ Dogs allowed in bar ~ Thurs evening quiz and monthly open mike first Weds evening of month ~ Open 11-3, 5-midnight; 11am-12.30am Fri, Sat; 12-midnight Sun ~ Bedrooms: £50S/£60S ~ www.horseandjockey.org

STONESFIELD

SP3917

White Horse

Village signposted off B4437 Charlbury–Woodstock; Stonesfield Riding; OX29 8EA

Attractively upgraded small country pub with good enjoyable food using local produce and a relaxed atmosphere

Handy for the Roman villa (English Heritage) at nearby North Leigh, this is a carefully run pub with quite an emphasis on food. There are contemporary artworks, restful colours (grey or off-white in the snug little bar, dark pink over a grey dado in the dining room) and nicely chosen furniture. One of their best touches is the little inner room with just a pair of sheraton-style chairs around a single mahogany table. Service is cheerful and efficient. The corner bar counter, with padded stools, has Ringwood Best and Boondoggle on handpump; open fire, daily papers, quiet background music. The dining room's french windows open on to a neat walled garden with picnic-sets; there's a skittle alley in the separate stone barn. As the pub is on the Oxfordshire Way there are good walks nearby. Please note the restricted opening times.

Free house ~ Licensees John and Angela Lloyd ~ Real ale ~ Bar food (12-2, 6.30-9; not Mon, Tues and Weds lunchtimes, Sun evening) ~ Restaurant ~ (01993) 891063 ~ Children welcome ~ Dogs allowed in bar ~ Open 12-3, 5(6 Sat)-11; 12-4 Sun; closed Mon, closed Tues and Weds lunchtimes, Sun evening ~ www.thewhitehorseinnatstonesfield.co.uk

SWINBROOK

SP2812

Swan

Back road a mile N of A40, 2 miles E of Burford; OX18 4DY

Rather smart old pub with handsome oak garden rooms, antique-filled bars, local beers and contemporary food using local and organic produce; bedrooms

As this civilised 17th-c pub is owned by the Dowager Duchess of Devonshire (the last of the Mitford sisters who grew up in the village) there are lots of interesting Mitford family photographs blown up on the walls. There's a little bar with simple antique furnishings, settles and benches, an open fire, and (in an alcove) a stuffed swan; locals do still drop in here for a pint and a chat. A small dining room leads off from the bar to the right of the entrance, and there are also two green oak garden rooms with high-backed beige and green dining chairs around pale wood tables, and views over the garden and orchard. Hook Norton Hooky Bitter and guests from breweries like Brakspears, Butcombe and Wye Valley on handpump, ten wines by the glass and Weston's organic cider. This is a lovely spot by a bridge over the River Windrush and seats by the fuchsia hedge make the best of the view. The bedrooms are in a smartly converted stone barn beside the pub. The Kings Head in Bledington (Gloucestershire) is run by the same first class licensees.

Free house ~ Licensees Archie and Nicola Orr-Ewing ~ Real ale ~ Bar food (12-2, 7-9) ~ Restaurant ~ (01993) 823339 ~ Children welcome ~ Dogs allowed in bar ~ Open 11(12 Sun)-11; 11-3, 6-11 in winter ~ Bedrooms: £90B/£120B ~ www.theswanswinbrook.co.uk

WOODSTOCK

SP4416

Kings Arms

Market Street/Park Lane (A44); OX20 1SU

Stylish hotel in centre of attractive town, well liked food using local produce where possible, enjoyable atmosphere and a wide choice of drinks; comfortable bedrooms

You can be sure of excellent service and a warm welcome from the well trained staff in this stylish town-centre hotel. The unfussy bar has a good mix of customers creating a relaxed and informal atmosphere, a happy mix of old and new furnishings including brown leather furniture on the stripped-wood floor, smart blinds and black and white photographs; at the front, there's an old wooden settle and an interesting little woodburner. In the bar leading to the brasserie-style dining room there's an unusual stained-glass structure used for newspapers and magazines; the restaurant is attractive, with its hanging lights and fine old fireplace. Brakspears Bitter and Oxford Gold and a guest like Banks's Mansfield Bitter on handpump, good coffees, 15 wines plus champagne by the glass and 21 malt whiskies; background music. The bedrooms are comfortable and the breakfasts very good. There are seats and tables on the street outside.

Free house ~ Licensees David and Sara Sykes ~ Real ale ~ Bar food (12-2, 6.30-9; all day Sun) ~ Restaurant ~ (01993) 813636 ~ Children welcome in bar and restaurant but no under-12s in bedrooms ~ Dogs allowed in bar ~ Open 11-11 ~ Bedrooms: £80S/£150B ~ www.kings-hotel-woodstock.co.uk

DOG FRIENDLY INNS, HOTELS AND B&Bs

BURFORD
SP2412

Lamb

Sheep Street, Burford, Oxfordshire OX18 4LR (01993) 823155
www.cotswold-inns-hotels.co.uk

£160; 17 comfortable rms. Lovely 500-year-old Cotswold inn with a classic, cosy bar, high-backed settles and old chairs on flagstones, a log fire and an extensive choice of drinks, a roomy beamed main lounge with distinguished elderly seats, rugs on wide flagstones or polished floorboards, winter log fire, and plenty of antiques; impeccable service, good enjoyable food, smashing breakfasts, and neatly kept lawns and terracing; walks in surrounding countryside; dogs anywhere except restaurant; bowls and treats; £10

CLIFTON
SP4931

Duke of Cumberlands Head

Clifton, Banbury, Oxfordshire OX15 0PE (01869) 338534 www.cliftonduke.com

£45; 5 cosy, good value rms. Pretty, thatched stone inn close to the canal (walks along the towpath and bridleways); warm bars with beams in low ceilings, rugs on bare boards, nice old furniture, church candles and a good log fire in a vast inglenook; real ales, wines by the glass and popular food; seats in the garden; dogs in bedrooms and bar

KINGHAM
SP2523

Mill House

Station Road, Kingham, Chipping Norton, Oxfordshire OX7 6UH (01608) 658188
www.millhousehotel.co.uk

£100; 23 light rms with country views. Carefully renovated, family-run 17th-c flour mill in 10 acres of grounds with a trout stream and plenty of original features; a cosy, bustling bar, a comfortable spacious lounge with books and magazines, an elegant restaurant where helpful, friendly staff serve inventive, modern dishes, popular afternoon teas and hearty breakfasts; dogs in some bedrooms; £10

KINGHAM
SP2624

Plough

The Green, Kingham, Chipping Norton, Oxfordshire OX7 6YD (01608) 658327
www.thekinghamplough.co.uk

£90; 7 pretty rms. Friendly restaurant-with-rooms combining an informal pub atmosphere with upmarket food; a properly pubby bar with nice old high-backed settles and brightly cushioned chapel chairs, candles on stripped tables, cheerful country prints, a log fire at one end and a woodburner at the other; spacious and raftered two-part dining room, highly enjoyable and inventive food (smashing breakfasts, too) and a thoughtful choice of drinks; dogs in annexe bedrooms and bar; £10

KINGSTON BAGPUIZE   SU3997
Fallowfields

Southmoor, Kingston Bagpuize, Abingdon, Oxfordshire OX13 5BH (01865) 820416
www.fallowfields.com

£155; 10 attractive rms. Delightful and beautifully kept gothic-style manor house with relaxing sitting rooms, open fires, imaginative food using home-grown produce in attractive conservatory dining room, courteous helpful service and 12 acres of pretty gardens and paddocks (where dogs may walk – countryside all around for longer walks); lots to see nearby; one resident cat (not in guest quarters); dogs in bedrooms; not in dining room; £5

MINSTER LOVELL   SP3211
Old Swan & Minster Mill

Old Minster Lovell, Minster Lovell, Witney, Oxfordshire OX29 0RN (01993) 774441
www.oldswanandminstermill.com

£195; 60 traditional and luxurious rms. Lovingly restored old place with much emphasis on the hotel and restaurant side but with a restful and unchanging bar at its heart; several attractive low-beamed rooms lead off here with big log fires in huge fireplaces, lots of sofas, armchairs and wooden dining chairs on bare boards or ancient flagstones, interesting antiques (bed-warming pans, swords, hunting horns and even a suit of armour) and fresh flowers; excellent, elaborate food using produce from their kitchen garden, delicious breakfasts and seats (and walks) in 65 acres of grounds (they have a mile of fishing on the River Windrush); chickens, ducks, guinea pigs; dogs in some bedrooms and snug; beds, bowls and special chicken dish; £20

OXFORD   SP5107
Old Parsonage

1 Banbury Road, Oxford OX2 6NN (01865) 310210 www.oldparsonage-hotel.co.uk

£225; 30 lovely rms. Handsome and civilised 17th-c parsonage with many fine original features, a little red-walled lounge with lots of prints and portraits, a cosy bar/restaurant with an open fire, very good modern british cooking, afternoon teas and smashing breakfasts, courteous staff and a pretty garden with seats on the terrace; walks in nearby parks; dogs welcome away from restaurant; bowls and basket on request

SHILLINGFORD   SU5991
Shillingford Bridge Hotel

Shillingford Road, Shillingford, Wallingford, Oxfordshire OX10 8LZ (01865) 858567
www.shillingfordbridgehotel.com

£89; 40 rms. Thames-side hotel with its own river frontage, terraced gardens, fishing and moorings; the spacious comfortable bars and attractive airy restaurant (all with fine views) have been refurbished recently with leather sofas and oak tables and chairs on new tiling, and the food served by helpful staff is enjoyable; walks along the Thames; dogs welcome away from restaurant; £7.50

SHIPLAKE   SU7779

Baskerville

Station Road, Lower Shiplake, Henley-on-Thames, Oxfordshire RG9 3NY (0118) 940 3332
www.thebaskerville.com

£96; 4 spotless rms. Particularly well run and friendly village pub with emphasis
on the imaginative food – but with a proper public bar, too; pale wooden tables
and chairs and plush banquettes, sporting memorabilia and pictures, log fires in
brick fireplaces, fresh flowers and house plants and a very good choice of drinks
served by well trained staff; the separate dining room offers impressive food using
organic produce and sustainably sourced fish and the breakfasts are very good;
the pretty garden has smart teak furniture under huge parasols and fun statues
made from box hedges; walks along nearby Thames Path; dogs in bedrooms (not
to be left unattended) and bar; bowls; £10

SHIPTON-UNDER-WYCHWOOD   SP2717

Shaven Crown

High Street, Shipton-under-Wychwood, Chipping Norton, Oxfordshire OX7 6BA
(01993) 830330 www.theshavencrown.co.uk

£85; 8 character rms. Densely beamed, ancient stone hospice built around a
striking medieval courtyard with seating by a lily pool and roses; impressive
medieval hall with a magnificent lofty ceiling, a sweeping stairway and old stone
walls, a log fire in the comfortable bar, a residents' lounge, an intimate candlelit
restaurant, good friendly service and a warm relaxed atmosphere; bowling green;
lots of walks not far away; dogs welcome away from restaurant; £10

TADPOLE BRIDGE   SP3200

Trout

Buckland Marsh, Faringdon, Oxfordshire SN7 8RF (01367) 870382 www.troutinn.co.uk

£130; 6 spacious, attractive rms. Busy, well run country inn by the River Thames
with walks along the Thames Path and seats in waterside gardens; L-shaped bar
with pink and cream-checked chairs on flagstones, two woodburning stoves, fresh
flowers, a friendly, civilised feel, well kept ales and carefully chosen wines, and
an appealing, candlelit restaurant; inventive and deservedly popular food, helpful
staff and particularly good breakfasts; dogs anywhere in the pub and in bedrooms

WOODSTOCK   SP4416

Feathers

Market Street, Woodstock, Oxfordshire OX20 1SX (01993) 812291 www.feathers.co.uk

£229; 21 individually decorated rms including five suites. Lovely old building
given a careful and tasteful contemporary makeover with bold coloured
furnishings, comfortable sofas and armchairs on pale wooden flooring or
rugs on flagstones, prints and pictures on the walls, open fires and courteous
staff, imaginative modern food from good breakfasts through light lunches
to afternoon teas and first class evening meals, and a sunny courtyard with
attractive seating; walks nearby; dogs in bedrooms and bar (not restaurant);
bedding, bowl, treats; £15

Shropshire

DOG FRIENDLY PUBS

BRIDGNORTH   SO7192
Old Castle
West Castle Street; WV16 4AB

Traditional town pub, relaxed and friendly, with generous helpings of good value pubby food, well kept ales and good-sized suntrap terrace

It's so nice to hear from a reader that this pretty little town pub consisting of two knocked-together cottages (you can really see this in its external appearance) is 'still bustling on market day [Saturday] with families and all sorts'. The low-beamed open-plan bar is properly pubby and genuinely characterful with tiles and bare boards, cushioned wall banquettes and settles around cast-iron-framed tables. Bar stools are arranged alongside the counter where the friendly landlord and his cheery staff serve well kept Hobsons Town Crier, Marstons EPA, Sharps Doom Bar and a guest such as Davenports Englands Glory on handpump. A back conservatory extension has darts and pool; background music and big-screen TV for sports events. A big plus here is the sunny back terrace, with shrub borders, big pots of flowers and children's playthings. The decking at the far end gives an elevated view over the west side of town. Do walk up the street to see the ruined castle, best seen before rather than after a drink: its 20-metre Norman tower tilts at such an extraordinary angle that it makes the leaning tower of Pisa look like a model of rectitude.

Punch ~ Tenants Bryn Charles Masterman and Kerry Senior ~ Real ale ~ Bar food (12-3, 6.30-8.30; not Sun evening except bank holidays) ~ (01746) 711420 ~ Children welcome ~ Dogs allowed in bar ~ Open 11.30-11 ~ www.oldcastlebridgnorth.co.uk

CARDINGTON   SO5095
Royal Oak
Village signposted off B4371 Church Stretton–Much Wenlock, pub behind church; also reached via narrow lanes from A49; SY6 7JZ

Lovely rural position, heaps of character inside and seasonal bar food

Dating from the 15th c, this ancient place (it's reputedly Shropshire's oldest continuously licensed pub) is packed with character and historical atmosphere. Gently frayed around the edges, its rambling low-beamed bar has a roaring winter log fire, a cauldron, black kettle and pewter jugs in its vast inglenook fireplace, the aged standing timbers of a knocked-through wall, and red and green tapestry seats solidly capped in elm; shove-ha'penny and dominoes; Hobsons Best, Marstons Pedigree and a couple of guests such as Three Tuns XXX and Salopian Hop Twister are on handpump. A comfortable dining area has exposed old beams and studwork. This is glorious country for walks, such as the one to the summit of Caer Caradoc, a couple of miles to the west (ask for directions at the pub), and the front courtyard makes the most of its beautiful position.

Free house ~ Licensees Steve and Eira Oldham ~ Real ale ~ Bar food (12-2(2.30 Sun), 6.30(7 Sun)-9) ~ Restaurant ~ (01694) 771266 ~ Children welcome ~ Dogs allowed in bar ~ Open 12-2.30, 6.30-11(midnight Fri, Sat); 12-3.30; 7-midnight Sun; closed Mon ~ www.at-the-oak.com

CHETWYND ASTON   SJ7517
Fox
Village signposted off A41 and A518 just S of Newport; TF10 9LQ

Civilised dining pub with generous helpings of well liked food and a fine array of drinks served by ever-attentive staff

The style of this handsome 1920s Brunning & Price pub, done up a few years ago, will be familiar to anyone who has visited other outposts in this successful chain. Though big and usually busy, it's intimate and friendly, with its welcoming atmosphere, helped along by kindly capable staff. A series of linked areas, one with a broad arched ceiling, has plenty of tables in all shapes and sizes, some quite elegant, and a loosely matching diversity of comfortable chairs, all laid out in a way that's fine for eating but serves equally well for just drinking and chatting. There are masses of attractive prints, three open fires and a few oriental rugs on polished parquet, boards or attractive floor tiling; big windows and careful lighting contribute to the relaxed atmosphere; board games. The handsome bar counter, with a decent complement of bar stools, serves an excellent changing range of about 18 wines by the glass and 50 malt whiskies; Phoenix Brunning & Price Original, Three Tuns XXX, Woods Shropshire Lad and three guests from brewers such as Newmans, Slaters and Titanic, are on handpump. Although highchairs are provided, pushchairs and baby buggies are not allowed; good disabled access. The spreading garden is quite lovely, with a sunny terrace, picnic-sets tucked into the shade of mature trees and extensive views across quiet country fields.

Brunning & Price ~ Manager Samantha Forrest ~ Real ale ~ Bar food (12-10(9.30 Sun)) ~ (01952) 815940 ~ Children welcome ~ Dogs allowed in bar ~ Open 12-11(10.30 Sun) ~ www.fox-newport.co.uk

MAESBURY MARSH   SJ3125
Navigation
Follow Maesbury Road off A483 S of Oswestry; by canal bridge; SY10 8JB

Versatile and friendly canalside pub with cosy bar and enjoyable food using local seasonal produce in a choice of dining areas

Dozens of watches, wrist and pocket, hang from the beams of the left-hand quarry-tiled bar, which has squishy brown leather sofas by the traditional black range blazing in its big red fireplace, and little upholstered cask seats around three small tables. A couple of steps lead up to a carpeted area beyond a balustrade, with dining chairs around a few more tables, and a piano; off to the left is a further dining room with cheerful prints. The main beamed dining room, with some stripped stone, is beyond another small bar with a coal fire – and an amazing row of cushioned carved choir-stalls complete with misericord seats. They have Stonehouse Station and a guest beer on handpump, ten wines by the glass and Weston's cider; very quiet background music. The terrace has picnic-table sets under cocktail parasols, safely fenced off from a restored stretch of the Montgomery Canal.

Free house ~ Licensees Brent Ellis and Mark Baggett ~ Real ale ~ Bar food (12-2, 6-8.30; not Sun evening or Mon, Tues lunchtimes) ~ Restaurant ~ (01691) 672958 ~ Well behaved children welcome ~ Dogs allowed in bar ~ folk open night last Fri of month ~ Open 12-2.30, 6-11; 12-6 Sun; closed Sun evening and Mon, Tues lunchtimes ~ www.thenavigation.co.uk

MUCH WENLOCK   SO6299
George & Dragon
High Street (A458); TF13 6AA

Bustling and atmospheric with plenty to look at, reasonably priced food and good beer selection; usefully open all day

In the centre of a charming town, this is a friendly and accommodating old place that's popular with both locals and visitors. It's filled with a fascinating collection of pub paraphernalia such as old brewery and cigarette advertisements, bottle labels, beer trays and George-and-the-Dragon pictures, as well as 200 jugs hanging from the beams. The front door takes you straight into a beamed and quarry-tiled room with wooden chairs and tables and antique settles all the way around the walls, and there are a couple of open fires in attractive Victorian fireplaces. At the back is a timbered dining room. As well as a wide choice of wines by the glass and a dozen decent malts, they keep five real ales like Black Sheep, Greene King Abbot, St Austell Tribute, Sharps Doom Bar, Wadworths 6X and Woodfordes Wherry on handpump; background music, dominoes, cards, board games and daily newspapers. There's a pay and display car park behind the pub.

Punch ~ Tenant James Scott ~ Real ale ~ Bar food (12-2.30, 6-9 (not Weds evening all year or Sun evening Oct-June)) ~ Restaurant ~ (01952) 727312 ~ Children welcome ~ Dogs allowed in bar ~ Open 12-11

SHREWSBURY   SJ4812
Armoury
Victoria Quay, Victoria Avenue; SY1 1HH

Vibrant atmosphere in interestingly converted riverside warehouse, enthusiastic young staff, good tempting food all day, excellent drinks selection

An impressively long run of big arched windows at this warehouse conversion gives views across the broad River Severn. Light and fresh, the spacious open-plan interior combines eclectic décor with nicely intimate furniture settings, creating a personal feel despite the vast space. Mixed wood tables and chairs are grouped on stripped-wood floors, huge brick walls display floor-to-ceiling books, or masses of old prints mounted edge to edge, and there's a grand stone fireplace at one end. Colonial-style fans whirr away on the ceilings, which are supported by occasional green-painted columns, and small wall-mounted glass cabinets display smoking pipes. The long bar counter has a terrific choice of drinks including Bathams Best, Phoenix Brunning & Price, Salopian Shropshire Gold, Three Tuns XXX, Woods Shropshire Lad and four guests from brewers such as Goffs, Hobsons, Purple Moose and Six Bells on handpump, a great wine list (with

16 by the glass), around 50 malt whiskies, a dozen gins, lots of rums and vodkas, a variety of brandies, some unusual liqueurs and a good range of soft drinks. Hanging baskets and smart coach lights decorate the massive red brick frontage. The crowd is lively and there may be queues at the weekend. The pub doesn't have its own parking, but there are plenty of places nearby.

Brunning & Price ~ Manager John Astle-Rowe ~ Real ale ~ Bar food (12-10(9.30 Sun)) ~ (01743) 340525 ~ Dogs allowed in bar ~ Open 12-11(10.30 Sun) ~ www.armoury-shrewsbury.co.uk

DOG FRIENDLY INNS, HOTELS AND B&Bs

BISHOP'S CASTLE   SO3288
Castle Hotel

Market Square, Bishop's Castle, Shropshire SY9 5BN (01588) 638403
www.thecastlehotelbishopscastle.co.uk

£95; 10 spacious rms with fine views. On the site of the old castle keep, this enjoyable 18th-c hotel is surrounded by the Shropshire Hills and Welsh Borders and plenty of good walks; three convivial bars, log fires and a relaxed and friendly atmosphere, an oak-panelled restaurant, real ales and good bar and restaurant food; seats in the garden; resident dog, Milly; dogs in some bedrooms and back bar; welcome pack, bowls, food fridge

CLUN   SO2882
New House Farm

Clun, Craven Arms, Shropshire SY7 8NJ (01588) 638314 www.new-house-clun.co.uk

£90; 2 rms with thoughtful extras. Remote 18th-c farmhouse near the Welsh border with plenty of surrounding hillside walks and lovely views; a cosy sitting room with a woodburning stove, collections of china and farming artefacts, a dining room with breakfasts that include home-made preserves and muesli, a country garden and helpful, friendly owner; dogs in bedrooms but not dining room; £5; bring own bedding

CLUN   SO3080
White Horse

The Square, Clun, Craven Arms, Shropshire SY7 8JA (01588) 640305
www.whi-clun.co.uk

£55; 4 attractively refurbished rms. Friendly 18th-c pub with a cheerful atmosphere in the low-beamed front bar, a woodburning stove in the cosy inglenook, seven real ales including their own brews and good value traditional food served by attentive staff in separate small dining room; resident terrier, Tilly; can walk close by; dogs anywhere except dining room

HOPTON HEATH   SO3877

Hopton House

Hopton Heath, Craven Arms, Shropshire SY7 0QD (01547) 530885
www.shropshirebreakfast.co.uk

£110; 3 large, airy and very comfortable rms. Friendly converted granary with several walks from the door in lovely countryside; a comfortable sun room with seating facing the garden and shelves of books and games, and a dining room with an open fire and delicious breakfasts (served until 10am) using local sausages, their own eggs and home-made fruit compotes; two places nearby for evening meals or you can bring in take-aways to eat in the dining room; resident dogs Mitsi and Murphy; dogs in annexe rooms

HOPTON WAFERS   SO6376

Crown

Hopton Wafers, Kidderminster, Worcestershire DY14 0NB (01299) 270372
www.crownathopton.co.uk

£95; 18 charming rms. Attractive creeper-covered stone inn in pleasant countryside with nearby walks; an open fire, beams and stonework in the interestingly furnished bar, three restaurants serving enjoyable food, decent house wines and well kept real ales, friendly efficient service, and a streamside garden; dogs in cottage bedrooms; £15

LUDLOW   SO5174

Church Inn

Buttercross, Ludlow, Shropshire SY8 1AW (01584) 872174 www.thechurchinn.com

£80; 8 simple rms, 3 with balconies and views. Characterful town-centre inn with cheerful landlord, an impressive ten real ales on handpump and three appealingly decorated areas with hops on heavy beams, banquettes in cosy alcoves and pews from the nearby church; a long central area has a winter fire, daily papers and old black and white local photos and the civilised upstairs lounge bar has good views of the church and surrounding countryside; straightforward, tasty food and good breakfasts; dogs in bedrooms and bar and given treats and bowl of water

LUDLOW   SO5074

Dinham Hall

Dinham, Ludlow, Shropshire SY8 1EJ (01584) 876464 www.dinhamhall.co.uk

£145; 13 individually decorated rms, 2 in cottage. Late 18th-c manor house in quiet walled gardens opposite the ruins of Ludlow Castle, with restful lounges, open fires and period furnishings, modern british cooking in the glass-roofed restaurant, good breakfasts in the Georgian Morning Room with River Teme Valley views, friendly staff, and seats on pretty terraces; pool, sauna and treatment rooms at their nearby sister hotel; dogs in cottage bedrooms and lounge; £15

NORTON   SJ7200

Hundred House

Bridgnorth Road, Norton, Shifnal, Shropshire TF11 9EE (01952) 730353
www.hundredhouse.co.uk

£87.50; 9 rms with antiques, chandeliers, a swing hanging from the beams
and newly refurbished bthrms. Mainly Georgian, family-run inn with quite a
sophisticated feel, a neatly kept bar with old quarry-tiled floors, beamed ceilings,
oak panelling and handsome fireplaces, interesting evening meals using some
of the inn's 100 different herbs, good pubby lunches and hearty breakfasts, and
friendly service; delightful garden (dogs allowed here under owner's control) and
walks at Ironbridge Gorge; dogs in bedrooms and reception; £10

RHYDYCROESAU   SJ2430

Pen-y-Dyffryn Hall

Rhydycroesau, Oswestry, Shropshire SY10 7JD (01691) 653700 www.peny.co.uk

£126; 12 rms, 4 with terrace in coach house. Handsome stone-built Georgian
rectory in 5 acres with lovely views of the Shropshire and Welsh hills, and trout
fishing, hill-walking and riding (shooting can be arranged); log fires in both
comfortable lounges, excellent modern food using the best local ingredients,
delicious breakfasts, helpful staff and a relaxed friendly atmosphere; resident
spaniel; nearby 100-acre wood next door for walks; dogs welcome; not in public
areas after 6pm; bowls and food

SHREWSBURY   SJ4917

Albright Hussey

Ellesmere Road, Broad Oak, Shrewsbury, Shropshire SY4 3AF (01939) 290571
www.albrighthussey.co.uk

£120; 26 lovely rms. Fine moated medieval manor house, partly timber-framed
and partly stone and brick, in 4 acres of landscaped gardens, with particularly
good, interesting food in timbered and panelled formal restaurant with its open
fire, comfortable sitting room and excellent service; walks from the door; dogs in
bedrooms, reception and lounge; £5

WEM   SJ5430

Soulton Hall

Soulton Road, Wem, Shrewsbury, Shropshire SY4 5RS (01939) 232786
www.soultonhall.co.uk

£116; 8 large, comfortable rms, some in carriage house and lodge. Red brick
Tudor manor house in the same family since 1556 and at the heart of a 500-
acre working farm – plenty of walks here and nearby; charming, friendly
owners, a relaxed atmosphere, a lounge, study and dining room with much
genuine character, fine original features, antiques and open fires, and enjoyable,
beautifully presented evening meals, generous breakfasts and afternoon teas
using their own produce; dogs in carriage bedrooms; not in public rooms; £10

WORFIELD

SO7595

Old Vicarage

Hallon, Worfield, Bridgnorth, Shropshire WV15 5JZ (01746) 716497
www.oldvicarageworfield.com

£80; 14 pretty rms. Restful and carefully restored Edwardian rectory in 2 acres of grounds; two airy conservatory-style lounges, sophisticated country cooking using the best local produce in the restaurant, a fine wine list, a cosseting atmosphere and warmly friendly, helpful service; dogs in bedrooms; £10

WREKIN

SJ6309

Buckatree Hall

Wrekin, Telford, Shropshire TF6 5AL (01952) 641821 www.buckatreehallhotel.com

£100; 62 well appointed rms, several with own balconies and many with lake views. Comfortable, extended former hunting lodge dating from 1820 in large wooded estate at the foot of the Wrekin, with a comfortable bar and lounge, dark red leather sofas and armchairs on carpet, a big flat-screen TV, enjoyable food in the plush Lakeside restaurant, and helpful attentive service; dogs in lower level bedrooms; £10

WROCKWARDINE

SJ6212

Church Farm

Wrockwardine, Telford, Shropshire TF6 5DG (01952) 244917
www.churchfarmshropshire.co.uk

£75; 5 individual well equipped rms, most with own bthrm. Friendly Georgian farmhouse overlooking the attractive garden and church, and with walking on surrounding footpaths; a relaxed atmosphere, particularly good, caring service, beams and a log fire in the lounge, and super breakfasts and extremely well thought of modern british food in the traditionally furnished dining room; resident staffie, Basil; dogs in certain bedrooms; not in breakfast room; bed, bowl and treats; £10

Somerset

DOG FRIENDLY PUBS

ASHCOTT   ST4337
Ring o' Bells
High Street; pub well signed off A39 W of Street; TA7 9PZ

Friendly village pub with traditional décor in several bars, separate restaurant, tasty bar food and changing local ales

This is a fine place for a warming lunch before a visit to Ham Wall Nature Reserve. It's been run by the same friendly family for some years now and the three main bars are on different levels but all are comfortable. There are maroon plush-topped stools, cushioned mate's chairs and dark wooden pubby tables on the patterned carpet, horse-brasses along the bressumer beam above the big stone fireplace and a growing collection of hand bells. Butcombe Bitter, RCH Pitchfork and Teignworthy Maltsters Ale on handpump, eight wines by the glass and local farm and bottled cider. There's also a separate restaurant and a skittle alley/function room. The terrace and garden have plenty of picnic-sets.

Free house ~ Licensees John and Elaine Foreman and John Sharman ~ Real ale ~ Bar food (12-2, 7-10) ~ Restaurant ~ (01458) 210232 ~ Children welcome ~ Dogs allowed in bar ~ Live folk music first Sat and third Weds of month ~ Open 12-3, 7-11(10.30 Sun) ~ www.ringobells.com

BABCARY   ST5628
Red Lion
Off A37 S of Shepton Mallett; 2 miles or so N of roundabout where A37 meets A303 and A372; TA11 7ED

Thatched pub with informal atmosphere in comfortable rambling rooms, interesting daily-changing food and local beers; bedrooms

They've now opened up smart bedrooms in this well run stone-built thatched inn – we'd expect this to be a very enjoyable place to stay and would love news from readers. It remains as popular as ever with a relaxed, comfortable atmosphere and a good bustle of both drinkers and diners, and the landlord and his staff make everyone feel welcome. Several distinct areas work their way around the carefully refurbished bar. To the left of the entrance is a longish room with dark pink walls, a squashy leather sofa and two housekeeper's chairs around a low table by a woodburning stove, and a few well spaced tables and captain's chairs. There are elegant rustic wall lights, some clay pipes in a cabinet, local papers or magazines to read and board games. Leading off here, with lovely dark flagstones, is a more dimly lit public bar area with a panelled dado, a high-backed old settle and other more straightforward chairs; table skittles and background music. The good-sized dining room has a large stone lion's head on a plinth above the open fire (with a huge stack of logs to one side), a big rug on polished boards and formally set tables. Otter Bright, Teignworthy Reel Ale and a guest like Cheddar Ales Gorge Best on handpump, around ten wines by the glass, and two farm ciders. The long informal garden has picnic-sets and a play area for children. The pub is handy for the A303 and for shopping at Clarks Village in Street.

Free house ~ Licensee Charles Garrard ~ Real ale ~ Bar food (12-2.30, 7-9.30(8.30 Sun)) ~ Restaurant ~ (01458) 223230 ~ Children welcome ~ Dogs allowed in bar ~ Open 12-3, 6-midnight ~ Bedrooms: /£104S ~ www.redlionbabcary.co.uk

BATCOMBE   ST6839
Three Horseshoes
Village signposted off A359 Bruton–Frome; BA4 6HE

Handsome old inn with smart bar rooms, enjoyable well presented food, local ales and friendly owners; comfortable bedrooms

Reached down winding lanes in a quiet village – just head for the church with its striking tower. This inn is 400 years old and built of honey-coloured stone and the friendly landlord and his staff make all their customers welcome and comfortable. The long, rather narrow main room is smartly traditional: beams, local pictures, built-in cushioned window seats, solid chairs around a nice mix of old tables and a woodburning stove at one end with a big open fire at the other. There's also a pretty stripped-stone dining room; best to book to be sure of a table, especially at weekends. Blindmans Golden Spire, Butcombe Bitter, and Devilfish Best on handpump, around a dozen wines by the glass and several malt whiskies. This is a nice place to stay and the bedrooms are delightful; they sell local honey.

Free house ~ Licensee Kav Javvi ~ Real ale ~ Bar food (12-2.30, 6-9.30(9 Sun)) ~ Restaurant ~ (01749) 850359 ~ Children welcome ~ Dogs allowed in bar ~ Open 11-3, 6-11; 11-11 Sat; 12-10.30 Sun ~ Bedrooms: £60B/£85B ~ www.thethreehorseshoesinn.co.uk

BISHOPSWOOD   ST2512
Candlelight
Off A303/B3170 S of Taunton; TA20 3RS

Friendly, hard-working licensees in neatly refurbished dining pub with granite walls and pale wooden floors, candlelight and fresh flowers, real ales and farm cider, enjoyable imaginative food and seats in garden

Run by warmly friendly, hands-on licensees, this is a neatly refurbished pub in the Blackdown Hills. It's more-or-less open-plan inside but separated into different areas by standing stone pillars and open doorways, and the atmosphere throughout is relaxed and informal. The beamed bar has high chairs by the counter where they serve Bass, Branscombe Best, Otter Bitter and RCH East Street Cream tapped from the cask, nice wines by the glass, a couple of farm ciders and winter drinks like hot Pimms, whisky toddies and hot chocolate; also, captain's chairs, pews and cushioned window seats around a mix of wooden tables on the newly sanded boards and a small ornate fireplace. To the left is a comfortable area with a button-back sofa beside a big woodburner, and then wheelback chairs and cushioned settles around wooden tables set for dining, and country pictures and photos, a hunting horn and bugles on the granite walls; background music and shove-ha' penny. To the other side of the bar is a similarly furnished dining room. Outside, there's a decked area with picnic-sets and a neatly landscaped garden with a paved path winding through low walls set with plants.

Free house ~ Licensees Tom Warren and Debbie Lush ~ Real ale ~ Bar food (12-2(2.30 weekends), 7-9(9.30 weekends); not Mon) ~ Restaurant ~ (01460) 234476 ~ Well behaved children welcome ~ Dogs allowed in bar ~ Open 12-3, 6-11; 12-11 Sun; closed Mon ~ www.candlelight-inn.co.uk

BRISTOL   ST5873
Highbury Vaults
St Michael's Hill, Cotham; BS2 8DE

Cheerful town pub with up to eight real ales, good value tasty bar food and friendly atmosphere

A warm welcome, a fine range of real ales and proper home cooking are the mainstays of this extremely popular, unpretentious pub. The little front bar, with the corridor beside it, leads through to a series of small rooms – wooden floors, green and cream paintwork and old-fashioned furniture and prints, including lots of period Royal Family engravings and lithographs in the front room. There's a model railway running on a shelf the full length of the pub, including tunnels through the walls. Bath Ales Gem Bitter, St Austell Tribute, Wells & Youngs Bitter and London Porter, and guests such as Dorset Durdle Door and Teignworthy Reel Ale on handpump and several malt whiskies. The attractive back terrace has tables built into a partly covered flowery arbour. In early Georgian times this was used as the gaol where condemned men ate their last meal – the bars can still be seen on some windows.

Youngs ~ Manager Bradd Francis ~ Real ale ~ Bar food (12-2, 7-9) ~ No credit cards ~ (0117) 973 3203 ~ Children welcome ~ Dogs allowed in bar ~ Open 12-12(11 Sun) ~ www.highburyvaults.co.uk

CHARLTON HORETHORNE   ST6623
Kings Arms
B3145 Wincanton–Sherborne; DT9 4NL

Bustling inn with relaxed bars and more formal restaurant, plenty of drinkers and diners, a good choice of ales and wines and enjoyable food using local produce; comfortable bedrooms

I mposing and rather smart, this carefully furnished Edwardian inn has a really good mix of chatty drinkers and those here to eat the first-rate food or to stay in the comfortable contemporary bedrooms; there's a friendly welcome for all. The main bar has all manner of local modern art (all for sale) on the dark mulberry or cream walls, nice old carved wooden dining chairs and pine pews around a mix of tables on the slate floor, and a woodburning stove. Leading off here is a cosy room with sofas, and newspapers on low tables. Butcombe Bitter, Sharps Doom Bar and a changing guest on handpump are served from the rather fine granite bar counter and they keep 13 wines by the glass, ten malt whiskies and local draught cider. To the left of the main door is an informal dining room with Jacobean-style chairs and tables on the pale wooden floor and more local artwork. The back restaurant (you have to walk past the open kitchen which is quite fun to peek into) has decorative wood and glass mirrors, wicker or black leather high-backed dining chairs around chunky polished pale wooden tables on coir carpeting, and handsome striped curtains. At the back of the building, the attractive courtyard has chrome and wicker chairs around teak tables under green parasols and there's a good smokers' shelter overlooking the croquet lawn.

Free house ~ Licensee Tony Lethbridge ~ Real ale ~ Bar food (12-2.30, 7-9.30(9 Sun, 10 Fri, Sat)) ~ Restaurant ~ (01963) 220281 ~ Children welcome ~ Dogs allowed in bar ~ Open 10am-11pm; 10.30-10.30 Sun ~ Bedrooms: /£110S ~ www.thekingsarms.co.uk

CHURCHILL   ST4459
Crown
The Batch; in village, turn off A368 into Skinners Lane at Nelson Arms; BS25 5PP

Unspoilt and unchanging small cottage with friendly customers and staff, super range of real ales and homely lunchtime food

'One of my all-time favourites' is how one of our readers describes this simple pub with its untouched interior. As well as a fine choice of real ales, a roaring log fire and a genuinely warm welcome, the small and rather local-feeling stone-floored and cross-beamed room on the right has a wooden window seat, an unusually sturdy settle, built-in wall benches and chatty, and friendly customers. The left-hand room has a slate floor and some steps past the big log fire in its large stone fireplace that lead to more sitting space. No noise from music or games (except perhaps dominoes) and up to ten real ales tapped from the cask: Bath Ales Gem Bitter, Bass, Butcombe Bitter, Glastonbury Thriller, Palmers Best, RCH Hewish IPA, and PG Steam, St Austell Tribute and changing guest beers. Several wines by the glass and local ciders. Outside lavatories are basic. There are garden tables at the front, a smallish back lawn and hill views; the Mendip morris men visit in summer. There's no pub sign outside but no one ever seems to have a problem finding it. Some of the best walking on the Mendips is close by.

Free house ~ Licensee Tim Rogers ~ Real ale ~ Bar food (12-2.30; not evenings) ~ No credit cards ~ (01934) 852995 ~ Children welcome away from bar ~ Dogs allowed in bar ~ Open 11-11(midnight Fri and Sat); 12-10.30 Sun

CLAPTON-IN-GORDANO   ST4773
Black Horse
4 miles from M5 junction 19; A369 towards Portishead, then B3124 towards Clevedon; in north Weston opposite school, turn left signposted Clapton, then in village take second right, may be signed Clevedon, Clapton Wick; BS20 7RH

Old-fashioned pub with lots of cheerful customers, friendly service, real ales and cider, and simple lunchtime food; pretty garden

Very pretty in summer with its hanging baskets and tubs, this unspoilt local is popular with locals, farmers and walkers with their dogs – but visitors are made equally welcome. The partly flagstoned and partly red-tiled main room has winged settles and built-in wall benches around narrow, dark wooden tables, window seats, a big log fire with stirrups and bits on the mantelbeam, and amusing cartoons and photographs of the pub. A window in an inner snug is still barred from the days when this room was the petty-sessions gaol; high-backed settles – one a marvellous carved and canopied creature, another with an art nouveau copper insert reading, East, West, Hame's Best – lots of mugs hanging from black beams and plenty of little prints and photographs. There's also a simply furnished room which is the only place families are allowed; darts. Butcombe Bitter, Courage Best, Exmoor Gold, Otter Ale, St Austell Tribute and

Wadworths 6X on handpump or tapped from the cask, several wines by the glass and farm ciders. There are some old rustic tables and benches in the garden, with more to one side of the car park, whose summer flowers are quite a sight. Paths from the pub lead up Naish Hill or to Cadbury Camp.

Enterprise ~ Lease Nicholas Evans ~ Real ale ~ Bar food (12-2; not evenings, not Sun) ~ (01275) 842105 ~ Children in plain family room only ~ Dogs allowed in bar ~ Open 11-11; 12-10 Sun ~ www.thekicker.co.uk

COMBE FLOREY   ST1531

Farmers Arms

Off A358 Taunton–Williton, just N of main village turn-off; TA4 3HZ

Pretty pub with delightful garden, open fire and real ales in cosy bar, popular food using local produce in little dining room and friendly landladies

Run by a mother and daughter team, this is a friendly and pretty thatched pub in attractive countryside that's popular with our readers. The charming cottagey garden is a big draw in warm weather with picnic-sets under white parasols and lovely flowering tubs and beds – you may hear the whistle of a steam train as the Taunton-Minehead line runs close by. Inside, it's a small place so you would be wise to book a table at peak times. The bar has a log fire in the big stone fireplace with lanterns on either side, cushioned pubby chairs and a settle around wooden tables on the flagstones and stools against the bar where they serve Cotleigh Tawny, Exmoor Ale and Gold and St Austell HSD on handpump and several wines by the glass. The cosy dining room leads off here with traditional seats and tables on the red patterned carpet and heavy beams. Evelyn Waugh lived in the village, as did his son Auberon.

Free house ~ Licensee Patricia Vincent ~ Real ale ~ Bar food (12-2.30, 6.30-9; only curry or chilli on Sun quiz evening) ~ Restaurant ~ (01823) 432267 ~ Children welcome ~ Dogs allowed in bar ~ Open 12-11 ~ www.farmersarmsatcombeflorey.co.uk

COMBE HAY   ST7359

Wheatsheaf

Village signposted off A367 or B3110 S of Bath; BA2 7EG

Smart and cheerful country dining pub perched prettily above steep wooded valley; first class food using game and fish caught by the landlord and locally foraged produce; attractive bedrooms

As befits a pub so highly rated for its food, most of the space here is devoted to dining; the exception in one central area by a big fireplace which has sofas on dark flagstones, with daily papers and current issues of magazines such as The Field and Country Life on a low table. All the other parts have stylish high-backed grey wicker dining chairs around chunky modern dining tables, on parquet or coir matting. It's all fresh and bright, with block-mounted photo prints, contemporary artwork, and mirrors framed in colourful ceramic mosaics (many for sale) on white-painted stonework or robin's-egg blue plaster walls. The sills of the many shuttered windows house anything from old soda siphons to a stuffed kingfisher and a Great Lakes model tugboat, and glinting glass wall chandeliers (as well as nightlights in entertaining holders) supplement the ceiling spotlights. They have a very good if not cheap choice of wines, Butcombe Bitter and Adam Hensons Rare Breed on handpump, and Cheddar Valley cider; staff are friendly and informal, the background music faint enough and the cheerful springer is called Brie.

Picnic-sets in the two-level front garden have a fine view down over the church and valley; you can walk from the pub. The bedrooms are stylishly simple and spacious.

Free house ~ Licensee Ian Barton ~ Real ale ~ Bar food (12-2, 7-9; not Sun evening, not Mon) ~ (01225) 833504 ~ Children welcome ~ Dogs allowed in bar ~ Open 10.30-3, 6-11; closed Sun evening, all day Mon ~ Bedrooms: /£120S ~ www.wheatsheafcombehay.co.uk

CROSCOMBE   ST5844
George
Long Street (A371 Wells–Shepton Mallet); BA5 3QH

Carefully renovated old coaching inn, warmly welcoming, informative canadian landlord, highly thought of bar food cooked by landlady, good local beers, attractive garden; bedrooms

This is a thoroughly enjoyable place and a true all-rounder and we get warm praise from our readers on all aspects – the terrific food, the local beers, the comfortable bedrooms (there are now two) and of course for the interested and genuinely warm welcome from Mr Graham, who is a first-rate landlord. The main bar has some stripped stone, dark wooden tables and chairs and more comfortable seats, winter log fires in inglenook fireplaces and the family grandfather clock; a snug area has recently been added with a stone fireplace and woodburning stove. The attractive dining room has more stripped stone, local artwork and photographs on the burgundy walls and high-backed cushioned dining chairs around a mix of tables. The back bar has canadian timber reclaimed from the local church and there's a family room with games and books for children. King George the Thirst (brewed exclusively for them by Blindmans), Butcombe Bitter, Cheddar Ales Potholer, and Devilfish Stingray on handpump or tapped from the cask, four farm ciders and ten wines by the glass. Darts, shut the box, a canadian wooden table game called crokinole, shove-ha'penny, background music and separate TV room. The friendly pub dog is called Tessa and the slightly more aloof cat, DJ. The attractive, sizeable garden has seats on a heated and covered terrace, flower borders and a grassed area; children's swings.

Free house ~ Licensees Peter and Veryan Graham ~ Real ale ~ Bar food (12-2, 6-9) ~ Restaurant ~ (01749) 342306 ~ Children welcome ~ Dogs allowed in bar ~ Open 12-2.30, 6-11 ~ Bedrooms: £35S/£70S ~ www.thegeorgeinn.co.uk

DULVERTON   SS9127
Woods
Bank Square; TA22 9BU

Smartly informal place with exceptional wines, real ales, first rate food using their own home-bred meat and a good mix of customers

Our readers love this place and since many others do too, it's best to book a table in advance. It's run by a charming landlord and his helpful, courteous staff and attracts a really good mix of both locals and visitors. Many are here for the top-class food but the local beers and, particularly, the exceptional wines draw customers from far and wide. They will open any of their 400 wines for just a glass from the quite extraordinarily good list and there's also an unlisted collection of about 500 well aged, new world wines which Mr Groves will happily chat about. St Austell Dartmoor Best, Otter Head and a changing guest beer tapped from the cask, a farm cider, many sherries and some unusual spirits. As the pub is on the edge of Exmoor, there are plenty of good sporting prints on

the salmon pink walls, some antlers, other hunting trophies, stuffed birds and
a couple of salmon rods. There are bare boards on the left by the bar counter
and daily papers to read, tables partly separated by stable-style timbering and
masonry dividers and a bit on the right which is carpeted and has a woodburning
stove in the big fireplace; maybe unobjectionable background music. Big windows
keep you in touch with what's going on out in the quiet town centre (or you
can sit out on the pavement at a couple of metal tables). A small suntrap back
courtyard has a few picnic-sets.

Free house ~ Licensee Patrick Groves ~ Real ale ~ Bar food (12-2, 7-9.30) ~ Restaurant ~
(01398) 324007 ~ Children welcome ~ Dogs allowed in bar ~ Open 11-3, 6-midnight; 12-3,
7-11 Sun ~ www.woodsdulverton.co.uk

HALLATROW   ST6357
Old Station

A39 S of Bristol; BS39 6EN

**Friendly former railway hotel with extraordinary knick-knacks, popular
food, Pullman carriage restaurant and friendly licensees**

The forest of bric-a-brac hanging from the ceiling and on the walls in this
friendly 1920s former railway hotel will amaze you. It includes anything from
musical instruments to half an old Citroen, from china cows to post boxes from
sailing boats to hundreds of beer badges and so forth. The rather handsome island
bar counter has Brains Rev James and Butcombe Bitter on handpump, and a
mix of furnishings includes a sofa, high chairs around big cask tables, and small
settles and dining or library chairs around more orthodox tables. The more formal
(and opulent) dining room is actually a Pullman carriage and photographs in the
bar show the hair-raising difficulty of getting it here. The garden alongside has
modern seats and tables on decking and there are picnic-sets on the grass. The
bedrooms are in a converted outbuilding (they don't offer breakfast).

Brains ~ Managers Neville and Debbie King ~ Real ale ~ Bar food (12-2.30, 6-9
(9.30 Fri, Sat); all day Sun) ~ Restaurant ~ (01761) 452228 ~ Children welcome ~ Dogs
allowed in bar ~ Open 12-3, 5-11; 12-midnight Fri, Sat; 12-10.30 Sun ~ Bedrooms: /£57B ~
www.theoldstationandcarriage.co.uk

HINTON ST GEORGE   ST4212
Lord Poulett Arms

*Off A30 W of Crewkerne and off Merriott road (declassified – former A356, off B3165) N of
Crewkerne; TA17 8SE*

**Thatched 17th-c stone inn with antique-filled rooms, top class food
using home-grown vegetables, good choice of drinks and a pretty garden;
pretty bedrooms**

A great many of our readers use this charming pub as a civilised break from the
busy A30 as they know they will get a genuinely friendly welcome and some
delicious food. Several attractive cosy linked areas have rugs on bare boards
or flagstones, open fires (one in an inglenook and one in a raised fireplace that
separates two rooms), walls of honey-coloured stone or painted in bold Farrow
& Ball colours, hop-draped beams, antique brass candelabra, fresh flowers and
candles, and some lovely old farmhouse, windsor and ladderback chairs around
fine oak or elm tables. Branscombe Branoc, Otter Ale and a guest such as Dorset
Tom Brown's on handpump, 14 wines by the glass, jugs of Pimms and home-made
cordial; the pub cat is called Honey. Outside, under a wisteria-clad pergola, there

are white metalwork tables and chairs in a mediterranean-style lavender-edged gravelled area and picnic-sets in a wild flower meadow; boules. The bedrooms are pretty and cottagey. This is a peaceful village and with nice surrounding walks.

Free house ~ Licensees Steve Hill and Michelle Paynton ~ Real ale ~ Bar food (12-2.30(4 Sun), 7-9.15; pizzas 3(5 Sun)-6.30) ~ (01460) 73149 ~ Children welcome ~ Dogs allowed in bar ~ Live music every other Sun Jun-Sept ~ Open 12-11 ~ Bedrooms: £65B/£95B ~ www.lordpoulettarms.com

HUISH EPISCOPI ST4326
Rose & Crown
Off A372 E of Langport; TA10 9QT

Unchanging old place in the same family for over a century, local cider and beers, simple reasonably priced food and a friendly welcome

Known locally as Eli's (after the present licensees' grandfather), this quite unspoilt old place has been in the same friendly family for over 140 years. There's no bar as such, just a central flagstoned still room with casks of Teignworthy Reel Ale and a couple of guests such as Hop Back Crop Circle and Palmers 200; also local Burrow Hill farm cider and cider brandy. The casual little front parlours, with their unusual pointed-arch windows, have family photographs, books, cribbage, dominoes, shove-ha'penny , bagatelle, and a good mix of both locals and visitors. A much more orthodox big back extension family room has pool, games machine and a juke box; skittle alley. There are tables in a garden and a second enclosed garden has a children's play area; you can camp (free by arrangement to pub customers) on the adjoining paddock. Summer morris men, fine nearby walks and the site of the Battle of Langport (1645) is close by.

Free house ~ Licensees Maureen Pittard, Stephen Pittard, Patrick O'Malley ~ Real ale ~ Bar food (12-2, 5.30-7.30; not Sun evening) ~ No credit cards ~ (01458) 250494 ~ Children welcome ~ Dogs allowed in bar ~ Live folk music third Sat of month, irish music last Thurs of month ~ Open 11.30-3, 5.30-11; 11.30-11.30 Fri, Sat; 12-10.30 Sun

PITNEY ST4527
Halfway House
Just off B3153 W of Somerton; TA10 9AB

Bustling, friendly local with up to ten real ales, local ciders and good simple food

As delightful and as unchanging as ever, this remains an honest village local with an excellent range of real ales. Tapped from the cask and changing regularly, they might include Butcombe Bitter, Cheddar Totty Pot, Crouch Vale Brewers Gold, Exmoor Fox, Forge Litehouse, Hop Back Summer Lightning, Moor Southern Star, Otter Bright, RCH Pitchfork, and Teignworthy Reel Ale. They also keep five local farm ciders, a dozen malt whiskies and several wines by the glass. No music or games machines. A good mix of people are usually found chatting at communal tables in the three old-fashioned rooms, all with roaring log fires, and there's a homely feel underlined by a profusion of books, maps and newspapers; cribbage, dominoes and board games. There are tables outside.

Free house ~ Licensee Mark Phillips ~ Real ale ~ Bar food (12-2.30, 7-9.30; some sort of food all day Sun) ~ (01458) 252513 ~ Children welcome ~ Dogs allowed in bar ~ Open 11.30-3, 5.30-11(midnight Sat); 12-11 Sun ~ www.thehalfwayhouse.co.uk

PRIDDY   ST5250
Queen Victoria
Village signed off B3135; Pelting Drove; BA5 3BA

Stone-built country pub with lots of interconnecting rooms of some character, open fires and woodburners, a friendly atmosphere and staff, real ales and honest food; seats outside

There's a lot of character in the various dimly-lit rooms and alcoves in this creeper-clad stone pub and plenty of original features, too. One room leading off the main bar has a log fire in a big old stone fireplace with a huge cauldron to one side and there are two woodburners as well – one in a raised fireplace. The floors are flagstoned or of slate or composition, the walls are bare stone (though the smarter dining room is half panelled and half painted) and hung with Queen Victoria photographs, horse tack and farm tools, and the customers are chatty and cheerful. Furniture is traditional: cushioned wall settles, farmhouse and other solid chairs around all manner of wooden tables, one nice old pew beside a screen settle making a cosy alcove and high chairs beside the bar counter where they serve Butcombe Bitter and Gold and Fullers London Pride on handpump, two farm ciders, 20 malt whiskies and ten wines by the glass. There are seats on the front courtyard and more across the lane where there's a children's playground.

Butcombe ~ Manager Mark Walton ~ Real ale ~ Bar food (12-3(4 winter Sun), 6-9; all day Sat and from Easter-October; not winter Sun evening) ~ (01749) 676385 ~ Children welcome ~ Dogs allowed in bar ~ Open 12-11(10.30 Sun) ~ www.queenvictoria.butcombe.com

STANTON WICK   ST6162
Carpenters Arms
Village signposted off A368, just W of junction with A37 S of Bristol; BS39 4BX

Bustling, warm-hearted dining pub in country setting with enjoyable, popular interesting food, friendly staff and a fine choice of drinks; comfortable bedrooms

Once you've found this attractive little stone inn, you will tend to come back again and again. The landlord and his staff are friendly and helpful, the food is highly enjoyable and there are good country walks close by. Coopers Parlour on the right has one or two beams, seats around heavy tables on the tartan carpet and attractive curtains and window plants; on the angle between here and the bar area, there's a fat woodburning stove in an opened-through corner fireplace. The bar has wood-backed wall settles with cushions, stripped-stone walls and a big log fire in an inglenook. There's also a snug inner room (brightened by mirrors in arched recesses) and a restaurant with leather sofas and easy chairs in a comfortable lounge area at one end. Butcombe Bitter, Courage Directors and Sharps Doom Bar on handpump, ten wines by the glass (and some interesting bin ends), and several malt whiskies; TV in the snug. There are picnic-sets on the front terrace and pretty flower beds, hanging baskets and tubs. The bedrooms are comfortable and well equipped.

Free house ~ Licensee Simon Pledge ~ Real ale ~ Bar food (12-2.30, 6-9.30(10 Fri, Sat); sandwiches all afternoon Sat; 12-9 Sun) ~ Restaurant ~ (01761) 490202 ~ Children welcome ~ Dogs allowed in bar ~ Open 11-11; 12-10.30 Sun ~ Bedrooms: £72.50B/£105B ~ www.the-carpenters-arms.co.uk

STOKE ST GREGORY

ST3527

Rose & Crown

Woodhill; follow North Curry signpost off A378 by junction with A358 – keep on to Stoke, bearing right in centre, passing church and follow lane for 0.5 miles; TA3 6EW

Friendly, family-run pub with quite a choice of popular food and a fine choice of drinks; comfortable bedrooms

With lots of events happening throughout the year, this bustling pub is always fun to visit and it's been run by the same hands-on, welcoming family for well over 30 years now. The interior is more or less open-plan and the bar area has wooden stools by a curved brick and pale wood-topped counter with Exmoor Ale, Otter Ale and a guest like Butcombe Bitter on handpump, local farm cider and several wines by the glass. This leads into a long, airy dining room with all manner of light and dark wooden dining chairs and pews around a mix of tables under a high-raftered ceiling. There are two other beamed dining rooms as well, with similar furnishings and photographs on the walls of the village and the recent fire damage to the pub; one room has a woodburning stove and another has an 18th-c glass-covered well in one corner. Throughout, there are flagstoned or wooden floors. The sheltered front terrace has plenty of seats. They have three ensuite bedrooms, two of which can connect to make a family room.

Free house ~ Licensees Stephen, Sally, Richard and Leonie Browning ~ Real ale ~ Bar food (12-2, 7-9) ~ Restaurant ~ (01823) 490296 ~ Children welcome ~ Dogs allowed in bar ~ Open 11-3, 6-11; 12-3, 6.30-10.30 Sun ~ Bedrooms: £55B/£85B ~ www.browningpubs.com

WRINGTON

ST4762

Plough

2.5 miles off A370 Bristol–Weston, from bottom of Rhodiate Hill; BS40 5QA

Welcoming, popular pub with bustling bar and two dining rooms, good food using local produce and well kept beer and seats outside

Only ten minutes from Cheddar Gorge and handy for Bristol Airport, this is a neatly kept and friendly pub in a picturesque village, and our readers enjoy their visits here very much. There's a chatty bar with stools against the counter where they serve Butcombe Bitter (the brewery is in the village), St Austell Tribute and Wells & Youngs Bitter on handpump and 18 wines by the glass, and two distinct dining rooms – one at the back with lots of big windows that overlook the gazebo and garden. The rooms are linked by open doorways and throughout there are three winter fires, slate or wooden floors, beams and standing timbers, plenty of pictures on the planked, red or yellow walls and all manner of high-backed leather or wooden dining or farmhouse chairs around many different sizes of table; fresh flowers, a games chest, table skittles and helpful service. There are picnic-sets at the front and on the back grass; boules. They hold a farmers' market on the second Friday of the month. This is sister pub to the Rattlebone at Sherston (Wiltshire).

Youngs ~ Tenant Jason Read ~ Real ale ~ Bar food (12-2.30, 6-9.30; 12-5 Sun; not Sun evening) ~ Restaurant ~ (01934) 862871 ~ Children welcome ~ Dogs allowed in bar ~ Open 12-3, 5-11; 12-12 Fri and Sat; 12-11 Sun ~ www.theploughatwrington.co.uk

DOG FRIENDLY INNS, HOTELS AND B&Bs

ALLERFORD   SS9047

West Lynch Farm

West Lynch, Allerford, Somerset TA24 8HJ (01643) 862816
www.exmoorfalconry.co.uk

£70; 3 rms with country views. Listed 15th-c National Trust farmhouse in 6 acres
of landscaped gardens and paddocks on the edge of Exmoor – no walking in the
grounds but lots in surrounding countryside; lots of original features, antiques
and persian rugs, homely lounge/dining room with woodburning stove, super
breakfasts with their own honey and home-made marmalade, and lots of animals;
falconry tuition and hawking all year, a collection of owls and birds of prey, clay
pigeon shooting and riding; dogs in bedrooms; towels, feeding tray and cover for
bed on request; £5

ASHILL   ST3016

Square & Compass

Windmill Hill, Ashill, Ilminster, Somerset TA19 9NX (01823) 480467
www.squareandcompasspub.com

£85; 8 spacious, comfortable rms. Friendly simple pub tucked away in the
Blackdown Hills with long-serving owners, chatty customers in little beamed
bar, upholstered window seats taking in the fine country view, heavy hand-made
furniture, an open winter fire, maybe the pub cat, Lily, good ales and wines and
well liked, generously served food; seats on a glass-covered walled terrace and in
the garden; dogs anywhere in the pub and in bedrooms

BABINGTON   ST7051

Babington House

Babington, Frome, Somerset BA11 3RW (01373) 812266 www.babingtonhouse.co.uk

£380; 28 individually decorated, well equipped contemporary rms, 12 in coach
house, 5 in stable block, 3 in lodge. Georgian mansion in 18 acres of lovely grounds
with cricket and football pitches, indoor and outdoor swimming pools, walled
garden, tennis courts and croquet; unusually decorated lounges, comfortable sofas
and an open fire in the bar, a library with books and games, a snooker room, a
wide range of modern food in the Deli Bar, Log Room and Orangery, a particularly
relaxed, informal atmosphere and helpful, friendly young staff; free cinema with
films five days a week and a spa with swimming pools, steam room sauna and gym;
dogs in some ground floor bedrooms, stable block and lodge

BARWICK   ST5613

Little Barwick House

Barwick, Yeovil, Somerset BA22 9TD (01935) 423902 www.littlebarwickhouse.co.uk

£160; 6 attractive rms. Carefully run Georgian dower house in 3.5 acres – you
can walk here and nearby; a relaxed atmosphere, two cosy sitting rooms with
log fires, an elegant restaurant with imaginative food using local produce, a

thoughtful wine list, super breakfasts, nice afternoon teas, and particularly good service; resident dog, Ellie, three cats and two horses; walks in grounds and nearby; dogs by prior arrangement; £10

BATH   ST7365

Bath Priory

Weston Road, Bath BA1 2XT (01225) 331922 www.thebathpriory.co.uk

£325; 31 lovely rms. Just a stroll from the city centre, this Georgian hotel has the feeling of a country house in its own grounds; the lounge and sitting room are elegant and full of antiques, chandeliers, oil paintings, and fresh flowers and have french windows opening on to the garden, the atmosphere is welcoming and warm, the modern european cooking is excellent and served in two restaurants (one light and spacious, the other cosy and sumptuous), the breakfasts are delicious, and the dedicated staff and courteous and helpful; indoor and outdoor swimming pools, spa and fitness centre; dogs in two bedrooms; £10

BATH   ST7465

Royal Crescent Hotel

16 Royal Crescent, Bath BA1 2LS (01225) 823333 www.royalcrescent.co.uk

£199; 45 luxurious rms. Elegant Georgian hotel in a glorious curved terrace and made up of five buildings; comfortable antique-filled drawing rooms, open fires and lovely flowers, excellent and imaginative modern cooking in the Dower House restaurant overlooking the 1-acre secluded gardens, a lighter all-day menu, delicious afternoon teas and breakfasts, and impeccable service; health spa, gym and croquet; dogs in bedrooms; they provide beds, baskets, balls and so forth

BRISTOL   ST5873

Hotel du Vin & Bistro

Narrow Lewins Mead, Bristol BS1 2NU (0117) 925 5577 www.hotelduvin.com

£199; 40 loft-style rms with spacious bthrms. Attractively converted former Sugar House with big pillars and arched cellars, wine prints, posters and empty bottles, comfortable armchairs on stripped wooden floors and a bustling but relaxed dining room with white napery; particularly good imaginative bistro-style cooking, helpful efficient staff and an interesting wine list; dogs in some bedrooms; £10

COMBE HAY   ST7359

Wheatsheaf

Combe Hay, Bath BA2 7EG (01225) 833504 www.wheatsheafcombehay.co.uk

£120; 4 stylishly simple, spacious rms. Smart and cheerful country dining pub perched prettily above a steep wooded valley with walks from the front door; a small bar with sofas on dark flagstones, daily papers and magazines, and a big log fire, and other fresh, bright areas leading off with stylish high-backed dining chairs around chunky modern dining tables on parquet or coir matting, contemporary artwork, and lots of interest on the sills of the many shuttered windows; a very good choice of drinks, first class food using game and fish caught by the landlord and locally foraged produce and friendly, informal staff; dogs anywhere in the pub and in bedrooms

CORTON DENHAM   ST6322

Queens Arms

Corton Denham, Sherborne, Dorset DT9 4LR (01963) 220317 www.thequeensarms.com

£110; 8 comfortable rms with country views. Civilised stone inn with friendly young staff, a plain high-beamed bar with a woodburner in the inglenook, rugs on flagstones, old pews, barrel seats and a sofa, church candles and fresh flowers, and a super choice of drinks; the enterprising food uses their own pork and eggs from their hens and is served in the bustling dining room; fresh bread and home-made preserves for breakfast; some fine surrounding walks; dogs in bedrooms and bar; bed and bowl; £15

EXFORD   SS8538

Crown

Exford, Minehead, Devon TA24 7PP (01643) 831554 www.crownhotelexmoor.co.uk

£139; 17 attractive rms. Comfortably upmarket coaching inn on the village green in Exmoor National Park with a delightful water garden – a lovely summer spot with trout stream, gently sloping lawns, tall trees and plenty of tables; brightly furnished lounge with very relaxed feel, hunting prints on cream walls, old photographs of the area and smart cushioned benches; real ales, a good wine list, and enjoyable modern cooking in candlelit dining room with simpler meals in the bar; a good base for walking; dogs welcome away from restaurant; £12

HATCH BEAUCHAMP   ST3020

Farthings

*Hatch Beauchamp, Taunton, Somerset TA3 6SG (01823) 480664
www.farthingshotel.co.uk*

£80; 12 pretty rms with thoughtful extras. Charming 18th-c house in 2 acres of pretty gardens with open countryside nearby for walks; open log fires in the comfortable lounge, a convivial, well stocked bar, good varied food using their own grown and other local produce in three elegant dining rooms, and breakfasts using eggs from their hens; resident dogs, Sasha and Aonghas, lambs, pigs and lots of fowl; dogs in some bedrooms; not in restaurant; £8

HOLFORD   ST1541

Combe House

Holford, Bridgwater, Somerset TA5 1RZ (01278) 741382 www.combehouse.co.uk

£89; 15 rms. Warmly friendly former tannery (still with a waterwheel) in a pretty spot with walks in the Quantock Hills; comfortable rooms, log fires, good home-made food using home-grown and other local produce in a light and airy modern dining room, and a relaxed atmosphere; health and beauty centre; dogs in some bedrooms and on lead in public areas and bar; £10

LANGFORD BUDVILLE   ST1024

Bindon Country House

Langford Budville, Wellington, Somerset TA21 0RU (01823) 400070 www.bindon.com

£149; 12 individually styled rms and suites. Tranquil 17th-c house designed as
a bavarian hunting lodge and set in 7 acres of formal and woodland gardens;
comfortable, elegant drawing room, a panelled bar and intimate restaurant,
enjoyable modern cooking and a thoughtful wine list; outdoor swimming pool,
tennis, croquet and boules; dogs in some bedrooms

LUXBOROUGH   SS9738

Royal Oak

Luxborough, Watchet, Somerset TA23 0SH (01984) 640319
www.theroyaloakinnluxborough.co.uk

£90; 10 neat, cottagey rms. Unspoilt and interesting old pub in idyllic spot,
marvellous for exploring Exmoor with many wonderful walks; compact bar of
character with some fine settles on ancient flagstones, a log fire in a huge brick
fireplace, plenty of locals (often with their dogs) and a genuinely warm welcome;
several dining rooms have attractive old pine and more formal chairs around nice
tables, there's quite a bit of country décor, real ales, farm ciders and 15 wines
by the glass, and reliably good food using seasonal local game and lamb and
beef from nearby farms; two resident dogs in owners' house opposite; dogs in
bedrooms, bar and one restaurant area; £5

Charlie

NETHER STOWEY   ST1939
Old Cider House

25 Castle Street, Nether Stowey, Bridgwater, Somerset TA5 1LN (01278) 732228
www.theoldciderhouse.co.uk

£60; 5 individually decorated rms. Carefully restored Edwardian house (previously used to produce cider – they now brew their own beers) in a secluded garden, with a big comfortable lounge and log fire, delicious breakfasts using their own bread, eggs and preserves, and interesting, candlelit evening meals using home-grown and local produce; plenty of walks and dog friendly beaches nearby; well behaved dogs in some bedrooms; away from dining room; welcome pack; £3

PORLOCK   SS8647
The Café

Porlock Weir, Minehead, Somerset TA24 8PB (01643) 863300
www.thecafeatporlockweir.co.uk

£88; 5 rms, some with sea view. Victorian villa housing a restaurant-with-rooms overlooking the harbour; country-house-style décor, imaginative modern british cooking using first class local produce (lovely fish and seafood), super breakfasts and a well chosen wine list; closed Mon and Tues, 2 weeks in Feb, 1 week in Oct; dogs in bedrooms; also allowed in café till 6pm

SELWORTHY   SS9346
Hindon Farm

Selworthy, Minehead, Somerset TA24 8SH (01643) 705244 www.hindonfarm.co.uk

£80; 3 pretty rms. 18th-c house on an organic Exmoor hill farm of 500 acres with sheep, pigs, cattle, donkeys and ducks; lovely walks from the door to the heather moors (must be on a lead on the farm until away from stock animals); a quiet, homely sitting room with lots of paintings and antiques, fine breakfasts in the comfortable dining room using their own organic bacon, sausages, eggs and fresh-baked bread, and seats in the garden; self-catering cottage with free organic produce hamper on arrival; own organic farm shop; several resident dogs; dogs in bedrooms if well house trained; £5

SOMERTON   ST4828
Lynch Country House

4 Behind Berry, Somerton, Somerset TA11 7PD (01458) 272316
www.thelynchcountryhouse.co.uk

£90; 9 prettily decorated rms, 4 in coach house. Carefully restored and homely Georgian house with a friendly welcome, books in the comfortable lounge and delicious breakfasts (no evening meals) in the airy Orangery overlooking the tranquil grounds and lake with black swans and exotic ducks; self-catering, too; lots of nearby walks; dogs in the coach-house rooms only; £10

STON EASTON
ST6254

Ston Easton Park

Ston Easton, Bath BA3 4DF (01761) 241631 www.stoneaston.co.uk

£150; 22 really lovely rms. Majestic Palladian mansion of Bath stone with beautifully landscaped 18th-c gardens and 36 acres of parkland; elegant day rooms with antiques and flowers, a library and billiard room, an attractive and elegant restaurant with imaginative food using kitchen garden produce and local game, fine afternoon teas and extremely helpful, friendly and unstuffy service; resident chocolate spaniel, Oscar; walks in the grounds and surrounding countryside; dogs in bedrooms and some other areas; £15

TAUNTON
ST2224

Castle

Castle Green, Taunton, Somerset TA1 1NF (01823) 272671 www.the-castle-hotel.com

£169; 44 lovely rms, some overlooking the garden. Appealingly modernised, partly Norman castle with comfortable sitting rooms, imaginative food including lighter meals in both the restaurant and grill, good breakfasts, a range of good value wines from a thoughtful list, and efficient friendly service; seats in the pretty garden and walks in the nearby park; dogs in bedrooms; £15

WATERROW
ST0525

Rock

Waterrow, Taunton, Somerset TA4 2AX (01984) 623293 www.rockinn.co.uk

£85; 8 attractive rms. Striking timbered inn with a civilised but friendly atmosphere, a small bar with a leather sofa in front of the log fire in its big stone fireplace, dining chairs and wooden tables on wood or carpeted floors, local beers, farm cider and good wines by the glass, and particularly good, interesting food using beef from their own farm in heavily beamed restaurant; the welsh collie is called Meg; dogs in bedrooms and bar

WHEDDON CROSS
SS9238

North Wheddon Farm

Wheddon Cross, Somerset TA24 7EX (01643) 841791 www.go-exmoor.co.uk

£80; 3 charming rms. Friendly farmhouse with open fires, an attractive, comfortable sitting room with fine fabrics, bold colours and cosy sofas, lovely breakfasts and good dinner party-style meals (on request) using their own produce; seats in the neatly kept garden and surrounding grounds; self catering also; dogs in bedrooms; £5

Staffordshire

MAPS 4 & 7

DOG FRIENDLY PUBS

CAULDON   SK0749
Yew Tree
Village signposted from A523 and A52 about 8 miles W of Ashbourne; ST10 3EJ

Treasure-trove of fascinating antiques and dusty bric-a-brac, simple good value snacks and bargain beer; very eccentric

Alan East, the jovial landlord at this uniquely idiosyncratic place, recently celebrated his 50th anniversary here. Much loved for its unusual charm (it's been affectionately described as a junk shop with a bar and it's not exactly what you'd call spic and span), it's filled with a museum's worth of curiosities. The most impressive pieces are perhaps the working polyphons and symphonions – 19th-c developments of the musical box, some taller than a person, each with quite a repertoire of tunes and elaborate sound-effects. But there are also two pairs of Queen Victoria's stockings, ancient guns and pistols, several penny-farthings, an old sit-and-stride boneshaker, a rocking horse, swordfish blades, a little 800BC greek vase, and even a fine marquetry cabinet crammed with notable early staffordshire pottery. Soggily sprung sofas mingle with 18th-c settles, plenty of little wooden tables and a four-person oak church choir seat with carved heads that came from St Mary's church in Stafford; above the bar is an odd iron dog-carrier. As well as all this, there's a choir of fine tuneful longcase clocks in the gallery just above the entrance, a collection of six pianolas (one of which plays most nights) with an excellent repertoire of piano rolls, a working vintage valve radio set, a crank-handle telephone, a sinuous medieval wind instrument made of leather and a Jacobean four-poster that was once owned by Josiah Wedgwood and still has his original wig hook on the headboard. Clearly, it would be almost an overwhelming task to keep all this sprucely clean. The drinks here are very reasonably priced so it's no wonder that it's popular with locals. You'll find well kept Bass, Burton Bridge and Rudgate Ruby Mild on handpump or tapped from the cask, along with about a dozen interesting malt whiskies; background music (probably Radio 2), darts, shove-ha'penny, table skittles, dominoes and cribbage. When you arrive, don't be put off by the plain exterior, or the fact that the pub is tucked unpromisingly between enormous cement works and quarries and almost hidden by a towering yew tree.

Free house ~ Licensee Alan East ~ Real ale ~ Bar food ~ No credit cards ~ (01538) 308348 ~ Children in polyphon room ~ Dogs allowed in bar ~ Folk music first Tues of month ~ Open 12-3, 7-12

WRINEHILL

Hand & Trumpet

A531 Newcastle-Nantwich; CW3 9BJ

Big attractive dining pub with good food all day, professional service, nice range of real ales and wines; pleasant garden

One of the most liked pubs in the Brunning & Price chain, this substantial dining pub is a relaxing place for an enjoyable meal. It's done out in typical light and airy open-plan style with a gentle mix of dining chairs and sturdy tables on polished tiles or stripped-oak boards and several warming oriental rugs that soften the acoustics. There are lots of nicely lit prints on cream walls between mainly dark dado and deep red ceilings. Original bow windows and, in one area, a large skylight keep it light and airy, and french windows open on to a spacious balustraded deck whose teak tables and chairs look down over ducks swimming on a big pond in the sizeable garden, which has plenty of trees. At the heart of the pub is a long solidly built counter, where friendly attentive staff serve Caledonian Deuchars IPA, Phoenix Brunning & Price Original, Salopian Oracle and guests from brewers such as Tatton, Wincle and Woodlands as well as a dozen wines by the glass and about 70 whiskies; good disabled access and facilities; board games.

Brunning & Price ~ Manager John Unsworth ~ Real ale ~ Bar food (12-10(9.30 Sun)) ~ (01270) 820048 ~ Children welcome ~ Dogs allowed in bar ~ Open 11.30-11(10.30 Sun) ~ www.handandtrumpet-wrinehill.co.uk

Teddy and Rupert – bedlington terriers; owners Greg and Bob

DOG FRIENDLY INNS, HOTELS AND B&Bs

HOPWAS   SK1704
Oak Tree Farm
Hints Road, Hopwas, Tamworth, Staffordshire B78 3AA (01827) 56807
www.oaktreefarmhotel.co.uk

£75; 14 comfortable, spacious and pretty rms, 10 in annexe. Carefully restored
farmhouse with an elegant little lounge – inglenook fireplace with a woodburning
stove, antiques and fresh flowers – an attractive adjoining breakfast room, a
friendly atmosphere and owners, and enjoyable breakfasts; gardens overlooking
the River Tame and an indoor swimming pool and steam room; dogs in some
bedrooms

PENKRIDGE   SJ9113
Mercure Stafford South Hatherton House
Pinfold Lane, Penkridge, Staffordshire ST19 5QP (01785) 712459
www.hotels-stafford.com

£67; 51 well equipped rms. Surrounded by countryside but handy for Stafford,
this sizeable, well run hotel has several comfortable lounge areas with leather
sofas and armchairs, a bar, an attractive restaurant with interesting modern food,
afternoon tea and good buffet-style breakfasts, and helpful, friendly staff; health
club with an indoor swimming pool, sauna and steam room, and gym; dogs in
bedrooms

ROLLESTON ON DOVE   SK2327
Brookhouse Hotel
Station Road, Rolleston on Dove, Burton upon Trent, Staffordshire DE13 9AA
(01283) 814188 www.brookhousehotel.co.uk

£115; 20 comfortable rms with Victorian brass or four-poster beds. Handsome
ivy-covered William & Mary brick building in 5 acres of lovely gardens, with
comfortable antique-filled rooms and good food using seasonal local produce in
the elegant little candlelit dining room; resident cat; walks on open farmland; dogs
in annexe bedrooms only; £10

Suffolk

MAP 5

DOG FRIENDLY PUBS

BOXFORD   TL9640
Fleece
Broad Street (A1071 Sudbury–Ipswich); CO10 5DX

Attractively restored partly 15th-c pub flourishing under new ownership, good food and splendid beer range

The Star Award is for the Corder Room on the right. The pub's new owners, Mill Green Brewery (at the White Horse, Edwardstone), have done it up beautifully, with dark panelled wainscoting, handsome William Morris wallpaper under a high delft shelf, sweeping heavy red curtains, and a handful of attractive period dining tables with good chairs and a built-in wall settle. With its chatty companionable atmosphere, this is as nice a room for enjoying a good pub meal as any we have seen this year. The beamed bar on the left has a woodburning stove in the terracotta-tiled front part, a big fireplace under a wall-hanging at the back, a couple of rugs on the boards there, and a mix of pews, winged settle and other seats around old stripped tables. Centre of attraction is the serving counter, with local farm cider, and well kept changing ales on handpump – on our visit Crouch Vale Golden Nugget, Harwich Town Ganges, and their own Mill Green Loveleys Fair, Mawkin Mild, Stella and Red Barn.

Free house ~ Licensees Jarred and Clare Harris ~ Real ale ~ Bar food (12-2(2.30 weekends), 6-9; not Sun evening, not Mon) ~ (01787) 211183 ~ Children welcome ~ Dogs allowed in bar ~ Open 12-3, 5-11; 12-midnight Fri, Sat; 12-11 Sun ~ www.boxfordfleece.com

CHELMONDISTON   TM2037
Butt & Oyster
Pin Mill – signposted from B1456 SE of Ipswich; IP9 1JW

Chatty, old riverside pub with pleasant views, good food and drink and seats on the terrace

Now that some of the old boat hulks have been removed, the views from this simple old bargemen's pub over the bustling River Orwell are even better; to make the most of the water activity try to bag a window seat inside or one of chairs and tables on the terrace. The half-panelled little smoke room is pleasantly worn and unfussy and has high-backed and other old-fashioned settles on the tiled floor. There's also a two-level dining room with country-kitchen furniture on bare boards and pictures and artefacts to do with boats and the water on the walls above the dado. Adnams Best, Broadside, Old and a changing guest beer on handpump or tapped from the cask, several wines by the glass and local cider; board games. The annual Thames Barge Race (end June/beginning July) is fun. The car park can fill up pretty quickly.

Adnams ~ Lease Steve Lomas ~ Real ale ~ Bar food (12-9.30) ~ Restaurant ~ (01473) 780764 ~ Children welcome in dining rooms ~ Dogs allowed in bar ~ Open 11-11 ~ www.debeninns.co.uk/buttandoyster

EARL SOHAM   TM2263
Victoria
A1120 Yoxford–Stowmarket; IP13 7RL

Nice beers from brewery across the road in this friendly, informal local; bar food

Unspoilt and easy-going this simple pub is best known for the ales from the Earl Soham brewery just across the road and for its home-cooking. Fairly basic and definitely well worn, the bar is sparsely furnished with kitchen chairs and pews, plank-topped trestle sewing-machine tables and other simple scrubbed pine country tables, and has stripped panelling, tiled or board floors, an interesting range of pictures of Queen Victoria and her reign, and open fires; board games. Earl Soham Brandeston Gold, Sir Rogers Porter, and Victoria Bitter on handpump. There are seats on a raised back lawn, with more out in front. The pub is quite close to a wild fritillary meadow at Framlingham and a working windmill at Saxtead.

Earl Soham ~ Licensee Paul Hooper ~ Real ale ~ Bar food (12-2, 7-10) ~ (01728) 685758 ~ Children welcome ~ Dogs allowed in bar ~ Open 11.30-3, 6-11; 12-3, 7-10.30 Sun

EASTBRIDGE   TM4566
Eels Foot
Off B1122 N of Leiston; IP16 4SN

Country local with hospitable atmosphere, fair value food using their own eggs, and Thursday evening folk sessions; bedrooms

This is a popular spot with bird-watchers, cyclists and walkers and the fresh water marshes bordering the inn offer plenty of opportunity for watching the abundance of birds and butterflies; a footpath leads you directly to the sea. It's a friendly, simple pub and the upper and lower parts of the bar have light modern furnishings on stripped wood floors, a warming fire, and Adnams Bitter, Broadside, Ghost Ship and a changing guest on handpump, around a dozen wines by the glass and several malt whiskies; darts in a side area, board games, cribbage and a neat back dining room. There are seats on the terrace and benches out in the lovely big back garden. The bedrooms (one with wheelchair access) in the newish building are comfortable and attractive.

Adnams ~ Tenants Julian and Alex Wallis ~ Real ale ~ Bar food (12-2.30, 7-9 (6.30-8.30 Thurs)) ~ Restaurant ~ (01728) 830154 ~ Children welcome ~ Dogs allowed in bar ~ Live folk music Thurs evening and last Sun of month ~ Open 12-3, 6-11(12-11 Fri); 11.30-11(10.30 Sun) Sat ~ Bedrooms: £80B/£99B ~ www.theeelsfootinn.co.uk

GRUNDISBURGH
TM2250

Dog

The Green; off A12 via B1079 from Woodbridge bypass; IP13 6TA

Civilised, friendly pub with enjoyable food, excellent choice of drinks and a log fire; garden with play area

Close to the village green, this pink-washed pub is a cosy place with friendly, cheerful staff. Nicely villagey, the public bar on the left has an open log fire and oak settles and dark wooden carvers around a mix of tables on the tiles. The softly lit and relaxing carpeted lounge bar has comfortable seating around dark oak tables; it links with a similar bare-boards dining room, with some attractive antique oak settles; darts. The impressive array of ten real ales includes Adnams, Earl Soham and guests from brewers like Cliff Quay, Nethergate and Woodfordes on handpump, half a dozen wines by the glass, ciders, local lager and good espresso coffee. There are several picnic-sets out in front by flowering tubs and the wicker-fenced back garden has a mediterranean feel with herbs for the kitchen, an olive tree and a grape vine and comfortable seats under white parasols; there's also a play area.

Free house ~ Licensees Charles and Eilir Rogers ~ Real ale ~ Bar food (12-2, 5.30-9) ~ Restaurant ~ (01473) 735267 ~ Children welcome away from bar ~ Dogs allowed in bar ~ Open 12-3, 5.30-11; 12-11 Fri and Sat; 12-10.30 Sun; closed Mon ~ www.grundisburghdog.co.uk

LAVENHAM
TL9149

Angel

Market Place; CO10 9QZ

Handsome old inn with emphasis on dining, good, if not cheap, food, a range of drinks, character rooms and sizeable back garden; comfortable bedrooms

Although this Tudor inn places firm emphasis on dining, there's a proper bar and they do keep Adnams Bitter, Greene King Abbot and a beer named for Marco Pierre White brewed for them by Lees on handpump; also, quite a few wines by the glass and several malt whiskies. This light and airy long bar area has a big inglenook log fire under a heavy mantelbeam and some attractive 16th-c ceiling plasterwork (even more elaborate pargeting in the residents' sitting room upstairs). Other dining areas have elegant dark wooden dining chairs around white-clothed tables, more heavy beams and panelling and cartoons and David Bailey celebrity photographs on the walls. There are seats and tables in a large sheltered back garden and picnic-sets out in front make the most of the setting in the former market square of this delightful small town. A good base for the area.

Free house ~ Licensee Rob Jackson ~ Real ale ~ Bar food (12-2.30(3.30 Sun), 6-9.30) ~ (01787) 247388 ~ Children welcome ~ Dogs allowed in bar ~ Open 11am-11.30pm ~ Bedrooms: £70S/£115S ~ www.wheelersangel.com

LEVINGTON
TM2339

Ship

Gun Hill; from A14/A12 Bucklesham roundabout take A1156 exit, then first sharp left into Felixstowe Road, then after nearly a mile turn right into Bridge Road at Levington signpost, bearing left into Church Lane; IP10 0LQ

Plenty of nautical trappings and character, in a lovely rural position; interesting modern cooking

It's worth arriving early at this attractively placed pub as ramblers and bird-watchers like coming here at lunchtime. The theme inside tends towards the nautical, with lots of ship prints and photographs of sailing barges, a marine compass under the serving counter in the middle room and a fishing net slung overhead. As well as benches built into the walls, there are comfortably upholstered small settles (some of them grouped around tables as booths) and a big black round stove. The flagstoned dining room has more nautical bric-a-brac and beams taken from an old barn. Adnams Bitter, Broadside and Sole Star on handpump or tapped from the cask and several wines by the glass. The pub is by a little lime-washed church and has views (if a little obscured) over the River Orwell estuary.

Adnams ~ Lease Adrian and Susan Searing ~ Real ale ~ Bar food (12-2.30(3 Sun), 6.30-9) ~ (01473) 659573 ~ Children welcome ~ Dogs allowed in bar ~ Open 11.30-3, 6-11; 11.30-11 Sat; 12-10.30 Sun ~ www.theshipinnlevington.co.uk

LINDSEY TYE   TL9846
Red Rose
Village signposted off A1141 NW of Hadleigh; IP7 6PP

Handsome 15th-c hall house with a couple of neat bars, enjoyable popular food, real ales and plenty of outside seating

Our readers enjoy their visits to this neatly kept and well run pub and there's always a warm and inviting atmosphere and plenty of contented chatty customers. The main bar has low beams and some standing timbers, a mix of wooden tables and chairs, red-painted walls and dried teasels in glass jugs on the window sills. In front of a splendid log fire in its old brick fireplace are a couple of squashy red leather squashy sofas, a low table and some brass measuring jugs. A second room is furnished in the same way, again with a big brick fireplace but is much simpler in feel, and perhaps quieter; background music. Adnams Bitter, Mauldons Moletrap Bitter and maybe a guest beer on handpump and ten wines by the glass. There are flowering tubs and a few picnic-sets in front , with more picnic-sets at the back – where there's also a children's play area, a football pitch and an animal pen with chickens and sheep.

Free house ~ Licensee Peter Miller ~ Real ale ~ Bar food (12-2.30(3 Sun), 6.30-9.30(7-9 Sun)) ~ (01449) 741424 ~ Children welcome ~ Dogs allowed in bar ~ Open 11-3, 5.30-11; 11-11 Sun ~ www.thelindseyrose.co.uk

MIDDLETON   TM4267
Bell
Off A12 in Yoxford via B1122 towards Leiston, also signposted off B1125 Leiston–Westleton; The Street; IP17 3NN

Thatch and low beams, friendly chef/landlord, good beer, popular good value food – a peaceful spot

Our readers love their visits to this well run pub and the courteous licensees make all their customers, regulars or visitors, feel warmly welcomed. There's always a cheerful bustle and the traditional bar on the left has a log fire in a big hearth, old local photographs, a low plank-panelling ceiling, bar stools and pew seating, Adnams Bitter, Broadside and a seasonal ales tapped from the cask, and darts. On the right an informal two-room carpeted lounge/dining area has padded mate's and library chairs around the dark tables below its low black beams, with pews by a big woodburning stove, and cheery modern seaside brewery prints. Dogs are welcomed with treats and a bowl of water. It's a pretty cream-washed building, with picnic-sets under cocktail parasols out in front, and camping available in the broad meadow behind. Walks on the coast and the RSPB Minsmere bird reserve are nearby.

Adnams ~ Tenants Nilmonas and Trish Musgrove ~ Real ale ~ Bar food (12-2.15, 6-9.15; 12-5 Sun; not Mon evening or winter Mon lunchtime – except bank holidays) ~ Restaurant ~ (01728) 648286 ~ Children welcome away from bar ~ Dogs allowed in bar ~ Open 12-3, 6-11; 12-12(11 Sun) Sat; closed winter Mon lunchtime

NAYLAND   TL9734
Anchor

Court Street; just off A134 – turn off S of signposted B1087 main village turn; CO6 4JL

Friendly riverside pub with seats by the water, newly refurbished bar and dining rooms, up to five ales and good interesting food

This is a lovely spot in summer when you can sit at picnic-sets beside the peaceful River Stour and watch the ducks. Inside, the new landlord has given the pub a careful refurbishment adding contemporary touches to the classic styling. The bare-boards bar has a mix of wooden dining chairs and tables, a big gilt mirror on silvery wallpaper at one end of the room with another mirror above the pretty brick fireplace at the other, fresh flowers on the bar, Adnams Bitter, Greene King IPA, Nethergate Growler and a beer named for them brewed by Hadleigh on handpump and several wines by the glass. Another room behind has individually chosen furniture and an open fire, and leads into the River Room with its elegant tables and chairs. Up some quite steep stairs is a cosy, candlelit restaurant and a small stylish room for private parties.

Free house ~ Licensee James Haggar ~ Real ale ~ Bar food (12-2.30(3 Sat, 4 Sun), 6-9.30) ~ Restaurant ~ (01206) 262313 ~ Children welcome ~ Dogs allowed in bar ~ Open 10am-11pm ~ www.anchornayland.co.uk

SIBTON   TM3570
White Horse

Halesworth Road; IP17 2JJ

Particularly well run inn, nicely old-fashioned bar, good mix of customers, real ales and imaginative food using produce from their own kitchen garden; comfortable bedrooms

Our readers really enjoy staying in the comfortable bedrooms here and the breakfasts are excellent. Mr and Mrs Mason are hard-working, hands-on licensees who welcome their guests with genuine friendliness and they've cleverly struck a balance between village pub and first class restaurant. The comfortable bar has horsebrasses and tack on the walls, old settles and pews, and a large inglenook fireplace with a roaring log fire. Adnams Bitter, Woodfordes Once Bittern and a changing guest beer on handpump (they hold a June beer festival with around 16 ales), several wines by the glass and a dozen malt whiskies are served from the old oak-panelled counter, and there's a viewing panel showing the working cellar and its Roman floor. Steps take you up past an ancient partly knocked-through timbered wall into a carpeted gallery and there's a smart dining room, too. The big garden has plenty of seats.

Free house ~ Licensees Neil and Gill Mason ~ Real ale ~ Bar food (12-2, 7-9) ~ Restaurant ~ (01728) 660337 ~ Well behaved children welcome but must be over 13 for accommodation ~ Dogs allowed in bar ~ Quiz every Mon (not bank holidays) ~ Open 12-2.30, 6.30-11; 12-3.30, 7-10.30 Sun ~ Bedrooms: £70S/£90B ~ www.sibtonwhitehorseinn.co.uk

SNAPE TM3957

Plough & Sail

The Maltings, Snape Bridge (B1069 S); IP17 1SR

Nicely placed dining pub extended airily around an older bar, real ales and well liked food using local seasonal produce; seats outside

Twin brothers have taken over this 16th-c former smugglers' haunt and are running it with enthusiasm and friendliness; Alex is front of house and Oliver is head chef. As it's part of the Snape Maltings they offer both pre- and post- concert menus. The pub is mostly open-plan and is a clever blend of the traditional and modern with wicker and café-style furnishings around an older heart with a woodburning stove, high bar chairs by the serving counter and rustic pine dining chairs and tables on terracotta tiling; another cosy little room has comfortable sofas and low coffee tables. Most diners head for the simply furnished bar hall and spacious airy dining room with blue-cushioned chairs around straightforward tables on light, wood-strip flooring and high ceilings with A-frame beams; motifs illustrating the history of the Maltings decorate the walls. Another restaurant upstairs has similar furnishings; background music. Adnams Bitter, Woodfordes Wherry and a couple of guest beers on handpump and several wines by the glass. The flower-filled terrace has plenty of teak chairs and tables and there are some picnic-sets at the front. The shops and other buildings in the attractive complex are interesting to wander through.

Suffolk Dining Ltd ~ Lease Alex Burnside ~ Real ale ~ Bar food (12-3, 5.30-9) ~ Restaurant ~ (01728) 688413 ~ Children welcome ~ Dogs allowed in bar ~ Open 11-11; 12-10.30 Sun ~ www.theploughandsailsnape.co.uk

SOUTHWOLD TM5076

Crown

High Street; IP18 6DP

Comfortable hotel with relaxed bars, a fine choice of drinks, papers to read, excellent imaginative food and seats outside; refurbished bedrooms

As this smart and civilised hotel is a favourite with so many of its customers, you really do have to arrive promptly to be sure of a table as they run a first-come first-served system. And whether you're popping in for a pint and a chat or a light lunch or staying in the lovely bedrooms you'll be genuinely welcomed by the courteous and extremely efficient staff. Many of our readers are very fond of the cosy, oak-panelled back locals' bar (reserved for drinkers) which has a proper pubby atmosphere, red leatherette wall benches on red carpeting, Adnams Bitter, Broadside and a seasonal guest on handpump, 20 wines by the glass from a splendid list and several hand-crafted spirits. The elegant beamed front bar has a relaxed, informal atmosphere, a stripped curved high-backed settle and other dark varnished settles, kitchen and other chairs, and a carefully restored rather fine carved wooden fireplace; maybe newspapers to read. The tables out in a sunny sheltered corner are very pleasant.

Adnams ~ Manager Francis Guildea ~ Real ale ~ Bar food (12-2, 7-9) ~ (01502) 722275
~ Children welcome ~ Dogs allowed in bar ~ Open 11-11; 9am-11pm Sun ~ Bedrooms:
£135B/£175B ~ www.adnams.co.uk/stay-with-us/the-crown

SOUTHWOLD   TM4975

Harbour Inn

Blackshore, by the boats; from A1095, turn right at the Kings Head, and keep on past the
golf course and water tower; IP18 6TA

Great spot down by the boats, lots of outside tables – interesting inside,
too; popular food with emphasis on local seafood

The back bar is nicely nautical, with its dark panelling, built-in wall seats
around scrubbed tables, low ceiling draped with ensigns, signal flags, pennants
and a line strung with ancient dried fish, quaint old stove, rope fancy-work, a
plethora of local fishing photographs, even portholes with water bubbling behind
them. It's still well used by locals as well as the many visitors, and cheerful staff
serve a good choice of wines by the glass along with Adnams Bitter, Southwold,
Broadside and Ghost Ship on handpump. They have their own weather station
for walkers and sailors. The tiled-floor lower front bar, also panelled, is broadly
similar, and the large, elevated dining room has panoramic views of the harbour,
lighthouse, brewery and churches beyond the marshes. Teak tables out behind
look out over the marshy commons to the town, and green picnic-sets on the front
terrace, by a big cannon, face the moored boats of the Blyth estuary. This is under
the same good management as the Bell in Walberswick.

Adnams ~ Tenant Nick Attfield ~ Real ale ~ Bar food (12-9) ~ (01502) 722381 ~ Children
welcome away from top bar ~ Dogs allowed in bar ~ Open 11-11 ~
www.harbourinnsouthwold.co.uk

SOUTHWOLD   TM5076

Lord Nelson

East Street, off High Street (A1095); IP18 6EJ

Bow-windowed town pub with long-serving owners, well liked pubby food
and a good choice of drinks; seats outside

With a happy mix of both locals and visitors, this is a well run pub with
a buoyant atmosphere and friendly, helpful staff. The partly panelled
traditional bar and its two small side rooms are kept spotless, with good lighting,
a small but extremely hot coal fire, light wood furniture on the tiled floor, lamps
in nice nooks and corners, and some interesting Nelson memorabilia, including
attractive nautical prints and a fine model of HMS Victory. They serve the whole
range of Adnams beers alongside Aspall's cider and several good wines by the
glass; board games. There are seats out in front with a sidelong view down to the
sea and more in a sheltered (and heated) back garden, with the Adnams brewery
in sight (and often the appetising fragrance of brewing in progress). Disabled
access is not perfect but is possible.

Adnams ~ Tenants David and Gemma Sanchez ~ Real ale ~ Bar food (12-2, 7-9) ~ (01502)
722079 ~ Children welcome in snug and family room ~ Dogs allowed in bar ~ Open 10.30am-
11pm; 12-10.30 Sun ~ www.thelordnelsonsouthwold.co.uk

STOKE-BY-NAYLAND

TL9836

Angel

B1068 Sudbury–East Bergholt; CO6 4SA

Elegant, comfortable inn with attractive bars, enterprising modern food including breakfasts, decent choice of drinks and neat uniformed staff; bedrooms

This elegant place has been offering hospitality to customers since the 17th c and today serves a good mix of both locals and visitors. The lounge area has handsome Elizabethan beams, some stripped brickwork and timbers, leather chesterfields and wing armchairs around low tables by the pile of logs in the non-working fireplace (there are working log fires, too), and paintings and prints of the pub, the village and the surrounding area. The chatty bar has farmhouse pine chairs and tables and high tables and stools on the red tiled floor, and more stools against the counter where they keep Greene King IPA, Hellhound Dirty Blond and Nethergate Barfly on handpump and ten wines by the glass (including champagne). The high-beamed and timbered Well Room (which has a glass cover over its 16-metre well) is more formal and carpeted with all sorts of cushioned dining chairs around polished dark tables, and a central lamp-style chandelier; staff are neatly uniformed and friendly. There are seats and tables on a sheltered terrace. The individually styled bedrooms are comfortable and the breakfasts very good.

Free house ~ Licensee James Haggar ~ Real ale ~ Bar food (12-2.45, 6-9.30; all day weekends; breakfast from 8am; morning coffee and afternoon tea) ~ Restaurant ~ (01206) 263245 ~ Children welcome ~ Dogs allowed in bar ~ Open 8am-11pm; 12-10.30 Sun ~ Bedrooms: /£95B ~ www.angelinnsuffolk.co.uk

STOKE-BY-NAYLAND

TL9836

Crown

Park Street (B1068); CO6 4SE

Smart dining pub with attractive modern furnishings, imaginative food using local produce, real ales and a great wine choice; good bedrooms

This civilised and chatty place is well laid out to give several distinct-feeling areas in its extensive open-plan dining bar – a sofa and easy chairs on flagstones near the serving counter, a couple more armchairs under heavy beams by the big woodburning stove, one sizeable table tucked nicely into a three-sided built-in seat, a lower side room with more beams and cheerful floral wallpaper. Tables are mostly stripped veterans, with high-backed dining chairs, but there are more modern chunky pine tables at the back; contemporary artworks, mostly for sale, and daily papers. Friendly informally dressed staff bustle happily about, and they have Aspall's cider as well as Adnams Bitter, Crouch Vale Brewers Gold, Woodfordes Wherry and a guest beer on handpump. Wine is a big plus, with more than three dozen by the glass, and hundreds more from the glass-walled 'cellar shop' in one corner – you can buy there to take away, too. Disabled access is good. The sheltered flagstoned back terrace has comfortable teak furniture, with heaters, big terracotta-coloured parasols, and a peaceful view over rolling lightly wooded countryside. Beyond is the very well equipped separate bedroom block (breakfasts are first class).

Free house ~ Licensee Richard Sunderland ~ Real ale ~ Bar food (12-2.30, 6-9.30(10 Fri, Sat); all day Sun) ~ (01206) 262001 ~ Children welcome ~ Dogs allowed in bar ~ Open 11-11; 12-10.30 Sun ~ Bedrooms: £90S(£110B)/£120S(£145B) ~ www.crowninn.net

WALDRINGFIELD   TM2844
Maybush
Off A12 S of Martlesham; The Quay, Cliff Road; IP12 4QL

**Busy pub with tables outside by the riverbank; nautical décor and a fair
choice of drinks and traditional fair value bar food**

In fine weather the many seats outside this popular family pub makes the most
of the view over the lovely River Deben, and if you arrive early enough, you
might be able to bag a window table inside. The spacious knocked-through bar is
divided into separate areas by fireplaces or steps. There's a nautical theme, with
an elaborate ship's model in a glass case and a few more in a light, high-ceilinged
extension – as well as lots of old lanterns, pistols and aerial photographs;
background music and board games. Adnams Bitter and Old and a changing guest
on handpump and a fair choice of wines by the glass. There are river cruises
available nearby but you have to pre-book; this is a haven for bird-watchers and
ramblers.

Adnams ~ Lease Steve and Louise Lomas ~ Real ale ~ Bar food (12-9.30) ~ Restaurant ~
(01473) 736215 ~ Children welcome ~ Dogs allowed in bar ~ Open 11-11 ~
www.debeninns.co.uk/maybush

WHEPSTEAD   TL8258
White Horse
Off B1066 S of Bury; Rede Road; IP29 4SS

**Charmingly reworked country pub with attractively furnished rooms and
well liked food and drink**

Although this popular pub was built in the 17th c there are several Victorian
additions and plenty of space for a drink or a meal. The dark-beamed bar has
a woodburning stove in the low fireplace, little stools around pubby tables on the
tiled floor and boards listing the menu. Linked rooms have sturdy, country kitchen
tables and chairs on beige carpet or antique floor tiles, with some attractively
cushioned traditional wall seats and some rather fine old farmhouse chairs.
Landscape paintings (for sale) and old prints decorate walls painted in soft canary
yellow or sage; the bookshelves have books that are actually worth reading.
Adnams Bitter and Broadside on handpump and eight wines by the glass. A tuck
shop sells sweets, chocolates and ice-creams; the resident westie is called Skye.
A neat sheltered back terrace is brightened up by colourful oilcloth tablecloths,
and at the picnic-sets out on the grass, birdsong emphasises what a peaceful spot
this is.

Free house ~ Licensees Gary and Di Kingshott ~ Real ale ~ Bar food (; 12-2, 7-9; not Sun
evening) ~ (01284) 735760 ~ Children welcome ~ Dogs allowed in bar ~ Open 11.30-3, 7-11;
closed Sun evening ~ www.whitehorsewhepstead.co.uk

DOG FRIENDLY INNS, HOTELS AND B&Bs

ALDEBURGH   TM4656

Cross Keys

Crabbe Street, Aldeburgh, Suffolk IP15 5BN (01728) 452637
www.aldeburgh-crosskeys.co.uk

£89.50; 3 attractively furnished rms. Cheerful, 16th-c pub near the beach (dogs can walk here) with views from seats on the sheltered back terrace across the promenade to the water; a buoyant atmosphere, low-ceilinged, interconnecting bars with antique and other pubby furniture, the landlord's collection of oils and Victorian watercolours, paintings by local artists and roaring log fires in two inglenook fireplaces; real ales and decent wines by the glass and tasty, traditional food; two resident dogs; dogs anywhere in the pub and in bedrooms

ALDEBURGH   TM4657

Wentworth

Wentworth Road, Aldeburgh, Suffolk IP15 5BD (01728) 452312
www.wentworth-aldeburgh.com

£189; 35 rms, some with sea view, 7 in Darfield House opposite (more spacious but no sea view). Comfortable and tranquil hotel, family run for 85 years, overlooking the fishing huts, boats and beach (where you can walk); a couple of lounges (one with a log fire), a convivial bar, good enjoyable food (plenty of fish) in the red-walled, candlelit restaurant, hearty breakfasts and a sunny terrace for light lunches; dogs in bedrooms and lounges; £2

BILDESTON   TL9949

Crown

High Street, Bildeston, Ipswich, Suffolk IP7 7EB (01449) 740510
www.thebildestoncrown.co.uk

£150; 12 pretty, individually furnished rms. Lovely timber-framed Tudor inn with log fires and stripped wooden floors in the spacious and convivial beamed bar, a comfortable, heavily beamed lounge, elegant restaurant, enjoyable modern cooking, well kept real ales and welcoming, courteous staff; seats in the central courtyard and on the heated terrace; dogs welcome; £10

BUNGAY   TM3088

Earsham Park Farm

Old Railway Road, Earsham, Bungay, Suffolk NR35 2AQ (01986) 892180
www.earsham-parkfarm.co.uk

£82; 4 lovely sunny rms. Light and airy Victorian farmhouse with an attractive garden on 600 acres of working farmland – lots of lovely walks; plenty of original features, super Aga-cooked breakfasts with their own sausages and bacon and home-made bread taken around a large family table in the prettily decorated dining room, and friendly, helpful owners; resident weimeraner, Woggle; dogs in bedrooms (not to be left unattended) and lounge only; towels; £5

BURY ST EDMUNDS

TL8564

Angel

3 Angel Hill, Bury St Edmunds, Suffolk IP33 1LT (01284) 714000 www.theangel.co.uk

£120; 74 individually decorated rms with bold colours and fabrics. Thriving town-centre Georgian hotel given a contemporary make-over, with all manner of artwork on the walls, interesting curios from all over the world dotted among comfortable sofas in the log-fire lounge, a relaxed bar with all-day light meals, interesting modern british food using the best local produce in the easy-going and elegant bare-boards restaurant, good breakfasts and friendly, helpful staff; gardens to walk in 50 metres away; dogs in bedrooms; £5

CAMPSEY ASH

TM3255

Old Rectory

Station Road, Campsey Ash, Woodbridge, Suffolk IP13 0PU (01728) 746524
www.theoldrectorysuffolk.com

£110; 7 most attractive rms. Very relaxed and welcoming Georgian house in 3 acres of gardens, with charming staff, a log fire in the comfortable and restful drawing room, quite a few Victorian prints, enjoyable food (using their own produce) either in the airy summer conservatory or winter dining room with its log fire, and good breakfasts; dogs in Coach House and Garden Cottage bedrooms only; not in main house

DUNWICH

TM4770

Ship

St James's Street, Dunwich, Saxmundham, Suffolk IP17 3DT (01728) 648219
www.shipatdunwich.co.uk

£97.50; 15 recently refurbished rms, some with marsh and sea views. Pleasant old pub by the sea with a welcome for regulars and visitors – and dogs, who are given a treat and bowl of water; the traditionally furnished main bar has benches, pews, captain's chairs and wooden tables on floor tiles, a woodburning stove (left open in cold weather) and lots of sea prints, and there's a simple conservatory; local beers, cider and wines by the glass and enjoyable food including their famous fish and chips; the RSPB reserve at Minsmere and Dunwich Museum are nearby – as are lots of coastal walks; dogs in bedrooms and bar; home-made treats; £5

HADLEIGH

TM0242

Edge Hall

2 High Street, Hadleigh, Ipswich, Suffolk IP7 5AP (01473) 822458 www.edgehall.co.uk

£85; 8 pretty rms, 2 in Lodge. Friendly Georgian house with an attractive walled garden where you can have afternoon tea or play croquet; a comfortable, elegant lounge with chandeliers, personal service, and traditional english cooking and good breakfasts using home-grown produce in the stately dining room; self-catering also; dogs in certain bedrooms; £5

HINTLESHAM
TM0843

Hintlesham Hall

Hintlesham, Ipswich, Suffolk IP8 3NS (01473) 652334 www.hintleshamhall.co.uk

£155; 33 lovely rms. Magnificent mansion, mainly Georgian but dating from
Elizabethan times, in 175 acres with big walled gardens, 18-hole golf course,
outdoor heated swimming pool, croquet, and tennis; restful and comfortable day
rooms with books, antiques and open fires, fine modern cooking in three smart
restaurants (lighter all-day options, too), a marvellous wine list, popular afternoon
teas (taken on the terrace in fine weather), and exemplary service; a newly
refurbished spa and treatment rooms; dogs in certain bedrooms; £15

HOPTON
TL9979

Old Rectory

Hopton, Suffolk IP22 2QX (01953) 688135 www.theoldrectoryhopton.com

£110; 3 attractive rms. 16th-c house in walled gardens with friendly, hospitable
owners, a cosy snug and relaxing drawing room, winter fires, home-made
cake and tea on arrival, delicious breakfasts in elegant dining room and seats
on terrace; resident labrador and border terrier; good walks close by; dogs in
bedrooms; £10

HORRINGER
TL8161

Ickworth

Horringer, Bury St Edmunds, Suffolk IP29 5QE (01284) 735350 www.ickworthhotel.com

£194.25; 27 rms plus 11 apartments in Dower House. Lovely 18th-c house in
marvellous parkland on an 1,800 acre National Trust estate (formerly owned
by the Marquess of Bristol), the east wing of which is a luxury hotel; elegant
and traditional décor mixes with more contemporary touches, the atmosphere
is relaxed and informal, and staff are friendly and helpful; excellent modern
cooking in dining conservatory and more formal restaurant and good, extensive
breakfasts; riding, tennis, indoor swimming pool, spa and treatment rooms, and
lots of surrounding walks; dogs in bedrooms; £10

IPSWICH
TM1644

Salthouse Harbour Hotel

Neptune Quay, Ipswich, Suffolk IP4 1AX (01473) 226789 www.salthouseharbour.co.uk

£130; 70 chic modern rms. Converted Victorian warehouse overlooking the
marina that's now a boutique hotel with contemporary furnishings and décor in
the open-plan bar and lounge, lots of artwork, attentive, courteous staff, inventive,
brasserie-style food in the clubby-feeling restaurant, good breakfasts (served until
10am) and beauty treatment rooms; dogs in bedrooms and lounge; £5

LAVENHAM

TL9149

Swan

High Street, Lavenham, Sudbury, Suffolk CO10 9QA (01787) 247477
www.theswanatlavenham.co.uk

£195; 45 smart rms. Handsome and comfortable Elizabethan hotel that
incorporates several fine half-timbered buildings; lots of cosy seating areas,
interesting historic prints and alcoves with beams, timbers, armchairs and settees,
an intriguing small bar, good food in lavishly timbered restaurant with a minstrels'
gallery (actually built only in 1965) or more informal brasserie, afternoon teas,
generous breakfasts and friendly helpful staff; dogs welcome anywhere except
restaurant; £10

LONG MELFORD

TL8645

Bull

Hall Street, Long Melford, Sudbury, Suffolk CO10 9JG (01787) 378494
www.thebull-hotel.com

£85; 25 comfortable rms. An inn since 1580, this fine black and white hotel was
originally a medieval manorial hall, and has handsome and interesting carved
woodwork and timbering, and an old weavers' gallery overlooking the courtyard;
the old-fashioned front lounge has antique furnishings and a log fire in a huge
fireplace, a spacious back bar has sporting prints and real ales, the food from
the Old English Inns menu in the restaurant is reasonably priced, and staff are
friendly; seats in an attractive courtyard; dogs in bedrooms (not on beds); not in
food service areas; £5

ORFORD

TM4249

Crown & Castle

Orford, Woodbridge, Suffolk IP12 2LJ (01394) 450205 www.crownandcastle.co.uk

£190; 21 thoughtfully designed, stylish rms. Red brick and high gabled Victorian
hotel by the Norman castle in this seaside village – they think of themselves more
of a restaurant-with-rooms; a lovely relaxed atmosphere, courteous staff, a small,
smartly minimalist bar and an open fire in the comfortable lounge, exceptionally
good modern british cooking using the best local ingredients in the informal
restaurant (lighter lunches and excellent breakfasts, too), 20 wines by the glass
and seats in the garden; lots of nearby walks; resident wire haired fox terriers,
Annie and Teddy; dogs in some bedrooms, bar and one table in restaurant; home-
made treats and towels; £5.50

ORFORD

TM4249

Kings Head

Front Street, Orford, Woodbridge, Suffolk IP12 2LW (01394) 450271
www.thekingsheadorford.co.uk

£95; 4 cosy rms. Likeable, partly 700-year-old pub surrounded by fine walks
and lovely coastline; plenty of authentic atmosphere in the snug main bar with
straightforward furniture on red carpeting, heavy low beams and local beers, a
candlelit dining room with stripped brick walls and rugs on the ancient bare

boards, popular bar food and two pub dogs called Sam and Teddy; dogs anywhere in the pub and in one bedroom

ROUGHAM   TL9063
Ravenwood Hall

Rougham, Bury St Edmunds, Suffolk IP30 9JA (01359) 270345
www.ravenwoodhall.co.uk

£125; 14 comfortable rms (some in mews) with antiques. Tranquil Tudor country house in 7 acres of carefully tended gardens and woodland; log fire in comfortable lounge, a cosy bar, good food in the timbered restaurant with big inglenook fireplace (home-preserved fruits and veg, home-smoked meats and fish), a good wine list, and helpful service; croquet and heated swimming pool; lots of animals, a resident dog and walks in the grounds; dogs welcome anywhere except restaurant

SNAPE   TM4058
Golden Key

Priory Lane, Snape, Saxmundham, Suffolk IP17 1SA (01728) 688510
www.goldenkeysnape.co.uk

£75; 3 rms. 16th-c village pub, surrounded by plenty of walks, with a traditional low-beamed lounge bar, winter log fire, a mix of pubby tables and chairs, local beer and cider and a dozen wines by the glass, a small snug, two dining rooms with open fireplaces, settles and scrubbed pine tables, and likeable bar food served by friendly staff; dogs anywhere in the pub and in bedrooms; dog treats and bowl

SOUTHWOLD   TM5076
Swan

Market Place, Southwold, Suffolk IP18 6EG (01502) 722186
www.adnams.co.uk/hotels/the-swan

£175; 42 well appointed rms, some overlooking the market square and a short stroll to the beach. 17th-c hotel with a comfortable lounge, a convivial bar, interesting, enjoyable food in elegant dining room, fine wines, well kept real ales (the hotel backs on to Adnams Brewery) and polite, helpful staff; dogs in ground floor bedrooms; £10

THORPENESS   TM4759
Dolphin

Thorpeness, Leiston, Suffolk IP16 4NB (01728) 454994 www.thorpenessdolphin.com

£95; 3 airy rms. Neatly kept extended pub in an interesting village – a fascinating early 20th-c curio built as a small-scale upmarket holiday resort; scandinavian-feeling main bar with pale wooden tables and chairs on broad modern quarry tiles, a winter log fire, fresh flowers, local beers, 18 wines by the glass and several whiskies and bourbons, a smaller public bar with pubby furniture and a sizeable dining room with enjoyable food; plenty of seats outside, and you can hire electric bikes; walks on beach; dogs anywhere except restaurant; £10

WALBERSWICK

TM4974

Bell

Ferry Road, Walberswick, Southwold, Suffolk IP18 6TN (01502) 723109
www.bellinnwalberswick.co.uk

£100; 6 newly refurbished, well equipped rms. Thriving 16th-c inn with a charming, rambling bar, antique curved settles, cushioned pews and scrubbed tables on bare boards, flagstones or black and red tiles, two huge fireplaces, good beers and wines served by friendly staff, and interesting food using free-range lamb and pork and local fish; a newly opened Barn Café serves tea and cakes (and takeaways); seats in the neat garden have a view over dunes to the sea; dogs in bedrooms and bar

WESTLETON

TM4469

Crown

The Street, Westleton, Saxmundham, Suffolk IP17 3AD (01728) 648777
www.westletoncrown.co.uk

£120; 34 comfortable rms in main inn or converted stables and cottages. Stylish old coaching inn with an attractive little bar at its heart – log fire, plenty of original features, local ales, a thoughtfully chosen wine list and a chatty, informal atmosphere; also a parlour, a dining room and conservatory, a nice mix of wooden dining chairs and tables, and old photos on some fine old bare-brick walls, interesting modern cooking and enjoyable breakfasts; seats in charming terraced garden; beach and heath walks; dogs in some bedrooms, bar, snug and lounge; biscuits, bowl, sausage and walk map; £7.50

WOODBRIDGE

TM2548

Seckford Hall

Seckford Hall Road, Great Bealings, Woodbridge, Suffolk IP13 6NU (01394) 385678
www.seckford.co.uk

£183.90; 22 well equipped, comfortable rms plus 10 in courtyard. Handsome red brick Tudor mansion in 34 acres of gardens and parkland with a carp-filled lake and putting; fine linenfold panelling, huge fireplaces, heavy beams, plush furnishings and antiques in comfortable day rooms, good bistro-style food (lovely teas with home-made cakes) in two restaurants, and helpful service; indoor heated pool, spa/leisure club in converted tithe barn; dogs in courtyard bedrooms; £10

Surrey

DOG FRIENDLY PUBS

BUCKLAND   TQ2250
Jolly Farmers
Reigate Road (A25 W of Reigate); RH3 7BG

Unusual place that sells and serves a wide range of local produce; fun to eat or shop in and atmospheric, too

Our readers enjoy their visits to this unusual place which is part pub, part restaurant and part delicatessen and serves some sort of food all day. The flagstoned bar is beamed and timbered with an informal, relaxed atmosphere, brown leather sofas and armchairs, Dark Star Hophead and Pilgrim Surrey Bitter on handpump, local wines and home-made cordials. A little brick fireplace separates the bar from the small wooden-floored dining room. The shop stretches across three little rooms and stocks fresh vegetables, deli meats, cheeses, cakes, chocolates and their own range of preserves; they hold a weekly food market with stalls outside (Saturdays 9am-3pm) and organise several food festivals and events throughout the year. There are tables out on a back terrace overlooking the car park.

Free house ~ Licensees Jon and Paula Briscoe ~ Real ale ~ Bar food (12-3, 5.30-9.30; breakfast 9.15-11.15am Sat, Sun; 12-9.30 Sat; 12-8.30 Sun) ~ Restaurant ~ (01737) 221355 ~ Children welcome ~ Dogs allowed in bar ~ Open 9.15am-11.30pm(10.30 Sun) ~ www.thejollyfarmersreigate.co.uk

CHIDDINGFOLD   SU9635
Crown
The Green (A283); GU8 4TX

Lovely old inn by village green with several bars and dining rooms, fine old woodwork and stained glass windows, five real ales and enjoyable, fairly priced food; well equipped and comfortable bedrooms

The sense of history is strong here – based on a 13th-c hospice for Winchester monks on the pilgrimage to Canterbury, it's the oldest licensed house in Surrey and one of the oldest in the country. The bar and connected dining rooms (just right size for a private party) have massive beams – some over two feet thick – oak panelling, a magnificently carved inglenook fireplace and huge chimneys; do note the lovely stained glass windows. There are mates' and other pubby chairs, comfortable cushioned wall seats, leather dining chairs with wooden barley-twist arms around fine antique tables, and lots of portraits. The simple, two-level back public bar has an open fire. Fullers London Pride, Hogs Back TEA, Ringwood Bitter, Sharps Doom Bar and a guest beer on handpump and several wines by the glass; service is helpful and friendly. Seats outside look across the village green to the interesting church, and there are more tables in a sheltered central courtyard. The well equipped bedrooms have a great deal of character, with sloping floors and heavy beams, and several have four-posters.

Free house ~ Licensee Daniel Hall ~ Real ale ~ Bar food (7am-10pm; breakfast is offered to non-residents) ~ Restaurant ~ (01428) 682255 ~ Children welcome ~ Dogs allowed in bar ~ Open 7am-11pm; 8am-11pm(10.30 Sun) Sat ~ Bedrooms: £100S/£145S ~ www.thecrownchiddingfold.com

CHIPSTEAD   TQ2757
White Hart
Hazelwood Lane; CR5 3QW

Neatly kept 18th-c pub with antique tables and chairs in open-plan rooms, lots to look at, real ales and several wines by the glass, good bistro-style food and friendly staff

Opposite rugby playing fields and with distant country views, this is a nicely kept pub with an informal, friendly atmosphere. The rooms are open-plan with a raftered dining room to the right, elegant metal chandeliers, rough-plastered walls, an open fire in the brick fireplace and a couple of carved metal standing uprights. The central bar has stools at it's panelled bar counter, where helpful, friendly staff serve Fullers London Pride, Harveys Sussex, Sharps Doom Bar and three guests from brewers such as Hepworth, Hopback and Tring from handpump, around 16 good wines by the glass and up to 80 malt whiskies; board games. The long room to the left is light and airy with lots of windows overlooking the seats on the terrace, some wall panelling at one end, and a woodburning stove. Throughout, there's a fine mix of antique dining chairs and settles around all sorts of tables (each set with a church candle), rugs on bare boards or flagstones, hundreds of interesting cartoons, country pictures, cricketing prints and rugby team photographs, large, ornate mirrors and, on the window sills and mantelpieces, old glass and stone bottles, clocks, books and plants.

Brunning & Price ~ Manager Damian Mann ~ Real ale ~ Bar food (12-10(9.30 Sun)) ~ Restaurant ~ (01737) 554455 ~ Children welcome ~ Dogs allowed in bar ~ Open 11.30-11; 12-10.30 Sun ~ www.brunningandprice.co.uk/whitehartchipstead

ESHER   TQ1566
Marneys
Alma Road (one-way), Weston Green; heading N on A309 from A307 roundabout, after Lamb & Star pub turn left into Lime Tree Avenue (signposted to All Saints Parish Church), then left at T junction into Chestnut Avenue; KT10 8JN

Country-feeling pub with good value traditional food and attractive garden

Cottagey and rather charming, this friendly little pub feels surprisingly rural for the area and the front terrace has seats and wooden tables and views over the wooded common, village church and duck pond; there are more seats on the decked area in the pleasantly planted sheltered garden. Inside, there are just two rooms. The small snug bar has a low-beamed ceiling, Fullers London Pride, Sharps Doom Bar and Wells & Youngs Bitter on handpump, about a dozen wines by the glass and perhaps horseracing on the unobtrusive corner TV. To the left, past a little cast-iron woodburning stove, a dining area has big pine tables, pews, pale country kitchen chairs and cottagey blue-curtained windows; background music. The pub is only a mile from Hampton Court Palace.

Free house ~ Licensee Thomas Duxberry ~ Real ale ~ Bar food (12-2.30(3 Sun), 6-9; not Fri-Sun evenings) ~ (020) 8398 4444 ~ Children welcome away from bar ~ Dogs allowed in bar ~ Open 11-11; 12-10.30 Sun ~ www.marneys.com

LEIGH   TQ2147
Seven Stars
Dawes Green, South of A25 Dorking–Reigate; RH2 8NP

Popular country dining pub with enjoyable food and good wines

A lways beautifully kept and homely, this tile-hung 17th-c tavern has plenty of traditional atmosphere, and serves well kept beer and jolly good food. The comfortable saloon bar has fine flagstones, beams, a 1633 inglenook fireback showing a royal coat of arms and dark wheelback chairs, and there's a plainer public bar. Greene King Old Speckled Hen, Fullers London Pride and Wells & Youngs Bitter are served from handpump from the glowing copper counter, alongside decent wines with about a dozen by the glass. The sympathetic restaurant extension at the side incorporates 17th-c floor timbers from a granary. Outside, there's plenty of room in the beer garden at the front, on the terrace and in the side garden.

Punch ~ Lease David and Rebecca Pellen ~ Real ale ~ Bar food (12-2.30(4 Sun), 6-9) ~ Restaurant ~ (01306) 611254 ~ Dogs allowed in bar ~ Open 12-3, 5.30-10.30(10 in winter); 12-11 Sat; 12-7.30 Sun; closed Sun evening ~ www.thesevenstarsleigh.co.uk

MICKLEHAM   TQ1753
Running Horses
Old London Road (B2209); RH5 6DU

Upmarket pub with elegant restaurant and comfortable bar, and food from sandwiches through to very imaginative smart dining

T his terrific place is an accomplished all-rounder that's equally popular as a local drinking haunt, walkers' stop and graceful dining destination. The spacious bar is timelessly stylish with a cheerfully smart atmosphere, hunting pictures, racing cartoons and Hogarth prints, lots of race tickets hanging from a beam, fresh flowers or a fire in an inglenook at one end and cushioned wall settles and other dining chairs around straightforward pubby tables and bar stools. Fullers London Pride, Wells & Youngs Bitter, Sharps Doom Bar and a guest such as Shepherd Neame Spitfire are on handpump alongside good wines by the glass from a serious wine list; background music. The extensive restaurant is quite open to the bar and although set out fairly formally with crisp white cloths and candles on each table, it shares the relaxing atmosphere of the bar. A terrace in front with picnic-sets and lovely flowering tubs and hanging baskets takes in a peaceful view of the old church with its strange stubby steeple. You may be asked to leave your credit card if you run a tab, and it's best to get here early, both to secure parking in the narrow lane (though you can park on the main road) and for a table. A notice by the door asks walkers to remove or cover their boots.

Free house ~ Licensees Steve and Josie Slayford ~ Real ale ~ Bar food (12-2.30(3 Sat, Sun), 7-9.30; 6.30-9 Sun) ~ Restaurant ~ (01372) 372279 ~ No children under 10 in bar area ~ Dogs allowed in bar ~ Open 12-11.30(10.30 Sun) ~ Bedrooms: £95S(£110B)/£110S(£135B) ~ www.therunninghorses.co.uk

MILFORD   SU9542
Refectory
Portsmouth Road; GU8 5HJ

Handsome building with plenty of interest inside, beams, timbering, fine stone fireplaces and so forth, lots of room, real ales and well liked food

The interesting interior of this most attractive golden stone and timbered building – thought to have be a former cattle barn, and a tea and antique shop – feels extremely spacious. It's essentially L-shaped and mainly open-plan, with strikingly heavy beams, lots of timbering, exposed stone walls, stalling and standing timbers creating separate seating areas and a couple of big log fires in handsome stone fireplaces. A two-tiered and balconied part at one end has a wall covered with huge brass platters; the rest of the walls are hung with some nice old photographs and a variety of paintings. Dining chairs and dark wooden tables are grouped on the wooden, quarry-tiled or carpeted flooring and rugs, bookshelves, big pot plants, stone bottles on window sills and fresh flowers. High wooden bar stools line the long counter where they serve Hogsback TEA, Phoenix Brunning & Price and four guests from brewers such as Adnams, Andwell and Hammerpot from handpump, around 16 wines by the glass and around 80 malt whiskies. There are teak tables and chairs in the back courtyard adjacent to the characterful pigeonry.

Brunning & Price ~ Manager Katie Dallyn ~ Real ale ~ Bar food (12-10(9.30 Sun)) ~ (01483) 413820 ~ Children welcome ~ Dogs allowed in bar ~ Open 11.30-11; 12-10.30 Sun ~ www.brunningandprice.co.uk/refectory

SHAMLEY GREEN   TQ0343
Red Lion
The Green; GU5 0UB

Pleasant dining pub with popular tasty food and nice gardens

In fine weather there's plenty of outside seating both at the back of this friendly pub where there are hand-made rustic tables and benches on a heated terrace and a lawn, and at the front, which overlooks the village green and cricket pitch. Inside, it's fairly traditional with real fires in its two connected bars, a mix of new and old wooden tables, chairs and cushioned settles on bare boards and red carpet, stripped standing timbers, fresh white walls and deep red ceilings; background music. They serve Youngs, a couple of guests such as Ringwood Fortyniner and Sharps Doom Bar, and over a dozen wines by the glass.

Punch ~ Lease Debbie Ersser ~ Real ale ~ Bar food (12-2.30(3 Sat, Sun), 6.30-9.30(8.30 Sun); not winter Sun evening) ~ Restaurant ~ (01483) 892202 ~ Children welcome ~ Dogs allowed in bar ~ Open 11.30-11; 12-10.30 Sun ~ www.redlionshamleygreen.com

THURSLEY   SU9039

Three Horseshoes

Dye House Road, just off A3 SW of Godalming; GU8 6QD

Civilised country village pub with a broad range of good food

Well placed for heathland walks – ask at the bar for a walking map – this is a pretty tile-hung pub jointly owned by a consortium of villagers who rescued it from closure. It has the feel of a gently upmarket country local. The convivial beamed front bar has a winter log fire, Hogs Back TEA and a guest such as Sharps Doom Bar or Surrey Hills Shere Drop on handpump, a farm cider and perry; background music. The art on the walls in the dining room is for sale. Tables in the attractive 2-acre garden take in pleasant views over Thursley Common and Thursley's 1,000-year-old Saxon church. On the terrace are smart comfortable chairs around tables with parasols. A separate area has a big play fort, a barbecue and a charcoal spit-roast that they use on bank holidays. Visiting dogs and horses might get offered a biscuit or carrot.

Free house ~ Licensees David Alders and Sandra Proni ~ Real ale ~ Bar food (12.15-2.15, 7-9; 12-3; no food Sun evening) ~ Restaurant ~ (01252) 703268 ~ Well behaved children welcome ~ Dogs allowed in bar ~ Open 12-3, 5.30-11; 12-11 Sat; 12-8 Sun ~ www.threehorseshoesthursley.com

WEST END   SU9461

Inn at West End

Just under 2.5 miles from M3 junction 3; A322 S, on right; GU24 9PW

Clean-cut dining pub with prompt friendly service, excellent wines, popular inventive food using village-reared pork, game shot by the landlord and their own vegetables and pretty terrace

Around 500 wines, mostly from Spain and Portugal, are now stocked in the wine shop here and the landlord holds regular tastings. At least 15 are served in three sizes of glass, and there are quite a few sherries, sweet wines and ports, too. The pub is open-plan and café-like with bare boards, attractive modern prints on canary-yellow walls above a red dado, and a line of dining tables with crisp white linen over pale yellow tablecloths on the left. The bar counter, with Fullers London Pride and a guest such as Exmoor Ale on handpump, and around 30 whiskies, is straight ahead as you come in, with chatting regulars perched on the comfortable bar stools. The area on the right has a pleasant relaxed atmosphere, with blue-cushioned wall benches and dining chairs around solid pale wood tables, broadsheet daily papers, magazines and a row of reference books on the brick chimneybreast above an open fire. This leads into a garden room, which in turn opens on to a terrace shaded by a grape and clematis-covered pergola, and a very pleasant garden; boules.

Enterprise ~ Lease Gerry and Ann Price ~ Real ale ~ Bar food (12-2.30, 6-9.30; 12-3, 6-9 Sun) ~ Restaurant ~ (01276) 858652 ~ Children welcome if seated and dining ~ Dogs allowed in bar ~ Open 12-3, 5-11; 11-11 Sat; 12-10.30 Sun ~ www.the-Inn.co.uk

DOG FRIENDLY INNS, HOTELS AND B&Bs

BAGSHOT   SU9062
Pennyhill Park
College Ride, Bagshot, Surrey GU19 5ET (01276) 471774 www.pennyhillpark.co.uk

£226; 123 individually designed luxury rms and suites. Impressive Victorian
country house in 123 acres of well kept gardens and parkland – nine-hole golf
course, tennis courts, outdoor heated swimming pool, clay pigeon shooting,
archery and an international rugby pitch; friendly, courteous staff, a tranquil
wood-panelled bar, a comfortable two-level lounge and reading room, open
fires and fresh flowers, exceptional, imaginative food in the smart Latymer
restaurant and stylish brasserie, indulgent afternoon teas, delicious breakfasts,
Sun lunchtime jazz, and seats on the terraces overlooking the golf course; dogs in
bedrooms and some other areas; £30

BRAMLEY   TQ0044
Jolly Farmer
*High Street, Bramley, Guildford, Surrey GU5 0HB (01483) 893355
www.jollyfarmer.co.uk*

£80; 5 cosy rms. Family-owned pub handy for Winkworth Arboretum and walks
up St Martha's Hill; the bars have a homely miscellany of wooden tables and
chairs, collections of enamel advertising signs, sewing machines, antique bottles,
prints and old tools, and the timbered semi-partitions, mix of brick and timbering
and open fireplace give the place a snug, cosy feel; eight real ales, six continental
lagers and two ciders and a range of tasty bar food; self-catering flat, too; dogs in
bedrooms and bar

CHOBHAM   SU9563
Pembroke House
*Valley End Road, Chobham, Surrey GU24 8TB (01276) 857654
www.pembrokebandb.co.uk*

£90; 4 light, airy rms. Lovely house in pretty gardens surrounded by rolling fields,
with a warm welcome from the owners, a rather fine entrance hall, a gracious
sitting room and good breakfasts in a charming dining room with spreading views;
tennis court; dogs welcome by arrangement

CRANLEIGH   TQ0539
Richard Onslow
*113-117 High Street, Cranleigh, Surrey GU6 8AU (01483) 274922
www.therichardonslow.co.uk*

£85; 10 well equipped rms. Bustling town-centre pub usefully open all day
from 7am for good breakfasts; public bar with leather tub chairs and sofa and
a slate-floored drinking area with real ales, two dining rooms with open fires,
local photos and tartan tub chairs, and a sizeable restaurant with pale tables and
chairs on wooden flooring and a good choice of interesting modern food served

by friendly, efficient staff; walks in the Surrey Hills; dogs in one bedroom and bar; bowls and treats; £10

HASLEMERE SU9232
Lythe Hill Hotel & Spa
Petworth Road, Haslemere, Surrey GU27 3BQ (01428) 651251 www.lythehill.co.uk

£129; 42 individually styled rms, a few in the original house. Lovely partly 15th-c building in 22 acres of parkland and bluebell woods (adjoining the National Trust hillside) with floodlit tennis court, croquet lawn and jogging track; plush, comfortable and elegant lounges, a relaxed bar, two restaurants (one is oak-panelled, the other overlooks the lake) serving first class modern food, afternoon teas, and delicious breakfasts, and good attentive service; spa with swimming pool, sauna, steam and beauty rooms and gym; dogs in some bedrooms; £20

HORLEY TQ2842
Lawn Guest House
30 Massetts Road, Horley, Surrey RH6 7DF (01293) 775751
www.lawnguesthouse.co.uk

£65; 5 attractive rms. Handsome Victorian house with a friendly, relaxed atmosphere, helpful owners and good breakfasts in attractive dining room; no evening meals but plenty of places nearby; dogs in bedrooms; £5

Winnie; owner Emily Auclair

Sussex

DOG FRIENDLY PUBS

ALCISTON   TQ5005
Rose Cottage
Village signposted off A27 Polegate–Lewes; BN26 6UW

Old-fashioned cottage with cosy fires and country bric-a-brac, several wines by the glass, well liked food and local beers; bedrooms

It's really worth a stroll around this charming small village (and the church, too) and then dropping into this extremely popular pub afterwards; get there early on Sunday lunchtimes as it does get packed then. There are half a dozen tables with cushioned pews, winter log fires and quite a forest of harness, traps, a thatcher's blade and lots of other black ironware; more bric-a-brac on the shelves above the stripped pine dado or in the etched-glass windows and maybe Jasper the parrot (only at lunchtimes – he gets too noisy in the evenings). The restaurant area has a lunchtime overflow as they don't take bookings in the bar then. Dark Star Hophead, Harveys Best and a guest beer on handpump and several wines by the glass; background music, darts and board games. For cooler evenings, there are heaters outside and the small paddock in the garden has ducks and chickens; boules. Nearby fishing and shooting. They take self-catering bedroom bookings for a minimum of two nights. There are bracing South Downs walks nearby.

Free house ~ Licensee Ian Lewis ~ Real ale ~ Bar food (12-2, 6.30-9.30(9 Sun)) ~ Restaurant ~ (01323) 870377 ~ Children welcome ~ Dogs allowed in bar ~ Open 11.30-3, 6.30-11; 12-3, 6.30-10.30 Sun ~ Bedrooms: /£60S ~ www.therosecottageinn.co.uk

ASHURST   TQ1816
Fountain
B2135 S of Partridge Green; BN44 3AP

16th-c country pub with beams, flagstones and open fires, good enjoyable food and drink and seats outside

'Always busy and always good,' commented one of our many contented readers after visiting this welcoming 16th-c country pub. The neatly kept and charmingly rustic tap room on the right has a couple of high-backed wooden, cottagey armchairs by the log fire in its brick inglenook, country dining chairs around polished wooden tables, a few bar stools on the fine old flagstones and horsebrasses on the bressumer beam. The opened-up snug has wonky walls, more flagstones, heavy beams, simple furniture, and its own inglenook fireplace; an oak-beamed skittle alley doubles as a function room.

Harveys Best, Courage Directors, Fullers London Pride and Sharps Doom Bar on handpump and 23 wines by the glass; service is friendly and attentive. The garden is prettily planted, there are seats on the front brick terrace, raised herb beds at the back, an orchard and a duck pond.

Free house ~ Licensee Elizabeth Fry ~ Real ale ~ Bar food (12-2.30(3 Sun), 6-9.30(9 Sun)) ~ Restaurant ~ (01403) 710219 ~ Children welcome ~ Dogs allowed in bar ~ Open 11-11(10.30 Sun) ~ www.fountainashurst.co.uk

CHARLTON   SU8812
Fox Goes Free
Village signposted off A286 Chichester–Midhurst in Singleton, also from Chichester–Petworth via East Dean; PO18 0HU

Comfortable old pub with beamed bars, popular food and drink and big garden; bedrooms

Being so close to Goodwood, this friendly, bustling pub can get packed on race days but as it's open all day you can easily avoid peak times then; the Weald and Downland Open Air Museum and West Dean Gardens are nearby, too. In fine weather, you can sit at one of the picnic-sets under the apple trees in the attractive back garden with the downs as a backdrop and there are also rustic benches and tables on the gravelled front terrace. Inside, the bar is the first of the dark and cosy series of separate rooms: old irish settles, tables and chapel chairs and an open fire. Standing timbers divide a larger beamed bar which has a huge brick fireplace with a woodburning stove and old local photographs on the walls. A dining area with hunting prints looks over the garden. The family extension is a clever conversion from horse boxes and the stables where the 1926 Goodwood winner was housed; darts, games machine, background music and board games. Ballards Best, a beer named for the pub brewed by Arundel and a guest such as Otter Bitter on handpump, several wines by the glass and Addlestones cider. There are good surrounding walks including one up to the prehistoric earthworks on the Trundle.

Free house ~ Licensee David Coxon ~ Real ale ~ Bar food (12-2.30, 6.30-9.30; all day weekends) ~ Restaurant ~ (01243) 811461 ~ Children welcome ~ Dogs allowed in bar ~ Live music every second Weds evening ~ Open 11-11(11.30 Sat); 12-10.30 Sun ~ Bedrooms: £65S/£90S ~ www.thefoxgoesfree.com

CHIDDINGLY   TQ5414
Six Bells
Village signed off A22 Uckfield–Hailsham; BN8 6HE

Lively, unpretentious village local with good weekend live music, extremely good value bar food and a friendly long-serving landlord

Even when this cheerfully village pub is packed out, the hard-working, hands-on landlord keeps everything running smoothly. There's a great deal of unpretentious character in the many small interconnected bars with their interesting bric-a-brac, local pictures, photographs and posters – as well as solid old wood pews, antique chairs and tables and cushioned window seats; log fires, too. A sensitive extension provides some much-needed family space; board games. Courage Directors, Harveys Best and a guest beer on handpump and decent wines by the glass. Outside at the back, there are some tables beyond a big raised goldfish pond and a boules pitch; the church opposite has the interesting Jefferay monument. Popular weekend live music and vintage and kit car meetings outside the pub every month. This is a pleasant area for walks. Note that dogs are allowed in one bar only.

Free house ~ Licensee Paul Newman ~ Real ale ~ Bar food (12-2.15; 6-9.30; all day Fri-Sun) ~ (01825) 872227 ~ Children allowed away from main bar ~ Dogs allowed in bar ~ Live music Fri-Sun evenings and Sun lunchtime ~ Open 11-3, 6-11; 11am-midnight Fri and Sat; 12-10.30 Sun

CHILGROVE   SU8116
Royal Oak
Off B2141 Petersfield–Chichester, signed Hooksway; PO18 9JZ

Unchanging and peaceful country pub with welcoming licensees, honest food and big pretty garden

Down a wooded track in a lovely rural position, this unspoilt country pub has been run by the same friendly licensees for 21 years. The two simple, cosy bars have huge log fires, plain country-kitchen tables and chairs, and Gales HSB, Hammerpot Shooting Star, Sharps Doom Bar and a guest beer on handpump. There's also a cottagey dining room with a woodburning stove and a plainer family room; background music, cribbage, dominoes and shut the box. Twiglet and Amber are the pub staffies and there's a parrot called Gilbert. Outside, the big pretty garden has plenty of picnic-sets under parasols. The South Downs Way is close by.

Free house ~ Licensee Dave Jeffery ~ Real ale ~ Bar food (12-2, 7-9; not Sun evening and Mon) ~ Restaurant ~ (01243) 535257 ~ Children in family room ~ Dogs allowed in bar ~ Live music last Fri evening of month ~ Open 11.30-2.30, 6-11; 12-3 Sun; closed Sun evening and Mon; last 2 weeks of Oct, first 2 weeks of Nov ~ www.royaloakhooksway.co.uk

DANEHILL   TQ4128
Coach & Horses
Off A275, via School Lane towards Chelwood Common; RH17 7JF

Bustling dining pub with bustling bars, welcoming staff, enjoyable food and ales and a big garden

Our readers enjoy their visits to this well run country pub very much and you can be sure of a warm welcome from the helpful staff. There's a little bar to the right with half-panelled walls, simple furniture on polished floorboards, a small woodburner in the brick fireplace and a big hatch to the bar counter: Harveys Best, Kings Old Ale and a guest such as Sharps Doom Bar on handpump and several wines by the glass including prosecco and champagne. A couple of steps lead down to a half-panelled area with a mix of dining chairs around characterful wooden tables (set with flowers and candles) on the fine brick floor and artwork on the walls that changes every couple of months; cribbage, dominoes and cards. Down another step to a dining area with stone walls, beams, flagstones and a woodburning stove. There's an adult-only terrace under a huge maple tree and picnic-sets and a children's play area in the big garden which has fine views of the South Downs.

Free house ~ Licensee Ian Philpots ~ Real ale ~ Bar food (12-2(2.30 Sat, 3 Sun), 7-9(9.30 Fri, Sat); not Sun evening) ~ Restaurant ~ (01825) 740369 ~ Well behaved children welcome but not on adult terrace ~ Dogs allowed in bar ~ Open 12-3, 5-11; 12-11 Sat; 12-11 Sun; evening opening 6 in winter; ~ www.coachandhorses.danehill.biz

DIAL POST

Crown

Worthing Road (off A24 S of Horsham); RH13 8NH

Extended village pub with interesting extremely popular food, real ales and plenty of space in the bar and two dining rooms; bedrooms

Particularly in the evening, there's a lively, friendly atmosphere here and a good mix of both drinkers and diners. The beamed bar has a couple of standing timbers, brown squashy sofas and pine tables and chairs on the stone floor, a small woodburning stove in the brick fireplace, and Harveys Best and Old and a changing guest beer on handpump from the attractive herringbone brick counter. The pub dog is called Chops. The straightforwardly furnished dining conservatory, facing the village green, is light and airy. To the right of the bar, the restaurant (with more beams) has an ornamental woodburner in a brick fireplace, a few photographs on the walls, chunky pine tables, chairs and a couple of cushioned pews on the patterned carpet, and a shelf of books; steps lead down to a further dining room. The bedrooms are in the converted stables and there are picnic-sets on grass behind the pub.

Free house ~ Licensees James and Penny Middleton-Burn ~ Real ale ~ Bar food (12-2, 6-9(9.30 Fri, Sat); not winter Sun evening) ~ Restaurant ~ (01403) 710902 ~ Children welcome but must be dining after 7pm ~ Dogs allowed in bar ~ Open 11.30-3, 6-11; 12-10; 12-4 winter Sun; closed winter Sun evening ~ www.floatingcrown.co.uk

DUNCTON

Cricketers

Set back from A285; GU28 0LB

Charming old coaching inn with friendly licensees, real ales, popular food and suntrap back garden

Ideally situated for the Goodwood horse-racing and motorsports, this pretty 16th-c coaching inn is also a good option for walkers and families. There are some picnic-sets out in front beneath the flowering window boxes and more on decked areas and under parasols on the grass in the picturesque back garden, which make the most of the pub's position in the Goodwood Hills. The friendly, traditional bar has a few standing timbers, simple seating, cricketing memorabilia and an open woodburning stove in the inglenook fireplace. Steps lead down to the dining room which is simply furnished with wooden tables and chairs. Gribble Fuzzy Duck, King Horsham Best Bitter and Skinners Betty Stogs on handpump, several wines by the glass and Thatcher's cider.

Inn Company ~ Lease Martin Boult ~ Real ale ~ Bar food (12-2.30, 6-9; 12-9 weekends and during summer holidays) ~ Restaurant ~ (01798) 342473 ~ Children welcome ~ Dogs allowed in bar ~ Open 11-11; 12-10.30 Sun ~ www.thecricketersduncton.co.uk

EAST CHILTINGTON

Jolly Sportsman

2 miles N of B2116; Chapel Lane – follow sign to 13th-c church; BN7 3BA

Excellent modern food in civilised, rather smart place, small bar for drinkers, contemporary furnishings, fine wine list and huge range of malt whiskies; nice garden

This civilised dining pub has a first class, innovative menu, whether for bar snacks or a three-course meal, and It's a favourite with many of our readers. The bar may be small but it's light and full of character, and has a roaring winter fire, a mixture of furniture on the stripped wood floors and Dark Star Hophead and Harveys Best tapped from the cask. They also have a remarkably good wine list with around a dozen by the glass, over 100 malt whiskies, an extensive list of cognacs, armagnacs and grappa and quite a choice of bottled Belgian beers. The pub is extremely well run, the charming staff have had good training. The larger restaurant is smart but cosy and welcoming, with contemporary light wood furniture and modern landscapes on coffee-coloured walls; there's also a new garden room. The cottagey front garden is pretty, with rustic tables and benches under gnarled trees on the terrace and on the front bricked area, and there are more on a large back law. There's a children's play area, and views towards the downs, as well as good walks and cycle rides nearby.

Free house ~ Licensee Bruce Wass ~ Real ale ~ Bar food (12-2.30(3 Sat, 3.30 Sun),7-9) ~ Restaurant ~ (01273) 890400 ~ Children welcome ~ Dogs allowed in bar ~ Open 12-3, 6-11; 12-11(10.30 Sun) Sat; closed winter Sun evening ~ www.thejollysportsman.com

EAST DEAN   TV5597
Tiger
Off A259 Eastbourne–Seaford; BN20 0DA

Charming old pub by cottage-lined village green, two little bars and a dining room, and an informal and friendly atmosphere, much liked food; bedrooms

This friendly, popular pub can get busy, and with something of a premium on space, it does pay to get here early if you want a seat, but the staff are always welcoming and the service attentive. As popular with drinkers as it is with diners, the atmosphere here is always chatty and relaxed. The focal point of the little beamed main bar is the open woodburning stove in its brick inglenook, surrounded by polished horsebrasses, and there are just a few rustic tables with benches, simple wooden chairs, a window seat and a long cushioned wall bench. The walls are hung with fish prints and a stuffed tiger's head, there are a couple of hunting horns above the long bar counter. Harveys Best and Old and their own-brewed Beachy Head Legless Rambler and Original are available on handpump, and several wines by the glass. Down a step on the right is a second small room with an exceptionally fine high-backed curved settle and a couple of other old settles, nice old chairs and wooden tables on the coir carpeting, and an ancient map of Eastbourne and Beachy Head and photographs of the pub on the walls; the dining room to the left of the main bar has a cream woodburner and hunting prints. There are picnic-sets on the terrace among the window boxes and flowering climbers, or you can sit on the delightful cottage-lined village green. The South Downs Way is close by and the lane leads on down to a fine stretch of coast culminating in Beachy Head, so the pub is a natural choice for walkers. The bedrooms are comfortable and the breakfasts good.

Free house ~ Licensee Jacques Pienaar ~ Real ale ~ Bar food (12-3, 6-9) ~ Restaurant ~ (01323) 423209 ~ Children welcome ~ Dogs allowed in bar ~ Open 11am-midnight(1am Sat) ~ Bedrooms: /£95S ~ www.beachyhead.org.uk

EAST LAVANT

SU8608

Royal Oak

Pook Lane, off A286; PO18 0AX

Bustling and friendly dining pub with proper drinking area, excellent food, extensive wine list and real ales; super bedrooms

Very handy for Goodwood and with plenty of nearby walks, this is a pretty little white house that manages to be both a proper village pub and somewhere for a fine meal in relaxed surroundings. It's all open plan with low beams and exposed brickwork, crooked timbers, winter log fires, and church candles. The well used drinking area at the front has wall seats and sofas, Arundel Gold and Sharps Doom Bar or Skinners Betty Stogs tapped from the cask, 20 wines by the glass from an extensive list, and a friendly welcome from the attentive staff. The attached seating area is focused on dining and sensitively furnished with brown suede and leather dining chairs around scrubbed pine tables, and pictures of local scenes and of motor sport on the walls; background music. Outside, there are cushioned seats and tables under green parasols on the flagstoned front terrace and far-reaching views to the Downs; rambling around the side and back are terraced, brick and grass areas with more seats and attractive tubs and baskets. The bedrooms are stylish and well equipped and they also have self-catering cottages. The car park is across the road.

Free house ~ Licensee Charles Ullmann ~ Real ale ~ Bar food (12-2.30, 6-9(9.30 Sat); 12-3, 6.30-9 Sun) ~ Restaurant ~ (01243) 527434 ~ Well behaved children welcome ~ Dogs allowed in bar ~ Open 11-11 (midnight Sat); 12-11 Sun ~ Bedrooms: £90S(£99B)/£125S(£140B) ~ www.royaloakeastlavant.co.uk

ERIDGE GREEN

TQ5535

Nevill Crest & Gun

A26 Tunbridge Wells–Crowborough; TN3 9JR

Handsome 500-year-old building with lots of character, beams and standing timbers, hundreds of pictures and photographs, three real ales, enjoyable modern food and friendly, efficient staff

Standing on the estate of the Nevill family (whose crest can be still be seen on the building), this fine 16th-c former farmhouse has plenty of interesting local history. It has been carefully and cleverly opened up inside with standing timbers and doorways keeping some sense of separate rooms. Throughout there are heavy beams (some carved), panelling, rugs on wooden floors, woodburning stoves and an open fire in three fireplaces (the linenfold carved bressummer above one is worth seeking out), all manner of individual dining chairs around dark wood or copper-topped tables and lots of pictures, maps and photographs, many of them local to the area. The window sills are full of Toby jugs, stone and glass bottles and plants, there are daily papers, board games and a happy mix of customers of all ages; the atmosphere is civilised but informal. Beers from Tunbridge Wells, Westerham and Phoenix Brunning & Price are on handpump and good wines by the glass; efficient, friendly staff. In front of the building are a few picnic-sets with teak furniture on a back terrace, beside the more recent dining extension with its large windows, light oak rafters, beams and coir flooring.

Brunning & Price ~ Manager Adam Holland ~ Real ale ~ Bar food (12-10(9.30 Sun)) ~ (01892) 864209 ~ Children welcome ~ Dogs allowed in bar ~ Open 11.30-11; 12-10.30 Sun ~ www.nevillcrestandgun.co.uk

FLETCHING

TQ4223

Griffin

Village signposted off A272 W of Uckfield; TN22 3SS

Busy, gently upmarket inn with a fine wine list, bistro-style bar food, real ales and big garden with far-reaching views; bedrooms

Staff get consistently positive reviews from our readers at this civilised, lively and well run inn who offer a genuinely warm welcome to all – children and dogs included. The pub also has an appealing and very spacious 2-acre back garden with plenty of seats for outside diners on the sandstone terrace and grass, as well as lovely views towards Sheffield Park Gardens; regular summer Sunday barbecues. The beamed and quaintly-panelled bar rooms have blazing log fires, old photographs and hunting prints, straightforward close-set furniture including some captain's chairs and china on a delft shelf. There's a small bare-boarded serving area off to one side and a snug separate bar with sofas and a TV. Harveys Best, Hogs Back TEA, King's Horsham Best and a guest beer on handpump, a fine wine list with 20 (including champagne and sweet wine) by the glass and farm cider. The bright, airy bedrooms are comfortable and the breakfasts are good; the inn is handy for Glyndebourne. There are ramps for wheelchairs.

Free house ~ Licensees James Pullan and Samantha Barlow ~ Real ale ~ Bar food (12-2.30, 7-9.30) ~ Restaurant ~ (01825) 722890 ~ Children welcome ~ Dogs allowed in bar ~ Open 12-11(midnight Sat) ~ Bedrooms: £80B/£85S(£95B) ~ www.thegriffininn.co.uk

HEATHFIELD

TQ5920

Star

Church Street, Old Heathfield, off A265/B2096 E; TN21 9AH

Pleasant old pub with bustling, friendly atmosphere, good mix of locals and visitors, well liked food and decent choice of drinks; pretty garden

Turner thought this 14th-c inn fine enough to paint. These days it's a smashing and bustling country pub of real character, with a good mix of both locals and visitors. The building has ancient heavy beams, built-in wall settles and window seats, panelling, inglenook fireplaces and a roaring winter log fire; a doorway leads to a similarly-decorated room more set up for eating with wooden tables and chairs (one table has high-backed white leather dining chairs) and a woodburning stove. There's also an upstairs dining room. Harveys Best, Shepherd Neame Spitfire and Wells & Young's Bitter are on handpump and the pub has an extensive wine list, including several by the glass; good food; friendly, helpful staff; background music. The garden is very prettily planted, there's rustic furniture under smart umbrellas and lovely views of rolling oak-lined sheep pastures.

Free house ~ Licensees Mike and Sue Chappell ~ Real ale ~ Bar food (12-2.30, 7-9.30; 12-3, 6.30-8.30 Sun) ~ Restaurant ~ (01435) 863570 ~ Children welcome ~ Dogs allowed in bar ~ Open 11.30-11; 12-10.30 Sun ~ www.starinnoldheathfield.co.uk

HORSHAM

TQ1730

Black Jug

North Street; RH12 1RJ

Bustling town pub with wide choice of drinks, efficient staff and good bar food

This well run old town pub has friendly, knowledgeable and attentive staff and a wide mix of customers. The one large open-plan, turn-of-the-century room has a long central bar, a nice collection of sizeable dark wood tables and comfortable chairs on the stripped-wood floor, board games, bookcases and interesting old prints and photographs above a dark wood-panelled dado on the cream walls. A spacious, bright conservatory has similar furniture and lots of hanging baskets. Caledonian Deuchars IPA and Harveys Best with guests such as Old Mill Old Priory Mild and Sharps Doom Bar on handpump, 20 wines by the glass, around 100 malt whiskies and Weston's cider. The pretty flower-filled back terrace has plenty of garden furniture. The small car park is for staff and deliveries only but you can park next door in the council car park.

Brunning & Price ~ Tenant Alastair Craig ~ Real ale ~ Bar food (12-10(9.30 Sun)) ~ (01403) 253526 ~ Children welcome ~ Dogs allowed in bar ~ Open 11.30-11; 12-10.30 Sun ~ www.blackjug-horsham.co.uk

HURST GREEN   TQ7326

White Horse

Silverhill (A21); TN19 7PU

Friendly, well run pub with relaxed bar, elegant dining room, enjoyable well liked food and seats in garden

In fine weather, the sizeable terrace at the back of this former Georgian farmhouse is a lovely place for a drink or a meal and there are attractive white metal tables and chairs looking across the lawn and over the Weald. The relaxed bare-boards bar has a few leather armchairs and white-painted dining chairs around various wooden tables (laid with nightlights and wooden candlesticks), game trophies, prints and photographs on the walls, fresh flowers and an open fire. Harveys Best on handpump and 14 nice wines by the glass; background music. An open doorway leads through to a second bar room with built-in leather wall seats and similar tables and then through again to the dining room. This is an elegant but informal room with similar furniture, oil paintings and ornate mirrors on modern paintwork, chandeliers and some panelling.

Free house ~ Licensee Anthony Panic ~ Real ale ~ Bar food (12-3, 6-10) ~ Restaurant ~ (01580) 860235 ~ Children welcome ~ Dogs allowed in bar ~ Live jazz last Fri of month ~ Open 12-3, 6-11; 12-8 Sun ~ www.thewhitehorsehurstgreen.com

LODSWORTH   SU9321

Halfway Bridge Inn

Just before village, on A272 Midhurst–Petworth; GU28 9BP

Restauranty coaching inn with contemporary décor in several dining areas, log fires, local real ales and interesting modern food using local and foraged produce; lovely bedrooms

This is a nice place to stay with stylish and comfortable bedrooms in a former stable yard and the breakfasts are good, too. Much emphasis is on the dining side of things – the tables are mostly set for eating – but regulars do still pop in for a pint and chat. The various bar rooms have plenty of intimate little corners and are carefully furnished with good oak chairs and an individual mix of tables; one of the log fires is a well polished kitchen range. The interconnecting restaurant rooms have beams, wooden floors and a cosy atmosphere. Long Blonde Ale, Langham Hip Hop, and Sharps Doom Bar on handpump and 25 wines by the glass; background music. At the back, there are seats on a small terrace.

Free house ~ Licensee Sam Bakose ~ Real ale ~ Bar food (12-2.30, 6-9.30; all day weekends) ~ Restaurant ~ (01798) 861281 ~ Children welcome ~ Dogs allowed in bar ~ Open 11-11 ~ Bedrooms: £90B/£130B ~ www.halfwaybridge.co.uk

LODSWORTH

SU9223

Hollist Arms

Off A272 Midhurst–Petworth; GU28 9BZ

Friendly and civilised village pub with local beers, good choice of wines, enjoyable bar food and seats outside

This smart 200-year-old village pub is just the place to head for after enjoying one of the pretty nearby walks. In fine weather the cottagey back garden has picnic-sets on the terrace, or you can sit underneath the huge horse chestnut tree on the green. The pub is open all day and you're sure to get a warm welcome from the cheerful landlord and his team. A small snug room on the right has a sofa and two tables by an open fire – just right for a cosy drink. The public bar area on the left has stools against the pale wooden counter, more around a few tables and a comfortable built-in window seat. Langhams Hip Hop, Skinners Betty Stogs and Timothy Taylors Landlord on handpump and a decent choice of wines. The L-shaped dining room has a couple of big, squidgy sofas facing each other in front of the inglenook fireplace and plenty of elegant spoked dining chairs and wheelbacks around tables on the wood-strip floor; the pale blue walls are completely covered with genuinely interesting prints and paintings.

Free house ~ Licensee Damian Burrowes ~ Real ale ~ Bar food (12-3, 6-9) ~ Restaurant ~ (01798) 861310 ~ Children welcome ~ Dogs allowed in bar ~ Live music every second Sat of month ~ Open 11-11(midnight Sat); 12-10.30 Sun ~ www.thehollistarms.com

LURGASHALL

SU9327

Noahs Ark

Off A283 N of Petworth; GU28 9ET

Busy old pub in nice spot with neatly kept rooms, real ales and pleasing food using local produce

Picnic-sets make the most of this 15th-c tile-hung pub's position, overlooked by Blackdown Hill and with views of the village green and cricket pitch; there are more tables in the large side garden. The simple, traditional bar is popular locally and has leather-topped bar stools by the counter where they serve Greene King IPA and Abbot and a guest such as Thwaites Wainwright on handpump, several wines by the glass, farm cider and a special bloody mary. Beams, a mix of wooden chairs and tables on the parquet flooring and an inglenook fireplace are also features. Open right up to its apex, the dining room is spacious and airy with church candles and fresh flowers on light wood tables; a couple of comfortable sofas face each other in front of an open woodburning stove. The pub border terrier is called Gillie and visiting dogs may get a dog biscuit.

Greene King ~ Lease Henry Coghlan and Amy Whitmore ~ Real ale ~ Bar food (12-2.30, 7-9.30; 12-3.30 Sun; not Sun evening) ~ Restaurant ~ (01428) 707346 ~ Children welcome ~ Dogs allowed in bar ~ Open 11-11(11.30 Sat); 12-10.30(8 in winter) Sun ~ www.noahsarkinn.co.uk

RINGMER

Cock

Uckfield Road – blocked-off section of road off A26 N of village turn-off; BN8 5RX

16th-c country pub with a wide choice of popular bar food, real ales in character bar and plenty of seats in the garden

The roaring log fire in the inglenook fireplace (lit from October to April) makes this family-run place a welcome refuge, particularly on a chilly evening. It's 16th c and weatherboarded and the unspoilt bar is cosy with traditional pubby furniture on flagstones, heavy beams, Harveys Best and a couple of guests from breweries like Hammerpot and Hogs Back on handpump, 11 wines by the glass, 12 malt whiskies and Weston's summer cider. There are also three dining areas; background music. Outside on the terrace and in the garden are lots of picnic-sets with views across open fields to the South Downs; the sunsets are pretty. Visiting dogs are offered a bowl of water and a chew, and the owners' dogs are called Bailey and Tally. Atmosphere and service are good; background music.

Free house ~ Licensees Ian, Val and Matt Ridley ~ Real ale ~ Bar food (12-2.15(2.30 Sat), 6-9.30; all day Sun) ~ Restaurant ~ (01273) 812040 ~ Well behaved children welcome away from bar ~ Dogs allowed in bar ~ Open 11-3, 6-11.30; 11-11.30 Sun ~ www.cockpub.co.uk

ROBERTSBRIDGE

George

High Street; TN32 5AW

Friendly former coaching inn with local beers in bustling bar, good food using seasonal produce in dining room and seats outside; good bedrooms

Popular locally but with a warm welcome for visitors too, this is a well run former coaching inn. There's a log fire in the handsome brick inglenook fireplace with a leather sofa and a couple of armchairs in front of it — just right for a quiet pint and a chat – high bar stools by the counter where they serve Harveys Best, Old Dairy Red Top and Rother Valley Level Best on handpump and several wines by the glass, friendly staff and an easy-going atmosphere; Stanley the basset hound may appear but please don't feed him. The dining area leads off here with elegant high-backed pale wooden chairs around a mix of tables (each with fresh flowers and a nightlight) on stripped floorboards, photographs or block paintings of local scenes, and big church candles in the small fireplace; background music. In warm weather there are plenty of seats and tables outside on the back terrace. The bedrooms are comfortable and the breakfasts good.

Free house ~ Licensees John and Jane Turner ~ Real ale ~ Bar food (12-2.30, 6.30-9, 12-3 Sun; not Sun evening or Mon) ~ Restaurant ~ (01580) 880315 ~ Children welcome but must by with adults at all times ~ Dogs allowed in bar ~ Live music last Sun of the month (not summer) ~ Open 11-11; 12-8 Sun; closed Mon; occasionally closed 3-6 winter Weds ~ www.thegeorgerobertsbridge.co.uk

RYE

Ypres Castle

Gun Garden; steps up from A259, or down past Ypres Tower; TN31 7HH

Traditional pub with several real ales, quite a choice of bar food (they make their own bread and chutneys) and seats in sheltered garden

New licensees took over this pleasant and bustling pub recently. It's in an interesting spot – perched beneath the ramparts of Ypres Tower and above the river in a quiet corner of the historic town. Conveniently open all day, the bars have various old tables and chairs – the informal, almost scruffy feel adds to the pub's character. There are comfortable seats by the winter log fire, local artwork, quite a mix of customers and a restaurant area serving local seafood apart from on Friday and Sunday nights; background music at other times. Harveys Best, Larkins Best, Old Dairy Copper Top and Timothy Taylors Landlord on handpump. The sheltered garden is a pleasant place to sit or play or watch boules. The resident dog is called Spud.

Free house ~ Licensee Jon Laurie ~ Real ale ~ Bar food (12-3, 6-9(8 Fri); all day Sat; best to phone for Sun evening) ~ (01797) 223248 ~ Children welcome ~ Dogs allowed in bar ~ Open 12-11(midnight Fri, Sat; 10.30 Sun) ~ www.yprescastleinn.co.uk

SALEHURST   TQ7424

Salehurst Halt

Village signposted from Robertsbridge bypass on A21 Tunbridge Wells–Battle; Church Lane; TN32 5PH

Relaxed small local in quiet hamlet, chatty atmosphere, real ales, well liked and fairly priced bar food and seats in pretty back garden

Come early to secure a seat at this bustling, friendly and informal little family-run pub, which is very popular with locals and visitors alike. To the right of the door, there's a small stone-floored area with a couple of tables, a piano, a settle, TV and an open fire. To the left, there's a nice long scrubbed-pine table with a couple of sofas, a mix of more ordinary pubby tables and wheelback and mate's chairs on the wood-strip floor. Occasional background music, board games and high-brow bookshelves. Dark Star American Pale Ale, Harveys Best and Old Dairy Silver Top on handpump, several malt whiskies and decent wines by the glass. The back terrace has metal chairs and tiled tables and there are more seats in the lovely landscaped garden with stunning views out over the Rother Valley; outdoor table tennis.

Free house ~ Licensee Andrew Augarde ~ Real ale ~ Bar food (12-2.30, 7-9; not Mon or winter Tues and not Sun evenings) ~ (01580) 880620 ~ Children welcome ~ Dogs allowed in bar ~ Live music 2nd Sun of month ~ Open 12-11(12-3, 5-11 Tues, Weds); closed Mon ~ www.salehursthalt.co.uk

SUTTON   SU9715

White Horse

The Street; RH20 1PS

Opened-up country inn, contemporary décor, real ales, good wines by the glass and popular modern food; smart bedrooms

Close to Bignor Roman villa, this quietly set pub is a friendly place with popular food and real ales. The bar has a couple of little open brick fireplaces at each end, nightlight candles on mantelpieces, cushioned high bar chairs, Harveys Best and a guest such as Timothy Taylors Landlord on handpump, good wines by the glass and helpful service. The wooden-topped island servery separates the bar from the two-room barrel-vaulted dining area (coir carpeting here) and throughout, the minimalist décor is a contemporary clotted cream colour, with modern hardwood chairs and tables on stripped wood and a few small photographs; there's another little log fire, church candles and fresh flowers.

Outside, steps lead up to a lawned area with plenty of picnic-sets and there are more seats out in front. Good walks in lovely surrounding countryside right from the door.

Enterprise ~ Lease Nick Georgiou ~ Real ale ~ Bar food (not Sun evening or Mon) ~ Restaurant ~ (01798) 869221 ~ Children welcome ~ Dogs allowed in bar ~ Open 11.30-2.30, 6-11; 12-3 Sun; closed Sun evening, Mon ~ Bedrooms: £65S/£85B ~ www.whitehorse-sutton.co.uk

WARNINGLID   TQ2425

Half Moon

B2115 off A23 S of Handcross or off B2110 Handcross–Lower Beeding; RH17 5TR

Good modern cooking in simply furnished pub with an informal chatty atmosphere, real ales, lots of wines by the glass and seats in sizeable garden

The friendly staff in this bustling 18th-c village pub work hard to ensure that the emphasis here is placed equally on dining and drinking – which suits their many customers very well. The lively locals' bar has straightforward pubby furniture on the bare boards and a small Victorian fireplace and a room just off here has oak beams and flagstones. A couple of steps lead down to the dining areas with a happy mix of wooden chairs, cushioned wall settles and nice old tables on floorboards, plank panelling and bare brick, and old photographs of the village; there's also another open fire and a glass-covered well. Dark Star Hophead, Greene King Old Speckled Hen, Harveys Best and a weekend guest beer on handpump and 20 wines by the glass. There are quite a few picnic-sets outside on the lawn in the sheltered, sizeable garden, which has a most spectacular avenue of trees, with uplighters that glow at night.

Free house ~ Licensees Jonny Lea and James Amico ~ Real ale ~ Bar food (12-2, 6-9.30; not Sun evening) ~ Restaurant ~ (01444) 461227 ~ Children welcome but under 4's in own area ~ Dogs allowed in bar ~ Open 11.30-3, 5.30-11; 11.30-11 Sat; 12-10.30 Sun ~ www.thehalfmoonwarninglid.co.uk

WEST HOATHLY   TQ3632

Cat

Village signposted from A22 and B2028 S of East Grinstead; North Lane; RH19 4PP

Popular 16th-c inn with old-fashioned bar, airy dining rooms, real ales, good food cooked by one of the landlords, and seats outside; lovely bedrooms

It's worth booking ahead for meals at this attractive and bustling 16th-c tile-hung inn and the hands-on licensees, a genuinely warm welcome for all and very highly thought of food (including first rate vegetarian options) all add to its appeal. There's a lovely old bar with beams, proper pubby tables and chairs on the old wooden floor, a fine log fire in the inglenook fireplace. With a focus on local breweries, Harveys Best and Old and Larkins Traditional Ale are available on handpump, as well as Hertfordshire cider and several wines by the glass; look out for a glass cover over the 75-foot deep well. The dining rooms are light and airy with a nice mix of wooden dining chairs and tables on the pale wood-strip flooring and throughout there are hops, china platters, brass and copper ornaments and a gently upmarket atmosphere. The contemporary-style garden room has glass doors that open on to a terrace with teak furniture. This is a comfortable and enjoyable place to stay (some of the pleasant rooms overlook the church) and the breakfasts are very good. The Bluebell Railway is nearby in this lovely hilltop village, as well as a host of other appealing walks. Parking is limited.

Free house ~ Licensee Andrew Russell ~ Real ale ~ Bar food (12-2(2.30 Fri-Sun), 6-9 (9.30 Fri, Sat); not Sun evening) ~ (01342) 810369 ~ Children welcome if over 7 ~ Dogs allowed in bar ~ Open 12-11.30; 12-4 Sun; closed Sun evening ~ Bedrooms: /£110B ~ www.catinn.co.uk

DOG FRIENDLY INNS, HOTELS AND B&Bs

ALFRISTON — TQ5203

George

High Street, Alfriston, Polegate, East Sussex BN26 5SY (01323) 870319
www.thegeorge-alfriston.com

£100; 6 recently refurbished beamed rms. Venerable inn in lovely village with comfortable, heavily beamed bars, massive hop-hung beams, lots of copper and brass, open fires (one in a huge stone inglenook), several real ales, a comfortable lounge with standing timbers and sofas, and good, interesting food in the candlelit restaurant; the South Downs Way and Vanguard Way cross here and Cuckmere Haven is close by; dogs anywhere; treats

BATTLE — TQ7414

Powder Mills

Powdermill Lane, Battle, East Sussex TN33 0SP (01424) 775511
www.powdermillshotel.com

£125; 42 individually decorated rms, some in annexe. Attractive 18th-c creeper-clad manor house in 150 acres of park and woodland with four lakes and outdoor swimming pool, and next to the 1066 battlefield; country-house atmosphere, log fires and antiques in elegant day rooms, attentive service and good modern cooking in Orangery restaurant; resident dogs; dogs in ground floor bedrooms; not in restaurant; £10

Mynti; owner Alastair MacKinnon

BEPTON
SU8618

Park House Hotel

Bepton, Midhurst, West Sussex GU29 0JB (01730) 812880 www.parkhousehotel.com

£160; 21 attractive rms, some in cottages. Quietly set, family-run country house near Goodwood and Cowdray Park, with outdoor and indoor swimming pools, grass tennis courts, croquet and putting; a comfortable drawing room, an honesty bar and good homely cooking in the formal dining room – particularly good breakfasts, too; spa, gym and fitness centre; dogs in two bedrooms

BRIGHTON
TQ3004

Grand

97-99 Kings Road, Brighton, East Sussex BN1 2FW (01273) 224300 www.devere-hotels.com

£115; 200 newly refurbished rms, many with sea views. Famous Victorian hotel with marble columns and floors and fine moulded plasterwork in the luxurious and elegant day rooms (undergoing a programme of careful updating); courteous, helpful service, very good contemporary british cooking in several restaurants, fine wines, popular afternoon tea in the sunny conservatory, extensive breakfasts and a luxurious new spa; walks for dogs on the beach (not during the summer); dogs in bedrooms; away from food areas; £20

BRIGHTON
TQ3004

Granville

124 Kings Road, Brighton, East Sussex BN1 2FA (01273) 326302 www.granvillehotel.co.uk

£100; 24 individually themed rms, some with sea views. Seafront boutique hotel with contemporary furnishings, a stylish restaurant and sleek bar on the lower ground floor, attentive, friendly service, traditional breakfasts and international dishes, and seats and tables on the summer terrace; dogs welcome in bedrooms

BRIGHTON
TQ3004

Hotel du Vin & Bistro

2-6 Ship Street, Brighton, East Sussex BN1 1AD (01273) 718588 www.hotelduvin.com

£180; 49 well equipped and comfortable rms and suites. Close to the seafront in the popular Lanes area, this hotel is housed in an unusual collection of part gothic-styled buildings; lots of wood, brick, glass and a feeling of space, a bustling bar area and newish wine bar, good bistro food using the freshest of local ingredients in the clubby-style restaurant, a fine wine list and helpful young staff; attached pub, too; dogs in bedrooms, bowl and bed included; £20

CHARLTON
SU8812

Woodstock House

Charlton, Chichester, West Sussex PO18 0HU (01243) 811666 www.woodstockhousehotel.co.uk

£118; 13 rms. 18th-c country house in the South Downs and close to Goodwood, with a friendly, relaxed atmosphere, a log fire in the homely sitting room, a small bar and a sun trap inner courtyard garden; nearby inns and restaurants for evening meals; lots to see nearby and plenty of walks; dogs in ground floor bedrooms; £15

CHICHESTER SU8601
Spire Cottage

Church Lane, Hunston, Chichester, West Sussex PO20 1AJ (01243) 778937
www.spirecottage.co.uk

£80; 4 pretty rms, one in annexe with private entrance and garden. Country cottage built from the old spire of the cathedral with a relaxed and friendly atmosphere, a comfortable lounge and good breakfasts with home-made preserves and home-squeezed juice in the pretty dining room with its winter log fire; dogs in garden bedroom; £5

CLIMPING TQ0000
Bailiffscourt

Climping Street, Climping, Littlehampton, West Sussex BN17 5RW (01903) 723511
www.hshotels.co.uk

£250; 39 lovely rms, many with four-poster beds, winter log fires and super views. Mock 13th-c manor built only 60 years ago but with tremendous character – fine old iron-studded doors, huge fireplaces, heavy beams and so forth – in 30 acres of coastal pastures and walled gardens: open fires, antiques, tapestries and fresh flowers, elegant furnishings, enjoyable modern english food in the mullion-windowed restaurant and courteous, helpful staff; spa with indoor swimming pool, gym and treatment rooms, plus outdoor swimming pool, tennis and croquet; dogs in bedrooms and lounges; bowl, biscuits and mat; £13.50

CUCKFIELD TQ3024
Ockenden Manor

Ockenden Lane, Cuckfield, Haywards Heath, West Sussex RH17 5LD (01444) 416111
www.hshotels.co.uk

£265; 22 individually decorated, pretty rms. Dating from 1520, this carefully extended manor house has antiques, fresh flowers and an open fire in the elegant sitting room, a well stocked, cosy bar, beautifully presented modern cooking in the panelled restaurant and super views of the South Downs from the neatly kept, 9-acre garden; spa with indoor and outdoor linked swimming pools, sauna, steam room, gym and treatment rooms; dogs in some bedrooms; £15

EAST HOATHLY TQ5116
Old Whyly

Halland Road, East Hoathly, Lewes, East Sussex BN8 6EL (01825) 840216
www.oldwhyly.co.uk

£120; 3 quiet rms. Handsome 17th-c manor house in a lovely garden with a tennis court and swimming pool; fine antiques, paintings and an open fire in the restful drawing room, delicious food (by arrangement) in the elegant dining room and super breakfasts with their own honey and duck and chicken eggs; plenty of walks nearby and fairly close to Glyndebourne (hampers can be provided); dogs by arrangement

EASTBOURNE
Grand

TV6198

King Edwards Parade, Eastbourne, East Sussex BN21 4EQ (01323) 412345
www.grandeastbourne.co.uk

£230; 152 individually designed rms, many with sea views. Gracious and very well run Victorian hotel with views of the sea and the cliffs at Beachy Head; a genuinely friendly atmosphere, spacious, comfortable lounges with lots of fine original features and lovely flower arrangements, imaginative food in two smart but unstuffy restaurants, popular afternoon teas and courteous, helpful service; spa with treatment, sauna and steam rooms, a gym and indoor and outdoor swimming pools; dogs in bedrooms; bed and meal provided; £7

EWHURST GREEN
White Dog

TQ7924

Ewhurst Green, Robertsbridge, East Sussex TN32 5TD (01580) 830264
www.thewhitedogewhurst.co.uk

£85; 2 rms. Friendly, family-run village pub with magnificent views of Bodiam Castle from seats in garden; a bustling bar with hop-draped beams, wood panelling, farm implements and horsebrasses, a log fire in the inglenook and real ales on handpump, and a flagstoned dining room with murals of the local area, well liked lunchtime and evening food using local seasonal produce, and tasty breakfasts; walks in surrounding fields and footpaths; two resident dogs; dogs in bedrooms and bar; water bowls and treats; £10

FAIRLIGHT
Fairlight Cottage

TQ8611

Warren Road, Fairlight, Hastings, East Sussex TN35 4AG (01424) 812545
www.fairlightcottage.co.uk

£65; 3 rms, one with a four-poster. Comfortable and very friendly house in pretty countryside with views over Rye Bay and plenty of rural and clifftop walks; a big, comfortable guest lounge with nice views, and good english or continental breakfasts in the elegant dining room or on the balcony; resident dog; dogs anywhere

GRAFFHAM
Forresters Arms

SU9217

The Street, Graffham, Petworth, West Sussex GU28 0QA (01798) 867202
www.forestersgraffham.co.uk

£85; 3 rms. 16th-c pub with heavy beams, a log fire in a huge brick fireplaces, pews and pale windsor chairs around light modern tables, and well liked tasty food; a second log fire and more beams in two other bars, real ales, monthly live jazz and seats in a sunny back garden; good local walks; dogs welcome anywhere (must be on lead); bowls, biscuits and towels

LEWES
TQ4109
Shelleys
High Street, Lewes, East Sussex BN7 1XS (01273) 472361 www.the-shelleys.co.uk

£130; 19 homely rms. Once owned by relatives of the poet, this stylish and spacious 17th-c town house is warm and friendly, with good food, nice breakfasts and bar lunches in an elegant dining room, popular morning coffee and afternoon teas and seats in the quiet back garden; dogs in bedrooms; £10

MIDHURST
SU8821
Spread Eagle
*South Street, Midhurst, West Sussex GU29 9NH (01730) 816911
www.hshotels.co.uk/hotels/spread-eagle.html*

£99; 39 pretty, well equipped rms. Historic 15th-c coaching inn with log fires in inglenook fireplaces, stained glass windows, beams and sloping floors, lots of sofas and armchairs, and very good modern british food in the candlelit restaurant or summer conservatory; picturesque grounds with plenty of seats, scandinavian-style spa with its indoor swimming pool, gym and sauna, steam and treatment rooms; dogs in some bedrooms; bed, bowl and food; £15

NEWICK
TQ4219
Newick Park Hotel
Newick, Brighton, East Sussex BN8 4SB (01825) 723633 www.newickpark.co.uk

£165; 16 individually decorated, spacious rms. Charming and carefully restored Georgian building in a huge estate of open country and woodland with fishing lakes, outdoor swimming pool, tennis and croquet; comfortable and spacious bar area, study and library, antiques and open fires, enjoyable, inventive food using home-grown produce and local game in the smart restaurant, and good breakfasts and afternoon teas; dogs in some bedrooms, one in the main house; £15 for first night, then £5 per night

PETWORTH
SU9721
Angel
*Angel Street, Petworth, West Sussex GU28 0BG (01798) 344445
www.angelinnpetworth.co.uk*

£110; 6 newly refurbished, comfortable rms. Carefully renovated and opened up inn on the edge of a lovely market town, with several interconnected bars, all manner of nice old chairs and tables on slate or wooden flooring, three open fires, genuinely friendly service, well kept local beers, very good breakfasts, lunches and evening meals, and seats in the pretty two-level garden; dogs in bedrooms and bar; £10

RUSHLAKE GREEN
TQ6218
Stone House
*Rushlake Green, Heathfield, East Sussex TN21 9QJ (01435) 830553
www.stonehousesussex.co.uk*

£148; 6 rms with antiques and lovely fabrics, some with four-posters, plus 2 in coach house. In 1,000 acres of pretty countryside (with plenty of walks and country sports) and surrounded by an 18th-c walled garden, this lovely house was built at the end of the 15th c and extended in Georgian times; log fires, antiques and family heirlooms in the drawing room, a quiet library, interesting dinner party-style food in the panelled dining room and good breakfasts; dogs in bedrooms; not in public rooms

RYE   TQ9120
Jeakes House
Mermaid Street, Rye, East Sussex TN31 7ET (01797) 222828 www.jeakeshouse.com

£114; 11 lovely rms overlooking the rooftops of this medieval town or across the marsh to the sea. Fine 16th-c building, well run and friendly, with good breakfasts in the galleried dining room, much character in the honesty bar and parlour with period furnishings and antiques, swagged curtains and a warm fire, and a peaceful atmosphere; nearby fields for walking; dogs welcome away from dining room; £5

RYE   TQ9220
Rye Lodge
Hilders Cliff, Rye, East Sussex TN31 7LD (01797) 223838 www.ryelodge.co.uk

£125; 18 rms. Family-run hotel close to the town and with fine views across the estuary and Romney Marsh; caring, friendly service, an elegant and comfortable lounge, a convivial bar, enjoyable food in marble-floored, candlelit restaurant and leisure centre with indoor swimming pool, sauna and steam room; well behaved dogs; not in restaurant; £8

RYE   TQ9120
Ship
The Strand, Rye, East Sussex TN31 7DB (01797) 222233 www.theshipinnrye.co.uk

£100; 10 cheerfully decorated rms. Appealingly quirky 16th-c pub with a comfortable, easy-going atmosphere in opened up rooms, beams and timbers, comfortable armchairs and sofas and other traditional seats and tables on stripped boards, flagstones and some carpeting, a log fire in a stripped-brick fireplace, a stuffed boar's head, real ales and local cider and perry, and a short choice of interesting dishes; lots of footpath and beach walks; dogs anywhere in the pub and in bedrooms; breakfast sausage included; £10

SEAFORD   TV4899
Silverdale
21 Sutton Park Road, Seaford, East Sussex BN25 1RH (01323) 491849
www.silverdaleseaford.co.uk

£100; 4 individually decorated rms. Extremely friendly guest house carefully run by the owners, who really care about their guests and their dogs and offer particularly good, generous breakfasts in the airy dining room; Bill is the resident brindle staffie; dogs very welcome; treats, bowls, towels and dog sitting service; £3

TICEHURST
TQ6830

Bell

High Street, Ticehurst, Wadhurst, East Sussex TN5 7AS (01580) 200234
www.thebellinticehurst.com

£90; 7 quirky rms each with a silver birch tree. Sensitively restored former coaching inn with heavy beams and timbering in two main rooms, a log fire in the inglenook, a happy jumble of wooden chairs around tables of various sizes, some unusual decorations, real ales and good wines by the glass; interesting food in the relaxed adjoining dining room, a comfortable sitting room with another open fire and, in what was the carriage room, benches on either side of a very long table; seats in back terraced garden; dogs in bedrooms and bar; £10 (which goes to a dog charity)

TILLINGTON
SU9622

Horse Guards

Tillington, Petworth, West Sussex GU28 9AF (01798) 342332
www.thehorseguardsinn.co.uk

£115; 3 cosy rms. 18th-c dining pub prettily set in a lovely village, with a neatly kept beamed front bar, good country furniture on bare boards, a log fire and thoughtfully chosen drinks; other rambling rooms, similarly furnished, have more open fires and original panelling, fresh flowers and a gently civilised atmosphere; food is delicious using some home-grown produce and service is genuinely welcoming and helpful; resident cat and chickens; the 800-year-old church opposite is worth a visit; walks in Petworth Park and South Downs National Park; dogs anywhere in the pub and in bedrooms; treats, bowls and basket; £10

WINCHELSEA
TQ9017

Strand House

Tanyards Lane, The Strand, Winchelsea, East Sussex TN36 4JT (01797) 226276
www.thestrandhouse.co.uk

£175; 13 low-beamed, character rms, 3 in cottage. Warmly friendly little hotel in two ancient buildings with a log fire in the comfortable sitting room, a quiet reading room with books and games, delicious afternoon teas, enjoyable country-house-style evening meals in the elegant candlelit dining room and nice breakfasts; resident cat; towpath and beach walks; closed first 3 weeks of Jan; dogs in two bedrooms; not in public rooms; treats; £7.50

Warwickshire
with Birmingham and West Midlands

MAP 4

DOG FRIENDLY PUBS

ALDERMINSTER   SP2348
Bell
A3400 Oxford–Stratford; CV37 8NY

Handsome coaching inn with contemporary décor mixing easily with original features, real ales, a good choice of wines, excellent modern cooking and helpful service; individually decorated bedrooms

Top notch attention to detail marks this stylish Georgian inn – part of the Alscot Estate – as somewhere rather special. Gently refurbished in an attractive, contemporary style, the open-plan layout, beams, standing timbers, flagstones or wooden floors and fresh flowers give an easy-going atmosphere. A small, bustling bar – with Alscot Ale (brewed for them by Warwickshire Beer Co), a couple of guest beers such as Sharps Doom Bar, a good range of wines by the glass, proper cocktails (including a special bloody mary) – has comfortable brown leather armchairs in front of the open fire, high bar chairs by the blue-painted counter and daily papers; background music The restaurant has an eclectic mix of furniture including painted dining chairs and tables, and leads into the conservatory which shares the same Stour Valley views as the modern chairs and tables in the attractive courtyard. The four boutique-style bedrooms are comfortable and individually decorated.

Free house ~ Licensee Emma Holman-West ~ Real ale ~ Bar food (12-2, 6.30-9; 12-3, 6.30-9.30 Fri, Sat; 12-3 Sun, not Sunday evening) ~ Restaurant ~ (01789) 450414 ~ Children welcome ~ Dogs allowed in bar ~ Open 9.30-3, 6-11; 9.30-11 Fri, Sat; 9.30-4 Sun; closed Sun evening all year and winter Mon (Jan-March) ~ Bedrooms: £75(£100S) (£100B)/£115(£125S)(£135B) ~ www.thebellald.co.uk

ARDENS GRAFTON   SP1153
Golden Cross
Off A46 or B439 W of Stratford, corner Wixford Road/Grafton Lane; B50 4LG

Friendly relaxed beamed bar and attractive dining room in good country dining pub with pleasing well thought of food

Rugs on the ancient dark flagstones, the woodburning stove in the large old fireplace, and the warm buff colour of the walls – hung with attractive contemporary photographs – all give a glow to this place, even without the staff's friendly efficiency. They have Wells & Youngs Eagle and Bombardier and a guest such as Purity UBU on handpump, a decent choice of wines by the glass, and – by a fine antique curved-back settle – a table of daily papers including the Racing Post. There are other character seats too, among the chapel chairs around the country-kitchen tables. The carpeted dining room has fruit prints, an unusual coffered ceiling, and a big mullioned bay window. The good-sized, neatly planted back garden has picnic-sets, with big canopied heaters on the terrace, and a pleasant country outlook.

Charles Wells ~ Lease Debbie Honychurch ~ Real ale ~ Bar food (12-2.30, 5-9; 12-9 Sat; 12-8 Sun) ~ Restaurant ~ (01789) 772420 ~ Children welcome ~ Dogs allowed in bar ~ Live music Thurs evening ~ Open 12-12(1am Fri-Sun) ~ www.thegoldencross.net

BARFORD   SP2660
Granville
1.7 miles from M40 junction 15; A429 S (Wellesbourne Road); CV35 8DS

Civilised, attractive respite from the motorway, for fireside comfort or a good meal

With friendly, helpful service and enjoyable imaginative food, it's not surprising that so many people leave the M40 to come here. It's an attractive place with a gently up-to-date feel with its sage-green paintwork, berber-pattern hangings on the end walls and contemporary lighting. Soft art-deco style leather sofas nestle by the fire in the angle of the L-shaped main bar. You can eat here at pale wooden tables and chairs on floorboards or at a mix of simpler tables and chairs in a carpeted section or you can head through to a more formal, raftered and stripped-brick restaurant. Hook Norton Old Hooky and Purity Mad Goose and UBU on handpump, and decent wines by the glass; background music and TV for major events. A floodlit back terrace has smart rattan chairs and loungers under huge retractable awnings, and the grass beyond rises artfully to a hedge of pampas grass and the like, which neatly closes the view. There's a rustic play area tucked away.

Enterprise ~ Lease Val Kersey ~ Real ale ~ Bar food (12-2.30, 6-9.30; 12-9.30 Sat; 12-5 Sun; not Sun evening) ~ Restaurant ~ (01926) 624236 ~ Children welcome ~ Dogs allowed in bar ~ Open 12-3, 5-11(11.30 Fri); 12-11.30 Sat, Sun ~ www.granvillebarford.co.uk

BARSTON   SP1978
Malt Shovel
3 miles from M42 junction 5; A4141 towards Knowle, then first left into Jacobean Lane/ Barston Lane; B92 0JP

Well run country dining pub full of happy eaters enjoying the delicious carefully prepared food, attractive layout, good service

The light and airy bar, its big terracotta tiles neatly offset by their dark grouting, rambles extensively around the zinc-topped central counter, which is painted blue to match the dado and other panelling, and has good wines by the glass, and Adnams and Sharps Doom Bar on handpump. It's comfortably furnished, with informal dining chairs and scatter-cushioned pews around stripped-top tables of varying types and sizes. Cheerful fruit and vegetable paintings decorate the cream walls, and at one end brown slatted blinds give a glimpse of the kitchen; efficient service by neat young staff. The sheltered garden behind, with a weeping willow, has picnic-sets, and teak seats for the terrace and verandah tables have cushions in summer.

Free house ~ Licensee Helen Somerfield ~ Real ale ~ Bar food (12-2, 6-9.30; 12-4 Sun; not Sun evening) ~ Restaurant ~ (01675) 443223 ~ Children welcome ~ Dogs allowed in bar ~ Open 12-12(10 Sun) ~ www.themaltshovelatbarston.com

FARNBOROUGH   SP4349

Inn at Farnborough

Off A423 N of Banbury; OX17 1DZ

Snug bar in civilised dining pub with wide choice of enjoyable food, both traditional and more elaborate

The cosy bar on the right of this popular golden stone house has dark beams and flagstones, some honey-coloured stripped stone, bucket armchairs with scatter cushions and matching window seats, racing car pictures and a log fire in the big stone fireplace. They have Hook Norton Hooky and an occasional guest on handpump, local spirits, about 20 wines by the glass and enterprising bar nibbles – charcuterie, whitebait and crayfish tails, for example; background music. A second fireplace, open on two sides, with a seat built in around it, divides off a compact two-room dining area with sturdy stripped kitchen tables and high-backed leather chairs; the carpeted inner room has wallpaper imitating shelves of books. There are blue picnic-sets and other seats in the neat sloping garden, which has a big yew tree and a canopied deck. Not a lot of nearby parking.

Free house ~ Licensees Anthony and Jo Robinson ~ Real ale ~ Bar food (12-2.30, 6-10; 12-10(9 Sun)) ~ Restaurant ~ (01295) 690615 ~ Children welcome ~ Dogs allowed in bar ~ Open 10-3, 5.30-10.30; 10-midnight Sat; 10-10.30 Sun ~ www.innatfarnborough.co.uk

GAYDON   SP3654

Malt Shovel

Under a mile from M40 junction 12; B4451 into village, then over roundabout and across B4100; Church Road; CV35 0ET

In a quiet village just off the M40; nice mix of pubby bar and smarter restaurant, tasty food cooked by the chef/landlord and four real ales

Spotlessly kept and friendly, this reliable place offers a tasty meal and a range of particularly well kept mainstream beers – Fullers London Pride, Hook Norton Best, Marstons Pedigree, Wadworths 6X, – along with a dozen or so wines, most available by the glass. Mahogany-varnished boards through to bright carpeting link the entrance, the bar counter on the right and the woodburning stove on the left at this bustling pub. The central area has a high-pitched ceiling, milk churns and earthenware containers in a loft above the bar. Three steps take you up to a little space with some comfortable sofas overlooked by a big stained-glass window with reproductions of classic posters on the walls. A busy eating area has fresh flowers on a mix of kitchen, pub and dining tables; background music, darts and games machine. They will keep your credit card if you run a tab outside. The springer spaniel is called Rosie and the jack russell is Mollie.

Enterprise ~ Lease Richard and Debi Morisot ~ Real ale ~ Bar food (12-2, 6.30-9) ~ Restaurant ~ (01926) 641221 ~ Children welcome ~ Dogs allowed in bar ~ Open 11-3, 5-11, 11-11 Fri, Sat; 12-10.30 Sun ~ www.maltshovelgaydon.co.uk

HUNNINGHAM SP3768
Red Lion

Village signposted off B4453 Leamington–Rugby just E of Weston, and off B4455 Fosse Way 2.5 miles SW of A423 junction; CV33 9DY

Informal, characterful and civilised, good individual food; fine riverside spot

The enterprising landlord at this spacious pub runs it with imagination and a sense of fun. He employs a house magician, hosts events such as a beer and film festival and is designing a comic book wine list. In fact, vintage comics are a passion and his dazzling collection of 320 brightly coloured examples crammed on the bright white walls leave a lasting impression. His enthusiastic lead imbues to the welcoming staff with a positive, interested approach. The light and airy open-plan yet cleverly sectioned layout is an easy-going mix of old and new, with warming red ceilings, a mix of seating from varnished chapel chairs to a variety of dining chairs, various mainly stripped tables, rugs on bare boards and chunky old-fashioned radiators. Windows at one end take in views of the garden with a charmingly arched 14th-c bridge over the gurgling River Leam and a 1948 Massey Ferguson tractor that's been converted into a fun children's climbing frame; good coal fires, and the day's Times, background music and board games. Drinks include an enterprising changing choice of about 25 wines by the glass, a good range of spirits including 45 single malts, Greene King IPA and Abbot and a couple of guests such as Butcombe Best and Titanic Iceberg on handpump, and home-made elderflower cordial.

Greene King ~ Lease Sam Cornwall-Jones ~ Real ale ~ Bar food (12-9.30 Sun) ~ (01926) 632715 ~ Children welcome but no prams or pushchairs ~ Dogs allowed in bar ~ Open 12-11(10.30 Sun) ~ www.redlionhunningham.co.uk

OFFCHURCH SP3665
Stag

North of Welsh Road, off A425 at Radford Semele; CV33 9AQ

Characterful refurbishment, good imaginative food and lively atmosphere

Sensitive refurbishments have kept the ancient character of this 16th-c thatched village pub intact but added a contemporary spark. Walkers and their dogs enjoy the relaxed atmosphere in the low-beamed oak-floored bar with its warming log fires, or you can be a little more formal in the cosy beamed restaurants which have bold wallpaper, deer antlers, animal heads, big mirrors and striking fabrics. The slightly unusual décor is continued on to the terrace with its black furniture. Lots of customers, enthusiastic licensees and friendly busy young staff generate a lively atmosphere. Purity Mad Goose and Warwickshire Best and Darling Buds are on handpump and about a dozen wines are offered by the glass.

Free house ~ Licensee Lizzie King ~ Real ale ~ Bar food (12-2.30(3 Sat, 3.30 Sun), 6-9.30(10 Sat, 9 Sun)) ~ Restaurant ~ (01926) 425801 ~ Children welcome ~ Dogs allowed in bar ~ Open 12-11(10.30 Sun) ~ www.thestagatoffchurch.com

PRESTON BAGOT   SP1765
Crabmill
A4189 Henley-in-Arden–Warwick; B95 5EE

Cider mill conversion with comfortable décor, relaxed atmosphere, a good choice of drinks and smart imaginative food

This rambling old cider mill is a lovely building with an easy-going atmosphere and extremely popular food. It's been attractively decorated with contemporary furnishings and warm colour combinations, and the smart two-level lounge area has comfortable sofas and chairs, low tables, big table lamps and one or two rugs on bare boards. The elegant and roomy low-beamed dining area has caramel leather banquettes and chairs at pine tables and a beamed and flagstoned bar area has some stripped-pine country tables and chairs and snug corners. From the gleaming metal bar they serve Greene King Abbot, the very local Purity Gold and St Austell Tribute on handpump and nine wines by the glass; background music is well chosen and well reproduced. There are lots of tables (some of them under cover) out in a large, attractive, decked garden.

Free house ~ Licensee Sally Coll ~ Real ale ~ Bar food (12-2.30(5 Fri and Sat), 6.30-9.30; 12-3.30 Sun; not Sun evening) ~ Restaurant ~ (01926) 843342 ~ Children welcome ~ Dogs allowed in bar ~ Open 11-11; 12-6 Sun; closed Sun evening ~ www.thecrabmill.co.uk

STRATFORD-UPON-AVON   SP2054
Encore
Bridge Street; CV37 6AB

Well run relaxed modern bar with enjoyable food all day, good river views from upstairs dining room

The building's old, but the style inside is contemporary – and enjoyed by people of all ages, thanks partly to the efficient, pleasantly informal staff. The main area has well spaced scrubbed-top cast-iron tables with bucket armchairs or fat soft square stools, stripped beams and broad oak boards or polished pale flagstones, big windows and two sides and big charcoal sketches of local sights on its butter-coloured walls. A softly lit dark-walled back area with barrel and other rustic tables has stairs up to the long comfortable dining room, which looks down over the road to the river. They have good coffees and plenty of wines by the glass, as well as Purity UBU and Sharps Doom Bar on handpump; log fire, well reproduced background music.

Mitchells & Butlers ~ Manager Matthew Skidmore ~ Real ale ~ Bar food (9.30am-10pm) ~ Restaurant ~ (01789) 269462 ~ Children welcome ~ Dogs allowed in bar ~ Open 9am-11pm(midnight Sat, 10.30 Sun) ~ www.theencorestratford.co.uk

DOG FRIENDLY INNS, HOTELS AND B&Bs

ARMSCOTE   SP2444
Fox & Goose
Armcote, Stratford-upon-Avon, Warwickshire CV37 8DD (01608) 682635
www.foxandgooseamscote.co.uk

£75; 4 bright rms named after Cluedo characters. Nicely modernised former blacksmith's forge with a small flagstoned bar with an open fire, a larger dining area with a woodburning stove, real ales, a good wine list, competent, friendly staff and a varied choice of enjoyable food; seats on decking overlooking the lawn; dogs in two bedrooms; £10

BIRMINGHAM
SP0687
Hotel du Vin & Bistro
25 Church Street, Birmingham, Warwickshire B3 2NR (0121) 200 0600
www.hotelduvin.com

£175; 66 stylish, contemporary rms. A converted eye hospital, this early Victorian building is right in the old city centre and has a friendly, informal atmosphere, helpful young staff, bistro-style food in the club-like restaurant with its wine bottles lining the window sills (the wine list is exceptional), and real ales and pubby food in the basement 'pub'; dogs in bedrooms; £10

BUBBENHALL
SP3771
Bubbenhall House
Pagets Lane, Bubbenhall, Coventry, Warwickshire CV8 3BJ (02476) 302409
www.bubbenhallhouse.co.uk

£70; 6 rms of character, looking over the gardens. A much loved family home, this mainly Edwardian house in 5 acres of mature woodland with marvellous wildlife (including one of only two dormouse sanctuaries in the UK) and once the home of the Mini's designer; beams and a fine staircase, open fires and comfortable sofas and armchairs, home-cooked meals (you can bring your own wine) and hearty breakfasts in the elegant dining room, and a friendly atmosphere; resident dogs – Zippy is the black labrador bitch and Amber the jack russell; Kitty is the cat; walks in nearby country park; dogs in bedrooms; not dining rooms

GREAT WOLFORD
SP2434
Fox & Hounds
Great Wolford, Shipston on Stour, Warwickshire CV36 5NQ (01608) 674220
www.thefoxandhoundsinn.com

£80; 3 rms. Delightful, unspoilt 16th-c inn with low hop-strung beams, an appealing collection of old furniture on flagstones, antique hunting prints and vintage photographs, real ales from an old-fashioned tap room, creative cooking and good breakfasts with home-made bread and home-grown produce, and seats on the terrace; dogs in bedrooms and bar; bring own bedding

HAMPTON IN ARDEN
SP2080
White Lion
10 High Street, Hampton-in-Arden, Solihull, West Midlands B92 0AA (01675) 442833
www.thewhitelioninn.com

£75; 9 nice rms. Former farmhouse with a relaxed atmosphere, a mix of furniture trimly laid out in the carpeted bar, low-beamed ceilings and some local memorabilia on the fresh cream walls, real ales on handpump and airy, modern dining areas with light wood and cane chairs on stripped floorboards, popular food and tasty breakfasts; the church opposite is mentioned in the Domesday Book; nearby walks; dogs anywhere in the pub and in bedrooms

---

LONG COMPTON
SP2832

Red Lion

Main Street, Long Compton, Shipston-on-Stour, Warwickshire CV36 5JS (01608) 684221
www.redlion-longcompton.co.uk

£90; 5 pretty, recently refurbished rms. Lovely old coaching inn with a warmly welcoming landlady and lots of original features to look out for – exposed stone, flagstones, beams and rambling corners with old-fashioned built-in settles and leather armchairs and a woodburning stove in the roomy lounge, a simpler public bar with real ales, and good, popular food; resident chocolate labrador, Cocoa; walks in surrounding countryside; dogs anywhere in the pub (on a lead); £10

STRATFORD-UPON-AVON
SP2054

Bear

Bridgefoot, Stratford-upon-Avon, Warwickshire CV37 7LT (01789) 265540
www.thebearfreehouse.co.uk

£129; 68 elegant rms in the adjoining Swans Nest Hotel. Properly pubby bar of a large comfortable riverside hotel with an impressive row of handpumps and fine wines by the glass, china and other bric-a-brac on the delft shelf, a couple of wing armchairs by the fire, a variety of other carefully chosen seats including sofas and scatter-cushioned banquettes, and good value popular bar food plus adjoining brasserie menu; thoroughly professional staff, big windows looking out to the swans on a reach of river, and seats on the waterside lawn; dogs anywhere in the pub and in the hotel bedrooms; £15

STRATFORD-UPON-AVON
SP2054

Melita

37 Shipston Road, Stratford-upon-Avon, Warwickshire CV37 7LN (01789) 292432
www.melitahotel.co.uk

£90; 12 well equipped rms. Family-run Victorian hotel, close to the theatres and town centre, with a pretty, carefully laid-out garden, a comfortable lounge with an open fire and extensive breakfasts; free leisure facilities at Alveston Manor hotel 2 mins away; dogs in bedrooms only; £8

STRATFORD-UPON-AVON
SP2054

Mercure Shakespeare

Chapel Street, Stratford-upon-Avon, Warwickshire CV37 6ER 0871 663 0627
www.accorhotels.com/gb/hotel-6630-mercure-stratford-upon-avon-shakespeare-hotel

£110; 74 individually named, contemporary rms. Smart hotel based on a handsome, lavishly modernised Tudor merchants' houses, with a convivial bar, a bar/lounge (both of which are popular for morning coffee, light lunches and afternoon teas), blazing log fires, quick friendly service, brasserie-style food in the newly refurbished restaurant, enjoyable breakfasts, and seats in the terraced garden; 3 mins walk from theatres; dogs in bedrooms only; £10

Wiltshire

MAP 2

DOG FRIENDLY PUBS

ALDBOURNE
SU2675
Blue Boar
The Green (off B4192 in centre); SN8 2EN

Bags of character in chatty, low-beamed, traditional pub with popular honest food

This character-filled and quintessential country village pub is a favourite with our readers – and with locals, too. The US' 506th Parachute Infantry Regiment of the 101st Airborne Division (made famous in the book and TV series Band of Brothers) became Blue Boar regulars when they were stationed in the village during World War II, and the pub had a further moment of glory when it was featured in a 1971 episode of Doctor Who. It's right at the heart of a quaint and pretty village, opposite the green, and has an easy-going atmosphere and a friendly welcome for all – dogs included. The left-hand bar is homely, with pubby seats around rustic tables on the bare boards or flagstones, lots of low black beams in the ochre ceiling, a boar's head above the bigger of the two log fires, a stuffed pine marten over one table; darts, board games and a corner cupboard of village trophies. Lots of unusual bottled beers line the rail above the dark pine dado. Reasonably priced Wadworths IPA and 6X and a changing guest beer on handpump and 15 malt whiskies. A separate bare-boards dining bar on the right, stretching back further, has more table space and is rather more modern in style (though with the same pubby atmosphere). There are picnic-sets and a couple of tall hogshead tables under big green canvas parasols in front of the pub.

Wadworths ~ Tenants Jez and Mandy Hill ~ Real ale ~ Bar food (12-2, 7-9) ~ Restaurant ~ (01672) 540237 ~ Children welcome ~ Dogs allowed in bar ~ Open 11.30-3, 5.30-11.30; 11.30am-midnight Fri and Sat; 12-11 Sun ~ www.thepubonthegreen.com

BERWICK ST JOHN
ST9422
Talbot
Village signed from A30 E of Shaftesbury; SP7 0HA

Unspoilt and friendly pub in attractive village with simple furnishings and tasty food using local produce

In a pretty and peaceful Ebble Valley village, this is a friendly, unspoilt pub with reasonably priced food. The heavily beamed bar has plenty of character, and a huge inglenook fireplace with a good iron fireback and bread ovens and is simply furnished with solid wall and window seats, spindleback chairs and a high-backed built-in settle at one end. Ringwood Best, Wadworths 6X and a guest like Ringwood Fortyniner on handpump and several wines by the glass; darts. There are seats outside and the pub is well placed for choice walks southwards through the deep countryside of Cranborne Chase and towards Tollard Royal.

Free-house ~ Licensees Pete and Marilyn Hawkins ~ Real ale ~ Bar food (12-2, 7-9; not Sun evening or Mon) ~ Restaurant ~ (01747) 828222 ~ Children welcome ~ Dogs allowed in bar ~ Open 12-2.30, 6.30-11; 12-4 Sun; closed Sun evening, Mon

BRINKWORTH   SU0184
Three Crowns
The Street; B4042 Wootton Bassett–Malmesbury; SN15 5AF

Busy dining pub, under new owners, with good range of beers and a carefully chosen wine list

Despite being best-known as a dining pub, this well run place still ticks all the boxes as a good old-fashioned local. The bar part of the building is the most traditional with big landscape prints and other pictures, some horse brasses on dark beams, a log fire in winter, a dresser with a collection of old bottles, big tapestry-upholstered pews, a stripped deal table and a couple more made from gigantic forge bellows. Bath Ales Gem bitter, Greene King IPA, Timothy Taylors Landlord, Weighbridge Best Bitter (from the owner's microbrewery) and a beer named for the village on handpump, 40 wines by the glass from a carefully chosen, extensive list, local cider and several malt whiskies. Most people choose to eat in the conservatory or the light and airy garden room. There's a terrace with outdoor heating to the side of the conservatory and more seats and tables in the garden, which stretches around the side and back and looks across to the church and on to rolling farmland.

Enterprise ~ Real ale ~ Bar food (12-2, 6-9.30; 12-8 Sun) ~ Restaurant ~ (01666) 510366 ~ Children welcome before 8pm ~ Dogs allowed in bar ~ Open 11-11(midnight Sat); 12-11 Sun ~ www.threecrowns.co.uk

BROAD HINTON   SU1176
Barbury
A4361 Swindon–Devizes; SN4 9PF

Refurbished roadside pub with a friendly, informal atmosphere, enjoyable food; a mix of comfortable and contemporary furnishings, and a good balance between eating and drinking

Not far from M4 junction 16, this well run roadside pub has been saved from dereliction by the professional team that run the Vine Tree at Norton. It's been completely refurbished inside and is welcoming to all its customers (dogs included) whether they are dropping in for a drink and a chat or for a meal. There's a long room with a comfortable sofa and two stumpy armchairs in pale brown leather beside the woodburner at one end, a few high-backed wicker armchairs around a couple of tables on bare boards, some attractive hound paintings, and a flat-screen TV on the wall above the fireplace. The bar area has regency-striped modern armchairs and tables opposite the dark grey-painted counter where there are usually cheerful locals sitting at the high chairs enjoying the well kept St Austell Trelawny and Tribute on handpump; good wines by the glass and helpful, willing service. Beside the second woodburner at the other end of the room are leather-cushioned chairs around polished tables (set for dining) – a step leads from here to the carpeted dining room with high-backed black wicker or wooden dining chairs around plain or painted-legged dining tables; throughout there are basket weave lamp shades, some ornate mirrors and planked ceilings. Also, newspapers to read and background music; it's all very easy-going and friendly. There are seats and tables on a partly covered back terrace.

Free house ~ Licensees Charles Walker and Tiggi Wood ~ Real ale ~ Bar food (12-2.30, 7-9.30(10 Fri and Sat); 12-3, 6.30-9 Sun) ~ Restaurant ~ (01793) 731510 ~ Children welcome ~ Dogs allowed in bar ~ Open 11.30am-midnight; 11-11 Sun ~ www.thebarburyinn.co.uk

BROUGHTON GIFFORD   ST8763
Fox
Village signposted off A365 to B3107 W of Melksham; The Street; SN12 8PN

Comfortably stylish pub with good, interesting food using their own bred pigs and home-grown vegetables, real ales and several wines by the glass and a nice garden

You can be sure of a genuinely warm welcome from the helpful landlord and his courteous staff in this relaxed but civilised pub. Each of the interconnected areas has a chatty atmosphere, and the big bird and plant prints, attractive table lamps and white-painted beams contrast nicely with its broad dark flagstones. You can sink into sofas or armchairs by a table of daily papers or another with magazines and board games, take one of the padded stools by the pink-painted bar counter, or go for the mix of gently old-fashioned dining chairs around the unmatched stripped dining tables, which have candles in brass sticks. Bath Ales Gem Bitter, Butcombe Bitter, Fullers London Pride and Otter Bitter on handpump, lots of wines by the glass, 24 malt whiskies and a good choice of spirits, and a log fire in the stone fireplace. The terrace behind has picnic-sets, and leads out on to a good-sized sheltered lawn. They have biscuits behind the bar for dogs.

Free house ~ Licensee Derek Geneen ~ Real ale ~ Bar food (12-2.30(3 Sat), 6-9.30; 12-5.30 Sun; not Sun evening or Mon lunchtime) ~ Restaurant ~ (01225) 782949 ~ Children welcome ~ Dogs allowed in bar ~ Open 12-midnight; 5-11 Mon; 12-10 Sun; closed Mon lunchtime ~ www.thefox-broughtongifford.co.uk

CRUDWELL   ST9592
Potting Shed
A429 N of Malmesbury; The Street; SN16 9EW

Appealing variation on the traditional country tavern theme, a fine choice of drinks, interesting inventive food and friendly staff

Consistently enthusiastic reports from our readers once again for this extremely well run Cotswolds inn – and all are welcomed. Thankfully, it remains very much a proper country pub rather than just another pub/restaurant, with cheerful and efficient young staff and a fine range of drinks such as Bath Ales Gem Bitter, Butcombe Bitter, Woodfordes Wherry and a changing guest beer on handpump, as well as an excellent range of 30 wines and champagne by the glass, home-made seasonal cocktails using local or home-grown fruit, local fruit liqueurs, good coffees and popular winter mulled wine. Low-beamed rooms ramble around the bar with mixed plain tables and chairs on pale flagstones, log fires (one in a big worn stone fireplace), some well worn easy chairs in one corner, and a couple of blacktop daily papers. Four steps take you up into a high-raftered further area with coir carpeting, and there's one separate smaller room ideal for a lunch or dinner party. The quirky, rustic decorations are not overdone: a garden-fork door handle, garden-tool beer pumps, rather witty big black and white photographs; visiting dogs may meet Barney and Rubble (the pub dogs) and be offered biscuits. Well chosen background music and board games. They have summer barbecues on fine Saturdays; there are sturdy teak seats around cask tables as well as picnic-sets out on the side grass among weeping willows. The pub's 2 acres of gardens supply a lot of the ingredients used in the food. They have also donated ten raised beds to villagers, and these are pleasant wander through. Good access for those in need of extra assistance. They also own the hotel across the road.

Enterprise ~ Lease Jonathan Barry and Julian Muggridge ~ Real ale ~ Bar food (12-2.30(3 Sun), 7-9.30(9 Sun)) ~ Restaurant ~ (01666) 577833 ~ Children welcome ~ Dogs allowed in bar ~ Open 11am-midnight(11pm Sun) ~ www.thepottingshedpub.com

EAST CHISENBURY   SU1352

Red Lion

At S end of village; SN9 6AQ

Thatched country inn run by a hard-working and enthusiastic couple (both are chefs), informal, friendly atmosphere, contemporary décor, delicious food including home-baked bread, own sausages and smoked meats, real ales and home-made cordials and seats in garden

With two top chefs running this thatched inn, the emphasis is of course on the exceptional food. But this not a straightforward dining pub, it's also a proper local selling ales from breweries such as Cottage and Keystone on handpump and regulars do drop in for a pint and a chat. If you don't fancy a beer, they make a rather special bloody mary (pressing the tomato juice themselves) and their own lime and other seasonal cordials, keep a thoughtful little wine list and offer unusual choices like brown rice sake and rare Kentucky bourbons. It's basically one long room split into different areas by brick and green-planked timbers. One end has a big woodburner in a brick inglenook and the other a comfortable black leather sofa and armchairs, and in between, there are painted or wooden dining chairs around chunky pale oak tables on bare boards or stone and wine bottles and candles on the window sills; drinkers tend to congregate at the high chairs by the bar counter. There's a further dining room, too. Décor includes a huge string of chillies and country and other pictures on the walls; background music, table skittles. Outside, there are picnic-sets on a terrace and tables and chairs on grass above; you can also go into the upper garden where they keep bantams. The bedrooms will be opened by the time this book is published; they make their own dog treats.

Free house ~ Licensees Britt and Guy Manning ~ Real ale ~ Bar food (12-2.30(3.30 Sun), 6.30-9.30(9 Sun)) ~ Restaurant ~ (01980) 671124 ~ Children welcome ~ Dogs allowed in bar ~ Open 12-3, 6-11; 12-12(11 Sun) Sat ~ www.redlionfreehouse.com

EAST KNOYLE   ST8731

Fox & Hounds

Village signposted off A350 S of A303; The Green (named on some road atlases), a mile NW at OS Sheet 183 map reference 872313; or follow signpost off B3089, about 0.5 miles E of A303 junction near Little Chef; SP3 6BN

Beautiful thatched village pub with splendid views, welcoming service, good beers and popular enjoyable food

This lively 15th-c pub, in a pretty spot by the village green, is a reliable choice for a warm welcome, good food and real ale. The three linked areas are on different levels around the central horseshoe-shaped servery and have big log fires, plentiful oak woodwork and flagstones, comfortably padded dining chairs around big scrubbed tables with vases of flowers, and a couple of leather sofas; the furnishings are all very individual and uncluttered. There's also a small light-painted conservatory restaurant. Hop Back Summer Lightning, Plain Ales Sheep Dip and guests like Palmers Copper Ale and St Austell Tribute on handpump, 20 well chosen wines by the glass and farm cider. Background music and skittle alley. The nearby woods are good for a stroll, and the Wiltshire Cycleway passes through the village; there are fine views of Blackmore Vale.

Free house ~ Licensee Murray Seator ~ Real ale ~ Bar food (12-2.30, 6-9.30) ~ (01747) 830573 ~ Children welcome ~ Dogs allowed in bar ~ Open 11.30-3, 5.30-11(10.30 Sun) ~ www.foxandhounds-eastknoyle.co.uk

FONTHILL GIFFORD
ST9231

Beckford Arms

Off B3089 W at Fonthill Bishop; SP3 6PX

18th-c coaching inn with refurbished bar and restaurant, unfailingly excellent interesting food, real ales and an informal but civilised atmosphere; bedrooms

Our readers love every aspect of this elegant and civilised old coaching inn which is on the edge of the lovely rolling parkland of the Fonthill Estate. The bustling main bar has a huge fireplace, bar stools beside the counter, various old wooden dining chairs and tables on parquet flooring, Butcombe Bitter, Keystone Phoenix (brewed especially for them) and a changing guest on handpump, several wines by the glass, local cider, mulled wine and cider in the winter and cocktails using home-grown ingredients; staff are cheerful and helpful. The stylish but cosy sitting room has comfortable sofas facing each other across a low table of newspapers, a nice built-in window seat and other chairs and tables, and an open fire in a stone fireplace with candles in brass candlesticks and fresh flowers on the mantelpiece. There's also a separate restaurant and charming private dining room. Much of the artwork on the walls is by local artists. They host film nights on occasional Saturdays and will provide water and bones for dogs (the pub dog is called Elsa.). The mature rambling garden has seats on a brick terrace, hammocks under trees, games for children, a dog bath and boules. This is a lovely place to stay: the bedrooms are luxurious and stocked with home-made toiletries, and the breakfasts (featuring home-made jams) are highly enjoyable.

Free house ~ Licensees Dan Brod and Charlie Luxton ~ Real ale ~ Bar food (12-3(3.30 weekends), 6-9.30; they open between 8-10 for breakfast) ~ Restaurant ~ (01747) 870385 ~ Children welcome ~ Dogs allowed in bar ~ Open 8am-11pm ~ Bedrooms: /£95B ~ www.beckfordarms.com

GRITTLETON
ST8680

Neeld Arms

M4 junction 17, follow A429 to Cirencester and immediately left, signed Stanton St Quinton and Grittleton; SN14 6AP

Bustling village pub with popular food and beer and friendly staff; comfortable bedrooms

This is a proper village pub with a good, bustling atmosphere and plenty of chatty locals – though visitors are made just as welcome. It dates back to the 17th c and is now largely open-plan with Cotswold-stone walls and a pleasant mix of seating ranging from bar stools, a traditional settle, window seats and pale wooden dining chairs around a mix of tables. The little brick fireplace houses a woodburning stove and there's an inglenook fireplace on the right. Wadworths IPA and 6X and guests such as Hook Norton Old Hooky and a seasonal ale from Wickwar are on handpump, served from the blue-painted panelled and oak-topped bar counter. The back dining area has another inglenook with a big woodburning stove; even back here, you still feel thoroughly part of the action. There's an outdoor terrace with a pergola. The comfortable bedrooms have a lot of character.

Free house ~ Licensees Charlie and Boo West ~ Real ale ~ Bar food (12-2, 6.30-9.30; 12-4, 7-9 Sun) ~ (01249) 782470 ~ Children welcome ~ Dogs allowed in bar ~ Open 12-3, 5.30(7 Sun)-11.30 ~ Bedrooms: £50B/£80B ~ www.neeldarms.co.uk

LACOCK   ST9367
Rising Sun
Bewley Common, Bowden Hill – out towards Sandy Lane, up hill past abbey; OS Sheet 173 map reference 935679; SN15 2PP

Unassuming stone pub with welcoming atmosphere, well liked food and great views from garden

The big two-level terrace here (where there are plenty of modern steel and wood tables and chairs) has a stunning 25-mile view over the Avon Valley, and the sunsets can be glorious. Inside, three welcoming little rooms have been knocked together to form one simply furnished area with a mix of wooden chairs and tables on stone floors, country pictures and open fires; there's also a conservatory with the same fantastic view as the terrace. Moles Best Bitter, Barleymole and Mole Catcher on handpump, several wines by the glass and maybe farm cider.

Moles ~ Managers Adam McGregor and Sarah Delancy ~ Real ale ~ Bar food (12-2.30(2 Sun), 5-9(7 Sun); 12-9 Fri, Sat and bank holidays) ~ Restaurant ~ (01249) 730363 ~ Children welcome ~ Dogs allowed in bar ~ Live entertainment last Weds of month ~ Open 12-3, 5-11; 12-11 Fri-Sun ~ www.therisingsunlacock.com

MANTON   SU1768
Outside Chance
Village (and pub) signposted off A4 just W of Marlborough; High Street; SN8 4HW

Popular dining pub, civilised and traditional, nicely reworked with sporting theme; interesting modern food

A new licensee recently took over this bustling dining pub but early reports from our readers suggest things are going well. The three small linked rooms have flagstones or bare boards, hops on beams, and mainly plain pub furnishings such as chapel chairs and a long-cushioned pew; one room has a more cosseted feel, with panelling and a comfortable banquette. The décor celebrates unlikely winners, such as 100-1 Grand National winners Coughoo and Foinavon, Mr Spooner's Only Dreams (a 100-1 winner at Leicester in 2007), or the odd-gaited little Seabiscuit who cheered many thousands of Americans with his dogged pursuit of victory during the Depression years. There's a splendid log fire in the big main fireplace and maybe fresh flowers and candlelight; background music and board games. Wadworths IPA, 6X, Bishops Tipple and a guest like Horizon on handpump, quite a few good wines by the glass, nicely served coffees, and neatly dressed young staff. A suntrap side terrace has contemporary metal-framed granite-topped tables and the good-sized garden has sturdy rustic tables and benches under ash trees; they have private access to the local playing fields and children's play area.

Wadworths ~ Tenant Howard Spooner ~ Real ale ~ Bar food (12-2.30(3 weekends), 6(7 Sun)-9) ~ (01672) 512352 ~ Children welcome ~ Dogs allowed in bar ~ Open 12-3, 5.30-11; 12-11 Sun and Sat ~ www.theoutsidechance.co.uk

NEWTON TONY   SU2140

Malet Arms

Village signposted off A338 Swindon–Salisbury; SP4 0HF

Smashing village pub with no pretensions, a good choice of local beers and highly thought of food

Nicely situated on the banks of the River Bourne, this 16th-c former coaching inn receives consistently positive praise from our readers for its relaxed atmosphere and unpretentious charm – and the cheerful landlord continues to run it with much friendly enthusiasm. The outside has been repainted and tidied up, as has the small front terrace, which has new garden seats; more on grass and in the back garden. Inside, there have been some changes to the snug, too, which now has a fantastic collection of photographs and prints celebrating the local aviation history of Boscombe Down together with archive photographs of Stonehenge festivals of the seventies and eighties. The other low-beamed interconnecting room has nice furnishings, including a mix of tables of different sizes with high-winged wall settles, carved pews, chapel and carver chairs, and lots of pictures, mainly from imperial days. The main front windows are said to be made from the stern of a ship, and there's a log and coal fire in a huge fireplace. At the back is a homely dining room. Four real ales are well kept on handpump from breweries such as fff, Fullers, Itchen Valley, Palmers, Plain Ales, Ramsbury and Stonehenge; they also have 31 malt whiskies, 11 wines by the glass and Weston's Old Rosie cider. Getting to the pub takes you through a ford and it may be best to use an alternative route in winter, as it can be quite deep. There's now an all-weather cricket pitch on the village green. The pub policy of no background music or games machines helps to maintain the peaceful atmosphere.

Free house ~ Licensees Noel and Annie Cardew ~ Real ale ~ Bar food (12-2.30, 6.30-10 (6-9 Sun)) ~ Restaurant ~ (01980) 629279 ~ Children in restaurant or snug only ~ Dogs allowed in bar ~ Open 11-3, 6-11; 12-3, 7-10.30 Sun ~ www.maletarms.com

NORTON   ST8884

Vine Tree

4 miles from M4 junction 17; A429 towards Malmesbury, then left at Hullavington, Sherston signpost, then follow Norton signposts; in village turn right at Foxley signpost, which takes you into Honey Lane; SN16 0JP

Civilised dining pub, beams and candlelight, big choice of first class, seasonal food, super wines (also sold at their deli/farm shop) and a sizeable garden

Once this former mill served drinks through the front windows to passing travellers. Nowadays, it serves thirsty visitors to Westonbirt Arboretum and other fine gardens, houses and racecourses in the area – and to riders following the county's official cycle route, too. But there are always lots of loyal locals as well and with its lovely atmosphere, friendly welcome and delicious food, it's always pretty busy. Three neatly-kept small rooms open into each other, with aged beams, some old settles and unvarnished wooden tables on the flagstone floors, big cream church altar candles, a woodburning stove at one end of the restaurant and a large open fireplace in the central bar, and limited edition and sporting prints; look out for Clementine, the friendly and docile black Labrador. Butcombe Bitter and St Austell Tribute and a couple of guests like Bath Ales Gem Bitter and Stonehenge Pigswill on handpump, 48 wines by the glass including sparkling wines and champagne (and they have their own wine shop, too), and quite a choice of malt whiskies and armagnacs, as well as mulled wine in the winter and award-winning bloody marys year-round. There are picnic-sets and a children's play area in a 2-acre garden, plus a pretty suntrap terrace with teak furniture under big cream umbrellas, and an attractive smokers' shelter. Pets (including horses!) are welcomed and provided for. Look out for the two ghosts that some visitors have spotted. They also run the Barbury at Broad Hinton.

Free house ~ Licensees Charles Walker and Tiggi Wood ~ Real ale ~ Bar food (12-2.30(3.30 Sun), 7-9.30(10 Fri and Sat)) ~ Restaurant ~ (01666) 837654 ~ Children welcome ~ Dogs allowed in bar ~ Open 12-3, 6-midnight; 12-midnight Sun and Sat; closed winter Sun evenings ~ www.thevinetree.co.uk

PITTON   SU2131
Silver Plough
Village signed from A30 E of Salisbury (follow brown tourist signs); SP5 1DU

Bustling country dining pub with popular, reasonably priced bar food, good drinks and nearby walks; bedrooms

A farmhouse until the World War II, this bustling, friendly place is surrounded by woodland and downland paths and makes a good stop for a pre- or post-walk meal. The comfortable front bar has plenty to look at as the black beams are strung with hundreds of antique boot-warmers and stretchers, pewter and china tankards, copper kettles, toby jugs, earthenware and glass rolling pins, and so forth. Seats include half a dozen cushioned antique oak settles (one elaborately carved, beside a very fine reproduction of an Elizabethan oak table) around rustic pine tables and they keep Badger Bitter, Gold and Tanglefoot on handpump and 13 wines by the glass served from a bar made from a hand-carved Elizabethan over-mantle. The back bar is simpler, but still has a big winged high-backed settle, cases antique guns, and substantial pictures; there are two woodburning stoves for winter warmth; background music. The skittle alley is for private use only. The quiet, south-facing lawn has picnic-sets and other tables under cocktail parasols and there are more seats on the heated terrace; occasional barbecues. If you stay overnight and don't have breakfast, the prices will be cheaper than those given below. They keep dog biscuits on the bar in the snug bar.

Badger ~ Tenants Stephen and Susan Keyes ~ Real ale ~ Bar food (12-2, 6-9; 12-8 Sun) ~ Restaurant ~ (01722) 712266 ~ Children welcome ~ Dogs allowed in bar ~ Open 12-3, 6-11; 12-9.30 Sun ~ Bedrooms: £60S/£70S ~ www.silverplough-pitton.co.uk

POULSHOT   ST9760
Raven
Off A361; SN10 1RW

Pretty village pub with friendly licensees, enjoyable food (cooked by the landlord) and beer and seats in back garden

J ust across from village green this is a pretty half-timbered pub with friendly, welcoming licensees who take great care of both their pub and their customers. The two cosy black-beamed rooms are spotlessly kept and have comfortable banquettes, pubby chairs and tables, an open fire and Wadworths IPA and 6X plus a seasonal guest beer tapped from the cask; background music in the dining room only. The jack russell is called Faith and the Doberman, Harvey. There are picnic-sets under parasols in the walled back garden.

Wadworths ~ Tenant Jeremy Edwards ~ Real ale ~ Bar food (12-2(2.30 Sun), 6-9; not winter Mon) ~ Restaurant ~ (01380) 828271 ~ Children welcome ~ Dogs allowed in bar ~ Open 11.30-3, 6.30-11; 12-3, 7-10.30 Sun; closed winter Mon ~ www.ravenpoulshot.co.uk

SALISBURY   SU1429
Haunch of Venison
Minster Street, opposite Market Cross; SP1 1TB

Ancient pub oozing history, with tiny beamed rooms, unique fittings and a famous mummified hand

A friendly new landlord recently took over this ancient pub and it's the sort of place that customers return to on a regular basis. Both the tiny downstairs rooms have a great deal of character and atmosphere and date back to 1320 when the place was used by craftsmen working on the cathedral spire. There are massive beams in the white ceiling, stout oak benches built into the timbered walls, black and white floor tiles, and an open fire. A tiny snug (popular with locals, but historically said to be where the ladies drank) opens off the entrance lobby. Courage Best, Hop Back Summer Lightning, Ringwood Fortyniner and a changing guest beer on handpump from a unique pewter bar counter, and there's a rare set of antique taps for gravity-fed spirits and liqueurs. They've also up to 100 malt whiskies and several wines by the glass. Halfway up the stairs is a panelled room they call the House of Lords, which has a small-paned window looking down on to the main bar and a splendid fireplace that dates back to the building's early years; behind glass in a small wall slit is the smoke-preserved mummified hand of an 18th-c card sharp still clutching his cards.

Scottish Courage ~ Lease Alex Marshall ~ Real ale ~ Bar food (12-2.30, 6-9.30; 12-4 Sun; not Sun evening) ~ Restaurant ~ (01722) 411313 ~ Children welcome ~ Dogs allowed in bar ~ Open 11-11(midnight Sat); 12-6 Sun; closed Sun evening ~ www.haunchofvenison.uk.com

SANDY LANE   ST9668
George
A342 Devizes–Chippenham; SN15 2PX

Friendly licensees at immaculately kept old pub with open fires, Wadworths ales and well liked tasty food

In a charming thatched village surrounded by the lovely Bowood Estate, this neatly kept and handsome Georgian pub is run by friendly, helpful licensees who have known it since childhood. The cosy bar area has an open fire, plush stools and a mix of chairs around pubby tables on the wooden flooring, Wadworths IPA and 6X on handpump and 16 wines by the glass. There's also a back dining room and a wooden-framed conservatory with farmhouse and red-plush dining chairs around dark tables on more pale floorboards. Outside, the terrace has rattan furniture and picnic-sets, with more on the lawn, and flower beds in the old piggery. The pub overlooks a small green.

Wadworths ~ Tenants Mark and Harriet Jenkinson ~ Real ale ~ Bar food (12-9.30; 12-3 Sun;

not Sun evening or Mon) ~ Restaurant ~ (01380) 850403 ~ Children welcome ~
Dogs allowed in bar ~ Open 12-10.30(11 Sat); 12-4 Sun; closed Sun evening, Mon ~
www.georgeinnsandylane.co.uk

SHERSTON   ST8585
Rattlebone
Church Street; B4040 Malmesbury–Chipping Sodbury; SN16 0LR

**Village pub with lots of atmosphere in rambling rooms, good bar food
using local and free-range produce, and real ales; friendly staff**

There's plenty of bustling atmosphere and buckets of character in this 17th-c
pub, named after the Saxon warrior John Rattlebone, who apparently haunts
it to this day. The public bar has a good mix of locals and visitors and the other
softly-lit rambling rooms – including the long back dining room – have beams,
standing timbers and flagstones, pews, settles and country-kitchen chairs around
a mix of tables, armchairs and sofas, and roaring fires. Butcombe Bitter, St
Austell Tribute and Wells & Youngs Bitter on handpump, local cider, home-made
lemonade and several wines by the glass on a thoughtful list; background music,
board games, TV and games machine. Outside there's a skittle alley, two boules
pitches, often in use by one of the many pub teams, a boules festival in July and
mangold hurling (similar to boules but using cattle feed turnips), as well as other
events. The two pretty gardens include an extended terrace where they hold
barbecues and spit roasts. Wheelchair access.

Youngs ~ Tenant Jason Read ~ Real ale ~ Bar food (12-2.30(3 Sun), 6-9.30(8.30 Sun)) ~
Restaurant ~ (01666) 840871 ~ Children welcome ~ Dogs allowed in bar ~ Monthly acoustic
music evenings ~ Open 12-3, 5-11(midnight Fri); 12-midnight(11 Sun) Sat ~
www.therattlebone.co.uk

SOUTH WRAXALL   ST8364
Longs Arms
Upper S Wraxall, off B3109 N of Bradford-on-Avon; BA15 2SB

**Friendly licensees at well run old stone inn, plenty of character, real ales
and first class food using local seasonal produce**

Carefully refurbished a year ago by its friendly licensees, this is a handsome
and partly 17th-c stone inn by the village church. The bar has windsor and
other pubby chairs around wooden tables on flagstones, horsebrasses on beams,
a woodburning stove in the fireplace and high chairs by the counter, where they
keep Wadworths IPA and 6X and a changing guest beer on handpump and several
wines by the glass. Another room has cushioned and other dining chairs, a nice
old settle and a wall banquette around a mix of tables on carpeting, fresh flowers
and lots of prints and paintings, and a further room has nice little boxy settles
and other seats on pale oak flooring; the skittle alley is much used in season – at
other times it can be used as extra dining space. There are seats in the pretty little
walled back garden. They keep dog biscuits behind the bar.

Wadworths ~ Tenants Rob and Liz Allcock ~ Real ale ~ Bar food (12-3, 5.30-9.30; 12-9.30
Fri-Sun) ~ Restaurant ~ (01225) 864450 ~ Children welcome ~ Dogs allowed in bar ~ Open
12-3, 5.30-11; 12-11 Fri-Sun ~ www.thelongsarms.com

WARMINSTER   ST8745

Weymouth Arms

Emwell Street; BA12 8JA

Charming backstreet pub with panelled rooms, a roaring winter fire in snug bar, candlelight and fresh flowers, real ales, friendly staff and well liked imaginative food; seats in courtyard; bedrooms

Tucked away down a quiet back street, this handsome old pub comes as quite a surprise. The snug, panelled entrance bar has a roaring log fire in a fine stone fireplace with a copper coal bucket and big log basket to one side and ancient leather books on the mantelpiece. Leather tub chairs around a fine walnut and satinwood table make the most of the fire's warmth, with more seats and tables against the walls and high stools by the counter; on our visit, locals were dropping in for a pint and a chat and to read the daily papers. Butcombe Bitter and Wadworths 6X on handpump and good wines by the glass are served by cheerful, friendly staff. Leading off here is another heavily panelled room with a smaller fireplace and brass candlesticks on the mantelpiece, similar furniture on wide bare boards, and a chandelier. The dining room (also panelled) on the other side of the bar, is on two levels and stretches back to the open kitchen. The lower part has banquette wall seating, spindleback dining chairs and candles on tables and the upper part is more contemporary. There are seats in the flower-filled back courtyard. Bedrooms are well equipped and comfortable.

Free house ~ Licensee Shane Goodway ~ Real ale ~ Bar food (12-2.30, 6-9) ~ Restaurant ~ (01985) 216 995 ~ Children welcome ~ Dogs allowed in bar ~ Open 12-2.30, 6-midnight; closed Mon lunchtime ~ Bedrooms: £65S/£75S ~ www.weymoutharms.co.uk

WEST LAVINGTON   SU0052

Bridge Inn

Church Street (A360); SN10 4LD

Friendly village pub with good bar food cooked by the landlord, real ales and a light, comfortable bar

This is a thoroughly nice pub and run by new enthusiastic licensees. It's quietly civilised and easy-going and the comfortable spacious bar mixes contemporary features with firmly traditional fixtures such as the enormous brick inglenook that may be filled with big logs and candles; at the opposite end is a smaller modern fireplace, in an area set mostly for eating. The cream-painted or exposed brick walls are hung with local pictures of The Lavingtons and there are fresh flowers and evening candlelight; timbers and the occasional step divide the various areas. Sharps Doom Bar and Wadworths IPA on handpump, nine wines by the glass and several malt whiskies; background music. A raised lawn at the back makes a pleasant place to spend a summer's afternoon, with several tables under a big tree; boules.

Enterprise ~ Lease Emily Robinson and James Stewart ~ Real ale ~ Bar food (12-3, 7-9.30; 12-4, 6-8 Sun; not Mon) ~ (01380) 813213 ~ Children welcome ~ Dogs allowed in bar ~ Open 12-3, 6-midnight; 12-4, 6-1am Sat; 12-10 Sun; closed Mon ~ www.the-bridge-inn.co.uk

WINSLEY
Seven Stars
ST7960

Off B3108 bypass W of Bradford-on-Avon (pub just over Wiltshire border); BA15 2LQ

Handsome old stone pub with attractive bars, imaginative highly thought of food, good real ales and friendly staff; seats outside

On a quiet lane in a pretty village, this early 18th-c stone building has plenty of picnic-sets and tables and chairs under parasols on the terrace or on neat grassy surrounds with flowering borders looking across to the bowling green opposite. Inside, the low-beamed linked areas have stripped stone walls and light pastel paintwork, candlelight, farmhouse chairs and wooden tables on flagstones and carpeting and a couple of stone fireplaces – one with a sizeable hearth. Helpful managers and cheerful young staff serve Bath Ales Gem Bitter, Devilfish Bomb Shell (one of the landlords, Mr Metz, also founded and co-owns the Devilfish Brewery), Wadworths 6X and Yeovil Summerset on handpump and several wines by the glass; background music and board games.

Free house ~ Licensees Claire Spreadbury and Evan Metz ~ Real ale ~ Bar food (12-2(2.30 Sun), 6-8; not winter Sun evening) ~ Restaurant ~ (01225) 722204 ~ Children welcome ~ Dogs allowed in bar ~ Open 12-2.30(3 Sat), 6-10.30(11 Sat); 12-3.30, 6-10 Sun; closed winter Sun evening ~ www.sevenstarswinsley.co.uk

DOG FRIENDLY INNS, HOTELS AND B&Bs

BRADFORD-ON-AVON
Woolley Grange
ST8361

Woolley Green, Bradford-on-Avon, Wiltshire BA15 1TX (01225) 864705
www.woolleygrangehotel.co.uk

£140; 25 very individual rms of character. Civilised Jacobean manor house with a relaxed, informal atmosphere, lovely flowers, log fires and antiques in comfortable, panelled sitting rooms, plenty of original features, genuinely friendly, helpful staff, interesting modern food using home-grown and other local produce in the restaurant, and marvellous breakfasts and light lunches in the Orangery; outdoor swimming pool, and a spa with treatment, steam and sauna rooms and indoor swimming pool; dogs welcome away from restaurant; bed, bowl and biscuits; £10

CASTLE COMBE
Manor House
ST8477

Castle Combe, Chippenham, Wiltshire SN14 7HR (01249) 782206 www.manorhouse.co.uk

£205; 48 sumptuous rms, some in mews cottages just 50m from the house. 14th-c manor house in 360 acres of countryside with an italian garden and parkland, an 18-hole golf course (with its own club house and restaurant), croquet and fishing; panelling, antiques, log fires and fresh flowers, a warm, friendly atmosphere, the convivial Clubhouse bar where the extensive breakfasts, light lunches and afternoon teas are taken, exceptional food in the smart Bybrook restaurant, and courteous, helpful staff; dogs in cottage bedrooms; bowl and bed; £25

CHICKSGROVE

ST9730

Compasses

Lower Chicksgrove, Tisbury, Salisbury, Wiltshire SP3 6NB (01722) 714318
www.thecompassesinn.com

£90; 4 attractive rms. Lovely thatched 14th-c inn with plenty of surrounding country walks and an unchanging bar of real character; old bottles and jugs hang from beams, there are farm tools and traps on the partly-stripped stone walls, high-backed wooden settles forming snug booths around tables on the mainly flagstoned floor, a log fire, real ales and interesting food (and smashing breakfasts) served by helpful, friendly young staff; self-catering cottage also; dogs anywhere and in bedrooms, but not on the beds

CHITTOE

ST9566

Glebe House

Chittoe, Chippenham, Wiltshire SN15 2EL (01380) 850864 www.glebehouse-chittoe.co.uk

£80; 3 pretty rms. Peacefully set former chapel with fine views and seats on terraces and in pretty garden; welcoming owners (tea and home-made cake on arrival), antiques and pictures in a comfortable drawing room, and carefully cooked breakfasts and evening meals in the candlelit dining room using home-grown and local produce; dogs in bedrooms by arrangement; £5

Bru and Waffle Braithwaite

CRICKLADE

SU1093

Red Lion

74 High Street, Cricklade, Swindon, Wiltshire SN6 6DD (01793) 750776
www.theredlioncricklade.co.uk

£85; 5 newly decorated, attractive rms. Well run 16th-c inn with nearby walks along the Thames Path; all sorts of bric-a-brac and old street signs on the stone walls of the bar, an open fire, traditional seats and tables on red carpet, ten real ales, 63 interesting bottled beers, farm cider and their own ginger beer; the more formal dining rooms, with pale wooden farmhouse and chairs and a woodburning stove, serve the popular, imaginative food (they make their own butter, bread, ice-creams, chutneys and jellies); dogs in two bedrooms and bar

CRUDWELL

ST9592

The Rectory

Crudwell, Malmesbury, Wiltshire SN16 9EP (01666) 577194 www.therectoryhotel.com

£125; 12 light and airy rms. Elegant, welcoming country-house hotel, formerly the rectory to the Saxon church next door, in 3 acres of lovely landscaped Victorian gardens with an outdoor swimming pool; a comfortable sitting room and bar, open fires and antiques, interesting and enjoyable food in the panelled restaurant, a relaxed atmosphere, and unpretentious service; their sister establishment, the Potting Shed pub across the road, is excellent; lots of nearby footpaths and bridleways; dogs in bedrooms but not restaurant; welcome box (treats, blanket, bowl)

HINDON

ST9132

Lamb

High Street, Hindon, Salisbury, Wiltshire SP3 6DP (01747) 820573
www.boisdale.co.uk/lamb-at-hindon

£95; 19 refurbished rms. Smart, attractive old hotel with a long, roomy log-fire bar, two flagstoned lower sections with a very long polished table, pews and settles, bold red walls with pictures and prints, a comfortable sitting room, a good choice of drinks including 100 malt whiskies, polite service from smartly dressed staff, enjoyable bar and restaurant food, and good breakfasts; tables on the terrace and in the garden across the road; boules; dogs in two bedrooms and in bar; £10

LACOCK

ST9168

At the Sign of the Angel

Church Street, Lacock, Chippenham, Wiltshire SN15 2LB (01249) 730230
www.lacock.co.uk

£129; 6 charmingly old rooms with antiques. Fine 15th-c house in a lovely National Trust village, lots of character, heavy oak furniture, beams and big fireplaces, a restful oak-panelled lounge, good english cooking in three candlelit restaurants using their own and other local produce, and generous breakfasts with home-made bread and their own eggs; dogs in bedrooms only

LOWER CHUTE

SU3153

Hatchet

Lower Chute, Andover, Hampshire SP11 9DX (01264) 730229 www.thehatchetinn.com

£80; 7 cottagey rms. Neatly kept, 13th-c thatched country pub with a convivial landlord and a very low-beamed bar with a splendid 16th-c fireback in the huge fireplace (and a roaring winter log fire), a mix of captain's chairs and cushioned wheelbacks around oak tables, a peaceful local feel, real ales, seven farm ciders and wines by the glass; bar food is well liked and the breakfasts are hearty; resident jack russell, Maxwell; plenty of nearby footpaths; dogs in some bedrooms; bring own bedding; bowls can be provided; £10

MALMESBURY

ST9387

Old Bell

Abbey Row, Malmesbury, Wiltshire SN16 0BW (01666) 822344 www.oldbellhotel.com

£115; 33 attractive rms, some in coach house. With some claim to being one of England's oldest hotels and standing in the shadow of the Norman abbey, this fine wisteria-clad building has traditionally furnished rooms with open fires (one in an early 13th-c hooded stone fireplace), plenty of comfortable sofas and armchairs, helpful service, good, attractively presented food, afternoon teas and nice breakfasts, and seats in the garden; dogs welcome but not in restaurant; £10

MARLBOROUGH

SU1869

Lamb

5 The Parade, Marlborough, Wiltshire SN8 1NE (01672) 512668
www.thelambinnmarlborough.com

£80; 7 light and cottagey rms. Friendly former coaching inn, tucked away from the high street, with a good mix of customers in its bustling bar, lots of hop bines, straightforward pubby seats and tables, a two-way gas-effect log fire, real ales tapped from the cask, candles in bottles and maybe the easy-going bulldog, Ludo, poddling about; large helpings of popular food cooked by the landlady and hearty breakfasts; 5 mins to River Kennet walks and 5 mins drive to Savernake Forest; dogs anywhere in the pub and in bedrooms

NETTLETON

ST8378

Fosse Farmhouse Hotel

Nettleton, Chippenham, Wiltshire SN14 7NJ (01249) 782286 www.fossefarmhouse.com

£95; 3 pretty rms. Friendly, 18th-c Cotswold stone house filled with decorative french antique furniture and english chintzes; a comfortable drawing room, a homely dining room and good food cooked by the owner; seats in the garden; nearby walks; self-catering also; dogs in bedrooms; £10

PURTON   SU0987
Pear Tree
Church End, Purton, Swindon, Wiltshire SN5 4ED (01793) 772100
www.peartreepurton.co.uk

£119; 17 pretty rms. Impeccably run former vicarage with elegant day rooms, fresh flowers, a conservatory restaurant with creative modern english cooking using home-grown herbs, helpful, caring staff and 7 acres of grounds; dogs in bedrooms (not to be left unattended); welcome pack including bowl, chews and towels

TEFFONT EVIAS   ST9931
Howards House
Teffont Evias, Salisbury, Wiltshire SP3 5RJ (01722) 716392
www.howardshousehotel.co.uk

£190; 9 pretty, pastel coloured rms, some overlooking the grounds. Partly 17th-c house in 2 acres of pretty gardens with ancient box hedges, croquet and kitchen gardens; fresh flowers, beams and an open fire in the restful sitting room, delicious modern cooking, fine breakfasts and impeccable service; walks all round; dogs in bedrooms; £11

WARMINSTER   ST8944
Bishopstrow House
Bishopstrow, Warminster, Wiltshire BA12 9HH (01985) 212312 www.bishopstrow.co.uk

£140; 32 recently decorated rms. Charming ivy-clad Georgian house in 27 acres of grounds with an outdoor swimming pool, indoor and outdoor tennis courts and fishing on River Wylye; a very relaxed friendly atmosphere, two comfortable lounges (where afternoon tea is taken) with original features, chandeliers, log fires, and paintings, and delicious inventive food in the stylish main restaurant with more informal meals in the conservatory; spa with treatment, sauna and steam rooms, a gym, and an indoor swimming pool; walks in the grounds and nearby; dogs welcome away from restaurants; £10

WHITLEY   ST8866
Pear Tree
Top Lane, Whitley, Melksham, Wiltshire SN12 8QX (01225) 709131
www.wheelerspeartree.com

£95; 8 lovely rms. Attractive honey-coloured stone farmhouse with a charming pubby front bar, cushioned window seats, some stripped shutters, an open fire, simple furniture on flagstones, real ales, farm cider and wines by the glass; the big back formal restaurant has cartoons on the walls, some interesting stained glass windows, fresh flowers, candlelight and inventive food; plenty of seating in the carefully maintained gardens; dogs in bedrooms and bar; £10

Worcestershire

MAP 4

DOG FRIENDLY PUBS

BEWDLEY   SO7875
Little Pack Horse
High Street; no nearby parking – best to park in main car park, cross A4117 Cleobury
road and keep walking on down narrowing High Street; DY12 2DH

Friendly town pub tucked away in side street with a bustling
atmosphere, decent beer and tasty bar food

Always chatty and with helpful, friendly staff, this 450-year-old town pub is
tucked away in a historic street among other similar-looking houses. It's much
bigger than its unassuming exterior suggests and is nicely timbered inside with
reclaimed oak panelling and floorboards and has various items of memorabilia on
the walls and a warming woodburning stove. Alongside Bewdley Worcestershire
Way, they keep a couple of guests from brewers such as St Austells and Timothy
Taylors on handpump, a selection of bottled ciders and perries and just under two
dozen wines; background music and TV. An area outside has heaters. No parking.

Punch ~ Tenant Mark Payne ~ Real ale ~ Bar food (12-2(4 Sat), 6-9(9.30 Sat); 12-4, 5.30-8
Sun) ~ Restaurant ~ No credit cards ~ (01299) 403762 ~ Children welcome ~ Dogs allowed
in bar ~ Open 12-3, 6-11; 12-midnight Sat; 12-11 Sun; closed Mon lunchtime ~
www.littlepackhorse.co.uk

BIRLINGHAM   SO9343
Swan
Church Street; off A4104 S of Pershore, via B4080 Eckington Road, turn off at sign to
Birlingham with integral 'The Swan Inn' brown sign (not the 'Birlingham (village only)'
road), then left; WR10 3AQ

Thatched charmer offering interesting beers, enjoyable reasonably
priced food and good-sized country garden

A mass of hops hang from the beams in the black-beamed quarry-tiled
bar of this pretty black and white timbered cottage. Popular with chatty
locals and genuinely welcoming, it's comfortably old-fashioned with copper-
topped tables, darts, a woodburning stove in the big stone fireplace and a snug
inner carpeted area by the smallish counter. This serves Wye Valley Bitter and
three guests from brewers such as Butcombe, Malvern Hills and Woods and
three ciders. They also hold beer festivals in May and September; background
music, cribbage, dominoes and poker. The back dining conservatory is simple
but comfortable, with creepers scrambling overhead. Service is quick and polite.

Somebody here loves gardening, as the pub is prettily covered with roses, and the garden behind is beautifully kept. It's divided into two parts by shrubs, with a variety of tables and chairs under parasols; we liked the mini watering can cutlery holders – and the birdsong.

Free house ~ Licensees Imogen and Nicholas Carson ~ Real ale ~ Bar food (12-2.30, 6.30-8.30(not Sun evening)) ~ Restaurant ~ (01386) 750485 ~ Children welcome ~ Dogs allowed in bar ~ Open 12-3, 6.30-11(10.30 Sun) ~ www.theswaninn.co.uk

BRANSFORD   SO8052

Bear & Ragged Staff

Off A4103 SW of Worcester; Station Road; WR6 5JH

Cheerfully run dining pub with pleasant places to sit both inside and out; well liked food using some of their own vegetables

Welcoming and friendly, this nice country dining pub offers the same menu in the formal restaurant (with its proper tablecloths and linen napkins) and the more relaxed bar. Its interconnecting rooms give fine views of attractive rolling country (as do the pretty garden and terrace) and in winter there's a warming open fire; background music and darts. They carry a good range of wines, with about a dozen by the glass, lots of malt whiskies, quite a few brandies and liqueurs, Hobsons Twisted Spire and a guest such as Sharps Doom Bar on handpump; good disabled access and facilities.

Free house ~ Licensee Lynda Williams ~ Real ale ~ Bar food (12-2(2.30 Sun), 6.30-9) ~ Restaurant ~ (01886) 833399 ~ Children welcome ~ Dogs allowed in bar ~ Open 11.30-2, 6(6.30 Sat)-11; 12-3 Sun; closed Sun evening ~ www.bear.uk.com

BRETFORTON   SP0943

Fleece

B4035 E of Evesham: turn S off this road into village; pub is in central square by church; there's a sizeable car park at one side of the church; WR11 7JE

Marvellously unspoilt medieval pub owned by the National Trust

Before becoming a pub in 1848 this lovely old farmhouse was owned by the same family for nearly 500 years, and many of the furnishings, such as the great oak dresser that holds a priceless 48-piece set of Stuart pewter, are heirlooms passed down through the generations. Its almost museum-like little rooms are atmospherically dim, with massive beams, exposed timbers and marks scored on the worn and crazed flagstones to keep out demons. There are two fine grandfather clocks, ancient kitchen chairs, curved high-backed settles, a rocking chair and a rack of heavy pointed iron shafts (probably for spit roasting) in one of the huge inglenook fireplaces, and two more log fires. Plenty of oddities include a great cheese-press and set of cheese moulds, and a rare dough-proving table; a leaflet details the more bizarre items. Four or five real ales on handpump are from brewers such as Cannon Royall, Hook Norton, Purity, Uley and Woods, alongside two farm ciders (one made by the landlord), local apple juices, german wheat beer and fruit wines, and ten wines by the glass; darts. At the end of May, as part of the Vale of Evesham Asparagus Festival they hold an asparagus auction, and they host the village fête on August bank holiday Monday. The calendar of events also includes morris dancing, and the village silver band plays here regularly, too. The lawn, with its fruit trees around a beautifully restored thatched and timbered barn is a lovely place to sit, and there are more picnic-sets and a stone pump-trough in the front courtyard. They may want to keep your credit card if you run a tab outside. If you're visiting to enjoy the famous historic interior try and go mid-week as it can be very busy at weekends.

Free house ~ Licensee Nigel Smith ~ Real ale ~ Bar food (12-2, 7-9) ~ Restaurant ~ (01386) 831173 ~ Children welcome ~ Dogs allowed in bar ~ Open 11-11; 11-3, 6-11 Mon, Tues in winter ~ Bedrooms: /£97.50S ~ www.thefleeceinn.co.uk

HANLEY CASTLE   SO8342
Three Kings
Church End, off B4211 N of Upton upon Severn; WR8 0BL

Timeless hospitable gem with five real ales and simple snacks

You can take an enjoyable step back in time at this unspoilt country local that's been run by the same characterful family for over a hundred years. It's the cheerful welcome, rather than the housekeeping, that counts in the eyes of those readers who like it, so we've certainly no quibbles with their happy relaxed approach. A homely little tiled-floor tap room on the right is separated from the entrance corridor by the monumental built-in settle that faces its equally vast inglenook fireplace. A hatch serves very well kept Butcombe Bitter, Hobsons and three guests on handpump from smaller brewers such as Church End and St Georges, with around 75 malt whiskies and farm cider. On the left, another room has darts, dominoes, cribbage and other board games. A separate entrance leads to a timbered lounge with another inglenook fireplace and a neatly blacked kitchen range, little leatherette armchairs and spindleback chairs around its tables, and another antique winged and high-backed settle. Bow windows in the three main rooms and old-fashioned wood-and-iron seats on the front terrace look across to the great cedar that shades the tiny green.

Free house ~ Licensee Sue Roberts ~ Real ale ~ Bar food (12-2; not weekends or evenings) ~ No credit cards ~ (01684) 592686 ~ Children welcome ~ Dogs allowed in bar ~ Jam sessions Fri lunchtime, Sun evening ~ Open 12-3, 7-11

HOLY CROSS   SO9278
Bell & Cross
4 miles from M5 junction 4: A491 towards Stourbridge, then follow Clent signpost off on left; DY9 9QL

Super well liked food, staff with a can-do attitude, delightful old interior and pretty garden

Successful as a dining pub yet still extremely welcoming if you're just popping in for a drink, this charmingly well kept place is run with meticulous attention to every detail to ensure that you have a most enjoyable visit. It has an unspoilt early 19th-c layout with five beautifully decorated little rooms and a kitchen opening off a central corridor with a black-and-white tiled floor. Rooms offer a choice of carpet, bare boards, lino or nice old quarry tiles, a variety of mood, from snug and chatty to bright and airy, and individual décor in each: theatrical engravings on red walls, nice sporting prints on pale green walls, and racing and gundog pictures above a black panelled dado. Most of them have coal fires and two have small serving bars, with Enville, Kinver Edge, Wye Valley6 and a guest such as Timothy Taylors Landlord on handpump, around 50 wines (with 14 by the glass), organic soft drinks and a range of coffees; daily papers; background music. A lovely garden has a spacious lawn, and the terrace offers pleasant views.

Enterprise ~ Tenants Roger and Jo Narbett ~ Real ale ~ Bar food (12-2(7 Sun), 6.30-9; not Sun evening) ~ (01562) 730319 ~ Children welcome ~ Dogs allowed in bar ~ Open 12-3, 6-11; 12-10.30 Sun ~ www.bellandcrossclent.co.uk

MALVERN   SO7845

Nags Head

Bottom end of Bank Street, steep turn down off A449; WR14 2JG

Remarkable range of real ales, delightfully eclectic layout and décor, tasty lunchtime bar food and warmly welcoming atmosphere

Few pubs can have as many real ales as this popular little place. If you struggle to choose from the range of 14, the cheery staff will happily offer you a taster. House beers are Banks's, Bathams, St Georges Charger, Friar Tuck and Dragons Blood, Sharps Doom Bar, Woods Shropshire Lad and Wychwood Hobgoblin, and they've seven changing guests – last year they got through over 500. They also keep two farm ciders, over two dozen malt whiskies and ten gins. A series of snug individually decorated rooms, with one or two steps between and two open fires, have an easy-going chatty atmosphere. Each is characterfully filled with all sorts of chairs including leather armchairs, pews sometimes arranged as booths, a mix of tables with sturdy ones stained different colours, bare boards here, flagstones there, carpet elsewhere, and plenty of interesting pictures and homely touches such as house plants, shelves of well thumbed books and broadsheet newspapers, board games. There are picnic-sets and rustic tables and benches on the front terrace (with heaters and umbrellas) and in the garden.

Free house ~ Licensees Clare Keane and Alex Whistance ~ Real ale ~ Bar food (12-2(2.30 Sun), 6.30(7 Sun)-8.30) ~ Restaurant ~ (01684) 574373 ~ Children welcome ~ Dogs allowed in bar ~ Open 11-11.15(11.30 Fri, Sat); 12-11 Sun ~ www.nagsheadmalvern.co.uk

NEWLAND   SO7948

Swan

Worcester Road (set well back from A449 just NW of Malvern); WR13 5AY

Popular creeper-clad pub with straightforward food, five real ales and big garden

The dimly lit dark-beamed bar at this attractive old place is quite traditional, with a forest canopy of hops, whisky-water jugs, beakers and tankards. Several of the comfortable and clearly individually chosen seats are worth a close look for their carving, and the wall tapestries are interesting. The carved counter has well kept St Georges Dragons Blood, Friar Tuck and Sharps Doom Bar, Wychwood Hobgoblin and a guest such as Butcombe Best on handpump. On the right is a broadly similar red-carpeted dining room, and beyond it, in complete contrast, an ultra-modern glass cube of a garden room; background music, bar billiards and board games. The garden itself is as individual as the pub, with a cluster of huge casks topped with flowers, even a piano doing flower-tub duty, and a set of stocks on the pretty front terrace.

Free house ~ Licensee Nick Taylor ~ Real ale ~ Bar food (12-2.30, 6.30-9; 12-3, 7-9 Sun) ~ Restaurant ~ (01886) 832224 ~ Children welcome ~ Dogs allowed in bar ~ Open 12-11

DOG FRIENDLY INNS, HOTELS AND B&Bs

AB LENCH   SP0151
Manor Farm House
Ab Lench, Evesham, Worcestershire WR11 4UP (01386) 462226
www.wolseylodges.com/Lodge/view.aspx?LodgeID=227

£40; 2 rms. Comfortable 250-year-old house in a rural spot with a lovely fenced
half-acre garden; two reception rooms (one has beams and a huge inglenook
fireplace), a study with TV, interesting objects collected from around the world
by the friendly owners and nice breakfasts; three little resident dogs; two resident
maltese dogs and one cat; plenty of surrounding fields for walks; dogs welcome
anywhere; treats and water bowl

BROADWAY   SP0937
Broadway Hotel
The Green, Broadway, Worcestershire WR12 7AA (01386) 852401
www.cotswold-inns-hotels.co.uk/property/the_broadway_hotel

£160; 19 beautifully furnished rms. Lovely 15th-c half-timbered building, once
a monastic guest house, with a galleried and timbered bar of real character, a
cosy sitting room with an inglenook fireplace (morning coffee and afternoon teas
are served here), an elegant, light brasserie restaurant with its contemporary
furnishings and imaginative food, attentive staff and seats outside on the terrace;
plenty of nearby walks; dogs welcome away from brasserie; must be on lead; £10

BROADWAY   SP0937
Crown & Trumpet
14 Church Street, Broadway, Worcestershire WR12 7AE (01386) 853202
www.cotswoldholidays.co.uk

£70; 4 cosy rms. Unreconstructed honest local with a warm welcome for all; a
bustling beamed and timbered bar with a down-to-earth feel, antique dark high-
backed settles, large solid tables, a blazing log fire, four real ales alongside farm
cider, wines by the glass and winter hot toddies and mulled wine; straightforward
bar food, old-fashioned pub games and seats on a raised front terrace; dogs in one
bedroom and bar

BROADWAY   SP0937
Lygon Arms
High Street, Broadway, Worcestershire WR12 7DU (01386) 852255
www.pumahotels.co.uk/hotels/central-england/barcelo-the-lygon-arms-hotel-cotswolds

£173; 77 rms, many with period features and some more modern, including 7
suites. Handsome hotel where Oliver Cromwell and King Charles I once stayed
with interesting beamed rooms, timber and flagstone floors, oak panelling,
antiques and log fires; a well stocked, cosy bar, a brasserie and a restaurant (in
the Great Hall with its minstrels' gallery and heraldic frieze) serving light lunches
and imaginative evening meals, excellent service and seats in the charming
garden; spa with treatment, sauna and steam rooms, a heated indoor pool and

gym; croquet, tennis and archery in the grounds; dogs in bedrooms and some public areas; £15

EVESHAM   SP0443
Evesham Hotel

Coopers Lane, Off Waterside, Evesham, Worcestershire WR11 1DA (01386) 765566
www.eveshamhotel.com

£129; 40 individually furnished rms – many are themed. Small, friendly hotel with eccentric touches and run with a sense of fun; two lounges, a well stocked bar, a dining room serving good breakfasts and enjoyable, interesting lunches and evening meals, and caring staff; indoor swimming pool and 2.5 acres of grounds – croquet and putting; dogs can walk in the garden or along the nearby River Avon; dogs in bedrooms and reception

GREAT MALVERN   SO7647
Cowleigh Park Farm

Cowleigh Park, Cradley, Malvern, Worcestershire WR13 5HJ (01684) 566750
www.cowleighparkfarm.co.uk

£70; 3 rms. Charming black and white timbered 17th-c farmhouse in an acre of grounds surrounded by lovely countryside – it's on the Worcestershire Way; carefully restored and furnished with beams and an inglenook fireplace in the sitting room, and serving good breakfasts with home-made bread and preserves; resident collie; self-catering also; dogs welcome; £3

HIMBLETON   SO9459
Phepson Farm

Phepson, Droitwich, Worcestershire WR9 7JZ (01905) 391205 www.phepsonfarm.co.uk

£75; 6 attractive rms, 4 in renovated farm buildings. Relaxed and friendly 17th-c farmhouse on a 50-acre sheep farm with a sizeable fishing lake and walks both on the farm and along the nearby Wychavon Way; a comfortable guests' lounge and very good breakfasts using their own conserves in a separate dining room; self-catering also; resident dogs and cats; dogs in some bedrooms (not to be left unattended)

KEMPSEY   SO8548
Walter de Cantelupe

34 Main Road, Kempsey, Worcester, Worcestershire WR5 3NA (01905) 820572
www.walterdecantelupe.co.uk

£65; 3 rms. Traditional inn with a friendly landlord, a carpeted bar with beams and an inglenook fireplace, a pleasant mix of furniture, four real ales on handpump plus summer cider, enjoyable food and seats in the walled garden; dogs in bedrooms and bar; £5

KNIGHTWICK

SO7355

Talbot

Bromyard Road, Knightwick, Worcester, Worcestershire WR6 5PH (01886) 821235
www.the-talbot.co.uk

£100; 11 good rms. Rambling country hotel with a heavily beamed and extended traditional lounge bar, a winter log fire, a variety of seats from small carved or leatherette armchairs to winged settles by the windows and a vast stove in a big central stone hearth; their own-brewed Teme Valley ales, farm cider and a number of malt whiskies, and a sedate dining room popular for the inventive food (using some of their own vegetables, home-reared pigs and home-made bread, pickles and jam); they hold a farmers' market here every second Sunday; there are tables and seats by the River Teme and lots of fantastic nearby walks; dogs anywhere except restaurant; beds, blankets, food, bowls (on request); £10

MALVERN WELLS

SO7742

Cottage in the Wood

Holy Well Road, Malvern, Worcestershire WR14 4LG (01684) 575859
www.cottageinthewood.co.uk

£198; 31 pretty rms, some in separate nearby cottages. Family-run Georgian dower house with quite splendid views across the Severn Valley and marvellous walks from the grounds; antiques, log fires, and comfortable seats in the public rooms, modern english cooking and an extensive wine list in the attractive restaurant; dogs in ground floor bedrooms; bedding, bowl and biscuits; £9

Coco; owner David Jackman

Yorkshire

DOG FRIENDLY PUBS

ADDINGHAM   SE0749
Fleece
Main Street (B6160, off A65); LS29 0LY

Enterprising new management with strong sense of style; good food cooked by the landlord and his team, using local produce

The smart bar on the right of this creeper-covered stone-built inn has a cool décor of dark flagstones, polished floorboards, crisp cream paintwork and some wallpaper based on antique fish prints above a charcoal-grey high dado. A pair of grey plaid tub armchairs stand by a great arched stone fireplace, and down a few steps is the civilised dining room (occasionally given over to their cookery classes). The interesting black-beamed village bar on the left has a good log fire in its high-manteled fireplace, comfortably worn easy chairs as well as well cushioned wall benches and window seats, and some most unusual substantial tables on its broad floorboards. Nicely framed local photographs include a series devoted to former landlord 'Heapy', hero survivor of a 1944 torpedoing. A massive choice of wines by the glass includes champagnes and four rosés; Copper Dragon Golden Pippin, Greene King Old Speckled Hen, Ilkley Mary Jane, Saltaire Blonde and Timothy Taylors Landlord on handpump. The flagstoned front terrace has neat tables under giant parasols, and a further dining terrace looks out over the garden. They have a cookery school and a deli next door.

Punch ~ Lease Craig Minto ~ Real ale ~ Bar food (12-2.15, 5-9; 12-8 Sun) ~ Restaurant ~ (01943) 830491 ~ Children welcome ~ Dogs allowed in bar ~ Open 12-11(midnight weekends) ~ fleeceinnaddingham.co.uk

BLAKEY RIDGE   SE6799
Lion
From A171 Guisborough–Whitby follow Castleton, Hutton le Hole signposts; from A170 Kirkby Moorside–Pickering follow Keldholm, Hutton le Hole, Castleton signposts; OS Sheet 100 map reference 679996; YO62 7LQ

Extended pub in fine scenery and open all day; popular food; bedrooms

Situated at the highest point of the North York Moors National Park (1,325 feet from sea level), this extended pub always has a good crowd of customers, despite being so remote. The views over the valleys of Rosedale and Farndale are breathtaking and there are also lots of surrounding hikes; the Coast to Coast path is nearby. The low-beamed and rambling bars have warm open fires, a few big high-backed rustic settles around cast-iron-framed tables, lots of small dining chairs, a nice leather sofa, and stone walls hung with some old engravings and photographs of the pub under snow (it can easily get cut off in winter; 40 days is the record so far). A fine choice of beers might include Black Sheep Best, Copper Dragon Golden Pippin, Greene King Old Speckled Hen, Theakstons Best and Old Peculier, and Thwaites Wainwright on handpump; background music and games machine. If you're thinking of staying, you must book well in advance. This is a regular stop-off for coach parties.

Free house ~ Licensees Barry, Diana, Paul and David Crossland ~ Real ale ~ Bar food (12-10) ~ Restaurant ~ (01751) 417320 ~ Children welcome ~ Dogs allowed in bar ~ Open 10am-11pm(midnight Sat) ~ Bedrooms: £23(£44.50B)/£78B ~ www.lionblakey.co.uk

BROUGHTON   SD9450
Bull
A59; BD23 3AE

Handsome, carefully refurbished inn making good use of pale oak and contemporary paintwork, good choice of drinks and enjoyable bar food

Overlooking the grounds of Broughton Hall, this handsome stone inn is now under the Ribble Valley Inn umbrella. The various carefully-furnished rooms have lots of pale oak, handsome flagstones, exposed stone walls, built-in wall seats and a mix of dining chairs around polished tables, contemporary paintwork hung with photographs of local suppliers and open log fires. Bowland Sawley Tempted, Copper Dragon Scotts 1816, Dark Horse Hetton Pale Ale, and Moorhouses Pride of Pendle on handpump, several malt whiskies and around a dozen wines (including champagne) by the glass. Outside, there are solid benches and tables on the attractive terrace; you can walk through the Hall Estate's 3,000 acres of beautiful countryside and parkland.

Ribble Valley Inns ~ Manager Leanne Richardson ~ Real ale ~ Bar food (12-2, 5.30-8.30(9 Fri, Sat); 12-8 Sun) ~ (01756) 792065 ~ Children welcome ~ Dogs allowed in bar ~ Open 12-11(10.30 Sun); closed Mon ~ www.thebullatbroughton.com

HALIFAX   SE1027
Shibden Mill
Off A58 into Kell Lane at Stump Cross Inn, near A6036 junction; keep on, pub signposted from Kell Lane on left; HX3 7UL

Tucked-away 300-year-old mill with cosy rambling bar, four real ales and inventive, highly thought of bar food; comfortable bedrooms

Tucked away at the bottom of a peaceful wooded valley and full of nooks and crannies, this 17th-c restored mill has the feel of a hidden treasure. Offering excellent food and friendly service and surrounded by stunning countryside, there's a happy mix of both locals and visitors. The rambling bar has a bustling atmosphere, cosy side areas with banquettes heaped with cushions and rugs, well spaced attractive old tables and chairs, and the candles in elegant iron holders give a feeling of real intimacy; also, old hunting prints, country landscapes and so forth, and a couple of big log fires. Cross Bay Nightfall, Little Valley Withens IPA, Moorhouses Premier Bitter and a guest beer on handpump and 18 wines by the glass from a wide list. There's also an upstairs restaurant; background music and TV. Outside on the attractive heated terrace, there are plenty of seats and tables, and the building is prettily floodlit at night. The bedrooms are well equipped and individually decorated.

Free house ~ Licensee Glen Pearson ~ Real ale ~ Bar food (12-2(2.30 Fri, Sat), 6-9.30; 12-7.30 Sun) ~ Restaurant ~ (01422) 365840 ~ Children welcome ~ Dogs allowed in bar ~ Open 12-2.30, 5.30-11; 12-11(10.30 Sun) Sat ~ Bedrooms: £85B/£105B ~ www.shibdenmillinn.com

HEATH
SE3520

Kings Arms

Village signposted from A655 Wakefield–Normanton – or, more directly, turn off to the left opposite Horse & Groom; WF1 5SL

Old-fashioned gas-lit pub in interesting location with dark-panelled original bar, up to 11 real ales and well liked bar food; seats outside

In a lovely spot opposite the village green and the 19th-c stone merchants' houses surrounding it, this remains an old-fashioned and unspoilt pub with a lot of genuine character. The original bar has gas lighting giving it a cosy feel, a fire burning in the old black range (with a long row of smoothing irons on the mantelpiece), plain elm stools, oak settles built into the walls, and dark panelling. A more comfortable extension has carefully preserved the original style, down to good wood-pegged oak panelling (two embossed with royal arms) and a high shelf of plates; there are also two other small flagstoned rooms and a conservatory that opens on to the garden. Ossett Silver King, Yorkshire Blonde and a beer named for the pub from Ossett, as well as Fuller's London Pride and four guest beers on handpump. There are some sunny benches facing the green and picnic-sets on a side lawn and in the nice walled garden.

Ossett ~ Manager Angela Cromack ~ Real ale ~ Bar food (12-2, 5-9; 12-8.45 Fri, Sat; 12-5 Sun; not Sun evening) ~ Restaurant ~ (01924) 377527 ~ Children welcome ~ Dogs allowed in bar ~ Open 12-11(midnight Fri, Sat) ~ www.thekingsarmsheath.co.uk

KIRKBY FLEETHAM
SE2894

Black Horse

Village signposted off A1 S of Catterick; Lumley Lane; DL7 0SH

Attractively reworked country inn with good enterprising food, cheerful atmosphere and stylish comfortable bedrooms

The long softly lit beamed and flagstoned bar on the right has some cosy little settles and high-backed dining chairs by the log fire at one end (blazing even for breakfast), and wrought-iron chairs a good deal more comfortable than they look the other. They have a good choice of wines by the glass, and well kept Black Sheep Best and All Creatures, Pennine Real Blonde and a beer brewed for them by Moorhouses on handpump; plenty of local regulars congregate at the counter's leather bar stools. The dining room on the right is light and open, with big bow windows each side, and a casual contemporary look – loose-covered dining chairs or pastel garden settles with scatter cushions around tables painted pale green. There's also a dark and intimate private dining room. Service is friendly and very attentive; Abba-era background music. Teak tables on a flagstoned side terrace have one with a couple of toffs dressed for a country outing – you have to look twice to see that they're models. A neat sheltered back lawn has a guinea pig hutch. Breakfasts are excellent; they don't start till 9, but if you can't wait the bedrooms have good continental breakfast hampers.

Free house ~ Licensee Philip Barker ~ Real ale ~ Bar food (12-2.30, 5-9(9.30 Fri, Sat); 12-7 Sun; not Sun evening) ~ Restaurant ~ (01609) 749011 ~ Children welcome ~ Dogs allowed in bar ~ Open 12-11.30(10.30 Sun) ~ Bedrooms: /£100S ~ www.blackhorsekirkbyfleetham.com

LEDSHAM   SE4529

Chequers

1.5 miles from A1(M) junction 42: follow Leeds signs, then Ledsham signposted; Claypit Lane; LS25 5LP

Friendly village pub, handy for the A1, with hands-on landlord, log fires in several beamed rooms, real ales and interesting, very popular food; pretty back terrace

Run by a friendly landlord and his helpful staff, this 16th-c stone inn is much enjoyed by both locals and visitors – the pub is very handy for the A1. There are several small, individually-decorated rooms with low beams, lots of cosy alcoves, Toby jugs and all sorts of knick-knacks on the walls and ceilings, and log fires. From the old-fashioned little central panelled-in servery they offer beers from breweries such as Brown Cow, John Smiths, Theakstons and Timothy Taylors, and a dozen wines by the glass. A lovely sheltered two-level terrace behind the house has plenty of tables among roses and the hanging baskets and flowers are very pretty. RSPB Fairburn Ings reserve is close by and the ancient village church is worth a visit.

Free house ~ Licensee Chris Wraith ~ Real ale ~ Bar food (12-9 Mon-Sat; not Sun) ~ Restaurant ~ (01977) 683135 ~ Children until 8pm ~ Dogs allowed in bar ~ Open 11-11; closed Sun ~ www.thechequersinn.f9.co.uk

LEVISHAM   SE8390

Horseshoe

Off A169 N of Pickering; YO18 7NL

Friendly village pub run by two brothers, neat rooms, real ales, very good food cooked by one of the landlords, and seats on the village green; bedrooms

In a pretty village on the North York Moors National Park, this 19th-c pub is a perfect place to relax after enjoying one of the lovely surrounding walks in gorgeous scenery. It' s a busy but friendly, traditional pub, run by two jovial brothers and our readers like staying in the smart, comfortable bedrooms – some with fine views. The bars have beams, smart blue banquettes, wheelback and captain's chairs around a variety of tables on the polished wooden floors, vibrant landscapes by a local artist on the walls, and a log fire in the stone fireplace; an adjoining snug has a woodburning stove, comfortable leather sofas and old photographs of the pub and the village. Black Sheep Best and a couple of guests like Cropton Endeavour Ale and Yorkshire Moors Bitter on handpump, home-made elderflower cordial, 20 malt whiskies and a farm cider; board games and background music. There are seats on the attractive green, with more in the back garden.

Free house ~ Licensees Toby and Charles Wood ~ Real ale ~ Bar food (12-2, 6-8.30) ~ (01751) 460240 ~ Children welcome but bedrooms not ideal for them ~ Dogs allowed in bar ~ Open 11am-11pm(10.30 Sun) ~ Bedrooms: £40/£80S ~ www.horseshoelevisham.co.uk

LOW CATTON
Gold Cup

SE7053

Village signposted with High Catton off A166 in Stamford Bridge or A1079 at Kexby Bridge; YO41 1EA

Pleasant pub with attractive bars, real ales, decent dependable food, seats in garden and ponies in paddock

This is a proper village pub with chatty locals, a helpful and informative landlord, and spic and span bars – and as it's open all day at weekends (and serves food all day then, too) it' s just the place to head for after a walk. These neat, beamed bars have a country feel with coach lights on the rustic-looking walls, smart tables and chairs on the stripped wooden floors, an open fire at one end opposite the woodburning stove, and quite a few pictures. The restaurant has solid wooden pews and tables (said to be made from a single oak tree) and pleasant views of the surrounding fields. John Smiths and Theakstons Black Bull on handpump; background music and pool. The garden has a grassed area for children and the back paddock houses Cinderella and Polly the ponies. The pub has fishing rights on the adjoining River Derwent.

Free house ~ Licensees Pat and Ray Hales ~ Real ale ~ Bar food (12-2, 6-9; all day weekends; not Mon lunchtime) ~ Restaurant ~ (01759) 371354 ~ Children welcome ~ Dogs allowed in bar ~ Open 12-2.30, 6-11; 12-11(10.30 Sun) Sat; closed Mon lunchtime ~ www.goldcuplowcatton.com

MARTON CUM GRAFTON
Punch Bowl

SE4263

Signed off A1 3 miles N of A59; YO51 9QY

Refurbished 16th-c inn in lovely village, with beams and standing timbers, character bar and dining rooms, real ales, interesting food using seasonal local produce and seats outside

This handsome inn, dating back to the 16th c, has re-opened after a recent refurbishment and is under new management. It's been carefully done without stripping away the character and the atmosphere throughout is relaxed and easy-going. The main bar is beamed and timbered with a built-in window seat at one end, lots of red leather-topped stools, cushioned settles and church chairs around pubby tables on the flagstones or bare floorboards, Black Sheep Best and Timothy Taylors Landlord on handpump and lots of wines by the glass served by friendly staff. Open doorways from here lead to five separate dining areas, each with an open fire, heavy beams, red walls covered with photographs of vintage car races and racing drivers (a previous owner was obsessed with vintage cars and the new owners have carried on with the theme), sporting cartoons and old photographs of the pub and village, and an attractive mix of cushioned wall seats and wooden or high-backed red dining chairs around antique tables on the oak flooring. Up a swirling staircase is a coffee loft and a private dining room. There are seats and tables on the back courtyard where they hold summer barbecues. The pub is part of Provenance Inns.

Free house ~ Licensee Michael Ibbotson ~ Real ale ~ Bar food (12-2.30(3 Sun), 5.30-9.30(8.30 Sun)) ~ Restaurant ~ (01423) 322519 ~ Children welcome ~ Dogs allowed in bar ~ Open 12-11 ~ www.thepunchbowlmartoncumgrafton.com

ROBIN HOOD'S BAY

NZ9505

Laurel

Bay Bank; village signed off A171 S of Whitby; YO22 4SE

Charming little pub in unspoilt fishing village, neat friendly bar and real ales; no food

Quite unchanging and unspoilt, this little local has a charming landlord and is at the heart of one of the prettiest and most unspoilt fishing villages on the north-east coast. The beamed and welcoming main bar is neatly kept and decorated with old local photographs, Victorian prints and brasses, and lager bottles from all over the world. There's an open fire and Adnams Best and Theakstons Best and Old Peculier on handpump; darts, board games and background music. In summer, the hanging baskets and window boxes are lovely. They have a self-contained apartment for two people.

Free house ~ Licensee Brian Catling ~ Real ale ~ No credit cards ~ (01947) 880400 ~ Children in snug bar only ~ Dogs allowed in bar ~ Open 2-11 Mon-Thurs; 12-11 Fri-Sun

ROECLIFFE

SE3765

Crown

Off A168 just W of Boroughbridge; handy for A1(M) junction 48; YO51 9LY

Smartly updated and attractively placed pub with a civilised bar, excellent enterprising food and a fine choice of drinks; lovely bedrooms

Under the hard-working and friendly Mainey family, this deservedly popular and attractive pub goes from strength to strength, and there's always a wide mix of both locals and visitors keen to enjoy a chat and a drink, a top class meal or an overnight stay in the cosy, country-style bedrooms. Of course much emphasis is on the food but they do keep Ilkley Gold and Mary Jane, Theakstons Best and Timothy Taylors Landlord on handpump, a couple of belgian beers on tap, 20 wines by the glass, and fruit ciders. The bar has a contemporary colour scheme of dark reds and near-whites with pleasant prints carefully grouped and lit; one area has chunky pine tables on flagstones and another part, with a log fire, has dark tables on plaid carpet. For meals, you have a choice between a small candlelit olive-green bistro with nice tables, a long-case clock and one or two paintings, and a more formal restaurant. The village green is opposite.

Free house ~ Licensee Karl Mainey ~ Real ale ~ Bar food (12-2.30, 6-9.15; 12-7 Sun) ~ Restaurant ~ (01423) 322300 ~ Children welcome ~ Dogs allowed in bar ~ Open 12-3, 5-12; 12-9 Sun ~ Bedrooms: £82B/£97B ~ www.crowninnroecliffe.com

WASS

SE5579

Wombwell Arms

Back road W of Ampleforth; or follow brown tourist-attraction sign for Byland Abbey off A170 Thirsk–Helmsley; YO61 4BE

Consistently enjoyable village pub with a friendly atmosphere, good mix of locals and visitors, interesting bar food (using the best local produce) and real ales; bedrooms

'Everything a pub should be,' says one of our readers – and many agree with him. It's a bustling 17th-c place and handy for Byland Abbey so it does get busy at lunchtimes in particular. The two bars are neatly-kept with plenty of simple character, pine farmhouse chairs and tables, some exposed stone walls, and log fires; the walls of the Poacher's Bar (in which dogs are welcome) are hung with brewery memorabilia. From the panelled bar counter, the friendly staff serve Theakstons Best, Timothy Taylors Landlord and a guest like Rudgate Viking on handpump, nine wines by the glass (quite a few from Mrs Walker's South Africa) and several malt whiskies; darts. The two restaurants are incorporated into a former granary and there are seats outside.

Free house ~ Licensees Ian and Eunice Walker ~ Real ale ~ Bar food (12-2(2.30 Sat), 6.30-9(9.30 Fri, Sat); 12-3, 6-8 Sun) ~ Restaurant ~ (01347) 868280 ~ Children welcome ~ Dogs allowed in bar ~ Folk music second Thurs of month ~ Open 12-3, 6-11; 12-11 Sat; 12-10.30 Sun; 12-4 winter Sun in winter; closed winter Sun evening, Mon ~ Bedrooms: £59S/£79S ~ www.wombwellarms.co.uk

WIDDOP   SD9531
Pack Horse

The Ridge; from A646 on W side of Hebden Bridge, turn off at Heptonstall signpost (as it's a sharp turn, coming out of Hebden Bridge road signs direct you around a turning circle), then follow Slack and Widdop signposts; can also be reached from Nelson and Colne, on high, pretty road; OS Sheet 103 map reference 952317; HX7 7AT

Friendly pub high up on the moors and liked by walkers for generous, tasty honest food, five real ales and lots of malt whiskies; bedrooms

Perfect for walkers on the Pennine Way or horse riders on the Mary Townley Loop, this isolated, traditional inn is popular with our readers. The bar has welcoming winter fires, window seats cut into the partly-panelled stripped-stone walls that take in the beautiful moorland views, sturdy furnishings and horsey mementoes. Black Sheep Best, Copper Dragon Golden Pippin, Thwaites Bitter and a guest like Cottage Norman Conquest on handpump, around 130 single malt whiskies and some Irish ones as well, and a dozen wines by the glass. The friendly golden retrievers are called Padge and Purdey and the alsatian Holly. There are seats outside in the cobblestone beer garden, and pretty summer hanging baskets. As well as the comfortable bedrooms (the breakfasts are very good), they also offer a smart self-catering apartment.

Free house ~ Licensee Andrew Hollinrake ~ Real ale ~ Bar food (12-2, 7-9; 12-8 Sun; not Mon or lunchtimes as below) ~ (01422) 842803 ~ Children in eating area of bar ~ Dogs allowed in bar ~ Open 12-3, 7-11; 12-11 Sun; closed Mon and lunchtimes Tues-Sat Oct-Easter ~ Bedrooms: £43S/£48S(£69B) ~ www.thepackhorse.org)

DOG FRIENDLY INNS, HOTELS AND B&Bs

AUSTWICK   SD7668
Traddock

Austwick, Settle, Yorkshire LA2 8BY (01524) 251224 www.thetraddock.co.uk

£115; 12 individually decorated rms, many with views. Surrounded by the Yorkshire Dales National Park and fantastic walks, this is a warmly friendly and homely country house; two warm and comfortable lounges with sofas, open fires, antiques and brocade curtains, a little bar, smashing breakfasts, light lunches, afternoon teas and interesting evening meals in the traditionally furnished restaurant, helpful, courteous service and seats on the terrace and in the garden; dogs welcome anywhere apart from two dining rooms; towel on request; £5

BAINBRIDGE   SD9390
Rose & Crown

Bainbridge, Leyburn, North Yorkshire DL8 3EE (01969) 650225
www.theprideofwensleydale.co.uk

£68; 11 pretty rms. 15th-c coaching inn overlooking the lovely village green, with antique settles and other old furniture in the beamed and panelled bars, open log fires, a cosy residents' lounge and enjoyable pubby food in both the bars and restaurant; walks nearby; dogs in bedrooms

BOLTON ABBEY   SE0753
Devonshire Arms

Bolton Abbey, Skipton, North Yorkshire BD23 6AJ (01756) 710441
www.thedevonshirearms.co.uk

£185; 40 individually furnished rms with thoughtful extras. Close to the priory itself and on the Duke of Devonshire's 30,000-acre Estate, this civilised former coaching inn is carefully furnished with fine antiques and paintings from Chatsworth; three comfortable lounges serving all-day light snacks and afternoon teas, beautifully presented, excellent food in two smart, formal restaurants, super breakfasts and faultless service; tennis, mountain bike hire and health barn with swimming pool, treatment, sauna and steam rooms, and gym; dogs in bedrooms and some public areas; welcome pack, treats, bedding; £10

BOROUGHBRIDGE   SE3966
Black Bull

6 St James Square, Boroughbridge, York, North Yorkshire YO51 9AR (01432) 322413
www.blackbullboroughbridge.co.uk

£68; 6 rms. A handy stop-off point from the A1, this is an attractive town pub with plenty of cheerful locals; the main bar area has a big stone fireplace and comfortable seats, there's a cosy snug with traditional wall settles, a tap room, a lounge bar and a restaurant; a good choice of drinks and pubby food that includes lots of hot and cold sandwiches and a pie of the day; the borzoi is called Spot and the two cats Kia and Mershka; nearby walks; dogs in bar and bedrooms; bowls, treats

BRADFIELD   SK2290
Strines Inn

Strines, Bradfield, Sheffield, South Yorkshire S6 6JE (0114) 285 1247
www.thestrinesinn.webs.com

£80; 3 rms with four-posters and a dining table (breakfasts are served in your room). A pub since the 18th c but actually five centuries older, this friendly place is surrounded by superb scenery and many customers are walkers with their dogs; the main bar has black beams liberally decked with copper kettles and so forth, quite a menagerie of stuffed animals, homely red plush-cushioned traditional wooden wall benches and small chairs, and a coal fire in the rather grand stone fireplace; two other rooms to the right and left are similarly furnished and serve real ales and reasonably priced food; dogs anywhere in the pub and in bedrooms; £5

CONSTABLE BURTON   SE1690
Wyvill Arms
Constable Burton, Leyburn, North Yorkshire DL8 5LH (01677) 450581
www.thewyvillarms.co.uk

£85; 3 rms. Well run, 18th-c former farmhouse with a small bar area, a winter fire in an elaborate stone fireplace, a mix of seating and a finely worked plaster ceiling with the Wyvill family's coat of arms; a second bar has various alcoves, leather seating around old oak tables, a model train on a railway track running around the room and a reception area with a huge leather sofa, another open fire and an old leaded church stained-glass window partition; imaginative food using home-grown produce and game from the estate across the road, and enjoyable breakfasts; Constable Burton Gardens are opposite; dogs in bedrooms and bar

COXWOLD   SE5377
Fauconberg Arms
Coxwold, York YO61 4AD (01347) 868214 www.fauconbergarms.com

£95; 8 comfortable rms. Friendly, family-run 17th-c inn with a heavily beamed and flagstoned bar, log fires in both linked areas, attractive oak chairs plus more usual furnishings, nicely chosen local photographs and other pictures on contemporary paintwork, 28 malt whiskies, real ales and thoughtful choice of wines; the candlelit dining room is quietly elegant and the extremely popular food (including smashing breakfasts) is cooked by the landlord and his daughters; they have a shop selling home-baked bread and their own cheese; resident labrador, Bramble, and terrier Phoebe; lots of walks nearby; dogs bedrooms and bar (not dining room); welcome pack, bowl and blanket; £10

CRAYKE   SE5670
Durham Ox
West Way, Crayke, York YO61 4TE (01347) 821506 www.thedurhamox.com

£100; 5 comfortable rms. Friendly, well run inn the on the hill up which the Grand Old Duke of York marched his men; the old-fashioned, relaxed lounge bar has a huge inglenook fireplace, interesting satirical carvings in the panelling, polished copper and brass and venerable furniture on flagstones, the bottom bar has a large framed print of the original famous Ox, and the Burns Bar has a woodburning stove, exposed brickwork, real ales, ten wines by the glass and several malt whiskies; helpful staff serve the imaginative food (they bake their own bread and make the petits fours); the courtyard has plenty of seats and tables and fantastic views over the Vale of York; dogs in bedrooms

CROPTON

SE7588

New Inn

Cropton, Pickering, North Yorkshire YO18 8HH (01751) 417330
www.croptonbrewery.com

£85; 9 rms. Modernised village pub with famous own-brewed beers (six at any one time) and a genuinely warm welcome; the bar has traditional seats and tables, wood panelling and a small fire, there's a downstairs conservatory with historical posters and an elegant restaurant with straightforward pubby food; the brewery shop and tours are popular; dogs in bedrooms and bar

DOWNHOLME

SE1197

Bolton Arms

Downholme, Richmond, North Yorkshire DL11 6AE (01748) 823716
www.boltonarmsdownholme.com

£60; 2 rms. This little stone-built inn is one of the last pubs in Britain to be owned by the Ministry of Defence; the black-beamed bar is friendly and carpeted, with a log fire, comfortable plush wall banquettes, lots of gleaming brass and drinks advertisements on the walls, fairly priced drinks and efficient service; there's also a dining room and a conservatory and the tasty pubby dishes are cooked by the landlord; dogs in bedrooms

EAST WITTON

SE1486

Blue Lion

East Witton, Leyburn, North Yorkshire DL8 4SN (01969) 624273 www.thebluelion.co.uk

£94; 15 individually decorated rms. Warmly civilised former coaching inn with an informal little bar, a good mix of drinkers and their dogs mingling happily with those waiting to eat, high-backed settles and old windsor chairs on rugs and flagstones, a log fire, daily papers, sporting caricatures and other pictures, real ales and excellent wines by the glass; the delicious, inventive food is served by courteous, charming and attentive service; nearby walks; dogs in bedrooms and bar; £10

ELSLACK

SD9249

Tempest Arms

Elslack, Skipton, North Yorkshire BD23 3AY (01282) 842450 www.tempestarms.co.uk

£89.95; 21 comfortably modern rms. 18th-c stone pub with three log fires in stylish rooms and a wide mix of customers (plenty of dog walkers); cushioned armchairs, built-in wall seats with comfortable cushions and all sorts of tables, amusing prints on cream walls, half a dozen real ales, wines by the glass and highly enjoyable and generously served food; resident dogs Milly and Lottie; lots of surrounding walks; dogs in bar and one of the bedrooms; bedding, bowl and treats

FELIXKIRK

SE4684

Carpenters Arms

Felixkirk, Thirsk, North Yorkshire YO7 2DP (01845) 537369
www.thecarpentersarmsfelixkirk.com

£165; 10 lodge-style rms, most built around the garden. Carefully refurbished and pretty village pub surrounded by both short and long distance walks; dark beams and joists, candlelight and fresh flowers, a relaxed atmosphere, real ales and 15 wines by the glass; a snug seating area has tartan armchairs in front of the double-sided woodburner, the red-walled dining room had traditional prints and antique and country kitchen chairs around scrubbed tables, and a new dining extension will open shortly; food is inventive and well presented; good nearby walks; dogs in bedrooms and bar; £8

GRINTON

SE0498

Bridge Inn

Grinton, Richmond, North Yorkshire DL11 6HH (01748) 884224
www.bridgeinngrinton.co.uk

£82; 5 neat rms. Former coaching inn with lovely surrounding walks in a pretty Swaledale village; traditional, comfortable bars, leather armchairs and sofas in front of two log fires, a relaxed atmosphere, several real ales and malt whiskies and an extensive two-part dining room with mint green and brown décor and a modicum of fishing memorabilia; bar food is tasty and the breakfasts are good; the church opposite is known as the Cathedral of the Dales; resident labrador, Teale, and cat, Timmy; dogs welcome away from restaurant; bowls and treats; £7

HALIFAX

SE0829

Holdsworth House

Holmfield, Halifax, West Yorkshire HX2 9TG (01422) 240024 www.holdsworthhouse.co.uk

£95; 40 individually decorated, quiet rms. Lovely, immaculately kept 17th-c house a few miles outside Halifax in its own neatly kept grounds; antiques, fresh flowers and fires in comfortable lounges, lots of sitting areas in the two bar rooms, friendly, particularly helpful staff and three carefully furnished dining rooms serving enjoyable, inventive food, brasserie-style lunches, very popular afternoon teas and delicious breakfasts; dogs in bedrooms and some public areas; £10

HAROME

SE6481

Pheasant

Mill Street, Harome, Helmsley, North Yorkshire YO62 5JG (01439) 771241
www.thepheasanthotel.com

£155; 12 lovely rms. Carefully converted from a 17th-c village smithy and barns and overlooking the village duck pond, this is owned by the same people who run the Star Inn (close by); the beamed bar has stuffed pheasants and an inglenook fireplace, the cosy sitting room opens on to a pretty terrace, and the elegant restaurant serves beautifully presented inventive food using the best local produce; also, light lunches, quite a choice of afternoon teas and excellent breakfasts; indoor heated swimming pool and nearby walks; dogs in courtyard rooms only; £26

HARROGATE   SE2955
Alexa House

26 Ripon Road, Harrogate, North Yorkshire HG1 2JJ (01423) 501988
www.alexa-house.co.uk

£94; 13 rms, some in former stable block. Attractive Georgian house with friendly staff, a comfortable lounge with an honesty bar, complimentary afternoon tea and cakes, marvellous breakfasts in the bright dining room and lots of pubs and restaurants nearby for evening meals; dogs in stable room bedrooms only; not in main building; walk map

HARROGATE   SE3055
Hotel du Vin

Prospect Place, Harrogate, North Yorkshire HG1 1LB (01423) 856800
www.hotelduvin.com/hotels/harrogate

£189; 44 stylish rms plus 4 airy loft suites. Made up of eight Georgian-styled houses and close to the town centre, this relaxed and informal hotel has a bustling atmosphere, a cellar snug, a billiard room, a sleek, comfortable brasserie serving imaginative bistro-style food and superb wines, and well informed, helpful staff; spa with treatment rooms and seats in the courtyard garden; dogs welcome away from restaurant; £10

HAWNBY   SE5690
Laskill Grange

Easterside, Helmsley, York, North Yorkshire YO62 5NB (01439) 798268
www.laskillgrange.co.uk

£80; 6 rms, some in beamy converted outside building. Attractive and welcoming creeper-covered stone house on a big sheep and cattle farm near Rievaulx Abbey and with lots of nearby walks; an open fire, antiques and books in the comfortable lounge, a conservatory overlooking the garden and super breakfasts using home-grown produce (evening meals on request); free trout fishing on their lake, and self-catering, too; resident labrador Tosh, swans and ducks; dogs in bedrooms; not dining room

HELMSLEY   SE6183
Black Swan

Market Place, Helmsley, North Yorkshire YO62 5BJ (01439) 770466
www.blackswan-helmsley.co.uk

£142; 45 attractive, contemporary rms. Striking Georgian house and adjoining Tudor rectory given a careful modern makeover though keeping many original features like beams, panelling and big open fireplaces; a convivial bar for pubby lunches, a tearoom/brasserie where their world famous afternoon teas are served, and a more formal restaurant serving enjoyable modern food from lunches to evening meals and six-course tasting menus; seats in the charming sheltered garden; dogs in some bedrooms; £10

HELPERBY
SE4370

Oak Tree

Raskelf Road, Helperby, York YO61 2PH (01423) 789189 www.theoaktreehelperby.com

£120; 6 well equipped rms. Pretty brick pub with slate, oak and weathered brick retaining some original character in the informal bar; church chairs and elegant wooden dining chairs, open fires, bold red walls, real ales and a friendly atmosphere, and a main dining room with a large woodburner in a huge brick fireplace and first class food served by helpful staff; breakfasts (available to non-residents, too) and popular morning coffee with pastries; walks by river and in woodland nearby; dogs in one bedroom and in bar after food service

KILBURN
SE5179

Forresters Arms

Kilburn, York, North Yorkshire YO61 4AH (01347) 868386 www.forrestersarms.com

£80; 9 clean rms. Friendly old coaching inn opposite the pretty village garden, with traditional pubby furnishings in the carpeted lounge, a big log fire in the cosy lower bar, a second bar in what was the stable with the manger and stalls still visible, real ales and wines by the glass, and enjoyable food in the separate restaurant; dogs welcome away from dining room; £10

KNARESBOROUGH
SE3457

Best Western Dower House

Bond End, Knaresborough, North Yorkshire HG5 9AL (01423) 863302 www.dowerhouse-hotel.co.uk

£139; 29 well equipped rms. Creeper-clad 15th-c former dower house with a contemporary bar and reception lounge where you can take morning coffee, afternoon teas and light lunches, a second lounge with an open fire, an informal restaurant with enjoyable food served by helpful staff, and plenty of seats and tables outside in the garden; spa with treatment rooms, an indoor swimming pool and gym, and walks along the River Nidd; dogs welcome by arrangement; £10

KNARESBOROUGH
SE3556

Newton House Hotel

5-7 York Place, Knaresborough, North Yorkshire HG5 0AD (01423) 863539 www.newtonhouseyorkshire.com

£105; 12 very well equipped rms. Elegant family-run 18th-c house close to the river and market square, with a warm welcome for guests of all ages, a comfortable sitting room with books, Freeview TV and daily papers, a licensed bar and good generous english breakfasts in the dining room; no evening meals but plenty of places close by; they provide a list of local walks; dogs in two bedrooms; home-made biscuits, towels, beds and bowls; £10

LASTINGHAM

SE7390

Lastingham Grange

High Street, Lastingham, York YO62 6TH (01751) 417345 www.lastinghamgrange.com

£199; 11 rms. Attractive, family-run stone-walled country house in 12 acres of neatly kept gardens and fields – with the moors beyond (marvellous walks); a relaxed homely atmosphere in the traditionally furnished lounge where complimentary afternoon tea is served, open fires, well liked food generously served in the airy dining room, good breakfasts and extremely helpful service; dogs in bedrooms only; not in public rooms

LEEDS

SE3033

42 The Calls

Leeds, West Yorkshire LS2 7EW (0113) 244 0099 www.42thecalls.co.uk

£124.50; 41 attractive, contemporary rms incorporating interesting original features. Stylish modern hotel in a converted riverside grain mill in a surprisingly peaceful spot overlooking the River Aire; genuinely friendly staff, super breakfasts with a dozen varieties of sausage and home-made conserves, room service for light snacks but can eat next door in Brasserie Forty-Four restaurant (a separate business); dogs in bedrooms

LEEDS

SE3033

Malmaison

Sovereign Quay, Leeds, West Yorkshire LS1 1DQ (0113) 398 1000 www.malmaison.com

£163; 100 well equipped, slinky rms. Stylish hotel, once a bus company office, with bold, modern furnishings, a comfortable, contemporary bar, a busy brasserie with leather booths and an open fireplace, good english dishes given an up-to-date twist, decent breakfasts, popular Sunday brunches and helpful, friendly service; gym; dogs in bedrooms; £10

LEYBURN

SE1190

Sandpiper

Railway Street, Leyburn, North Yorkshire DL8 5AT (01969) 622206
www.sandpiperinn.co.uk

£90; 2 charming rms. 17th-c cottage in lovely spot with a warmly friendly landlord, a cosy bar with chatty locals, a log fire, cushioned wall seats around a few tables, local ales and 100 malt whiskies; also, a back snug, an attractive restaurant with fresh flowers and excellent food cooked by the landlord, who also makes his own bread and ice-creams; pretty summer hanging baskets and flowering climbers on the front terrace; walks nearby; closed Mon; dogs in bedrooms, bar and snug; not in restaurant; £7.50

LINTON IN CRAVEN

SD9962

Fountaine

Linton, Skipton, North Yorkshire BD23 5HJ (01756) 752210 www.individualinns.co.uk

£99; 5 newly opened rms in converted barn. Neatly kept pub in a charming village with civilised bar rooms, attractive wall benches and stools around copper-topped tables, lots of wall prints, log fires (one in a beautifully carved heavy wooden fireplace), five real ales and popular food usefully served all day; resident cocker spaniel, Fudge; super surrounding walks in the Yorkshire Dales National Park; dogs in bedrooms and bar; bowl, bed and dog wash

LONG PRESTON
SD8355
Maypole

Main Street, Long Preston, Skipton, North Yorkshire BD23 4PH (01729) 840219
www.maypole.co.uk

£75; 6 quiet, clean rms. Comfortable village pub, a good base for walkers, with a jovial long-serving landlord, a carpeted two-room bar with traditional seats and tables, plenty of local photos, real ales, farm ciders and a good choice of wines and whiskies; there's a separate dining room, a tap room, and well liked pubby food and tasty breakfasts served by friendly staff; dogs in bedrooms and bar; £6

MALHAMDALE
SD9062
Miresfield Farm

Malham, Skipton, North Yorkshire BD23 4DA (01729) 830414 www.miresfield-farm.com

£65; 10 rms. Spacious old farmhouse with good freshly prepared breakfasts in the beamed dining room, a lounge with an open fire and Sky TV, and a lovely garden by a stream and the village green; walks along the Pennine Way; dogs in bedrooms

MASHAM
SE2179
Swinton Park

Masham, Yorkshire HG4 4JH (01765) 680900 www.swintonpark.com

£185; 31 well equipped, huge rms with estate views. Grand luxury castle hotel dating in part from 17th c and still an ancestral home; quite a choice of sumptuously decorated day rooms (though the atmosphere is relaxed and friendly) plus a bar in the former family museum/chapel, a private cinema and a snooker and Victorian games room; imaginative food in elegant restaurant using seasonal produce from the extensive walled garden and estate; 200 acres of parkland and gardens, falconry, fishing, spa with treatment rooms, Jacuzzi and sauna, gym and popular cookery school; dogs in bedrooms only; not in public rooms; £25

MONK FRYSTON
SE5029
Monk Fryston Hall

Main Street, Monk Fryston, Leeds, West Yorkshire LS25 5DU (01977) 682369
www.monkfrystonhallhotel.co.uk

£99; 29 comfortable rms. Benedictine manor house in 30 acres of secluded gardens with a lake and mature woodland; many original features such as inglenook fireplaces, oak panelling and stone mullioned windows, a lounge and bar with antiques, paintings and fresh flowers, interesting modern cooking in the elegant restaurant, lighter pubby-style lunches, hearty breakfasts and friendly helpful staff; well behaved dogs in bedrooms and public areas; not in restaurant; £5

OTLEY   SE2143
Chevin Country Park Hotel
Yorkgate, Otley, West Yorkshire LS21 3NU (01943) 467818
www.crerarhotels.com/ourhotels/chevin_hotel

£89; 49 rms, some in log lodges deep in the woods. Built of finnish logs and offering walks through 50 acres of birchwood (lots of wildlife), this comfortable hotel has a lounge with leather sofas, an informal, cosy bar, a conservatory bar and lakeside restaurant, a wide choice of food from good breakfasts through light lunches and afternoon teas to smart, contemporary evening meals, and friendly, helpful staff; spa with treatments rooms, hot tub, sauna and steam room, indoor swimming pool and gym; dogs in some bedrooms; £10

PICKERING   SE7984
White Swan
Market Place, Pickering, North Yorkshire YO18 7AA (01751) 472288
www.white-swan.co.uk

£150; 21 luxurious rms. Smart, civilised 16th-c coach inn on the edge of the North York Moors National Park; the little bar is relaxed and has a log fire, comfortable sofas, some wood panelling, an extensive (and very good) wine list and local beers, smart lounges have more open fires, attractive prints, and all sorts of seats and tables on bare boards or carpet, the attractive restaurant has yet another fire and ancient flagstones, and the residents' lounge is in a converted, beamed barn; excellent food and delicious breakfasts served by courteous, efficient staff; dogs in bedrooms and bar; £12.50

PICKHILL   SE3483
Nags Head
Pickhill, Thirsk, North Yorkshire YO7 4JG (01845) 567391 www.nagsheadpickhill.co.uk

£80; 12 well equipped, comfortable rms. Neatly kept dining pub, handy for the A1, with an enthusiastic long-serving landlord and a bustling tap room decorated with jugs, coach horns and ale-yards hanging from beams and masses of ties; also, a smarter lounge with plush seating and an open fire, a library-themed restaurant, local beers, a thoughtful choice of wines, whiskies and vintage armagnacs, and consistently good food using local game (some shot by the landlord); boules, quoits and a nine-hole putting green; dogs in bedrooms (not to be left unattended); £5

RAMSGILL   SE1171
Yorke Arms
Ramsgill, Harrogate, North Yorkshire HG3 5RL (01423) 755243 www.yorke-arms.co.uk

£320, including dinner; 14 fine rms plus two-storey apartments. Enjoyable former shooting lodge that's now a restaurant-with-rooms, with antique furnishings, log fires, exceptionally good imaginative cooking in elegant dining rooms, flagstoned sitting areas (walkers are welcome here for a drink or snack), fine wines, real ales, courteous service and lovely surrounding walks; dogs only by special request

REETH   SE0399

Arkleside Country Guest House

Reeth, Richmond, North Yorkshire DL11 6SG (01748) 884200 www.arklesidereeth.co.uk

£80; 9 cosy rms including a suite. Former row of 17th-c lead miners' cottages with lovely Swaledale views, a friendly atmosphere, a comfortable lounge, good breakfasts in the airy restaurant and helpful, polite service; little garden and plenty of good walks; dogs in bedrooms; £5

RICHMOND   NZ1700

Millgate House

Millgate, Richmond, North Yorkshire DL10 4JN (01748) 823571 www.millgatehouse.com

£145; 4 rms, 2 overlooking the garden. Georgian town house with lots of interesting antiques and lovely plants, a peaceful drawing room, warm, friendly owners offering meticulous attention to detail, and good breakfasts in charming dining room which overlooks the award-winning and really special garden (no dogs here but riverside walks nearby); three resident whippets; dogs in bedrooms (not to be left unattended)

RIPLEY   SE2860

Boars Head

Ripley, Harrogate, North Yorkshire HG3 3AY (01423) 771888 www.boarsheadripley.co.uk

£100; 25 individually decorated rms, 10 in courtyard. Smart coaching inn with a friendly bar/bistro and an informal, relaxed atmosphere; warm yellow walls are hung with golf clubs, cricket bats and jolly little drawings of cricketers or huntsmen and a boar's head (part of the family coat of arms), and some furniture came from the attic of next-door Ripley Castle; real ales, 20 wines by the glass and malt whiskies, and good, popular food using produce from their kitchen garden; dogs in bedrooms and bar; not in dining areas; dog bed, bowl and Bonio; £10

RIPON   SE3171

Old Deanery

Minster Road, Ripon, North Yorkshire HG4 1QS (01765) 600003
www.theolddeanery.co.uk

£125; 10 stylish rms. Carefully modernised 17th-c hotel built on the site of a former monastery, with a fine old oak staircase, comfortable leather sofas and log fire in the lounge, a convivial bar, imaginative modern food in the attractive, candlelit dining room, bistro-style lunches and popular afternoon teas, good breakfasts, attentive service and a 1-acre garden; canal and River Ure walks nearby; dogs in bedrooms and reception area; £5

SEDBUSK   SD8790

Stone House

Hawes, North Yorkshire DL8 3PT (01969) 667571 www.stonehousehotel.com

£125; 23 rms, 5 in conservatory style. Small, warmly friendly Edwardian hotel in a stunning setting with magnificent views and marvellous walks; a country-house atmosphere, log fires and appropriate furnishings, an attractive oak-panelled drawing room, a library/billiard room, and a pleasant extended dining room with good, honest food served by helpful staff; P G Wodehouse stayed here as a guest of the original owner who employed a butler called Jeeves – it was on him that Wodehouse based his famous character; dogs in bedrooms, on lead in lounges; bowls and blankets; no charge for good dogs

---

SKIPSEA   TA1655

Village Farm

Back Street, Skipsea, E Yorkshire YO25 8SW (01262) 468479
www.villagefarmskipsea.co.uk

£80; 3 quiet, attractive rms. Carefully renovated traditional farmhouse and outbuildings set around a central courtyard with nearby walks along 40 miles of beach; their Tea Room serves sandwiches, all sorts of teas and home-made cakes and scones all day and is turned into a candlelit dining room at night – good hearty breakfasts, too; resident labrador, Katie, and cat, Wilf; dogs in bedrooms; towels; £5

STUDLEY ROGER   SE2970

Lawrence House

Studley Roger, Ripon, North Yorkshire HG4 3AY (01765) 600947
www.lawrence-house.co.uk

£120; 3 spacious, lovely rms with peaceful views. Attractive Georgian house in 2 acres of lovely gardens on the edge of Studley Royal and Fountains Abbey where there are 100 acres to walk in; fine antiques and paintings, a roaring log fire in the drawing room, enjoyable breakfasts and a cosseting atmosphere; resident labrador Boris, and Beetle, Mole and Rattie the border/lakeland terriers; dogs in bedrooms; not in public rooms

---

THORNTON WATLASS   SE2385

Buck

Thornton Watlass, Ripon, North Yorkshire HG4 4AH (01677) 422461 www.buckinn.net

£90; 7 rms. Honest village pub and very much the heart of the community with a friendly welcome for all from long-serving licensees; a pleasantly traditional bar has ancient bottles on shelves, mounted fox masks and an open fire in the brick fireplace, and the lounge (overlooking the cricket green) has large prints of the pub's cricket teams, signed bats and so forth, well kept beers and 40 malt whiskies; popular Sun jazz, generously served honest food and particularly good breakfasts; quoits; walks nearby; dogs in bedrooms and residents' lounge; not bars or restaurant; water bowl; £5

WEST WITTON   SE0688

Wensleydale Heifer

West Witton, Leyburn, North Yorkshire DL8 4LS (01969) 622322
www.wensleydaleheifer.co.uk

£140; 9 rms. Stylish restaurant-with-rooms with log fires, oak beams and comfortable leather sofas, a cosy, informal food bar and extensive main, formal restaurant, particularly good, interesting food, big breakfasts and attentive, helpful service; dogs in superior bedrooms; dog bed and treats; £10

WILLERBY   TA0230
Best Western Willerby Manor
Well Lane, Willerby, Hull, East Yorkshire HU10 6ER (01482) 652616
www.willerbymanor.co.uk

£128; 51 individually decorated rms. Originally the home of an Edwardian shipping merchant, this carefully extended hotel is surrounded by 3 acres of gardens; a friendly modern bar, enjoyable breakfasts, lunches, afternoon teas and evening meals in the attractive Figs brasserie, helpful service, lots of seats and tables on the terrace, and health club with swimming pool; dogs in ground floor bedrooms; £10

YORK   SE5952
Grange Hotel
1 Clifton, York YO30 6AA (01904) 644744 www.grangehotel.co.uk

£146; 36 individually decorated rms. Close to the Minster, this Regency town house has elegant and deeply comfortable lounges with open fires, handsome oil paintings, gilt-edged mirrors and fresh flowers, a grill room in the original brick vaulted cellars with red leather wall seating and evening candlelight, a stylish modern brasserie restaurant with brown leather chairs and beige wall seating on pale wooden flooring, interesting, contemporary cooking, afternoon tea and good breakfasts, and warmly, friendly staff; nearby riverside walks and gardens; dogs in bedrooms; not public areas; £20

YORK   SE5951
Hotel du Vin
89 The Mount, York YO24 1AX (01904) 557350 www.hotelduvin.com

£215; 44 stylish rms and suites. Fine early 19th-c building, once an orphanage, close to the historic city centre; stylish brasserie and attractive, informal area with wicker armchairs and navy sofas, chatty bar, modern, bistro-style french-influenced food including a popular Sunday brunch, a good choice of wines by the glass, friendly, helpful young staff and seats and tables in the courtyard, terrace and inner forum; dogs in bedrooms; £10

YORK   SE5947
Middlethorpe Hall
Bishopthorpe Road, Middlethorpe, York YO23 2GB (01904) 641241
www.middlethorpe.com

£199; 29 elegant rms with pretty fabrics, most in the adjoining courtyard. Lovely, immaculately restored William III country house in 20 acres of neat gardens and parkland; antiques, paintings and fresh flowers in comfortable, quiet day rooms (plenty of fine original features), excellent, imaginative food in the panelled dining rooms, afternoon tea, very good breakfasts and courteous, helpful service; spa with indoor swimming pool, treatment rooms, sauna and gym; dogs in some bedrooms

London

MAP 3

DOG FRIENDLY PUBS

CENTRAL LONDON
Lamb & Flag

Rose Street, off Garrick Street; ✆ *Leicester Square, Covent Garden; WC2E 9EB*

Historic yet unpretentious, full of character and atmosphere and with six real ales and pubby food; especially busy in the evening

The eight real ales and friendly efficient service continue to draw huge numbers of cheerful customers to this tucked-away pub. It's an unspoilt and, in places, rather basic old tavern and the more spartan front room leads into a snugly atmospheric low-ceilinged back bar with high-backed black settles and an open fire; in Regency times this was known as the Bucket of Blood thanks to the bare-knuckle prize-fights held here. As the pub is owned by Fullers they keep many of their beers plus a guest like Adnams Ghost Ship on handpump, as well as ten wines by the glass and 16 malt whiskies. The pub cat is called Beautiful. The upstairs Dryden Room is often less crowded and has more seats (though fewer beers). The pub has a lively and well documented history: Dryden was nearly beaten to death by hired thugs outside, and Dickens made fun of the Middle Temple lawyers who frequented it when he was working in nearby Catherine Street.

Free house ~ Licensee Christopher Buckley ~ Real ale ~ Bar food (12-7(Sun 12-5)) ~ Restaurant ~ (020) 7497 9504 ~ Children in upstairs dining room only ~ Dogs allowed in bar ~ Live jazz Sun evening ~ Open 11-11; 12-10.30 Sun ~ www.lambandflagconventgarden.co.uk

CENTRAL LONDON
Star

Belgrave Mews West, behind the German Embassy, off Belgrave Square; ✆ *Knightsbridge, Hyde Park Corner; SW1X 8HT*

Bustling local with restful bar, upstairs dining room, Fullers ales, well liked bar food and colourful hanging baskets

Tucked away in a cobbled mews in the heart of Belgravia, this classy but friendly pub is covered with an astonishing array of hanging baskets and flowering tubs – a lovely sight in summer. The small bar is a pleasant place with sash windows, stools by the counter on the wooden floor, a restful feel outside peak times and Fullers ESB, Summer Ale and Wild River on handpump, good wines by the glass and 35 malt whiskies. An arch leads to the main seating area with well polished tables and chairs, and good lighting; there's also an upstairs dining room. It's said that this is the pub where the Great Train Robbery was planned.

Fullers ~ Managers Jason and Karen Tinklin ~ Real ale ~ Bar food (12-4(5 Sun, 7 Sat), 5-9) ~ Restaurant ~ (020) 7235 3019 ~ Children welcome ~ Dogs allowed in bar ~ Open 11(12 Sat, Sun)- 11(10.30 Sun) ~ www.star-tavern-belgravia

NORTH LONDON
Duke of Cambridge

St Peters Street; ⊖ *Angel, though 15 minutes walk away; N1 8JT*

Trail-blazing organic pub with carefully sourced, imaginative food, excellent range of organic drinks and a nice, chatty atmosphere

The atmosphere in this busy, friendly pub is warmly inviting and it's the kind of place that somehow encourages conversation, with a steady stream of civilised chat from the varied customers. This was London's first organic pub and they try and reuse and recycle as much as possible and source organic drinks and organic produce for the food. Little Valley Tods Blonde and Withens Pale Ale, St Peters Best Bitter and a guest from Pitfield on handpump, organic draught lagers and cider, organic spirits (including a new ethical whisky list), a wide range of organic wines (many of which are available by the glass), quite a few teas and coffees, and a spicy ginger ale. The big, busy main room is simply decorated and furnished with lots of chunky wooden tables, pews and benches on bare boards. A corridor leads off past a few tables and an open kitchen to a dining room, more formally set for eating, and a conservatory. It's worth arriving early to eat, as they can get very busy.

Free house ~ Licensee Geetie Singh ~ Real ale ~ Bar food (12.30-4, 6.30-11(10.30 Sun)) ~ Restaurant ~ (020) 7359 3066 ~ Children welcome ~ Dogs allowed in bar ~ Open 12-11(10.30 Sun) ~ www.dukeorganic.co.uk

NORTH LONDON
Holly Bush

Holly Mount; ⊖ *Hampstead; NW3 6SG*

Unique village local, with good food and drinks and lovely unspoilt feel

Once the stable block of a nearby house, this is a proper local with a friendly welcome for all from the efficient, helpful staff. The old-fashioned front bar has a dark sagging ceiling, brown and cream panelled walls (decorated with old advertisements and a few hanging plates), open fires, bare boards, and secretive bays formed by partly glazed partitions. Slightly more intimate, the back room, named after the painter George Romney, has an embossed red ceiling, panelled and etched glass alcoves, and ochre-painted brick walls covered with small prints; lots of board and card games. Fullers London Pride, Discovery and ESB on handpump, as well as 23 whiskies and 16 wines by the glass from a good wine list. The upstairs dining room has table service at the weekend, as does the rest of the pub on a Sunday. There are benches on the pavement outside.

Fullers ~ Manager Hannah Borkulak ~ Real ale ~ Bar food (12-4, 6-10; 12-5, 6-9 Sun) ~ Restaurant ~ (020) 7435 2892 ~ Children welcome till 7pm ~ Dogs allowed in bar ~ Open 12-11(10.30 Sun)

SOUTH LONDON

Greenwich Union

Royal Hill; ✆ ⇌ *Greenwich; SE10 8RT*

Enterprising pub with distinctive beers from small local Meantime Brewery, plus other unusual drinks and good, popular food

This nicely renovated, friendly pub is still one of just two taps for the small Meantime Brewery (which has moved to Greenwich now) and they stock all their distinctive unpasteurised beers. The range includes a traditional pale ale (served cool, under pressure) a mix of proper pilsners, lagers and wheat beers, one a deliciously refreshing raspberry flavour, and a stout. The knowledgeable, helpful staff will generally offer small tasters to help you choose. They also have Adnams Best and Dark Star Hop Head on handpump, and a draught cider, as well as a helpfully annotated list of around 150 bottled beers. The rest of the drinks can be unfamiliar too, as they try to avoid the more common brands. Perhaps feeling a little more like a bar than a pub, the long, narrow stone-flagged room has several different parts: a simple area at the front with a few wooden chairs and tables, a stove and newspapers, then, past the counter with its headings recalling the branding of the brewery's first beers, several brown leather cushioned pews and armchairs under framed editions of Picture Post on the yellow walls; background music, TV. Beyond here a much lighter, more modern-feeling conservatory has comfortable brown leather wall benches, a few original pictures and paintings, and white fairy lights under the glass roof; it leads out to an appealing terrace with green picnic-sets and a couple of old-fashioned lamp posts. The fence at the end is painted to resemble a poppy field, and the one at the side a wheat field. Though there are plenty of tables out here, it can get busy in summer (as can the whole pub on weekday evenings). In front are a couple of tables overlooking the street. The pub is slightly removed from Greenwich's many attractions and there's a particularly good traditional cheese shop as you walk towards the pub.

Free house ~ Licensee Andrew Ward ~ Real ale ~ Bar food (12-10(9 Sun); 11-10 Sat) ~ (020) 8692 6258 ~ Children welcome ~ Dogs allowed in bar ~ Open 12-11; 11-11 Sat; 12-10.30 Sun ~ www.greenwichunion.com

SOUTH LONDON

Royal Oak

Tabard Street/Nebraska Street; ✆ ⇌ *Borough, London Bridge; SE1 4JU*

Old-fashioned corner house with particularly well kept beers and honest food

When Harveys – the only London pub belonging to the Sussex brewer – took over this enjoyable corner house, they transformed it, painstakingly re-creating the look and feel of a traditional London alehouse; you'd never imagine it wasn't like this all along. The two busy little L-shaped rooms meander around the central wooden servery, which has a fine old clock in the middle. They're done out in a cosy, traditional style with patterned rugs on the wooden floors, plates running along a delft shelf, black and white scenes or period sheet music on the red-painted walls, and an assortment of wooden tables and chairs. They keep the full range of Harveys ales plus a guest from Fullers on handpump and Thatcher's cider. There's a disabled ramp on the Nebraska Street entrance.

Harveys ~ Tenants John Porteous, Frank Taylor ~ Real ale ~ Bar food (12-2.30, 5-9.15; 12-8 Sun) ~ (020) 7357 7173 ~ children welcome until 9pm ~ Dogs allowed in bar ~ Open 11-11; 12-9 Sun; closed 26 Dec ~ www.harveys.org.uk/theroyaloaklondon.htm

WEST LONDON
Churchill Arms

Kensington Church Street; ✛ *Notting Hill Gate, Kensington High Street; W8 7LN*

Cheery irish landlord at bustling and friendly local with very well kept beers and excellent thai food; even at its most crowded, it stays relaxed and welcoming

The enthusiastic and friendly irish landlord has now been running this bustling local for 28 years and there's always a warm welcome for both locals and visitors. Mr O'Brien is a great collector and loves butterflies – you'll see a variety of prints and books on the subject dotted around the bar. He doesn't stop there though – the pub is also filled with countless lamps, miners' lights, horse tack, bedpans and brasses hanging from the ceiling, a couple of interesting carved figures and statuettes behind the central bar counter, prints of american presidents, and lots of Churchill memorabilia. Well kept Fullers Chiswick, ESB, London Pride and Fullers seasonal beers on handpump and two dozen wines by the glass. The spacious and rather smart plant-filled dining conservatory may be used for hatching butterflies, but is better known for its big choice of excellent thai food. Look out for special events and decorations around Christmas, Hallowe'en, St Patrick's Day, St George's Day, and Churchill's birthday (30 November) – along with more people than you'd ever imagine could feasibly fit inside this place; they have their own cricket and football teams. There can be quite an overspill on to the street, where there are some chrome tables and chairs. The façade is quite a sight in summer as it almost disappears behind the glorious display of 85 window boxes and 42 hanging baskets.

Fullers ~ Manager Gerry O'Brien ~ Real ale ~ Bar food (12-10(9.30 Sun)) ~ Restaurant ~ (020) 7727 4242 ~ Children welcome ~ Dogs allowed in bar ~ Open 11-11(midnight Thurs-Sat); 12-10.30 Sun

WEST LONDON
Colton Arms

Greyhound Road; ✛ *Barons Court, West Kensington; W14 9SD*

Unspoilt little pub kept unchanged thanks to its dedicated landlord; it's peaceful and genuinely old-fashioned with well kept beer; no food

This unspoilt little gem is like an old-fashioned country tavern and is run by a friendly long-serving landlord who has been here since 1963 – though his son now helps out, too. The main U-shaped front bar has a log fire blazing in winter, highly polished brasses, a fox's mask, hunting crops and plates decorated with hunting scenes on the walls and a remarkable collection of handsomely carved antique oak furniture. That room is small enough, but the two back rooms, each with their own little serving counter with a bell to ring for service, are tiny. Fullers London Pride, Sharps Doom Bar and a guest such as Adnams Lighthouse on handpump. When you pay, note the old-fashioned brass-bound till. Pull the curtain aside for the door out to a charming back terrace with a neat rose arbour. The pub is next to the Queens Club tennis courts and gardens.

Enterprise ~ Lease Norman and Jonathan Nunn ~ Real ale ~ Bar food ~ No credit cards ~ (020) 7385 6956 ~ Children must be over 4 and welcome till 7pm ~ Dogs allowed in bar ~ Open 12-3(4 Sat), 6(7 Sat)-11.30; 12-4, 7-11 Sun

WEST LONDON
Duke of Sussex

South Parade; ⊖ *Chiswick Park* ⇌ *South Acton; W4 5LF*

Attractively restored Victorian local with interesting bar food, a good choice of drinks and a lovely big garden

With a new landlord and some recent refurbishment, this sizeable Victorian pub is extremely popular. Once through the intriguing entrance lobbies with their cut glass, mahogany and mosaics you enter the classy, simply furnished bar. This has huge windows, some original etched glass, chapel and farmhouse chairs around scrubbed pine and dark wood tables on the new floorboards and a big horseshoe-shaped counter lined with high bar stools where they serve Cottage IPA, Nethergate Essex Border and Trumans Seek and Save on handpump and several wines by the glass. Leading off is a room mainly for eating, again with plenty of simple wooden furnishings on parquet, but also a few little booths, chandeliers and a splendid skylight framed by colourfully painted cherubs; there are a couple of big mirrors, one above a small tiled fireplace. The lighting is mostly modern but there are a few standard lamps and table lamps which, at night, create a warm yellow glow that from the street makes the place look warmly inviting. A huge bonus is the most unexpected big back garden. With plenty of tables under parasols, nicely laid out plants, heaters and carefully positioned lighting, it's a real oasis – though it can get packed on sunny days.

Greene King ~ Manager Claude Levi ~ Real ale ~ Bar food (12-10.30(9.30 Sun)) ~ Restaurant ~ (020) 8742 8801 ~ Children welcome ~ Dogs allowed in bar ~ Open 12-11(11.30 Fri and Sat, 10.30 Sun) ~ www.thedukeofsussex.co.uk

WEST LONDON
White Horse

Parsons Green; ⊖ *Parsons Green; SW6 4UL*

Cheerfully relaxed local with big terrace, an excellent range of carefully sourced drinks and imaginative food

Even when this easy-going pub is at its busiest, the well trained and friendly staff remain as efficient as ever. The stylishly modernised U-shaped bar has a gently upmarket and chatty atmosphere, plenty of sofas and wooden tables, huge windows with slatted wooden blinds, and winter coal and log fires – one in an elegant marble fireplace. An impressive range of drinks takes in regular real ales like Adnams Broadside, Harveys Best, Oakham JHB, Roosters Yankee and up to four guests from breweries such as Brodies, Fyne Ales, Goddards, Harviestoun, Twickenham and Weltons on handpump, imported keg beers from overseas (usually belgian and german but occasionally from further afield), six of the seven trappist beers, around 177 other foreign bottled beers, several malt whiskies and 22 good wines by the glass. They have quarterly beer festivals, often spotlighting regional breweries. The pub overlooks the green and has plenty of seats on the front terrace with something of a continental feel on summer evenings and at weekends; they have barbecues out here most sunny evenings.

Mitchells & Butlers ~ Manager Jez Manterfield ~ Real ale ~ Bar food (9.30am-10.30pm; brunch 9.30-12) ~ Restaurant ~ (020) 7736 2115 ~ Children welcome ~ Dogs allowed in bar ~ Open 9.30am-11.30pm(midnight Thurs-Sat) ~ www.whitehorsesw6.com

OUTER LONDON   TQ0490
Old Orchard
Off Park Lane; Harefield UB9 6HJ; UB9 6HJ

Wonderful views from the garden in front of this Edwardian house, a good choice of drinks, friendly staff and well liked, interesting brasserie-type food

In fine weather you have to arrive early at this former country house to bag one of the much prized tables on the front terrace – the view is stunning. You look down over the longboats on the canal and on to the lakes that make up a conservation area known as the Colne Valley Regional Park; it's a haven for wildlife. Seats from the gazebo and picnic-sets in the garden have the same fantastic view. Inside, the knocked-through open-plan rooms have an attractive mix of cushioned dining chairs around all size and shape of dark wooden tables, lots of prints, maps and pictures covering the walls, books on shelves, old glass bottles on window sills and rugs on wood or parquet flooring. One room is hung with a sizeable rug and some tapestry. There are daily papers to read, three cosy coal fires, big pot plants and fresh flowers. Half a dozen real ales on handpump include Fullers London Pride, Phoenix Brunning & Price, Tring Side Pocket for a Toad, alongside guests from brewers such as Adnams, St Austell and Windsor & Eton; also about two dozen wines by the glass and over 100 whiskies; friendly, helpful staff. The atmosphere is civilised and easy-going. There's a bowl of water for visiting dogs.

Brunning & Price ~ Manager Dan Redfern ~ Real ale ~ Bar food (12-10(9.30 Sun)) ~ (01895) 822631 ~ Children welcome ~ Dogs allowed in bar ~ Open 11.30-11; 12-10.30 Sun ~ www.oldorchard-harefield.co.uk

DOG FRIENDLY INNS, HOTELS AND B&Bs

Chesterfield
35 Charles Street W1J 5EB (020) 7491 2622 www.chesterfieldmayfair.com

£216; 107 well equipped, pretty rms. Charming hotel with particularly courteous helpful staff, a relaxed club-style bar with a resident pianist, a light and airy conservatory for lunches and afternoon teas, and a smart, attractive restaurant for fine dining; Hyde Park is close by for walks; dogs in bedrooms and public areas; bowls, treats, bed, dog sitting and walking service

Levin
28 Basil Street SW3 1AS (020) 7589 6286 www.thelevinhotel.co.uk

£360; 12 comfortable, carefully furnished rms. Family-run small hotel in the heart of Knightsbridge, with a comfortably modern entrance hall and reception/lounge, an honesty bar, a bustling basement brasserie for continental breakfasts and simple all-day food, and helpful, friendly staff; dogs in bedrooms; £50

Malmaison

Charterhouse Square EC1M 6AH (020) 7012 3700 www.malmaison.com/locations/london

£346; 97 stylish, modern, very well equipped rms. Large, elegant red-brick Victorian hotel converted from a nurses' residence for St Bartholomew's hospital and set in the cobbled courtyard of leafy Charterhouse Square; imaginative modern cooking in the brasserie, a chic bar off the spacious lobby with comfortable sofas, and helpful, attentive service; the Thames Path for walks is just under a mile away; dogs in bedrooms; bed and blanket; £10

Portobello

22 Stanley Gardens W11 2NG (020) 7727 2777 www.portobellohotel.com

£354; 21 rms decorated in very individual styles. Relaxed and informal hotel (liked by music and show business celebrities) on a quiet residential street, with plenty of eccentric character, big plants and flower arrangements, a little bar, a reception/lounge with comfortable sofas and armchairs, and a drawing room for the enjoyable breakfasts and small choice of bistro-type meals (residents get a discount at the owners' restaurant nearby, Julie's); dogs in patio bedrooms

Rubens

39-41 Buckingham Palace Road SW1W 0PS (020) 7834 6600 www.rubenshotel.com

£230; 161 luxurious rms, 8 Royal Rooms and 10 suites. Opposite Buckingham Palace and near Victoria Station, this attractive hotel has comfortable lounges, a couple of bars, one restaurant with a popular and extensive buffet-style carvery and a library restaurant with à la carte classics, and views of the Royal Mews; nearby parks for walks; dogs in bedrooms; bowls, bed, welcome hamper and other services available

The Draycott

22-26 Cadogan Gardens SW3 2RP (020) 7730 6466 www.draycotthotel.com

£365; 35 rms with a 24-hour room service menu. Made up of three Edwardian houses with fine staircases, this is an informal and enjoyable small hotel with a library, a drawing room for afternoon tea, a breakfast room (the breakfasts are of real quality), genuinely helpful staff, and a 1-acre garden; no restaurant; dogs in three bedrooms

Scotland

DOG FRIENDLY PUBS

EDINBURGH   NT2574
Abbotsford
Rose Street; E end, beside South St David Street; EH2 2PR

Lively city pub with period features, changing beers and bar and restaurant food

This handsome Edwardian pub was purpose built in 1902 and remains virtually unaltered since its construction. Perched at its centre, on a sea of red carpet, is a hefty highly polished Victorian island bar ornately carved from dark spanish mahogany, serving up to six changing real ales (on air pressure tall founts) from independent Scottish brewers such as Fyne, Harviestoun, Highland, and Stewart; and around 50 malt whiskies. At lunchtime you'll usually find an eclectic mix of business people and locals occupying stools around the bar and long wooden tables and leatherette benches running the length of the dark wooden high-panelled walls. Above all this there's a rather handsome green and gold plaster-moulded high ceiling. The smarter upstairs restaurant, with its white tablecloths, black walls and high ornate white ceilings, looks impressive too.

Stewart ~ Licensee Daniel Jackson ~ Real ale ~ Bar food (12-9) ~ Restaurant (12-2.15, 5.30-9.30) ~ (0131) 225 5276 ~ Children in restaurant ~ Dogs allowed in bar ~ Open 11-11(midnight Fri, Sat); 12.30-11 Sun ~ www.theabbotsford.com

EDINBURGH   NT2574
Kays Bar
Jamaica Street West; off India Street; EH3 6HF

Cosy, enjoyably chatty backstreet pub with good value lunchtime food and an excellent choice of well kept beers

The interior of this cheery pub is unpretentious but warmly welcoming, with long well worn curving red plush wall banquettes and stools around cast-iron tables on red carpets, and red pillars supporting a red ceiling. It's simply decorated with big casks and vats arranged up along the walls, old wine and spirits merchant notices and gas-type lamps. A quiet panelled back room (a bit like a library) leads off, with a narrow plank-panelled pitched ceiling and a collection of books ranging from dictionaries to ancient steam-train volumes for boys; there's a lovely coal fire in winter. The seven real ales include Caledonian Deuchars IPA and Theakstons Best, plus guests like Atlas (Orkney) Tempest, Cairngorm Trade Winds, Houston Texas, Summer Wine Apache and Timothy

Taylors Landlord on handpump; they also stock more than 70 malt whiskies between eight and 50 years old, and ten blended whiskies. TV and board games. In days past, the pub was owned by John Kay, a whisky and wine merchant; wine barrels were hoisted up to the first floor and dispensed through pipes attached to nipples still visible around the light rose.

Free house ~ Licensee David Mackenzie ~ Real ale ~ Bar food (12(12.30 Sun)-2.30) ~ (0131) 225 1858 ~ Dogs allowed in bar ~ Open 11am-midnight(1am Sat); 12.30-11 Sun ~ www.kaysbar.co.uk

HOUSTON   NS4066

Fox & Hounds

South Street at junction with Main Street (B789, off B790 at Langbank signpost E of Bridge of Weir); PA6 7EN

Village pub with award-winning beers from own brewery and tasty food

This 18th-c pub – now run by the second generation of the same friendly family – is most notable as the home to the Houston Brewery and their beers are as popular as ever. The six constantly changing ales include a guest beer plus their own Barochan, Killellan, Peters Well and Warlock Stout – you can look through a window in the bar to the little brewery where they are produced. They hold a couple of Best of Scotland beer festivals during the summer. You can try a fantastic choice of other drinks too including more than 100 malt whiskies, a dozen wines by the glass and 12 rums and 12 gins. The clean, plush, hunting-theme lounge has beams, comfortable seats by a fire and polished brass and copper; background music. Popular with a younger crowd, the lively downstairs bar has a large-screen TV, pool, juke box and fruit machines. At the back is a covered and heated area with decking.

Own brew ~ Licensee Jonathan Wengel ~ Real ale ~ Bar food (12-10(9 Sun)) ~ Restaurant ~ (01505) 612448 ~ Children welcome ~ Dogs allowed in bar ~ Open 11am-midnight(1am Sat); 12-12 Sun ~ www.foxandhoundshouston.co.uk

PITLOCHRY   NN9459

Moulin

Kirkmichael Road, Moulin; A924 NE of Pitlochry centre; PH16 5EH

Attractive 17th-c inn with own-brewed beers and well liked traditional food; a nicely pubby bar and comfortable bedrooms

Reasonably priced food and four own-brew beers ensures the popularity of this enjoyably bustling pub. The beers (Ale of Atholl, Braveheart, Light and the stronger Old Remedial) are brewed in the little stables across the street and served on handpump. They also keep around 40 malt whiskies and a good choice of wines by the glass and carafe. Although much extended over the years, the lively bar, in the oldest part of the building, still seems an entity in itself, nicely down-to-earth and pubby and with plenty of traditional character. Above the fireplace in the smaller bare-boarded room is an interesting painting of the village before the road was built (Moulin used to be a bustling market town, far busier than upstart Pitlochry), while the bigger carpeted area has a good few tables and cushioned banquettes in little booths divided by stained-glass country scenes, another big fireplace, some exposed stonework, fresh flowers, antique golf clubs, and local and sporting prints around the walls; bar billiards, board games and a 1960s one arm bandit; there's also a restaurant. On a gravelled area surrounded by tubs of flowers, picnic-sets outside look across to the village kirk; there are excellent walks nearby.

Own brew ~ Licensee Heather Reeves ~ Real ale ~ Bar food (12-9.30) ~ Restaurant ~ (01796) 472196 ~ Children welcome till 8pm ~ Dogs allowed in bar ~ Open 11(12 Sun)-11 ~ Bedrooms: £57B/£72B ~ www.moulinhotel.co.uk

PLOCKTON   NG8033
Plockton Hotel
Village signposted from A87 near Kyle of Lochalsh; IV52 8TN

Lovely views from this family-run loch-side hotel; very good food with emphasis on local seafood and real ales; bedrooms

This enjoyable family-owned hotel is in the centre of a lovely National Trust for Scotland village and part of a long, low terrace of stone-built houses. It's a great place for a break (it's worth booking well ahead), with most of the comfortable bedrooms in the adjacent building). Half of them have extraordinary views over the loch and the rest, some with balconies, over the hillside garden; good breakfasts. The welcoming comfortably furnished lounge bar has window seats looking out to the boats on the water, as well as antiqued dark red leather seating around neat Regency-style tables on a tartan carpet, three model ships set into the woodwork and partly panelled stone walls. The separate public bar has pool, board games, TV, a games machine and background music. Two real ales might be from breweries like Hebridean, Houston, Orkney or Plockton and are served on handpump; also, 30 malt whiskies and several wines by the glass. Tables in the front garden look out past the village's trademark palm trees and colourful shrub-lined shore and across the sheltered anchorage to the rugged mountainous surrounds of Loch Carron; a stream runs down the hill into a pond in the attractive back garden. There's a hotel nearby called the Plockton, so don't get the two confused.

Free house ~ Licensee Alan Pearson ~ Real ale ~ Bar food (12-2.15, 6-9) ~ Restaurant ~ (01599) 544274 ~ Children welcome ~ Dogs allowed in bar ~ Local musicians Weds evening ~ Open 11-12(11.30 Sat); 12.30-11 Sun ~ Bedrooms: £55B/£130B ~ www.plocktonhotel.co.uk

SCOTTISH ISLANDS

SLIGACHAN   NG4930
Sligachan Hotel
A87 Broadford–Portree, J with A863; IV47 8SW

Summer-opening mountain hotel in the Cuillins with walkers' bar and plusher side, hearty food served all day, impressive range of whiskies and useful children's play area

'If I was descending from the Cuillins after an exhausting day of walking I would like to know this place was waiting for me,' says one reader who thoroughly enjoyed his visit here. The huge modern pine-clad main bar, falling somewhere between a basic climbers' bar and a plusher more sedate hotel side, is spaciously open to its ceiling rafters and has geometrically laid out dark tables and chairs on neat carpets; pool. The splendid range of 350 malt whiskies makes a most impressive display behind one end of the bar counter where they keep their own Cuillin Black Face, Eagle, Glamaig, Pinnacle and Skye, and a scottish guest on handpump. It can get quite lively in here some nights, but there's a more sedate lounge bar with leather bucket armchairs on plush carpets and a coal fire; background highland and islands music. A feature here is the little museum charting the history of the island, and children should be delighted with the big play area which can be watched from the bar. There are tables out in a garden, and as well as self-catering accommodation there's a campsite with caravan hook-ups across the road. Dogs are only allowed in this main bar and not in the hotel's cocktail bar.

Own brew ~ Licensee Sandy Coghill ~ Real ale ~ Bar food (8am-11pm) ~ Restaurant ~ (01478) 650204 ~ Children welcome ~ Dogs allowed in bar ~ Open 8am-midnight; 11-11 Sun; closed Nov-Feb (for the hotel side); the separate attached pubby bar is closed beginning Oct-some time in May – best to phone ~ Bedrooms: £55S/£110S ~ www.sligachan.co.uk

DOG FRIENDLY INNS, HOTELS AND B&Bs

ACHILTIBUIE   NC0208
Summer Isles Hotel

Achiltibuie, Ullapool, Ross-shire IV26 2YQ (01854) 622282 www.summerisleshotel.co.uk

£190; 10 comfortable rms and 2 suites. Beautifully placed above the sea towards the end of a very long and lonely road and with plenty of surrounding walks; warm, friendly, well furnished hotel with delicious set menus using fresh local ingredients (some hydroponically grown), lovely puddings and excellent selection of scottish cheeses; also a locals' bar well stocked with malt whiskies; self-catering cottage; closed Nov-Apr; dogs in bedrooms (not to be left unattended)

ALYTH   NO2448
Tigh Na Leigh

22-24 Airlie Street, Alyth, Perthshire PH11 8AJ (01828) 632372 www.tighnaleigh.com

£110; 5 comfortably furnished, well equipped rms (all with spa baths). Former Victorian doctor's house with friendly, helpful owners, an informal and relaxing atmosphere and interesting contemporary décor; three different lounges – one with a log fire, one for TV and another with books, daily papers and a computer – super breakfasts (home-made bread and preserves) and good meals using local, seasonal produce (some home grown) in conservatory dining room; cats Tom and Bunny; landscaped gardens, dog walks in nearby park; closed Dec and Jan; dogs in bedrooms; not in dining room; treats, bowls and towels; £7.50

ARDEONAIG   NN6634
Ardeonaig Hotel

Ardeonaig, Killin, Perthshire FK21 8SY (01567) 820400 www.ardeonaighotel.co.uk

£160; 17 rms including cottage suites. Extended 16th-c farmhouse on south shore of Loch Tay, with log fire in snug and lounge, library with fine views, lunchtime bar food and more formal evening dining using fresh local produce; salmon fishing rights on the loch – trout fishing, too – a drying and rod room, shooting/stalking can also be arranged, lots of surrounding walks; dogs in some bedrooms (not to be left unattended)

ARDUAINE   NM7910

Loch Melfort Hotel

Arduaine, Oban, Argyll PA34 4XG (01852) 200233 www.lochmelfort.co.uk

£144; 25 rms with stunning sea views over Asknish Bay. Comfortable modern hotel popular in summer with passing yachtsmen (own moorings), nautical charts and marine glasses in airy bar, good food in bistro and restaurant including excellent local seafood; pleasant foreshore walks, outstanding springtime woodland gardens; two resident dogs; closed 2 weeks in Jan; dogs in several ground floor rooms; beds, food and water bowls; £8.50

AUCHENCAIRN   NX8149

Balcary Bay

Auchencairn, Castle Douglas, Kirkcudbrightshire DG7 1QZ (01556) 640217 www.balcary-bay-hotel.co.uk

£160; 20 rms with fine views. Once a smugglers' haunt, this charming hotel has wonderful views over the bay, neat grounds running down to the water, comfortable public rooms (one with log fire), a relaxed atmosphere and good food; lots of walks; closed Dec-Feb; dogs in bedrooms only, bring own bedding

BALQUHIDDER   NN4318

Monachyle Mhor

Balquhidder, Lochearnhead, Perthshire FK19 8PQ (01877) 384622 www.mhor.net

£195; 15 rms with fine views, some overlooking Voil and Doine lochs. Remote 18th-c farmhouse/hotel 4 miles west of Balquhidder on 2,000-acre estate with prettily furnished rooms and good food using own game, cured meats and herbs; private fishing and stalking for guests; two resident dogs; closed 2 weeks in Jan; dogs in four bedrooms, bar and lounge; £10

BRIDGE OF CALLY   NO1551

Bridge of Cally Hotel

Bridge of Cally, Blairgowrie, Perthshire PH10 7JJ (01250) 886231 www.bridgeofcallyhotel.com

£95; 18 rms. Adjoining 1,500 acres of private moorland, this former drovers' inn is a friendly family-run place with good value home-made food including seasonal game in popular restaurant and comfortable chatty bar; salmon fishing, stalking, shooting, golf and skiing are all locally available; dogs welcome in four rooms but must be well behaved

CALLANDER   NN6207

Highland Guesthouse

South Church Street, Callander, Perthshire FK17 8BN (01877) 330269 www.thehighlandguesthouse.co.uk

£60; 9 rms, some recently refurbished. Georgian house just off the main street with friendly owners, homely residents lounge and cosy bar, good scottish breakfasts; pleasant back garden (no dogs), plenty of surrounding walks and outdoor activities; dogs welcome if small and well behaved; not in public rooms

CALLANDER   NN6208

Poppies

Leny Road, Callander, Perthshire FK17 8AL (01877) 330329 www.poppieshotel.com

£95; 9 rms. Small private hotel with excellent food in popular and attractive candlelit dining room including a very good value early evening menu, comfortable lounge, cosy bar with some 125 malt whiskies, helpful friendly owners, seats in the front garden; closed most of Jan; dogs in two bedrooms

DULNAIN BRIDGE   NH9923

Auchendean Lodge

Dulnain Bridge, Grantown-on-Spey, Morayshire PH26 3LU (01479) 851347 www.auchendean.com

£90; 3 comfortable rms. Edwardian hunting lodge with wonderful views over the Spey Valley to the Cairngorms; two homely lounges with plenty of pictures and knick-knacks, a piano for guests' use and a warm log fire; enthusiastic owners, good, traditional cooked scottish breakfast (home-made marmalade and jams); pretty grounds with nine-hole pitch-and-putt course; Bess, the owner's border collie, loves taking other dogs for walks in the nearby woods and moors; self-catering apartment; closed Nov-Easter; dogs in bedrooms and lounges; bring own bedding; £5

EAST HAUGH   NN9656

East Haugh House

East Haugh, Pitlochry, Tayside PH16 5TE (01796) 473121 www.easthaugh.co.uk

£138; 13 rms, 5 in converted bothy, some with four-posters and 1 with open fire. Turreted stone house with lots of character, delightful fishing-themed bar, house-party atmosphere and particularly good food including local seafood, game in season and home-grown vegetables cooked by chef/proprietor; excellent shooting, stalking and salmon and trout fishing on surrounding local estates (own River Tay beat); three resident dogs and lots of good walks; two self-catering cottages (dogs welcome); dogs in porch of ground floor bedrooms – cars can be parked directly outside; £10

EDINBURGH   NT2776

Malmaison

1 Tower Place, Leith, Edinburgh EH6 7DB (0131) 468 5000 www.malmaison.com

£120; 100 stylish, well equipped rms, some with harbour views. Converted baronial-style seamen's mission in the fashionable docks area of Leith with very good food in the downstairs brasserie (wrought iron-work, leather banquettes and candlelight), cheerful, airy café bar with terrace, and friendly service; gym; free parking, dog walks in nearby Leith Links; dogs in bedrooms and lobby; £10

ERISKA

NM9041

Isle of Eriska Hotel

Ledaig, Oban, Argyll PA37 1SD (01631) 720371 www.eriska-hotel.co.uk

£345; 24 refurbished rms. In a wonderful position on small island linked by bridge to mainland, impressive baronial hotel with very relaxed country-house atmosphere, log fires, pretty drawing room, excellent food, comprehensive wine list and exemplary service; leisure complex with indoor swimming pool, sauna, gym and so forth, nine-hole golf course, clay pigeon shooting and lovely surrounding walks, plenty of wildlife including tame badgers who come nightly to the library door for their bread and milk; two resident labradors; self-catering house; closed Jan; dogs in most bedrooms (not to be left unattended); not in public rooms; food available

FORTROSE

NH7256

Anderson

Union Street, Fortrose, Inverness, Highland IV10 8TD (01381) 620236 www.theanderson.co.uk

£90; 9 rms. Seaside hotel with friendly, enthusiastic owners, a homely bar with a vast collection of belgian beers and 200 malt whiskies, a light, airy dining room with an open fire and good food using the best local ingredients (smashing fish and shellfish), and walks on the nearby beach; resident dog and cats; closed mid Nov-mid Dec; dogs in some bedrooms and in bar; bowls, biscuits, lots of attention

GAIRLOCH

NB8075

Old Inn

Gairloch, Ross-shire IV21 2BD (01445) 712006 www.theoldinn.net

£95; 17 rms; Quietly positioned old inn in charming waterside setting with a chatty and relaxed public bar, their own-brewed beers, over 20 malt whiskies, paintings and murals on exposed stone walls, traditional tables and chairs, and a warming woodburning stove, another woodburner in the residents' lounge; well liked food using local fish and game, they also smoke their own meats, fish and cheese; you can sit by trees lining the stream, and there are good walks from the door; dogs in bedrooms and bar; not in residents' lounge; £5

GATEHOUSE OF FLEET

NX6056

Cally Palace

Gatehouse of Fleet, Castle Douglas, Kirkcudbrightshire DG7 2DL (01557) 814341 www.callypalace.co.uk

£150; 56 rms. 18th-c country mansion, a hotel since 1934, with marble fireplaces and ornate ceilings in the public rooms, relaxed cocktail bar and sunny conservatory, enjoyable food in elegant dining room (smart dress required), evening pianist and helpful, friendly staff; 18-hole golf course, croquet and tennis, indoor leisure complex with heated swimming pool; plenty of walks; closed Jan and weekdays in Feb; dogs in bedrooms (not be left unattended); £5

GIFFORD
NT5367

Tweeddale Arms

Gifford, Haddington, East Lothian EH41 4QU (01620) 810240

£80; 14 rms. Civilised late 17th-c inn in quiet village; comfortable sofas and chairs in tranquil lounge, gracious dining room, wide choice of good daily changing food and charming service; nice walks nearby; dogs must be well behaved; not in lounge or restaurant

GIGHA
NR6551

Gigha Hotel

Isle of Gigha PA41 7AA (01583) 505254 www.gigha.org.uk

£60; 12 rms. Traditional community-run hotel, small and attractive with bustling bar (popular with yachtsmen and locals), neatly kept, comfortable residents' lounge and local seafood in restaurant; fields for dogs to exercise in; self-catering cottages; dogs in most bedrooms

GLASGOW
NS5567

Hotel du Vin

One Devonshire Gardens, Glasgow G12 0UX (0141) 339 2001
www.hotelduvin.com/hotels/glasgow/glasgow.aspx

£140; 49 opulent rms. Elegant, cosseting hotel a little way out from the centre; luxurious Victorian furnishings, fresh flowers, exemplary staff and fine modern cooking in the stylish restaurant; parks nearby for dogs to exercise; dogs in bedrooms; £10

GLASGOW
NS5865

Malmaison

278 West George Street, Glasgow G2 4LL (0141) 572 1000 www.malmaison.com

£120; 72 well equipped, individually decorated rms, some with french windows. Stylishly converted 19th-c church with greek façade, striking central wrought-iron staircase, a well stocked bar in vaulted crypt and enjoyable modern food in attractive brasserie, relaxed contemporary atmosphere and friendly staff; gym; nearby park for exercising dogs; dogs in bedrooms and in other rooms not serving food; beds and food

GLENFINNAN
NM9080

Glenfinnan House

Glenfinnan, Fort William, Highland PH37 4LT (01397) 722235
www.glenfinnanhouse.com

£130; 14 homely rms. In lovely grounds beside Loch Sheil (plenty of surrounding walks), this Victorian hotel has a comfortable drawing room, a bustling bar with traditional furnishings and local music, log fires, particularly good breakfasts, light bar lunches and french/scottish-influenced evening meals using the best local produce, and genuinely friendly, helpful service; closed Nov-mid-March; dogs welcome away from restaurant

GLENROTHES
NO2802
Balbirnie House
Markinch, Glenrothes, Fife KY7 6NE (01592) 610066 www.balbirnie.co.uk

£210; 30 rms. Fine Georgian country-house hotel in 400-acre park landscaped in Capability Brown style; fresh flowers, open fires and antiques in gracious public rooms, good bistro food or more creative cooking in evening Orangery restaurant, comprehensive wine list; dogs in bedrooms; £20

INNERLEITHEN
NT3336
Traquair Arms
Innerleithen, Peebles-shire EH44 6PD (01896) 830229 www.traquairarmshotel.co.uk

£80; 15 comfortable rms. Friendly hotel with good food in attractive dining room, cosy lounge bar, plenty of malt whiskies and good Traquair Bear ale brewed nearby; pretty little garden, and three self-catering apartments in converted stables; lots of local walks; dogs in two bedrooms, away from restaurant

INVERNESS
NH6343
Loch Ness Country House Hotel
Inverness IV3 8JN (01463) 230512 www.lochnesscountryhousehotel.co.uk

£195; 11 rms including 6 suites with own lounge and 2 garden cottages. 18th-c italianate mansion in 6 acres of well tended gardens and woodland, a short walk from the River Ness and Caledonian Canal; comfortably elegant with log fires and fresh flowers, enterprising food using local ingredients (some home-grown), generous breakfasts, around 200 malt whiskies; a popular wedding venue; lots of walks and golf courses nearby; closed first 2 weeks in January; dogs in garden cottages; £10

ISLE OF IONA
SM2874
Argyll Hotel
Iona, Argyll and Bute PA76 6SJ (01681) 700334 www.argyllhoteliona.co.uk

£136; 16 attractive rms, some with water views. Family-run former croft house looking over the Sound of Iona (beach and hill walks just 5 mins away), with three traditionally furnished lounges, a TV room, log fires and lots of books, good wholesome food in the dining room using seasonal organic produce from their kitchen garden, and a friendly, relaxed atmosphere; closed end Oct-end Mar; dogs in bedrooms; not in dining areas; beanbag bed and bowl; £10

ISLE OF WHITHORN
NX4736
Steam Packet
Harbour Row, Isle of Whithorn, Newton Stewart, Wigtownshire DG8 8LL (01988) 500334 www.steampacketinn.biz

£80; 7 rms, several with sea views. Friendly family run inn with big picture windows over the picturesque working harbour and a comfortable low-ceilinged bar with plush banquettes, stripped-stone walls and a woodburner; the lower beamed dining room has excellent wildlife photographs, rugs on wooden floor and quite a choice of bar food, there's also a small eating area off the lounge bar and a conservatory; you can walk from here to the remains of St Ninian's kirk; dogs in bedrooms and bar

ISLE ORNSAY
NG7012

Eilean Iarmain

Isle Ornsay, Isle of Skye IV43 8QR (01471) 833332 www.eileaniarmain.co.uk

£120; 16 individual rms including 4 suites (those in main hotel best), all with fine views. Sparkling white hotel on sheltered bay overlooking the Sound of Sleat, some Gaelic-speaking staff and locals, cheerful bar with open fire, dining conservatory and restaurant with lovely sea views, and very good food including local fish/seafood, real ales from Skye plus own range of whiskies; two self-catering cottages; well behaved dogs welcome; £5

ISLE ORNSAY
NG7315

Kinloch Lodge

Isle Ornsay, Isle of Skye IV43 8QY (01471) 833214 www.kinloch-lodge.co.uk

£340; 19 rms. Surrounded by rugged mountain scenery at the head of Loch Na Dal, this charming white stone hotel has a relaxed atmosphere in its comfortable and attractive drawing rooms, antiques, portraits, flowers, log fires and good imaginative food; cookery demonstrations; plenty of surrounding walks; children by arrangement; closed 2 weeks in Jan; dogs welcome in bedrooms; £20 (£10 winter)

KELSO
NT7233

Ednam House

Ednam, Kelso, Roxburghshire TD5 7HT (01573) 224168 www.ednamhouse.com

£150; 32 rms (the original ones are the nicest) including 2 suites. Large Georgian manor house by the River Tweed with 3 acres of gardens and owned by the same family since 1928; three distinctive lounges with antiques and plenty of comfortable seating, good choice of whiskies in log-fire bar, excellent food (own rare-breed pigs, smokery, bakery and bee hives) in large candlelit dining room overlooking the river, a lovely informal atmosphere and particularly good, friendly service; shooting and fishing by arrangement; dogs in bedrooms (not to be left unattended); not in restaurant

KILBERRY
NR7267

Kilberry Inn

Kilberry, Tarbert, Argyll PA29 6YD (01880) 770223 www.kilberryinn.com

£200; 5 ground floor rms. Homely and warmly welcoming inn on west coast of Knapdale with fine sea views, old-fashioned character, very good traditional home cooking relying on fresh local ingredients; resident jack russell; closed Jan-Feb; dogs in one bedroom; £10

KILCHRENAN · NN0723

Ardanaiseig

Kilchrenan, Taynuilt, Argyll PA35 1HE (01866) 833333 www.ardanaiseig.com

£268; 16 lovely big, themed rms with views of the loch or gardens. Scottish baronial mansion quietly set in its own natural gardens and woodland right on Loch Awe; antique-filled reception areas, comfortable squashy sofas, bold décor and colours, marvellous modern cooking, super afternoon tea and very friendly young staff; open-air theatre, bathing, fishing, and rowing boat; dogs in bedrooms; £20

KILCHRENAN · NN0422

Taychreggan Hotel

Kilchrenan, Taynuilt, Argyll PA35 1HQ (01866) 833211 www.taychregganhotel.co.uk

£160; 18 rms. Civilised hotel on the shores of Loch Awe with fine garden and 40 acres of grounds where dogs can walk; comfortable airy bar serving light lunchtime and early evening food, polite, efficient staff, good six-course dinner and Sun lunch in restaurant, a carefully chosen wine list and dozens of malt whiskies; pretty inner courtyard; activities such as falconry, clay-pigeon shooting, canoeing and fishing; dogs in some bedrooms (must be well behaved), and away from dining areas; £10

KILNINVER · NM8727

Knipoch

Knipoch, Oban, Argyll PA34 4QT (01852) 316251 www.knipochhotel.co.uk

£150; 21 rms. Elegant very well kept Georgian hotel in lovely countryside overlooking Loch Feochan; fine family portraits, log fires, fresh flowers and polished furniture in comfortable lounges, restaurant and bar, carefully chosen wines and fine selection of whiskies (some pre-war), excellent seasonal food including their own smoked salmon; resident hungarian wiesler, lovely walk from the door; dogs in bedrooms, but not bar or restaurant

KINCLAVEN BY STANLEY · NO1437

Ballathie House

Stanley, Perth PH1 4QN (01250) 883268 www.ballathiehousehotel.com

£220; 42 pretty rms, some luxurious and some in newer building with river views from balconies. Turreted Victorian mansion on vast estate with fine salmon fishing on the River Tay (lodge accommodation and facilities for fishermen) and plenty of sporting opportunities; comfortable and relaxed drawing room, separate lounge, dining room and bar, good modern scottish cooking; croquet, putting and lots of space for dogs to walk; dogs in some bedrooms (not to be left unattended); £20

KIRK YETHOLM   NT8228

Border

The Green, Kirk Yetholm, Kelso, Roxburghshire TD5 8PQ (01573) 420237
www.theborderhotel.com

£80; 5 rms. Welcoming and comfortable village-green hotel at one end of the
Pennine Way; cheerfully unpretentious bar, beams and flagstones, a log fire,
Borders scenery etchings and murals; snug side rooms and a comfortable lounge
with a another fire, neat conservatory and spacious dining room with fishing-
themed décor and enjoyable food; Jura is the resident jack russell and Scree the
lakeland terrier; walks from the front door; dogs in bedrooms and bar; treats and
bowls; £6

KIRKTON OF GLENISLA   NO2160

Glenisla Hotel

Glenisla, Blairgowrie, Perthshire PH11 8PH (01575) 582223 www.glenisla-hotel.com

£75; 6 cosy rms. Old coaching inn in lovely quiet position with lots of country
pursuits all around; convivial, traditionally furnished beamed bar with open fire,
drawing room with comfortable sofas, flowers and books, games room, enjoyable
seasonal food and hearty scottish breakfasts in elegant dining room, well kept
real ales; closed to non residents on Mon and Tues lunchtimes; dogs in bedrooms
and bar (outside of mealtimes); £5

MELROSE   NT5433

Burts Hotel

Market Square, Melrose, Roxburghshire TD6 9PL (01896) 822285 www.burtshotel.co.uk

£140; 20 immaculate little rms. Welcoming 18th-c family-run hotel close to abbey
ruins in delightfully quiet village; warming fire, classic pubby furniture on carpet,
scottish prints on pale green walls and

Aggie and puppy Mynti – border collies; owner Alastair MacKinnon

real ales, farm cider and around 80 malt whiskies served by particularly helpful staff; the restaurant is elegant and the food most enjoyable (good breakfasts, too); dogs in some bedrooms and bar/bistro; walk map

MINNIGAFF NX4165
Creebridge House
Creebridge, Newton Stewart, Wigtownshire DG8 6NP (01671) 402121
www.creebridge.co.uk

£120; 18 rms (most of them refurbished). Attractive country-house hotel in 3 acres of gardens; relaxed friendly atmosphere, open fire in comfortable drawing room, cheerful bar with woodburner and wide choice of delicious food including fine local fish and seafood in garden restaurant; good forest walks, closed first 3 wks Jan; dogs in bedrooms and public rooms (not restaurant)

MUIR OF ORD NH5251
Dower House
Highfield, Muir of Ord, Ross-shire IV6 7XN (01463) 870090 www.thedowerhouse.co.uk

£135; 4 rms with fresh flowers and garden views. Gabled 18th-c cottage in lovely wooded gardens with a family-home atmosphere, friendly owners, cosy lounge with log fire, ornaments, books and antiques, attractive dining room, wholesome and interesting british cooking, and generous scottish breakfasts using their own eggs and local honey; dogs in bedrooms; not in public rooms

NEWTON STEWART NX4266
Kirroughtree Hotel
Newton Stewart, Wigtownshire DG8 6AN (01671) 402141 www.kirroughtreehouse.co.uk

£180; 17 comfortable rms with fine views, some with own sitting room. Early 18th-c mansion with lavish Victorian/Edwardian extension, in large grounds close to the Galloway Forest Park; oak-panelled lounge with open fire, oil paintings, antiques and french windows leading on to the garden, particularly helpful, personal service, elegant dining rooms and excellent food; pitch and putt, croquet and plenty to do nearby; dogs in lower ground floor bedrooms; not in public rooms

NEWTONMORE NN6892
Crubenbeg House
Falls of Truim, by Newtonmore PH20 1BE (01540) 673300 www.crubenbeghouse.com

£75; 4 individually decorated, well equipped rms. Carefully run guest house with wonderful views from all rooms, charming, friendly owners, lots of teddy bears (Mrs England collects them), open fire in comfortable, homely guest lounge and good breakfasts around large antique table in light and airy dining room; can arrange packed lunches and light suppers (not Mon or Tues evenings, or July, Aug); elderly resident dog; lots of surrounding walks and activities; dogs in bedrooms (not to be left unattended) and other areas; not in restaurant

PITLOCHRY   NN9162
Killiecrankie House
Killiecrankie, Pitlochry, Perthshire PH16 5LG (01796) 473220
www.killiecrankiehotel.co.uk

£230; 10 spotless rms. Comfortable country hotel in spacious grounds with
splendid mountain views; modernised green panelled bar, cosy sitting room with
books and games, a relaxed atmosphere and friendly owners; excellent, well
presented, locally sourced food and good wine list in elegant restaurant; resident
cocker spaniel; fine nearby walks; closed Jan–mid-Mar; dogs in some bedrooms
(must not be left unattended) and bar; £10

PORT APPIN   NM9045
Airds Hotel
Port Appin, Appin, Argyll PA38 4DF (01631) 730236 www.airds-hotel.com

£350; 11 lovely rms including 3 suites. Instantly relaxing 18th-c inn with fine
views of Loch Linnhe and the island of Lismore, blissfully comfortable day rooms,
professional, courteous staff and charming owners; the food is exceptional (as is
the wine list), there are lots of surrounding walks, with more on Lismore (small
boat every hour), clay pigeon shooting and riding, self-catering cottage; closed
first 2 weeks of Dec; dogs in bedrooms (must not be left unattended); £10

PORT CHARLOTTE   NR2558
Port Charlotte Hotel
Port Charlotte, Isle of Islay (01496) 850360 www.portcharlottehotel.co.uk

£190; 10 rms, most with sea views. Made up of former cottages by the water
in a lovely Georgian village with sweeping views over Loch Indaal, this bustling
hotel has a civilised bare-boards pubby bar with padded wall seats and modern
art, a comfortable back bar, a separate restaurant and roomy conservatory, an
exceptional collection of about 140 Islay malt whiskies, enjoyable food using local
seafood and good breakfasts; walks nearby and on the beach; well behaved dogs
in bedrooms only

PORTPATRICK   NX0252
Knockinaam Lodge
Portpatrick, Stranraer, Wigtownshire DG9 9AD (01776) 810471
www.knockinaamlodge.com

£230; 10 individual rms. Neatly kept little country-house hotel with comfortable,
pretty rooms, open fires, wonderful food and friendly, caring service, panelled
whisky bar with over 120 malts; 30 acres of grounds stretching down to private
beach, dramatic surroundings and fine cliff walks; dogs in three bedrooms by
prior arrangement; £20

SCARISTA   NG0192
Scarista House
Scarista, Harris, Isle of Harris HS3 3HX (01859) 550238 www.scaristahouse.com

£220; 3 rms in main house, 3 suites in annexe. Wonderful wild countryside and empty beaches surround this small, isolated hotel (a former manse), antiques-furnished rooms, open fires and a warm friendly atmosphere, plenty of books and CDs (no TV); impressive wine list and good food in candlelit dining room using organic home-grown vegetables and herbs, hand-made cheeses, their own eggs, home-made bread, cakes, yoghurt and marmalade, and lots of fish and shellfish; excellent for wildlife, walks and fishing; resident pug, Maud, and Misty the cat; self-catering cottage, closed mid-Dec-Mar; dogs in bedrooms and one sitting room

SCONE
NO1526
Murrayshall House
Perth PH2 7PH (01738) 551171 www.murrayshall.co.uk

£150; 41 rms including 14 suites, plus lodge sleeping 6. Handsome mansion set in 350 acres of park and woodland where dogs may walk, very popular with golfers (it has two courses); comfortable elegant public rooms and a friendly, relaxed atmosphere; imaginative food and good wines; dogs in bedrooms only

SCOURIE
NC1544
Scourie Hotel
Scourie, Lairg, Sutherland IV27 4SX (01971) 502396 www.scourie-hotel.co.uk

£90; 20 rms, some with views to Scourie Bay. A haven for anglers, with 46 exclusive beats on 25,000-acre estate; snug bar and cocktail bar, two comfortable lounges and good food using plenty of local game and fish in smart dining room; fine walks on the doorstep; closed Oct-Apr; dogs in bedrooms and lounge

SHIEL BRIDGE
NG9419
Kintail Lodge
Glenshiel, Kyle, Ross-shire IV40 8HL (01599) 511275 www.kintaillodgehotel.co.uk

£130; 12 big rms. Pleasantly informal and fairly simple former shooting lodge on Loch Duich, with magnificent views, four acres of walled gardens, residents' lounge bar and comfortable sitting room, good well prepared food including local seafood in conservatory restaurant and fine collection of malt whiskies; there's also a separate locals' bar, bunkhouse and trekkers' lodge; resident spaniel, good variety of local walks; closed Mon and Tues in winter; dogs in bedrooms; not in restaurant or breakfast room; bring own bedding

SHIELDAIG
NG8153
Tigh an Eilean
Shieldaig, Strathcarron, Ross-shire IV54 8XN (01520) 755251 www.tighaneilean.co.uk

£150; 11 tranquil rms. Attractive hotel in outstanding position with lovely view of the pine-covered island and the sea, and within easy reach of NTS Torridon Estate, Beinn Eighe nature reserve and the Applecross peninsula; the two storey bar is separate from the hotel and is gently contemporary and relaxed with lots of timbering, scottish ales and a dozen wines by the glass; you can eat in the first floor dining room or on the decked balcony and the local fish and seafood is delicious; they also have several sitting rooms with guidebooks, a restaurant and seats in sheltered courtyard; closed Jan 4-Feb 4; dogs in bedrooms, one sitting room and bar; food available

SPEAN BRIDGE
NN2891
Letterfinlay Lodge
Letterfinlay, Spean Bridge, Inverness-shire PH34 4DZ (01397) 712622
www.letterfinlaylodgehotel.co.uk

£95; 18 rms including 3 suites. Secluded and genteel country house with picture window in extensive modern bar overlooking loch, comfortable reading room, good popular food in sun lounge and conservatory, friendly attentive service; grounds run down through rhododendrons to the jetty and Loch Lochy (dogs may walk here), fishing can be arranged; dogs in one bedroom only

SPITTAL OF GLENSHEE
NO0672
Dalmunzie Castle
Glenshee, Blairgowrie, Perthshire PH10 7QG (01250) 885224 www.dalmunzie.com

£205; 17 rms with fine views and named after local families. Old-fashioned turreted Victorian shooting lodge peacefully set in huge estate among spectacular mountains, plenty of walks within it, and golf course; comfortable drawing room, open fires in two other lounges, cosy, informal bar and antique-filled library, good inventive country-house cooking in candlelit restaurant using local produce, and hearty breakfasts; disabled access and lift, large self-catering property; dogs in bedrooms (must be well behaved); £5

STEIN
NG2656
Stein Inn
Stein, Waternish, Isle of Skye IV55 8GA (01470) 592362 www.steininn.com

£74; 5 rms, all with sea views. Skye's oldest inn standing just above a sheltered inlet with views out to the Hebrides and quite glorious sunsets; the unpretentious bar has much character, sturdy country furnishings, flagstones, panelled and stripped-stone walls, a double-sided stove, scottish ales, and over 125 malt whiskies; smartly uniformed staff serve a short menu of good, simple food using local fish and highland meat – breakfasts are good too; self-catering apartment; dogs in bar (not 6-9.30pm) and bedrooms

STRONTIAN
NM7961
Kilcamb Lodge Hotel
Strontian, Acharacle, Argyll PH36 4HY (01967) 402257 www.kilcamblodge.co.uk

£270; 10 rms. Warm, friendly little hotel in 22 acres by Loch Sunart, with log fires in two lounges, carefully cooked food using fresh ingredients, good choice of malt whiskies in small bar and a relaxed atmosphere; dogs welcome in grounds and on beach, resident terrier, Milly; no young children, closed Jan; dogs in some bedrooms only; beds, treats and towels; dog sitting available; from £6

TARBERT   NR8571
Stonefield Castle
Stonefield, Tarbert, Argyll PA29 6YJ (01880) 820836
www.celticcastles.com/castles/stonefield

£120; 32 rms. With wonderful Loch Fyne views and 60 acres of surrounding
wooded grounds where dogs can walk, this 1837 baronial mansion has a panelled
lounge bar and other comfortable sitting areas, good food and super views in the
restaurant, and a separate snooker room; fishing and riding can be arranged; dogs
in bedrooms; not in bar or restaurant; £10

THORNHILL   NX8893
Trigony House
Closeburn, Thornhill, Dumfriesshire DG3 5EZ (01848) 331211
www.countryhousehotelsscotland.com

£105; 9 individually decorated rms (each with a little teddy on the bed). In 4
acres of garden and woodland, this friendly Edwardian shooting lodge is now
a country-house hotel with wonderful walks just 5 mins' drive away; a cosy
lounge and bar with open fires, traditional furniture and games, light bar lunches,
delicious, interesting food using home-grown produce in the pretty dining
room with its french windows on to the garden, and hearty breakfasts; resident
miniature dasch, Kit, and golden retriever, Roxy; can arrange riding, falconry,
shooting, fishing and cycling; dogs welcome away from dining room; £5.50;
bedding, bowls, treats and food

TIRORAN   NM4828qq
Tiroran House
Tiroran, Isle of Mull PA69 6ES (01681) 705232 www.tiroran.com

£180; 11 comfortable rms, some in annexe. Friendly hunting lodge in 17 lovely
acres of grounds on the shores of Loch Scridain (lots of walks); two cosy sitting
rooms, a log fire, helpful guidebooks, a candlelit dining room and vine-covered
conservatory, tea and home-made cakes on arrival, excellent, beautifully
presented evening meals and hearty scottish breakfasts; resident border terrier,
Penny, and two cats, Pixie and Paddy, closed mid Nov-Mid March; dogs in three
bedrooms (not to be left unattended); not in public rooms; treats and towels

TOBERMORY   NM5055
Highland Cottage
24 Breadalbane Street, Tobermory, Isle of Mull, Highland PA75 6PD (01688) 302030
www.highlandcottage.co.uk

£150; 6 cosy, comfortable rms. Spotlessly kept small hotel rebuilt from an old
cottage run by friendly, helpful, hands-on owners (Mrs Currie also cooks the
highly enjoyable food); a sitting room with views over Tobermory Bay, an honesty
bar, an attractive dining room and hearty breakfasts; self-catering house also;
closed end Oct-end March; dogs in bedrooms; not in public rooms

TORRIDON

NG8854

The Torridon

Torridon, Achnasheen, Ross-shire IV22 2EY (01445) 791242 www.thetorridon.com

£190; 18 comfortably refurbished rms including separate cottage. Built in 1887 as a shooting lodge, this turreted stone house is spectacularly placed in 58 acres at the foot of Ben Damph by Upper Loch Torridon; unusual ornate ceilings, panelling and log fires; innovative cooking, whisky bar with 350 malts; they also run the dog-friendly Torridon Inn nearby as a cheaper alternative; closed Jan; dogs in cottage; not in main hotel

ULLAPOOL

NH1293

Ceilidh Place

12-14 West Argyle Street, Ullapool, Ross-shire IV26 2TY (01854) 612103
www.theceilidhplace.com

£145; 13 simply furnished rms, most with own bthrm, plus 11 in bunkhouse across road. White-painted hotel in quiet street, attractive conservatory dining room and café-bar with modern prints, plants and central woodburner, also a comfortable living room with honesty bar and balcony to sit out on; good locally sourced food all day and nice choice of wines and whiskies; relaxed, friendly atmosphere; books and radios in bedrooms rather than TV, art exhibitions, live music and theatre, book shop; resident border collie, Rieff; river walk from the door; dogs in bedrooms; not in dining areas; £8

WALKERBURN

NT3637

Windlestraw Lodge

Galashiels Road, Tweed Valley, Walkerburn, Scottish Borders EH43 6AA (01896) 870636
www.windlestraw.co.uk

£150; 6 lovely rms. Handsome little Edwardian hotel looking over the River Tweed and surrounding forests, with marvellous nearby walks; several lounges and a bar with plenty of original features, open fires, comfortable seating and family photographs, an elegant restaurant offering beautifully presented, inventive food (cooked by the owner using the best local produce) and extensive breakfasts; resident black labrador and cocker spaniel; dogs in some bedrooms (not to be left unattended) and in bar after dinner; bowls and treats

WEEM

NN8449

Ailean Chraggan

Weem, Aberfeldy, Perthshire PH15 2LD (01887) 820346 www.aileanchraggan.co.uk

£107; 5 comfortable rms. Family-owned inn with 2 acres of grounds and fine views of the mountains; homely, simple bar with scottish ales, 100 malt whiskies and good wines, a comfortably carpeted modern lounge and adjoining neatly old-fashioned dining room, inventive food and good breakfasts; nice walks from the door; dogs in bedrooms and bar

Wales

MAPS 6 & 7

DOG FRIENDLY PUBS

EAST ABERTHAW   ST0366
Blue Anchor
B4265; CF62 3DD

Character-laden thatched pub with five real ales and good value bar food

Deeply atmospheric with its cosy range of low-beamed little rooms, this relaxed medieval tavern makes a memorable spot for a drink, with five real ales on handpump: Brains Bitter, Theakstons Old Peculier, Wadworths 6X and Wye Valley Hereford Pale Ale, alongside a changing guest from a brewer such as Cotleigh, as well as Gwynt y Ddraig farm cider. The building has massive walls, low-beamed rooms and tiny doorways, with open fires everywhere, including one in an inglenook with antique oak seats built into its stripped stonework. Other seats and tables are worked into a series of chatty little alcoves, and the more open front bar still has an ancient lime-ash floor. Rustic seats shelter peacefully among tubs and troughs of flowers outside, with stone tables on a newer terrace. The pub can get very full in the evenings and on summer weekends, and it's used as a base by a couple of local motorbike clubs. A path from here leads to the shingly flats of the estuary.

Free house ~ Licensee Jeremy Coleman ~ Real ale ~ Bar food (not Sun evening) ~ Restaurant ~ (01446) 750329 ~ Children welcome ~ Dogs allowed in bar ~ Open 11-11; 12-10.30 Sun ~ www.blueanchoraberthaw.com

GRESFORD   SJ3453
Pant-yr-Ochain
Off A483 on N edge of Wrexham: at roundabout take A5156 (A534) towards Nantwich, then first left towards the Flash; LL12 8TY

Thoughtfully run, gently refined dining pub in the Brunning & Price chain, good food all day, very wide range of drinks, pretty lakeside garden

This elaborately gabled black and white 16th-c former manor house is an absolute delight, with exemplary service and an enchanting garden with herbaceous borders, mature trees and thriving box-edged herb beds; solid wooden furniture overlooks a lake frequented by waterfowl. The light and airy rooms are stylishly decorated, with a wide range of interesting prints and bric-a-brac, and a good mix of individually chosen country furnishings, including comfortable seats for relaxing as well as more upright ones for eating, and there's a recently rebuilt conservatory as well as a good open fire; one area is set out as a library, with floor-to-ceiling bookshelves. Their terrific range of drinks includes Flowers Original, Phoenix Brunning & Price Original, and four to six guest ales including Snowdonia and Weetwood, farm cider, a good range of decent wines (strong on up-front new world ones), with 15 by the glass, and around 100 malt whiskies. Disabled access is good.

Brunning & Price ~ Licensee James Meakin ~ Real ale ~ Bar food (12-9.30(9 Sun)) ~ (01978) 853525 ~ Children welcome ~ Dogs allowed in bar ~ Open 11.30-11; 12-10.30 Sun ~ www.brunningandprice.co.uk/pantyrochain/

MAENTWROG SH6640

Grapes

A496; village signed from A470; LL41 4HN

Lively inn with good mix of customers and well liked bar food, pleasant garden views; bedrooms

You may well get greeted in Welsh as you enter this welcoming inn in the Vale of Ffestiniog, within sight and tooting distance of the quaint steam trains of the Ffestiniog Railway. Its three bars are each furnished with stripped pitch-pine pews, settles, and pillars and carvings, mostly salvaged from chapels; elsewhere are soft furnishings. Warming woodburning stoves are on the go in winter, with one in the great hearth of the restaurant. Four beers on handpump are all from Evan Evans – Best, Cwrw, Warrior, and they bring in a seasonal guest; background music, TV, darts; disabled lavatories. There are views from the good-sized conservatory, as well as a pleasant back terrace and walled garden.

Evan Evans ~ Manager Callisa Smith ~ Real ale ~ Bar food (12-2, 5.30-8.30(6-8 Sun)) ~ Restaurant ~ (01766) 590208 ~ Children welcome ~ Dogs allowed in bar ~ Open 12-11(midnight Sat) ~ Bedrooms: £45B/£80B ~ www.grapeshotelsnowdonia.co.uk

MOLD SJ2465

Glasfryn

N of the centre on Raikes Lane (parallel to the A5119), just past the well signposted Theatr Clwyd; CH7 6LR

Open-plan bistro-style pub with inventive, well prepared upmarket food available all day, nice décor, wide choice of drinks

With Theatr Clwyd just over the road, this cheery and enthusiastically run Brunning & Price bistro-style dining pub is often full of the buzz of theatregoers in the evening, while in the day there may be families happily enjoying a meal. Decorated in this fine chain's trademark successful style, its open-plan interior is cleverly laid out to create plenty of nice quiet corners. It has a mix of informal attractive country furnishings, turkey-style rugs on bare boards, deep red (some high) ceilings, a warming fire and plenty of homely close-hung pictures; board games. Besides 30 wines by the glass, local apple juice, farm cider and around 70 malt whiskies, they've a wide choice of beers on handpump, with Flowers Original, Phoenix Brunning & Price Original and Purple Moose Snowdonia, alongside several swiftly changing guests from brewers such as Timothy Taylors and Titanic. On warm days, the large terrace in front of the pub makes an idyllic place to sit out by the wooden tables, from which you get sweeping views of the Clwydian hills.

Brunning & Price ~ Manager Graham Arathoon ~ Real ale ~ Bar food (12-9.30(9 Sun)) ~
(01352) 750500 ~ Children welcome ~ Dogs allowed in bar ~ Open 11.30-11; 12-10.30 Sun ~
www.glasfryn-mold.co.uk

OVERTON BRIDGE   SJ3542

Cross Foxes

A539 W of Overton, near Erbistock; LL13 0DR

**Terrific river views from well run 18th-c coaching inn with good carefully
prepared bar food and extensive range of drinks**

Immediately below this substantial 18th-c coaching inn sweeps the River Dee;
big windows all round the walls of an airy dining room give a great view of it.
The ancient low-beamed bar, with its red tiled floor, dark timbers, a warm fire in
the big inglenook and built-in old pews, is more traditional than most pubs in the
Brunning & Price group, though the characteristic turkey rugs and frame-to-frame
pictures are present, as they are in the dining areas; board games and newspapers.
Friendly competent staff serve Brakspear, Jennings Cumberland and a couple of
guests from brewers such as Evan Evans and Ringwood from handpumps, a farm
cider, 50 malts, an excellent range of armagnacs and a changing choice of around
15 wines by the glass. Good oak chairs and tables on a raised terrace make the
most of the riverside position; picnic-sets down on a lawn are even closer to the
water.

Brunning & Price ~ Manager Ian Pritchard-Jones ~ Real ale ~ Bar food (12-9.30(9 Sun))
~ (01978) 780380 ~ Children welcome ~ Dogs allowed in bar ~ Open 12-11(10.30 Sun) ~
www.crossfoxes-erbistock.co.uk

PANTYGELLI   SO3017

Crown

*Old Hereford Road N of Abergavenny; off A40 by war memorial via Pen Y Pound, passing
leisure centre; Pantygelli also signposted from A465; NP7 7HR*

**Prettily placed country pub, attractive inside and out, with good food
and drinks**

A lovely place to arrive at after a walk up the nearby Sugar Loaf, this well kept
free house is just inside the Brecon Beacons National Park. The neat and
efficient staff take their cue from the friendly hands-on owners, giving a warmly
welcoming atmosphere. The dark flagstoned bar, with sturdy timber props and
beams, has a piano at the back, darts opposite, a log fire in the stone fireplace,
and – from its slate-roofed counter – well kept Bass, Rhymney Best, Wye Valley
HPA and a guest such as Celt Native Storm on handpump, Stowford Press and
Gwatkin's farm cider, good wines by the glass, local organic apple juice, and good
coffees. On the left are four smallish, linked, carpeted dining rooms, the front
pair separated by a massive stone chimneybreast; thoughtfully chosen individual
furnishings and lots of attractive prints by local artists make it all thoroughly
civilised; background music, darts and board games. Comfortable wrought-iron
and wicker chairs on the flower-filled front terrace look up from this lush valley to
the lower slopes of the Black Mountains; a smaller back terrace is surrounded by
lavender.

Free house ~ Licensees Steve and Cherrie Chadwick ~ Real ale ~ Bar food (12-2, 7-9; not
Sun evening or Mon) ~ Restaurant ~ (01873) 853314 ~ Children welcome ~ Dogs allowed in
bar ~ Open 12-2.30(3 weekends), 6-11(10.30 Sun); closed Mon lunchtime ~
www.thecrownatpantygelli.com

PENNAL

SH6900

Riverside

A493; opposite church; SY20 9DW

Fresh refurbishment with tasty bar food and local beers

One reader arrived at this cheerfully run dining pub in the Dovey Valley with a group of muddy walkers and the friendly owners made them feel very welcome. It has been neatly refurbished with fresh green and white walls, slate flooring tiles, a woodburning stove, modern light wood dining furniture and some funky fabrics. High-backed stools are lined up along the stone-fronted counter where they serve three changing beers such as Purple Moose Dark Side of the Moose and Sharps Doom Bar, several malts and around a dozen wines by the glass; background music, TV and garden.

Free house ~ Licensees Glyn and Corina Davies ~ Real ale ~ Bar food (12-2.30, 6-9.30) ~ Restaurant ~ (01654) 791285 ~ Children welcome ~ Dogs allowed in bar ~ Open 12-11(midnight Sat); closed 2 weeks in Jan ~ www.riversidehotel-pennal.co.uk

PONTYPRIDD

ST0790

Bunch of Grapes

Off A4054; Ynysangharad Road; CF37 4DA

A fine choice of drinks in friendly, relaxed pub, delicious inventive food and a warm welcome for all

Our readers love this pub. It's a late 18th-c building , backs on to the remnants of the Glamorganshire Canal and was given a modern refurbishment a couple of years ago. There's a cosy bar with an informal, relaxed atmosphere, comfortable leather sofas, wooden chairs and tables, a roaring log fire, newspapers to read, Otley O1 and two guests plus another five quickly changing guest beers from breweries far and wide on handpump, continental and American ales on draught or in bottles, a couple of local ciders or perrys, seven wines by the glass and good coffee; service is knowledgeable, friendly and efficient. There's also a restaurant with elegant high-backed wooden dining chairs around a mix of tables and prints on pale contemporary paintwork; some seats outside on decking. They also have a deli with home-baked bread and chutneys, home-cooked ham, local eggs, quite a choice of welsh cheeses, and so forth, and hold cookery classes and regular themed evenings.

Free house ~ Licensee Nick Otley ~ Real ale ~ Bar food (11.30-2.30(3 Sat), 6.30-9.30; 12-3.30 Sun; not Sun evening) ~ Restaurant ~ (01443) 402934 ~ No children after 8pm unless dining in restaurant ~ Dogs allowed in bar ~ Open 11am-11.30pm; 12-11 Sun ~ www.bunchofgrapes.org.uk

STACKPOLE

SR9896

Stackpole Inm

Village signed off B4319 S of Pembroke; SA71 5DF

Impressive food, good accommodation, friendly service and usefully placed for exploring the Stackpole Estate

Within walking distance of the Pembrokeshire Coast Path and the Bosherston Lily Ponds, this efficiently run pub has attractive gardens, with colourful flowerbeds and mature trees around the car park. One area around the bar has pine tables and chairs, but the major part of the pub, L-shaped on four different levels, is given over to diners, with neat light oak furnishings, and ash beams and low ceilings to match; background music and board games. Brains Rev James, Felinfoel Chwerw Gorau and Double Dragon a guest from a brewer such as Rhymney are on handpump, with several wines by the glass and farm cider. The spotless bedrooms are comfortable and readers have enjoyed the breakfast.

Free house ~ Licensees Gary and Becky Evans ~ Real ale ~ Bar food (12-2(2.30 Sun), 6.30-9) ~ Restaurant ~ (01646) 672324 ~ Children welcome ~ Dogs allowed in bar ~ Open 12-3, 6-11; 12-11 Sat; 12-11 Sun ~ Bedrooms: £60S/£90S ~ www.stackpoleinn.co.uk

USK
SO3700

Nags Head

The Square; NP15 1BH

Spotlessly kept by the same family for 45 years, traditional in style with hearty welcome and good fair value food and drinks

'What all pubs should aspire to' is typical of the praise heaped on this supremely well run pub, where families are made to feel very welcome. The beautifully kept traditional main bar is cheerily chatty and cosy, with lots of well polished tables and chairs packed under its beams (some with farming tools), lanterns or horsebrasses and harness attached, as well as leatherette wall benches, and various sets of sporting prints and local pictures – look out for the original deeds to the pub. Tucked away at the front is an intimate little corner with some african masks, while on the other side of the room a passageway leads to a new dining area converted from the old coffee bar; background music. There may be prints for sale, and perhaps a group of sociable locals. They do ten wines by the glass, along with Brains Rev James and SA, Sharps Doom Bar and a guest such as Brains Arms Park on handpump. The church here is well worth a look. The pub has no parking and nearby street parking can be limited.

Free house ~ Licensees the Key family ~ Real ale ~ Bar food (12-2, 5.30-9.30) ~ Restaurant ~ (01291) 672820 ~ Children welcome ~ Dogs allowed in bar ~ Open 10.30-2.30(3 Sun), 5.30-11(10.30 Sun)

DOG FRIENDLY INNS, HOTELS AND B&Bs

ABERDOVEY
SN6196

Penhelig Arms

27-29 Terrace Road, Aberdovey, Gwynedd LL35 0LT (01654) 767215
www.penheligarms.com

£100; 15 comfortable rms, 4 in impressively furnished annexe, with lovely views. In fine spot overlooking the Dovey estuary, this 18th-c hotel has a fisherman's bar with log fire, panelling and traditional furnishings, real ales, 20 wines by the glass and a dozen malt whiskies served by efficient, friendly staff, well thought of food using local fresh fish in bar or more formal restaurant, good breakfast; walks on five miles of beach; dogs in all but one bedroom; not in restaurant; £10

ABERGAVENNY   SO2914

Angel Hotel

15 Cross Street, Abergavenny, Monmouthshire NP7 5EN (01873) 857121
www.angelabergavenny.com

£110; 35 well equipped, contemporary rms, some in mews and cottages. A
former coaching inn with a Georgian façade, this family-run hotel is on the edge
of the Brecon Beacons (marvellous walks); a bustling bar (liked by locals, too),
a comfortable lounge where their award-winning afternoon teas are served,
smart restaurant with excellent modern european dishes, and particularly good
breakfasts; pre-theatre menus also; walks along river Usk 2 mins away; dogs in
bedrooms and bar; not in restaurant; bedding and bowls; £10

ABERSOCH   SH3226

Porth Tocyn Hotel

Bwlch Tocyn, Pwllheli, Gwynedd LL53 7BU (01758) 713303 www.porthtocynhotel.co.uk

£160; 17 attractive cottagey rms, most with sea views. On a headland
overlooking Cardigan Bay, this comfortable and homely place – converted from
a row of lead miners' cottages – has been run by the same hard-working family
for 60 years; several cosy interconnecting sitting rooms with antiques, books and
fresh flowers, sunny conservatory, most enjoyable cooking from light lunches
through an imaginative dinner menu to huge Sun buffet lunch, helpful young staff;
lots of space in the pretty garden, heated swimming pool in summer, hard tennis
court; closed Nov to mid-Mar; self-catering cottage also; dogs in some bedrooms;
not in public rooms

ANGLE   SM8703

Old Point House

Angle Village, Angle, Pembroke, Dyfed SA71 5AS (01646) 641205

£75; 3 rms, 1 with own bthrm. Simple, welcoming seafarers' pub on the
Pembrokeshire Coast Path, with walks west around the peninsula to the beach
at West Angle Bay, and charming views over the water from some snug little
windows and picnic-sets on the big gravelled terrace; tiny spartan bar with simple
wooden settles, a warming fire in lovely old fireplace, welsh ales, a lounge bar,
and a dining room with likeable, honest food; resident bearded collie, Ki; dogs in
bedrooms and two bars; bowls, food and venison treats (when available)

BETWS-Y-COED   SH7955

Ty Gwyn

Betwys-y-Coed, Gwynedd LL24 0SG (01690) 710383 www.tygwynhotel.co.uk

£56; 12 comfortable rms and a holiday cottage. 17th-c coaching inn in the heart
of the Snowdonia National Park, beamed lounge bar with ancient cooking range,
easy chairs, antiques, silver, cut glass, old prints and interesting bric-a-brac, really
good interesting food in bar and restaurant using local produce including own
fruit and vegetables, real ales, friendly professional service; closed Mon-Weds in
Jan; dogs in two bedrooms; £5

BRECHFA

SN5230

Ty Mawr

Brechfa, Carmarthen SA32 7RA (01267) 202332 www.wales-country-hotel.co.uk

£113; 6 simple rms. A former farmhouse and school, this tranquil hotel is on the edge of the Brechfa forest (lots of walks), and has rambling rooms with beams, exposed stone walls and open fires; friendly, helpful owners and staff, and good, honest food including generous breakfasts, and packed lunches (on request); dogs not in restaurant or breakfast room

BROAD HAVEN

SM8616

Druidstone Hotel

Broad Haven, Haverfordwest, Dyfed SA62 3NE (01437) 781221 www.druidstone.co.uk

£180; 11 rms some with sea views, some with shared bthrms. Alone on the coast above a fine beach with exhilarating cliff walks, this roomy and informally friendly hotel (run by the same family since the 1940s) has something of a folk-club and Outward Bound feel at times; it's extremely winning and relaxing if you take to its unique combination of good wholesome and often memorably inventive food (including themed nights), slightly fend-for-yourself approach amid elderly furniture and glorious seaside surroundings; resident parsons terrier, Dash, and eight cats; self-catering cottages also; dogs welcome away from restaurant; £5

CAERNARFON

SH4859

Plas Dinas

Bontnewydd, Caernarfon, Wales LL54 7YF (01286) 830214 www.plasdinas.co.uk

£129; 9 individually furnished and well equipped rms overlooking the garden. A lovely former gentleman's residence between the mountains and the sea (fantastic walks) in 15 acres of grounds; friendly, helpful owners (he also cooks the top class food), a comfortable big drawing room with its open fire, afternoon tea with home-made chocolate brownies, a gun room with interesting royal memorabilia and a smart restaurant; resident miniature schnauzer, Patsy; self-catering also; small dogs in some bedrooms and drawing room; treats; £10

CONWY

SH7577

Sychnant Pass House

Sychnant Pass Road, Conwy, Gwynedd LL32 8BJ (01492) 596868
www.sychnant-pass-house.co.uk

£155; 12 rms including 2 suites. Victorian house in 2 acres among the foothills of the Snowdonia National Park; big comfortable sitting rooms, log fires, a relaxing, friendly atmosphere and enjoyable food (the restaurant is open to non-residents, too); spa with heated swimming pool; dogs in bedrooms; £20

CRICCIETH   SH5039

Mynydd Ednyfed Country House

Caernarfon Road, Criccieth, Gwynedd LL52 0PH (01766) 523269 www.criccieth.net

£100; 8 individually decorated rms, some with four-posters. Beautifully set 400-year-old house in 8 acres of garden, orchard, paddock and woods with lovely views overlooking Tremadog Bay, and once home to Lloyd George's family; traditional lounge bar with leather chesterfields and inglenook woodburner, enjoyable food using local produce (some home grown) in comfortable dining room and airy conservatory, friendly staff; resident chocolate labrador, Poppy, black cat, Bertie, and several ponies and chickens; all-weather tennis court and a treatment room; surrounding walks by rivers and on beaches; small and well behaved dogs in bedrooms only; £7

CRICKHOWELL   SO2118

Bear

High Street, Crickhowell, Powys NP8 1BW (01873) 810408 www.bearhotel.co.uk

£135; 34 appealing rms. Interesting inn run by the same convivial family for many years, with a splendid, old-fashioned bar area, real ales, 40 malt whiskies and vintage and late-bottled ports, heavily beamed lounge with roaring log fire, plenty of fine antiques, fresh flowers; comfortable reception rooms, too; imaginative food and enjoyable breakfasts served by genuinely helpful staff; river and canal walks within 10 mins; dogs in bedrooms and bar; bowl and treat

EGLWYSFACH   SN6796

Ynyshir Hall

Eglwysfach, Machynlleth, Dyfed SY20 8TA (01654) 781209 www.ynyshirhall.co.uk

£315; 8 individually decorated rms, one with a four-poster. Carefully run Georgian manor house in 14 acres of landscaped gardens adjoining the Ynyshir coastal bird reserve; particularly good service, antiques, log fires and paintings in the light and airy public rooms, extremely good food using home-grown vegetables, and delicious breakfasts; resident bernese mountain dog; lots to do nearby; dogs in ground floor bedrooms

FELINFACH   SO0933

Griffin

Felinfach, Brecon, Powys LD3 0UB (01874) 620111 www.eatdrinksleep.ltd.uk

£130; 7 tastefully decorated rms. Classy, relaxed dining pub with a proper back bar, scrubbed kitchen tables on bare boards, leather sofas by log fire, real ales, local cider, welsh spirits and fine wines by the glass; two smallish, attractive dining rooms with white-painted stone walls, excellent, imaginative food using local produce (some from own kitchen garden), breakfasts are hearty and nicely informal; the resident dog Max is ready for a game any time; dogs in bedrooms and bar

GELLILYDAN

SH6939

Tyddyn-du Farm

Gellilydan, Blaenau Ffestiniog, Gwynedd LL41 4RB (01766) 590281
www.snowdoniafarm.com

£90; 4 ground floor, private stable and long barn suites with Jacuzzi baths, fridges and microwaves, one with airbath – lovely country and mountain views. 400-year-old farmhouse on working farm in the heart of Snowdonia, with beams and exposed stonework, and big inglenook fireplaces in lounge; children can help bottle-feed the lambs and look at goats, sheep, alpacas and shetland ponies; two sheepdogs, Pero and Gel; fine walks, including short one to their own Roman site; dogs welcome away from dining room; must bring own bedding; £4

GLYNARTHEN

SN3049

Penbontbren Farm

Glynarthen, Llandysul, Dyfed SA44 6PE (01239) 810248 www.penbontbren.com

£110; 5 lovely suites with own sitting room area and terrace. Former farmhouse, now a luxury B&B, in 32 acres of grounds with nearby beaches for walks; charming, helpful owners, exceptional breakfasts (using their own eggs) in the carefully converted barn with crisply clothed tables and pretty flowers (and plenty of places close by for evening meals); resident king charles spaniels; dogs welcome away from breakfast room; £3

LLANABER

SH5919

Llwyndu Farmhouse

Llanaber, Barmouth, Gwynedd LL42 1RR (01341) 280144 www.llwyndu-farmhouse.co.uk

£94; 3 charming rms, 2 with four-posters, 4 more in nicely converted 18th-c granary. Most attractive 16th-c farmhouse just above Cardigan Bay, with a warm welcome from friendly owners, big inglenook fireplaces, oak beams and mullioned windows, relaxing lounge, good imaginative food in candlelit dining room, enjoyable breakfast, too; plenty of walks; dogs in granary bedrooms; not in public rooms

LLANARMON DYFFRYN CEIRIOG

SJ1532

Hand

Llanarmon Dyffryn Ceiriog, Llangollen, Clwyd LL20 7LD (01691) 600666
www.thehandhotel.co.uk

£107; 13 rms (some in converted stables). Comfortable rural hotel in remote valley looking out to the Berwyn Mountains; black-beamed carpeted bar with good inglenook log fire, mixture of chairs and settles and old prints on cream walls, local beers, fair-priced wines by the glass and malt whiskies; the largely stripped-stone dining room has a woodburner and tasty food served by friendly staff (satisfying breakfasts, too); there's also an attractive residents' lounge; resident dogs, Pero and Rosie; walks from the door among sheep; dogs anywhere away from dining room; towels and treats; £5

LLANARMON DYFFRYN CEIRIOG   SJ1532

West Arms

Llanarmon Dyffryn Ceiriog, Llangollen, Clwyd LL20 7LD (01691) 600665
www.westarms.com

£110; 16 comfortable character rms. Charming 16th-c beamed and timbered
inn in lovely surroundings, cosy atmosphere in picturesque upmarket lounge bar
full of antique settles, sofas, even an elaborately carved confessional stall, good
original bar food strong on local produce, friendly staff, nice range of wines, malt
whiskies and three well kept local ales, more sofas in old-fashioned entrance hall,
comfortable back bar, too, roaring log fires, good restaurant; pretty lawn running
down to River Ceiriog (fishing for residents), good walks; dogs welcome away
from restaurant; £7.50

LLANDELOY   SM8527

Lochmeyler Farm

Llandeloy, Haverfordwest, Dyfed SA62 6LL (01348) 837724 www.lochmeyler.co.uk

£80; 4 cottage suites. Attractive creeper-covered 16th-c farmhouse on 220-acre
working dairy farm; lounge and pleasant dining room for welsh breakfast; mature
garden, can walk around the farm trails and coast path is 3 miles away; dogs in
bedrooms only (not to be left unattended)

LLANDRILLO   SJ0337

Tyddyn Llan

Llandrillo, Corwen, Clwyd LL21 0ST (01490) 440264 www.tyddynllan.co.uk

£160; 12 pretty rms and a garden suite. Elegant and relaxed Georgian house with
3 acres of lovely gardens surrounded by the Berwyn mountains; fresh flowers in
comfortable public rooms, enterprising food including gourmet and tasting menus
using the best ingredients, and an impressive wine list; fine forest walks and
watersports; two resident cats; closed 2 weeks Jan; dogs in bedrooms; £10, then
£5 for subsequent nights

LLANDUDNO   SH7882

St Tudno

15 North Parade, Llandudno, Gwynedd LL30 2LP (01492) 874411 www.st-tudno.co.uk

£156; 18 individually decorated rms, some with sea view. Opposite the pier, this
well run, smart seaside hotel (in same ownership for over 40 years) has genuinely
helpful and friendly staff; Victorian-style décor in restful sitting room, a convivial
bar lounge, relaxed coffee lounge for good light lunches and dinner, and an
attractive italian-style restaurant; small indoor pool; dogs in bedrooms (not to be
left unattended) and coffee lounge; £10

LLANFAIR D C   SJ1355

Eyarth Station

Llanfair Dyffryn Clwyd, Ruthin, Clwyd LL15 2EE (01824) 703643
www.eyarthstation.co.uk

£78; 6 pretty rms. Carefully converted old railway station with quiet gardens and wonderful views; friendly relaxed atmosphere, log fire in airy and comfortable beamed lounge, good breakfast in dining room (more lovely views); sun terrace and heated swimming pool, lots of walks; dogs in bedrooms (not to be left unattended); not in dining room; food and bowls; £7

LLANFERRES
SJ1860
Druid
Ruthin Road, Llanferres, Mold, Clwyd CH7 5SN (01352) 810225 www.druidinn.com

£75; 6 rms; Friendly extended 17th-c whitewashed inn in choice walking country; fine views from civilised, smallish plush lounge and bigger beamed back bar, with its two handsome antique oak settles, pleasant mix of more modern furnishings, quarry-tiled area by the log fire; real ales, 30 malt whiskies and reasonably priced, generously served food; dogs anywhere except dining room

LLANGAMMARCH WELLS
SN9447
Lake
Llangammarch Wells, Powys LD4 4BS (01591) 620202 www.lakecountryhouse.co.uk

£195; 30 charming, pretty rms. Particularly well run 1860s half-timbered hotel in 50 acres with plenty of wildlife, well stocked trout lake, tennis, riding and walking; two friendly labradors; deeply comfortable tranquil drawing room with antiques, paintings and log fire, wonderful afternoon teas (in summer under the chestnut tree overlooking the river), courteous service, fine wines and good modern british cooking in elegant candlelit dining room, breakfast served in the orangery; spa with four treatment rooms and swimming pool; dogs in some bedrooms; not in public rooms; £10

LLANWDDYN
SJ0219
Lake Vyrnwy Hotel
Llanwddyn, Oswestry, Powys SY10 0LY (01691) 870692 www.lakevyrnwy.com

£174; 52 individually furnished rms – some overlooking the lake. Large, impressive Tudor-style mansion in a 26,000-acre estate – 16,000 acres are dedicated to the RSPB; conservatory looking over the water, log fires and sporting prints in the comfortable and elegant public rooms, convivial bar, a relaxed atmosphere and good food using their own lamb and game from the estate and home-made preserves, chutneys, mustards and vinegars, enjoyable teas, too; dogs allowed in grounds on lead; dogs in some bedrooms and bar; £10; they also have free heated kennels

LLANWRTYD WELLS
SN8746
Carlton Riverside
Irfon Crescent, Llanwrtyd Wells, Powys LD5 4ST (01591) 610248
www.carltonriverside.com

£90; 4 well equipped rms. Warmly friendly owners run this restaurant-with-rooms; two lounges with large squishy sofas and modern glass coffee tables, a well stocked bar, contemporary restaurant overlooking the River Irfon and old stone bridge, exceptionally good modern british cooking using top quality local produce, super breakfasts with home-made bread and marmalade, and a thoughtful wine list; good walks straight from the door, self-catering apartment; dogs welcome away from public rooms

MONTGOMERY
SO2296
Dragon

Market Square, Montgomery, Powys SY15 6PA (01686) 668359 www.dragonhotel.com

£99; 20 rms. 17th-c black and white timbered, family-run hotel with a pleasant grey-stone tiled hall, comfortable residents' lounge, beamed bar and restaurant using local produce; indoor swimming pool, sauna; countryside walks; dogs welcome away from drink and food areas

NANTGWYNANT
SH6555
Pen-y-Gwryd

Nantgwynant, Caernarfon, Gwynedd LL55 4NT (01286) 870211 www.pyg.co.uk

£80; 16 rms, some with own bthrm. In 2 acres, this cheery hotel (in same family for 70 years) is by the Llanberis Pass in Snowdonia National Park; warm log fire in simply furnished panelled residents' lounge, rugged slate-floored bar that doubles as mountain rescue post; lots of climbing mementoes and equipment, games room, hearty enjoyable food, big breakfasts and packed lunches; sauna in the trees and outdoor swimming pool, table tennis; private chapel; closed Nov-Dec and midweek Jan-Feb; dogs in bedrooms and bar; £2

NEWPORT
SN0539
Golden Lion

East Street, Newport, Dyfed SA42 0SY (01239) 820321
www.goldenlionpembrokeshire.co.uk

£90; 13 well appointed rms. Stylishly refurbished, welcoming village inn with a nice balance of comfortable dining and pubby character; cosy beamed rooms with distinctive old settles, four changing beers, local cider, wines by the glass and malt whiskies; the dining room has elegant blond wood oak furniture, whitewashed walls and potted plants and serves enjoyable, carefully presented food; walks from the door to the sea; dogs in one bedroom and bar; not in dining room; £15

NEWPORT
SN0539
Llys Meddyg

East Street, Newport, Fishguard, Pembrokeshire SA42 0SY (01239) 820008
www.llysmeddyg.com

£100; 8 large, bright rms. A former coaching inn and now a restaurant-with-rooms in the Pembrokeshire Coast National Park, with extensive walks from the front door; warmly welcoming owners and staff, a comfortable sitting room, a cosy and informal flagstoned cellar bar, good artwork and open fires, a wooden-shuttered restaurant with fresh flowers and candlelight, first class, imaginative food using local seasonal ingredients (home-smoked, foraged or shot) and excellent breakfasts; closed first week Jan; dogs in three bedrooms and bar

OLD RADNOR · SO2559

Harp

Old Radnor, Presteigne, Powys LD8 2RH (01544) 350655 www.harpinnradnor.co.uk

£90; 5 pretty rms. Welcoming 15th-c inn in superb hilltop position with lovely views and good walks nearby; traditional bars with log fires, some slate flooring and antique settles, real ales, local cider and quite a few malt whiskies, lots of local books and guides for residents; character dining room, good food from sensibly short menu using home-grown produce; closed weekday lunchtimes and Mon; dogs in bedrooms and bar

OXWICH · SS4986

Oxwich Bay Hotel

Oxwich, Swansea, West Glamorgan SA3 1LS (01792) 390329 www.oxwichbayhotel.co.uk

£110; 26 rms. Comfortable hotel on edge of beach in a lovely area, restaurant/ lounge bar with panoramic views, summer outdoor dining area, food served all day, friendly staff and a welcome for families; 8 acres of grounds in which dogs can walk; dogs in cottage bedrooms; £5

PRESTEIGNE · SO3164

Radnorshire Arms

High Street, Presteigne, Powys LD8 2BE (01544) 267406 www.radnorshirearmshotel.com

£95; 19 rms, some in garden lodges. Rambling handsomely timbered hotel dating from the 16th-c with many later additions, elegantly moulded beams and fine dark panelling in the lounge bar, latticed windows, enjoyable food (including morning coffee and afternoon tea), separate restaurant, well kept real ales and politely attentive service; resident dog and cat; walks nearby (or in the garden); dogs in garden lodges, public areas outside of food times; £15

RAGLAN · SO3608

Clytha Arms

Clytha, Abergavenny, Gwent NP7 9BW (01873) 840206 www.clytha-arms.com

£90; 4 comfortable rms. Rural inn, beautifully placed in parkland, and well located for walks along the Usk (footpaths run from the garden); comfortable, light and airy with scrubbed wood floors, pine settles and a good mix of old country furniture, a couple of warming fires and an impressive array of drinks (they hold cider and beer festivals); can eat in the bar, lounge or contemporary linen-set restaurant, part-welsh and part-spanish tapas menu plus other enjoyable dishes, good breakfasts, too; six resident dogs; dogs welcome; bed and bowl

REYNOLDSTON · SS4691

Fairyhill

Reynoldston, Swansea, West Glamorgan SA3 1BS (01792) 390139 www.fairyhill.net

£180; 8 rms. 18th-c hotel in 24 wooded acres with croquet, trout stream and wild ducks on the lake; log fire in comfortable drawing room, cosy bar, lovely food in attractive dining room using local produce (some from own walled garden), hearty breakfasts, a leafy terrace and personal friendly service; closed 1-25 Jan; dogs in bedrooms

RHAYADER   SN9969
Beili Neuadd

Rhayader, Powys LD6 5NS (01597) 810211 www.midwalesfarmstay.co.uk

£70; 3 rms with log fires, and converted stone barn with 3 bunkhouse rms. Charming, partly 16th-c stone-built farmhouse with panoramic views set in quiet countryside; beams, polished oak floorboards, log fires and nice breakfasts in garden room; own dogs, cats, pigs, sheep and chickens, walks in paddocks, garden and surrounding area; self-catering chalet; dogs in bunkhouse, chalet and farmhouse public rooms

SKENFRITH   SO4520
Bell

Skenfrith, Abergavenny, Gwent NP7 8UH (01600) 750235 www.skenfrith.co.uk

£170; 11 rms, some with four-posters. Elegant but relaxed inn by bridge over the River Monnow and close to the impressive medieval ruin of Skenfrith Castle; flagstones and canary-yellow walls in linked areas with settees, pews and carved settles among more conventional pub furniture, church candles on tables, a log fire in big fireplace; good wines by the glass,

Casper – weimaraner, and Charlie – border terrier; owners Jacqui and Alan Davies.

real ales and interesting food using the best local produce (including their own vegetables and pigs) in both bar and extensive bare-boards restaurant, generous breakfasts; picnic-sets out on the terrace, good nearby walks (they have leaflets); well behaved dogs in bedrooms (not to be left unattended); not in restaurant; £5

ST BRIDES WENTLOOG   ST2982

West Usk Lighthouse

St Brides Wentloog, Newport, Gwent NP10 8SF (01633) 810126
www.westusklighthouse.co.uk

£160; 4 rms. Unusual ex-lighthouse – squat rather than tall – that was on an island in the Bristol Channel (the land has since been reclaimed); modern stylish furnishings, lots of framed record sleeves (Mr Sheahan used to work for a record company), informal atmosphere, good big breakfasts and can be driven to local restaurants in their Rolls Royce (£30 each way); aromatherapy, reflexology and other treatments, large roof terrace with barbecue and hot tub (Tardis changing room – there's also a Dalek downstairs); resident border collie; lots of nearby walks; dogs in one bedroom; £10

ST DAVID'S   SM7524

Warpool Court

St David's, Haverfordwest, Dyfed SA62 6BN (01437) 720300 www.warpoolcourthotel.com

£140; 22 attractive rms, some with sea views. Originally built as St David's cathedral school in 1870 and bordering National Trust land, this popular hotel has lovely views over St Bride's Bay; Ada Williams' collection of lovely hand-painted tiles can be seen in the public rooms and some bedrooms, food in the elegant restaurant is imaginative (good for vegetarians, too) and staff are helpful; attractive quiet gardens (walks here and in surrounding fields), heated summer swimming pool, tennis and croquet, games room with table tennis and pool; closed Nov-March; dogs in bedrooms; £10

TALSARNAU   SH6135

Maes-y-Neuadd

Talsarnau, Gwynedd LL47 6YA (01766) 780200 www.neuadd.com

£100; 15 individually decorated, cosy rms, 4 in adjacent coach house. Looking out across Snowdonia, this attractive extended 14th-c country-house hotel stands in 25 acres of landscaped hillside (dogs welcome to walk on lead); flowers, plants, antiques and log fires, peaceful atmosphere, very good food (herbs and vegetables from their own garden), charming staff; resident sheepdog and cat; dogs in two coach-house bedrooms; £7.50

TAL-Y-BONT   SH7669

Lodge

Tal-y-bont, Conwy, Gwynedd LL32 8YX (01492) 660766 www.thelodgehotelconwy.co.uk

£85; 12 rms. Friendly little modern hotel in 4 acres on the edge of Snowdonia, family owned, with comfortable lounge, open fire, generous helpings of popular food using lots of home-grown produce in restaurant, good service; plenty of walks; closed Jan; dogs in some bedrooms; £10

TINTERN PARVA

SO5200

Parva Farmhouse

Tintern, Chepstow, Gwent NP16 6SQ (01291) 689411 www.parvafarmhouse.co.uk

£80; 8 comfortable rms, most with river view. Friendly 17th-c stone farmhouse, leather chesterfields, woodburner and honesty bar in large beamed lounge, books (no TV downstairs); very good food and wine (some from local vineyard) in cosy inglenook restaurant; 50 metres from River Wye, Tintern Abbey nearby, lovely surrounding countryside; elderly resident dog, Frodo; dogs in two bedrooms and residents' lounge; £3

TY'N-Y-GROES

SH7773

Groes

Ty'n-y-groes, Conwy, Gwynedd LL32 8TN (01492) 650545 www.groesinn.com

£138; 14 well equipped rms, some with terraces or balconies. Delightful 15th-c former drovers' inn of much character; rambling, low-beamed and thick-walled rooms with antique settles, old clocks, portraits, hats and tins hanging from walls, cheerful log fires, own-brewed beers, wines by the glass and maybe a harpist playing; several options for enjoying the good food (using local lamb, salmon and game) include an airy conservatory and a smart white linen restaurant; seats in idyllic back garden and on terracing; dogs in some ground floor bedrooms and bar; bowl and treats; £10

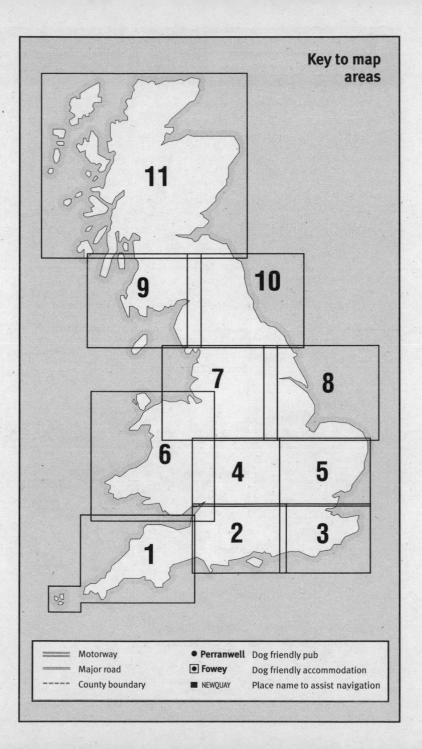

Key to map areas

	Motorway	● **Perranwell**	Dog friendly pub
	Major road	�⊡ **Fowey**	Dog friendly accommodation
	County boundary	■ NEWQUAY	Place name to assist navigation

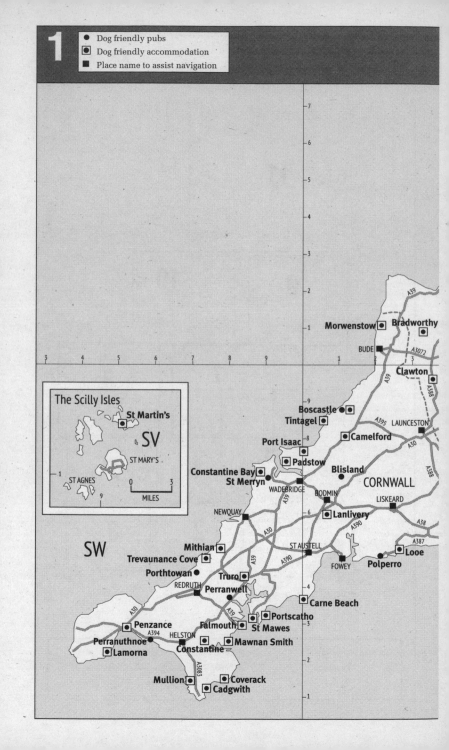

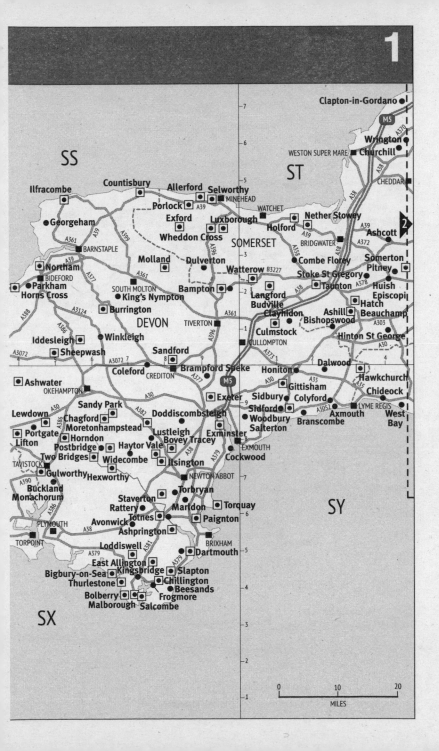

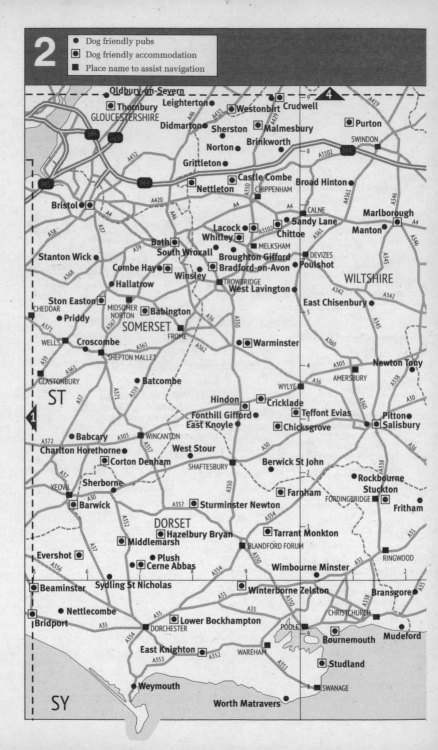

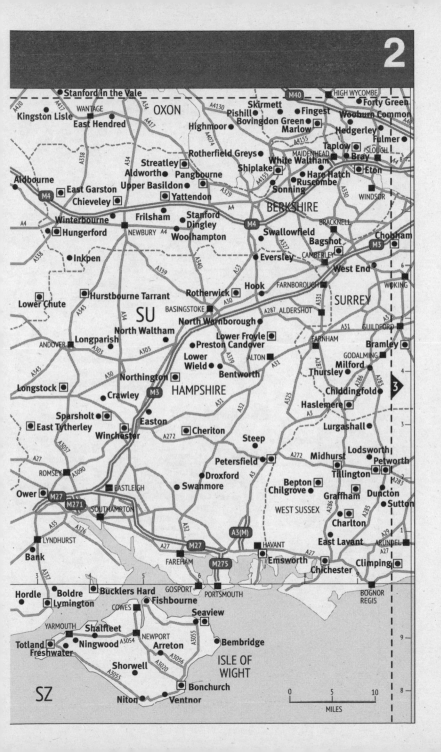

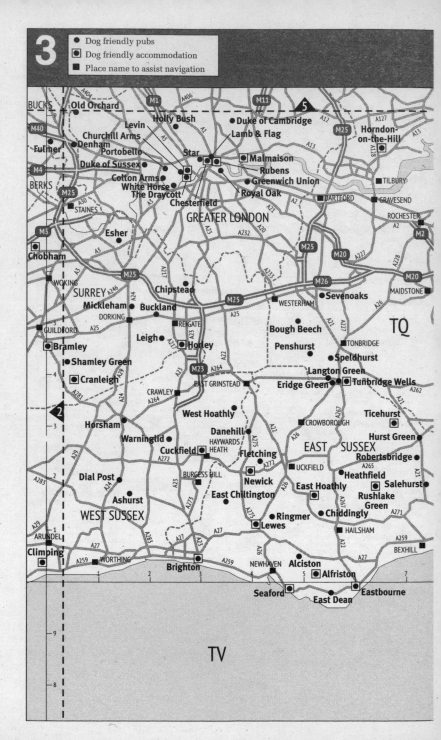

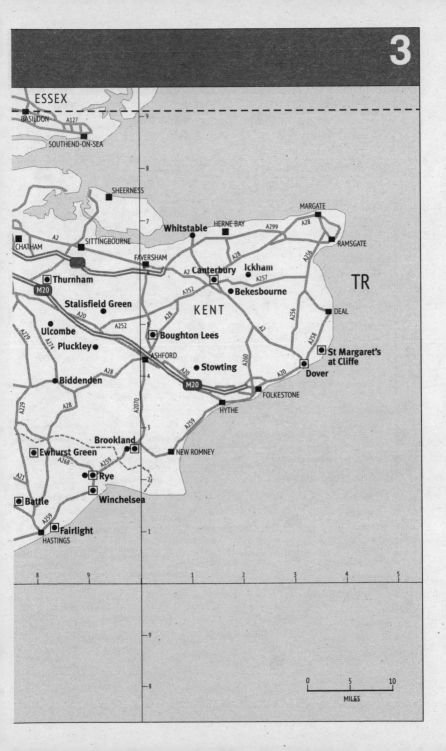

3

ESSEX

BASILDON ■ A127

SOUTHEND-ON-SEA

SHEERNESS ■

CHATHAM ■ A2 SITTINGBOURNE ■

FAVERSHAM

Whitstable HERNE BAY A299 A28 MARGATE ■

RAMSGATE ■

● **Thurnham** M20

A2 **Canterbury** **Ickham** ●

A256 **TR**

● **Bekesbourne**

Stalisfield Green A20 A252 A28

KENT

A257

DEAL ■

A256

Ulcombe ● A274

Pluckley ● A252 ● **Boughton Lees**

A259 ASHFORD

A258

● **St Margaret's at Cliffe**

A28 M20 ● **Stowting** A260 A20 ● **Dover**

● **Biddenden** A2070 A20

A229 A28 FOLKESTONE

3 A259 HYTHE

Brookland ●

● **Ewhurst Green** A268 A259 ● NEW ROMNEY

A21 ● **Rye** 2

● **Battle** ● **Winchelsea**

A259 ● **Fairlight** 1

HASTINGS

8   9   1   2   3   4   5

9

8

0   5   10
MILES

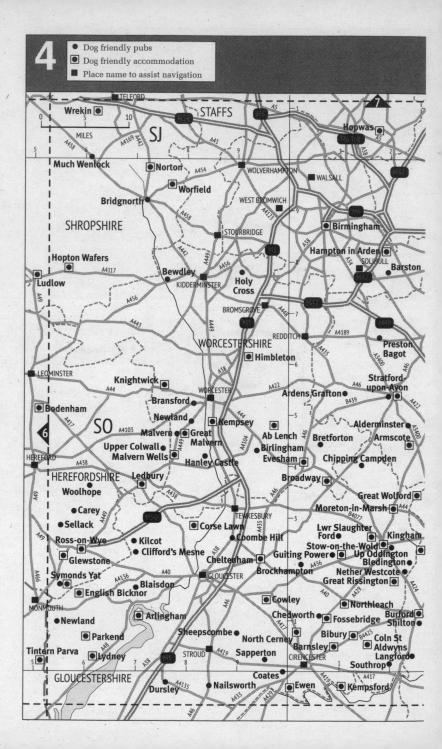

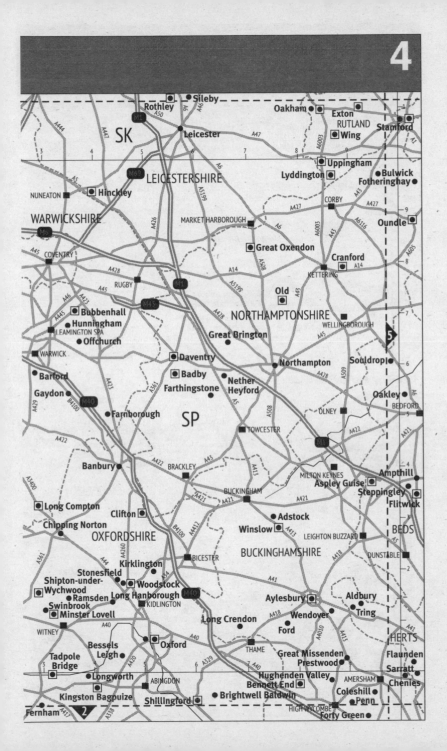

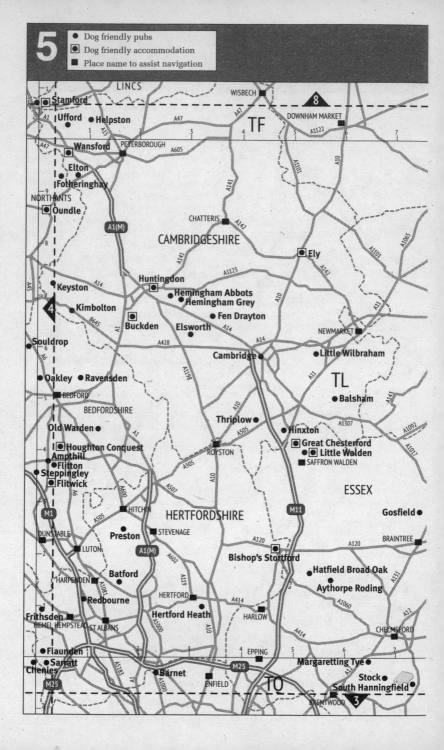

5

- ● Dog friendly pubs
- ◉ Dog friendly accommodation
- ■ Place name to assist navigation

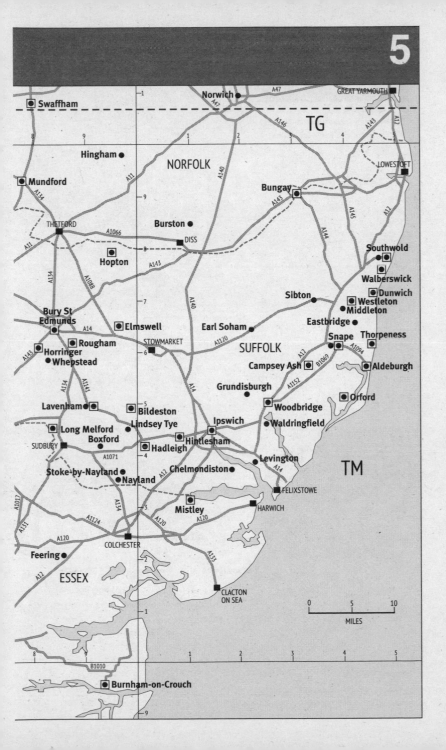

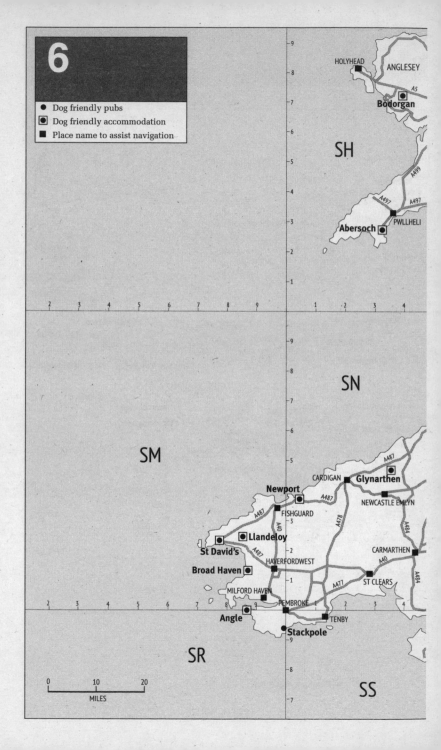

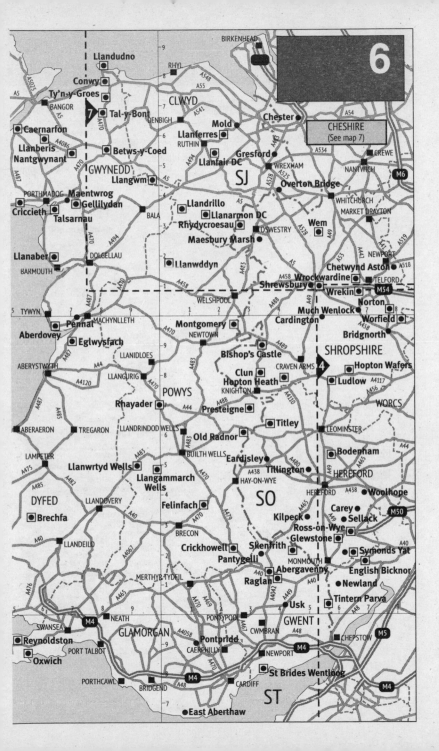

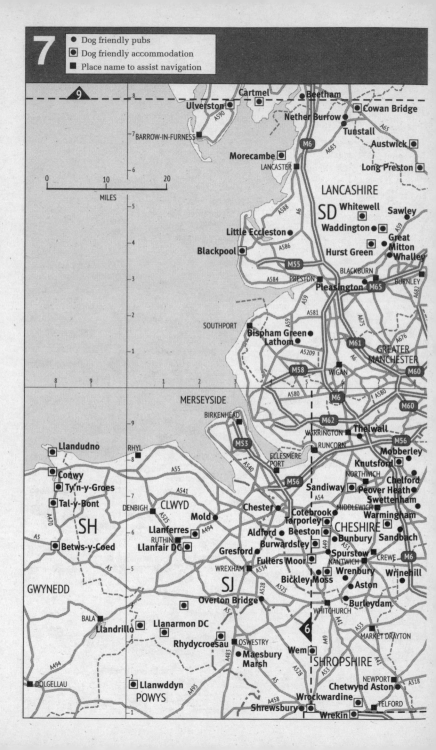

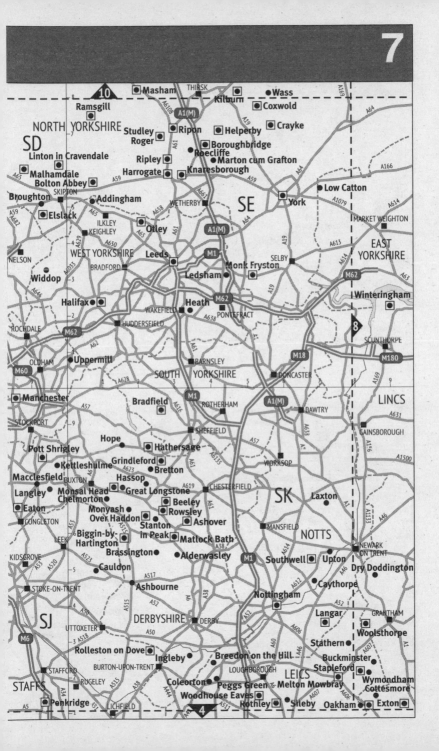

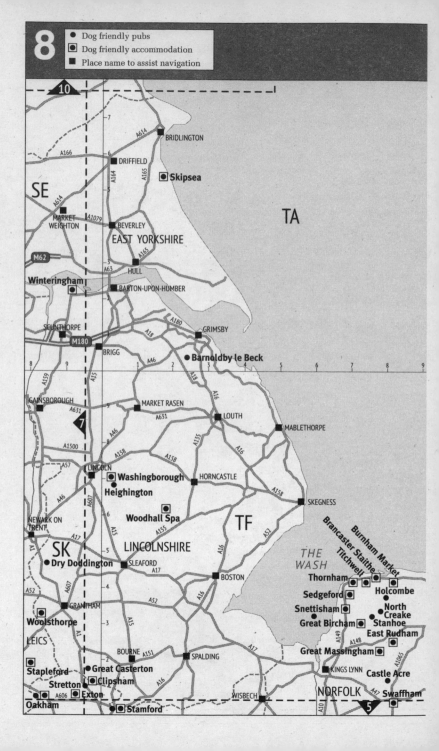

8

● Dog friendly pubs
◉ Dog friendly accommodation
■ Place name to assist navigation

10

SE

A166
A614
7
6
A164
A1079

BRIDLINGTON
■ DRIFFIELD
◉ **Skipsea**

TA

■ MARKET WEIGHTON
■ BEVERLEY
EAST YORKSHIRE

M62
A165
A63
5
A1079

HULL

Winteringham
◉

■ BARTON-UPON-HUMBER

SCUNTHORPE
M180
A180
A18

■ BRIGG
A46
A18

■ GRIMSBY
● **Barnoldby le Beck**

A159
8 9
A631
A15
1 2 3 4 5 6 7 8 9

GAINSBOROUGH
7
A1500
A57
A46

■ MARKET RASEN
A631
8
A46
A158
A135
A158

■ LOUTH
A16
A16

■ MABLETHORPE

■ LINCOLN
◉ **Washingborough**
● **Heighington**

■ HORNCASTLE
A158

■ SKEGNESS

NEWARK ON TRENT
A607
A17
6
A15
5
◉ **Woodhall Spa**
A155

TF

SK
● **Dry Doddington**
■ SLEAFORD
A17

LINCOLNSHIRE
A16
A52

■ BOSTON

THE WASH

Brancaster Staithe
Burnham Market
Titchwell
■ **Thornham** ◉ ◉ ◉
◉ **Holcombe**
◉ **Sedgeford**
● **Snettisham**
● **North Creake**
Great Bircham ◉ ● **Stanhoe**
East Rudham

A52
GRANTHAM
A1
4
A15
A52
A16
A17

Woolsthorpe
◉

LEICS
3
A15

BOURNE
A151
■ SPALDING
A17

A149
A148
Great Massingham ◉

Stapleford
◉
Stretton
◉ **Great Casterton**
◉ **Clipsham**
A606 ◉ **Exton**

■ KINGS LYNN
Castle Acre
NORFOLK **Swaffham**

Oakham
◉ **Stamford**
A16
■ WISBECH
A10
A47

5

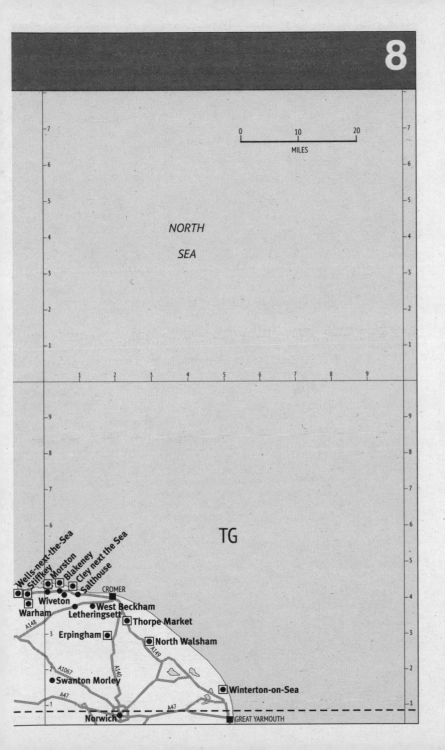

8

0   10   20

MILES

NORTH

SEA

TG

Wells-next-the-Sea
Stiffkey
Morston
Blakeney
Cley next the Sea
Salthouse

CROMER

Wiveton

Warham

West Beckham

Letheringsett

Thorpe Market

A148

Erpingham

North Walsham

A149

A1067

A140

Swanton Morley

A47

Winterton-on-Sea

A47

Norwich

GREAT YARMOUTH

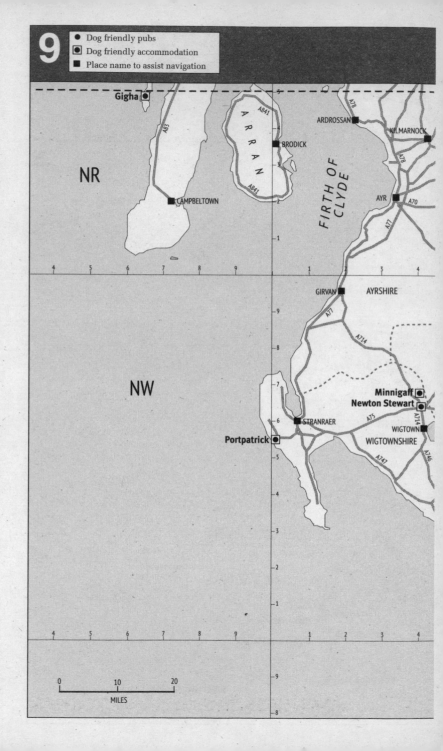

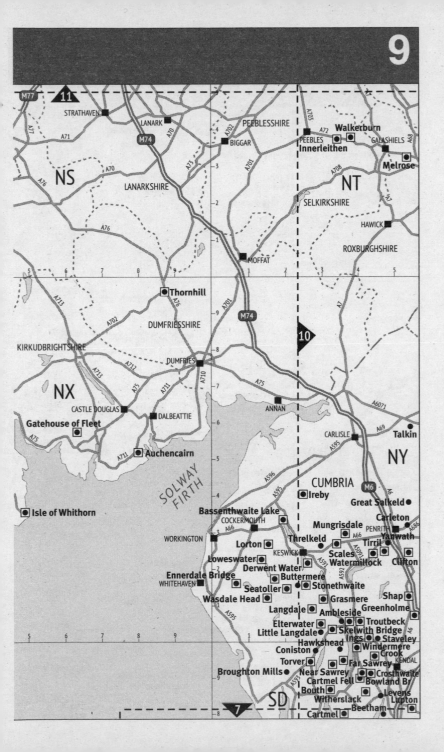

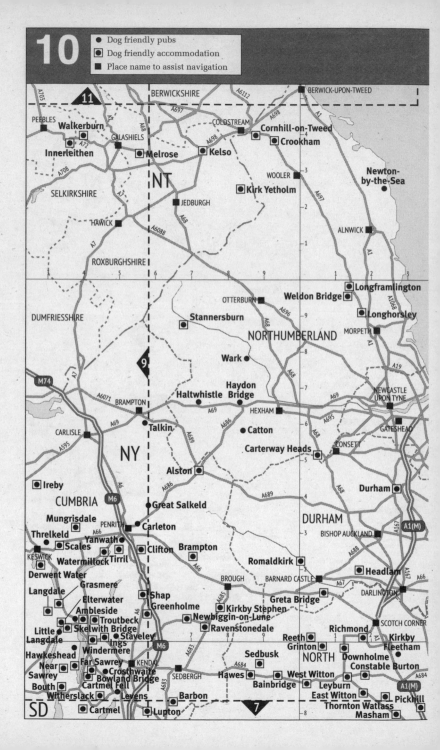

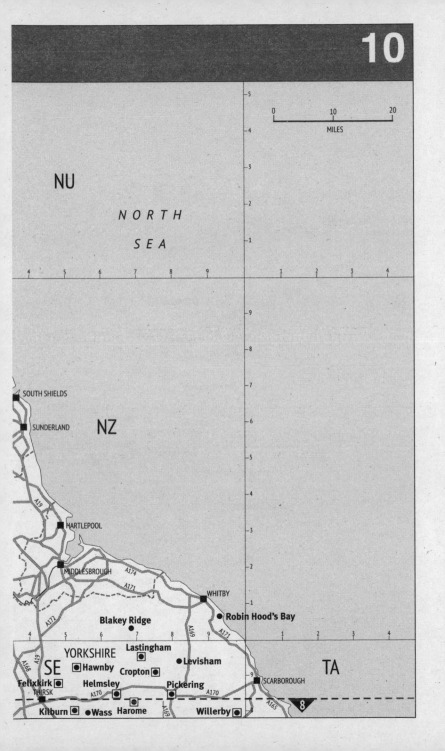

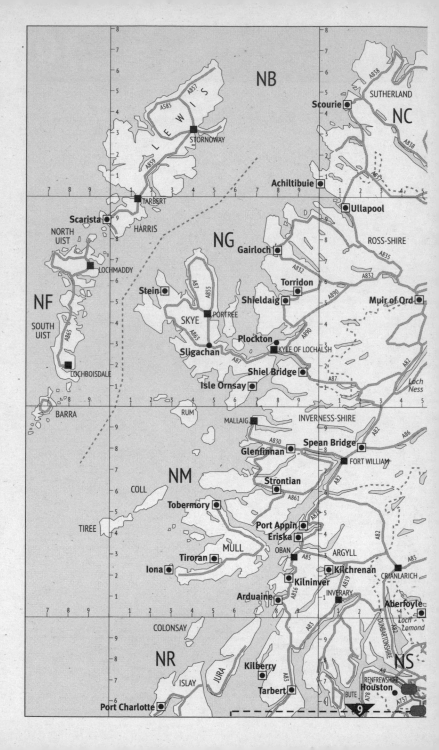

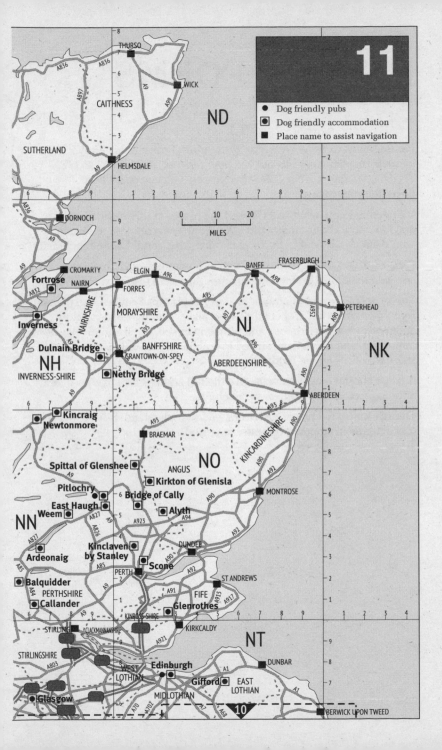

REPORT FORMS

Please report to us: you can use the tear-out forms in this book, or write on plain paper to our freepost address, Dogs, FREEPOST TN1569, Wadhurst, TN5 7BR. Alternatively you can email us at **dogs@goodguides.com**.

We need to know what you think of the places in this edition, and we need to know about other places you think are worthy of inclusion. It would also be helpful to know about ones that should *not* be included.

Please tell us how welcome you felt with your dog, and about any special facilities or welcoming touches that were provided for your dog.

The atmosphere and character are very important features – so please try to describe what is special about a place. And we need to know about any changes in décor and furnishings, too. Food and drink is also important, and if you have stayed overnight, please tell us about the standard of the accommodation.

It helps enormously if you can give the full address for anywhere new, although just its postcode is very helpful.

Though we try to answer all letters, please understand if there is a delay (particularly in summer, our busiest period).

I have been to the following places in the *Good Guide to Dog Friendly Pubs, Hotels and B&Bs* in the last few months, found them as described, and confirm that they deserve continued inclusion:

continued overleaf

PLEASE GIVE YOUR NAME AND ADDRESS ON THE BACK OF THIS FORM

Report on continued..........

By returning this form, you consent to the collection, recording and use of the information you submit, by The Random House Group Ltd. Any personal details which you provide from which we can identify you are held and processed in accordance with the Data Protection Act 1998 and will not be passed on to any third parties. The Random House Group Ltd may wish to send you further information on their associated products.

Please tick box if you do not wish to receive any such information. ☐

Your own name and address (block capitals please)

....

....

....

Postcode...

In returning this form I confirm my agreement that the information I provide may be used by The Random House Group Ltd, its assignees and/or licensees in any media or medium whatsoever.

Please return to

Dog Friendly Guide
FREEPOST TN1569
WADHURST
East Sussex
TN5 7BR

IF YOU PREFER, YOU CAN SEND
US REPORTS BY EMAIL:

dogs@goodguides.com

Report On

....(establishment's name)

Establishment's address

....

....

postcode ....

☐ YES, My dog was welcome   ☐ NO, My dog was not welcome

Please tick one of these boxes to show your verdict, and give reasons,
descriptive comments, prices and the date of your visit

continued overleaf

PLEASE GIVE YOUR NAME AND ADDRESS ON THE BACK OF THIS FORM

Report on continued..........

Your own name and address (block capitals please)

....

....

....

Postcode..

Please return to

Dog Friendly Guide
FREEPOST TN1569
WADHURST
East Sussex
TN5 7BR

IF YOU PREFER, YOU CAN SEND
US REPORTS BY EMAIL:

dogs@goodguides.com

Report On

....(establishment's name)

Establishment's address

....

....

postcode ....

☐ YES, My dog was welcome ☐ NO, My dog was not welcome

Please tick one of these boxes to show your verdict, and give reasons, descriptive comments, prices and the date of your visit

continued overleaf

PLEASE GIVE YOUR NAME AND ADDRESS ON THE BACK OF THIS FORM

Report on continued..........

Your own name and address (block capitals please)

....

....

....

Postcode..

Please return to

Dog Friendly Guide
FREEPOST TN1569
WADHURST
East Sussex
TN5 7BR

IF YOU PREFER, YOU CAN SEND
US REPORTS BY EMAIL:

dogs@goodguides.com

Report On

....(establishment's name)

Establishment's address

....

....

postcode ....

☐ YES, My dog was welcome   ☐ NO, My dog was not welcome

Please tick one of these boxes to show your verdict, and give reasons, descriptive comments, prices and the date of your visit

continued overleaf

PLEASE GIVE YOUR NAME AND ADDRESS ON THE BACK OF THIS FORM

Report on continued..........

Your own name and address (block capitals please)

....

....

....

Postcode..

Please return to

Dog Friendly Guide
FREEPOST TN1569
WADHURST
East Sussex
TN5 7BR

IF YOU PREFER, YOU CAN SEND
US REPORTS BY EMAIL:

dogs@goodguides.com

Report On

.... (establishment's name)

Establishment's address

....

....

postcode ....

☐ YES, My dog was welcome   ☐ NO, My dog was not welcome

Please tick one of these boxes to show your verdict, and give reasons, descriptive comments, prices and the date of your visit

continued overleaf

PLEASE GIVE YOUR NAME AND ADDRESS ON THE BACK OF THIS FORM

Report on continued...........

Your own name and address (block capitals please)

....

....

....

Postcode...

Please return to

Dog Friendly Guide
FREEPOST TN1569
WADHURST
East Sussex
TN5 7BR

IF YOU PREFER, YOU CAN SEND
US REPORTS BY EMAIL:

dogs@goodguides.com

Report On

....(establishment's name)

Establishment's address

....

....

postcode ....

☐ YES, My dog was welcome   ☐ NO, My dog was not welcome

Please tick one of these boxes to show your verdict, and give reasons, descriptive comments, prices and the date of your visit

continued overleaf

PLEASE GIVE YOUR NAME AND ADDRESS ON THE BACK OF THIS FORM

Report on continued..........

Your own name and address (block capitals please)

....

....

....

Postcode..

Please return to

Dog Friendly Guide
FREEPOST TN1569
WADHURST
East Sussex
TN5 7BR

IF YOU PREFER, YOU CAN SEND
US REPORTS BY EMAIL:

dogs@goodguides.com

Report On

.... (establishment's name)

Establishment's address

....

....

postcode ....

☐ YES, My dog was welcome   ☐ NO, My dog was not welcome

Please tick one of these boxes to show your verdict, and give reasons,
descriptive comments, prices and the date of your visit

continued overleaf

PLEASE GIVE YOUR NAME AND ADDRESS ON THE BACK OF THIS FORM

Report on continued..........

Your own name and address (block capitals please)

....

....

....

Postcode..

Please return to

Dog Friendly Guide
FREEPOST TN1569
WADHURST
East Sussex
TN5 7BR

IF YOU PREFER, YOU CAN SEND
US REPORTS BY EMAIL:

dogs@goodguides.com

Report On

....(establishment's name)

Establishment's address

....

....

postcode ....

☐ YES, My dog was welcome ☐ NO, My dog was not welcome

Please tick one of these boxes to show your verdict, and give reasons, descriptive comments, prices and the date of your visit

continued overleaf

PLEASE GIVE YOUR NAME AND ADDRESS ON THE BACK OF THIS FORM

Report on continued:.........

By returning this form, you consent to the collection, recording and use of the information you submit, by The Random House Group Ltd. Any personal details which you provide from which we can identify you are held and processed in accordance with the Data Protection Act 1998 and will not be passed on to any third parties. The Random House Group Ltd may wish to send you further information on their associated products.

Please tick box if you do not wish to receive any such information. ☐

Your own name and address (block capitals please)

....

....

....

Postcode..

In returning this form I confirm my agreement that the information I provide may be used by The Random House Group Ltd, its assignees and/or licensees in any media or medium whatsoever.

Please return to

Dog Friendly Guide
FREEPOST TN1569
WADHURST
East Sussex
TN5 7BR

IF YOU PREFER, YOU CAN SEND
US REPORTS BY EMAIL:

dogs@goodguides.com

Report On

....(establishment's name)

Establishment's address

....

....

postcode ....

☐ YES, My dog was welcome   ☐ NO, My dog was not welcome

Please tick one of these boxes to show your verdict, and give reasons,
descriptive comments, prices and the date of your visit

continued overleaf

PLEASE GIVE YOUR NAME AND ADDRESS ON THE BACK OF THIS FORM

Report on continued..........

Your own name and address (block capitals please)

....

....

....

Postcode..

Please return to

Dog Friendly Guide
FREEPOST TN1569
WADHURST
East Sussex
TN5 7BR

IF YOU PREFER, YOU CAN SEND
US REPORTS BY EMAIL:

dogs@goodguides.com